Human–Information Interaction and Technical Communication:

Concepts and Frameworks

Michael J. Albers
East Carolina University, USA

T0344301

Information Science
REFERENCE

Managing Director:	Lindsay Johnston
Senior Editorial Director:	Heather Probst
Book Production Manager:	Sean Woznicki
Development Manager:	Joel Gamon
Development Editor:	Michael Killian
Acquisitions Editor:	Erika Gallagher
Typesetter:	Lisandro Gonzalez
Cover Design:	Nick Newcomer, Lisandro Gonzalez

Published in the United States of America by

Information Science Reference (an imprint of IGI Global)
701 E. Chocolate Avenue
Hershey PA 17033
Tel: 717-533-8845
Fax: 717-533-8661
E-mail: cust@igi-global.com
Web site: http://www.igi-global.com

Library of Congress Cataloging-in-Publication Data

Human-information interaction and technical communication: concepts and frameworks / by Michael J. Albers.
    p. cm.
  Includes bibliographical references and index.
  Summary: "This book works to provide practical knowledge based on a sound theoretical foundation for allowing people to engage in a meaningful dialogue as they make decisions with respect to designing that communication"--Provided by publisher.
  ISBN 978-1-4666-0152-9 (hardcover) -- ISBN 978-1-4666-0153-6 (ebook) -- ISBN 978-1-4666-0154-3 (print & perpetual access) 1. Interpersonal communication. 2. Information technology. I. Albers, Michael J.
  BF637.C45H86 2012
  302.2'4--dc23
                    2011046563

British Cataloguing in Publication Data
A Cataloguing in Publication record for this book is available from the British Library.

All work contributed to this book is new, previously-unpublished material. The views expressed in this book are those of the authors, but not necessarily of the publisher.

Table of Contents

Section 1
People and Interactions of Situation and Information

Section 2
People and Information Presentation

Chapter 10

Section 3
People and Information Use

Chapter 11

Chapter 12

Detailed Table of Contents

Chapter 1 defines what the author means by human-information interaction and how it fits within the overall communication process and within user-centered design. It also describes the model which forms the basis for the remainder of the book. It sets up how people need to move from technology-centric views of information interaction to human-centric views.

Section 1
People and Interactions of Situation and Information

Chapter 2 considers the information as it exists in the world. It presents a high level view of the information within a situation and how it moves toward the people who need it. In any particular situation, some information is relevant and some isn't (with no arrows). Of the relevant information, some is more salient. The design goal is to ensure the reader receives only relevant information and most relevant is the most salient. It reviews how information has both content and context, the importance of meeting each, and how people handle incomplete information.

Chapter 3 considers the cognitive aspects that people bring to the situation. A design team has no influence over them, but instead must work within the limitations of how the human mind operates. It reviews how human memory works, cognitive resource theory, biases in interpreting information, mental models, and attention theory.

Chapter 4

Chapter 4 considers some of those factors that influence how people approach and interpret information which they have found. Depending on people's goals and information needs, information interaction and interpretation can differ. These differing goals and information needs means what information is important and how hard people work to understand it can differ radically between people. The chapter reviews the factors inherent in human nature, which come into play when interacting with information, such as: cognitive effort, multitasking, information salience, and age-related factors.

Chapter 5

Chapter 5 considers how people approach and interact with technology. HII in the modern world, and as viewed within this book, almost always consists of a computer-based interaction. The computer itself influences how people interact with the information. This chapter examines some of the major ways technology exerts its influence, such as: models of accepting technology, technology factors driving user satisfaction, and motor control factors relevant to HII.

Section 2
People and Information Presentation

Chapter 6

Chapter 6 considers the information as it moves from the situation to the person and some of the factors driving how people form that first impression. A design team must ensure their material leaves a good impression within the first two seconds or so of looking at a page, the time during which people evaluate the appearance and begin to read and comprehend the text. The first glance evaluation of an information display sets people's expectations; if they believe it will be highly usable, they will tend to continue to believe that. The chapter reviews perception and preattentive processing, page appearance, Gestalt theory, optical illusions, and change blindness.

Chapter 7

Chapter 7 considers how the typography used for presenting the information exerts a profound effect on the effectiveness of the communication. A design team must ensure that the typography gives proper salient to the important information and does not distract the reader with poor readability. It reviews font design, font legibility and readability, and how people perceive different fonts.

Chapter 8

Chapter 8 considers how the graphics used for presenting information exert a strong affect on how the information is perceived. Use of graphics helps people interpret a situation more quickly. However, even if they find information that is accurate and reliable, that information is essentially useless unless they are able to interpret and apply it to their current situation. It reviews the cognitive processing of graphics, how text and graphics work as an integrated pair, and the factors influencing how people comprehend a graphic.

Chapter 9

Chapter 9 considers how people interact with quantitative information, numbers, statistics, and probabilities, as they work to gain an understanding of a situation. It reviews issues of numeracy (number literacy), how people interpret statistics, and how they interpret risk information.

Chapter 10

Chapter 10 considers how the presentation of information on a display affects the HII. The type and order of the presentation exert a strong influence on how people perceive and interpret information. This chapter connects and integrates the information of the previous three chapters as it reviews issues of information presentation, how people mentally handle presentation, and the effects of different ways of presenting the same information.

Section 3
People and Information Use

Chapter 11

Chapter 11 considers how people read and comprehend information. The underlying psychological concepts of how people read can help design teams make clear content decisions and evaluate problematic usability test results of technical information. It reviews basic reading and comprehension theory, how people form coherent mental images of a text, and how they make inferences.

Chapter 12

Chapter 12 considers how people search for information across different texts and different display formats. It focuses on the forces that drive people to search for information and what mental processes are involved as they evaluate the findings in the course of reaching a stopping point. The chapter reviews models of how people search and the strategies they use.

Chapter 13

Chapter 13 considers the factors that influence how a people use that information to make a decision. In the end, effective communication depends on people doing something with the information; a decision needs to be made and actions need to be taken. Decisions within an HII context never exist in isolation, but are embedded in the larger tasks that the decision maker is trying to accomplish. The chapter reviews how presentation affects decision making, different models of decision making, and the strategies people use.

Chapter 14
Conclusion 459

Chapter 14 provides a conclusion that expands and fleshes out the HII model presented in chapter 1 based on the content of the book.

Preface

Human-Information Interaction provides a systematic tour of the domain of knowledge of fields concerned with producing and communicating written information. A major goal of this book is to take a step toward a laying a theoretical foundation that would enable designers and writers to use empirically grounded principles for predicting the effects of design alternatives within a specific environment. This book works to provide a framework that establishes a solid theoretical foundation that allows the designers and content developers to predict people's needs and behavior in order to make well-informed decisions about the content they must communicate. And notice that it is "content they must communicate," not "content they must create." Human-information interaction revolves around communicating, not creating information.

Human-Information Interaction emphasizes communicating information, not writing documents or designing websites, nor methods of generating content. An express purpose of this book is to take the theoretical and applied research that has been done across several different fields and turn it into a form which is accessible to the generalist or student. The book works to provide practical knowledge based on a sound theoretical foundation for allowing design teams to engage in a meaningful dialogue as they make decisions with respect to designing that information. In the process, they can move forward with better designs and better communication because they have a more solid foundation on which to make decisions about how to communicate information, and people will interact with that information.

In their introduction to special issue of *Technical Communication* on visualization, Gribbons and Elsar (1998) say "Researchers in the cognitive, neurological, and communication fields are conducting basic research that explains the interaction of visualization with human cognition" (p. 467). They were discussing visualization, but the problem they describe is much wider than just visualization research. Unfortunately, a significant part of most of the basic research knowledge that impacts communicating information is not yet a standard part of either the technical communication curriculum or professional design team knowledge or at least not in a structured, integrated way that is useful for creating content. This book works to provide that integration and helps design teams understand how communication happens (or doesn't happen) at a much deeper level as it connects the research findings of a range of research fields in a way that fits the needs of the people creating technical content.

In an era long past, technical information meant writing for closed-ended questions, such as procedures. But now, most texts and web pages are created with an intent of providing complex information for open-ended questions with a goal of communicating information that address questions such as "How are X and Y affecting Z?" Modern design teams need a much deeper understanding of how effective communication occurs than a procedure writer needed. Design teams are increasingly being called upon to address information needs that go beyond providing simple answers or step-by-step instructions and those that involve communicating information for open-ended questions and problems. Questions and problems that can only be addressed by providing information specific to a situation and presenting it in a way that supports various users' goals, information needs, and cognitive processing strategies. Woods and Roth (1988) define cognitive engineering as "about human behavior in complex worlds" (p. 417). In the same vein, technical communication is about creating content that is comprehendible and properly conforms to the expected human behavior in complex situations. Technical communication does not operate within a clean, simple world; this is a faulty assumption that has lead to many impossible to read texts and endless jokes about poorly written computer manuals. Instead, it operates within a highly complex and dynamic world (Albers, 2003, 2004; Mirel, 1998, 2003). High quality technical communication and HII means developing information that fits people's needs. Accomplishing this goal requires understanding how people think and what drives their decision processes.

Clear communication requires understanding readers from perspectives of technical communication, cognitive psychology, usability, human-computer interaction, information design, and information science. Designing and clearly communicating information involves understanding multiple perspectives of the readers' experiences and understanding their motivations and rationale that drives their behavior. The research in diverse areas has all examined the issue though different lenses. However, there has not been an attempt at transforming the academic studies into a form accessible to technical communication students or to practitioners charged with designing and creating the content. There are no clear-cut, correct/incorrect answers in this domain of communicating technical content. There are only tradeoffs; the ever-present "it depends" answer. It is the job of the professionals working within their field to identify those tradeoffs and know the benefits and costs of each side in the tradeoff. A major goal of this book is to provide the foundation which a design team can use to judge and explain those tradeoffs and benefits.

Human-Information Interaction focuses on communicating information, not creating information. Developing information which clearly communicates and fits people's needs requires understanding how people think and what drives their decision processes. To help achieve that goal, this book works to:

- Lay a theoretical foundation that would enable design teams to use empirically grounded principles for predicting the effects of design alternatives on comprehension within a specific environment. In the process, it synthesizes technical communication, cognitive psychology, socio-technical system, and interface design research as it applies to people working to gain an understanding of a situation.
- Provide a framework that establishes a solid theoretical foundation that allows the design teams to predict people's needs and behavior in order to make well-informed decisions about how to structure the content they must communicate.
- Provide an understanding of how people interact with and understand information at a much deeper level as it communicates multi-disciplinary research findings in a way that fits the needs of design teams tasked with creating technical information.
- Bring into focus the many issues that impede a reader along the path from comprehending data and transforming it into information relevant to the current situation.

The writing style is a long, detailed literature review, which connects the research across a range of fields with the skills required by a people practicing within the fields devoted to producing and communicating technical information. The book works to provide practical knowledge based on a sound theoretical foundation for allowing people to engage in a meaningful dialogue as they make decisions with respect to designing that communication. Besides being a reference for the academic researcher or practicing technical communicator, the book is written so it can be used as a graduate textbook for either a foundational or theories of technical communication course.

Most books are written from the viewpoint of the designer or writer. They constantly make comments such as: "the designer needs to consider how…" or they provide specific guidelines for how to design a page. But this book does not take that approach. It is written from the viewpoint of how a reader interacts with text, not from the viewpoint of how to design that text. That viewpoint is then connected back to what a design team needs to consider to allow a reader to comprehend the text. There are many books that explain how to design and create content; there does not seem to be any other book thaty focuses on explaining how people read, comprehend, and use that content. It may seem trivial; people pour a cup of coffee, sit down, and read what is placed before them. But that is not even close to reality. For a designer to understand what will motivate people to read, comprehend, and properly use information in a specific content, they need to understand the factors which go into people interacting with a text. This book strives to provide that understanding.

Throughout the book, I use the terms "people" and "reader" and rarely refer to them as "user." The only time I say "user" is when I'm very specifically talking about the interaction with a computer system. I'm not one of the militant anti-user terminology people; you'll find I use the term constantly in various articles and in my previous book *Communicating Complex Information* (Albers, 2004a). But this book is focused on people and the factors that determine how effectively information gets communicated to them; interaction with a system is a secondary, albeit essential, part of that communication process. An underlying assumption of many books and articles about people and technology is that people want to use the technology. In general, this is a wrong assumption. People do not want to use a Web-based Information System or a computer application; they want to accomplish a real-world goal. The computer just happens to provide the most efficient means of achieving that goal.

Many of the sections and topics within them have multiple books written about the subject. Obviously, I cannot possibly do more than touch on the surface in the page or so spent on the topic. Plus, the audience for this book is a person engaged in communicating information to another person, not as being a researcher. The information needs of these two groups are different in both overall content and in the details. All of the topics have much more that could be said, and often I knew more specific details, but I had to select and choose based on what would be appropriate for the audience. In addition, this book deals with people as individuals interacting with information; I specifically avoid the exploding amount of social interaction research since it would more than double the page count. However, I do not see this as a serious shortcoming. The complex interactions of a group are still based on and arise from the complexity of individual interactions. A design team needs to consider how an individual will react to and approach information before they can consider how the group in which that individual is embedded will react to the information.

In the foreword of *Reshaping Technical Communication*, Redish (2002) considers Borland's chapter where he "urges technical communicators in both academia and industry to learn about interaction design, to understand contemporary technologies and tools, to learn the principles, practices, and nuances of the knowledge domains about which they write" (p. vii). She then considered this problem from the educational viewpoint.

Technical communication teachers already realize that their students need more than a background in rhetoric and a deep understanding of the writing process. They realize that technical communication is also about understanding users (from cognitive psychology, usability [from ethnography, anthropology, and human-computer interaction], and information architecture [from information science]), as well as understanding information about information design and graphic design, technology, and so on (p. viii).

How well the related fields Redish mentions have moved into the classroom or are known/applied by practitioners in the field is a different story. This book reflects part of my mental image of the map of the landscape as it now stands and how a design team needs to navigate within that landscape as the field moves from writing text to helping the reader interact with and comprehend information. Hart-Davidson (2001) echoed Redish's concerns when he discussed theory in technical communication.

With this claim, I risk rekindling a familiar and (to some) tiresome debate about the place and value of "theory" in technical communication. My claim, put another way, is that at least part of what has held technical communicators—both in the workplace and in the academy—back is the lack of adequate theory that makes our expertise sufficiently portable in time of technological change (Hart-Davidson, 2001, p. 146).

Besides being a reference for the academic researcher, this book is written so it can be used as a graduate textbook for either a foundational or theories of technical communication course. I have constructed this book with a strong eye on its use as a graduate textbook. One reason I'm undertaking this book is to help remedy a problem Davis (2001) describes by saying "If we remain locked into the image of educating writers who lack the broad-based technical grounding to succeed in the next 50 years, then we are shortchanging the future of technical communication" (Davis, 2001, quoted in Spilka, 2002, p. 100). The world of communicating information is changing; design and content based on a "looks good to me" or "that's how I've always written it" philosophy is no longer appropriate. Nor should design teams have an attitude that the most important task is generating finely-crafted prose: the content of that prose and its ability to support people interacting with and understanding it is the most important task.

The major goal of this book is to bring into focus the many issues that impede people from comprehending information and understanding a situation as they move along the path of transforming data to information. It works to clarify the issues which must be considered by design teams tasked with communicating information so they can maximize the reader's comprehension of that information.

ORGANIZATION OF THE BOOK

The book is organized into fourteen chapters. A brief description of each of the chapters follows:

Chapter 1 defines what I mean by human-information interaction and how it fits within the overall communication process and within user-centered design. It also describes the model which forms the basis for the remainder of the book. It sets up how people need to move from technology-centric views of information interaction to human-centric views.

Chapter 2 considers the information as it exists in the world. It presents a high level view of the information within a situation and how it moves toward the people who need it. In any particular situation, some information is relevant and some isn't (with no arrows). Of the relevant information, some is more salient. The design goal is to ensure the reader receives only relevant information and most relevant is the most salient. It reviews how information has both content and context, the importance of meeting each, and how people handle incomplete information.

Chapter 3 considers the cognitive aspects people bring to the situation. A design team has no influence over them, but instead must work within the limitations of how the human mind operates. It reviews how human memory works, cognitive resource theory, biases in interpreting information, mental models, and attention theory.

Chapter 4 considers some of those factors that influence how people approach and interpret information which they have found. Depending on people's goals and information needs, information interaction and interpretation can differ. These differing goals and information needs means what information is important and how hard people work to understand it can differ radically between people. The chapter reviews the factors inherent in human nature, which come into play when interacting with information, such as: cognitive effort, multitasking, information salience, and age-related factors.

Chapter 5 considers how people approach and interact with technology. HII in the modern world, and as viewed within this book, almost always consists of a computer-based interaction. The computer itself influences how people interact with the information. This chapter examines some of the major ways technology exerts its influence, such as: models of accepting technology, technology factors driving user satisfaction, and motor control factors relevant to HII.

Chapter 6 considers the information as it moves from the situation to the person and some of the factors driving how people form that first impression. A design team must ensure their material leaves a good impression within the first two seconds or so of looking at a page, the time during which people evaluate the appearance and begin to read and comprehend the text. The first glance evaluation of an information display sets people's expectations; if they believe it will be highly usable, they will tend to continue to believe that. The chapter reviews perception and preattentive processing, page appearance, Gestalt theory, optical illusions, and change blindness.

Chapter 7 considers how the typography used for presenting the information exerts a profound effect on the effectiveness of the communication. A design team must ensure that the typography gives proper salient to the important information and does not distract the reader with poor readability. It reviews font design, font legibility and readability, and how people perceive different fonts.

Chapter 8 considers how the graphics used for presenting information exert a strong affect on how the information is perceived. Use of graphics helps people interpret a situation more quickly. However, even if they find information that is accurate and reliable, that information is essentially useless unless they are able to interpret and apply it to their current situation. It reviews the cognitive processing of graphics, how text and graphics work as an integrated pair, and the factors influencing how people comprehend a graphic.

Chapter 9 considers how people interact with quantitative information, numbers, statistics, and probabilities, as they work to gain an understanding of a situation. It reviews issues of numeracy (number literacy), how people interpret statistics, and how they interpret risk information.

Chapter 10 considers how the presentation of information on a display affects the HII. The type and order of the presentation exert a strong influence on how people perceive and interpret information. This chapter connects and integrates the information of the previous three chapters as it reviews issues of information presentation, how people mentally handle presentation, and the effects of different ways of presenting the same information.

Chapter 11 considers how people read and comprehend information. The underlying psychological concepts of how people read can help design teams make clear content decisions and evaluate problematic usability test results of technical information. It reviews basic reading and comprehension theory, how people form coherent mental images of a text, and how they make inferences.

Chapter 12 considers how people search for information across different texts and different display formats. It focuses on the forces that drive people to search for information and what mental processes are involved as they evaluate the findings in the course of reaching a stopping point. The chapter reviews models of how people search and the strategies they use.

Chapter 13 considers the factors that influence how a people use that information to make a decision. In the end, effective communication depends on people doing something with the information; a decision needs to be made and actions need to be taken. Decisions within an HII context never exist in isolation, but are embedded in the larger tasks that the decision maker is trying to accomplish. The chapter reviews how presentation affects decision making, different models of decision making, and the strategies people use.

Chapter 14 provides a conclusion that expands and fleshes out the HII model presented in chapter 1 based on the content of the book.

Michael J. Albers
East Carolina University, USA

REFERENCES

Albers, M. (2003). Complex problem solving and content analysis. In Albers, M., & Mazur, B. (Eds.), *Content and complexity: Information design in software development and documentation* (pp. 263–284). Mahwah, NJ: Erlbaum.

Albers, M. (2004). *Communication of complex information: User goals and information needs for dynamic Web information*. Mahwah, NJ: Erlbaum.

Davis, M. T. (2001). Becoming a profession. In Mirel, B., & Spilka, R. (Eds.), *Reshaping technical communication* (pp. 97–109).

Gribbons, W., & Elsar, A. (1998). Visualizing information: An overview of this special issue. *Technical Communication, 45*(4), 467–472.

Hart-Davidson, W. (2001). On writing, technical communication, and Information Technology: The core competencies of technical communication. *Technical Communication, 48*(2), 145–155.

Mirel, B. (1998). Applied constructivism for user documentation. *Journal of Business and Technical Communication, 12*(1), 7–49. doi:10.1177/1050651998012001002

Mirel, B. (2003). *Interaction design for complex problem solving: Developing useful and usable software*. San Francisco, CA: Morgan Kaufmann.

Redish, J. (2002). Foreword. In Mirel, B., & Spilka, R. (Eds.), *Reshaping technical communication* (pp. vii–xiii). Mahwah, NJ: Erlbaum.

Spilka, R. (2002). Becoming a profession. In Mirel, B., & Spilka, R. (Eds.), *Reshaping technical communication* (pp. 97–109). Mahwah, NJ: Erlbaum.

Woods, D., & Roth, E. (1988). Cognitive engineering: Human problem solving with tools. *Human Factors, 30*(4), 415–430.

Acknowledgment

Many people had an indirect influence on bringing this book about. Specifically, there is my wife Linda, and my dogs who patiently lay around my desk while I write.

I started writing in early 2005 after completing *Communication of Complex Information*. I was expecting to complete it in 2, maybe 3 years. Obviously that schedule proved overly optimistic. I received a Professional Development Assignment (sabbatical) from the University of Memphis in Spring 2006 during which I read a substantial amount of the research incorporated into the book and wrote the first draft. Then I moved to East Carolina University where the department nicely kept me off committees and allowed me time to write.

For the final stages of writing, there are the anonymous reviewers. Their comments were instrumental shaping the book into its final form. A thanks to my development assistant at IGI Global, Michael Killian, for his fast responses to all my questions as I finished up the manuscript.

I also must acknowledge the local coffee shops, especially the Daily Grind, where I spent too many afternoons drinking too much coffee while writing a large portion of this book.

Finally, my thanks to everyone who takes an interest, either as a researcher or practitioner, in the communication of complex information and the need for quality human-information interaction. Technical communication needs to address these issues as it moves forward, and you are the people who will make it happen.

Michael J. Albers
East Carolina University, USA
June 2011

Chapter 1
Introduction

ABSTRACT

Decisions on what content to include and how to design that content are major decisions that profoundly influence the overall communication of any text. In the course of arriving at how to communicate the information, alternatives are narrowed down until a final design, content, and interaction strategy is reached. Information is not a commodity to be simply transferred from person to person, nor is it something that can be poured into someone's head. Instead, it is inherently value laden, and the situational context and presentation strongly influence people's comprehension and the content's overall effectiveness. Different choices of media affect readers differently and change how they interpret a text (Nisbet et al., 2002). Printed reports get interpreted differently than an identical online report. Changing the color schemes or adding audio can change it again. There is no single answer to what is the best method; it depends on the readers. Communicating clearly to that reader requires the design teams understands those readers.

"The skill of writing is to create a context in which other people can think."— *Edwin Schlossberg*

INTRODUCTION

In the end, design teams need to consider all of the reader's information needs, text constraints, and content options, which make up the text's problem space, map those onto the design space, and then map both of these onto a person's goal space. All three of the spaces: problem space,

design space, and user's goal space need to be explored and charted until the final product is produced. (Albers, 2008). "Understanding and facilitating information interaction requires considering the process of interaction, as well as the resultant changes in both the human-information seeker and the information objects" (Marchionini, 2008, p. 171).

Nickerson and Landauer (1997) suggest that a better understanding of how humans conceptualize information spaces should increase software usability. They want to shift the design focus from technology to people. Likewise, a significant increase in information communication effec-

DOI: 10.4018/978-1-4666-0152-9.ch001

tiveness could result if design teams had a better understanding of how readers conceptualize and interpret information. Explicitly missing from much discussion of communicating technical information are the nitty-gritty issues of how people approach, interpret, and use information. Improving the ability to communicate complex technical information requires understanding the situations people work within and the information needs of the tasks performed in those situations (Ash, Berg, & Coiera, 2004; Mirel, 1998; Stary, 1999).

Many of the communication failure issues we consistently see have a root cause not based on human-computer interaction (HCI) and how people interact with computers, nor on the completeness of the information, nor the writing quality of the text. Instead, it fails because of a failure to understand how information is communicated to people and how those people interact with and interpret that information to accomplish their goals. Essentially every modern business and technical communication textbook starts with statements about how the writer must understand the user, but fails to provide much information about what we know about how people mentally process text. Generally missing from most of the design and writing literature are the underlying concepts about how people actually understand and interact with information. This book works to develop a coherent presentation of *human-information interaction* (HII) which strives to address that shortcoming.

Discussing software system design, Malhotra and Galletta (2004) state "Even the best-designed information systems are not used if they are not aligned with the system users' motivations and commitment" (p. 89). They were talking about typical computer systems, but the same applies even more strongly to systems designed primarily to communicate information, such as most web sites. Consider the huge amount of information which must be condensed down by a design team to allow people to achieve their goals. With the wide range of potential people and varying needs, this becomes a highly complex problem.

To help ensure that users' interactions with a system are successful, preparation of content and its presentation to users must take into account (a) what information needs to be extracted, (b) the way in which this information should be stored and organized, (c) the methods for retrieving the information, and (d) how the information should be displayed (Proctor et al., 2002, p. 26).

Most design teams can create a consistent interface and well-written content, but that same content too often fails to consider how people really interact with the information. As a consequence, it fails at supporting high quality HII. A goal of this book is to help design teams bring those considerations into the design process and to improve overall HII.

I heard a ballet choreographer in a TV interview say "It's not that I love to dance, but that I want to create good dancing." He gets it; too many designers and writers don't get it. It's not about creating carefully, meticulously crafted designs or sentences, it's about communicating information and enabling people to comprehend and use that information. It's about motivating people to fully use the information which needs to be considered throughout the design (Selker, 2005). The primary focus must be the information content and the ability of that information to be communicated to the audience. The goal of this book is to consider how people approach, interact with, and use information for understanding situations, for making decisions and for solving problems.

HUMAN-INFORMATION INTERACTION

The opening section laid out the importance of supporting how people interact with information. Human-information interaction (HII) is the title

Box 1.

> **Major disasters and HII**
> The space shuttle Challenger explosion has the subject to many studies. Tufte's (1997) analysis of the PowerPoint slides showed that the vital information was hidden and that it would be almost impossible for NASA management had fully understanding the information. Herndl, Fennell, and Miller (1991) compared both Challenger and Three Mile Island and exposed similar problems with information flow.
>
> From an HII perspective, there is no question that the data was available to the decision makers. However, it was presented in the wrong manner and was not designed in a way that would let NASA management or the Three Mile Islands operators comprehend it and build relationships between it and other parts of the situation. For Challenger, the Morton Thiokol engineers had created technically correct presentation which failed to account for HII issues and, as a result, failed to communicate its content.

of this book, but I have yet to define what I mean. The 119-word elevator definition of HII, as used in this book, is:

HII develops an understanding of how people use and react to information so that a design team can make informed evaluations of what constitutes "meaningful and appropriate" information and information delivery in a specific situation. HII builds on cognitive and social psychology, HCI, human factors, and technical communication theories, and reworks them into a basis for evaluating the tradeoffs inherent in creating effective communication. Understanding the underlying theory behind how people interact with information supports making predictions about reader response and making design decisions matching those predictions. It also helps the design team articulate what is being improved or given up as design and content decisions change during project development, as well as provide the basis for developing the usability test plans.

Human-information interaction is not my term. Like the terms in the following section, many different definitions can be found in the literature (Marchionini, 2008). For example, one of the

long-standing leading laboratories in HCI, Xerox PARC, now uses the term human–information interaction. It has been used in the information science literature for many years where it is used in relation to organizing, categorizing, and finding information. At least one information science program has a course titled *Human-Information Interaction*. On the other hand, this book focuses on issue of creating content which supports how people, approach and use information within situations.

Just as user-centered design puts the focus on people rather than the system, this book's definition of HII starts and ends with people. HII focuses on the interactions between people and information within the context of a situation and a system (Toms, 2002). It's never a matter of just picking the technology or tool to solve a problem; it's a matter of understanding how people will interact with the information and designing accordingly. And understanding that the HII changes between situations; there is no one-size-fits-all for either the people or the information.

HII works to support an understanding of how people use the information and how they react so that the designer and writer can make informed evaluations of what "meaningful and appropriate" mean in their specific situation. HII takes as its starting point cognitive and social psychology theories and reworks them for technical communication, which gives a basis for evaluating the tradeoffs in effective communication. Understanding the underlying theory behind how people interact with information supports making predictions about reader response when making design decisions. It helps the designer and writer articulate what is being given up as design and content emerges during project development (Albers, 2008). It considers how people find, interpret, and use information to best achieve their goals. At one level, this may seem like "ok to know, but not essential" information for people involved in design and communicating information, but in reality; it is totally essential. A major problem of

Box 2.

Complex software systems

A usability study on C2PC, a US Marine Corps command and control software product, found the Marines were able to perform simple tasks, but had difficulty combining those simple tasks into realistic tasks (Albers, 2010). The purpose of the system is to maintain the situation awareness of the battlefield commanders. It does accomplish that task, but makes the operator (who is not the battlefield commander) perform extra steps and move slower. Like many complex systems, it technically functioned according to design, but failed to adequately support people solving open-ended, unstructured, complex problems which require extensive and recursive decision-making or problem solving (Albers, 2003).

Unfortunately, this is not an isolated example, but one that occurs many times (Albers & Still, 2010). Poor HII is reflected in designs which fail to support effectively rolling up the individual tasks into the complex interactions that people must perform. Or they fail to provide information presented in a form which meets people needs. Any complex information system involves complex situations; design teams must consider what factors influence how people perceive the information in their contextual environment and then build on those perceptions to enable the selection of relevant information to support judgments, decisions, and actions.

---

many designs is they display a lack of understanding of how people interact with information. I'm not claiming the design teams do not care about the reader, but, instead, lack the foundational knowledge to make the design choices required to ensure the design fits a reader's needs.

Shneiderman (2000) claimed one of the key problems people have is overly complex systems and poorly-crafted interfaces which lead to high levels of frustration and errors. Too often a design gets put forth as solving a problem, when only part of the communication problem is solved. The design problems with C2PC explained in the sidebar are one example of a development team coming up with a technology solution to a highly complex problem which works, but which forces people bend to the system presentation. Avoiding these problems requires that from the beginning, the design team needs to be identifying and asking questions about all the parts, how they fit within people's situational context, and the sequence of events which lead to them looking at the information in the first place. A route to over-

coming the problem lies in understanding and closing the gap between what people know and what they need to know. Shneiderman was thinking in HCI terms, but the idea is easy to generalize to HII where the problem is redefined from being a poorly-crafted interface (although that may be a symptom of the problem) to poorly-crafted information design and content for the current situation. Interestingly, this allows for a very finely-crafted interface to still fail if it fails to be suitable for the current situation (which also fits well with, to paraphrase Norman, "if the person can't find it, it's not there"). People's goals and information needs are highly situational and imbedded in their current context (Albers, 2004a). People must be able to identify information needs, to locate corresponding information sources, to extract and organize relevant information from each source, and to synthesize information from a variety of sources into cogent, productive uses (Moore, 1995). HII strives to capture those situational and contextual requirements and provide information that can be manipulated to achieve them.

The poorly-crafted interfaces which Shneiderman was complaining about were probably not buggy, nor did they fail to perform as the developer wanted. Typically, they fully met what the development team set out to create and what the client ordered. However, on one side we have what was ordered and the design team set out to create and on the other side we have what people need to understand a situation, unfortunately these are often two very different things. Both a finely-crafted interface and well-written prose can fail because, in most situations, information does not "exist" and merely needs to be placed on a platter and passed to a reader. (Thankfully, that is a belief whose time is long past, at least for most communication professionals.) Communication does not happen because a writer took stuff from a subject matter expert, either wrote it down or cleaned up the grammar, and placed it before a reader. Instead, people take information about the situation, combine it with other information, and then mentally reshape that combination into knowledge (Hughes, 2002). People work with information in context and shape their understanding based on prior knowledge, evaluation of the source quality, and their current needs. Statements such as "I read something about that yesterday" or "Maybe we can modify the second part of this to work here" shows how communication is not simply a matter of providing content. Without knowing the situation and interpreting the information in context, sentences such as these make no sense. In the same vein, situation comedies depend on misunderstanding overheard information as a major plot element; information heard out of context gets misinterpreted and results in actions inappropriate for the situation.

Written texts form the major method of communicating information, as Bazerman (2001) points out (Note that this book deals exclusively with written text. It makes no attempt to discuss the extensive literature of oral communication, although I acknowledge it plays a part in how people gain an understanding of the situation.):

Information, for most purposes, takes the form of a written record, of signs inscribed on durable medium. This information may then be displayed in graphic, oral, or tactile formats, particularly as digital technologies facilitate the transformation of the archived inscriptions into various means of gaining human attention (p. 260).

With most information now in digital form, the primary communication method is assumed to be via a computer, although the interaction with the computer itself is secondary (Here is where HII and HCI have a level of split with HCI more deeply focused on the interface-based interaction.). People typically interact with a computer system to access and manipulate the information, but simply having this ability is neither necessary nor sufficient to accomplish their goals and meet their information needs (Mirel, 1998; Marchionini,

2008). A computer interface communicates with people and, as Gulliksen and Lantz (2003) point out, "communication is identified as one of the key issues that needs to be addressed to achieve well- functioning user-centered design" (p. 5). I'll even go beyond "one of the key issues" and claim communication with a goal of maximizing comprehension is the most important issue. Designing that communication involves a focus on a human interacting with information, not a computer, and thus a need for dedicated study of HII.

The ultimate test of whether or not information is communicated is whether or not people can comprehend it and relate it to their situation. Also important, but as will be discussed later, a somewhat problematical metric, is what decisions or actions are initiated after reading it. HII deals with ensuring the content supports people in achieving their goals; this requires close attention to the presentation, interaction methods, and content as it relates to the dynamics of the situation itself. This will be a huge change for many designers and writers who see the end objective as the actual development and completion of the content itself (McGovern, 2005).

The problem of information overload has a long history (Miller, 1960) and forms a significant problem facing design teams as current computer systems provide too much data. The systems can collect and regurgitate huge amounts data, but people's ability to digest it and transform it into useful information has not changed. This results in what Woods, Patterson, and Roth (2002) call a "data availability paradox." Technology is providing access to every increasing amount of data, but people are having a harder and harder time making sense of all that data. They need a flow from a garden hose and are receiving a flow from a fire hose of ever-increasing diameter. A substantial problem is that systems tend to end up with acontextualized data, but people need it in context:

The cognitive activity of focusing in on the relevant or interesting subset of the available data is a difficult task because what is interesting depends on context. What is informative is context sensitive when the meaning or interpretation of any change (or even the absence of change) is quite sensitive to some but not all the details of the current situation or past situations. (Woods, Patterson, & Roth, 2002, p. 26)

Some people have described today's business environment as managing by PowerPoint bullet lists. The managers and executives expect everything to be boiled down to a five-point bullet list. The interesting HII question is why this has evolved. A significant part of the answer probably comes from having read too many poorly written reports which dumped the data. Those report writers ignored their responsibilities of creating information which was appropriate for and properly presented to the audience. The design teams forgot they were communicating information about a situation to their bosses and, instead, wrote a report for them. A subtle difference, but one which brings the needs for HII into focus.

As part of the transfer from laboratory-based cognitive psychology to a set of usable principles, Woods and Roth (1988) introduced the idea of cognitive engineering, which they define as "about human behavior in complex worlds" (p. 417). Cognitive engineering works to understand the principles behind human activities and to design systems that supports these activities. It developed around the necessity of making sure that systems that humans use to accomplish tasks do not hinder or make it impossible to complete those tasks. People should be able to perform the intended tasks with minimal cognitive effort (Jaspers et al., 2004). Although in general, cognitive engineering has focused on areas such as controls panel design and other complex human factors issues, most of its concepts apply to HII and its goals of communicating information to people. Methods such as the think aloud method, protocol analysis

Box 3.

> **HII and police information systems**
> The San Jose police department rolled out a laptop-based system for computer-aided dispatch in their patrol cars which rapidly caused problems. Although the system gave the officers the ability to quickly look up what they had to previously call the dispatcher for (such as checking on a car's license plate), the overall usability was very poor. It required the officer to drive and type on a laptop at the same time; however, both require two hands and focused attention. Dividing someone's attention between a critical task (driving) and any other factor is dangerous. In the resulting grand jury investigation and lawsuits, problems with the technology and how it communicated with people were a major factor (Santa Clara, 2005).

or cognitive task analysis are used to analyze in detail the way in which humans perform tasks and comprehend situations.

Redish (2007) considers the complex usability aspects and the complications that complex information interactions incur for both the people doing the interacting and the design teams tasked with developing it. HII deals with these same aspects. A full theory of HII requires synthesizing a wide range of research from technical communication and related research areas. Many of these ideas structure cognitive psychology, HCI and human factors fields already, but those fields cover areas outside the scope of communicating technical information. What this book strives to accomplish is transferring the pertinent aspects of all related fields and reshaping them into a form applicable to a design team to efficiently communicate content. The goal of this book is to bring into focus some of the issues that impede a reader along the path to comprehending and using information and to put forth the need to develop methods that people tasked with communicating information can use to overcome those issues. It strives to take a step toward defining the necessity of a theoretical foundation that would enable design teams to use empirically grounded principles for predicting the effects of design alternatives within specific environments and situations. The end result will be a solid theoretical foundation that allows design teams to predict people's needs and behavior in order to make well-informed decisions about the information they must communicate. And notice the previous sentence says "information they must communicate," not "content they must create." HII revolves around communicating, not displaying or creating content.

Definitions

This section defines the major terms will be used throughout the book. Each of them has multiple potential definitions and each academic field seems to define them slightly differently. Thus, this section works to lay out my definitions to avoid later confusion.

Content: The actual words and images which are presented to the readers.

Context: The entire real-world situation in which the situation exists and the information gets presented. It includes any mitigating factors within the information presentation, social interactions, and overall environment.

Goals: The real-world change of the current situation or understanding of the current situation that people are trying to achieve. HII views goals from a person-situation viewpoint (what is happening and what does it mean), rather than the system viewpoint (how the system displays a value for x). Goals can consist of sub-goals, which are solved in a recursive manner.

Information: 'Information' denotes data that has been processed from its raw form. It is not about analyzing streams of signals as defined in information theory (Shannon, 1948). When people work toward achieving their goals, they look at maps, text reports, photographs, books, web pages, and so on (Scholtz 2006). That information has to be mentally integrated and transformed to make sense with respect to the current situation.

Information theory allows people to calculate the minimum number of bits to transmit a certain amount of information. Although it works for efficient compression of computer-computer communications, people are not computers, they are too prone to missing some of the transmitted bits or not remembering the conversion algorithms (does bit space bit mean roast beef for dinner or pick up the dry cleaning?). In real-world situations, people are very hard pressed to understand or work with information in such a minimalist form. Unlike computer communication, human language is a highly redundant medium. When dealing with information from an HII viewpoint, the concern is not how to minimize the amount of transmitted data, but on how to maximize communicating content and comprehension to a person.

Information needs: The information required by a people to achieve a goal. Information needs typically require information both to initially understand the situation and to access goal achievement.

Interaction: Most human-information interaction of interest to a design team is highly repetitive: text is read multiple times or there is a sequence of click-read-click. The interaction between a person and the information results in changes to the information or overall understanding of the situation. Marchionini (2008) reserves the term interaction for situations where people engage in several cycles of action with the information, with both the people and the situation changing as a result.

Situation: The current world state which people need to understand. People interact with information (normally via a computer system) to gain the necessary information in order to understand the situation. In most situations, after understanding the situation, they interact with the situation, resulting in a change which must be reflected in updated information.

User-Centered Design Meets HII and Communicating Information

Design of technical information has become a science and art of user-centered design (UCD). To achieve working within that sphere, design decisions need to be based on how people approach and interact with information. The design team needs to have an understanding of what goes on in people's minds. Many design teams have been criticized for basing their designs on what they know or want, instead of on what people using the information are likely to know or want. The move to UCD is in direct opposition to this attitude and developed as a way to prevent it.

The HCI community has strongly embraced the move toward UCD and putting the focus on people and their interaction with information rather than on people manipulating computer interfaces (Marchionini, 2008). People working within technical communication and related areas tasked with developing content also realize the need to consider audience, and have moved toward UCD. On top of this movement to UCD, it's splintering into various areas with names like experience design and interaction design, all different views and different paths to reach essentially the same goal. They all realize that communicating information requires having a deep understanding of people's information needs and the situational context in which they will use that information.

The information interaction is a human-centered action with all of the complexities borne out by years of psychology and sociology research. Old school HCI and information development took a highly rational view and assumed that people would be as logical as the computers they were interacting with. Computers will always give the same answers; humans will not. The interactions are highly non-linear: their past history with the situation matters, slight changes in their goals matters, the path taken to an answer can vary (Albers, 2004a).

People are not computers. We forget. We cannot search our mental databases. Our thinking and memory are not disconnected from acting and sensing. The two are engrained and inseparable. Yet computers are increasingly driving our day-to-day lives and pushing their paradigms into our human experience. We are rapidly moving to a world where everything is always stored—in many different locations—and everything is always accessible. Life would be easy for us if we just thought like computers. But we don't. We feel bombarded with data, but we can't find what we need, we can't make sense of it. So what are human-centered data? How should they be presented, stored, organized, visualized, so that they are relevant for us, and not (just) for a computer? What does that mean for such varied fields as car design, mobile device software, or digital signage? (Vanderbeeken, 2009, p. 56).

Diaper and Sanger (2006) claim that HCI developed in an ad hoc manner focused on solving the current pressing problem, rather than developing any general theories. Although their claim can be strongly argued both for and against, UCD is also suffering the same ad hoc development. The HII discussed in this book strives to provide a base level of theory as it relates that theory to practices which consider the different ways in which people approach information and the different factors which affect that approach and subsequent interaction. In the end, it feeds back into UCD by providing an enhanced base from which to make design decisions.

Two HII Examples

These two examples help show the range of situations of interest to HII. In the situations described in the following examples, people cannot track all the required information without assistance, thus some type of computer system is required. A system that must present coherent information that is relevant to the situation and their goals.

Before UCD, the design assumptions would have focused on either (1) defining the path to the optimal answer or (2) simply collecting what information people needed and dumping it. A design which Allen (1996) criticizes, "much information-system design emphasizes the data contained in the system rather than the users of the system and what they want to do, and that is why there are so many bad information systems" (p. xxi). With UCD, the design assumptions focused on providing sufficient information to address the user's information needs in a manner which makes sense to that individual user (Albers, 2003). With the addition of HII on top of UCD ideas, the design team can get a clearer understanding of what motivates people and how they need the information presented for effective use.

Report Analysis

Consider the design of the typical reports a manager receives. Rather than providing any help with interpreting the information in the reports, the report designers normally take the view of just asking what information is desired and providing a collection of reports that contain it somewhere. The issues surrounding how the managers interpreted and worked with the reports each month was deemed too difficult to address and, thus, outside the scope of report design. On the other hand, here is an example (Mirel, 2002, p. 258) gives of how managers and analysts really work with reports.

For example, if a marketing analyst for a coffee manufacturer is inquiring into whether a new espresso product is likely to succeed in this specialized market, she needs to view, process, and interact with a wide range of multi-scaled data....She will assess how espresso has fared over past and current quarters in different channels of distribution, regions, markets, and stores, and impose on the data her own knowledge of seasonal effects and unexpected market conditions....She

will arrange and rearrange the data to find trends, correlations, and two-and three-way causal relationships; she will filter data, bring back part of them, and compare different views. Each time she will get a different perspective on the lay of the land in the "espresso world."

By considering report analysis as a form of HII and using dynamic online reports, the report interpretation methods do not have to be outside of scope. Instead, it can support the needs of the manager and the analyst as they work with their monthly reports. The problem is not a lack of data, but a lack of data shaped into an integrated presentation that fits how they interact and manipulate information to achieve their goals.

Healthcare Information

After a diagnosis of a chronic disease, a patient or care-provider will be given several brochures describing the disease. Each one may cover a specific aspect such as general explanation, nutrition, lifestyle changes, etc. Since each one is written as a stand-alone document, they impose several problems with the patient getting a clear picture: overlap and repetition of information, some irrelevant information (such as only relevant for infants), not directly relevant to the disease (such as general low-fat nutrition information), possibly contradictory information, and probably written for a low-literacy reader to address all patients in one document. In additions, there can be a fundamental communication problem that the brochures focus on the discourses used by health professionals rather than patients (Payne, 2002), a discourse which can be almost unintelligible to the patients and often containing material they consider irrelevant.

Now consider what people really want from the medical brochures. They expect and need more than general descriptions. In addition, the information medical people want and what patient or care-provider wants are very different. The medical people want diagnostic and treatment information while the patient wants to understand outward disease progression and how to care for themselves. They want information written at a detail level and knowledge level that fits their needs (Albers, 2003). For example, does the person want to understand a disease in detail or just know the high points? Coupled with this detail level is the person's general medical knowledge. The writing appropriate for a person with no knowledge and a person with college level biology is different. However, in all cases, the health question itself is highly open-ended. The amount of information is immense and people can continue to collect information until they decide to stop.

Fallowfield (2001) argued that "Patients cannot participate in decision making to their desired extent unless they have the right types of information, given in ways optimal for their own level of understanding" (p. 1144). HII strives to give the design teams the tools to help the patients participate in that decision-making. And notice the goal is to help the patient, not to develop a brochure. Although the result in both cases may be a brochure, the viewpoint of the design team and the factors defining success can be very different.

FROM TECHNOLOGY TO CONTENT TO COMMUNICATION

The view of how people interact with information has changed radically in the last couple of decades, primarily driven by the increased number of general readers being exposed to technical documents. The readers of pre-computer technology texts and early computer technology texts had a high training level and could get by with very system-centered documentation. With the rise of the PC, documentation had to be aimed at the non-technical reader. Now, with huge amounts of technical information available via the World Wide Web, the need for user-centered, rather than system-centered, documents is even more important. HII stresses the reader as the center of the document comprehension and use.

Gribbons (1991) succinctly summed up a problem with information design, a problem which still exists, although not as severe as when he wrote it.

The design community has failed to resolve this problem by incorporating the latest findings from the perceptual and cognitive sciences. Instead, they continue to employ 18th and 19th century design conventions to solve 20th century information problems. The results: a flood of poorly designed, inefficient, and ineffective information products (p. 42).

Gribbons accused design teams of having a very document or technology centered view (Figure 1). Much of the design was either based on the designer's past experience ("it worked before, so it must be good" or "the user wants what I'd want") or is based/modified from research on how to design for print. Using past experience only works if the new design is sufficiently like the old design. If it is too different (and what makes it too different can be hard to pin down), then the design fails to communicate. "The user's model is not formed from the design model, but from the way the user interprets the system image. It should be realized that everything the user interacts with helps to form that image" (Gulliksen & Lantz, 2003, p. 8). Design teams (actually in the past it was often a single writer, not a team) produced documents that people could read, but the document itself was the end product. How well it communicated or how well the reader could comprehend it was not a major design goal. With the rise of the Internet, that attitude has changed, but there is still the problem of what it really means to consider how people approach and interact with information.

It is less apparent what it means for people to interact with information. On one hand, since digital forms of information are so ubiquitous and require some kind of technology to facilitate hu-

Figure 1. Technology centric view. For teams focused on technology, the information in the bubble simply exists and will be pulled as needed and passed out to a user. Neither the information nor the users are a concern for the design team; they focus on the technology (adapted from Marchionini, 2008, p. 166).

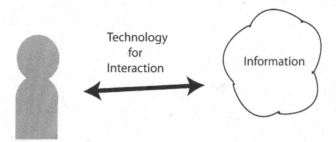

man perception, people interact with the technology as an intermediary. This intermediate interaction with technology is tangible and necessary (but not sufficient) to accomplish information goals. Because early electronic technologies were so foreign to common human experience, human–computer interaction has classically addressed interaction with the technology (Marchionini, 2008, p. 170).

The arrow in the center of Figure 1 reveals a technology-centered mindset. An approach which often results in low communication or low comprehension because of information overload or information dumping. I once worked on a project where a programmer said it was user friendly because it used windows and a mouse rather than the old system's text interface. She also didn't understand why it was cancelled because it technically worked. She was right, it did work technically, but it was such an HCI horror that the regional vice presidents refused to let it be installed in their regions. It was a design solely focused on the technology and it ignored the people aspects.

With a strong HII focus, the drawing can be redone as Figure 2, which downplays the technology to a means of communicating the information and elevates the information to the most important element. Communicating information is not a matter of having technology to provide data, but having a means of helping people interact with

contextually relevant information so they can build relationships within that information and relate it to their situation (Albers, 2008; Woods, Patterson, & Roth, 2002).

A significant part of designing for more effective HII lays in changing the view of audience. Most print-based communication was a single author and a single reader. With modern web-based designs, much of communication involves complex social interactions. The single author has expanded to multiple authors and information drawn from multiple databases. The reader has expanded to many readers each of whom bring a different set of goals and information needs to their reading of the text. There has been a move from simple text-to-person or even computer-to-person, to a complex interplay of person-to-computer-to-person-to-person. That person-to-person must be considered as part of creating a design (Whitworth & Moor, 2003). Unfortunately, it is difficult for a design team to fully grasp the implications of that move when designing a document; it is easy to fall into a simple text-to-person mindset since that is how it has always been done. However, in the final evaluation, to be considered successful, the information must be effectively communicated to all of the readers. This is a very difficult, but imperative goal for the success of the design.

Figure 2. HII centric view. The focus is the communication interaction which occurs along the heavy arrow between the person and the information cloud. The technology's task is to support that interaction, but is secondary to the communication itself.

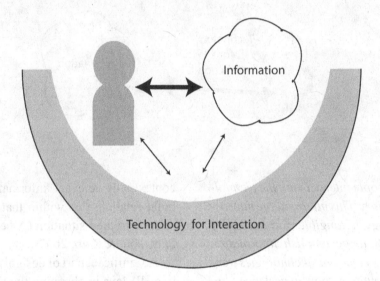

Clear and Simple Writing

In the TV interview with a ballet choreographer, he said "Choreography isn't about steps; it's about coordination." Likewise, design and writing technical information isn't about designing layout or architecture or writing perfectly constructed sentences, it's about communicating usable information; information which fits people's goals and needs and which arrives when and how they need it.

I have known writers in both literary and business settings who don't give the reader a second thought. They are in fact oblivious to the fact that what they write might actually be read. In fact, in my experience, a large percentage of organization content is created without any real focus on who might read it, or why they might want to read it, or what they might do after they read it. (McGovern, 2005)

Maintaining that communication flow is what HII is all about. HII is a philosophy and process

Box 4.

> **Clear healthcare writing**
> Most written patient information is produced by health professionals for patients. A typical problem is that these writers assume that patients want and need to know about the medical, pathological and physiological aspects of their disease, rather than aspects of living with a condition or simply dealing with a medical procedure. For example:
> In summary, health professionals create texts that explain: (Payne, 2002)
>
> - older women are potentially vulnerable to hypocalcaemia
> - older people are more likely to fall
> - hip protectors prevent serious injury.
>
> While older people might prefer texts which address concerns such as:
>
> - falling is not a sign of incompetence
> - falling is not moral failure
> - padded hips violate desirable social norms relating to body image, especially for women.
>
> These very fundamental content issues are then overlaid with writing issues, such as having texts which are too complicated for easy comprehension (Hochhauser, 1998). Many of the studies measured the writing's grade level, itself a problematical measurement, but regardless, a low grade level well written text is still useless if it contains the wrong information to fit a person's needs (Rowan, 1991).

Table 1. Characteristics of simple, complicated, and complex situations (adapted from Albers, 2004a, p. 16)

	Characteristics	**Examples**
Simple	Single path to a solution exists. Information requirements to answer a question can be predefined. Effect on the overall system of a change to one factor can be predicted.	ATM (user view) Mall store-finder kiosk Software menu description
Complicated	Total system is a sum of its parts (a complete description can be given). Multiple paths to a solution exists. Information requirements to answer a question can be predefined.	Tax software Computers Chess Jet engine repair manual Telecommunications switch documentation Mandelbrot set
Complex	Total system is more than just the sum of the parts (a complete description cannot be given). Multiple paths to a solution exist. Information requirements to answer a question cannot be predefined. Effect on the overall system of a change to one factor cannot be predicted (nonlinear response). Part of an open system. Difficult to break out and study a section in isolation.	Car buying Report analysis Medical patient records System design of any realistic complexity Traffic flow on a highway

that is greater than the sum of the individual information/people/technology components which compose it (Marchionini, 2008).

In order to develop effective communication, we need to know what the reader is thinking, what they are looking to do, what they need, what is easy to understand, what is difficult to understand, how easy and difficult vary between audiences, and why they need the information in the first place. The design team cannot set a goal of producing clear-concise simple information, but must have a goal of producing information which, within a person's specific situation, is easy to use in a manner which makes sense with respect to that specific situation. From a writer's point of view, the goal of creating content should not be to make it simple, but rather to make the highly complex issues manageable and complicated things meaningful.

In non-learning situations, people do not come to a situation as a blank slate waiting to be filled, but instead approach and interact with information using significant amounts of prior knowledge.

They interpret new information in terms of the knowledge they already have, building their understanding of the situation by connecting new information to what they already believe. Design teams need to develop information which supports this type of interaction, not one which assumes the reader knows nothing.

Simple and Complex Situations

No one would claim that all situations are the same, although some design seems to treat them that way. The situations people face can be broken down into three classes: simple, complicated, and complex. HII as a design philosophy works best with complicated and complex situations. It still applies to simple situation interactions, but with their more straightforward information needs and interactions, HII risks being overly complicated for the return. The main difference between the three situation types is whether or not the situation and its solution paths can be fully described, as shown in Table 1.

Box 5.

Car company vehicle comparison charts
All of the major car companies place a comparison chart someplace on their web site which compares their various models. They present a table containing categories such as: price, power train, dimensions, exterior, interior, safety, fuel economy, and warranty. Each category contains several different characteristics relevant to that category.

Compression Ratio	✓	11.3	9.7	10.0
Turning Diameter (Left)	✓	37.7	33.4	38.9
Turning Diameter (Right)	✓	37.7	33.4	38.9
Rear Suspension	✓	Independent	Live	Independent
Length (inches)	✓	190.4	188.1	197.7
Width (inches)	✓	75.5	73.9	75.7
Wheelbase (inches)	✓	112.3	107.1	116.0
Height (inches)	✓	54.2	55.6	57.1

Excerpt from a table comparing three car models.
These tables are hard to use for several reasons:
- They are long and require scrolling, which makes it difficult to compare categories widely separated on the table.
- They assume people want to see every model and category. Potential economy car and sports car buyers have very different interests in what they want to see in the table.
- They assume people want the engineering specifications. Values such the car's overall dimensions, power train details, etc. are useful from an engineering or car buff perspective and are easy to pour into the table, but are meaningless to most car buyers. The is all technical information which is easy to provide, but is not what the potential buyers need. For example, size of the car might be a purchase factor, but few people have a clue about the size of their current car and would have trouble interpreting size in inches and relating to their needs.

Poor designs that fail to communicate often try to treat all situations as simple. Often because after performing a task analysis, the tasks are broken down to the point that each resulting task is simple. A substantial problem is that in the process of analyzing the task analysis, the tasks have lost their situational context. Once that is considered, and people will always place them in context, in many situations the tasks cannot simply be chained together in a linear fashion.

Complex situations address information needs which go beyond step-by-step instructions and involve communicating information for open-ended questions and problems (Mirel, 1998, 2002). This basically includes any situation that has lots of complex information which people need to understand. Open-ended questions and problems can only be addressed by providing information specific to a situation and presenting it in a way

Box 6.

Creating pull quotes
An assignment I give my students is to write a set of instructions for creating a pull quote in Word. They need to explain how to insert and format the text box, how to insert a graphic, and how to insert the text. In Word each of those actions are separate and nothing connects them. In many software packages, the early task analysis may have defined that the users needed to insert pull quotes. It then broke that down into the individual steps which are given to different programmers. As a result, nothing in the final product lets the user understand how to insert the pull quote. It supports doing it, but doesn't provide any guidance. Even the help will only explain how to use the individual options. Some place in the transition from the early design analysis to the final product, the user's goal of inserting a pull quote gets lost.

that supports various goals, information needs, and cognitive processing strategies (Albers, 2004a).

HII analysis and design considers the communication needs in the highly dynamic situational context complex situations (Albers, 2000), with a goal being to support building the information interrelationships and contextual awareness required for people to achieve their goals. As Mirel (2002) states, "people's actual approaches to complex tasks and problems….are contextually conditioned, emergent, opportunistic, and contingent. Therefore, complex work cannot be formalized into formulaic, rule-driven, context-free procedures" (p. 259). HII designs address those information needs which require understanding the complexity of the entire contextual situation.

In general, complex situations are the norm, not the exception. A complex situation contains too many factors to be completely analyzed since they contain lots of ambiguity and subtle information nuances, so it is essentially impossible to provide a complete set of information or fully define paths through the situation. That fact, if nothing more, moves the emphasis of the information interaction from the computer to the human since computers cannot handle ambiguity (although research areas such as fuzzy logic are working on the issue). The easiest design methods, ones that are still too prevalent but going away as design moves to user-centered methods, never try to address the ambiguity. The system displays the information and leaves it up to the 'system user'—a user considered as external to the design—to sort out the ambiguity. An HII design philosophy, on the other hand, works to create information that provides proper support for those people. Computers and people both excel at different tasks, effective design must balance the two and let each do what they do best.

WHY USE AN HII VIEW?

With the movement of information onto the Internet, the increased volume of information resulted in a major upheaval in how information was created and presented, in both good and bad ways. New professions have appeared; people who now hold titles such as information architect, usability specialist, and information designer. The field of technical communication expanded to include these areas while at the same time, other areas such as library science and human factors also expanded to include them. In the end, although people's early training helps shape how they approach problems (impose assumptions on a design), each of these areas has developed into its own area, independent of its origins. Communication has moved from a single person driven by artistic impulses or a craftsman mentality to a team project focused on meeting an audience's goals and information needs. But much of that communication still uses the same mindset that giving people all of the information in grammatically accurate prose is sufficient and they can sort it out. I acknowledge that view is shifting, but the shift is rather ad hoc; HII can help underpin the shift (Albers, 2008).

"People actively create tools out of their texts" (Swarts, 2004, p. 68). They use the texts as a means of understanding their situations and accomplishing their goals. Design teams need to ensure the texts they provide support people in creating tools and not in hindering them. It can be the difference between handing someone an ax and handing them an ax head, a block of wood, and a knife to carve the ax handle. Really poor design only provides the ax head and the block of wood and expects a usable ax to simply appear.

Part of the issue is that people interact with information content, but too many projects ignore the low-level content and work at higher levels. For example, the wireframe in Figure 3 is typical of what gets produced for a project. A single page; other pages would be connected with an arrow showing architecture flow paths. It focuses on the HCI, not on the HII. Not that wireframes are bad; they are an essential element of the design product. But they allow the design team to shift the view from human-information interaction to information arrangement. Likewise, the wireframe diagram fails to explicitly show the

Figure 3. An all too typical design mock up of a web page. This design ignores the content, the actual information which people want and need to accomplish their goals. The design team can ignore the user text and assume it magically appears from the database. But communication (and success/failure) of the design depends on the user text, not of the navigation or page layout.

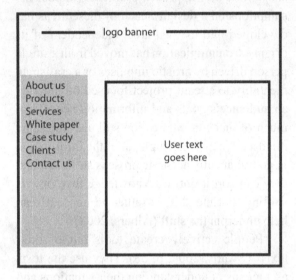

reader, the writer, the content, or how the reader should interact with the content—which isn't even displayed (it will magically be provided later). Yet, obviously, all are required for a high quality design. Ultimately, information quality and usability comes from proper content supported by the format, and never from a high quality format with so-so content. For effective HII, the information must be clearly thought out to enable people to easily comprehend the content.

Information science has considered information-seeking as a human problem-solving process (Marchionini, 2008). On the other hand, information-seeking research tends to stop at the point where people find the information. The bigger picture aspects of comprehending and using the information are outside of their scope. In this book, the chapter on information finding is second to last; a huge number of factors need to be considered before considering how people search for information. The ultimate test of whether or not information communicates is what people do with it after reading it. This will be a huge change for many design teams who see the end objective as the actual completion of the content itself (McGovern, 2005). Understanding how to help readers accomplish their goals requires shifting the conception of designing and writing to one of being a constant problem-solving and decision-making process. An HII view strongly supports this problem solving approach.

Gains from Using an HII View

Human-computer interaction, technical communication, or information architecture, are rarely presented through a problem-solving lens; not that the problem-solving does not occur, but the information they work with are not designed from this viewpoint. The focus is too often on people interacting with computers, not on people interacting with information and solving problems (Hegland, 2006). Unfortunately, the move to online information has often done little more than speed up information search. The online information presentation has not better addressed people's problems or information needs (Tomasi & Menlenbacker, 1999). Basically, our understanding of how humans mentally represent the information available to them and learn to navigate within hypertext systems has not kept up with the technology (Nilsson & Mayer, 2002). In addition, explicitly missing from much discussion of communicating information are the human issues: "Human-centered design process for interactive systems. In addition to the design, knowledge of the human being is essential" (Gulliksen & Lantz, 2003, p. 10). High quality HII must address how human psychology drives the information interaction and comprehension in problem-solving situations.

HII provides the underlying theories which a design team can use to either develop a high quality design, or to understand why a design failed to communicate its information and how to improve it. HII helps to provide guidance for answering the question "did the usability test result show the problem or a symptom." Fixing symptoms will not fix problems; at best, it may hide them.

Morrison, Pirolli, and Card (2001) analyzed the methods people use for obtaining the information they needed to accomplish their critical tasks.

- **Collect:** 71%. Users searching for multiple pieces of information. They are driven by a specific goal, but are not looking for one particular answer. Instead, achieving their goal requires them to collect and mentally integrate multiple pieces of information.
- **Find:** 25%. Users searching for something specific. Many usability tests operate on this principle when they ask people to find X and then time them or count clicks.
- **Explore:** 2%. Users looking around without a specific goal. This is similar to the general browsing of the early web days when people didn't have a real reason to visit the site other than to see how it looked.
- **Monitor:** 2%. Users repeatedly visiting the same website to view updated information. Visits are triggered by routine behavior rather than a particular goal. Examples are visiting a new web site. (Morrison, Pirolli, & Card, 2001)

Notice how in these findings, 71% of the people needed multiple pieces of information. They had to interact with that information, mentally manipulate it, and build relationships between multiple pieces of information on the way to fully comprehending how it all applied to their goal. Yet, information sources such as search engines do not let people compare multiple pieces of information (Nielsen, 2001). HII works to help this 71% of the people who need multiple information elements which they must comprehend and integrate before they can take action. A design succeeds or fails on how well people can comprehend and use its information. A design which ignores the intricacies

of HII risks poor usability, poor communication, and poor human performance in the situations for which the information is most needed. In almost every case, these 71% are operating in a complex situation while the 25% finding information are in a simple situation. Designs which confuse the two are problematical.

Nickerson and Landauer (1997) suggest that a better understanding of how humans conceptualize information spaces should increase software usability. A significant part of that increase arises from design methods more focused on people (the basic idea of UCD) rather than the technology. Likewise, and more importantly, a significant increase in information communication could result if design teams had a better understanding of how people conceptualize and interpret information. The acceptance and use of UCD has significantly shifted the design view toward people since Nickerson and Landauer wrote their text. However, explicitly missing from much UCD discussion of information design and content creation are the nitty-gritty cognitive issues of how people interact with, interpret, and use information at the textual level. HII leads information design and development in a shift from data modeling to understanding the situations people work within and the information needs of the tasks performed in those situations (Albers, 2004a; Ash et al, 2004; Mirel, 1998; Stary, 1999).

Unlike more typical user and task analysis, an analysis based on HII stresses how people react differently to information in different situations and what type of behavior is exhibited by people with different levels of ability and knowledge. HII analysis operates at a much finer grained and more comprehensive level than is typical of current development projects—although it operates at the level advocated by many sources, such as Hackos and Redish (1998). Rather than a generic description of how people react, HII works to consider how the defined audience groups will react across time within the situations of interest.

Figure 4. Information required by different groups. The shaded areas correspond to the knowledge a person has on a topic and what they need. This project has three very different audience groups which must be considered. For a graph that looks like this one, it cannot be assumed that one design will work for all three audience. Whether they can all effectively use the same information presentation will require usability testing.

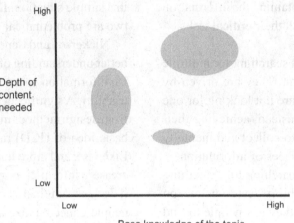

People's information needs can be described in the graph in Figure 4, which shows how different people's needs vary (Albers, 2003). Each person fits into one point on the graph; an audience group forms cloud of closely related points. Once graphs such as this are created, the design team can understand what content must be created and have a basis for matching the presentation to a person's needs. The various personas used by the design team do not map to single points, but to cloud shapes. More importantly, the graph helps trying to present information for any point on the graph (everyone) or for a single point (the mythical average user).

Even in the same situation, different audience groups can react in very different ways and even the people working in the same role (which may be grouped into a single persona) may approach and react to similar situations with different behaviors (Korzenko, Robins, & Holmes, 2008). Issues such as time stress, environmental variables, multitasking requirements, etc. all have a profound effect on how people interpret and comprehend information. Thus, what HII can give is a path to

a high quality design which takes these factors into account and avoids providing a generic design which supports only a mythical average user rather than real people.

Risks of Not Using an HII View

Discussing software system design, Malhotra and Galletta (2004) state "even the best-designed information systems are not used if they are not aligned with the system users' motivations and commitment" (p. 89). Likewise, much of the information produced sits unread on dusty shelves or dusty computer drives because it too misses addressing people's motivations and needs. The movement to online information has not caused a shift from unread printed manuals to read online text; instead, we have large amounts of unread online text. The presentation of the information has not better addressed a user's problems or information needs. Many web sites have huge quantities of useless and unread information which fails to address a reader's goals and needs. From the viewpoint of helping people understand their situation, little has changed with separate files (such as launching a web browser) containing help information or the needed information spans multiple pages of a web site or the information answers single simple answers, but does not help people looking for multiple information elements.

People's information needs, text constraints, and content decisions make up a text's problem space, which must be mapped onto its design space and both of these must be mapped onto the person's goal space. The content analysis and design is, essentially, performing that mapping. The quality of the communication directly reflects the quality of the mapping. Decisions on information architecture, information design, and content are major decisions which profoundly influence the overall communication of any text. Any design will forever have to live with and be limited by its initial assumptions. HII helps to effectively define those initial assumptions.

Information is not a commodity to be transferred from expert to another person. It is inherently value-laden and the social and political framing of the source strongly influences the overall presentation (Payne, 2002). For example, too much of web design is focused on the individual page, rather than the overall website, or the overall user experience (reflected in wireframes such as Figure 3). The design field needs to continue its ongoing shift in focus from people interacting with computers, to a focus on people interacting with information and solving problems (Hegland, 2006). At the same time, different media effect readers differently and change how they interpret a text (Nisbet et al., 2002). Unfortunately, many current designs get side-tracked by external issues, such as corporate politics or time, and fail to fully appreciate the full social and cognitive framing that enhancing reader comprehension requires.

MODELS OF HUMAN-INFORMATION INTERACTION

The purpose of any representation or model is to allow one to abstract over much of the complexity of real world behavior while retaining an unambiguous description of the essential elements needed to explain that behavior (Monk, 1999). A model attempts to capture in a general sense the concepts and structures which comprise the entity being modeled which, in turn, helps people organize their view and understanding (De Angeli et al., 2003).

Multiple models have been put forth to help explain how people interact with information. Many of them come from the cognitive sciences. Early models took a view of a person as a computer interacting with information in a highly logical manner. Unfortunately, people do not interact in highly logical manners and these models were less than helpful for designing for HII. As Toms (2002) describes it:

The complexity of information interaction is not well expressed in typical models of human–computer interaction. The range of tasks general supported by computer systems extend from routine tasks to problem-solving tasks that require extensive backtracking and digressions (p. 856).

Toms' concerns can be seen in the shift of cognitive psychology from viewing people as "general-purpose computational systems" to viewing them as "adaptive and adapted organisms whose whole computational mechanisms are specialized and contextualized" to a particular environment (Medin, Lynch, & Solomon, 2000, p. 136). Later, more useful models, shifted to viewing people as actors working within a situation, with Suchman's (1987) situated activity theory work as an early example. Her theory was one of the first to view people as not forming and rigorously following a full set of logical plans up front and then carrying them out, but rather forming a basic plan then continuously updating it in response to the results of the current action.

Early Models of Information Interaction

Suchman's work spawned numerous different models that considered different aspects of how people responded to and interacted with the information within a situation. Toms (2002) presented a cyclic model (Figure 5) of human-information interaction which starts with people and focuses on how they integrate through information to comprehend and reach a decision point. This model, like the HII of this book, privileges the human-information interaction and places it at the center.

Basing his model on education and technical communication concepts, rather than cognitive psychology, Carliner (2000) put forth a three part model that, although developed for information design, describes how the major aspects of interacting with information is highly human-centered with the major issues being not finding the information, but understanding it (cognitive) and wanting to actually use it (affective).

- *Physical*, the ability to find information
- *Cognitive* (intellectual), the ability to understand information
- *Affective* (emotional), the ability to feel comfortable with the presentation of the information (comfort with the information itself might not be possible, depending on the message) (Carliner, 2000, p. 564).

An express purpose of Carliner's model is to help shift design teams from focusing on the physical interaction with information (typically the button-pushing or link-clicking aspects of the interface) to considering the cognitive and affective aspects of people's problem-solving and decision-making processes, which for the real reason for their information interaction.

Figure 5. Iterative model of information interaction. "The user scans the text, although it may be graphical as well. When a cue is noted, the user stops to examine the text, and may or may not extract and integrate the information. The user may recycle in multiple, nonlinear ways through category selection, cues, and extraction.... Thus, the same set of items could be presented to the user, but different choices might be selected at different times. The state of the user changes with time; a single instance is unlikely ever to be the same for the same person or for different people" (adapted from Toms, 2002, p. 857).

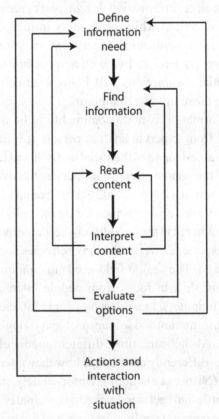

Situation Interaction

Other researchers, notably Redish (2007) and Mirel (1998, 2003) considered how people interact with complex information and how dealing with complex information had fundamental differences from dealing with simple information. Albers

Figure 6. Interactions in complex situations. People have goals and information needs which require them to interact with the system and other people in the situation to collect sufficient information to understand the situation. (adapted from Albers, 2004a).

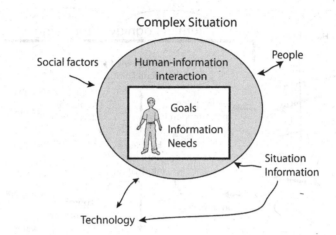

(2004a) developed a model of interactions with complex situations (Figure 6) based around user goals and information needs with the information interaction occurring to achieve the goals.

Model of Human-Information Interaction

This book develops the model in Figure 7 which shifts the focus from dealing with information as both Toms' and Albers early' models, to one relating comprehension of a situation. The model shows the interaction of:

- Information in the environment which is available to a person.
- Movement of information via gate-keeping functions of a system or, principally, human perception, which selects the information which will receive consideration.
- Prior knowledge and mental models a person brings to the situation
- Evaluation and comprehension of the information and the construction of relationships between information elements.
- Effects of how people approach information

- Effects of how different presentations can change how people interact with information.
- Decisions and performance of actions which change both the situation and the information which a person must understand.

The basic diagram is cyclic. In actual operation, it would contain many internal cycles. For example, all of the necessary information will probably not be collected initially. Instead, as people build the relationships, they realize based on their mental model that more information is required. The interaction then goes back to collecting information from the world.

In the bigger picture, a model should help people better understand how the varies pieces interact and to use empirically grounded principles to make informed predictions about the outcomes of those interactions. It is not so much the model presented here which allows the predictions, but the instantiated situation-specific models design teams build around this model which allows for understanding of and predictions of people's information interaction. In the case of an HII model, the model needs to work within the complex set

Figure 7. Model of human-information interaction. This model of HII is developed throughout this book. It extends the models just discussed by including a strong focus on information salience and information relationships to allow the person to build their contextual awareness.

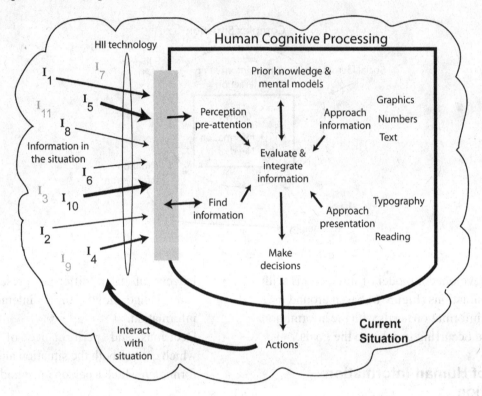

of information and situations to enable the design team to understand a audience group's goals, information needs, how they interact with the information to achieve those goals, and how the information needs and interactions vary between audiences. Basic design ideas can be tested with the model, exposing problems early before they enter the actual design.

Any model must live with its limitations, caused by the simplifications which went into making the model. These arise both from unknown information, which can be incorporated as it is understood, and known but overly complex information which must be simplified to make the model manageable. Of course, it's the limitations and simplifications which went into the model which also make it useful. A model with no limitations is essentially a duplicate of the real situation

and would be as difficult to fully grasp. Instead, through proper choice of limitations, the model can focus on the areas of interest without being overwhelmed by other areas and provide design support that is adequate for good design decisions.

The design team needs to make informed trade-off of what to simplify and how much to simplify what they put into the HII model. Too much and the model fails to help them understand the entire design problem and too much and the model collapses under its own complexity. In the end, every model has limitations on its prediction ability. A design teams goals must be to build a model with the major limitations occurring outside of the area of interest.

Information in the World

The relevant information about a situation exists in the world. As part of comprehending a situation, people have to take in the relevant information. Thus, the first part of comprehending a situation is identifying which information exists and which is relevant. Unfortunately, the relevant information is mixed with lots of irrelevant information which makes it difficult for people to extract the relevant information.

The information comes in many forms: structured, unstructured, people. The information in databases is structured and is the easiest for a computer system to work with. Unstructured information exists in text documents where it cannot be easily extracted and manipulated by a computer, but is easy for a human as long as they can find it. Finally, there is information which exists in people's heads; the type of information they knows but has never been written down.

People often have a difficult time sifting out the relevant from irrelevant information. Low signal to noise ratio (Albers, 2004b) makes it hard to distinguish and mentally rank the appropriate information. People are very good at pulling information out of a noisy environment if they know what information they need, but had difficulty if they do not know what they need or if the information even exists. Factors contributing to a low signal to noise ratio include:

- Lots of information exists online (especially in corporate intranets) which was placed there 'because someone might want it.' The result is lots of information of minimal relevance to anything. The trend has been to make more knowledge, such as best practices, success stories, policy books and training manuals available online. However, successfully using that information also means people must have access to the relevant knowledge in the context in which they need it. "Contextualized access means access to relevant task knowledge is immediate and within the problem-solving context rather than via searching in a separate context. Thus, there is no need to break the continuity of task performance to seek relevant domain knowledge" (Mao, & Benbasat, 2001, p. 788).

- Graphics tend to out-compete text for people's attention. The eye is naturally drawn to the graphical images and they tend to be remembered better. Of course, that does not mean they are more important.

- Many computer systems present lots of easy to obtain/display information which hides the much smaller amount of important or hard to display information.

- Poor design can give high salience to irrelevant information or give all information the same salience, which forces people to work harder identifying what they need. In Figure 7, the weight of the arrows represents the information's salience.

High quality design for HII starts with knowing what information, both good and bad, will be in the situation's information space and requires maximizing information salience and relevant information changes.

Initial or First Glance Evaluation

Figure 7 shows a gray box through which the information moves from the world to the person. It represents the first glance evaluation which acts as a gate keeping function for the movement of information so a person can process it. The gate keeping includes both the filtering which occurs via the system and via a person's perception and explicit information interaction.

Any situation contains too much information to process at once and most of that information is irrelevant. Unfortunately, people often cannot easily see that they either have too much or irrelevant information. Instead, they try to process all of it. The gate keeping controls the flow so only the relevant information for the current stage is processed. Processing too much information at once leads to cognitive overload and processing information in the wrong order/time impairs comprehension and interpretation. In both cases, decision making ability is seriously compromised.

The system has the first level of information filtering. This occurs when design teams decide what information exists in the system. The HCI provided by the system provides another level of filtering by controlling how the information gets displayed and how people can interact with it. For example, poor navigation or poor information architecture may require too much effort to make finding the information worthwhile. Within this model, HCI implementation details such as whether to use buttons, pull down menu, etc., which must be worked out later in development, can be ignored.

A second level of filtering occurs as the person reads the information. People are constantly bombarded with information all day; thus, they are very good at ignoring information. When looking at information, they only tend to see information which they feel is relevant. Other information is disregarded and never mentally processed. Obviously, all of the available information can be classified as relevant or irrelevant; poor designs lead to misclassifying information and letting improper information through the gates.

Prior Knowledge and Mental Models

People bring to a situation both a set of prior knowledge and a set of mental models for how the situation's information should be interpreted.

The prior knowledge is their current understanding of the situation (which may be minimal or incorrect). The prior knowledge has a profound effect on how new information gets interpreted, since it gets interpreted with respect to the prior knowledge and not as stand-alone information.

The mental models (Johnson-Laird, 1983) are dynamic models constructed from previous interactions with similar situations. It contains a stereotypical set of relationships and information needs for understanding the situation.

Constructing a situation model, which is an instantiated mental model, is a major element of understanding a situation. The situation model has shifted from the mental model's stereotypical description to one that contains the actual values and concepts for the current situation. One limitation of the situation model is that is built from a mental model. Misconceptions in the mental model are reflected in the situation model.

Making Sense of the Information

People search for information to meet specific needs which they think will enable them to meet their situational goals (Slone, 2002). They read, interact with, and interpret information as part of comprehending it and relating it to their current information needs.

As they develop a well-formed mental model of the information and its relationships and begin to comprehend the topic, they shift from needing general information to specific points to fill in gaps which exist in their mental model.

Availability of information alone is not sufficient for people to comprehend it; contextualized accessibility is the key for effective dissemination, proper comprehension, and subsequent performance enhancement (Albers, 2004a; Mirel, 1998; Mao & Benbasat, 2001). Information must be viewed in the proper context, information isolated from other relevant information leads to limited or distorted understanding (Ahn et al., 2005). Putting the found information in context is crucial for fully comprehending the information. A substantial part of developing an understanding of the information in a situation is to build the relationships between that information. Connecting the information to the situation exists more in the relationships than it does in the information itself (Albers, 2009).

Approach Information

Different groups of people or the same person at different time approach information differently. Depending on people's goals and information needs, information interaction and interpretation can differ. What they want and how they expect to acquire information differs. Understanding what information is desired and audience expectations are essential to meeting their information needs and communication goals. These differing goals and information needs means what information is important and how hard people work to understand it can differ radically between people. In any particular situation, even after the information has been found and is being considered, there are many factors inherent in human nature which comes into play.

Approach Presentation

The presentation of information becomes the crucial factor in maintaining the flow of information (Laplante & Flaxman, 1995). Norman (2002) and other researchers (such as Wilson & Rutherford, 1989) make the observation that for a computer user, their view of the display essentially constitutes the entire process. The presentation contains more than just the information; it exerts a strong influence on people's response to that information as they to gain an understanding of the situation (Robertson, Card, & Mackinlay, 1993). Thus, no matter how or why people interact with and reads information content, the quality of both the presentation strongly effects their satisfaction and performance (Mirani & King, 1994).

Decisions

After people understand a situation and have developed the information relationships, they are in a position to make informed decisions. Without good understanding, decisions tend to be reactions to current events without an understanding of how it will affect other parts of the situation or the situation's future.

Decisions lead to actions which change the information in the situation. This leads to a cyclic interaction with people having to comprehend the changed information and modify the relationships based on the changes so they can potentially engage in more decision-making/actions.

Good HII helps to both lead people to making decisions and to monitor the changes in the situation as a result of the actions following from the decisions.

REFERENCES

Ahn, H., Lee, H., Cho, K., & Park, S. (2005). Utilizing knowledge context in virtual collaborative work. *Decision Support Systems, 39*, 563–582. doi:10.1016/j.dss.2004.03.005

Albers, M. (2000). Information design for web sites which support complex decision making. *Proceedings of the STC 2000 Annual Conference*, Orlando FL. May 21–24, 2000.

Albers, M. (2003). Complex problem solving and content analysis. In Albers, M., & Mazur, B. (Eds.), *Content and complexity: Information design in software development and documentation* (pp. 263–284). Mahwah, NJ: Erlbaum.

Albers, M. (2004a). *Communication of complex information: User goals and information needs for dynamic Web information.* Mahwah, NJ: Erlbaum.

Albers, M. (2004b). Signal to noise ratio of information in documentation. *Proceedings of 22nd Annual International Conference on Computer Documentation* (pp. 41–44). New York, NY: ACM.

Albers, M. (2008). Human-information interaction. *Proceedings of 28th Annual International Conference on Computer Documentation* (pp. 117–124). New York, NY: ACM

Albers, M. (2009). Information relationships: The source of useful and usable content. *Proceedings of 29ᵗʰ Annual International Conference on Computer Documentation.* (pp. 171–178). New York, NY: ACM.

Albers, M. (2010). Design and usability: Beginner interactions with complex software. *Journal of Technical Writing and Communication.*, *41*(3), 273–289.

Albers, M., & Still, S. (2010). *Usability of complex Information Systems: Evaluation of user interaction.* Boca Raton, FL: CRC Press. doi:10.1201/EBK1439828946

Allen, B. (1996). *Information tasks: Toward a user-centered approach to Information Systems.* San Diego, CA: Academic Press.

Ash, J., Berg, M., & Coiera, E. (2004). Some unintended consequences of Information Technology in health care: The nature of patient care information system-related errors. *Journal of the American Medical Informatics Association*, *11*(2), 104–112. doi:10.1197/jamia.M1471

Bazerman, C. (2001). Nuclear information: One rhetorical moment in the construction of the information age. *Written Communication*, *18*(3), 259–295. doi:10.1177/0741088301018003002

Carliner, S. (2000). A three-part framework for information design. *Technical Communication*, *49*, 561–576.

De Angeli, A., Matera, M., Costabile, M., Garzotto, F., & Paolini, P. (2003). On the advantages of a systematic inspection for evaluating hypermedia usability. *International Journal of Human-Computer Interaction*, *15*(3), 315–335. doi:10.1207/S15327590IJHC1503_01

Diaper, D., & Sanger, C. (2006). Tasks for and tasks in human-computer interaction. *Interacting with Computers*, *18*, 117–138. doi:10.1016/j.intcom.2005.06.004

Fallowfield, L. (2001). Participation of patients in decisions about treatment for cancer. *British Medical Journal*, *323*, 1144. doi:10.1136/bmj.323.7322.1144

Gribbons, W. (1991). Visual literacy in corporate communication: Some implications for information design. *IEEE Transactions on Professional Communication*, *34*(1), 42–50. doi:10.1109/47.68427

Gulliksen, J., & Lantz, A. (2003). Design versus design—From the shaping of product to the creation of user experience. *International Journal of Human-Computer Interaction*, *15*(1), 5–20. doi:10.1207/S15327590IJHC1501_02

Hackos, J., & Redish, J. (1998). *User and task analysis for interface design.* New York, NY: Wiley.

Hegland, F. (2006). *Welcome page.* Retrieved June 12, 2006, from http://www.liquidinformation.org/index-fr.html

Herndl, C., Fennell, B., & Miller, C. (1991). Understanding failures in organizational discourse: The accident at Three Mile Island and the shuttle Challenger disaster. In Bazerman, C., & Paradis, J. (Eds.), *Textual dynamics of the profession* (pp. 279–305). Madison, WI: University of Wisconsin.

Hochhauser, M. (1998). Writing for staff, employees, patients, and family members. *Hospital Topics*, *76*(1), 5–12. doi:10.1080/00185869809596484

Hughes, M. (2002). Moving from information transfer to knowledge creation: A new value proposition for technical communicators. *Technical Communication*, *49*(3), 275–285.

Jaspers, M., Steen, T., Bos, C., & Geenen, M. (2004). The think aloud method: A guide to user interface design. *International Journal of Medical Informatics*, *73*, 781–795. doi:10.1016/j.ijmedinf.2004.08.003

Johnson-Laird, P. (1983). *Mental models*. Cambridge, UK: Cambridge UP.

Korzenko, J., Robins, D., & Holmes, J. (2008). *What are your users REALLY thinking? An objective way to uncover the subjective*. Presentation at IA Summit 2008.

Laplante, P., & Flaxman, H. (1995). The convergence of technology and creativity in the corporate environment. *IEEE Transactions on Professional Communication, 38*(1), 20–23. doi:10.1109/47.372389

Malhotra, Y., & Galletta, D. (2004). Building systems that users want to use. *Communications of the ACM, 47*(12), 89–94. doi:10.1145/1035134.1035139

Mao, J., & Benbasat, I. (2001). The effects of contextualized access to knowledge on judgment. *International Journal of Human-Computer Studies, 55*, 787–814. doi:10.1006/ijhc.2001.0507

Marchionini, G. (2008). Human–information interaction research and development. *Library & Information Science Research, 30*, 165–174. doi:10.1016/j.lisr.2008.07.001

McGovern, G. (2005). *Why it matters to focus on your reader*. Retrieved from http://www.gerrymcgovern.com/nt/2005/nt_2005_06_06_reader.htm

Medin, D., Lynch, E., & Solomon, K. (2000). Are there kinds of concepts? *Annual Review of Psychology, 51*, 121–147. doi:10.1146/annurev.psych.51.1.121

Miller, J. (1960). Information input overload and psychopathology. *The American Journal of Psychiatry, 116*, 695–704.

Mirani, R., & King, W. (1994). Impacts of end-user and information center characteristics on end-user computing support. *Journal of Management Information Systems, 11*(1), 141–160.

Mirel, B. (1998). Applied constructivism for user documentation. *Journal of Business and Technical Communication, 12*(1), 7–49. doi:10.1177/1050651998012001002

Mirel, B. (2002). Advancing a vision of usability. In Mirel, B., & Spilka, R. (Eds.), *Reshaping technical communication* (pp. 165–188). Mahwah, NJ: Erlbaum.

Mirel, B. (2003). *Interaction design for complex problem solving: Developing useful and usable software*. San Francisco, CA: Morgan Kaufmann.

Monk, A. (1999). Modeling cyclic interaction. *Behaviour & Information Technology, 18*(2), 127–139. doi:10.1080/014492999119165

Moore, P. (1995). Information problem solving: A wider view of library skills. *Contemporary Educational Psychology, 20*, 1–31. doi:10.1006/ceps.1995.1001

Morrison, J., Pirolli, P., & Card, S. (2001). *A taxonomic analysis of what World Wide Web activities significantly impact people's decisions and actions*. Presented at the Association for Computing Machinery's Conference on Human Factors in Computing Systems, Seattle, March 31–April 5, 2001.

Nickerson, R., & Landauer, T. (1997). Human-computer interaction: Background and issues. In Helander, M., & Landauer, T. K. (Eds.), *Handbook of human-computer interaction* (2nd ed., pp. 3–32). Amsterdam, The Netherlands: Elsevier Science B.V.

Nielsen, J. (2001). *The 3Cs of critical Web use: Collect, compare, choose*. Retrieved December 3, 2008, from http://www.useit.com/alertbox/20010415.html

Nisbet, M., Scheufele, D., Shanahan, J., Moy, P., Brossard, K., & Lewenstein, B. (2002). Knowledge, reservations, or promise? *Communication Research, 29*(5), 584–608. doi:10.1177/009365002236196

Norman, D. (2002). *The design of everyday things*. New York, NY: Basic Books.

Payne, S. (2002). Balancing information needs: Dilemmas in producing patient information leaflets. *Health Informatics Journal, 8*, 174–179. doi:10.1177/146045820200800402

Proctor, R. (2002). Content preparation and management for web design: Eliciting, structuring, searching, and displaying information. *International Journal of Human-Computer Interaction, 14*(1), 25–92. doi:10.1207/S153275901-JHC1401_2

Redish, J. (2007). Expanding usability testing to evaluate complex systems. *Journal of Usability Studies, 2*(3), 102–111.

Robertson, G., Card, S., & Mackinlay, J. (1993). Information visualization: Using 3D interactive animation. *Communications of the ACM, 36*(4), 57–71. doi:10.1145/255950.153577

Rowan, K. (1991). When simple language fails: Presenting difficult science to the public. *Journal of Technical Writing and Communication, 21*, 369–382. doi:10.2190/D3BD-32RC-FGW0-C5JB

Santa Clara Grand Jury. (2005). *Problems implementing the San Jose police computer aided dispatch system*. Retrieved June 12, 2006, from http://www.sccsuperiorcourt.org/jury/GJreports/2005/SJPoliceComputerAidedDispatch.pdf

Scholtz, J. (2006). Metrics for evaluating human information interaction systems. *Interacting with Computers, 18*, 507–527. doi:10.1016/j.intcom.2005.10.004

Selker, T. (2005). Fostering motivation and creativity for computer users. *International Journal of Human-Computer Studies, 63*, 410–421. doi:10.1016/j.ijhcs.2005.04.005

Shannon, C. (1948). A mathematical theory of communication. *The Bell System Technical Journal, 27*, 379–423.

Shneiderman, B. (2000). Universal usability. *Communications of the ACM, 43*(5), 85–91. doi:10.1145/332833.332843

Slone, D. (2002). The Influence of mental models and goals on user search patterns during Web interaction. *Journal of the American Society for Information Science and Technology, 53*(13), 1152–1169. doi:10.1002/asi.10141

Stary, C. (1999). Toward the task-complete development of activity-oriented user interfaces. *International Journal of Human-Computer Interaction, 11*(2), 153–182. doi:10.1207/S153275901102_5

Suchman, L. (1987). *Plans and situated actions: The problem of human-machine communication*. Cambridge, UK: Cambridge.

Swarts, J. (2004). Textual grounding: How people turn texts into tools. *Journal of Technical Writing and Communication, 34*(1 & 2), 67–89. doi:10.2190/EG0C-QUEY-F9FK-2V0D

Tomasi, J., & Menlenbacker, B. (1999). Re-engineering online documentation: Designing example-based online support systems. *Technical Communication, 46*(1), 55–66.

Toms, E. (2002). Information interaction: Providing a framework for information architecture. *Journal of The American Society for Information Science and Technology, 53.1*. 855–862.

Tufte, E. (1997). *Visual explanations: Images and quantities, evidence and narrative*. Cheshire, CT: Graphics Press.

Vanderbeeken, M. (2009). Taking a broader view of the human experience. *Interaction*, (March/April): 54–57. doi:10.1145/1487632.1487645

Whitworth, B., & Moor, A. (2003). Legitimate by design: Towards trusted socio-technical systems. *Behaviour & Information Technology*, *22*(1), 31–51. doi:10.1080/01449290301783

Wilson, J., & Rutherford, A. (1989). Mental models: Theory and application in human factors. *Human Factors*, *31*, 617–634.

Woods, D., Patterson, E., & Roth, E. (2002). Can we ever escape from data overload? A cognitive systems diagnosis. *Cognition Technology and Work*, *4*, 22–36. doi:10.1007/s101110200002

Woods, D., & Roth, E. (1988). Cognitive engineering: Human problem solving with tools. *Human Factors*, *30*(4), 415–430.

ADDITIONAL READING

Mirel, B. (2003b). *Interaction design for complex problem solving: Developing useful and usable software*. San Francisco, CA: Morgan Kaufmann.

Norman, D. (2002). *The design of everyday things*. New York, NY: Basic Books.

Redish, J. (2007). Expanding usability testing to evaluate complex systems. *Journal of Usability Studies*, *2*(3), 102–111.

Woods, D., Patterson, E., & Roth, E. (2002). Can we ever escape from data overload? A cognitive systems diagnosis. *Cognition Technology and Work*, *4*, 22–36. doi:10.1007/s101110200002

Woods, D., & Roth, E. (1988). Cognitive engineering: Human problem solving with tools. *Human Factors*, *30*(4), 415–430.

Section 1
People and Interactions of Situation and Information

Chapter 2
Information in the Situation

ABSTRACT

Although in an ideal form the information in the world would not involve people, in reality, it has no meaning without people observing and interacting with it. There is a widespread myth (a positivistic view) that information is something in the world that does not depend on people's point of view and that it is independent of the situation in which it occurs. But information never has fixed significance. The available data is simply the raw material that must be processed. Any particular information element gains significance only from its relationship to other information in the context in which it occurs (Woods, Patterson, & Roth, 2002). However, this chapter tries to minimize those interaction and interpretation aspects, deferring those for the later parts of the book. Instead, it concentrates on the issues of the information in the situation before it gets mentally processed.

BACKGROUND

Communication is rhetorical and "nothing can be taken out of its rhetorical context and that items in that context must work in harmony to achieve purpose" —Gribbons & Elsar, 1998, p. 471

This part of the book considers the information as it exists in the world. It presents a high-level view of the information within a situation and how it moves toward the people who need it. The white area in Figure 1 shows the area of the HII model relevant to this chapter. In any particular situation, some information is relevant (with arrows) and some is not (with no arrows). Of the relevant information, some is more salient (line weight). The design goal is to ensure that the reader receives only relevant information and to ensure that the most relevant is the most salient. In many failed designs, this simple concept fails to hold true.

DOI: 10.4018/978-1-4666-0152-9.ch002

Figure 1. Information in the world

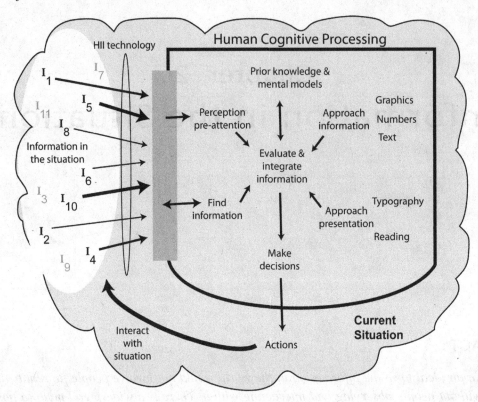

This chapter looks at:

Sources of information: People can obtain information from a variety of sources: books, brochures/leaflets, reports, technical manuals, the Internet, etc. With complex technical information, the kind of information which requires a high level of HII, there needs to be a high level of integration done by design teams. In these situations, large amounts of information are available and it must not cognitively overload them.

Information content: Content involves, besides the text itself, the type and scope of the information included in a system.

Information context: The context of the situation's information depends on both people's goals and information needs. People need access to relevant task information that is immediately

understandable and is properly positioned within the situation.

Incomplete, ambiguous or conflicting information: An underlying assumption of many design teams is that they will be supplying people with all of the information they need. However, this is rarely true. A major problem is that people cannot tell if the information is complete, incomplete, ambiguous, conflicting, or irrelevant. Yet, people try to work with this information and integrate it into their understanding of the situation.

INTRODUCTION

There exists a wide range of different definitions of information, with many authors presenting various overlapping views. In a survey of different definitions, Buckland (1991) found they fell into

Figure 2. Transformation of data to information to knowledge. The raw data needs to be placed into context so it can become useful information. The person then mentally integrates it with other information to form knowledge.

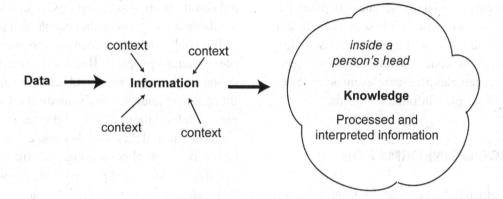

three groups, with Marchionini (2008) updating the list by adding a fourth.

- Information as process. The situational-based process of informing people about a set of facts or data. Whether or not something is information depends on the specific circumstances surrounding it and making the information relevant or irrelevant to the situation.
- Information as knowledge in the head. Personal and subjective evaluation of what people know or feel. This would be a combination of both new data and prior knowledge. How the information gets into the head tends to be glossed over.
- Information as thing. The information content in a text or other source which could be given to someone. In this view, a book, brochure, or hard drive could be considered information. This view sees information as a stand-alone object that exists independent of any reader.
- Information as temporal states in cyberspace (Marchionini's update). Information in this sense moves beyond being readable and includes the interactions and manipulations people can perform on it. Thus,

rather than just reading it, people can annotate or link it, or in other ways work to extend the information content provided by the original author.

In a related vein, there are the issues of defining and distinguishing information from data or knowledge (Figure 2).

- **Data.** Raw facts and figures in the environment without context. In general, facts and figures are meaningless unless they are applied to a specific situation.
- **Information.** Data in context. In addition to the data, information contains the relationships which connect it to the situation.
- **Knowledge.** Processed and interpreted information in the head. Very similar to Buckland's second form, it forms the basis on which people make decisions. As part of comprehending and interpreting information in a situation, people transform it into knowledge.

By these definitions, information existing in a situation consists of a mix of data and information. It can't become knowledge until after people mentally process it. The difference between data and information lies in how people see that particular piece of content. If it is seen as relevant to the situation, data becomes information or at least has the potential to combine with other data to become information; if it is seen as irrelevant, it remains just data and a potential distraction. Problems with understanding situations occur when what gets classified as relevant or irrelevant doesn't fit people's information needs.

SOURCE OF INFORMATION

People can obtain information from a variety of sources: books, brochures/leaflets, reports, technical manuals, the Internet, etc. For general communication, the list would expand to include newspapers, magazines, and such, but for complex technical information these don't tend to play a major part. In some cases, such as with a corporate report, the report context contains all of the available information, unless the reader wants to redo the report research. In other cases, there are a limited number of easy sources, such as when a physician gives a patient several brochures about a disease. However, patients could do further research on their own. In most other situations, people have to sort through potential sources and decide which ones they will use based on their experience.

With the rise of the web, there has been a shift toward putting all support information online. The logic is that people will never lose or lack access to the manual, can always access the information, and the information can be kept up to date. Many design teams work from the assumption that their content is the primary source of information. However, people tend first to look to other people before using any specific information source. Research into use of software manuals finds that asking people, and trial and error, come before looking for an answer either online or in printed manuals. This pushes the "official" information down the list and leads to potential conflicts, or to inaccurate information entering into people's understanding of the situation.

Although the information may be always available on the web, simply having the information available does not mean that people will process it. In a study which looked at the comprehension of information people had been given about medication, major gaps were found between what they thought they knew about the medication and the correct information. People had been given the information, and they said they had either read it or received verbal counseling, but still they did not clearly understand it (Kerzman, Baron-Spel, & Toren, 2005). This study didn't go into detail on what information the people were missing, but there is the chance it didn't fit their needs. To be useful and relevant, an information source needs to fit people's perceived needs. For example, the medical community is trying to give patients access to their medical records on the assumption that it will improve compliance and quality of care. Windleman, Leonard, and Rossos (2005) found that simply having access was of little value—most non-medical people can't understand it. Instead, people need their medical information integrated into their current healthcare support infrastructure.

In reality, for technical information, availability options are often rather limited. A corporation might produce only a single report. However, any time multiple sources are used there can be problems with conflicting information or extensive overlap. Some of the issues with multiple sources are:

- People assess the value of the information based on quantity rather than quality (Shenton & Dixon, 2004a). Websites with more content or larger books/reports are considered a better source. Quality is a difficult factor to measure unless people understand the topic well enough that they don't really need the information. Thus, most people substitute quantity for quality.

- People don't necessarily prefer the information source that gives them the easiest path to finding information (Hertzum & Frøkjaer, 1996). People may prefer a document based on factors such as better graphics or font choices, which may make a text look more inviting, but actually slows down search times or contains less relevant information.
- Sources can contain conflicting information. A later section of this chapter considers how people handle conflicts between information elements.
- People who are familiar with the contents of a document or website will tend to use it rather than using other sources, even when they admit the other source would be more appropriate.
- There can be "(re-occurring) hidden assumptions that cause a variety of problems that somehow seem random, but which actually are strongly connected to each other" (Müller, 2007. p. 110). People ignore the usual and focus on the unusual. If the cause of the problem is a slight change in the usual, then it might go unnoticed unless specifically pointed out.

With complex technical information, the kind of information which requires a high level of HII, there needs to be a high level of integration done by design teams. In these situations, large amounts of information are available and it must not cognitively overload people. Consider the fundamental difference between a small set of documents designed by one person and a large set designed by several writers working over many months or years. In the large document set, important concepts will often occur in multiple places in different forms since the documents were designed and written by different people. This is a major problem which must be overcome with proper integration, which requires intensive communication within design teams. In this example, all of the information was more or less controlled from a single point. In many situations, design teams only have control of a subset of the information available as different groups or departments supply content. The idea of using crowd outsourcing to build up a technical support database is one example in which control of a significant portion of the information has been given up.

Static vs. Dynamic vs. Real Time Information

People can receive three different types of information:

Static: The information does not change, or changes over a time period which is longer than the situation. Term definitions or operational procedures are two examples. The procedure may change in a few months, but it can be considered fixed for any specific situation. Books and brochures are also examples of static information, but the information they contain may be out-of-date. Websites claim to be easily updatable, but they too often are static with respect to any specific situation and can also contain out-of-date information. Unfortunately, most people reading them will not know parts are out-of-date.

Dynamic: The information can change on time scales short enough to influence how people interact with the situation. This may be an adaptation by the system to minimize redundant or repeated information which people already know, or may reflect status changes within the situation.

Real time: The information updates as the situation itself changes. Examples of real-time information are a stock market ticker or a car speedometer. The interface can display the current stock values with updates happening every few seconds. Other real-time displays are control systems which update at fixed intervals to allow an operator to monitor the system and respond to any changes. Human factor researchers and designers are very interested in real-time information in areas such as airplane cockpit design and plant control rooms. On the other hand, real-time information is typically not a major factor in many informational systems since the situations do not change on short time scales. Real-time and dynamic information differ in that dynamic may involve time delays in reflecting the situation, or there may be changes in the information presentation without significant changes to the content itself.

The use of dynamic and real-time information is increasing as the ability to provide it via web-based interfaces improves. An entire research area of adaptive hypertext is working at producing better methods of providing dynamic information to fit people's needs.

INFORMATION CONTENT

Content involves, besides the text itself, the type and scope of the information included in a system (Kim & Lee, 2002). "When designing a system it is important to know what users should be able to achieve using the system" (Van Schaik, 1999, p. 455). Although an obvious-sounding quote, it sums up an issue with many systems and their associated documentation, a problem which has grown worse with movement of information onto the web—information dumping, namely, dumping all available information and letting the reader sort it out. What the "users should be able to achieve" was not part of the design. Rather than conforming to people's goals, the information content provides raw data and stops, leaving it up the reader to select the appropriate data, decide out how it is relevant, and figure out how to apply it to the current situation. A data dump approach ignores the issues of type and scope of information and arranging it for effective interpretation. Tufte (1983) was

referring to essentially the same concept when he discussed data/ink ratio and chart junk.

It is very difficult to mentally transform a collection of data, and this transformation carries a high cognitive workload. As a result, people often shed the workload and don't do the transformation (Herbig & Kramer, 1992; Webster & Kruglanski, 1994). Rather than devising ways to efficiently handle the cognitive load, people often simply reduce cognitive load by dumping parts of the problem and reverting to previously learned conventions (cognitive load is discussed further in chapter 3: *What people bring with them*). Rather than working to understand information, people reduce their cognitive effort and ignore information because it isn't understood. Such is human nature: no design can change it, but must acknowledge it (Bettman, Johnson, and Payne, 1990; Wickens, 1992).

The huge number of documents on corporate intranets which were placed there "in case someone wants to read it" is one example of dumping information. McGovern (2006c) describes an intranet where 60,000 of 100,000 pages were deleted and no one noticed. Creating pages that no one looks at wastes both the design team's time and system resources, but as long as no one looks at them, they do not interfere with interpreting relevant information. Happily, writers who subscribe to data dumping are becoming fewer. However, many non-designers and non-writers still work from this view, which is but another variation on McGovern's comments about the large amount of useless stuff on corporate intranets.

The first step in any effective design, although one which is too often short-changed or skipped, is to clearly define who the audience is, what they should be able to accomplish, what information is needed, and the information relations that must be understood to accomplish people's goals. Defining the audience and what should be accomplished is relatively easy, compared to understanding the information needs and relationships, but high-

Figure 3. Mentally integrating information content. The situation contains a large collection different pieces of information. Gaining an understanding requires assembling them into a coherent picture. With the image assembled properly, the person has developed a good understanding. When the image is assembled incorrectly, although the person thinks he understands the situation, serious misunderstandings exist.

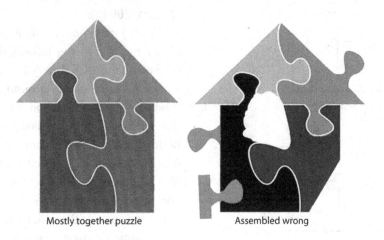

Mostly together puzzle   Assembled wrong

quality content must be designed with those two points forming a foundation (Albers, 2010).

Mentally, handling and integrating information content can be viewed as a jigsaw puzzle with each of the information elements being a piece of the puzzle (Figure 3). People develop an understanding of a situation in the same way they solve a puzzle. Matching pieces are found and attached. If they happen to fit into a place in the puzzle that is not yet assembled, then two or three connected pieces can be placed aside and inserted later.

Unfortunately, design teams often take an overly simplistic view of this information assembly as a puzzle.

- People have trouble putting together pieces and dealing with them later. Information must fit into the main puzzle.
- The information itself is often not static, which equates to solving a puzzle in which the pieces keep changing shape.
- Since connecting information tends to adjust the information needs, connecting

two pieces would change the other sides (Figure 4).

- The available information is more than required, similar to trying to solve a jigsaw puzzle with multiple puzzles mixed together.
- The available information may not be complete. The final puzzle will have holes in it.

Just like the dynamic jigsaw puzzle, real-world work is complex and is based on a collection of different systems that interact in complex ways—ways so complex that almost nobody understands the entire system (Beyer & Holtzblatt, 1998). Part of design teams' jobs are to ensure that the relevant information has proper salience and to minimize the movement of irrelevant information toward the people using the system.

Ignoring Relevant Content

People are given too much information all day long and the majority gets ignored, thus tend to ignore what they don't understand or don't know to be relevant. The alarm which constantly gives

Figure 4. Working a dynamic jigsaw puzzle. The pieces are not static; instead they change both over time and upon being fitted together (based on Albers, 2004a p. 3).

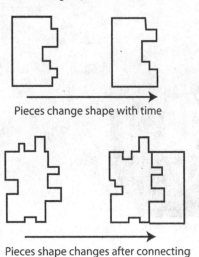

Pieces change shape with time

Pieces shape changes after connecting

false alarms gets ignored. The fine print in a contract gets ignored when people lack the legal knowledge to decipher it, even when they admit it probably contains important information. A problem indicator which doesn't fit into the current situational understanding gets ignored until people shift mental models, and then it becomes relevant and vital to explaining the real problem.

On the other hand, people can pull information from a very noisy source if they know what they want and are familiar with the information they seek. One example is a business analyst laboriously extracting bits and pieces of data from multiple reports into a spreadsheet to gain understanding of a serious production problem. Or when people listen to a song on a car radio with the window down; the words are clear only when they know the song. Mentally separating signal from noise requires an expert's viewpoint, someone who can differentiate the signal and noise of each individual piece. People with lower knowledge levels can't perform that task because although they can see what's in the reports, they lack the prior knowledge to make build the relationships

between the separate pieces. And most people using a system are not experts, so design teams must provide support for identifying relevant content and developing a clear view of a situation (Albers, 2004b).

In an interesting twist, people often fail to notice the usual—the information that a model of the situation is expected to present. There is so much "usual noise" around that people filter it out so they can focus on the unusual information (Müller, 2007), an issue related to change blindness, discussed in chapter 3: *What people bring with them.* Unfortunately, this filtering tends also to ignore new information if it is too closely combined with any expected information. If it appears as part of the usual, information will not be examined closely enough for differences to be noted. Consider in the early days of the web, major websites changed the background color of their website. People had a very rapid and vocal negative response to the color change and forced them to go back to the old color. However, they then started changing the color very slowly over a couple of month period and no one noticed. The usual/expected color of the site didn't noticeably change day to day, so people filtered out the change since it was the color they expected.

HII and Dynamic Information

Creating true dynamic documentation that updates in real time or adjusts for people's browsing habits or current information needs has been researched for several years and is the subject of major conferences, normally under the term *adaptive hypertext*. Dynamic information provides a clean way of providing answers to focused information. It deals with topics and information needs which can be defined beforehand as relevant to people, although the *actual* information content needed or presented will be dynamically changed. It deals with communicating integrated information to people rather than forcing them to build up the information set themselves from multiple sources. It breaks with the "one size fits all" model of information presentation and provides each person with a customized presentation of information they need.

With print documents, information is static. Once the document gets printed, it cannot change without physically replaced pages. One of the advantages of the web is that information can change, although many websites still contain essentially static information. Providing navigation via links rather than a turned page is not true interactivity. Instead, once a web page is developed, the information remains static until at some future time, someone rewrites the text. Having the ability to easily update information does not mean it will happen and is not equivalent to having dynamic information.

HII would benefit from dynamic information because the information remains relevant to people's needs, which change over time. For instance, Stoop, van't Riet, and Berg (2004) discuss medical information and how different patients present different information needs, and how the needs of a particular patient vary over time. As more is learned about a situation, more specific information is called for. In addition, information within the situation is rarely static, even as people interact with it; and it may actively undergo change at the hands of multiple people. In a collaborative environment, people need to know how changes made by other people are rippling through the situation (Johnson, May, & Johnson, 2003). Or, in the long term, as people gain general knowledge, they want information presented in a way that assumes they possess the needed background knowledge. Maximizing comprehension depends on presenting the information at the proper level (McNamara, 2001; McNamara & Kintsch, 1996).

Communicating information and supporting interaction with it requires dynamic interaction. As people gain a deeper understanding of the situation or the situation evolves, their information needs change, and thus the information they receive should change. Dynamic and adaptive

information can be restructured and presented differently for each person viewing it. The most relevant information fitting the current situation has changed, so the most salient information also changes. Dynamic information focuses on changing the content and/or presentation to fit current needs. It filters out details which are irrelevant (outside current interest) or fits the content to people's understanding (adjusting explanatory information based on people's knowledge level of the topic or situation). This definition of dynamic information goes well beyond simple template-based single sourcing, or single sourcing with conditionals for paper or online help. Rather, it works to fulfill the information needs for the situation based on experience and knowledge level.

Dynamic information does present the complication that people have trouble adjusting to displays that look different each time they view it. The use of dynamic menus in software caused confusion as the order of the items changed based on use. Although adaptation put the most-used items at the top, people had trouble because, from experience, they expected that menu item to be three-quarters of the way down from the top, not moving around. This complication with dynamic information comes from people's mental image of what a page (or menu, etc.) should look like, so they tend to get confused when the page looks different. This can be especially problematic when people are refinding information since they may remember its general location (e.g., it was right under the picture of big plane), but with the adaptive change, the information has moved.

INFORMATION CONTEXT

The context of the situation's information depends on people's goals and on their information needs. The trend has been to make more knowledge available online, such as best practices, success stories, policy books, and training manuals. However, successfully using that information also means people must have access to the relevant knowledge in the context in which they need it. "Contextualized access means access to relevant task knowledge is immediate and within the problem-solving context rather than via searching in a separate context. Thus, there is no need to break the continuity of task performance to seek relevant domain knowledge" (Mao & Benbasat, 2001, p. 788). Most situations contain an overabundance of information; that overabundance needs to be cut down based on context, formatted for proper salience, and presented so that it supports people's information needs.

In complex situations, information context often becomes more important than content since people seek information when they realize their knowledge about a situation is incomplete and they believe the information they need can be found within the system. The content represents information provided by the system. However, having content is not sufficient to support HII. The content must be placed within people's situational context in order to be usable. People search for information to meet specific needs which they think will enable them to meet their situational goals (Slone, 2002). Putting the found information in context is crucial for fully comprehending the information. Without being viewed in the proper context, information can be isolated from other relevant information, which limits or distorts understanding (Ahn et al., 2005). Taken together, these propositions support the view that availability of information alone is not sufficient; contextualized accessibility is key to effective dissemination, proper comprehension, and subsequent performance enhancement (Albers, 2004; Mirel, 1998; Mao & Benbasat, 2001).

A fundamental concept of putting information into context is defining people's goals and understanding of how they form connections between a situation and applicable information (Kammersgaard, 1988). This issue will be examined in greater detail in "Information Relationships." More than the technical or content requirements

Box 1.

> **Information integration in reports**
> Many student literature reviews suffer from "dumping found information" problem. The student doesn't sufficiently understand the topic to pick closely related articles, but finds articles that cover a much broader view of the topic. As a result, they tend to address each article individually since they don't fit together well. Of course, this is part of the student's learning process.
>
> Many business reports suffer from the same issues. The report writers gather a bunch of information, dump it together without clearly integrating it, and expect the reader to make sense of it. A reason why some reports are accepted and acted upon which others are rejected often comes down to the integration of the information and situational context. The less the mental effort the reader has to exert, the better received is the report.

of a design, the contextual requirements have a strong cognitive basis and must fit people's psychological needs and how they comprehend information (Bowie, 1996; Hefley, 1995).

This, of course, raises the question of how to decide on that context and which content is appropriate for the context. Working across many audiences and situations requires that a system contain a large amount of content. For any specific situation, the majority of that content should be hidden since it does not fit the context. Sprague (1995) claims that the major value of online information "derives from its ability to expand the scope of information management from facts in the form of data records and databases, to concepts and ideas that are generally captured, stored, and communicated in the form of documents" (p. 33). Implicit within his claim is the value-add of having information address complex situations by presenting itself to people when it is required, in the form required. In other words, it allows the content to be shaped by the context and molded to fit the situation in people's terms.

Some researchers have argued that design which allows for context-of-use will be intrinsically "better" than design which focuses only on cognitive issues, managerial requirements, or inspired guesswork (Berg, 1998). However, it is a complex matter, separating content (which is relatively easy to define) from the context (which varies by audience group and specific situation). A design starts with the content, but for maximum communication that content must be reshaped to fit each reader's context. People's goals and information needs must be considered, as well as the factors that transform content into contextually relevant information. Once people's goals and information needs have been identified and the appropriate information identified, that content must be organized to enable them to understand the situation with minimum effort (Rosenfeld & Morville 1998).

The activities that need to be understood and supported by design include multiple and collaborative tasks (Johnson, May, & Johnson, 2003). They do not always have single, clear goals, they often lack discrete start and end points, and sometimes the multiple goals are incompatible. Tasks are frequently carried out in parallel, with various levels of interweaving and interruption. People need help directly relevant to solving their needs to address real-world issues, often involving high-level reasoning and open-ended information needs. In these situations, it is hard for design teams to clearly define exactly what information is needed and when enough has been gathered. People face a complex situation that requires answers to open-ended questions, so any linear information presentation sequence breaks down. Forcing a linear sequence onto these situations creates major usability problems as it becomes harder for people to put the information into context. Conklin (2003) referred to these as "wicked problems, contrasting them with tame problems which have straightforward and clearly defined solutions.

Goals

People's goals form the foundation of the information context. As Norman and Draper (1986) point out, "There is a discrepancy between the person's *psychologically* expressed goals and the *physical* controls and variables of the task"

Box 2.

Timing of information presentation to meet information needs

Timing of information presentation has a significant influence on whether or not the information itself is actually useful. A study about the information men received about prostate cancer screening and possible treatments found that most men had already made their screening decisions (either yes or no) before receiving the information (Sheridan et al., 2004). Although the content may have been needed by the men, since it was given too late it was no longer appropriate to the context of their information needs. Helping these men achieve their health goals would require presenting the information to them sooner. Since they had already made their decision, no redesign or reformat of the information without a change in timing would affect the overall information communication outcomes. In a different study, of women who had chosen breast conserving surgery with radiotherapy as their breast cancer treatment, 26% said that they were dissatisfied with the pre-operative information they had used to make their treatment decisions. They claimed that quite basic information had been omitted, such as the need for post-operative radiotherapy and the need for post-operative arm exercises (Fallowfield, 1997). The medial people focused on the narrow situation they were responsible for (the surgery and immediate post-op) which the patient wanted the bigger picture. Poor HII had led them to see the surgery a single step to getting better when it was only a small piece.

Studies such as these show that information should be given systematically, at the right time and via several different routes, to maximize the chances for patients to understand the implications of treatment options, that they might make truly informed choices.

(p. 33). People come to a situation with a set of goals to be achieved, but to achieve them, they must translate those goals into tasks to perform and the information needed to accomplish those tasks. The ease which with people can achieve a goal directly maps on to how easily the design supports that translation into tasks and related information needs.

People's goals can be defined as follows:

The real-world change of the current situation or understanding of the current situation that the user is trying to achieve. Goals can consist of sub-goals, which are solved in a recursive manner. Goals should be considered from the user-situation viewpoint (what is happening and what does it mean to the user), rather than the system viewpoint (how can the system display a value for x). The system provides a pathway for the user to obtain the information to achieve the goal (Albers, 2004, p. 11).

Allen (1996) reminds us that people develop different goals, and that many systems do not support working to achieve those goals.

An individual facing one kind of problem may need to explore a topic area in a different way than an individual facing a different kind of problem. This kind of problem-based flexibility in the presentation of information is not frequently found in current information systems. In part, this inflexibility may be attributed to the data-centered approach, which focuses on the data rather than on the uses to which the data can be applied. It is also true that implementing information systems

that can tailor their functioning to the different problems faced by users is far more difficult than implementing systems with less flexibility (p. 115).

Design teams need to start with people's goals and work toward developing the flexible system which provides the information they need to achieve those goals. The interrelations of information within a situation's context must be considered because people are better viewed, not as users with clear goals (an unstated assumption of much task analysis, but not valid for situations with more than a minimal level of complexity (Albers, 2003a), but as users with fluid, ill-formed goals, constantly dealing with ambiguous information (Mumby, 1988).

Box 3.

Goals vary by audience

Health care is moving from a system in which all decisions are made by a physician with the patient as a passive receptor to one where the patient is expected to be actively involved in making treatment decisions. For chronic diseases, this type of shared decision making has been shown to greatly improve compliance (Payne, 2002). But, in order to participate and make informed decisions, the patient needs the proper information presented in the proper way. Information geared toward the experienced healthcare provider, or information which is too simplistic, will not give the patient the proper level of understanding (Fallowfield, 2001).

A significant part of the problem of meeting both patient and healthcare provider needs is that they have very different underlying goals. Decision factors and user goals sometimes compete: while the over-arching goal of the physician and patient may be the same—recovery from the disease—the sub-goals can be quite different.

- A patient is typically concerned with quality-of-life issues and wants to know what they need to do to recover or live with the disease. Information such as having high values on specific lab tests is irrelevant unless the situation is life-threatening.
- Healthcare professionals, by training, focus on the pathological and physiological aspects of the disease, factors which patients do not need to be as familiar with, but which drive treatment options. Healthcare professionals care about lab results, how the disease expresses itself on the body, and what drugs should be used for treatment.

The information context for any specific high-level healthcare concept differs for both the patient and the professional, even if their primary goal is the same.

Software manuals don't address people's goals

Software manuals are not used since they don't address a user's goals. A typical software manual reflects the menu structure of the application (and the online manuals have not deviated from this structure). It carefully explains all of the dialog boxes and menu functions starting at file-new and continuing through until help-about. Yet, no one uses these manuals. Interestingly, I was once told by a co-worker that "yes, no one will probably read it, but it's very important to have it documented."

The fundamental problem is that the manuals don't connect the menu options to bigger tasks. They don't address how people really work. They don't support people's real-world goals, but the low-level software tasks. People come to the software and the manual with a real-world problem defined in their terms. Performing the work and achieving the goal requires using multiple menu options for essentially every non-trivial task. These non-trivial tasks are people's real goals. Manuals should explain how to assemble tasks, rather than providing acontextual explanations with no information on using options together or why a menu option would be used. A substantial factor in the popularity of third party software books (the ones sold in a bookstore) arise from how they focus on using the product to do useful things rather than just describing the individual features.

Information Needs versus Information Wants

Achieving a goal requires obtaining the proper information to allow making proper decisions. Information may be needed, but people often do not *know* they need it nor may not want to actually know it (consider how people avoid bad news), or they may not even know that it is available. Fulfilling people's information needs is complicated since information wants and needs can radically differ.

The difference between information needs and information wants has generated much discussion among commentators. Gross (1998) suggests that the terms are often used interchangeably. Derr (1983), on the other hand, makes a strong argument that information needs do not equal information wants. In fact, an information want might be in conflict with the information need. What people want might be irrelevant to the situation; it might be too precise or too general—all of which impairs the HII. If a person wants a red car, she will refuse to look at any other color, even though they may be more than adequate for her transportation needs.

Albers (2004a, p. 12) defined information needs and wants as follows:

Information needs: The information required by the user to achieve a goal. These information needs often require both information to initially understand the situation and to access that the goal was achieved. A major aspect of good design is ensuring that the information is provided in an integrated format that matches the information needs required by the user goals. Although a perfect system always contains the information needed to meet a goal, in reality, the design must compensate for incomplete information.

Information wants: The information wanted by people to help them achieve a goal. Unfortunately, their needs and wants are often

Box 4.

Reader's expectations versus information wants
Many organizations are putting all of their information on the web; however, many people still prefer printed materials. Any communication channel must be appropriate for communicating the information and not simply rely on the easiest or cheapest method. Research into how to prepare material for medical patients found that they wanted written (not oral) materials (Hinds, Streater, & Mood, 1995) and that written material increased patient satisfaction (Grissom & Dunagan, 2001). Interestingly, while patients prefer written material, other research has shown that they have a difficult time understanding it (Johansson et al., 2004), often because it is written at much too high a reading level (Klingbeil et al., 1995; Murphy et al., 2001; Winslow, 2001). Except for Johansson et al., none of these studies looked at whether or not patients comprehended the material, but focused on what people wanted. There could be a strong influence at work, that the patient expected to be given something even if they had no real intention of reading it.

---

quite different, with people rarely knowing what they actually need. Too often wanted information is irrelevant to the situation or redundant with other information.

A person needs a car for driving to work. A used sub-compact car will meet that requirement. But the person wants a convertible or a two-seater sports car. Whether they can afford it, often forces close consideration of needs versus wants. In most information situations, the tradeoffs are not as clear and people refuse to carefully consider what is really a need and what is a want.

A significant part of the problem of defining information wants versus needs is that people don't realize what information they use to accomplish most tasks, especially the more subtle supporting information. With experience, their reasoning process becomes too deeply ingrained for them to explain it to a design team. On the other hand, in a situation they haven't encountered before or encounter infrequently, they often don't know what information they need so they don't know to ask for it. They may not realize that the information exists or may not realize that different information can lead to alternate paths to achieving their goal (Constantine & Lockwood, 1999).

Box 5.

> **Understanding what people want to know**
> Most patients want as much information as possible about their illness and potential treatments. An extremely important finding was that 98% of patients wanted to know whether the illness was cancer. Some healthcare professionals, on the other hand, may hold an old belief (myth?) that the patient would prefer not to know, a belief left over from an era when there were few effective cancer treatments. Furthermore, 95% of patients wished to know their chances of being cured, so information about prognosis needs to be discussed with the patient (Jenkins, Fallowfield, & Saul, 2001).

Box 6.

> **Seven points to "anything"**
> A common article type in magazines and websites have titles like "Seven points to a winning grant proposal" or "Five tips for perfect vacation planning." These articles are trying to convert an open-ended question into a closed question. The information they provide is not wrong, but is too general to be directly applied or fails to consider the various factors unique to the current reader's needs. In the short space they have, they really can't address that.
>
> The titles of these type of articles flag them as a specific genra. Although lacking the title flag, a substantial amount of information in corporate reports falls into the same problem as does part of management by PowerPoint bullets. There is a desire to convert open-ended questions (which are difficult to solve) into closed-ended questions (which are much easier). But this can compromise the quality of the resulting situational understanding and decisions.

Open versus Closed Information Needs

When people look for information, they will approach the matter from one of two different types of situations (open or closed), with different information needs.

Closed: An exact answer exists. At some point in the process of retrieving the information on a topic, the person knows the answer is complete. For example, they may be seeking instructions on completing a form or finding the part number for a piece of equipment.

Open: An exact answer does not exist. There is no precise definition of what constitutes an answer to an open-ended question. In general, people have a goal and a vague idea of what information will address it. The steps toward achieving the goal tend to involve collecting information to understand the topic. How much information to collect depends on many different factors, such as how much time people have and how much they want to know. In the end, even when possessing the information, it is hard to determine whether the goal is achieved since it is hard to judge the quality and completeness of the information. The boundary is fuzzy and more information can normally be found. Examples would be looking up information on buying a new car, or on a healthcare topic. There is no clear stopping point for either.

Marchionini (1989) found that people's information behavior differed depending on the type of information need. They needed to spend more time for the open task than for a closed task. In addition, the open task seemed to require a higher number of information elements to achieve a satisfactory answer. This is not surprising since an open-ended question has multiple answers, rather than a single answer. Plus, people normally have no way of knowing if the information they found is either complete or incomplete and, if incomplete, how incomplete it is. Post-event analysis can easily determine how complete the information is, but that involves hindsight and knowledge of how information interaction at one point will affect future events. In the end, people look for and interact with the information until they are satisfied with it.

Defining Information Needs

Even when people do know what information is available, they often will not look for what they really need. Most people quickly form an answer for how to address the current situation and do not want to see anything that contradicts that answer or their current beliefs (Klein, 1999). They may actively refuse to look at it (the equivalent of holding hands over ears and singing la-la-la to avoid bad news). In addition, as the situation becomes more complex and the amount of information increases, people respond by increasingly ignoring information incompatible with their preferred decision (Ganzach & Schul, 1995). In other words, they only want information which confirms that what they already believe is true, really is true.

The task analysis conflict is that if most people are asked what type of information they considered most salient, they answer something along the lines of "information to show I'm making the right choice," when that is the exact opposite of what they really need. The information people need is *not* the information which shows they made the right choice, but rather information which might show they made the wrong choice. For example, part of the miscommunication which contributed to the Three Mile Island accident was that operators ignored indicators which contradicted their current view of what was wrong with the nuclear reactor. Likewise, NASA managers ignored information on why not to launch Challenger in favor of reasons for their preferred choice, which was to launch (Herndl, Fennell & Miller, 1991).

People often must resolve personal conflicts between different goals, information needs, and time pressure. There are times when specific information wants get placed at a lower priority, which results in less information seeking. Although this behavior is understandable when people have other higher-priority goals which must be addressed first, an avoidance behavior toward some information does intrude. In addition, age and gender often influence the information people perceive as important. For example, Choi-Kwon et al. (2005) found strong correlations with respect to age for the amount and type of information stroke patients wanted, with younger patients wanting more medical information.

An information-seeking paradox arises where people seek less information as their need for it increases. Johnson, Andrews, and Allard (2001) noted this paradox in patients diagnosed with critical diseases. These patients must gain an understanding of their condition so they can discuss treatment options with their physician, yet some people preferred not to search for or gain any information about their condition. Savolainen (1995) described this problem in terms of an "unwanted guest" who is best ignored. Unresolved issues about the information-seeking paradox are whether this same behavior carries over to other high-stress environments.

Besides knowing what information people need, there is also the issue of how they mentally process it and how they intend to interact with it. Most discussions of task analysis ignore HII issues and focus on defining a hierarchal structure of information needs which becomes acontextual. Yet the HII drives both people's information needs and usability issues of the system. The closer the mapping of the presentation and interaction to their internal model of the situation, the easier the HII.

Capturing the information needs and wants, and the differences between them, requires a thorough audience analysis and task analysis, the importance of which cannot be overemphasized (Hackos & Redish, 1998). The analysis must focus on determining and defining people's informational and psychological needs (Lansdale & Ormerod, 1994) and how to provide the information to help people solve problems (Belkin, 1980). Redish (1994) argues that documentation should move up a level to address goals and task repertoires, and she recognizes that that emphasis on "higher than discrete task" is crucial for anyone doing everyday work. The driving force for this shift arises because people, rather than machines, are reading the information. Modern web interfaces frequently deal with the presentation of vast quantities of information, and often address complex situations. To complicate matters, basic information must meet diverse needs. Unfortunately, how well the interface addresses people's complex needs (as distinct from providing individual information elements) varies greatly among systems, with the focus too often on individual information elements.

Design teams can fall into a trap of making it easy to design/create rather than easy to use.

Accomplishing this requires us to view the creation and presentation of content and its subsequent communication from a humanistic viewpoint, rather than a mechanistic one (Whitburn, 1984). User goals and information needs must be placed within proper social and technical contexts and designed to assist people, rather than doing the work for them. Schriver (1997) looked at brochures created for a junior high anti-drug campaign. When she showed them to the intended audience, they laughed and saw nothing relevant in them. The comments clearly revealed that the design team had no understanding of how to communicate with inner-city junior high students. The brochures failed to address their information needs and failed to present it in a format which would communicate it.

Since people often do not know what information they need—or, with experts, a decision process is so ingrained they don't know all the information they use—it is hard to find out what information is needed. Simply asking people what information they want is likely to result in a few stock answers:

- An explanation of what the information will be used for.
- A statement of what information they expect to find.
- A statement of what information they always look for when facing the current situation. The list of information typically misses small but vital elements. The problem is that the response can miss information they use and does not explain how it is related to the problem or how it is used.
- A statement of what they think the researcher wants to hear or the textbook/official company response of what is needed in this situation.

Any of these bullet points can compromise the quality of the analysis. Instead, design teams must observe many interactions of people and see what information they really need and how they interact with it.

WHEN ALL NEEDED INFORMATION IS NOT AVAILABLE

An underlying assumption of many design teams is that they will be supplying people with all of the information they need. However, this rarely holds true. In most instances, people do not receive complete information and have to make decisions with incomplete information, either because the information simply isn't available or they could not take the time to find it. People do not expend cognitive effort dealing with a poorly designed system, but move forward to solve their task with the least possible effort (Müller, 2007).

A major problem is that people cannot tell if the information is complete, incomplete, ambiguous, conflicting, or irrelevant, except in hindsight. Consider how accident investigation teams typically find multiple points where people did not respond properly to a lack of information, or points where the information was misinterpreted. Lacking the hindsight of an investigation team, people working in real time within a situation often cannot make the proper judgment. If the information is confusing, people know they are confused and can react to that, but often they think they have all of the relevant information. Then they move forward believing they understand the situation when they don't. Any decisions made on the basis of confusing or misunderstood information are suspect.

In a fundamental conflict with effectively communicating information, any text's design inhibits effective information interaction at some level—one would hope, at a minimal level. Design teams might even be able to point out the needed

Box 7.

Lack of information for healthcare decisions
One study on how people searched for information looked
at people who had been diagnosed with cancer. Both men
with prostate cancer and their spouses spent significant time
researching the disease, but still reported feeling confused
by what they found (Feltwell & Rees, 2004). Obviously,
they felt a need to make treatment decisions, but they also
reported feeling panicked. The panicked feeling decreases
available cognitive resources and makes it harder to interpret
any information. Part of the problem leading to the confusion
and panic was that they still lacked information. They may
only have learned enough to understand how little information
they possessed and how complex the subject was. (I was once
told that "you know you are starting to understand a subject
when you realize how much you don't know.") However,
they still faced the need for a decision, had a strong desire to
make a decision, but knew they lacked information to make an
informed decision. The problem was that they knew so little,
they couldn't judge any information they found, resolve any
conflicts, define the most relevant information, and mentally
organize it into a coherent picture.

---

content within a text, but if people can't find it, then that information is *not* available.

A range of design issues can impair information availability. Obviously, all of these views are highly problematic with respect to a communication goal of having people comprehend the information.

- Many texts are written on the assumption that people read documents from beginning to end (recall the oft-seen admonition, "read all instructions before starting"). In fact, people do not so read. They skim, looking only for relevant information. They ask questions until the people around them can't help them anymore. They search for information until they reach an impasse. As a result, the text's fundamental design is at odds with the person's information interaction.

- Too much information exists with a system-based focus and was never created with an attempt to present it to fit people's goals. Instead, it expects people to perform that mental transformation, a conversion from the information provided to the information needed. However, people minimize the cognitive effort they expend (Simon, 1979); they resist the exertion of making that transformation (Johnson, Payne, & Bettman, 1988). If information is too hard to understand, they ignore it.

- Information is viewed as a commodity to be transferred from an expert to a lower-knowledge person. As a result, issues of people's goals and information needs are rendered moot. They get what an expert thinks they need to know, or what the expert thinks is important (Payne, 2002). Content is not a low-grade commodity which can be easily provided to anyone. Instead, transferring the information requires knowing how to present it and how people will interact with it.

- Many technical documents are too focused on being complete to the detriment of coherent writing or usable design. Documents need to contain what people require and must be in a format that effectively communicates that information. Completeness has no advantage if people are unable to extract the proper information at the proper time.

Resolve Incomplete Information

People rarely have complete information about a situation. In a dynamic situation, the information may be changing too fast to acquire a complete set. Or the easy-to-obtain information sources may be incomplete, with time pressure preventing their obtaining more. Even experts can have trouble handling incomplete information. When the situation is relatively static, they can adjust for the incomplete information, but in dynamic situations, they perform much poorer (Shanteau, 1992).

When people have incomplete information to understand the situation, they use their mental models to fill in the missing information and make inferences about unavailable information based on the information they do have. Depending on the quality of the mental model, which is very dependent on experience, and the available information they are extrapolating, the inferences may fail to reflect reality.

Insufficient information can fail to give readers what they need in order to limit possible interpretations and resolve ambiguity. Since specific information can indicate specific information relationships, they may ignore pertinent information or reject potential decisions which they would have considered if more complete information had been available (Wills & Moore, 1996). For example, instructions state to turn a knob to the desired level, but do not give any advice on what "desired level" means. Although this could be because of poor design, or because writing provided inadequate content, in many situations the information itself isn't available. In a design of a brochure, the design teams must make font choices which can depend on audience characteristics, but if they are working from a poor audience analysis, they lack the information to make a clear choice.

Resolve Ambiguous Information

Ambiguous information is susceptible to multiple possible interpretations which make sense within the situation. Writing guidelines state that information should strive to be clear and complete. However, information rarely is clear or complete. Instead, all communication contains some level of ambiguity and contains content which is not clear to the reader. Real-world information essentially always contains some element of ambiguity.

Some of the sources of multiple possible interpretations:

- Lack of reader knowledge can result in people's not being able to fully understand the nuances of the information.

Box 8.

> **Purchasing a product with incomplete information**
> People often need to purchase products which can be obtained from multiple suppliers, but each supplier differs in product quality and price. Obviously, the best purchase is the highest quality product at a reasonable price. The incomplete information problem is that people do not know the quality of the desired product, but only, at best, the past history of the supplier's different product lines. Stacks of roofing shingles sitting in a lumber yard may have big signs with their different warranties, all claiming to be the best. Yet, they have widely different prices. Lacking enough background knowledge in roofing, most people have no strong basis for making a decision on which product fits their needs. The result is often picking the cheapest, or the one with the most features just in case they are needed.

- Incomplete information does not give the reader enough to fully resolve how it applies to the situation.
- Poor information design fails to clearly connect information relationships as being relevant to the current situation (Albers, 2010). Reusing identical information designs across multiple situations can lead to this problem. The information is correct, but the needed items are too separated in the text for people to realize they go together.
- The text itself may have been written to be ambiguous, with the company trying to hide information or misdirect the reader, but still being able to claim that the document was misinterpreted. Granted, this is not an ethical approach, but it does occur.

To cope with the ambiguity problem, people have developed many skills at efficiently handling ambiguity. Unfortunately, these mental strategies often degrade effectiveness. Simon's (1979) work on sufficing and Klein's (1999) work on rational decision making both reflect how people respond to and handle ambiguous information. The "good enough" decisions which suffice for normal day-to-day life prove insufficient when interpreting technical or financial information. Rapid mental analysis and reaching a fast conclusion is efficient, but results in high error rates, which, in turn, leads to ineffective decisions. In typical day-to-day decisions, future problems can be identified as they occur and easily corrected, but in many situations with a strong HII, problems are harder to identify and respond to as they affect many facets of the overall situation.

To resolve ambiguity, in many instances, people resort to using a representativeness heuristic (Tversky & Kahneman, 1974) in which they evaluate a situation based on how closely available information matches a representation of the proposed decision or understanding which is contained in their mental model. (People very quickly form a desired solution.) The problem occurs because they accept a solution that fits their mental representation without considering the probability that the answer is correct. In other words, 4 out of 5 potential information points match, so the ambiguity is considered resolved, but the resolution is for a solution with a low chance of occurring. For example, a computer which refuses to turn on could have a bad power supply (low probability), but it might also be unplugged (higher probability). Likewise, physicians complain about patients who did Internet research and claim to have a disease which does somewhat fit their symptoms, but is transmitted by bug bites in the Amazon. The patient simply overlooked that aspect since the other symptoms fit.

The research into how people handle ambiguous information has found some interesting results which a designer needs to consider.

- People tended to judge ambiguous information as less important than nonambiguous information, probably because they judged it to be significantly more difficult to understand than nonambiguous information (Eylon & Allison, 2002). Since people try to minimize mental effort, it is easier to ignore the ambiguous information. Also, it is easier to accept what is clear at face value and ignore other information. Unless the information is deliberately being obscured, design teams do try to ensure that information is not ambiguous. Usability test results are sometimes surprising nonetheless.

- Reports may carefully lay out cause-effect relationships, but people do not take full advantage of causal information, even when given cues about its reliability (Lim & O'Connor, 1996).

- People confuse cause-effect relationships with correlation relationships and make decisions assuming cause-effect. They may also assume relationships exist because of close proximity in a report. Both topics are discussed in the same paragraph, thus they must be related.

Resolve Information Conflicts

When multiple sources of information are used, there is a significant chance they will conflict with one another. The information may also conflict with what people expect, or with their prior knowledge (Parush, 2004b). When an audience has a variety of backgrounds, the chance of conflict increases. It could be as subtle as two disciplines using the same word to mean two different things, or viewing the same problem from different angles.

It is possible for a mental model based on prior knowledge to be so strong that people are unable to consider alternate interpretations of the information. Kuhn's (1962) discussion of paradigms and having to wait for the old guard to die gives some extreme examples of people refusing to consider alternatives to resolve a conflict. Likewise, if any new information conflicts with what people are expecting, (e.g., a report shows a downward trend when an upward trend was expected), depending on how strongly they feel, the new, conflicting information may be rejected as incorrect or subjected to close scrutiny, that its apparent error might be discovered. Of course, the opposite occurs as well: information which agrees with a position is accepted without examination. Otero & Kintsch (1992) noted that people who read text containing contradicting information rarely noticed the conflict. In post-reading recall texts, they only recalled one side or explained away the discrepancy. Other research has that found people make more systematic errors in interpretation when their prior knowledge conflicts with the information in the graph. Thus, viewers' knowledge about content also influences their data interpretations (Shah & Hoeffner, 2002). For example, Lord, et al. (1979) gave people descriptions of studies that either supported or refuted their own prior beliefs about controversial topics like the death penalty. Overall, the people were more likely to notice problems in studies that were inconsistent with their beliefs than in studies that were consistent with their beliefs. These research findings were explained as showing that people depend on global text interpretation or prior knowledge.

Another way that conflicting information can enter a situation arises when people try to find more information. They will go to multiple sources and compare what various experts are saying. What they often find is that different experts on the subject are in conflict. For example, consider economists' discussions on how the stock market will behave over the next six months, or the controversy over global warming. The problem from a design team's perspective is that the message has a high chance of being disregarded. When experts conflict, people tend to ignore both of the experts and continue to believe what they originally believed. In this case, the conflict resolution is to simply ignore everything.

Whitmore (2003) found that many undergraduates working on their senior thesis said they were not too troubled by conflicting information. For the others, she found a split between people who carefully considered different views and those who went with the majority, or the more prestigious journal or author. In agreement with Ganzach and Schul (1995), some of the people she interviewed admitted to rejecting or ignoring any source which

disagreed with their position. The ability of people to handle information conflicts is directly tied to their level of epistemological development; unsurprisingly, those with higher stages being able to better fit information together (Whitmire, 2004). The differences were most profound when they encountered conflicting information.

From the review of the epistemological development theories, this study hypothesizes that individuals rated in the lower levels of epistemological development would reject conflicting information while believing that if something was in print or on the Web that it must be valid. Subjects rated in the medium range of epistemological development would begin to believe that uncertainty exists and that two authors can have differing views on the same subject and that both could be correct. These undergraduates would not reject conflicting information. They might believe, however, that knowledge reflects personal beliefs and not reasoned judgments and that the authors are entitled to their own beliefs. Undergraduates rated at the highest levels of epistemological beliefs would evaluate information based on the logical reasoning ability of the authors. These individuals would begin to think of themselves as capable of creating knowledge and using their own viewpoints to select or reject information sources. They would also consider the context in which the information was formulated and begin to recognize the credibility of particular publishers or journals, and so forth (Whitmire, 2003, p. 131).

In many situations, such as when design teams know their website will be only one of many from which people will obtain information, they need to consider how they will put the information together and how their information may conflict with other sites.

Resolve Irrelevant Information

Irrelevant information is information which is correct and may be important in a different situation, but not in the current one. Irrelevant information, at best, wastes people's time by the effort to process it, and at worst can mislead them. Unfortunately, people often cannot easily see that they have irrelevant information. Lacking knowledge of the situation, all of the information seems relevant. Thus, they try to process all of it, which leads to problems. In the hindsight provided by investigations of bad decisions (the type that led to millions of dollars in losses or damage), the irrelevant information is obvious, but it is never obvious during decision-making.

Normally, when considering factors that affect the decision process, most design teams only look at relevant factors. However, seemingly irrelevant factors often have a strong influence. Hsee (1996) found that, given a piece of information tempting to a decision maker but irrelevant to the problem, the decision maker would often rationalize using the irrelevant information—for example, using case color as a consideration for technical equipment (blue fits the office décor better). This behavior was especially prevalent when there was uncertainty associated with the factors relevant to the problem. Another example is picking a conference based on the location rather than quality of the program. People will tend to pick a conference in Orlando over one in Chicago, especially in January, even if the Chicago conference is better and more relevant to them. The weather should be an irrelevant factor when choosing a conference.

Often, irrelevant information comes from a design team's need to create a generic set of information, or when the team lacks a clear understanding of situational contexts. When design teams do not command a clear understanding of relevant information, there is a risk that highly salient but contextually irrelevant information which is easy to provide will overshadow the relevant information.

Box 9.

Conflicting information in medicine
People often report that written information (even brochures given to them by health professionals) was contradicted by health professionals. One study found over 50% of patients received conflicting information (Carpenter et al, 2010). Often, this is because the brochure is written in general terms and contains information which is not appropriate to their specific treatment.

I asked the doctor about that because I said shouldn't I be taking this because I've taken this and that tablet. 'Oh that's all right Mrs. P.' 'Well why do they put it on that leaflet?' 'Oh' she said 'don't take any notice of that.' I said 'Well why did they print it?' (Payne, 2002, p. 177).

The problem here is that the health professional must now try to explain the issue when the person is now predisposed to ignore any explanation. There is also a significant chance that the patient will start to ignore all written information given to her, since some of it conflicts, and then consider the healthcare provider as the primary source.

Detection of irrelevant information is connected with domain expertise (Kumsaikaew, Jackman, & Dark, 2006). Interestingly, experts do not always use all or a greater amount of relevant information to make a decision. However, the information used by experts is more relevant than information used by novices. People with different expertise levels differ significantly in their ability to evaluate what information is relevant in a given context. That is, they differ in terms of their ability to reduce the available information to only the most relevant (Haider & Frensch, 1999). Experts have learned to distinguish relevant from irrelevant information and to attend to or process only relevant information. Novices find it more difficult to separate irrelevant from relevant information in the process of completing their tasks (Shanteau, 1992).

Some other factors that can influence how people handle irrelevant information:

- People see trends in random data and, although it is both wrong and irrelevant, people will use it as part of their decision

Table 1. Three main audience groups and their goals

Knowledgeable amateur	Student researcher	General public
What parts of them are best for observing? What time during the year is best for observing. How do they form? How do they help understand star formation	How do they form? How do stars form in them? How are they arranged in the galaxy? Size and mass information.	What images can I see? Size and distance information. Why do the different telescope images vary?

making process since they think the trend exists.

- Age slows mental processing times and makes people more susceptible to distraction from irrelevant information (Hoyer et al, 1979).

EXAMPLES

At the end of each chapter, two longer examples using the design of an astronomical website and business reports will provide a discussion of the chapter's topics.

Astronomical Information

A design team has been assigned to create a large web site to provide the astronomical information. Although this example uses astronomy, it would be simple to rewrite most of it to apply to any web site focused on providing the general public with information. For example, medical information, museum exhibits or web sites, environmental information about the benefits of turtles or skunks, or the design of medieval cathedrals or baseball stadiums.

The astronomical website's overall goal is to provide information about various astronomical events and concepts. While an overall scope statement could be "astronomy information," that is much too broad. That equates to a reader saying "Tell me everything about astronomy." What does the person what know about astronomy and how does it need to be explained? People's goals and information needs are typically much more refined

in scope. The design teams needs to focus the scope to fit individual goals and information needs.

After performing an audience analysis, three main audience groups are defined with different goals (knowledgeable amateurs, students, general public). Each section of the site needs to provide content fitting the different audience group goals (Table 1). Consider how these three groups goals vary in the section on giant molecular clouds. Besides different information needs between the groups, even when the information needs overlap each group needs different detail level in the content to match their prior knowledge.

Business Reports

Simply having the information is not sufficient. Initial design analysis needs to reveal the general information needs and the potential goals the manager may address as they proceed to gaining an understanding. Business analysts use a set of heuristics for analyzing reports and spotting problems, but these must be adjusted for each individual situation or problem. Each new piece of data the business analyst uncovers affects the path taken and the eventual outcome of the analysis. The context provides the clues the business analyst needs to connect the integrated information into a coherent view of the situation.

This makes the context of the information at least as important, if not more important, the information content itself. Some potential contextual factors are:

Figure 5. Context of sales information. Depending on how the graph places the information into context, the perspective of the information can change dramatically. In A and B, the south seems to be the best performing region, but C reveals that it may need attention.

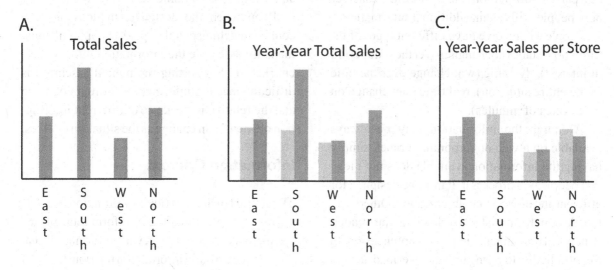

- How the numbers match against the long term company strategic plans.
- What business factors may have affected the numbers. A snow storm or other catastrophic event can make a set of number move to high or low for a short time period, but do not indicate significant trends. New stores or a new product line can cause an increase in total sales, but that increase may mask problems in some product areas.

Figure 5 shows three graphs. 5A one shows the south region has the highest sales, but that number has no context. 5B makes it look even better with the sales increase year-over-year, but it still lacks the full context of how many stores are contributing to the sales. If the company opened several stores in the south region, clearly total sales will increase. 2-5C shows that the per store values are substantially lower in the south and have decreased. Each view provides a different context for the information. Design teams must ensure they place the information into the proper context for the people's information needs and not simply provide the easy information. The report must provide integrated and interpreted information and not a data dump.

SUMMARY

This chapter examined information as it exists in the world and the factors that design teams need to consider as they work to create content. Information does not simply exist in the world; instead, it depends on both the reader's point of view and the situation in which it occurs. The available data is simply the raw material which must be mentally processed to comprehend the situation.

Sources of Information

People can obtain information from a variety of sources such as books, brochures/leaflets, reports, technical manuals, or the Internet. Regardless of the source, designs teams need consider how people will access the information and consider how they will integrate all of the information they receive. In most HII situations, the design teams are the main source of information about the topic, such as when they produce internal corporate information. In other situations, they will only be a partial information source and must consider how people will obtain additional information.

People can receive three different types of information: static (unchanging over the time period of interest), dynamic (will change over the time of the entire situation), real time (can change on time scales of minutes).

Although the information may be always available on a web or corporate intranet, simply having the information available does not mean that people will process it. It must be designed for efficient and effective communication. Otherwise, the design team risks overloading the reader, which will dramatically impair comprehension. In a contradiction to trying prevent overload, design teams face the problem that people assess the value of the information based on quantity rather than quality (Shenton & Dixon, 2004a). Sources that have more content or larger books/reports are considered a better source of information.

Information Content

Content involves the text itself, the type of the information, and scope of the information. The design team needs to ensure that the content supports the people using the system.

People are given too much information all day long and the majority gets ignored, thus tend to ignore what they don't understand or don't know to be relevant. The first step in any effective design, although one which is too often short-changed or skipped, is to clearly define who the audience is, what they should be able to accomplish, what information is needed, and the information relations that must be understood to accomplish people's goals.

The content must conform to people's goals because mentally transforming it is very demanding and requires a good understanding of the information. In general, since it is so mentally demanding, people often shed the workload and

don't do the transformation. As a result, their comprehension of the information is very poor and it fails to communicate.

Even when the design team does produce content matching people's goals, people still must mentally assemble the information into a coherent picture. Supporting the mental assembly is difficult since the information is often not static and the relative importance of different information elements can change as the situation evolves.

Information Context

The context of the situation's information depends on both people's goals and information needs. People need access to relevant information that allows them to build information relationships and comprehend the situation. In complex situations, information context often becomes more important than content since people seek information when they realize their knowledge about a situation is incomplete. Yet, understanding that situation means more that simply have the information, it means understanding the relationships within the information and how it relates to different aspects of the situation.

People come to a situation with a set of goals to be achieved, but to achieve them, they must translate those goals into tasks to perform and the information needed to accomplish those tasks. The ease which with people achieve a goal directly maps on to how easily the design supports that translation into tasks and related information needs. People's goals form the foundation of the information context. However, as Norman and Draper (1986) point out, "There is a discrepancy between the person's *psychologically* expressed goals and the *physical* controls and variables of the task" (p. 33).

Achieving a goal requires obtaining the proper information to allow making proper decisions. Information may be needed, but people often do not *know* they need it nor may not want to actually know it (consider how people avoid bad news), or they may not even know that it is available. Fulfilling people's information needs is complicated since information wants and needs can radically differ. Design teams need to understand both the wants and needs and resolve the differences between them. Capturing the information needs and wants, and the differences between them, requires a thorough audience analysis and task analysis, the importance of which cannot be overemphasized (Hackos & Redish, 1998). The analysis must focus on determining and defining people's informational and psychological needs (Lansdale & Ormerod, 1994) and how to provide the information to help people solve problems (Belkin, 1980)

Incomplete, Ambiguous, or Conflicting Information

An underlying assumption of many design teams is that they will be supplying people with all of the information they need. However, this is rarely true. A major problem is that people often cannot tell if the information is complete, incomplete, ambiguous, conflicting, or irrelevant. Instead, they assume the information is both complete and clear.

When people have incomplete information to understand the situation, they use their mental models to fill in the missing information and make inferences about unavailable information based on the information they do have.

Ambiguous information can be interpreted in multiple ways. Although writing guidelines state that information should strive to be clear, all communication contains some level of ambiguity. Design teams need to work to understand the points at which the ambiguity can occur.

When using multiple information sources, people will encounter information which conflicts with other sources. Besides conflicts between sources, the conflict may also occur between a source and what people expect based on their prior knowledge. Content creation may need to explicitly address potential sources of conflict.

Poor design can provide irrelevant information, information which is correct but not useful in the current situation. Irrelevant information, at best, wastes people's time by the effort to process it, and at worst can mislead them since they will try to use it as part of understanding the situation. Unfortunately, people often cannot easily see that they have irrelevant information. Detection of irrelevant information is connected with domain expertise. When the readers will have lower levels of domain knowledge, design teams must ensure the presented information is directly relevant to understanding the situation.

REFERENCES

Ahn, H., Lee, H., Cho, K., & Park, S. (2005). Utilizing knowledge context in virtual collaborative work. *Decision Support Systems, 39*, 563–582. doi:10.1016/j.dss.2004.03.005

Albers, M. (2003a). Complex problem solving and content analysis. In Albers, M., & Mazur, B. (Eds.), *Content and complexity: Information design in software development and documentation* (pp. 263–284). Mahwah, NJ: Erlbaum.

Albers, M. (2004a). *Communication of complex information: User goals and information needs for dynamic Web information.* Mahwah, NJ: Erlbaum.

Albers, M. (2004b). Signal to noise ratio of information in documentation. *Proceedings of 22nd Annual International Conference on Computer Documentation* (pp. 41–44). New York, NY: ACM.

Albers, M. (2009). Information relationships: The source of useful and usable content. *Proceedings of 29th Annual International Conference on Computer Documentation* (pp. 171–178). New York, NY: ACM.

Albers, M. (2010). Usability and information relationships: Considering content relationships when testing complex information. In Albers, M., & Still, B. (Eds.), *Usability of complex Information Systems: Evaluation of user interaction* (pp. 109–132). Boca Raton, FL: CRC Press. doi:10.1201/EBK1439828946-9

Allen, N. (1996). Ethics and visual rhetorics: Seeing's not believing anymore. *Technical Communication Quarterly*, 5(1), 87–105. doi:10.1207/s15427625tcq0501_6

Belkin, N. (1980). Anomalous states of knowledge as a basic for information retrieval. *The Canadian. Journal of Information Science*, 5, 133–143.

Berg, M. (1998). Medical work and the computer based patient record: A sociological perspective. *Methods of Information in Medicine*, 38, 294–301.

Bettman, J., Johnson, E., & Payne, J. (1990). A componential analysis of cognitive effort in choice. *Organizational Behavior and Human Decision Processes*, 45, 111–139. doi:10.1016/0749-5978(90)90007-V

Beyer, H., & Holtzblatt, K. (1998). *Contextual design: Defining customer-centered systems*. San Francisco, CA: Morgan-Kaufmann.

Booth, K., Beaver, K., Kitchener, H., O'Neill, J., & Farrell, C. (2005). Women's experiences of information, psychological distress and worry after treatment for gynecological cancer. *Patient Education and Counseling*, 56, 225–232. doi:10.1016/j.pec.2004.02.016

Bowie, J. (1996). Information engineering: Communicating with technology. *Intercom*, 43(5), 6–9.

Buckland, M. (1991). Information as thing. *Journal of the American Society for Information Science American Society for Information Science*, 42(5), 351–360. doi:10.1002/(SICI)1097-4571(199106)42:5<351::AID-ASI5>3.0.CO;2-3

Carpenter, D., DeVellis, R., Fisher, E., DeVallis, B., Hogan, S., & Jordan, J. (2010). The effect of conflicting medication information and physician support on medication adherence for chronically ill patients. *Patient Education and Counseling*, 81(2), 169–176. doi:10.1016/j.pec.2009.11.006

Choi-Kwon, S., Lee, S., Park, H., Kwon, S., Ahn, J., & Kim, J. (2005). What stroke patients want to know and what medical professionals think they should know about stroke: Korean perspectives. *Patient Education and Counseling*, 56, 85–92. doi:10.1016/j.pec.2003.12.011

Conklin, J. (2003). *Wicked problems and fragmentation*. Retrieved March 7, 2003, from http://www.cognexus.org/id26.htm

Constantine, L., & Lockwood, L. (1999). *Software for use: A practical guide to the models and methods of usage-centered design*. New York, NY: ACM Press.

Derr, R. (1983). A conceptual analysis of information need. *Information Processing & Management*, 19(5), 273–278. doi:10.1016/0306-4573(83)90001-8

Eylon, D., & Allison, S. (2002). The paradox of ambiguous information in collaborative and competitive settings. *Group & Organization Management*, 27, 172–208. doi:10.1177/10501102027002002

Fallowfield, L. (1997). Offering choice of surgical treatment to women with breast cancer. *Patient Education and Counseling*, 30, 209–214. doi:10.1016/S0738-3991(96)00947-0

Fallowfield, L. (2001). Participation of patients in decisions about treatment for cancer. *British Medical Journal*, 323, 1144. doi:10.1136/bmj.323.7322.1144

Feltwell, A., & Rees, C. (2004). The information-seeking behaviors of partners of men with prostate cancer: A qualitative pilot study. *Patient Education and Counseling*, 54, 179–185. doi:10.1016/S0738-3991(03)00212-X

Ganzach, Y., & Schul, Y. (1995). The influence of quantity of information and goal framing on decisions. *Acta Psychologica, 89*, 23–36. doi:10.1016/0001-6918(94)00004-Z

Gribbons, W., & Elsar, A. (1998). Visualizing information: An overview of this special issue. *Technical Communication, 45*(4), 467–472.

Grissom, S., & Dunagan, L. (2001). Improved satisfaction during rehabilitation after hip and knee arthroplasty: A retrospective analysis. *American Journal of Physical Medicine & Rehabilitation, 80*, 798–803. doi:10.1097/00002060-200111000-00002

Gross, M. (1998). The imposed query: Implications for library service evaluation. *Reference and User Services Quarterly, 37*, 290–299.

Hackos, J., & Redish, J. (1998). *User and task analysis for interface design*. New York, NY: Wiley.

Haider, H., & Frensch, P. (1999). Information reduction during skill acquisition: The influence of task instruction. *Journal of Experimental Psychology. Applied, 5*, 129–151. doi:10.1037/1076-898X.5.2.129

Halford, G., Baker, R., McCredden, J., & Bain, J. (2005). How many variables can humans process? *Psychological Science, 16*(1), 70–76. doi:10.1111/j.0956-7976.2005.00782.x

Hefley, W. (1995). Helping users help themselves. *IEEE Software, 12*(2), 93–95. doi:10.1109/52.368272

Herbig, P., & Kramer, H. (1992). The phenomenon of innovation overload. *Technology in Society, 14*, 441–461. doi:10.1016/0160-791X(92)90038-C

Herndl, C., Fennell, B., & Miller, C. (1991). Understanding failures in organizational discourse: The accident at Three Mile Island and the shuttle Challenger disaster. In Bazerman, C., & Paradis, J. (Eds.), *Textual dynamics of the profession* (pp. 279–305). Madison, WI: University of Wisconsin.

Hertzum, M., & Frøkjær, E. (1996). Browsing and querying in online documentation: A study of user interfaces and the interaction process. *ACM Transactions on Computer-Human Interaction, 3*(2), 136–161. doi:10.1145/230562.230570

Hinds, C., Streater, A., & Mood, D. (1995). Functions and preferred methods of receiving information related to radiotherapy. *Cancer Nursing, 18*, 374–383. doi:10.1097/00002820-199510000-00007

Hoyer, W., Rebok, G., & Sved, S. (1979). Effects of varying irrelevant information on adult age differences in problem solving. *Journal of Gerontology, 34*(4), 553–560.

Hsee, C. (1996). The evaluability hypothesis: An explanation of preference reversals between joint and separate evaluations of alternatives. *Organizational Behavior and Human Decision Processes, 67*(3), 247–257. doi:10.1006/obhd.1996.0077

Jenkins, V., Fallowfield, L., & Saul, J. (2001). Information needs of patients with cancer: Results from a large study of UK cancer centres. *British Journal of Cancer, 84*, 48–51. doi:10.1054/bjoc.2000.1573

Johansson, K., Salantera, S., Katajisto, J., & Leino-Kilpi, H. (2004). Written orthopedic patient education materials from the point of view of empowerment by education. *Patient Education and Counseling, 52*, 175–181. doi:10.1016/S0738-3991(03)00036-3

Johnson, E., Payne, J., & Bettman, J. (1988). Information displays and preference reversals. *Organizational Behavior and Human Decision Processes, 42*, 1–21. doi:10.1016/0749-5978(88)90017-9

Johnson, J. D., Andrews, J. E., & Allard, S. (2001). A model for understanding and affecting genetics information seeking. *Library & Information Science Research, 23*(4), 335–349. doi:10.1016/S0740-8188(01)00094-9

Johnson, P., May, J., & Johnson, H. (2003). Introduction to multiple and collaborative tasks. *ACM Transactions on Computer-Human Interaction, 10*(4), 277–280. doi:10.1145/966930.966931

Kammersgaard, J. (1988). Four different perspective on human-computer interaction. *International Journal of Man-Machine Studies, 28*, 343–362. doi:10.1016/S0020-7373(88)80017-8

Kerzman, H., Baron-Epel, O., & Toren, O. (2005). What do discharged patients know about their medication? *Patient Education and Counseling, 56*, 276–282. doi:10.1016/j.pec.2004.02.019

Kim, J., & Lee, J. (2002). Critical design factors for successful e-commerce systems. *Behaviour & Information Technology, 21*(3), 185–199. doi:10.1080/0144929021000009054

Klein, G. (1999). *Sources of power: How people make decisions*. Cambridge, MA: MIT.

Klingbeil, C., Speece, M., & Schubiner, H. (1995). Readability of pediatric patient education materials. Current perspectives on an old problem. *Clinical Pediatrics, 34*(2), 96–102. doi:10.1177/000992289503400206

Kuhn, T. (1962). *The structure of scientific revolutions*. Chicago, IL: University of Chicago Press.

Kumsaikaew, P., Jackman, J., & Dark, V. (2006). Task relevant information in engineering problem solving. *Journal of Engineering Education, 95*, 227–239.

Lansdale, M., & Ormerod, T. (1994). *Understanding interfaces: A handbook of human-computer dialogue*. London, UK: Academic Press.

Lim, J., & O'Connor, M. (1996). Judgmental forecasting with time series and causal information. *International Journal of Forecasting, 12*, 139–153. doi:10.1016/0169-2070(95)00635-4

Lord, C., Ross, L., & Lepper, M. (1979). Biased assimilation and attitude polarization: The effects of prior theories on subsequent evidence. *Journal of Personality and Social Psychology, 37*, 2098–2110. doi:10.1037/0022-3514.37.11.2098

Mao, J., & Benbasat, I. (2001). The effects of contextualized access to knowledge on judgment. *International Journal of Human-Computer Studies, 55*, 787–814. doi:10.1006/ijhc.2001.0507

Marchionini, G. (1989). Information-seeking strategies of novices using a full-text electronic encyclopedia. *Journal of the American Society for Information Science American Society for Information Science, 29*(3), 165–176.

Marchionini, G. (2008). Human–information interaction research and development. *Library & Information Science Research, 30*, 165–174. doi:10.1016/j.lisr.2008.07.001

McGovern, G. (2006c). *Is your content a waste of time and money?* Retrieved from http://www.gerrymcgovern.com/nt/2006/nt-2006-02-06-content-value.htm

McNamara, D. (2001). Reading both high and low coherence texts: Effects of text sequence and prior knowledge. *Canadian Journal of Experimental Psychology, 55*, 51–62. doi:10.1037/h0087352

McNamara, D., & Kintsch, W. (1996). Learning from text: Effects of prior knowledge and text coherence. *Discourse Processes, 22*, 247–287. doi:10.1080/01638539609544975

Mirel, B. (1998). Applied constructivism for user documentation. *Journal of Business and Technical Communication, 12*(1), 7–49. doi:10.1177/1050651998012001002

Müller, M. (2007). Being aware: Where we think the action is. *Cognition Technology and Work, 9*(2), 109–126. doi:10.1007/s10111-006-0047-7

Mumby, D. (1988). *Communication and power in organizations: Discourse, ideology, and domination.* Norwood, N J: Ablex.

Murphy, P., Chesson, A., Berman, S., Arnold, C., & Galloway, G. (2001). Neurology patient education materials: Do our education aids fit our patients' needs? *The Journal of Neuroscience Nursing, 2,* 99–104. doi:10.1097/01376517-200104000-00006

Norman, D., & Draper, S. (1986). *User centered system design: New perspectives on human-computer interaction.* Mahwah, NJ: Erlbaum.

Otero, J., & Kintsch, W. (1992). Failures to detect contradictions in a text: What readers believe versus what they read. *Psychological Science, 3*(4), 229–235. doi:10.1111/j.1467-9280.1992.tb00034.x

Parush, A. (2004). *Interview with Donald Norman on mental models.* Retrieved from http://www.carleton.ca/hotlab/hottopics/Articles/DonNormanInterview.html

Payne, S. (2002). Balancing information needs: Dilemmas in producing patient information leaflets. *Health Informatics Journal, 8,* 174–179. doi:10.1177/146045820200800402

Redish, J. (1994). Understanding readers. In Barnum, C., & Carliner, S. (Eds.), *Techniques for technical communicators* (pp. 15–41). New York, NY: Macmillan.

Rosenfeld, L., & Morville, P. (1998). *Information architecture for the World Wide Web.* Cambridge, MA: O'Reilly.

Savolainen, R. (1995). Everyday life information seeking: Approaching information seeking in the context of "way of life". *Library & Information Science Research, 17,* 259–294. doi:10.1016/0740-8188(95)90048-9

Schriver, K. (1997). *Dynamics in document design: Creating texts for readers.* New York, NY: Wiley.

Shah, P., & Hoeffner, J. (2002). Review of graph comprehension research: Implications for instruction. *Educational Psychology Review, 14*(1), 47–69. doi:10.1023/A:1013180410169

Shanteau, J. (1992). Competence in experts: The role of task characteristics. *Organizational Behavior and Human Decision Processes, 53*(2), 252–266. doi:10.1016/0749-5978(92)90064-E

Shenton, A., & Dixon, P. (2004a). Issues arising from youngsters' information-seeking behavior. *Library & Information Science Research, 26,* 177–200. doi:10.1016/j.lisr.2003.12.003

Sheridan, S., Felix, K., Pignone, M., & Lewis, C. (2004). Information needs of men regarding prostate cancer screening and the effect of a brief decision aid. *Patient Education and Counseling, 54,* 345–351. doi:10.1016/j.pec.2003.12.003

Simon, H. (1979). *Models of thought.* New Haven, CT: Yale UP.

Slone, D. (2002). The influence of mental models and goals on user search patterns during Web interaction. *Journal of the American Society for Information Science and Technology, 53*(13), 1152–1169. doi:10.1002/asi.10141

Sprague, R. (1995). Electronic document management: Challenges and opportunities for information system managers. *Management Information Systems Quarterly, 19*(1), 29–50. doi:10.2307/249710

Stoop, A., van't Riet, A., & Berg, M. (2004). Using information technology for patient education: Realizing surplus value? *Patient Education and Counseling, 54*, 187–195. doi:10.1016/S0738-3991(03)00211-8

Tufte, E. (1983). *The visual display of quantitative information*. Cheshire, CT: Graphics Press.

Tversky, A., & Kahneman, D. (1974). Judgment under uncertainty: Heuristics and biases. *Science, 185*, 1124–1130. doi:10.1126/science.185.4157.1124

Van Schaik, P. (1999). Involving users in the specification of functionality using scenarios and model-based evaluation. *Behaviour & Information Technology, 18*(6), 455–466. doi:10.1080/014492999118878

Webster, D., & Kruglanski, A. (1994). Individual differences in need. for cognitive closure. *Journal of Personality and Social Psychology, 67*(6), 1049–1672. doi:10.1037/0022-3514.67.6.1049

Whitburn, M. (1984). The ideal orator and literary critic as technical communicators: An emerging revolution in English departments. In Lundsford, A., & Ede, L. (Eds.), *Essays in classical rhetoric and modern discourse* (pp. 230–248). Carbondale, IL: Southern Illinois University Press.

Whitmire, E. (2003). Epistemological beliefs and the information-seeking behavior of undergraduates. *Library & Information Science Research, 25*, 127–142. doi:10.1016/S0740-8188(03)00003-3

Whitmire, E. (2004). The relationship between undergraduates' epistemological reflection, reflective judgment and their information seeking behavior. *Information Processing & Management, 40*(1), 97–111. doi:10.1016/S0306-4573(02)00099-7

Wickens, C. (1992). *Engineering psychology and human performance*. New York, NY: HarperCollins.

Wills, C., & Moore, C. (1996). Perspective-taking judgments of medication acceptance: Inferences from relative importance about the impact and combination of information. *Organizational Behavior and Human Decision Processes, 66*(3), 251–267. doi:10.1006/obhd.1996.0054

Winkleman, W., Leonard, K., & Rossos, P. (2005). Patient-perceived usefulness of online electronic medical records. *Journal of the American Medical Informatics Association, 12*, 306–314.

Winslow, E. (2001). Patient education materials. *The American Journal of Nursing, 10*, 33–39. doi:10.1097/00000446-200110000-00021

Woods, D., Patterson, E., & Roth, E. (2002). Can we ever escape from data overload? A cognitive systems diagnosis. *Cognition Technology and Work, 4*, 22–36. doi:10.1007/s101110200002

ADDITIONAL READING

Albers, M., & Still, B. (2010). *Usability of complex Information Systems: Evaluation of user interaction*. Boca Raton, FL: CRC Press. doi:10.1201/EBK1439828946

Beyer, H., & Holtzblatt, K. (1998). *Contextual design: Defining customer-centered systems*. San Francisco, CA: Morgan-Kaufmann.

Hackos, J., & Redish, J. (1998). *User and task analysis for interface design*. New York, NY: Wiley.

Chapter 3
What People Bring with Them

ABSTRACT

The psychology literature has many articles on how people react to information and the deeper cognitive process behind those reactions, but, unfortunately, this information has not transferred over to the litera-ture relevant to HII. This chapter provides a high level overview of some of those findings and connects them to HII needs. This chapter considers the cognitive aspects people bring to a situation. Design teams have no influence over them, but instead must work within the limitations of how the human mind oper-ates. The white area in figure 1 shows the area of the HII model relevant to this chapter. Comprehending any situation requires people to expend cognitive resources. Depending on the quality of the overall HII design, that expenditure may be high or low. Too high and they may reject the information as too hard or incomprehensible. The design team's goal must be to minimize the cognitive resources required, which in turn requires an understanding of what drives people's allocation of cognitive resources.

BACKGROUND

People's behavior makes sense if you think about it in terms of their goals, needs, and motives.—Thomas Mann

This chapter looks at:

How memory works: Describes a basic model of human memory and considers some of the factors about how people process informa-tion in memory.

How human vision works: Describes the basics of how the human eye works, eye movement during reading, visual acuity, and contrast effects.

Cognitive resources and how they are allocated to tasks: Describes cognitive load, theories of how people allocate cognitive resources, and how allocation affects comprehension.

Prior knowledge: The knowledge a person brings to a situation strongly influences how they

DOI: 10.4018/978-1-4666-0152-9.ch003

Figure 1. What people bring with them to a situation

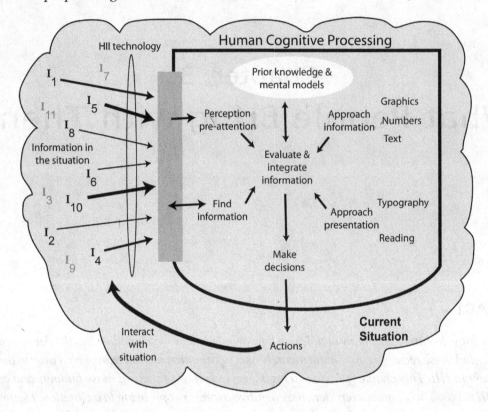

interpret the information and comprehend the situation.

Information biases: A bias is a systematic deviation from the expected path. Describes the various types of bias and how they affect comprehension.

Mental models: Describes mental model theory, how people develop and use mental models, and design factors which influence mental model activation.

Attention: Describes the types of human attention and how they affect understanding a situation.

INTRODUCTION

The research of cognitive psychology into how people process and interact with information plays a vital part in understanding how the human ele-

ment of HII operates or, in cases of poor design, does not operate. Gulliksen & Lantz, (2003) pointed out that explicitly missing from much discussion of communicating information are the human issues. The issues that are the focus of cognitive psychology research. Of course, a major hindrance to crossing over is the framing of the psychology research itself and the need for it to be translated and integrated into something meaningful for an audience focused on HII—a non-trivial task. Wickens and Hollands (2000) were able to perform that translation for engineering psychology and human factors, but their scope was too broad for HII and technical communication, with a significant portion of their research discussing plant control and aviation design issues of concern for industrial engineering and ergonomics.

In document design, Mirel, Feinberg, & Allmendinger (1991) found the "active learning needs are inseparable from task type and complexity"

(p. 82). Research on poorly designed interfaces and documents shows people getting frustrated with the basics and failing to conceptualize the appropriate principles for properly interacting with the system.

The poorly designed document fails to provide or support the necessary HII of the people interacting with the information. In complex tasks, the interactions operate along multiple dimensions and, during the interaction, changes occur along each of those multiple dimensions, but designers often fail to consider all dimensions. As a result, design failures occur because of problems in an unanalyzed dimension, often the dimension of the person's cognitive processes (Rasmussen, Pejtersen, & Goodstein, 1994). A dimension that often goes unanalyzed because design teams concentrate on tasks as a program concept, rather than a real-world action performed by a person. In other words, they define them as a computer task rather than an HII task. Design teams need to understand how the people think about information, the system and the decisions made with the system. They need to understand people's cognitive processes and what factors influence the mental processing of information. An understanding which must be viewed "in terms of the behavior-shaping goals and constraints that define the boundaries of a space within which actors are free to improvise guided by their local and subjective performance criteria" (Rasmussen, Pejtersen, & Goodstein, p. 23).

Many models of handling complex information assume the goals, constraints and interactions are simply the sum of the parts. For example, Card, Moran, and Newell's (1983) work took this view. But this view is simply wrong; the HII is an emergent feature and is much greater than the sum of the parts (Hutchins, 1995; Klein, 1999; Mirel, 1998; Suchman, 1987). However, before designers can see the forest, they must understand the trees. This chapter reviews the foundational elements of cognitive psychology and reinterprets them into a form applicable to a design team working to create high quality HII. Of necessity, it treats each area as an independent factor, although they all interact in real-world HII. Later chapters will deal with merging them all together.

MEMORY

Mentally processing information, to use a computer metaphor, consists of using memory both short term (RAM) and long term (hard drive). Information is moved around within memory and manipulated to arrive at an understanding. The RAM aspects of memory are very limited. Thus, HII depends on memory; words and images are processed in people's memory and stored there. Although this statement about of how people use their memory is obvious, when working on a computer, people frequently need to remember information while they change to another screen or scroll down for additional information. If the information is physically difficult to retrieve (slow access, etc.), people will use what they remember. Remembering the initial information can be cognitively taxing, increasing the chance of forgetting and making errors.

This section discusses a basic model of human memory and considers some of the factors that research has found about how people mentally process information.

Model of Human Memory

The human cognitive system has been modeled as a collection of various types of systems with different storing capacities and retrieval characteristics (Figure 2). There are two main parts of the human memory system. Both are discussed in the following sections. The areas in Figure 2 tend to be factors which feed information into one of these two areas.

- Working memory
- Long term memory

Figure 2. Model of human cognitive system (adapted from Jaspers et al, 2004, p. 784)

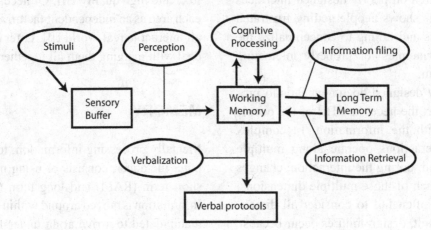

Working Memory

Working memory is the area of where people actively manipulate or store information for short time periods. Any information currently defined as "active" resides in working memory. Working memory contains the information which is immediately available and is the part of memory where people carry out their thought processes. Working memory is where a phone number is remembered between when it is looked up and dialed. It is also where mental processes such as math and information understanding occur. Working memory seems to play a critical role in most high-level cognitive tasks, such as learning,

reasoning, and comprehension (Ashby & O'Brien, 2005; McNamara & Scott, 2001).

Working memory is divided into four areas (Figure 3) that operate essentially independently of one another. Each can maintain its own limited amount of information with minimal interference from the others (Baddeley, 1986, 1995).

Auditory-verbal: Area which handles textual information. (Called the phonological loop in some sources.) Audio information is also processed in this area. If a person reads a set of directions, they would be processed in this area.

Figure 3. Working memory (adapted from Baddeley, 2000)

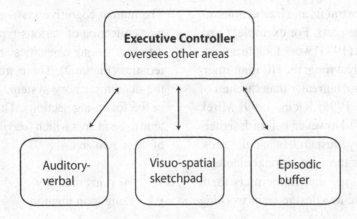

Visuo-spatial Sketchpad: Area which handles the information about what we see, and handles relations between objects and images. If a person is shown a map, the mental image would be processed in this area.

Episodic Buffer: Area which links information to form integrated units of visual, spatial, and verbal information with time sequencing. "The episodic buffer is assumed to be a limited-capacity temporary storage system that is capable of integrating information from a variety of sources" (Baddeley, 2000, p. 421).

Executive Controller: The executive controller works as the controller for the other three areas. It handles the multitasking aspects of using working memory by directing a person's attention to the specific task and when to shift tasks. It only seems to be active when a task requires conscious attention, but not on tasks that have been learned to automaticity. For example, having people generate a sequence of random numbers while performing another task requires the executive controller since thought must go into figuring out the next number, but counting for 1 to 10 repeatedly does not.

Working memory processes information by combining and integrating new inputs from the senses with information retrieved from long term memory. New knowledge is constructed from these two information sources and, depending on the situation, may be either used immediately or stored in long term memory.

A major limitation of working memory is that it can only maintain and manipulate limited amounts of information. People have a hard time remembering and manipulating multiple items in memory at the same time, with Miller's (1956) 7 +/- 2 being the seminal work. However, recent work by Halford et al. (2005) shows that when problem solving, people have difficulty with four variables and find five nearly impossible. Unlike Miller who had people memorize lists, Halford et al. (2005) had people analyzing graphical representations, a real-world task.

Working memory capacity seems to be a factor in reading ability. Skilled readers can recall more words in working memory tasks than can less skilled readers. The interpretation of this result is that a skilled reader can perform more complex operations for integrating and interpreting the text (McNamara & Scott, 2001).

Information in working memory has a short lifetime unless the person engages in active rehearsal (working to remember it). This rapid decay is what causes people to forget information quickly, such as looking up a phone number and then forgetting it if they are interrupted before dialing.

Dual Coding Theory

Dual coding theory considers how the brain seems to have two separate areas of working memory which gives provides seperate pathways for visual and aural processing. It explains how people can see and hear different things and still make sense of them or why hearing and seeing information results in better learning.

Dual coding theory (Paivio, 1971, 1986) postulates that there are two different channels in the brain which separately process visual and verbal information. Thus, visual and verbal information is processed both separately and differently as they get integrated into a situation model. Baddeley's (2000) working memory model of a two-part processing system with the Auditory-verbal and visuo-spatial sketchpad essentially maps to Paivio's theory. However, Baddely had the two working together and drawing from a single cognitive resource pool while Paivio sees them as working in fully separate processes within the brain, with their own independent cognitive resource pools.

One example of dual coding comes from the selective interference effect, which occurs when people try to perform two mental tasks that require manipulating similar information. People find it very difficult to deal with two visual inputs (watching two images at once) or two verbal inputs (listening to two people at once). On the other hand, if asked to perform a visual and a verbal task simultaneously, (viewing an image while listening to unrelated information), they perform both faster and with fewer errors. In all three of these interference cases, a single code channel can only handle one thing at a time, but separate channels can process information in parallel. The training research which finds people who both see and hear information learn better also stems from dual-coding theory. Providing redundant information in both channels helps to strengthen the mental integration.

Long Term Memory

Long term memory is the storage area for everything people know. It seems to be essentially infinite in size. Learning can be defined as moving information from working memory into long term memory. Once stored in long term memory, the content will tend to decay (be forgotten) if not repeated at some interval, but this is a much longer interval than with working memory. The decay rate of highly difficult or traumatic events or learning may have decay rates spanning years.

Long term memory is organized around categories (which depend on how the information was learned) and retrieval is based on the categories. Attempts to retrieve known information when the retrieval does not match a category are difficult (comparable to doing a keyword-based with the wrong keywords). Information retrieval from long term memory is much slower than retrieving it from working memory.

Long term memory seems to be stored as different memory types which people can access at various contextual levels, which cause these memory types to influence HII differently.

Declarative Memory: All memories that are consciously available. It can be divided into two types, although they overlap extensively in most instances.

Episodic Memory: Refers to memories of specific past events (Tulving, 2002). They are very context-rich and may include multiple senses. For example, the memories of fresh pine during a specific Christmas celebration.

Semantic Memory: Refers to memories of facts (Eichenbaum, 1997). Typically, they lack context. The fact can be recalled, but it is isolated from any other references. Last-minute cramming for an exam deals exclusively with semantic memory.

Procedural Memory: Procedural memory refers to memories of skills learned through practice (Ashby & O'Brien, 2005). Typically, these are motor skills, such as sports. Developing procedural memory is a slow process and requires immediate and constant feedback. Unlike other memories, there is little awareness of the details, which is reflected in people's inability to describe how they do a particular, highly learned action.

Retrieval and Recognition

Once information is stored in long term memory, it can be recalled as needed. It appears that memories of two major types are stored.

Explicit memory: Conscious memory of previous actions and information which people can recall as needed. Explicit memory tasks such as recall and recognition require people to think back to a previous event.

Implicit memory: Unconscious memory of previously learned procedural actions. Use of implicit memory allows people to perform actions without thinking about them, such a tying shoes or knowing the route to drive to work.

The use of cued recall and free recall in usability testing access different retrieval methods for explicit memory. Cued recall gives people the category label which, it is hoped, corresponds to how it was stored, making it much easier to recall. With a free recall, people lack that category help and must mentally develop their own. How people categorize objects influences how those objects are represented in long-term memory and how easily they can be recalled (Schyns & Rodet, 1997). Pictures are recalled or recognized better than words and concrete nouns are better remembered than abstract nouns on explicit memory tests such as free recall (Hamilton & Rajaram, 2001).

Once people learn which features are important for category membership, these diagnostic features become more salient than non-diagnostic features in long-term memory and object recognition (Wagar & Dixon, 2005). This shows why color is not important for classifying an animal such as a house cat, but would be for telling apart a cheetah and a leopard (at least for the non-cat expert).

The difficulty with which people learn a task seems to have a strong influence on how well they can recall it later, with high difficulty being most remembered. In a study of language learning, the more difficult the learning conditions, the easier it was for people to remember what they had learned (Schneider, Healy, & Bourne, 2002). If people exert little effort to learn a task, they may be doing essentially all of the work in working memory and never committing it to long term memory.

Interference

A significant factor in working memory is that both have an auditory-verbal and the visuo-spatial sketchpad, and they can operate in a cooperative fashion and not compete for resources or interfere with each other (Baddeley, 1995; Baddeley & Hitch, 1974). Thus, design teams should strive for designs which maximize both areas to minimize the disruptions caused by overloading one or the other. Although they do not interfere with each other, both of the areas do experience interference from many sources, which leads to problems with remembering information.

Interference means the loss of performance caused by any overlap of information process (this is different from overload where the brain lacks sufficient cognitive resources). Typically it manifests either by making the people forget information or by confusing the information between two tasks. When people have to hold multiple mental representations in working memory at once, they tend to overwrite each other because of limited available cognitive resources (Oberauer, Lange, & Engle, 2004). As would be expected, similar material tends to interfere with each other more than non-similar material (Oberauer & Kliegl, 2006).

VISION

This section looks at basic eye anatomy and the physiological factors of how the eye responds to reading text.

Structure of the Eye

This section describes the basic structures of the eye (Figure 4).

Iris: Iris regulates the amount of light that enters the eye. It forms the colored, visible part of the eye in front of the lens. Light enters through a central opening called the pupil.

Pupil: Pupil is the circular opening in the centre of the iris through which light passes into the lens of the eye. The iris controls widening and narrowing (dilation and constriction) of the pupil.

Cornea: Cornea is the transparent circular part of the front of the eyeball. It refracts the

Figure 4. Basic eye anatomy (adapted from National Eye Institute, National Institutes of Health)

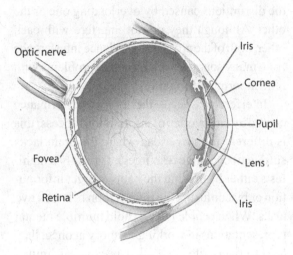

light entering the eye onto the lens, which then focuses it onto the retina. The cornea contains no blood vessels and is extremely sensitive to pain.

Lens: Lens is a transparent structure situated behind the pupil of the eye and it is enclosed in a thin transparent capsule. It helps to refract incoming light and focus it onto the retina. The lens can change its shape (and therefore its refractive power) rapidly and voluntarily. Using its ability to change shape, the lens allows the eye to change its focal point. Changes in the shape of the lens will allow a normal eye to focus on near objects. As a person ages, the lens loses some of its flexibility, which results in presbyopia—when a person needs reading glasses.

Fovea: Fovea area is very sensitive because essentially every photoreceptor has its own nerve cell. As the cones and rods move further toward the edge of the eye, a single nerve connects more and more of them.

Retina: Retina is a light-sensitive layer that lines the interior of the eye. It is composed of light-sensitive cells (the photoreceptors) known as rods and cones. The retina works much in the same way as film in a camera.

Optic nerve: Optic nerve leaves the eye at the optic disk, and transfers all the visual information to the brain.

Photoreceptors

Rods: Rod cells are one of the two types of photoreceptor cells in the retina. There are about 125 million rods. Rods respond to light, but not color. They are more light-sensitive than cones, which is why objects seen in low light tend to be seen in grayscale rather than color.

Cones: Cone cells are the second type of photoreceptor cells in the retina. They are sensitive to color, able to perceive finer detail and more rapid changes in an image. Cones come in three varieties that are sensitive to different wavelengths of light—red, green, or blue. The brain combines these to form all the other colors. The human retina contains 6 to 7 million cones which function best in bright light.

The distribution of cones and rods is not equal across the retina. They both become increasing dense approaching the fovea area, with cones being denser than rods. In the fovea, there are only cone cells. While only about four percent of the color-sensitive photoreceptors (cones) lining the retina are sensitive to short-wavelength light, they are distributed farther into the periphery than cones sensitive to medium and long wavelengths. As a result, blue-sensitive cones are far apart, so it is difficult to see distracting patterns in a blue background. At the edges of the retina, there are very few cones, giving people essentially black and white peripheral vision.

Color Blindness

Color blindness is a genetic problem caused when a person lacks one or more of the three types of cone cells. Which type is lacking determines which colors cannot be seen.

Red-green: Red and green appear the same. It affects eight percent of males and 0.5 percent of females of populations with Northern European ancestry, with a much lower percentages in other populations. It is the most common color blindness and design teams must consider it when using color.

Blue-yellow: Blue and yellow appear the same. It affects fewer than 1 in 10,000 people. Consistent across world populations and genders.

No color vision: No color perception; the person sees shades of gray. It affects fewer than 1 in 30,000 people.

Designs using color must consider the prevalence of color blindness among the audience and pick colors which will not cause interpretation issues. Many guidelines state to never use only color coding, but to always have a secondary coding that is color-independent, such as cross-hatching on a graph. In a design, green and red must have redundant coding because these colors will look the same to a person with red-green color blindness. Numerous websites provide tools that modify an image to show how it looks for the different types of color blindness.

Eye Movement

Only in a very small area at the center of vision, at about a two-degree visual angle, can objects be seen in detail. This small area is called the *fovea.* In order to read text, it typically must be in the fovea area—an area that corresponds to a few words long at normal reading distance. Eye movements during reading work to place the current set of words within this area (Figure 5).

Anything outside of the fovea is seen with lessening detail until it moves completely out of the visual field. The useful field of view (UFOV) is the area around the fixation points from which useful information can be extracted. In general, the UFOV to be about 1-4 degrees. The range is determined by factors such as the density of the information, the contrast, and overall task demands (Williams, 1989). The UFOV decreases as the information density increases, the contrast be-

Figure 5. Saccades when reading text. The eye focuses on each of the gray areas and moves across the line with a series of saccades. The area of the fovea roughly compares to the highlighted area. Large fonts put fewer letters within the area of sharpest vision, which make them slower to read. Outside of the central area, the ability to distinguish details falls off rapidly.

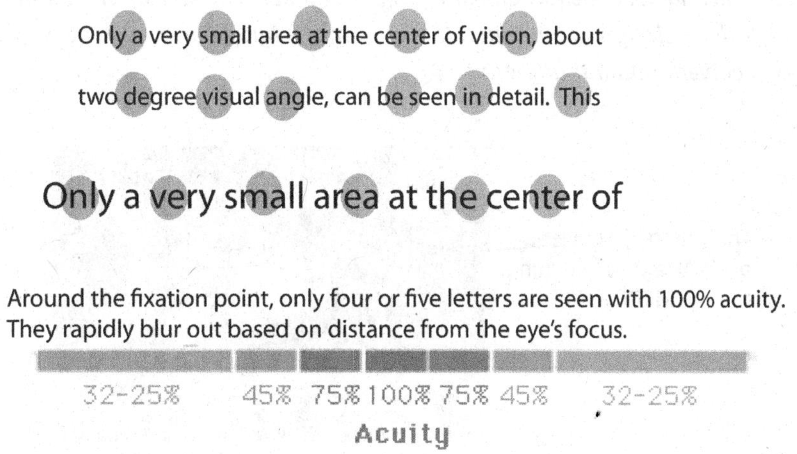

Only a very small area at the center of vision, about

two degree visual angle, can be seen in detail. This

Only a very small area at the center of

Around the fixation point, only four or five letters are seen with 100% acuity. They rapidly blur out based on distance from the eye's focus.

32-25%   45% 75% 100% 75% 45%   32-25%

Acuity

tween the foreground and background decreases (poor lighting or poor color combinations), or the task difficulty increases. In addition, age and training play a significant factor in the size of the UFOV.

Since the fovea covers such a small area of detailed vision, the eye needs to constantly move to capture details of the entire picture. There are two types of movement:

Pursuit movement: A relatively smooth movement used when tracking a moving object.

Saccadic movement: Discrete, jerky movements which are used to move the eye across stationary objects. Reading text uses a series of saccadic movements to transverse the line of text. Likewise, when viewing a web page, the head is held mostly steady and saccadic movements jump around the displayed page—eye trackers works by recording the pauses at the end of each jump. The pauses are called fixations; visual information is only processed during the fixation, not during the movement.

The flyback (returning the eye to the beginning of the next line) is a slow movement compared to a saccade (the eye jump which occurs during reading). Short lines require excess reading time because of the number of saccades. Long lines impair reading by making the flyback such a long movement, the eye can get lost and move to the wrong line. This also causes problems with posters with long lines. If a line extends the entire width of a five foot wide poster, the head must turn to read it when standing at a normal viewing distance.

Eye saccades occur at a rate of about 2-4 per second when reading or searching for information. This limits the reader to mentally processing 2-4 UFOV per second. Using an eye tracker allows for measuring both where a person looks and for how long (Figure 6). Besides the saccade rate, there is the dwell time for the fixation, how long the eye looks at a specific point. More important information, denser information, or information which impairs extraction (such as low contrast) all increase dwell time. In other words, areas that are important or hard to read are looked at longer. Areas which contain important information receive more fixations and they last longer than areas which contain less important information. What information is rated by a reader as highly important is driven more by the activated mental model and information salience than by the actual importance of the information to understanding

Figure 6. Eye dwell time and saccades when using an eye tracker. The size of the dot indicates the dwell time. With eye tracker data, design teams can tell where on the image or page a person spent time looking and what parts received minimal attention.

the situation. Thus, for efficient HII, design teams must ensure that these factors match.

There are also special cells in the eye periphery which only detect motion. They are very useful for detecting potential threats outside of the center of view; however, they are very counter-productive during focused reading. Any text motion is picked up, which interferes with processing information in the UFOV. These cells explain why motion of tickertapes on websites can prove so distracting. Of course, from an HII perspective, moving text is harder to read and should be avoided.

Visual Acuity and Angle

Visual acuity is how much an eye can differentiate one object from another in terms of visual angles. It is measured in cycles per degree (CPD), which measures an angular resolution.

Typically, human eyes with excellent acuity have a resolution of about 37 CPD (1.6 minute of arc per line pair, or a 0.47 mm line pair, at 1 m). Resolution in CPD can be measured by bar charts of different numbers of white–black stripe cycles. For example, if each pattern is 1.75 cm wide and is placed at 1 m distance from the eye, it will subtend an angle of 1 degree, so the number of white–black bar pairs on the pattern will be a measure of the cycles per degree of that pattern. The highest such number that the eye can resolve as stripes, or distinguish from a gray block, is then the measurement of visual acuity of the eye.

Visual acuity tests use black lines, but many designs use colored lines. Thus, it is important to consider how well people can detect color with closely spaced lines as well as resolving the separation. It is almost impossible for the human eye to identify the color of a line whose thickness is smaller than 0.06 inch. That actual width at which the color can be identified depends on the specific hue and saturation. Blues and light shades are the hardest to distinguish in narrow lines. Also, a black background has been shown to provide better color discrimination than a white background (Young & Miller, 1991).

Visual angle, which is the minimum gap a person can see, is directly related to visual acuity, Being able to see a gap of 1 arc minute corresponds to 20/20 vision. On an eye chart, a letter for 20/20 vision subtends an angle of 5 arc minutes. When designing text, as a rough estimate, characters should subtend at least 20 arc minutes and the preferred size is 20-22 arc minutes. For text, legibility begins to decrease with symbol heights less than 18 arc minutes (FAA). MIL Standard 1472 states that under office lighting conditions the visual angle subtended by height of black & white characters should be not less than 16 arc minutes with 20 arc minutes preferred as measured from the greatest anticipated viewing distance. The visual angle for colored characters should be at least 21 arc minutes. If the light level is lower (and even most homes have significantly lower lighting than an office), the size of the letters needs to increase since legibility decreases with decreased light levels.

Visual angle defines the size of the image on the retina. The relative size of an object depends on how close it is to the eye (Figure 7). While this is typically considered with respect to buildings or other material objects, in HII it becomes a critical factor for text size and readability. Obviously, the 10-12 point text on a printed page cannot be read down the hall. When designing posters or other such displays which will be viewed at a distance, the apparent size must be considered. A word on a page and large word on a poster down the hall may have the same visual angle. Table 1 shows how the relative size of a letter can be calculated. The interesting point is that if the visual angle of two letters is the same, the image size on the retina is the same, yet the brain is able to provide the relative distance based on other perception cues. Shinoda and Ikeda (1998) found that although the retina size remained the same, the perceived legibility of the letters decreased with perceived increasing distance. Thus, text which will be

Figure 7. Calculating relative letter size. The letters at points A and B are the same physical size on the retina, since they have the same visual angle. For the same perceived legibility between points A and B, the letter at A must be larger.

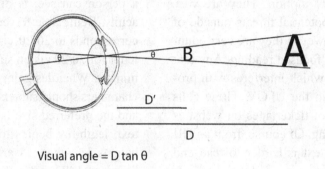

Visual angle = D tan θ

Table 1. Size versus distances for normal reading-size letters. Values are the required height so the letters appear to be the same size at the given distance.

Font size	18 inches	3 feet	6 feet	20 feet	100 feet
12	12 pt	24 pt	48 pt	2.25 in	11 in
14	14 pt	28 pt	56 pt	2.59 in	13 in
24	24 pt	48 pt	96 pt	4.45 in	22 in
36	36 pt	72 pt	144 pt	6.67 in	33 in

viewed at a distance, needs to be relatively larger than the same text viewed up close for people to perceive the same legibility.

Contrast of Foreground and Background

A significant element of text legibility is the contrast between the letters and the background (discussed in chapter 7: *How people approach typography*, "Legibility"). Contrast can be defined as the visual properties that distinguish a letter (or other objects) from the background. In general, this depends on both the color and the brightness difference of between the letter and the background. For human visual perceptions, contrast depends on the relative difference between the objects rather any absolute color or brightness.

Black and white provides the highest contrast of any color combination. Interestingly, black text on a white background and white text on a black ground are not the equivalent contrasts from a reading perspective. White text on a black background is a higher contrast. A black background has been shown to provide better visual discrimination than a white background (Young & Miller, 1991).

Text with low contrast is difficult to read since people have to work harder to distinguish the letters (Figure 8). Poor contrast is the problem with poorly designed web sites that use bad color combinations such as blue links on black backgrounds, red text on green a background, or yellow on a white background. These sites also demonstrate how people who know the text (the site designer) can read it with a much poorer contrast than people who do not (new readers).

Contrast issues are important for interpreting graphical information. Gray scale designs may provide 256 different shades of gray, but the human eye has a difficult time distinguishing one

Figure 8. Changing readability of text with different background contrast. Numbers in the first column are the percent grayscale for the row. The first column is a sans serif and the second column is serif; notice how the font style also affects the readability.

100%		Line of text
80%	Line of text	Line of text
60%	Line of text	Line of text
40%	Line of text	Line of text
20%	Line of text	Line of text
10%	Line of text	Line of text
0%	Line of text	

shade from another. Differences in color hue, on the other hand, are easy to distinguish. The use of false color images in the sciences exploits this feature. A false-color image is derived from a grayscale image by mapping each pixel value to a color (transform a gray to a color). A familiar example is the encoding of altitude in physical relief maps, where negative values (below sea level) are usually represented by shades of blue, and positive values by greens and browns. Although false-coloring does not increase the information contents of the original image, it can make some details more visible, by making it easier to distinguish small changes.

PowerPoint presentations have become one of the most common uses of color where people are not directly interacting with the system. A common element in slide design is the use of colored backgrounds. Research in the education field has examined how color affects learning, and found little long-term impact (Berry, 1991). However, some color combinations seem to work better than others (Mackiewicz, 2007a; 2007b). A comparison of colored symbols on black backgrounds found that the scores for white symbols were the highest, followed by three versions of yellow (Start,

1989). When black alphanumeric characters were presented on white, blue, and green backgrounds, black-on-white had higher recall both immediately and one hour after the presentation. Pett (1993) summarized the results of two unpublished studies on the legibility of white letters on colored backgrounds. Yellow and cyan backgrounds had significantly higher legibility than red or blue, and green was also significantly better than blue. With slides on computer monitors, magenta, blue, and yellow were significantly better than cyan or green, and red was significantly better than green. Both studies also asked subjects about their preferred color backgrounds, and cyan and blue were preferred to most other colors. However, these studies asked about user preferences and did not test for comprehension.

Color

Although color starts with the wavelengths of light reflected or emitted by an object, the actual color perceived is a result of how the eye's cones and the brain interpret it. Color detection is essentially an automatic process; it is processed in parallel and automatically during pre-attentive visual processes (Treisman, 1985). (Pre-attention is discussed in section "Attention" in this chapter.) Basically, this means people can detect and potentially respond to a color without having to devote any cognitive resources.

Color can be described by three different factors: hue, saturation, and intensity.

Hue: Hue is what is typically called color; technically a specific wavelength of light. A spectrum is made up of a range of hues.

Saturation: The purity of the color. For emitted colors, it is based on the amount of white light mixed with pure hue. For reflective colors, it is based on the amount of gray mixed with the pure hue. Pastels have a low saturation.

Intensity: The intensity of the color. High value colors appear bright.

Figure 9. Hue, intensity, saturation curve. All three curves have the same hue (they appear the same color). Curve A has the lowest saturation (widest spread) and would appear the palest. Curve B is the most saturated (smallest spread). Curve C has the highest intensity (highest peak) and would appear the brightest.

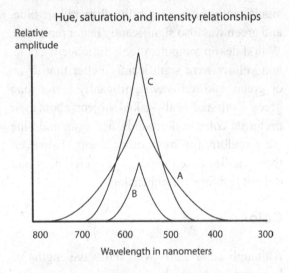

The three values can be described graphically in Figure 9. The hue is the color value at a single wavelength. The saturation is the amount of spread of the curve. Intensity is the height of the curve.

COGNITIVE LOAD

People possess a pool of cognitive resources which they devote to the various tasks they are performing (Figure 10). Without going into details on the different theories (which are generally similar enough for our purposes here), people seem to have a small fixed-size pool of cognitive resources. Cognitive load is the amount of cognitive resources which are actually being used at any specific time. High cognitive load results in increased errors as well as lower comprehension and performance; identifying and correcting for these places within a web design should improve the overall usability.

Cognitive Resources

Depending on the researcher and how a specific theory is constructed, the amount of cognitive resources and how they are allocated to tasks can vary, but across all models, the actual amount of available cognitive resources is very low (e.g., Baddeley, 2001; Chandler & Sweller, 1996; Wickens, 2002).

Figure 10. Cognitive resource allocated across various tasks. When working with a website, people typically have to allocate resources for answering the initial question which brought them to the site, then site navigation, and then reading and analyzing the content. Part A shows the cognitive load imposed by well-designed site. Part B shows the overload problem caused by poorly designed navigation which requires more resources.

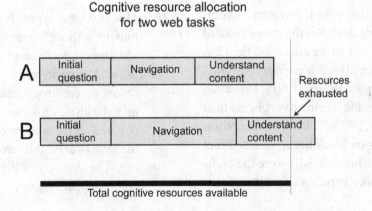

The cognitive resources people have available are not a fixed value for all situations, but vary based on many external factors. The external factors themselves could be considered to be consuming some of the cognitive resources, thus rendering them unavailable. Some of the factors which decrease available cognitive resources are:

- Emotional stress, including the general stress of a harried work environment or life.
- Time pressure to complete a task or make a decision.
- Lack of sleep.

Methods of measuring cognitive load are based on psychological research of the cognitive resources people possess and how they allocate them to tasks (Sweller, 1988). The NASA TLX test considers cognitive load as connected to a person and not to the task; it views cognitive load as a hypothetical construct that represents the cost incurred by people as they work to achieve a particular level of performance (Hart & Staveland, 1988). Rather than considering workload as an inherent property, it sees it as a factor which results from the process of performing a task. Regardless of the theory, essentially, a person has a very limited amount of resources which must be allocated across all tasks currently being performed. Miller's (1956) well-known work on 7 +/- 2 information chunks was early research into memory and can be interpreted as a reflection of limited cognitive resources. Remembering the chunks consumed resources; when the resources are exhausted, people can't remember a chunk's contents. It is the highly limited nature of cognitive resources and how people handle them which can be used as an explanation for issues such as difficulties in multitasking and forgetting previously read information.

Reducing the cognitive load on a reader requires that design teams control both the amount of information and its complexity so that it matches the specific situation and reader characteristics (Garrett & Caldwell, 2002). One significant factor is the amount of mental integration people must perform to transform the information content into something applicable to their situation (Albers, 2008). Even small cognitive transformations take effort away from the intended task and design teams should work to fit the information closely to the situation. Two methods which are used are mnemonics and memory aids, both help offload the work to the screen and minimize cognitive load (Hix & Hartson, 1993).

Cognitive Overload

Each mental task consumes cognitive resources, especially when tasks must be done in parallel. Once those resources are exhausted, people suffer from cognitive overload, shown in Figure 10). High cognitive load results in increased errors as well as lower comprehension and performance; identifying and correcting for these places within a design should improve overall performance and usability.

Because cognitive resources are very limited, unfortunately, cognitive overload can occur easily. People do not operate in a state of cognitive overload. Instead, they reduce the workload. When this occurs, several things can happen, all of which degrade efficient and effective information communication:

- Error rates dramatically increase. The failures that occur when playing the higher levels of Tetris occur because of cognitive overload from having to rapidly calculate and perform the required rotations.
- Frustration increases. People may quit performing the task or simply pick any answer to avoid further interactions. Frustration also leads to negative views of overall system usability and usefulness.

- Tasks are shed. Rather than trying to mentally juggle multiple tasks, people shed (stops doing) one or more tasks.
- Information may be accepted without evaluation of its quality.
- People shed tasks and try to mentally simplify the analysis. As the information increases in quantity and complexity, contrary to intuition, people do not increase the complexity of their analysis strategy but rely on heuristics (Fennema & Kleinmuntz, 1995; Thuring, Hannemann, & Haake 1995).
- Information is disregarded. Instead of working to incorporate new or updated information into the current mental model, information is ignored. This is basically a variation of task shedding.

Interestingly, until a person reaches cognitive overload, the level of cognitive load has minimal effect on task performance (Figure 11). After reaching the point of cognitive overload, performance decreases abruptly and dramatically. For example, the sudden onset of errors a person experiences on reaching a new level of Tetris or other such game results because the game requires more cognitive resources than are available. In other research, Wickens and Carswell (1995) point out that graphs reduce cognitive load by shifting the load to visual perception. Lohse (1997) claims that the effects of reducing cognitive loading will only be noticeable in complex tasks which are normally constrained by cognitive resources since it frees up resources for use elsewhere. In terms of Figure 1, the effect is only seen when the cognitive load point is exceeded.

In a study of driver guidance systems, the findings are a good example of how cognitive load level affects response:

The results showed that each of the guidance information representation factors— the number of exit roads, the presence or absence of a landmark and the types of intersections— has a significant influence on the mean maximum duration of glances. Moreover, below a raised threshold of complexity, the number of glances remains stable and independent of the quantity of information presented, whereas passing this threshold demands extra glances from the driver (Labiale, 2001, p. 149).

Figure 11. When the cognitive load level (increasing line) crosses the overload threshold (dotted line); the performance (heavy line) drops abruptly.

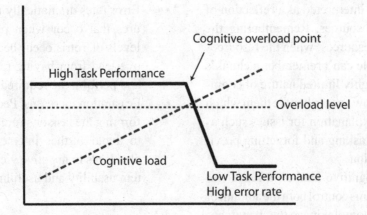

Until the driver suffered cognitive overload, the number of glances remained stable. After reaching cognitive overload, the glance pattern changed as the driver tried to adjust to handle all of the incoming information.

Measuring Cognitive Load

"An ever expanding array of complex systems is being found in both industry and the military. This increase in complexity is placing a larger burden on operators because interactions with these systems requires higher-level cognitive processes such as problem-solving and decision-making" (Fiore, Cuevas & Oser, 2003, p. 185). Meeting these needs for higher-level cognitive processes requires that the design and content consider the problem-solving and decision-making inherent in the situation, and support it. As a part of effective design, design teams must consider the cognitive load the design imposes and strive to minimize it.

Psychology and human factors researchers have a long history of using cognitive load measures to determine specific points of high cognitive load. For example, design of control panels in both aviation and industrial plants, especially nuclear control rooms, normally includes studies of operator cognitive load while interacting with the systems.

There are many different methods of measuring cognitive load, ranging from direct measurement of neuro-physiological response to post-event questions.

Measurements of physiology responses, such as EEG and pulse rates, vary according to the cognitive load level and provide a highly effective measurement method. However, these types of measurements are also expensive and require special equipment and training. Although these studies are typically only used for safety-critical systems, their expense and test time prohibit their application to most software or web-based interactions.

Post-event questionnaires, such as Subjective Mental Effort Questionnaire (SMEQ) and the NASA Task Load Index (TLX) provide a method to assess the workload situation once an action is complete. The NASA TLX test (considered by many the gold standard for cognitive load measurements) was developed to measure the overall work load of equipment operation in various human-machine environments such as aircraft cockpits and process control environments. The concept of the NASA TLX is to allow the user time to assess the workload situation once an action is complete. For example, the person would complete a NASA TLX form after each major step, such as after removing a panel cover and then after disconnecting a piece of equipment. To assess the workload experienced while completing multiple tasks, the person rates their effort on six scales: mental demand, physical demand, temporal demand, performance, effort, and frustration (JTAP). The user rates each of these on a Likert scale and then answers 15 questions that pairs two scales and asks the user to select the one that is the most important contributor to the workload of the task.

Secondary task interference tests impose a second task which reduces available cognitive resources and helps push people into cognitive overload. A standard variation is to have the person rhythmically tap, and measuring when the taps vary (Tracy & Albers, 2006). People are told to tap with their non-dominate hand with a steady rhythm of about one tap per second. When they suffer cognitive overload, the tap rate will slow or stop. There is also the Sternberg memory task (Sternberg, 1966), where people memorize a few numbers and then responds yes/no to whether a given number was one they memorized. People are give a small set of number (1-6) to memorize and then are given a sequence of probe numbers at regular intervals while they perform the primary task. For example, memorize 3 and 6. If the probe number is 8, people say "no" and if the probe number is 6, they say "yes.". When they suffer cognitive overload, there can be a substantial delay or out-right forgetting of memorized numbers.

Cognitive Resources and Computers Interfaces

Computer interfaces require both cognitive and physical interactions. People have to plan out their movements, figure out efficient ways of doing those movements, and actually execute them. There are two types of effort which come into play: cognitive effort for reading and deciding actions, and physical effort of manipulating the interface. Basden and Hibberd (1996) state that, "What this means is that at least some of user's cognitive effort is devoted to performing the interface action, as distinct from its [the interface content's] meaning" (p. 148). Any cognitive resources devoted to manipulating the interface are not available to mentally processing the information contained in that interface, thus the need to make the interface as transparent as possible. People's attention gets split between the needed information and the interface; psychology and human factors research have looked at split attention issues for many years, with a consistent finding that it impairs comprehension. The more complex the interaction, the harder time people have comprehending the information since too many resources are directed to manipulating the interface. "Every effort additional to reading reduces the mental resources available for comprehension. With respect to hyper-documents, such efforts primarily concern orientation, navigation, and user-interface adjustment" (Thuring, Hannemann, & Haake, 1995, p. 59). Designing for easy manipulation and assimilation of information requires minimizing cognitive effort of activities not directly tied to the information.

Halford et al. (2005) shows that when problem solving, people have difficulty with four variables and find five nearly impossible. The more variables the interface requires people to track, the fewer remain for the information of interest.

A poorly designed interface can consume those four variables, leaving scant cognitive resources for comprehending the content.

Hutchins, Hollan & Norman (1985) developed a model that explains the effectiveness of a direct manipulation interface (the normal Windows or Mac interface) as the result of the commitment of fewer cognitive resources in order to complete a given task. They point out that cognitive effort is minimized if the system interface maps directly onto people's mental model of a task. Thus, a command line interface shifts attention from the object to be manipulated (normally a file) to the command and any associated switches. A direct manipulation interface, on the other hand, allows the person to remain focused on the objects of interest. In a similar manner, research suggests, for instance, that reading hypertext materials imposes higher cognitive demand than reading print because of the extra effort of deciphering links and working to interact with the interface (Wenger & Payne, 1996).

PRIOR KNOWLEDGE

The knowledge people bring to a topic strongly influences how they interpret information. Prior knowledge provides a basis for making judgments about information quality and for prioritizing information. As such, prior knowledge is closely related to which mental model gets activated and used since the mental model determines which prior knowledge is deemed relevant. Later in this section, we will discuss how prior knowledge which contradicts the current information can override it. Thus, it is important that audience analysis give a clear understanding of the prior knowledge the various audience groups have, and how that knowledge varies among audience groups.

This section looks at how prior knowledge affects information comprehension, the types of prior knowledge people have, the comprehension problems that result if prior knowledge conflicts with the current information, and how people transfer knowledge across situations.

Prior Knowledge and Comprehension

Prior knowledge has a strong effect on how well people comprehend information. "In general, researchers have noted that prior knowledge can affect comprehension in two basic ways (Spyridakis & Wenger, 1992).

By activation of topic-relevant prior knowledge for learning: The proper information is activated and used to evaluate new information.

By inadequate activation and use of prior knowledge: If the current information is presented improperly, it risks activating the wrong prior knowledge, or not activating prior knowledge at all. If poor presentation prevents people from realizing they have prior knowledge, then it will not be activated. If the wrong prior knowledge is activated, then the entire situation will be interpreted incorrectly. For example, if a problem situation report focuses entirely on the problem costs, the reader's knowledge about people conflicts may not used, which is the real reason for the initial problem.

A reader's prior knowledge level affects the level of knowledge gained from a text. Low-knowledge readers tend to gain a surface level understanding and are not able to extract deeper levels of comprehension. This is detrimental to contextual awareness and interferes with gaining the deeper levels of comprehension required for effective decision making. For example, in a usability test, they can quote the text, but not explain it or put it into their own words. Or when people read information, they might understand individual words but cannot extract a concept. Even if words themselves are recognized and interpreted correctly, people have to grasp the underlying concept to understand the effects. For example, if a person is unfamiliar with the relationship of pressure, tube, and flow of fluid, even writing the text in low-literacy language will not clarify that leg muscles press on veins to move the blood, an important prevention principle to avoid venous blood clots during prolonged flights (Lukoscheka, Fazzarib, & Marantz, 2003). Or if the text explicitly states that "leg muscles press on veins to move blood," the person might simply commit that phrase to memory without understanding. As a result, the person forms a false concept of blood circulation and will not be able to apply it to related situations.

A fundamental principle of learning is repetition. However, most HII situations are not truly learning situations. The difference can be considered as learning new concepts or ideas (attending a class) versus gathering information to understand the specifics of a situation that is already understood in general terms. For example, consider how business analysts look at monthly reports to figure out why employee retention has decreased. They know how to analyze reports; what they don't know is the answer to their questions about current employee retention issues. Their prior knowledge includes how to analyze the information and may even contain some clues about what areas to look at specifically.

More influential than the general prior knowledge is specific guidance given just before reading the text. If people are given some guidance before they interpret the text, their interpretation or decision tends to reflect the guidance.. For example, if people are told about interpersonal conflicts damaging projects and then given case study, they will identify more of the interpersonal conflicts. This is called priming, which is discussed in detail in chapter 10: *How people interact with information presentation*, "Priming." With priming, the specific prior knowledge which is activated exerts a strong influence on interpreting the information.

Prior knowledge is relatively easy to activate through the use of titles, headings, subheadings, and lists of key words or concepts (Duin, 1991). A significant part of the usefulness of document headings and other advanced organizers is to activate proper prior knowledge and allow the reader to apply it to the text. However, although prior knowledge has a strong effect on reading comprehension, Rouet (2003) did not find a strong prior knowledge effect for search strategies with respect to either time or accuracy, although he did see trends in that direction. He did find greater learning of material (when people were given information search tasks) when the people had prior knowledge about the overall subject (i.e., when they were working within their discipline). With prior knowledge, people were able to mentally integrate the new information better.

The complication for design teams is that repeating unknown or new information can help with comprehension, but repeating the already known interferes with interpreting information. A person has to devote cognitive resources to evaluating it, to confirming that it is already known, and then deciding to ignore it. For example, inline definitions decreased performance when the readers knew those definitions, but they did help readers who do not know them (Chalmers, 2003). Thus, the value of repeating information or providing redundant information, such as inline definitions, is highly dependent on audience. And text written in the wrong way will impede comprehension. In one study, following a standard presentation of a newborn hearing screening test, comprising a leaflet and a brief description from the testers, a mother's knowledge of the test was good. An additional structured presentation about the test did not increase scores for the entire group, but did help people with lower levels of education (Baker, Uus, Bamford, & Marteau, 2004).

One major factor distinguishing expert- from novice-level interaction within a situation is that experts possess prior knowledge. This gives them an advantage over novices because they can supply

Box 1.

Different terms, same meaning

Think of the problem when a person is talking about a topic but is using terms the other person doesn't know. When I was in the Navy, I once overheard a conversation between an Engineer Officer and one of his senior chiefs about a planning drill that a nuclear-trained officer from the squadron wanted the diesel-powered ship to run as part of an inspection. The Engineer Officer was asking for a 'high delta temp alarm' drill, which had the chief baffled. Suddenly, the chief asked, "You mean a crankcase over-temperature alarm?" (Being a chief, he used a little more colorful phrase.) Once the terms were changed, it made sense to the chief and, as a result, the entire discussion made sense to both people. The problem was inadequate activation of the chief's prior knowledge. He knew how to plan the desired drill but he didn't understand the terminology in the request. Once he understood, he was able to apply his prior knowledge, he knew what type of drill he was supposed to run.

The basic problem here is that nuclear power plants and diesel power plants have different terminology for the same basic concept of a part of this system running too hot. Until the realization of the terms' equivalence and chief's mental translation from one to the other, there was little communication.

---

information based on experience and use heuristics to understand the current situation. Using prior knowledge, they know which information to pay attention to and which to ignore. With prior knowledge, experts are able to resolve ambiguity, identify subtle cause and effect relationships, and as a result, develop better contextual awareness more effectively than novices. "When the task requires problem structuring, interpretation of ambiguous cues within the expert's domain, and reliance on underlying causal models, experts surpass novices who lack the knowledge base to guide their performance" (Orasanu & Connolly, 1993, p. 11). On the other hand, an expert's prior knowledge only helps in situations where they either actually posses prior knowledge or can make use of positive transfer (discussed later in this section). In a situation where their prior knowledge does not apply, they perform no better than a novice. In addition, in some situations their prior knowledge can interfere (negative transfer) and then they may actually perform worse than a novice who lacks any prior knowledge to cause interference.

Tacit versus Explicit Knowledge

The prior knowledge that people possess exists in three different forms: tacit, semi-tacit, and explicit. Only explicit knowledge lends itself to easy capture (Desouza, 2003; Grice, 1975; Nicholson & Sahay, 2004). Yet, the other two forms tend to be the knowledge that is vital to making sense of information.

Tacit knowledge: Tacit knowledge is understood and used but can't be recorded. Making sense of the values on a report and acting properly is tacit knowledge. Filling in the gaps of incomplete information depends on the tacit knowledge possessed by the reader and often is a major factor in determining skill levels (Albers, 2004a). Examples include learning which occurs through experience with no actual teaching, such as knowing your car engine sounds wrong. Also, skills which were learned but which have since become so internalized that they are inaccessible without mental effort (Seger, 1994). For example, touch typists can perform type without looking at the keyboard, but typically find it difficult to answer questions such as "which key is to the left of 'g'?" Implicit learning is learning which occurs without any explicit or semi-tacit stage, and is therefore tacit throughout, making it inaccessible to introspection. For example, an experienced drivers will usually know how their car sounds and feels when it is operating properly, but will usually be unable to articulate this to someone else.

Consider how the tacit knowledge involved with design requirements, such as typography and color, are experience-based skills which are hard to capture at a level that can be communicated. Instead, the advice is more generic like "pick fonts that work for the audience"—a good bit of advice, but not one which allows an inexperienced designer to apply it to a design.

Semi-tacit knowledge: Semi-tacit knowledge is knowledge that can be accessed by some methods but not by others. It would not be mentioned in a verbal interchange; capturing it often requires an explicit probe. Semi-tacit knowledge is often taken-for-granted knowledge that a person assumes everyone knows. This normally occurs when the person is so familiar with the information, or it is so ingrained, that it makes no sense to mention it. For example, mentioning doing something at Christmas and assuming everyone knows about the Christmas break. Or describing how to perform an action on a computer and assuming the other person is using a PC and not a Mac. Semi-tacit knowledge can also be knowledge that depends on recognition as opposed to recall. For instance, most Word users recognize all the standard menu bar items, but have difficulty recalling them.

Explicit knowledge: Explicit knowledge has a tangible value and can be recorded. This makes it easy to capture and present back to a reader. The sum of all the information displayed on a screen is the explicit knowledge, as is watching a person perform a sequence of actions. (On the other hand, the logic the person used to decide that sequence of actions might be tacit knowledge.)

The goal of many information searches is either to make tacit knowledge into explicit knowledge (Hughes, 2002) or to gain explicit knowledge. Clearly defined daily routines and standard operating procedures are attempts at trying to make tacit knowledge explicit and to transfer that knowledge to other people (Cohen & Bacdayan, 1994). During the late 1980s and early 1990s, there was a strong knowledge engineering movement which tried to capture an expert's knowledge, codify that knowledge as a set of rules (transforming tacit into explicit) and build those rules into an expert system which anyone could use. Although there were success cases, the attempt failed in most instances. Essentially, it worked as an experiment to show that availability of information alone is not sufficient; contextualized accessibility is the key for effective dissemination, proper comprehension, and subsequent performance enhancement (Albers, 2004a; Mirel, 1998; Mao & Benbasat, 2001). Having explicit information available does not imply that the communication of useful information about the current situation will occur.

Some of difficulty of transforming tacit knowledge into explicit knowledge comes from the situational context in which the information is used. There is often an assumption that the information can be captured in one situation and used across many others; however, this assumption has proved problematic (Bechky 2003; 2000; Szulanski, 1996; von Hippel, 2001). Teaching by a case study method assumes that after examining management ideas/problems for a case, the person will be able to handle those ideas/problems in other situations. Other research has found that people are unable to describe the key elements of the task or verbalize the ways in which they used a system to make decisions (Berry & Broadbent, 1987, 1988). Such a lack of awareness, both of how they perform a task and how sub-tasks interrelate, demonstrate people's dependence on tacit knowledge (Gonzalez, 2005). Such knowledge is implicit, which is interpreted to mean that they never formed rules about how the system works (Dienes & Fahey, 1995). Design requirements are written with a tacit knowledge set which may or not be true for the people implementing those requirements; a problem especially prevalent in off-shored or out-sourced development (Nicholson, & Sahay, 2004). The writer may be assuming the design team understands the "this is how we do things here" assumptions of the functionality of some basic design features. This level of writing would be ok for requirements written for an in-house team, but the out-source team does not share that view and lacks the tacit knowledge to fill in the missing assumptions.

Standard design methods support the transformation of explicit to tacit knowledge at different levels of quality.

- Scenarios and personas have proven useful in defining communication needs because they provide a way to connect tacit and semi-tacit knowledge of design require-

ments, rather than the explicit declarative knowledge captured in a more conventional process (Carroll, 1995).
- Wizards have proven very useful for enabling users to accomplish complicated software tasks with minimal training. However, they have also been criticized because they provide no instruction. In other words, they conceal the tacit and most of the explicit knowledge required to perform the task without their assistance (Albers, 2004a; Farkas 1998). People never learn how to perform the task or how to vary the task beyond what the wizard provides.

Conflict between Current and Prior Knowledge

Prior knowledge helps people understand a current situation. People tend to interpret information in one distinct way, and such interpretation tends to be consistent with their prior knowledge. Although an obvious sounding statement, it has strong HII ramifications. Recht and Leslie (1988), grouping people by the strength of their mental model, found that strong prior knowledge overrode text-based information. In other words, if prior knowledge contradicted what a text said, then people assumed the text was wrong and went with prior knowledge. For example, if a report says monthly production was flat and the person had prior knowledge that said had increased, she would ignore the "flat production" and make decisions based on increased production. Interestingly, they also found that that when prior knowledge agreed with the text, it had no effect on improving performance over people with no prior knowledge. Outdated or incorrect information, even when people know it is outdated or incorrect, exerts an influence on overall understanding and comprehension (O'Brien, Cook, & Peracchi, 2004).

In general, the research has found that when current new information and prior knowledge conflict, people go with prior knowledge. Some examples follow:

- A change in the social or political situation may change what would be the proper decision based on the same information. But people privilege their prior knowledge and goes with the decision which worked before, ignoring the new information and changes to the situation.

- With instructions people have expectations, and those expectations and the real instructions can differ. Patel, Branch, and Arocha (2002) found "instructions which are incongruent with the user's intuitive representation of the application situation tend not to be followed, where people generally fall back on prior intuitions when uncertain about specific procedures" (p. 207). They looked at how people interpreted medication labels. Instructions such as "take two pills four to five times daily" were dismissed with comments such as "that's too often" or "that's too much." When people expect to take medications once or twice a day, they reject taking it more often. Sometimes the person will justify the action by claiming they recently heard about over-medication or drug overdose problems.

It is possible for a mental model based on prior knowledge to be so strong that people are unable to consider alternate interpretations of the information. Thus, when the audience has a variety of backgrounds, the chance of conflict increases. It could be as subtle as two disciplines using the same word to mean something different, or having different ways of viewing the same problem. Whitmire (2003, 2004) looked at how the information-seeking behavior of undergraduates depended on their level of epistemological development, with higher stages being able to make knowledge fit together. The differences were most profound when they encountered conflicting information. Some of the people she interviewed admitted to rejecting or ignoring any source which disagreed with their position.

Incorrect Prior Knowledge

A substantial issue with HII and prior knowledge conflicts is that there is no guarantee that the prior knowledge is correct. For example, when a person reads information about medications, missing from the patient's knowledge is the in-depth medical information about the rate at which a particular drug is broken down in the body, which drives the dosage frequency. This can lead patients to dismiss directions to take the drug every 4 hours, with comments such as "that is too often," or, "I only take my other drug once a day. Why the difference?" Likewise, information about newborn baby care suffers from the "grandma effect" where the current medical advice is often in conflict with what the new mother has been taught by her mother or grandmother. Healthcare campaigns focused on topics such as always having a newborn sleep on their back must address this effect.

Design teams typically either ignore people's prior knowledge or assume it is correct. However in many cases, the prior knowledge is not correct. People hold many misconceptions or they may have learned incorrectly in the past. Some examples may be:

- A person has obtained medical information from a web site which is just plain quacky.
- A business owner "knows" all of his employees are very happy to work for his company and he ignores information about employment issues.
- A person "knows" she shouldn't exercise in her medical condition, but then she receives new information from a medical website advising an hour of exercise each day.

Lipson (1982) found that people with no prior knowledge performed better than people with inappropriate prior knowledge. Combining Lipson's with Recht and Leslie's (1988) findings show that sometimes people may be better off not knowing anything rather than knowing incorrect information. Graphs also can be misinterpreted because of incorrect prior knowledge. People's estimation of correlations or co-variation between graph variables is highly influenced by prior knowledge. When they think that two variables are related to each other (such as height and weight), they overestimate the correlation compared to those who bring no prior knowledge about the variables' relationship (Shah & Hoeffner, 2002). People expect to see a relationship, so they do see one. The incorrect prior knowledge interferes with comprehending and interpreting the new information, a condition the person who initially knew nothing about the topic does not have to overcome. These issues are closely related to expectancy bias, which is discussed later in this chapter in section "Expectancy bias."

To overcome this problem, when communicating information which might conflict with prior knowledge, design teams must acknowledge the conflict and directly challenge potential misconceptions. If the conflicting information is simply presented as information, it has a high chance of being ignored. Instead, the text should explicitly point out the potential conflict and explain why the new information is correct. For example, Powe et al. (2005) found that breast cancer pamphlets did not explicitly challenge women's misperceptions, which greatly reduced their effectiveness. Many healthcare information sites are starting to create a myths section as a way of directly confronting misperceptions or incorrect prior knowledge.

Recently Acquired Information

People's judgments about situational information tend to be skewed toward recently accessed prior knowledge or recent experiences (Koriat, 1995).

Thus, people's prior knowledge works at different levels of importance. Recent events can cause the activation of a recently used mental model even if it is not the most appropriate. The problem here is that people expect the future to be similar to the recent past and that future situations will match past situations. So as soon as something happens which sort of resembles a recent event, then they will treat the two situations the same. In the decision making section of chapter 13: *How people make decisions and take action*, "Decision making influences and biases" this idea will be considered in more detail as part of biases.

Recent events, especially single, uncommon events, have a very profound effect on what prior knowledge is applied—even when people admit that they rationally know the event was a one-off situation. For example, after an airplane crash, people may be hesitant to fly. Or after something bad happens in a business or a friend's business, the managers will be hesitant to make that decision again. This applies even if the factor causing the earlier problem had nothing directly to do with the present problem. For example, twice a year the company has a big picnic for the employees and their families at a local park. One year a family gets in fatal car accident driving to the picnic. Or maybe, just before picking the picnic date, the manager hears about another company's picnic with a fatal car accident. Either way, she might decide to cancel the picnic to avoid risking an accident.

Transfer Effects

People use their prior knowledge to understand the information in a new situation. How well they are able to use that prior knowledge depends on how well they can transfer it to the new situation. In reality, people are rather poor at transferring knowledge to new situations; they do best if they have a strong conceptual model of the old situation and very poorly if they only possess a low-level

Box 2.

Negative transfer between Word and InDesign

Microsoft Word and Adobe InDesign work with different interaction models: Word is a fancy typewriter and InDesign is a fancy paste-up artist desk. Most people are familiar with Word and try to apply that knowledge to performing actions in InDesign. But they suffer from a negative transfer. They can't simply start typing text. They need to select the text tool, set the color, and create the text box. Since InDesign places the text into a movable/resizable text block, something Word does not do, people suffer a negative transfer when using their Word skills with in InDesign.

Part of the steep learning curve of InDesign is overcoming the negative transfer effects. Before people become proficient in InDesign, they must learn a new mental model which changes much of their prior knowledge about how a word processor is supposed to work.

---

model (such as knowing what buttons to push but not knowing why).

The use of prior knowledge for a new situation is called a transfer effect, which can be either positive or negative. Transfer effects address using the knowledge learned about one situation and applying it to another.

Positive-transfer effect: Skills or knowledge learned for one activity support the performance of another activity. The skill sets are similar and performed in the same manner, so after people learn one set they are able to do the other with minimal problems. An example is the standard use of CTRL+C and CTRL+V for copy and paste on Windows programs; early DOS programs did not have this standardization and each program's editing commands had to be learned separately. There is also high positive transfer between automobiles which allows a person to drive any car.

Negative-transfer effect: Skills or knowledge learned for one activity inhibit the performance of another activity. If the two activities are similar, but are performed differently (perhaps done in a different order) then people must mentally remap their view.

Negative transfer effect requires experience since the effect relies on people knowing about a specific domain (Schanteau, 1992). The two programs must show a set of specific features which a person assumes work similarly. Users of a PC/Mac suffer from negative transfer since their basic windows manipulation operations are very similar. On the other hand, users of a Quicken would not suffer negative transfer using the financial sections of SAP since they are so different, even though the person is dealing with accounts payable in both programs.

Changes often create more or new errors because of transfer effects. Part of the problem with people learning a new version of a software package comes from negative transfer. In many corporate settings, the new version of internal software may be more than just additional features, it may change the overall workflow of the tasks addressed by the software. The employees already know how to perform an action with the old system, and know how it fits within their work environment. When a system is upgraded, people must adapt their skills to reflect the changes. In other words, the intentions and actions they perform must change. From a business standpoint, the changes may have made the workflow more efficient, but from a user's point of view, they cause errors because although old knowledge no longer applies, they inadvertently tried to apply it.

Not surprisingly, error rates are also high for tasks which are procedurally consistent across related tasks or tasks which are similar but use different actions (Besnard & Cacitti, 2005; Park, Yoon, & Ryu, 2000). For example, the use of new information technology in health care often shows increases in medical errors—errors which normally arise from poor design (Ash, Berg, & Coiera, 2004; Kushniruk et al., 2005). Negative transfer makes people try to use the same actions that worked for related tasks. If the task operates slightly differently, errors result. To reduce errors

Box 3.

> **Negative transfer in an employee manual**
> One company decides to develop a new employee benefits handbook. They found that new employees quickly mastered using the handbook to find out about their benefits. Older employees, however, had considerable difficulty using the new handbook, since they had a deep knowledge of the old handbook. They knew how to use handbooks and forms, and they knew they had to sign up for benefits every year by filling out forms, but they did not know to use this new handbook and its forms. They were frustrated, confused, and antagonistic about the change (Hackos & Redish, 1998, p. 27).

in a revised design, Galliers, Sutcliffe and Minocha (1999) propose that the design analysis focus on re-designing the existing interfaces to avoid or reduce errors. Besnard and Cacitti (2005) go so far as to state that a new design should actively inhibit former modes of interaction to help prevent negative transfer effects.

All HII interactions depend on people's comparisons with a previous interaction. Design teams need to consciously relate their own expectations and prior knowledge with the expectations and prior knowledge of the audience. Otherwise, team members run a high risk of designing for themselves and not the audience (Øritsland & Buur, 2003), a problem which repeatedly has caused projects to fail.

BIAS IN INFORMATION COMPREHENSION

A bias is a systematic deviation from the expected path (Tversky & Kahneman, 1974). This section describes several different types of bias, but they all result in a tendency to skew the HII and to interfere with an impartial interpretation and comprehension of the information. In many cases, a bias can be considered to result in a "one-sided perception."

Any set of information interpretations or decisions show a random spread around the optimal, but a bias systematically shifts that spread. In-

formation biases are fundamental ways in which people's judgment is consistently affected to produce a non-optimal decision. In general, it is very difficult for people to adjust for most biases since biases are deeply rooted in the cognitive processes of information evaluation and decision making. The study of biases is an active area of psychology research which has indentified many more than the ones discussed here.

Design teams assume that the reader needs the information and will interpret it correctly. However, even properly presented information gets interpreted incorrectly or with a distinctive slant because any reader has a bias. Information salience plays a major factor in many types of bias since the salience determines what information people focus on and the mental weight assigned to it.

Biases exist because, in most cases, of day-to-day decision making, they work just fine and provide a fast, cognitively efficient method of reaching decisions. They exist as a side-effect of heuristic reasoning, which trades optimal performance for lower mental effort (Besnard & Cacitti, 2005). Unfortunately, as the HII aspects which people must comprehend grow in complexity, biases start to negatively affect the quality of many decisions.

Biases may be either explicit or inherent.

Explicit bias: A bias arising for the reader's personal agenda. The reader assigns values and interprets information to fit a predetermined mindset. It is very difficult, if not impossible, for a design team to have much influence over explicit biases. Some examples are:

- ° People from different political parties reading campaign material for a candidate. They will view the information very differently depending on whether they support that candidate.
- ° Academic journals use blind peer review to help focus the evaluation on the content and prevent articles from receiving better or worse evaluations

based on reviewer's personal or professional feelings toward the author.

° Evaluating a set of products when the reviewer (or the reviewer's boss) has decided the choice will be product A. The evaluation of products B and C will be skewed so that they compare poorly against product A. The reviewer may pick criteria which overemphasize the bad points of B and C or the good points of A.

Inherent bias: The bias arising from basic human cognitive processes. Designs teams can try to minimize them, and if readers know of their existence they can try to avoid them. The sources of bias discussed in this section are all inherent biases.

Cognitive Biases

Actor-observer bias: A tendency to attribute one's own action to external causes, while attributing other people's behaviors to internal causes. People attribute the blame or success differently depending upon whether they are the actor or the observer in a situation (Jones & Nisbett, 1971). In a situation where a person experiences something negative, the individual will often blame the situation or circumstances ("I couldn't do it because this system is bad"). When something negative happens to another person, people will often blame the individual for their personal choices, behaviors and actions ("She couldn't do it because she's too dumb to understand computers").

Anchoring bias: A tendency to rely too heavily on one information element. Sequential evaluation often suffers from anchoring since people pick what they consider as the most important feature of the first item and evaluates the other items based on this anchor point. It can also apply when people make judgments about changes which deviate from the current situation (such as evaluating a new software system). Their responses tend to be anchored in their view of the current system. Consider how people think of change in terms of how it affects what is happening how (anchored to current procedures) rather than how it will improve overall performance. Anchoring can occur because of how a text is written. For example, Tversky and Kahneman (1974) showed that when asked to guess the percentage of African nations which are members of the United Nations, people who were first asked "Was it more or less than 45%?" guessed lower values than those who had been asked if it was more or less than 65%. The people anchored on the percentage they were given, even though it had no relationship to the real value. Mussweiler (2002) found the anchoring effect can be easily manipulated to be stronger or weaker, and that it tends to be stronger when focusing on similarities rather than differences between tasks or potential changes.

Ambiguity bias: People prefer a known probability over an unknown one. When faced with making choices where the probability is only known for one of the options, most people pick the known one rather than risk that the unknown one will be lower.

Automation bias: Believing computers provide correct answers. People tend to believe computer recommendations and do not seek other information unless the recommendation conflicts with their desired decision. The recent observations about how people accept Internet medical information without verifying the source is one example. A stronger, and more problematical, issue of decision support systems is that people are willing to take a recommendation without subjecting it to a critical analysis and without understanding what factors went into the recommendation. In fault diagnosis research, when an intelligent agent presented a solution and a confidence level, people accepted high-confidence suggestions without review. However, they did review solutions with a low confidence level (Sundstrom & Salvador, 1994).

Availability heuristic: Using the information that is easiest to retrieve mentally. People judge the likelihood of events by their vividness. As a result, hearing a well-told story can distract people or make them put great weight on the information in the story. Recent information is mentally more available than older or less information; as result it gets used in a disproportional manner for evaluating information.

Base rate fallacy: Overall statistical probabilities are ignored and specific instances are privileged. If people have recently had or heard about a poor or good event in a similar situation, they tend to assume that the current situation will end with the same result. They may even acknowledge that the other event was exceptional, but will ignore that fact. These issues will be discussed in more detail in chapter 9: *How people approach numbers, statistics, and risk,* "Risk perception."

Certainty bias: People want absolute certainty in a decision. The bias comes from changes in wording or presentation of the statistics. People view a change of 10% as more with 100%–10% rather than 50%–10% (Tversky & Kahneman, 1981).

Confirmation bias: People tend to only seek information which confirms their beliefs or desired decision. Once a decision is reached, there is a tendency to seek evidence to support that decision and ignore disconfirming information. When asked to determine a rule for a sequence of items, people only look at or try sequences which conform to the expected rule. They do not try sequences which would refute the expected rule. Once a decision is made to buy product A, people look for reasons to support buying product

A and do not look for reasons not to buy it, or for reasons product B might be better.

Distinction bias: Evaluations of two items differ if the evaluation is done together (head to head comparison) or sequentially (Hsee & Zhang, 2004). Part of the difference is explained in that small differences are more obvious and weighted more when the evaluation is done together.

Expectancy bias: People see what they expect to see in a set of data. This bias has significant impacts on HII and is discussed in more detail in the next section.

Over confidence bias: Overestimating the accuracy of the decision. People tend to be very confident that they made the correct decision. They also tend to be optimistic that the situation will progress in the way they want. New information will be interpreted in a way to support that decision or view of the situation. Because they feel very confident in the choice, people tend not to look for more information. When they do look for information, confirmation bias will cause them to look only for confirming information. Overconfidence is not just found in research studies; it has been observed across a range of experts working within their domains. It has been observed in doctors, clinical psychologists, lawyers, engineers, and financial analysts.

Recent events bias: More recent information is given more weight than older information. Information which is more easily recalled (often more recent) gets more weight. Vivid events are more compelling than statistical information; baseline data is often ignored. A person who recently encountered a problem which occurs very infrequently will (a) interpret information expecting to find the problem again or (b) make decisions specifically to avoid a chance that the problem will reoccur. In both cases, they may ignore more frequent problems which they have not recently encountered. People over-react to recent poor or good information, assuming that the immediate past trend will continue (Remus, O'Connor, & Griggs, 1995). Typically, these are simply fluctuations around the overall trend, but people have difficulty mentally smoothing out trends. This effect is magnified when the information is sparse or ambiguous, or when it has random fluctuations (O'Connor, Remus & Griggs, 1993).

Small numbers bias: Accepting that a small sample is representative of the population. In user testing, the four people tested are often assumed to be representative of the entire user group. If the first four coin tosses come up heads, the coin would be considered biased toward heads. Since most HII tends to work with small information sets, design teams need to consider how it will affect people.

Statistical regression fallacy: Exceptional performance (good or bad) tends to regress toward the mean. Most measures fluctuate partly by chance so when there is an extremely good result or score, the next measurement is likely to be worse. This means that observed measures are the result of a 'true score' and an 'error component.' Very positive results on one test are likely to be followed by lower scores. Yet, people expect the results to be similar and trends, either up or down, to continue.

Expectancy Bias

When people look at information, expectancy bias causes them to see what they expect to see (Wickens & Hollands, 2000). Klein's research (1999) found that people tended to interpret a passage in one distinct way and that these interpretations were consistent with their backgrounds. When people read a report in which either good or bad results are expected, they will privilege the information which supports those good or bad expectations. In other words, they will see the report as supporting their expectations of good or bad results.

Unfortunately, identifying expectancy bias is difficult. It tends to build up over time and is only seen in hindsight (Klein, 1999). Expectancy bias helps explain why in many disaster or major accident situations, people made seemingly bad choices and ignored the correct data that was right in front of them (Klein, 1988). Post-incident findings which reveal a person had the information available but ignored it in favor of a desired set of information can often be attributed to expectancy bias. For example, a person who believes a company has a breakthrough product will ignore poor financial statements and focus only on the good aspects of a company when making investment decisions. Expectancy bias also comes into play with usability testing since it can result in the testers' seeing the problems they wish to see, or the usability report readers' only seeing problems they want to address, or seeing no major problems since they expect the product to be ready to ship.

People's prior knowledge about a subject affects how they evaluate information credibility. If their prior knowledge leads them to expect to find specific information, expectancy bias will often result in their finding that information. At the same time, they ignore other information which brings the reliability or validity of their preferred information or decision into question. Salient information which is outside of the information people expect to see must have a higher salience in order to capture their attention. If the writer believes the readers are looking for good news, then bad news needs to have a higher level of salience.

Stress or time pressure plays a major factor in strengthening the effects of expectancy bias. People do not (or are unable to) devote the necessary time to properly interpret the information. Instead, they will pick and choose the information, based on what they expect to see.

MENTAL MODELS

The basic framework for acquiring information in a situation is human-centered in that a person defines the task, controls the extent of the interaction with the information, defines what is relevant information, assesses the quality of the progress toward an acceptable understanding, and determines, based on having collected adequate information, when to stop acquiring information. Knowing what information to collect and how to analyze it with respect to the current situation is based on a person's mental model. According to Norman (1988, p 189), "The operation of any device—whether it be a can opener, a power generating plant, or a computer system—is learned more readily, and the problems are tracked down more accurately and easily, if the user has a good conceptual [mental] model." Wilson and Ruthorford (1989) define a mental model as:

A representation formed by a user of a system and/or task based on previous experience as well as current observations, which provides most (if not all) of their subsequent system understanding and consequently dictates the level of task performance (p. 619).

A mental model corresponds to the cognitive layout that people use to organize information in memory (Johnson-Larid, 1983). Mental models are high-level knowledge structures that support any aspect of knowledge and human skills (Reason, 1990). Satzinger (1998) has described mental model theory to include knowledge structures that store concepts in human memory, including procedural knowledge of how to use the concepts. A mental model can be viewed as a cognitive template of a person's knowledge meant to solve problems for which skills have already been built. The mental model helps simplify understanding a situation because it carries with it preformed ideas and so it helps build connections among disparate bits of information (Redish, 1994). In overly simplistic terms, a mental model is a stereotypical template in the mind, built on previous experience (Figure 12), that contains a collection of known information and relationships for a particular class of situations, not the specifics for any single situation (Cooke & Rowe, 1994). It lets people organize the information and go beyond simply knowing the information exists (Gery, 2002) to knowing how it relates to the situation.

Mental models support the fast processing of routine situations for which one acts virtually automatically from their identification. Without a mental model, people would lack a basis for understanding the information coming from a situation and would have to figure out all of the relationships for each situation from scratch. With the overabundance of information in essentially all real-world situations, they would be constantly suffer cognitive overload.

The literature also uses terms such as cognitive model, cognitive schema, mental schema (Rumelhart, 1980), frames (Minsky, 1975), or scripts (Schank & Abelson, 1977), and to make it more confusing, other authors often mix the use of these terms and apply them at varying levels of abstraction.

Figure 12. Mental model as a set of empty space. The mental model provides a collection of empty spaces which a person needs to fill. The advantage of the mental model is that it lays out which boxes need to be filled; information that does not fit into a box is not needed. If any empty space is not filled, then the mental model provides a default value.

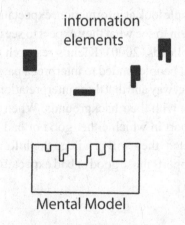

information elements

Mental Model

Mental models can be considered as a set of rules which define what information is relevant to a situation and the information relationships. On the basis of those rules, people know what information to examine and which to ignore as irrelevant (Rasmussen, 1986). People use a mental model as a basis for understanding the situation and making predictions about future events. The initial information people look for corresponds to information required to transform the mental model from a generic template into a specific instance fitting the current situation. All new information flowing into the situation gets interpreted with respect to and fitted into the mental model. It is also the basis of deciding what information to ignore. Any information not called for by the mental model is deemed irrelevant, no matter how salient. Simply put, people use a mental model to fit the current situation into past experiences.

Structural patterns inherent in mental models are essential to human knowledge representation; the identification and representation must carry over to the interaction with computer systems (Treu, 1992). Each time people encounter a similar situation, they initially set similar goals and expect similar information relationships. They use their mental model of the situation to define goals and relationships and to decide on which information they need in order to achieve those goals. Thus, people should receive information about the situation in a manner that matches their mental model.

One important point is to view a mental model as a stereotype of a situation, not a detailed description. It contains a typical representation of a situation, not a list of necessary and sufficient conditions for each particular situation (Wilson & Rutherford, 1989). Thus, a fast food mental model works across all the various fast food chains even though each handles food ordering in a slightly different way. As a stereotype, it contains the facts of buy food at a counter, find your own table, and eat food wrapped in paper. Although a specific chain's details differ, the chains are

consistent enough that a single mental model provides people with a structure into which they can place and interpret specific details. Consider how some of the new fast food chains use counter ordering, but deliver the food to the table, violates the fast food mental model and requires a mental adjustment during the first restaurant visit. By applying a mental model to a situation, people can quickly place everything within a context and make the proper response. The caveat to the previous sentence is that the proper mental model must be used; mistakes or cognitive dissidence results when an incorrect mental model is used. A person who walked into a fast food restaurant and was greeted by a host wearing a tux would be confused because this does not fit a fast food restaurant mental model. Likewise, a customer entering an expensive French restaurant would be confused if she found she was expected to place an order at a counter.

A major reason people develop and use mental models is that they allow for minimizing cognitive effort. Applying a mental model to the situation reduces the amount of effort required to understand it since a significant part of the understanding is contained within the stereotypical behavior of the mental model itself. As a consequence, people are strongly inclined to apply well-known solution procedures to new problems (Moray, 1987); in other words, they apply a mental model for known situation A to unknown situation B if they see anything which indicates it might be relevant. Accidents caused by changes in a work environment (e.g., implementing a new software system or a new piece of equipment) happen when people interact with the new system as if it will respond the same way as the old one (Besnard & Cacitti, 2005). People used their existing mental model which failed to conform to the changed reality.

Readers interpret information by applying their own knowledge and expectations to the mental model; the instantiated mental model is called a situation model. People's active mental model strongly influences how they view the

Box 4.

Microsoft Word and Adobe InDesign mental models
Microsoft Word and Adobe InDesign operate with very different underlying models. Word is essentially a fancy typewriter and InDesign uses text boxes which reflect the work of pre-computer graphic artists as a collection of individual pieces of paper which can be moved around on a paste-up table. When introducing students to InDesign, I give them a simple task, such as reproducing a one-page flyer. Many will type in all of the text and then try to format it. The students are using a mental model of word processing based on a typewriter and Word. They rapidly find that this model fails miserably when they try to format text with InDesign. From a cognitive viewpoint, they were working with a situation with the wrong mental model activated. On the other hand, since most have no experience with any packages except Word, they have no other mental model to activate. As they learn how to work efficiently with InDesign, they are developing a new mental model. Later, when they have to learn a new word processing, desktop publishing, or web design program, they will have two models to draw on.

---

world and how events or facts are interpreted. Situation comedies base much of their humor on a person's activating a wrong mental model and misinterpreting the actions of everyone around them. According to Anderson and Pearson (1984), mental models serve as networks linked by factors that imply order, such as chronology, function, topics, and so forth. If the design and presentation of information matches the mental model, it's easy to process. Comprehension of information requires that the presented information mesh with and complete the mental picture of the active mental model currently being used to represent information and its relationships. If the reader has to work to match the information to the mental model, it takes more time and information is much harder to understand. This view of mental model construction treats information coherence as a positive factor and cognitive overload as a negative factor (Thuring, Hannemann, & Haake, 1995).

On the other hand, Lansdale and Ormerod (1994) argue that the concept of mental models contributes little more than pointing out that people use their knowledge to make predictions about how an interface will work. Some researchers point out the lack of consensus on how

model elicitation is best accomplished or how to actually measure it (Cooke & Rowe, 1994). Even if evidence of mental models is observable, researchers point out that characterizing them cannot be easily done, and that mental models must be inferred from people's behavior (Norman, 1983; Sasse, 1992). Staggers & Norcio (1993) concluded that mental models are difficult for people to articulate, particularly models which are incomplete. Mental models, especially experts' mental models, contain a set of actions which happen without conscious thought, which makes them very hard to capture. For instance, Borgman (1985) believed her study participants had constructed models but that her methods were unable to capture clear evidence of those models. Unfortunately, observing behavior rarely captures why the choice was made and people have trouble giving detailed explanations of their actions. Often in interviews, people fall into a trap of giving the expected answers or what they think the interviewer wants to hear. Plus, many of their choices were based on implicit knowledge and they can't clearly verbalize the reasoning behind them. In the end, understanding a person's mental model requires both interacting with the person by watching him work and asking questions so that he explains why he is making his choices.

Understanding of a situation comes when people interpret information with the proper mental model, which means design teams must ensure that the information presentation matches the expectations of the readers as closely as possible. Properly developing those expectations can be a difficult task. A major goal of much training is to help people development an accurate and complete mental model of the system (at least one sufficient for the job) so they can use that mental model in future work (Patrick & Haines, 1988). The training relates the high-level structure of a person's goals and the information relationships contained in the system to help the person develop a mental model containing those relationships. The structure of the goals (i.e., order of address-

Box 5.

> **Uncovering mental models of physical and logical systems**
> Obtaining a mental model of a system within an industrial context may be possible since people can be asked to draw and explain how they think the system operates. With a physical system the actual layout of pumps, valves, and motors should match the mental image. With information systems, the task of capturing the mental model is more difficult. Issues of information flow and how close the model needs to map to reality depend on what people need to achieve. It is likewise for systems such as computer software. Although a system analyst needs a very detailed mental model of how the program interacts with the database, most users do not. And even the system analyst may be able to work effectively with only a rudimentary model of how the database engine interacts with the hardware since that is outside the scope of the software application. Casaday (1991) noted the logical versus physical design of human-computer interaction gives many software engineers problems. While they can work at a logical level with the program itself, they find it extremely difficult to work with the logical design of the interface and often require a physical, concretely drawn design. The difference is partially attributed to the quality of their mental model of the two different items.

Box 6.

> **Donald Norman interview on defining mental models**
> Parush provides this excerpt from an interview with Donald Norman about how designers can uncover a mental model and how they relate to understanding a situation.
>
> [Interviewer:] The industrial engineers kept telling me "there is no such thing as mental models—it all has to do with performance, what do we care about mental models?"
>
> [Norman:] I would ask them how they know what to do when there's an unexpected problem. In process control for instance, there might be an unexpected rise in temperature with a simultaneous decrease in pressure. So, you might ask these engineers "what do you think is going on?" The point being not whether their answer is right or wrong but how they reach their answer. I can tell you the way you answer this question is that you do a mental simulation. You take your knowledge of the way the process is working and imagine what could give rise to an increase in temperature and a decrease in pressure and since they are normally correlated (normally pressure increase is caused by temperature increase) they would have to do some clever simulation. This "imagining" process is what we mean by mental models; how people take their understanding of something to simulate what would happen in a novel situation (Parush, 2004).

ing goals, which sub-goals go with higher goals) forms a model of how people should view a situation. The information relationships show how information elements relate to goals and provide a framework for working toward goals.

Characteristics of Mental Models

Mental models seem to provide a very good abstraction of how people handle understanding a situation. They are invaluable in understanding what information needs to be communicated. Based on the mental model, people expect certain information and certain presentations. By understanding people's mental model, design teams can more easily meet those expectations.

Some of the characteristics of mental models are (Kearsley, 2006):

- They provide simplified explanations of complex phenomena. As a stereotype, they do not contain all of the information. Instead, they are designed to work across many similar situations, which requires models based on the similarities and consistencies.

- They are incomplete and constantly evolving. Thatcher and Greyling (1998) noted that with increasing experience a mental model carried with it increased detail and completeness.

- They often fail to be an accurate representation, but instead, contain errors and contradictions. A mental model of an "ideal" expert would be equivalent to the conceptual model of the system, but the actual mental models are generally fragmentary and include superstitious notions that decrease memory load at the expense of efficiency (Brazier & Veer, 1991). People may adjust their mental model if they encounter an error, but in many cases the errors make no difference. Major errors in a mental model of how a computer hard drive works do not matter to a typical computer user.

- They represent actions by rules which describe "if this occurs, then respond by that." In general, a person has learned the response, but often does not know why and has trouble determining whether the response is appropriate if the initiation condition is similar to the rule condition. Using the rules helps prevent errors or dangerous use of the system.

How People Develop a Mental Model

The literature is full of references to mental models and how people create them. Confusion can arise because different authors often interchange the mental models people form and the model of the person/situation that a designer creates. This section discusses the stereotypical mental image that a person builds in light of past experience. Ideally, that mental image closely matches the one design teams intend people to have.

People form a mental model based on their interaction with a system or situation, not based on what how the designer imagines the situation (Gulliksen & Lantz, 2003). "The designer has an obligation to provide an appropriate conceptual model for the way that the device works. It doesn't have to be completely accurate but it has to be sufficiently accurate that it will help in both the learning of the operation and also dealing with novel situations" (Parush, 2004). The initial mental model (actual conceptual model) may be substantially incorrect, but people will rapidly form one based on their prior knowledge and will use it to move forward with understanding the situation.

Kieras and Bovair (1984) studied how the mental model was initially formed while doing procedures and determined the formation was a comprehension process and not skill-learning. Unfortunately, most documentation fails to make this distinction and concentrates on presenting skills. Gribbons (1991) points out that design failures arise when a design is not sensitive to or fails to

match people's mental models. He then lists three different models which exist, only one of which (actual conceptual model) is held by the user and forms the basis for situation use and interaction. The other two are held by the designer.

- **Cognitive model:** model held by the design team of how the think the user's mind works
- **Intended conceptual model:** model of how the system should be used
- **Actual conceptual model:** how the user actually pictures the system working

When these models are different, people tend to have problems responding to and interpreting information in a situation because their expectations are not met.

The overall view people form of how a system operates or a situation unfolds and how easy it is to interact with arises from three points:

- People always have an active mental model.
- The product model should match the person's model or make a new one easy to form.
- The closer the match, the easier to the system is to learn and use (Rubin, 1996).

If people encounter a situation for which they do not have a mental model, they will always rapidly form one (Farris, Jones, & Elgin, 2002). "The user's model is not formed from the design model, but from the way the user interprets the system image. It should be realized that everything the user interacts with helps to form that image" (Gulliksen & Lantz, 2003, p. 8). This ability to develop mental models quickly must be addressed in the design of how to communicate information and in usability studies to test that communication (Nilsson & Mayer, 2002). Some points which impede the formation of a mental model are:

- Cognitive overload or disorientation (such as lost in hypertext) impairs the formation (Chalmers, 2003). The mental task of developing a mental model requires cognitive resources and if a person is already taxed, it is an easy task to slough off.
- Too close of a comparison between situations can cause problems because of making inappropriate assumptions arising from the differences between them (Halasz & Moran, 1983). The subtle interaction differences between a Mac and PC are one example.

Experience and Developing Mental Models

Both human mental models and the computer have structure. Effective HII occurs when the human mental model and the computer interface model match as closely as possible (Treu, 1992). Previous studies have shown that mental models of an expert and novice are different (Moray 1992, Newman & Lamming 1995). A beginner's mental model is built on spotty knowledge based on simple definitions and superficial concepts of the situation (Fiore, Cuevas & Oser, 2003). As people gain expertise, that spotty knowledge is fleshed out with a structured and coherent view. Mental models from experienced people show increased detail and completeness as structure is gained, connecting to prior knowledge (Thatcher and Greyling, 1998). The deeper mental model gained with experience provides a base from which to understand similar situations.

When a problem is unknown, people have little choice but to try to solve it by trial and error (Byrne, 1989; Liu, 1991) based on whatever past experience they have. Once a solution has been found, it forms the basis for creating a mental model or modifying an existing one. As people work with the same category of problems, they eventually build a generic solution which is their mental model. The source inputs which people use to build a mental model include observation, other people's explanations, and construction of models from a set of basic components or from analogous models (Johnson-Laird, 1989). Along with the rest of the mental model, the rules for responding to various conditions are built (Besnard & Cacitti, 2005).

Graphics can help create a mental model. Fiore, Cuevas, and Oser (2003) point out that graphics help because they make the relationship between abstract concepts or complex tasks explicit and easier to understand than a textual description of the same concepts. A graphic also helps to reduce the cognitive load required to establish the mental model, with high cognitive loads impairing mental model formation (Chalmers, 2003). On the other hand, a too-simplistic graphic will not accomplish the desired result. People will remember the graphic better than the text. So providing a simplistic graphic with extra details in the text will typically result in the formation of a mental model based on the graphic but without the text details added. Depending on the situations in which it will be used, this may not be effective. Likewise, a too-complex graphic, while realistic, will provide too much detail to remember and be ignored as too cognitively demanding.

It should not be surprising that the more accurate mental models (closer to an expert model) resulted in better performance in various tasks (Cuevas et al., 2004). What this points out is the substantial difference between a novice and expert mental model in how concepts are connected and how the person understands of those relationships. When people interact with a new situation, they inevitably reuse former interaction modes and actions. They use their experiences with old situations as a basis for developing expectations of how the new situation will react and what information they need. The development of expert-level experience could be considered the employment of mental models which support the reuse of previous accumulated experience (Song & Salvendy, 2003). The problems encountered by people with minimal experience in similar situations come from the lack of previous information to reuse; instead people are forced into trial and error with its high error rates.

The novice stage of use only lasts for a short period. As the mental model is developed and filled in, people quickly become intermediate users. Usability studies which attempt to capture differences in behavior between experience levels need to consider how quickly people can develop a mental model and how quickly they progress past a novice stage. Over-emphasis on communicating information to a novice will cause communication difficulties for people at both intermediate- and expert-level.

Activating and Using a Mental Model

People have a huge collection of mental models, and when exposed to a new situation they will activate a model that they consider appropriate to the current situation, based on a first impression. Mental model activation occurs rapidly and at a subconscious level. It gets activated so quickly that people do not have time to read or examine the content. Instead, it is based on their expectations and the overall display layout along with large scale items such as titles and major headings (Duin, 1989). These are all elements which they can mentally integrate at single glance with pre-attentive processing. Ensuring that the proper mental model gets activated means that the design must immediately provide a view of the information which fits with their expectations. A design always invokes a mental model; design teams must ensure it's the proper response. A person will always have an active mental model to interpret all the information they perceive. Whether or not the proper mental model is activated depends on the information they initially see. Improper information can cause the wrong mental model to be activated, leading to errors and misinterpretations.

Hollnagel (1988) suggested that the order and quantity of the situation's information has a strong influence on how people gain an understanding of the situation. The fundamental issue is that if the wrong mental model is activated, people interpret information correctly for the active mental model, but incorrectly for the situation. Mental models work because they provide a preset structure on which to interpret observations of a situation. They contain the structural patterns that define information relationships and information importance. The mental model allows people to apply it to various situations in order to make inferences and fill in missing information (Fawcett, Ferdinand, & Rockley, 1991; Smith & Goodman, 1984). Many of the bins in Figure 12 have default values and if the situation does not provide a value, the default is used.

The required clarity of the mental model depends on the type of system and how it is to be used. In general, if people tend to perform the same types of actions on a regular basis, then an unclear mental model may suffice. The real strength of mental models comes in novel situations. But for performing normal actions, they are not really used; the person knows that when A happens you do B (Parush, 2004). On the other hand, if the application requires people to understand and apply a wide range of different computer actions in unplanned and spontaneous ways, then a better mental model of the system would be helpful. The difference is that in a novel situation, people tend to use a goal-oriented approach, but in normal situations they use a set of rules based on what has previously worked (Rasmussen, 1986), with the rules contained in the mental model. Teaching based on explaining the proper mental model, rather than strictly the procedures, improves learning. People trained with a mental model of a control panel learned procedures faster and retained them better (Kieras & Bovair, 1984). Borgman (1986) found that they had better performance when required to extrapolate beyond basic system operation. In other research, students were taught to use a calculator, either by learning various procedures or by learning the model of how the calculator worked. Both groups performed well for normal situations, but the mental model group was better at novel situations (Halasz & Moran, 1983). Exposing students to variations on a problem helped them form better mental models. Interestingly, the students learned more slowly but gained a deeper understanding with a broader, more flexible mental model (Chen & Mo, 2004). The more experimentation with the system that is required, the clearer will be the mental model that a person develops (Bailey, 1989). The experimentation which forms the basis of minimal-manual documentation works on the principle that experimentation builds a better mental model (Carroll, 1985).

Difficulties in Switching Mental Models

The active mental model can so strongly impose an interpretation that people may be unaware of alternative interpretations. People may be so set in using their current active mental model, that they refuse to acknowledge that another valid one applies to the situation. As a result, once the wrong mental model is activated, people have a hard time switching to the correct one. The cognitive effort for a switch is very high and most people try to avoid the effort (Einhorn & Hogarth, 1981). It is difficult to get people to switch to a new mental model. They only switch when the disconnect between their current active model and reality becomes so strong that it can no longer ignored. The failure to change assessment strategy arises because people are very limited in their ability to handle multiple mental tasks (Wickens, 1992). It requires, at some level, significant cognitive resources to reevaluate the approach to understanding the situation and to come up with a new one.

Since the active mental model determines information interpretation, designs that initially invoke the wrong mental model pose trouble from the start. An interaction decision is based on the current mental model; an incorrect mental model

can cause a goal to be set which is incorrect for the situation (but correct for the active mental model). With the wrong mental model, misinterpretation of information becomes almost certain. The overall problem is that a mental model provides people with a set of expectations which anchor people to one view (Tversky & Kahneman, 1981). The issues of expectation bias and confirmation bias come into play. People see what they expect to see while ignoring unexpected information or information not considered relevant, in a phenomenon called *cognitive tunnel vision* (Woods & Cook, 1999). Plus, they tend to look only for confirming information and ignore information which might disprove their current line of thought (Einhorn & Hogarth, 1981). As a result, many errors or misinterpretation of information can occur with people ignoring or rationalizing away the conflicts between expectations and reality.

ATTENTION

Attention is the focus people put onto information or a task. Most attention research is focused on surveillance or monitoring, such as people monitoring plant control panels or radar operators. These are people who spend long periods of time watching relatively static displays and are required to detect and respond to changes immediately. Most human-information interactions do not require this type of monitoring; instead, people are trying to read and comprehend the information within a short time period. But external distractions that are part of a normal work environment and workload also affect the amount of attention people devote to dealing with textual information.

The cognitive driver of attention, as Simon (1976) points out, is that

The information-processing systems of our contemporary world swim in an exceedingly rich soup of information, of symbols. In a world of this kind, the scarce resource is not information; it is

the processing capacity to attend to information. Attention is the chief bottleneck in organizational activity (p. 294).

Many designs seem to assume that the basic problem is lack of information, when often it is lack of attention or inability of people to provide enough attention to the information (Simon, 1981). In these situations, increasing the amount of information will not improve performance and may impair it.

When people are trying to read information and perform other tasks, then attention issues come into play. Multitasking requires rapid shifting between multiple information sources. Research into handling different types of attention have found that comprehension is reduced when attention is not solely focused on a single task. Tracking multiple information sources results in decreased quality of the comprehension of all the sources. Understanding these factors can improve the quality of the audience and task analysis, and it can help ensure that the resulting design accounts for how people cognitively handle attention issues.

Often, people think they have taken in an entire scene when, in reality, they have only processed the area they were attending to and only gotten the gist of the scene. Attention is sometimes described with a searchlight metaphor (Wachtel, 1967), with the beam of the searchlight falling on the information currently being processed. Everything in the beam is processed whether it is relevant or not, and everything outside the beam is ignored. Shifting attention from one task to another can be viewed as shifting the spotlight focus from one spot to another. An indicator of expert performance is knowing where to direct the searchlight and knowing how wide the beam should be. People with lower experience can suffer from "attentional capture," where highly salient but task-irrelevant information or objects grab their focus.

Attention has been broken down into multiple types:

Pre-attentive: Rapid unconscious mental processing done before a person knows there is a stimulus.

Focused attention: Focusing on only one specific aspect, with the person trying to shut out all external stimulations.

Selective attention: Focusing on only specific aspects of an information set and ignoring the others.

Divided attention: An intentional effort to focus on two or more things simultaneously.

Split attention: Shifting focus between different tasks in a short period rotation. This differs from divided attention because the person gives full attention to the current task, but jumps between tasks.

Pre-Attentive

Pre-attentive processing is carried out automatically in the mind and organizes the visual image into groups of related objects (Kahneman, 1973). For example, color is detected and processed during pre-attentive visual processes (Treisman, 1982). After this initial organization, a person consciously begins to examine the various groups of objects. Actions such as ignoring flashing ads on a webpage are handled as part of pre-attention processing. Pre-attention processing can let some parts of the information be ignored so quickly that people will later not recall seeing them, and eye-trackers do not record any glances toward them.

The various Gestalt principles operate at the pre-attention level. Take for example the figure-ground perception, which gives rise to the optical illusion of having a figure look like one of two images. An important design aspect is to ensure that related information is close together so it can be properly pre-attentively grouped.

The organization of the elements must match people's information needs if the information is to be communicated effectively. In figure 13, the B image looks much better arranged and should support easier mental processing. However, that

Figure 13. Gestalt principles of organization. In this arrangement of grouping similar meters, pre-attention processing will group the various sets into units to be considered together. Of course, to be effective the groupings must match the system design and person's mental model of how to view it (adapted from Wikens & Hollands, 2000, p. 87).

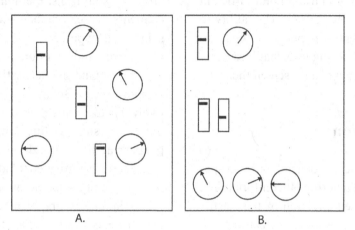

A.   B.

assumes that all the indicators in each group are related. What if the person was constantly comparing a dial on the upper left with one on the lower left? The A image might be the better designed one for some situations. If the indicators are clustered into the information groups that a person needs to understand the situation, then while the organization looks haphazard (some boundary lines would help) it might effectively support pre-attentive processing better than a panel neatly organized by gauge type.

Focused Attention

In focused attention, people consciously try to focus on only one specific information aspect and attempts to shut out all external stimulation. Unlike divided attention, with focused attention people only care about a single information element and attempt to read or analyze it without interruption.

The ability of people to focus depends on competing distractions. A person reading a document in a noisy environment has to use focused attention to block out the noise. A person reading a web page with inconsequential elements that are blinking or brightly colored must also use focused

Box 7.

Missing the gorilla suit
There are many variations on YouTube (for example, http://www.youtube.com/watch?v=hwCzasHBXNc or http://www.youtube.com/watch?v=47LCLoidJh4) of a classic psychology experiment where people are asked to focus their attention and miss something. In the video, two groups of people in white and black shirts are passing basketballs. You are asked to count the number passes for the white team. While counting passes, people miss a person in a black bear suit walking through the group of people. Attention is so focused on the white team's ball that everything else is blocked out and receives no attention. People ignore the black team and consequently ignore the black bear.

More interesting is people's reaction when the video asks if they saw the black bear. It tends to be shock and they make comments such as "no way would I have missed that." But they did because their attention was focused on one aspect of the scene; everything else was disregarded during pre-attentive processing.

attention to block out the flashing and focus on the text. People have gotten very good at ignoring many areas of a web page; the banner at the top is essentially always ignored no matter what it contains. Likewise, any flashing or blinking is ignored as being an advertisement even when it contains relevant information.

A failure of focused attention occurs when people are distracted. Some level of distracters exists in any situation. Simply instructing people to focus attention on a certain task is not sufficient to prevent distracter interference. The ability to maintain focused attention depends on the number of distracters, which suggests that it requires cognitive resources to mentally screen them out (Lavie, 2005).

Selective Attention

Selective attention means focusing only on specific information and ignoring other information. It differs from focused attention in that, while in focused attention distracters are consciously excluded, in selective attention the exclusion is unconscious. If the information given selective attention is the wrong information, or information is given too much attention, problems can occur. For example, missing information in a changing environment because the attention is directed at one highly salient piece of information. Cognitive tunnel vision is essentially the same as selective attention.

The cocktail party phenomenon in which a person focuses on specific aspects of a scene while ignoring others is one example of selective attention. Two people standing in a noisy room can carry on a conversation and retain nothing of the other conversations around them.

Divided Attention

Divided attention is an intentional effort to focus on two or more things simultaneously. It refers to the ability to process multiple tasks at once, such as being able to drive a car and carry on a conversation at the same time. Unlike split attention, discussed later in this section, with divided attention people try to operate in multiple communication channels at once rather than shifting from one to another. Driving and texting is one dangerous example of divided attention.

The ability to use divided attention is highly constrained by cognitive resources. With limited cognitive resources available to be split among all processing tasks, the number of information elements that can be handled simultaneously is small. With experience in the individual tasks and in using divided attention, people can improve in this ability. One characteristic of expert behavior is being able to use divided attention more effectively. Factors which reduce available cognitive resources (such as time pressure) also reduce people's ability to use divided attention.

Some research has concluded that no more than two physically separate areas of a multidimensional, animated, graphical display should be of concern to the viewer at a time (Lightner, 2001). Having three or more areas to monitor exhausts a person's cognitive resources and will result in sub-optimal use of the information.

Interestingly, while learning and comprehension are reduced, recalling previously learned information is minimally affected by divided attention (Naveh-Benjamin et al., 2000). People can recall information already stored in long-term memory with the same speed as during focused-attention tasks.

Box 8.

> **Divided attention and using a laptop while driving**
> Divided attention caused problems for the San Jose police department which rolled out a new system for computer-aided dispatch. Each patrol car had a laptop which allowed the officers to quickly look up information they previously had to call the dispatcher for (such as checking on a car's license plate). However, using the system required the officer to drive and type on a laptop at the same time. Worse, there was no way to operate it by feel; the officer had to look at the screen. In other words, it required divided attention, and dividing someone's attention between a critical task (driving) and any other factor is dangerous. In the resulting lawsuits, problems with the technology and how it communicated with people were a major factor (Santa Clara, 2005). But the flaws were not so much in the technology, as in the basic design and failure of the designers to consider the context of use and how people's cognitive abilities interact with that use.

Split Attention

Split attention describes the process by which people split their attention between multiple sources of information (Chalmers, 2003). It differs from divided attention because rather than simultaneously trying to process multiple information inputs, with split attention people devote their full attention to a task for a short period (normally a few seconds) before switching to another. They cycle through each of the tasks.

Various aspects of split attention are very important when it comes to performing tasks with the aid of a computer system. A task supported by a computer may be seen as consisting of three subtasks: the main task to be performed, the task of reading the information on the computer, and the subsidiary task of interacting with the computer system itself. All of these tasks require attention, and if too much attention is required for any one of them, performance in the others is likely to suffer compared with when only one of the tasks can be given full attention. Obviously, the less attention (cognitive resources and time) people must devote to the interface, the more they can devote to the comprehending the content. For example, scrolling text requires switching attention from reading to the interface, to find the scroll bar and ensure that the mouse is properly positioned, and then to watching the amount of text scroll.

Ash et al. (2004) showed that large sheets of paper were better than multiple screens for allowing intensive care nurses to remember and relate patient information. Having to split their attention between navigating and patient information interfered with their ability to form a clear mental picture of the patient's overall condition.

The problems people have with using documentation are an example of split attention. With people trying to use the interface and also comprehend the text, they are trying to do two things at once and suffering impairment in both. The reading of the help is distinct from the actions required to operate the computer program itself. Of course,

if the help screen blocks part of the application, screen manipulation also requires attention and distracts from the primary task of working with the computer program. "What this means is that at least some of user's cognitive effort is devoted to performing the interface action, as distinct from its meaning" (Basden & Hibberd, 1996, p. 148).

Problems with split attention will be particularly noticeable if computer tasks have to be performed under time pressure (Waern, 1989). People tend to adjust the time spent on a task to maintain high accuracy; thus, time pressure can cause problems with maintaining this trade-off. As a result, formats that give acceptable accuracy with no time pressure may result in unacceptable error rates under time pressure (Bettman & Zins, 1979).

EXAMPLES

Astronomical Information

The astronomical website has three main audience groups: knowledgeable amateurs, students, general public. Each of these groups brings substantially different prior knowledge. Amateur astronomers have a solid understanding and what to learn new information. Students and the general public typically have minimal knowledge and the site must provide that background. Design teams must allow for this wide range since the amateur astronomer's comprehension will be impaired with too much background and they will consider it noise. Likewise, too technical of information will become noise for the general reader.

The mental models used to interpret the information will vary. Some people will have a well-developed astronomical mental model, some a good science-based model, but lacking in astronomy knowledge, and other may have very poorly constructed (poor science background) or even a hostile one (anti-science). How a design team shapes the site to address these different mental models depends on the audience analysis. Chances are good that the hostile mental model can be ignored as those people will make up a minimal part of the audience, so the design team does not have to spend resources designing for them. Quality HII requires providing information for the audience and not information fit for "everyone".

Business Reports

Design teams have to allow for the basic cognitive aspects of how people interact with reports. The factors discussed in this chapter all have an influence on how they will interact with it, but are also factors outside of a design team's control. Thus, they must adjust the report design to address them.

The reports contain an excess of information and can rarely place it all on a single page. Instead, people often have to look at multiple reports or numbers on different pages of a long report. This requires them to remember values as they flip between pages, which depends on working memory. Working memory is limited and decays rapidly, thus the report design should strive for maximum integration and minimal remember/ look up another value. The interactive designs which computers support can minimize this by good integration design. Paper reports had to use multiple report formats; online reports should define the issues looked at and create integrated views for each.

The creation of integrated views will reduce the business analyst's cognitive load since only the relevant information will be displayed with proper salience. A one-size-fits-all design gives both irrelevant information and fails to give proper salience to information fitting the current situation or goal.

People have a mental model of how to interpret a report. Past experience with similar reports, generic business analysis, and knowledge of current business goals all help to shape the view of the report. The reports will be interpreted based on the business strategic goals and values and on their experience with interpreting similar reports.

Readers bring biases to the report analysis. They will know last month's (or report cycle) results and expect similar results. Or they might be expecting to see a strong upturn or downturn in the values. Either way, they will interpret the report in a manner consistent with what they expect to see and will tend to disregard information which contradicts their expectations. For example, if a major new promotion has started which should create a significant increase in sales, any higher values will be interpreted as supporting that increase. In reality, the increase may be within normal month-to-month variation of the values.

SUMMARY

This chapter considers the cognitive aspects which people bring to a situation. Design teams have no influence over them, but instead must work within the limitations of how the human mind operates. The design team's goal must be to minimize the cognitive resources required, which in turn requires an understanding of what drives people's allocation of cognitive resources.

How Memory Works

The human cognitive system has been modeled as a collection of various types of systems with different storing capacities and retrieval characteristics. There are two main parts of the human memory system: working memory and long term memory. Working memory is the area of where people actively manipulate or store information for short time periods. Any information currently defined as "active" resides in working memory. Long term memory is the storage area for everything people know. It seems to be essentially infinite in size. Learning can be defined as moving information from working memory into long term memory.

How Human Vision Works

Reading occurs at a very small area at the center of vision called the fovea which has about a two-degree visual angle. In order to read text, it must be in the fovea area—an area that corresponds to a few words long at normal reading distance. Reading text uses a series of saccades, discrete jerky eye movements, that move across the line of text with the text being read at each fixation. The flyback returns the eye to the beginning of the next line.

Visual acuity measures how well an eye can differentiate one object from another in terms of visual angles. It is typically measured by having people distinguish closely spaced lines. Visual angle, which is the minimum gap a person can see, is directly related to visual acuity, Being able to see a gap of 1 arc minute corresponds to 20/20 vision.

Contrast is the ability to distinguish a letter from the background. In general, this depends on both the color and the brightness. Black and white provides the highest contrast of any color combination. Text with low contrast is difficult to read since people have to work harder to distinguish the letters.

Cognitive Resources and How They Are Allocated to Tasks

People possess a pool of cognitive resources which they devote to the various tasks they are performing. Cognitive load is the amount of cognitive resources which are actually being used at any specific time. The available cognitive resources are very low and people can easily exhaust them. Cognitive overload results in increased errors as well as lower comprehension and performance.

Prior Knowledge

The prior knowledge people bring to a topic strongly influences how they interpret informa-tion. It helps people understand a current situation because it provides a basis for making judgments about information quality and for prioritizing information. People tend to interpret information in one distinct way, and that interpretation is consistent with their prior knowledge.

People use their prior knowledge to understand the information in a new situation. How well they are able to use that prior knowledge depends on how well they can transfer it to the new situation. They can experience either positive transfer (prior knowledge applies to the new situation) or negative transfer (prior knowledge conflicts with the new situation and hinders understanding it).

Prior knowledge is relatively easy to activate through the use of titles, headings, subheadings, and lists of key words or concepts. One major factor distinguishing expert-level from novice-level interaction is that experts possess prior knowledge and know how to apply it.

The prior knowledge that people possess exists in three different forms: tacit (understood, but can't be recorded), semi-tacit (can be recorded in some situations, but not others), and explicit (tangible value and can be recorded). Scenarios and personas help design teams transform tacit and semi-tacit knowledge to the explicit knowledge of the design requirements.

Information Biases

A bias is a systematic deviation from the expected path. Any set of information interpretations or decisions show a random spread around the optimal, but a bias systematically shifts that spread. Design teams assume that a reader will interpret the information in an unbiased manner, but this rarely occurs. Instead, the design team needs to understand the audience so they can allow for potential biases and create content which will minimize its affect.

Mental Models

A mental model corresponds to the cognitive layout that people use to organize information in memory. Mental models are built based on experience. Knowing what information to collect and how to analyze it with respect to the current situation is based on a person's mental model. The mental model can be considered a framework of the situation which the person populates with the current information. Without a mental model, people would lack a basis for understanding the information coming from a situation and would have to figure out all of the relationships for each situation from scratch. With a mental model, many of those relationships are part of the mental model.

Attention

Attention is the focus people put onto information or a task. They may focus on a single aspect or rapidly shift their attention between multiple different tasks or areas of an interface. The best comprehension occurs when a person can focus their attention and the more it is split, the lower the overall comprehension or task performance.

REFERENCES

Albers, M. (2000). Information design for web sites which support complex decision making. *Proceedings of the STC 2000 Annual Conference*, Orlando FL. May 21–24, 2000.

Albers, M. (2008). *Human-information interaction*. 28th Annual International Conference on Computer Documentation, Lisbon Portugal. Sept 22–24, 2008.

Anderson, R., & Pearson, P. (1984). A schema-theoretic view of basic processes in reading comprehension. In Pearson, P. (Ed.), *Handbook of reading research* (pp. 255–291). New York, NY: Longman.

Ash, J., Berg, M., & Coiera, E. (2004). Some unintended consequences of Information Technology in health care: The nature of patient care Information System-related errors. *Journal of the American Medical Informatics Association, 11*(2), 104–112. doi:10.1197/jamia.M1471

Ashby, F., & O'Brien, J. (2005). Category learning and multiple memory systems. *Trends in Cognitive Sciences, 9*(2), 83–89. doi:10.1016/j.tics.2004.12.003

Baddeley, A. (1986). *Working memory*. Oxford, UK: Oxford UP.

Baddeley, A. (1995). Working memory. In Gazzaniga, M. S. (Ed.), *The cognitive neurosciences* (pp. 755–764). Cambridge, MA: MIT Press.

Baddeley, A. (2000). The episodic buffer: A new component of working memory? *Trends in Cognitive Sciences, 4*(11), 417–423. doi:10.1016/S1364-6613(00)01538-2

Baddeley, A. (2001). Is working memory still working? *The American Psychologist, 56*, 851–864. doi:10.1037/0003-066X.56.11.851

Baddeley, A., & Hitch, G. (1974). Working memory. In Bower, G. (Ed.), *The psychology of learning and motivation: Advances in research and theory* (*Vol. 8*, pp. 47–89). New York, NY: Academic Press.

Bailey, R. (1989). *Human performance engineering*. New York, NY: Prentice-Hall.

Baker, H., Uus, K., Bamford, J., & Marteau, T. (2004). Increasing knowledge about a screening test: Preliminary evaluation of a structured, chart-based, screener presentation. *Patient Education and Counseling, 52*, 55–59. doi:10.1016/S0738-3991(02)00249-5

Basden, A., & Hibberd, P. (1996). User interface issues raised. by knowledge refinement. *International Journal of Human-Computer Studies, 45*, 135–155. doi:10.1006/ijhc.1996.0046

Bechky, B. (2003). Sharing meaning across occupational communities: The transformation of understanding on a production floor. *Organization Science*, *14*(3), 312–330. doi:10.1287/orsc.14.3.312.15162

Berry, D., & Broadbent, D. (1987). The combination of explicit and implicit learning processes in task control. *Psychological Research*, *49*(1), 7–15. doi:10.1007/BF00309197

Berry, D., & Broadbent, D. (1988). On the relationship between task performance and associated task knowledge. *The Quarterly Journal of Experimental Psychology. A, Human Experimental Psychology*, *36*, 209–231. doi:10.1080/14640748408402156

Berry, L. (1991). The interaction of color realism and pictorial recall memory. *Proceedings of Selected Research Presentations at the Annual Convention of the Association for Educational Communications and Technology*. (ERIC Document Reproduction Service No. ED334974.)

Besnard, D., & Cacitti, L. (2005). Interface changes causing accidents. An empirical study of negative transfer. *International Journal of Human-Computer Studies*, *62*, 103–125. doi:10.1016/j.ijhcs.2004.08.002

Bettman, J., & Zins, M. (1979). Information format and choice task effects in decision making. *The Journal of Consumer Research*, *6*(2), 141–153. doi:10.1086/208757

Borgman, C. (1985). The user's mental model of an information retrieval system. *Proceedings of the 8th International ACM Special Interest Group on Information Retrieval Conference*, (pp. 268–273). New York, NY: ACM.

Borgman, C. (1996). The user's mental model of an information retrieval system: An experiment on a prototype online catalog. *International Journal of Man-Machine Studies*, *24*, 47–64. doi:10.1016/S0020-7373(86)80039-6

Brazier, F., & Veer, G. (1991). Design decisions for a user interface. In Ackerman, D., & Tauber, M. (Eds.), *Mental models and human computer interaction* (pp. 159–178). Amsterdam, The Netherlands: North Holland.

Byrne, R. (1989). Human deductive reasoning. *The Irish Journal of Psychology*, *10*, 216–231.

Card, S., Moran, T., & Newell, A. (1983). *The psychology of human-computer interaction*. Hillsdale, NJ: Erlbaum.

Carroll, J. (1995). *Scenario-based. Design: Envisioning work and technology in system development*. New York, NY: Wiley.

Chalmers, P. (2003). The role of cognitive theory in human-computer interface. *Computers in Human Behavior*, *19*, 593–607. doi:10.1016/S0747-5632(02)00086-9

Chandler, P., & Sweller, J. (1996). Cognitive load while learning to use a computer program. *Applied Cognitive Psychology*, *10*, 151–170. doi:10.1002/(SICI)1099-0720(199604)10:2<151::AID-ACP380>3.0.CO;2-U

Chen, Z., & Mo, L. (2004). Schema induction in problem solving: A multidimensional analysis. *Journal of Experimental Psychology. Learning, Memory, and Cognition*, *30*, 583–600. doi:10.1037/0278-7393.30.3.583

Cohen, M., & Bacdayan, P. (1994). Organizational routines are stored as procedural memory: Evidence from a laboratory study. *Organization Science*, *5*(4), 554–568. doi:10.1287/orsc.5.4.554

Cooke, N., & Rowe, A. (1994). Evaluating mental model elicitation methods. *Proceedings of the Human Factors and Ergonomics Society 38th Annual Meeting*, (pp. 261–265).

Cuevas, H., Fiore, S., Bowers, C., & Salas, E. (2004). Fostering constructive cognitive and metacognitive activity in computer-based complex task training environments. *Computers in Human Behavior, 20*, 225–241. doi:10.1016/j. chb.2003.10.016

Desouza, K. (2003). Facilitating tacit knowledge exchange. *Communications of the ACM, 46*(6), 85–88. doi:10.1145/777313.777317

Dienes, Z., & Fahey, R. (1995). Role of specific instances in controlling a dynamic system. *Journal of Experimental Psychology. Learning, Memory, and Cognition, 21*(4), 848–862. doi:10.1037/0278-7393.21.4.848

Duin, A. (1989). Factors that influence how readers learn from test: Guidelines for structuring technical documents. *Technical Communication, 36*(2), 97–101.

Duin, A. (1991). Reading to learn and do. *Proceedings of 38th STC Conference.*

Eichenbaum, H. (1997). Declarative memory: Insights from cognitive neurobiology. *Annual Review of Psychology, 48*, 547–572. doi:10.1146/ annurev.psych.48.1.547

Einhorn, H. J., & Hogarth, R. M. (1981). Behavioral decision theory: Processes of judgment and choice. *Annual Review of Psychology, 32*, 53–88. doi:10.1146/annurev.ps.32.020181.000413

FAA. (n.d.). *Character and symbol size.* Retrieved November 25, 2008, from http://www.hf.faa.gov/ Webtraining/ VisualDisplays/text/size1a.htm

Farkas, G. (1998). Reading one-to-one: An intensive program serving a great many students while still achieving large effects. In Crane, J. (Ed.), *Social programs that work* (pp. 75–109). New York, NY: Russell Sage Foundation.

Farris, J., Jones, K., & Elgin, P. (2002). Users' schemata of hypermedia: What is so spatial about a website? *Interacting with Computers, 14*, 487–502. doi:10.1016/S0953-5438(02)00011-5

Fawcett, H., Ferdinand, S., & Rockley, A. (1991). *Organizing information.* Presented at the 38th STC Conference.

Fennema, M., & Kleinmuntz, D. (1995). Anticipation of effort and accuracy in multi-attribute choice. *Organizational Behavior and Human Decision Processes, 63*(1), 21–32. doi:10.1006/ obhd.1995.1058

Fiore, S., Cuevas, H., & Oser, R. (2003). A picture is worth a thousand connections: The facilitative effects of diagrams on mental model development and task performance. *Computers in Human Behavior, 19*(2), 185–199. doi:10.1016/S0747-5632(02)00054-7

Galliers, J., Sutcliffe, A., & Minocha, S. (1999). An impact analysis method for safety critical user interface design. *ACM Transactions on Computer-Human Interaction, 6*, 341–369. doi:10.1145/331490.331493

Garrett, S., & Caldwell, B. (2002). Describing functional requirements for knowledge sharing communities. *Behaviour & Information Technology, 21*(5), 359–364. doi:10.1080/0144929021000050265

Gery, G. (2002). Task support, reference, instruction, or collaboration? Factors in determining electronic learning and support options. *Technical Communication, 49*(4), 420–427.

Gonzalez, C. (2005). Decision support for real-time, dynamic decision-making tasks. *Organizational Behavior and Human Decision Processes, 96*, 142–154. doi:10.1016/j.obhdp.2004.11.002

Gribbons, W. (1991). Visual literacy in corporate communication: Some implications for information design. *IEEE Transactions on Professional Communication, 34*(1), 42–50. doi:10.1109/47.68427

Grice, H. (1975). Logic and conversation. In Cole, P., & Morgan, J. (Eds.), *Syntax and semantics* (pp. 41–58). New York, NY: Academic Press.

Gulliksen, J., & Lantz, A. (2003). Design versus design—From the shaping of product to the creation of user experience. *International Journal of Human-Computer Interaction, 15*(1), 5–20. doi:10.1207/S15327590IJHC1501_02

Hackos, J., & Redish, J. (1998). *User and task analysis for interface design.* New York, NY: Wiley.

Halasz, F. G., & Moran, T. P. (1983). Mental models and problem solving in using a pocket calculator. In *Proceedings of the Association for Computing Machinery, Special Interest Group on Computer and Human Interaction and the Human Factors Society,* (pp. 212–216). New York, NY: ACM.

Halford, G., Baker, R., McCredden, J., & Bain, J. (2005). How many variables can humans process? *Psychological Science, 16*(1), 70–76. doi:10.1111/j.0956-7976.2005.00782.x

Hamilton, M., & Rajaram, S. (2001). The concreteness effect in implicit and explicit memory tests. *Journal of Memory and Language, 44,* 96–117. doi:10.1006/jmla.2000.2749

Hart, S., & Staveland, L. (1988). Development of NASA-TLX (task load index): Results of empirical and theoretical research. In Hancock, P., & Meshkati, N. (Eds.), *Human mental workload* (pp. 239–250). Amsterdam, The Netherlands: North-Holland. doi:10.1016/S0166-4115(08)62386-9

Hix, D., & Hartson, R. (1993). *Developing user interfaces: Ensuring usability through product and process.* New York, NY: Wiley.

Hollnagel, E. (1988). Mental models and model mentality. In L. P. Goodstein, H. B. Andersen & S. E. Olsen (Eds.), *Task errors and mental models* (pp. 261–268). RisÃ National Laboratory, Denmark: Taylor & Francis.

Hsee, C. K., & Zhang, J. (2004). Distinction bias: Misprediction and mischoice due to joint evaluation. *Journal of Personality and Social Psychology, 86*(5), 680–695. doi:10.1037/0022-3514.86.5.680

Hughes, M. (2002). Moving from information transfer to knowledge creation: A new value proposition for technical communicators. *Technical Communication, 49*(3), 275–285.

Hutchins, E. (1995). *Cognition in the wild.* Cambridge, MA: MIT.

Hutchins, E., Hollan, J., & Norman, D. (1985). Direct manipulation interfaces. *Human-Computer Interaction, 1*(4), 311–338. doi:10.1207/s15327051hci0104_2

Jaspers, M., Steen, T., Bos, C., & Geenen, M. (2004). The think aloud method: A guide to user interface design. *International Journal of Medical Informatics, 73,* 781–795. doi:10.1016/j.ijmedinf.2004.08.003

Johnson-Laird, P. (1983). *Mental models.* Cambridge, UK: Cambridge UP.

Jones, E., & Nisbett, R. (1971). *The actor and the observer: Divergent perceptions of the causes of behavior.* New York, NY: General Learning Press.

Kahneman, D. (1973). *Attention and effort.* Englewood Cliffs, NJ: Prentice-Hall.

Kearsley, G. (2006). *Mental models.* Retrieved July 13, 2006, from http://tip.psychology.org/models.html

Kieras, D., & Bovair, S. (1984). The role of a mental model in learning to operate a device. *Cognitive Science, 8,* 255–273. doi:10.1207/ s15516709cog0803_3

Klein, G. (1988). Do decision biases explain too much? *Human Factors Society Bulletin, 32*(5), 1–3.

Klein, G. (1999). *Sources of power: How people make decisions.* Cambridge, MA: MIT.

Koriat, A. (1995). Dissociating knowing and the feeling of knowing: Further evidence for the accessibility model. *Journal of Experimental Psychology. General, 124*(3), 311–333. doi:10.1037/0096-3445.124.3.311

Kushniruk, A., Triola, M., Borycki, E., Stein, B., & Kannry, J. (2005). Technology induced error and usability: The relationship between usability problems and prescription errors when using a handheld application. *International Journal of Medical Informatics, 74,* 519–526. doi:10.1016/j. ijmedinf.2005.01.003

Labiale, G. (2001). Visual search and preferences concerning different types of guidance displays. *Behaviour & Information Technology, 20*(3), 149–158. doi:10.1080/01449290110048025

Lansdale, M., & Ormerod, T. (1994). *Understanding interfaces: A handbook of human-computer dialogue.* London, UK: Academic Press.

Lavie, N. (2005). Distracted and confused? Selective attention under load. *Trends in Cognitive Sciences, 9*(2), 75–82. doi:10.1016/j.tics.2004.12.004

Lightner, N. (2001). Model testing of users' comprehension in graphical animation: The effect of speed and focus areas. *International Journal of Human-Computer Interaction, 13*(1), 53–73. doi:10.1207/S15327590IJHC1301_4

Lipson, M. (1982). Learning new information from text: The role of prior knowledge and reading ability. *Journal of Reading Behavior, 14*(3), 243–261.

Liu, X. (1991). Hypotheses testing by fundamental knowledge. *International Journal of Man-Machine Studies, 35,* 409–427. doi:10.1016/ S0020-7373(05)80136-1

Lohse, G. (1993). A cognitive model for understanding graphical perception. *Human-Computer Interaction, 8,* 352–388. doi:10.1207/ s15327051hci0804_3

Lukoscheka, P., Fazzarib, M., & Marantz, P. (2003). Patient and physician factors predict patients' comprehension of health information. *Patient Education and Counseling, 50,* 201–210. doi:10.1016/S0738-3991(02)00128-3

Mackiewicz, J. (2007a). Audience perceptions of fonts in projected PowerPoint text slides. *Technical Communication, 54*(3), 295–307.

Mackiewicz, J. (2007b). Perceptions of clarity and attractiveness in PowerPoint graph slides. *Technical Communication, 54*(2), 145–156.

Mao, J., & Benbasat, I. (2001). The effects of contextualized access to knowledge on judgment. *International Journal of Human-Computer Studies, 55,* 787–814. doi:10.1006/ijhc.2001.0507

McNamara, D., & Scott, J. (2001). Working memory capacity and strategy use. *Memory & Cognition, 29*(1), 10–17. doi:10.3758/BF03195736

Miller, G. (1956). The magical number seven, plus or minus two: Some limits on our capacity for processing information. *Psychological Review, 63,* 81–97. doi:10.1037/h0043158

Minsky, M. (1975). A framework for representing knowledge. In Winston, P. (Ed.), *The psychology of computer vision* (pp. 211–277). New York, NY: McGraw-Hill.

Mirel, B. (1998). Applied constructivism for user documentation. *Journal of Business and Technical Communication, 12*(1), 7–49. doi:10.1177/1050651998012001002

Mirel, B., Feinberg, S., & Allmendinger, L. (1991). Designing manuals for active learning styles. *Technical Communication, 38*(1), 75–87.

Moray, N. (1987). Intelligent aids, mental models and the theory of machines. *International Journal of Man-Machine Studies, 27*, 619–629. doi:10.1016/S0020-7373(87)80020-2

Moray, N. (1992). Mental models of complex dynamic systems. Mental models and everyday activities. In P. A. Booth & A. Sasse (Eds.), *Proceedings of 2nd Interdisciplinary Workshop on Metal Models,* (pp. 103–131). Cambridge, UK: Robinson College.

Mussweiler, T. (2002). The malleability of anchoring effects. *Experimental Psychology, 49*(1), 67–72. doi:10.1027//1618-3169.49.1.67

Naveh-Benjamin, M., Craik, F., Perretta, J., & Tonev, S. (2000). The effects of divided attention on encoding and retrieval processes: The resiliency of retrieval processes. *The Quarterly Journal of Experimental Psychology, 53*(4), 609–625.

Newman, W. M., & Lamming, M. G. (1995). *Interactive system design.* Cambridge, MA: Addison-Wesley.

Nicholson, B., & Sahay, S. (2004). Embedded knowledge and offshore software development. *Information and Organization, 14*, 329–365. doi:10.1016/j.infoandorg.2004.05.001

Nilsson, R., & Mayer, R. (2002). The effects of graphic organizers giving cues to the structure of a hypertext document on users' navigation strategies and performance. *International Journal of Human-Computer Studies, 57*, 1–26. doi:10.1006/ijhc.2002.1011

Norman, D. (2002). *The design of everyday things.* New York, NY: Basic Books.

O'Brien, E. J., Cook, A. E., & Peracchi, K. A. (2004). Updating situation models: Reply to Zwaan & Madden. *Journal of Experimental Psychology. Learning, Memory, and Cognition, 30*, 289–291. doi:10.1037/0278-7393.30.1.289

O'Connor, M., Remus, W., & Griggs, K. (1997). Going up–going down: How good are people at forecasting trends and changes in trends? *Journal of Forecasting, 16*, 165–176. doi:10.1002/(SICI)1099-131X(199705)16:3<165::AID-FOR653>3.0.CO;2-Y

Oberauer, K., & Kliegl, R. (2006). A formal model of capacity limits in working memory. *Journal of Memory and Language, 55*, 601–626. doi:10.1016/j.jml.2006.08.009

Oberauer, K., Lange, E., & Engle, R. (2004). Working memory capacity and resistance to interference. *Journal of Memory and Language, 51*, 80–96. doi:10.1016/j.jml.2004.03.003

Orasanu, J., & Connolly, T. (1993). The reinvention of decision making. In Klein, G., Orasanu, J., Calderwood, R., & Zsambok, C. (Eds.), *Decision making in action: Models and methods* (pp. 3–20). Norwood, NJ: Ablex.

Øritsland, T., & Buur, J. (2003). Interaction styles: An aesthetic sense of direction in interface design. *International Journal of Human-Computer Interaction, 15*(1), 67–85. doi:10.1207/S15327590IJHC1501_06

Paivio, A. (1971). *Imagery and verbal processes.* New York, NY: Holt, Rinehart, and Winston.

Paivio, A. (1986). *Mental representations: A dual coding approach.* Oxford, UK: Oxford UP.

Park, J., Yoon, W., & Ryu, H. (2000). Users' recognition of semantic affinity among tasks and the effects of consistency. *International Journal of Human-Computer Interaction, 12*(1), 89–105. doi:10.1207/S15327590IJHC1201_4

Parush, A. (2004). *Interview with Donald Norman on mental models.* Retrieved from http://www.carleton.ca/hotlab/hottopics/Articles/DonNormanInterview.html

Patel, V., Branch, T., & Arocha, J. (2002). Errors in interpreting quantities as procedures: The case of pharmaceutical labels. *International Journal of Medical Informatics, 65,* 193–211. doi:10.1016/S1386-5056(02)00045-X

Patrick, J., & Haines, H. (1988). Training and transfer of fault-finding skills. *Ergonomics, 31,* 193–210. doi:10.1080/00140138808966661

Pett, D. (1993, October). *White letters on colored backgrounds: Legibility and preference.* Visual Literacy in the Digital Age: Selected Reading from the Annual Conference of the International Visual Literacy Association. ERIC Document Reproduction Service No. ED370559.

Powe, B., Daniels, E., Finnie, R., & Thompson, A. (2005). Perceptions about breast cancer among African American women: Do selected educational materials challenge them? *Patient Education and Counseling, 56,* 197–204. doi:10.1016/j.pec.2004.02.009

Rasmussen, J. (1986). *Information processing and human-machine interaction: An approach to cognitive engineering.* New York, NY: North-Holland.

Rasmussen, J., Pejtersen, A., & Goodstein, L. (1994). *Cognitive systems engineering.* New York, NY: Wiley.

Reason, J. (1990). *Human error.* Cambridge, UK: Cambridge UP.

Recht, D., & Leslie, L. (1988). Effect of prior knowledge on good and poor readers' memory of text. *Journal of Educational Psychology, 80,* 16–20. doi:10.1037/0022-0663.80.1.16

Redish, J. (1994). Understanding readers. In Barnum, C., & Carliner, S. (Eds.), *Techniques for technical communicators* (pp. 15–41). New York, NY: Macmillan.

Remus, W. E., O'Connor, M. J., & Griggs, K. (1995). Does reliable information improve the accuracy of judgmental forecasting? *International Journal of Forecasting, 11,* 285–293. doi:10.1016/0169-2070(94)00578-Z

Rouet, J. (2003). What was I looking for? The influence of task specificity and prior knowledge on students' search strategies in hypertext. *Interacting with Computers, 15,* 409–428. doi:10.1016/S0953-5438(02)00064-4

Rumelhart, D. (1980). Schemata: The building blocks of cognition. In Spiro, R., Bruce, B., & Brewer, W. (Eds.), *Theoretical issues in reading comprehension* (pp. 38–58). Hillsdale, NJ: Erlbaum.

Santa Clara Grand Jury. (2005). *Problems implementing the San Jose police computer aided dispatch system.* Retrieved June 12, 2006, from http://www.sccsuperiorcourt.org/jury/GJreports/2005/SJPoliceComputerAidedDispatch.pdf

Sasse, M. (1992). Users' models of computer systems. In Rogers, Y., Rutherford, A., & Bibby, P. A. (Eds.), *Models in the mind: Theory, perspective & application.* London, UK: Academic Press.

Satzinger, J., & Olfman, L. (1998). User interface consistency across end-user applications: The effects on mental models. *Journal of Management Information Systems, 14*(4), 167–194.

Schank, R., & Abelson, R. (1977). *Scripts, plans, goals and understanding.* Mahwah, NJ: Erlbaum.

Schanteau, J. (1992). Competence in experts: The role of tasks characteristics. *Organizational Behavior and Human Decision Processes, 53,* 252–266. doi:10.1016/0749-5978(92)90064-E

Schneider, V., Healy, A., & Bourne, L. (2002). What is learned under difficult conditions is hard to forget: Contextual interference effects in foreign vocabulary acquisition, retention, and transfer. *Journal of Memory and Language, 46,* 419–440. doi:10.1006/jmla.2001.2813

Schyns, P., & Rodet, L. (1997). Categorization creates functional features. *Journal of Experimental Psychology. Learning, Memory, and Cognition, 23,* 681–696. doi:10.1037/0278-7393.23.3.681

Seger, C. A. (1994). Implicit learning. *Psychological Bulletin, 115,* 163–196. doi:10.1037/0033-2909.115.2.163

Shah, P., & Hoeffner, J. (2002). Review of graph comprehension research: Implications for instruction. *Educational Psychology Review, 14*(1), 47–69. doi:10.1023/A:1013180410169

Shinoda, H., & Ikeda, M. (1998). Visual acuity depends on perceived size. *Optical Review, 5*(1), 65–68. doi:10.1007/s10043-998-0065-1

Simon, H. (1976). *Administrative behavior* (3rd ed.). New York, NY: Free Press.

Simon, H. (1981). *Sciences of the artificial* (2nd ed.). Cambridge, MA: MIT Press.

Smith, E., & Goodman, L. (1984). Understanding written instructions: The role of an explanatory schema. *Cognition and Instruction, 1*(4), 359–396. doi:10.1207/s1532690xci0104_1

Song, G., & Salvendy, G. (2003). A framework for reuse of user experience in Web browsing. *Behaviour & Information Technology, 22*(2), 79–90. doi:10.1080/0144929031000092231

Spyridakis, J., & Wenger, M. (1992). Writing for human performance: Relating reading research to document design. *Technical Communication, 39*(2), 202–215.

Staggers, N., & Norcio, A. (1993). Mental models: Concepts for human-computer interaction research. *International Journal of Man-Machine Studies, 38,* 587–605. doi:10.1006/imms.1993.1028

Start, J. (1989). The best colors for audio-visual materials for more effective instruction. *Proceedings of Selected Research Papers presented at the Annual Meeting of the Association for Educational Communications and Technology in Dallas, TX.* ERIC Document Reproduction Service No. ED308842.

Sternberg, S. (1966). High speed scanning in human memory. *Science, 153,* 652–654. doi:10.1126/science.153.3736.652

Suchman, L. (1987). *Plans and situated actions: The problem of human-machine communication.* Cambridge, UK: Cambridge.

Sundstrom, G., & Salvador, A. (1994). Cooperative human-computer decision making: An experiment and some design implications. *Proceedings of the Human Factors and Ergonomics Society 38th Annual Meeting,* (pp. 220–224). Nashville, Tennessee Oct. 24–28, 1994.

Sweller, J. (1988). Cognitive load during problem solving: Effects on learning. *Cognitive Science, 12,* 257–285. doi:10.1207/s15516709cog1202_4

Szulanski, G. (1996). Exploring internal stickiness: Impediments to the transfer of best practice within the firm. *Strategic Management Journal, 17,* 27–43.

Thatcher, A., & Greyling, M. (1998). The use and meaning of the "computer experience" variable. In Scott, P., & Bridger, R. (Eds.), *Global ergonomics* (pp. 541–546). Amsterdam, The Netherlands: Elsevier.

Thuring, M., Hannemann, J., & Haake, J. (1995). Hypermedia and cognition: Designing for comprehension. *Communications of the ACM, 38*, 57–66. doi:10.1145/208344.208348

Tracy, J., & Albers, M. (2006). *Measuring cognitive load to test the usability of web sites*. Society for Technical Communication 53rd Annual Conference, Las Vegas, NV. May 7–10, 2006.

Treisman, A. (1982). Perceptual grouping and attention in visual search for features and for objects. *Journal of Experimental Psychology. Human Perception and Performance, 8*(2), 194–214. doi:10.1037/0096-1523.8.2.194

Treisman, A. (1985). Preattentive processing in vision. *Computer Vision Graphics and Image Processing, 31*, 156–177. doi:10.1016/S0734-189X(85)80004-9

Treu, S. (1992). Interface structures: Conceptual, logical, and physical patterns applicable to human-computer interaction. *International Journal of Man-Machine Studies, 37*, 565–593. doi:10.1016/0020-7373(92)90024-F

Tulving, E. (2002). Episodic memory: From mind to brain. *Annual Review of Psychology, 53*, 1–25. doi:10.1146/annurev.psych.53.100901.135114

Tversky, A., & Kahneman, D. (1974). Judgment under uncertainty: Heuristics and biases. *Science, 185*, 1124–1130. doi:10.1126/science.185.4157.1124

Tversky, A., & Kahneman, D. (1981). The framing of decisions and the psychology of choice. *Science, 211*, 453–458. doi:10.1126/science.7455683

von Hippel, E. (2001). Innovation by user communities: Learning from open-source software. *MIT Sloan Management Review, 42*(4), 82–86.

Wachtel, P. (1967). Conceptions of broad and narrow attention. *Psychological Bulletin, 68*, 417–419. doi:10.1037/h0025186

Waern, Y. (1989). *Cognitive aspects of computer supported tasks*. New York, NY: Wiley.

Wagar, B., & Dixon, M. (2005). Past experience influences object representation in working memory. *Brain and Cognition, 57*, 248–256. doi:10.1016/j.bandc.2004.08.054

Wenger, M., & Payne, D. (1996). Human information processing correlates of reading hypertext. *Technical Communication, 43*, 51–60.

Whitmire, E. (2003). Epistemological beliefs and the information-seeking behavior of undergraduates. *Library & Information Science Research, 25*, 127–142. doi:10.1016/S0740-8188(03)00003-3

Whitmire, E. (2004). The relationship between undergraduates' epistemological reflection, reflective judgment and their information seeking behavior. *Information Processing & Management, 40*(1), 97–111. doi:10.1016/S0306-4573(02)00099-7

Wickens, C. (1992). *Engineering psychology and human performance*. New York, NY: HarperCollins.

Wickens, C., & Carswell, C. (1995). The proximity compatibility principle: Its psychological foundations and its relevance to display design. *Human Factors, 37*, 473–494. doi:10.1518/001872095779049408

Wickens, C., & Hollands, J. (2000). *Engineering psychology and human performance*. Upper Saddle River, NJ: Prentice Hall.

Williams, L. (1989). Foveal load affects the functional field of view. *Human Performance, 2,* 1–28. doi:10.1207/s15327043hup0201_1

Wilson, J., & Rutherford, A. (1989). Mental models: Theory and application in human factors. *Human Factors, 31,* 617–634.

Woods, D., & Cook, R. (1999). Perspectives and human error. In Durso, F. (Ed.), *Handbook of applied cognition* (pp. 141–172). West Sussex, UK: Cambridge UP.

Young, H., & Miller, J. (1991). Visual-discrimination on color VDTs at 2 viewing distances. *Behaviour & Information Technology, 10,* 191–205. doi:10.1080/01449299108924282

ADDITIONAL READING

Hix, D., & Hartson, R. (1993). *Developing user interfaces: Ensuring usability through product and process.* New York, NY: Wiley.

Johnson-Laird, P. (1983). *Mental models.* Cambridge, UK: Cambridge UP.

Klein, G. (1999). *Sources of power: How people make decisions.* Cambridge, MA: MIT.

Norman, D. (2002). *The design of everyday things.* New York, NY: Basic Books.

Paivio, A. (1971). *Imagery and verbal processes.* New York, NY: Holt, Rinehart, and Winston.

Chapter 4
How People Approach Information

ABSTRACT

Information interaction and interpretation will vary dependent on people's goals and information needs. These differing goals and information needs shape what information is actually deemed important, and how hard people will work to understand it. As a result, information importance can also differ radically between people. In any particular situation, even after the information has been found and is being considered, factors inherent in human nature come into play to influence the interpretation. This chapter considers some of those factors influencing the ways people approach and interpret information. The white area in Figure 1 shows the area of the HII model relevant to this chapter.

BACKGROUND

My definition of usability is identical to my definition of plain language, my definition of reader-focused writing, my definition of document design... We're here to make a the product work for people —Janice Redish

The main areas covered in this chapter are:

Reacting to Information: How people actually react to information. This can range from a very active to a very passive approach to interpreting it. Some people question all the information and some people prefer to avoid the information altogether.

Effort: How much effort people will put into understanding the information and what factors influence their decision to exert that effort.

Sufficing: People stop looking for and interpreting information when they are happy with the answer because it fits their information needs or understanding of the situation. The answer is not always sufficient, but people have a hard time judging sufficiency.

Multitasking: Multiple tasks pull people in different directions and they can rarely give full

DOI: 10.4018/978-1-4666-0152-9.ch004

Figure 1. HII model—approaching information

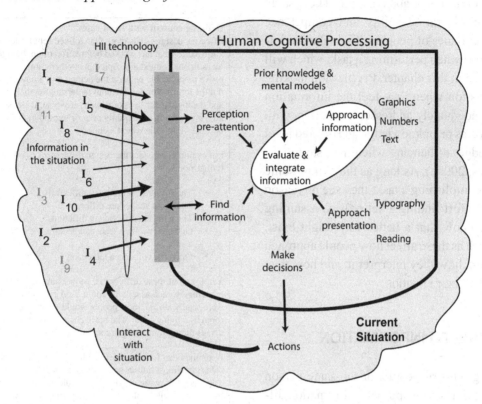

attention to interacting with information. Dealing with multiple simultaneous tasks creates its own problems.

Salience: Not all information carries the same level of importance. The most salient information needs to be identified and processed.

Information Quality: Information must meet a certain level of quality before people will trust it and people must trust it before they will use it. People judge quality based on their perception of its accuracy, completeness, authority, usefulness, and accessibility.

Age: Age and its associated changes in cognitive ability change how people interact with information.

Novice to Expert: Level of experience and background knowledge change how people interact with information.

INTRODUCTION

A common design idea is to create a web site (especially intranet sites) that contains a large collection of cases which people can use to share their experiences and prevent similar problems in the future. However, while most people see this idea as a potential benefit, research calls into question how much it is actually used. The provided information often gets viewed as a big pile of text people must search through and then convert/reshape for an answer to their situation. In general, people usually feel competent to go about their work without needing of additional information; they only resort to information searches when they don't know an answer (Kwan & Balasubramanian, 2003). Note the use of the word "feel" at the beginning of the previous sentence. Unfortunately, people "feel" they know more than they do; they tend to overrate their ability since they don't realize the extent of what they don't know about a topic. These same feelings of overrating ability and competence relate to the issues of people sufficing and minimizing effort when performing a task, which will be discussed in this chapter. People stop looking for information when they feel the information they have adequately addresses a question, with factors such as prior knowledge and desired level of knowledge influencing when they stop looking (Albers, 2004a). As long as they know some way of accomplishing a task, they see no reason to expend effort finding a better way, assuming they even know that a better way might exist. Factors such as these affect how people approach information, how they interpret it, and how they connect it to their situation.

REACTING TO INFORMATION

Different groups of people, or the same person at different times, will approach information differently. What they want and how they expect to acquire information differs. Understanding what information is desired and audience expectations are essential to meeting their information needs and communication goals. Therefore, design teams need to ensure that the information source conforms to both the situational context and the way people approach the information.

A design team often makes the assumption that the information can be captured in one situation and used across many others. Although it greatly simplifies content creation, the mindset that "information is information," and that what applies to one situation applies to all, seriously impedes HII. As may be expected, that assumption has proven problematic. Szulanski (1996) and Tyre and von Hippel (1997) have looked at transferring information internally within a corporation and found causal ambiguity to be a major impediment. Causal ambiguity puts information in terms or concepts which people cannot easily place within their current situation. People may

Box 1.

> **Defining content with fixed rules**
> Effective design needs more than a fixed set of rules or simple knowledge what has worked before. Too often, though, *good* ideas in one context are copied in another context in ways that prove inapplicable because the person only knows the rule, but not the logic behind it. Without understanding both the rule and the logic leads to poor design, or worse: it leads to simply copying existing (potentially poor or unusable) design ideas because "that's the way it's done."
>
> For example, consider the design differences between two living rooms.
>
> - The furniture is arranged differently.
> - The room shapes are different.
> - The paints and fabric are different.
> - One has two love seats and no sofa, the other has just a sofa.
> - Only one contains a television.
>
> Yet, for all of these differences, people have no trouble recognizing each as a living room. And even if the description were totally verbal, most people would be able recognize the room as a living room. The basic characteristics of living room versus dining room or bedroom are apparent.
>
> If, on the other hand, we defined living room as having green sofas, then most houses suddenly cease to have a living room. Likewise, following interior design rules for making paint contrast wonderfully with the upholstery, rug, and room accents is an exercise in futility unless the fundamental room layout fits the owner's needs and the floor joists properly support the weight. The structural needs for an antique grand piano are different from a sofa, as are the traffic flow paths around them.

even acknowledge that they are good ideas, but that they just don't see how to apply them to their situation. This can have major economic impacts, such as a failure to transfer best practices between work sites or rejecting a recommendation that would improve a process. Bechky (2003) points out that communication problems, such as those which occur between production workers, engineers, and management, arise from how they view the information differently. She also describes how factors as simple as where the interaction occurs (within an office/conference room or on the production floor) have a strong impact on how the information is approached and interpreted.

Information is useful only when it fits within the contextual constraints of the current situation and the reader can understand how it fits. Many post-incident reports find that people had the required information but failed to act on it. They either because they didn't realize its importance, they didn't perceive its relevance to the situation, or else too much effort was required to analyze and reshape the information. All of which directly result from poor HII and not "human error."

In explaining (or excusing) their failures to foresee crises in their businesses, executives and directors of large corporations have emphasized the difficulty of "knowing everything." With the pace of corporate life today, even the best intentioned must rely on knowledge that has been extracted, summarized, and reorganized. No business leader would claim "PowerPoint made me do it!" But the reduction— and occasional oversimplification— of a complex matter to a few bullet points on a PowerPoint slide epitomizes the way technology has changed how we know things (Gorry, 2005).

A significant factor that distinguishes good from poor information is how well the presentation takes into account contextual constraints and fits the information into a given situation. Consider how a report may explain why a change would be good for one department but ignores the affects of the recommended change on other departments. It has overly focused on one aspect of the situation and not the entire situation including how the department fits within the corporate structure.

Designing information which conforms to these constraints is difficult. The situational context of a person is a dynamic, continually evolving and open-ended process which contains all the cultural, social, and historical aspects of the situation. Any new information that people obtain must be transformed from its current form into one relevant to all of those aspects. Fortunately, people are adaptive in transforming their information (Payne, Bettman, & Johnson, 1993). The strategies they use are taken from a mixed bag, with frequent strategy shifts; people do not adhere to just one strategy (Navarro-Prieto, Scaife, M.

Box 2.

Approaches to health information

The Internet has become the major source of health information for non-medical people. In 2004, 56% of Internet users reported accessing the Internet for healthcare information, a number which is by now undoubtedly very low.

Access to information about disease ailments, their treatments, and their consequences for patients is clearly important, but how people actually approach that information varies.

- The information a patient privileges is different from that of a medical provider. Patients want information about how to care for themselves, not disease-specific medical details relevant to medical providers.
- Patients' ways of accessing information change over time. Hospital-linked, professional sources of information are generally used around the time of diagnosis. But within 6 months, many patients had begun using non-professional sources such as television, magazines, and newspapers (Booth et al., 2005).
- Information on the Internet supplements a physician's advice. Essays from the early days of the Internet expressed fear that people would ignore medical advice and try to define their own treatments via online means. This fear has not materialized. Most people use the Internet for finding general information and getting a second opinion, but not as a means of self-diagnosis. Online health information complements, but does not replace, interaction with a physician (Zeng et al., 2004).

All of these different approaches are valid and all are used by non-medical people looking for healthcare information. From the very beginning of considering the HII, design teams need to consider how different sections of each audience group will approach the information, how that approach affects the HII, and how to ensure that the design supports it.

& Rogers, 1999). The effectiveness of different approaches varies, of course, and a design team should strive for designs which lead the reader along the most effective paths. Of course, this complicates design teams' jobs since they cannot assume that any specific strategies will be used. They need to understand what information is needed and how it will be used, but this does not mean restricting people to a predefined, "correct" way (Albers, 2004a).

Usability testing is the current best method of determining if the HII is achieving project goals. Such testing can best determine whether people approach information as the design team expected (Redish, 2007). However, Russell (2005) considers how difficult it is to determine whether a design fits how people want to approach the information. He claims that testing must go beyond the typical observations of usability testing and include deeper techniques, such as eye-tracking, to capture the subtleties of people's interaction with the content. Some of the major problems requiring thought, apart from poor design or content, are that:

- People can approach information with either an active or passive intent, which changes how it needs to be presented.
- People tend to avoid information. Dealing with the content takes a lot of effort and people try to minimize that effort.
- People need to transform the text into a form that fits their current situation. Information may be of high quality by most standards, but if it does not lend itself to easy transformation, the content will not be successfully communicated.

Active versus Passive Approaches to Content

People can approach information with either an active or a passive view. The active-passive spectrum (Figure 2) forms a continuum with most people falling somewhere in the middle, and with their exact placement depending on the situation, their individual personality, and the external factors they bring to the situation.

Figure 2. Active-passive spectrum with examples of the various points (adapted from Retzinger, 2009, p. 249)

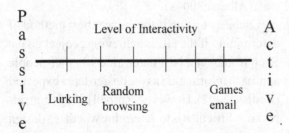

Active View: In the active view, people intend to actively interact with and manipulate information and expect to exert some level of effort to fully extract information from it. A business analyst sitting down with the monthly reports knows that the main points that senior management needs are not listed verbatim in those reports. The information must be manipulated to reveal the answers.

Passive View: In the passive view, people expect the information to be provided in a fully digested manner that requires no effort for understanding. An example is a couch potato sitting down in front of a television and thinking "I'm here; entertain me." From a documentation or web-content viewpoint, the passive approach could be the static presentation of a news site or any text which provides a fixed set of content with no provision for finding more or filling in missing details. A passive approach could also simply provide a fixed sequence of steps to accomplish a task with no explanation. Although people can use this to accomplish the task, next time they will be forced to follow the same steps again.

Older and mostly discredited design ideas viewed people as passive input/output devices that were empty containers into which information could be poured or from which it could be retrieved. Many data entry programs still take this view, that people are themselves nothing more than data entry devices. As long as the only function of the program is data entry, the concept of people as data entry devices is marginally workable. People's control over an interaction is a key factor in active approaches (Retzinger, 2009). However, control of the interaction needs to be real, not just a false sense of control gained via superficial interactivity.

A user can be presented with options that allow them to be in control of a text, yet those options can be seen as features that designers create and force users to use. Thus, a false sense of control can be seen as being created. This false sense of control can be seen specifically when a user uses a website where a user has control over how she navigates through a website, but she does not necessarily control the content of a website (Retzinger, 2009, p. 247).

When the HII requires interaction with or manipulation of the information, problems can arise. Issues of information salience and minimizing cognitive effort, which are discussed later in this chapter, can impact any conclusions drawn from the information.

Data dumping of corporate reports and other information, with the attitude of "here's the stuff, you sort it out," is an example of assuming active recipients, but failing to meet their needs. Data dumping views information as a commodity to be dumped on people. But effective HII requires that information be shaped and focused for each audience group to maximize comprehension. Mirel, Feinberg, and Allmendinger (1991) found that when active users are somewhat uncertain about their task goals, they seek instruction, but not in the form of rote, step-by-step procedures. Rather, they desire elaborated discussions on the implications of various commands and the conditions and cases that are associated with specific courses of action. A consistent disconnect is seen between design teams viewing the content itself as the important "thing" while people interacting with that content viewing their goal as the important "thing." People see information only as a means of achieving their goal and judge it on how well it helps they achieve that goal. Software training people consistently encounter users who do not wish to learn about software, but only to do something meaningful with it. They don't care about the software itself; they care about ways to accomplish their job.

Carroll and Rosson (1987) first described what they called "the paradox of the active user." Rather than learning new methods so they can efficiently interact with information, people are content with their current approaches. In reflecting on this paradox, Krug (2000) advocates against passive approaches to design and for active approaches which do not hinder the reader. He points out that the idealized rational human that a design team may think does not reflect the reality of a real person using the interface. Design teams must design for the real person, not an idealized one.

Carroll and Rosson (1987) have observed that the paradox of the active user is composed of a production bias and an assimilation bias.

Production Bias: The observation that people are often not discovering and using functions that could have been more efficient. People have a goal to complete a task and they approach the task focused on achieving that goal. Learning new functionality which may be useful later is not a current goal. People want to create a table of contents in a document. They may realize that learning and applying styles will make generating the table of contents easier, but refuse to invest the time since they want this documents table of contents now.

Assimilation Bias: The observation that people often figure out how to use what knowledge they already possess to achieve new goals. People use their prior knowledge as a basis for interacting with information. Assimilation bias is using what worked in the past to accomplish a new task. A person may center a heading with spaces rather than a center function because in the past that is what they used.

However, assimilation bias introduces a significant chance of negative transfer (see chapter 3: *What People Bring with Them*, "Transfer effects"), which can frustrate people. For example, learning to use a layout program, such as Adobe InDesign, which uses a paste-up board metaphor, conflicts

Box 3.

Approaching healthcare information

A significant amount of the work on how people (patients) approach information has occurred within the realm of health care. Many of the brochures that patients receive assume a passive recipient receiving information as a commodity (Payne, 2002). The writing style and information content level seems to assume that the patient only wants a minimal amount of material, an assumption which is not supported by the research. For example, "pregnant women either represented themselves as active information seekers or provided compelling reasons why they could or should not actively seek information" (McKenzie, 2002, p. 43).

Part of the design problem is the different mindsets of patient and healthcare provider. Patients want information about the disease. The healthcare provider wants to treat the disease and privileges information relevant to making treatment decisions (as well as already understanding the disease prognosis). People want healthcare information. They want to understand what is wrong with them and how it will affect their life; however, they do not necessarily want to make treatment decisions (Jenkins, Fallowfield, & Saul, 2001). The two types of information needs—the patient's and the provider's—are distinct, but people writing the information often take the healthcare provider's point of view.

---

with prior knowledge from word processors based on a typewriter metaphor. The negative transfer makes it difficult to learn to add text and, since it is not part of a typewriter, and people may never learn that objects can be moved off the page and onto the paste-up board for later reuse on different pages.

Fu and Gray (2004) looked deeper at the concept of how these biases affect the learning of new procedures and found that inefficient procedures continue to be used even when people seem to know about more efficient procedures. They explained their findings in terms of people offloading cognitive effort. People avoid using a procedure which forces them to keep information in their head and prefer procedures which offload that memory effort to the display. A series of inefficient steps with good feedback is preferred over a shorter/faster series that requires mental effort. A study that looked at how well people understood software functions they used constantly found many people could not describe how they used

them, but simply relied on system feedback while performing the action (Payne, 1991). Interpreting this approach as more than just minimizing mental effort, Fu and Gray also found that people justified this approach as giving better control over performance and errors. It allowed them to accomplish a task and ensure they were progressing in the desired direction.

Strong Tendency to Avoid Reading Information

Design teams try to create a highly usable design containing all of the information people need. However, many people don't really want to access a web page or use a manual. Ignoring information has a long history. The syndrome is often summed up comically as follows: "When all else fails, read the manual." Penrose and Seiford (1988) found less than 30% of the people in their survey looked at the manual before using the software. Those people viewed manuals as something to ignore until they had a problem. Only then would they search for information. The movement of information to the Internet has not changed this finding; it has only shifted the search venue from manuals to web pages. Nielsen (2001a) sums up this phenomenon by stating, "Nielsen's First Law of Computer Documentation is that people don't read it."

Simply providing information to people has never worked. It must match their mental models and situational needs (Mirel 1988). However, the way people avoid reading information raises profound implications design teams must consider.

- Design teams cannot assume that people have read any previous information, necessitating highly modular design.
- Design teams cannot assume that all of the text in the section will be read. For example, people routinely ignore written procedures and only follow examples (Lefevre & Dixon, 1986).

- Design teams cannot assume that any text not deemed essential to the current task will be read—what the reader deems essential, not the design team, which can often differ. Unfortunately, poor design can lead people to misjudge how essential a block of text is for achieving a goal.

- Design teams cannot assume that people read before they get into trouble. When a problem occurs, they want only enough information to get out of trouble and back on track.

Perversely, just when information can be most useful to people, they avoid it because of various, often personally unpleasant factors. Johnson, Andrews, and Allard (2001) discuss an information-seeking paradox in which people are less likely to look for cancer information as their proximity to cancer increases. This appears irrational because the proximity to cancer patients increases the information need and that information could result in reduced morbidity and mortality. Although design teams know that people need information, they must acknowledge that for various reasons, people will desire to avoid the content. The design must draw them into the content.

Transforming Information

Information as written is rarely directly usable for people; instead, it needs to be transformed and synthesized to be directly applicable to the situation. People are constantly faced with huge quantities of information of varying relevance and quality. However, they may find it difficult to mentally transform a collection of data because this transformation carries a high cognitive workload. As a result, poor design carries the risk that people will shed the workload and not do the transformation (Herbig & Kramer, 1992; Webster & Kruglanski, 1994). In simple terms, they ignore the information.

Depending on how closely the original information matches the reader's needs, the transformation can run from minimal changes to extensive reshaping. A potential issue with how people transform information is that they will change the problem to fit information presentation (Johnson, Payne, & Bettman, 1988). Thus, the wrong presentation can cause difficulty in relating the information to the situation. However, a later section of this chapter considers the amount of effort people put into tasks, and discusses that if the information requires extensive transformation, it will probably be ignored as mentally too demanding.

Software-based documentation requires significant transformation. The content explains how to perform a task with the software, but does not relate it to the situation. When the real-world goal requires using multiple software functions, people are forced to develop their own model of how to relate the software tasks to achieving the goal (Mirel, 1992; Redish and Schell, 1989). For example, inserting a pull quote into a Word document requires using a textbox. Although Word's documentation explains how to insert a textbox, it never provides any clues about why a textbox would be used. If people did not know to start with a textbox, they would be unable to transform the content into part of their "insert a pull quote" goal statement. One of the distinguishing differences between vendor manuals and third-party books found in bookstores is that the content of a third-party book requires less transformation. The writer has better fit the information to the reader's needs.

The difficulty of transforming content can be found in Dye's (1988) research, which found that over 70% of user comments about a product's documentation arose from errors in interpreting the documentation. Further analysis found that the documentation did correctly explain the software but failed to relate it to real-world tasks. System content might well contain the answers, but if poor HII intrudes—if people cannot transform that information into a form relevant to the current goal—the information will not be successfully communicated.

Another example: people find it easier to remember phone numbers formulated as words (555-CALL), but they also find them harder to dial than a full set of numbers. The problem is that people do not dial letters, but numbers; they have to transform CALL by searching the touchpad for the corresponding digits.

Factors affecting information transformation:

Credibility: How much credibility the information is *perceived* to have determines how much effort people are willing to put into the transformation. Content deemed only marginally credible will not be transformed. Credibility is based on perceived value, not actual value; with poor HII, the two can be substantially different.

Task Relevance: The content must be relevant to the current task. People need to be able to distinguish relevant from irrelevant information and to group information elements together. Information viewed as secondary will not be transformed. Research on instructions finds that people skip blocks of explanatory text (failing to transform it for their situation) since it does not help them complete the task. Relevant text must be cued so that readers know to transform it.

Availability: People tend to work only with information that is easily available. Rather than hunting down higher quality information, they will use what is at hand.

Systematic Arrangement: Information must be arranged to support connecting it to the current situation. People always impose structure on information, and they will interpret it and draw some type of conclusion. If the content fails to fit the context, that interpretation and conclusion can be wrong. "If something can be interpreted (no matter how specious the basis for this interpretation), then it will be interpreted. Ad hoc theories are hastily

Box 4.

> **Transformation of numbers versus graphs**
> One of the basic tenets of numerical design is to use tables for exact numbers and graphs for trends. Using the wrong presentation means that people will have a hard time transforming the information which is readily apparent in one into the other. Given a set of numbers in a table, people find it hard to see trends, other than trivial trends such as "increasing." It is also very difficult to discern trends within non-linear functions, or in data with high noise levels. Likewise, most graphs do not allow easy reading of exact values of various data points. In both of these cases, the proper presentation of the graphic minimizes the required transformation.

assembled out of these odds and ends of partially relevant and partially extraneous generalization. And these 'theories' are used for further prediction" (Carroll & Rosson, 1987, p. 81). Klein (1999) found that people evaluate information based on the order in which they receive it. This accentuates the importance of information salience, and that information be presented in an order relevant to situational understanding. Random data dumps of information fail to communicate since they require too much effort to transform.

Readability: Readability considerations such as font choice and page layout make a strong initial impression. Content will be ignored if it is presented in an uninviting design or unreadable fonts, even if the reader admits that the information is important.

Information Which is Not Understood is Ignored

People tend to ignore information they do not understand, or if they do not understand how it applies to the current goal. Content written at the wrong level, especially at a more expert level than the reader can handle, is typically skipped. People reading healthcare information will not read sections containing medical jargon. Since they don't understand the terms, the text makes no sense to them. Likewise, most people don't understand mathematics or statistics and will skip sections containing equations or statistical information.

Interestingly, text written at an inconsistent level, whether intentionally or unintentionally, bears the risk that readers will skip the entire text. After ignoring (skipping) some paragraphs, readers who have a hard time getting reoriented will just stop reading. Text which intentionally contains content written at various levels must clearly cue the level of each text block.

Information Which is Not Relevant is Ignored

Based on experience, people use their activated mental model to begin the search for information. The mental model provides the basic skeleton, which they fill in with information specific to the situation. The mental model provides the filter which allows them to sift through all of the information available and only focus on the relevant information. The mental model can lead to an expectancy bias (seeing what you expect to see rather than what is there) that exerts a strong effect on what information gets processed. Expectancy bias helps explain why, in many disaster or major accident situations, people made seemingly bad choices and ignored the correct data that was right in front of them (Klein, 1988; Woods, Patterson, & Roth, 2002). They were using a wrong mental model and did not see the relevance of information which turned out to be critical.

People mentally process only the information they view as relevant to the current situation. Most situations contain an overabundance of data, mostly irrelevant to current goals, that complicates the work of comprehending the content. People need to sift through the available text, decide what is relevant, and use it to achieve their goal. Unless the presentation effectively supports cueing of information to allow people to make proper choices, there is a strong risk that some relevant

information will be ignored and irrelevant information brought to the fore.

Relevant information gets ignored because people suffice. Rather than devising ways to efficiently handle the cognitive load, people often simply reduce cognitive load by dumping parts of the problem and reverting to previously learned conventions. Rather than working to understand information, people reduce their cognitive effort and ignore it because it isn't understood (Bettman, Johnson, and Payne, 1990; Wickens, 1992).

Interestingly, as the information flow increases in complexity, contrary to intuition, cognitive overload prevents people from increasing the complexity of their mental integration. Instead, they start to ignore increasingly larger amounts of information. Thus, while this seems to support that highly compact information presentation, Rubens and Rubens (1988) found that making the information too compact or concise hindered performance.

Good mental representations of the overall situation, and commanding a clear understanding of the current situation, are very important when dealing with complex or open-ended questions, since they lack any clear stopping point for acquiring information (Redish, 2007; Rouet, 2003). The design and analysis phases of development require working closely with the real users and understanding how they develop their understanding of a situation.

Known Information versus Need to Know Information

Casner (1994) found that with most commercial jet pilots, a large proportion of the mental processes used to fly a known route were environmental. With experience gained by repeated flying the route, the pilots learned what to look for and what to expect next. The commercial pilot knows what information is needed and knows when and where to look for specific information. Before looking at the specific information, the pilot will not be able to state its value, but will know it is needed, why it is needed now, and how it will fit into the current situation model. Likewise, a business analyst knows what to look for in the monthly financial or production reports. Good HII makes it easier to find and analyze that information.

Some uses of online information systems are no different. People with experience know what information is needed as well as how to find it (such as by reading monthly reports, or booking an airline flight). They simply need to access the proper information. People new to the situation lack this ability because they lack experience, but through interaction with a particular site (for instance, a corporate intranet) they build up a base of experiences which help them to remain oriented and to find information quickly. The faster and easier a design supports acquiring this experience, the more efficient the HII becomes across multiple interactions. Experience helps them build a good mental representation of the overall site and, consequently, lets them easily find the information which fits into their mental model of the current problem situation. The specifics of the desired information and their prior knowledge affect the coherence of the mental representation, which in turn, affects the quality of the final result (Rouet, 2003).

Finding information takes effort. Both the physical acts of interacting with a computer or paper manual, and mentally processing the text to integrate it into the current situation model, require effort. In general, people try to minimize the effort they put into searching for information. So if they already possess some knowledge, they will be willing to use imperfect knowledge they already have, rather than interact with a system to find better information (Gray & Fu, 2004). Going with previously acquired information is more error-prone, but less taxing on time and cognitive resources.

Information Relationships and Information Interaction

Connecting different goals and their associated information needs is key to understanding a situation and knowing what information is salient. Effective design focuses on providing information that allows people to achieve their goals. Building an understanding of the information requires forming the proper relationships between the salient information elements.

Understanding information relationships provides a solid foundation for understanding the cause of a problem and how to solve it (Casaday, 1991). Understanding these relationships places the entire situation in context (Endsley, 1995). Helping people achieve goals and comprehend information requires providing contextually relevant information that fits their goals and information needs, allowing for efficient interaction with that information, and making clear the interrelationships within that information. Designs must provide integrated information that demonstrates these relationships, not just a collection of information (Albers, 2009, 2010). The design goal behind showing the information relationships "is to help people solve problems, rather than directly to solve problems posed to them (e.g., question-answer systems)" (Belkin, 1980, p. 134). People must be made aware that the information exists and that they have easy access to it; but in addition, the overall information structure must permit easy construction of information relationships. Presenting too much information leads to cognitive overload, and trying to guide people along one path only frustrates them because it presents information they either already know or consider irrelevant, while failing to show the information relationships that fit the current situation.

The fundamental problem of many existing designs is poor handling of information relationships. The systems contain the information, but lack clear connections between information elements. The interrelationships that require a high salience that are often not clearly evident. Further complicating the design, these interrelationships can change as people's situational awareness improves or the situation evolves. Yet, design teams cannot be faulted for the lack of good design; we still lack clear methods of how to perform that design. Today we still lack easy ways of tracking, manipulating, and refinding multiple pieces of information on intranets and the Internet. A fundamental problem to overcome is that people have a hard time integrating information and relating various data points to each other. But even more importantly, they have a hard time remembering or considering subtle cause-and-effect, goal-oriented relationships that exist between the information being viewed and other relevant information.

For design teams to provide support for information relationships requires understanding both what the situation is and what it means to people: how do they view the situation, what previous knowledge do they bring, and what do they want to accomplish? Achieving the design goal of supporting people in understanding the relationships between goals involves:

- Finding the logical relationships between different goals and available information.
- Defining the information needs to make those relationships both easily visible and clearly understood.
- Defining how people will have to interact with the information to fully comprehend it.
- Defining how the social and cognitive aspects of interactions inherent in a situation affect both goal relationships.
- Showing why or when the connections between goals are relevant or when they are irrelevant (with the latter being just as important as the former).

Box 5.

Information relationships and improving writing
A major pharmaceuticals manufacturer wanted to improve the ability of their chemists to write reports. A typical report is an incident report, which describes where something went wrong, such as when part of the chemistry control went out of specifications. The report must document what happened and what corrective actions were taken and whether it affected the production batch quality and how such events would be prevented in the future.

The managers saw a need to "improve tech writing" and "have chemists write clearly" since the reports were not accomplishing what they desired. However, the writing consultants they hired saw the problem not as a lack of writing ability, but as a lack of building relationships within the report. The chemists were not having problems with sentences and grammar (the "improve technical writing" part), but with thinking through what happened, connecting the basic plant data with unintended results, and building those relationships within the text to present a well-formed argument on what occurred and what needed to change (Bernhardt, 2002). The chemists understood the problem but did not understand how to communicate it to management.

EFFORT EXPENDED TO UNDERSTAND INFORMATION

Effort has been mentioned multiple times in earlier sections of this chapter. This section takes a closer look at what is meant by effort and the different types of effort people engage in when approaching information.

When people engage in a task or read information, they engage in an effort trade-off between obtaining the desired information and expending the least acceptable effort. Depending on the situation, the least acceptable effort varies based on the perceived value of the information sought. People call the help desk first because they think it requires less effort. A consideration of this effort trade-off is a significant factor missing from many design analysis reports.

A misguided approach in many information systems is a focus on ensuring that the *maximum* amount of accurate content is available. Then, when the system is released, design teams are surprised to find that people are not extracting the maximum amount of information possible.

Instead, support requests how people asking for content which is already in the system. People are failing to interact with the system as intended. And often it is that design teams find people requesting information that is already available in the system. Because of poor design, they can't find it. This closely relates to reluctance to use help files (Scanlon, 1996; Spool 1997). Likewise, help desk research reveals that a majority of the answers for help desk questions are within the user-available online help and documentation. However, those people either couldn't find that information or, more likely, didn't bother looking since it seemed easier to call the help desk. People are reluctant to look for information because they believe their search will not succeed. Such a view may stem from a learned response because of past use of poor documentation. The information was not available in the past; why would it be there now?

Part of the problem is a design assumption that providing a maximal amount of information will result in people's extracting all of that information, or more typically, that they will have no trouble extracting specific, relevant points. In general, that doesn't happen because people don't want to expend the mental energy to transform that information into content applicable to their situation. Instead, people use strategies based on a trade-off between time and the amount of effort required to gain accurate and sufficient information (the next section, on sufficing, explains how obtaining complete information is rarely people's goal). People attempt to minimize both cognitive resources and time wasted by estimating the amount of effort required for a task and making strategic choices toward accomplishing the task based on that evaluation (Fennema & Kleinmuntz, 1995). At the same time, they tend to make choices in terms of immediate, rather than long-term, efficiency and effort (Payne, Howes, & Reader, 2001). In turn, choices which lead to minimizing effort lead to sufficing and accepting inadequate information. Either way, people do not extract all of the information that they should or that they need.

Box 6.

Failure to use system features

Most people only use a small subset of the features in a product, which is interesting since they buy the product on the basis of the whole feature set. One explanation of the scant use of most features is the effort required to learn how to use them.

Consider learning to use a new camera. The camera itself is the size of a deck of cards. Its accompanying documentation contains three manuals: a "Direct Print User Guide" at 77 pages; a "Camera User Guide" at 225 pages; and a "Software Starter Guide" at 80 pages.

The manuals explain all of the 23 shooting modes with an additional 34 functions that could be used within the various shooting modes. Although people will acknowledge that they may be able to take better pictures if they learn how to use those modes, it is simpler and adequate for their needs to just figure out how to point and shoot while relying on autofocus and autoflash. The extra effort required to learn the 23 modes and 34 functions is not worth their time.

Since people try to minimize the amount of physical and mental effort they expend, an effective and efficient design must minimize both the physical and mental exertion required to interact with the information. Many interfaces, especially those which provide information in complex situations, impose a high cognitive demand. Of course, at times the high cognitive demand was the result of poor design decisions (which are often easier for the development team)—products such as data dumps for reports. The goal for quality HII is to minimize both cognitive and physical interaction demands, which means people get a better design. Design teams need to consider three different types of effort:

Perceived Effort: People make decisions to minimize effort based on their estimates of the effort (what they perceive the effort will be) rather than the actual effort.

Physical Effort: Clicking and typing on an interface and manipulating information requires physical effort.

Cognitive Effort: The mental effort required to synthesize and transform the content into information applicable to the situation.

Box 7.

Online prescription writing

Physicians work under high time pressure and want to accomplish their tasks as fast as possible. Thus, the slower time for using an online clinical order entry system (online prescription writing) gets translated to requiring extra effort, causing initial resistance to using the system. Plus, the major benefits are to the hospital system as a whole and not to the individual physician.

Studies of online clinical order entry have found a few consistent aspects associated with the effort expended by physicians. The use of the system is typically mandated by hospital administration, leaving the physician little choice about using the system. In general, online prescriptions take longer than writing by hand, with only a modest offset in time savings from looking in charts and the decrease in pharmacy inquiries from unintelligible handwriting (Bell et al., 2004). There tends to be a strong emotional reaction to using the system—probably the only response available since hospital administration mandates that physicians use it. On the other hand, speed does improve with experience. In the longer term, after becoming reliant on the system, any downtime causes chaos and greatly slowed-down responses. After becoming proficient with the system, the physician has trouble writing prescriptions any other way (Ash et al., 2007). The physical and cognitive effort required to hand-write prescriptions is revealed to be greater than using the system, but only after the system is well-learned.

Perceived Effort

When starting a task, people select a strategy and make a mental estimate of the amount of effort it will require. Estimates which fail to closely fit reality can misdirect people's efforts. If the estimate calls for too much effort, they may forgo the task and make do with other information which they have estimated to result in lower effort. However, the effort used for strategy selection is not the actual effort required, but their perception of the anticipated effort (in other words, how hard does the task *seem* to be if a particular strategy is used). Page design guidelines say to use lots of white space and graphics—often summed up as making the page look inviting—with the intent of making the page appear to require less effort to read. A page that does not look inviting will cause people to form an opinion that the text requires a lot of effort to read and understand. If the perceived

effort level exceeds the potential return, people will not read the page.

Unfortunately, the correlation between anticipated and actual effort is low; people find it very hard to judge accurately how much effort a task will require (Fennema & Kleinmuntz, 1995). This leads them to pick strategies which *seem* low-effort but which in fact might be highly sub-optimal, ultimately requiring more effort than was really necessary had a wise strategy been followed from the start. For people to make a reasonable effort estimate requires that information have a coherent structure which they are able to distinguish (Thuring, Hannemann, & Haake, 1995). People must be able to grasp the relationships between the information elements (Albers, 2010). Simply having a coherent structure from the design team's perspective is not enough if people can't relate it to their situation.

People's perceptions of effort depend on task complexity, or on how difficult they assume a task will be to accomplish—a judgment that varies depending on prior knowledge. Kieras and Polson (1985) showed that perceived task complexity correlates with people's knowledge of the task, not the actual complexity. This means that a task about which people know very little will be perceived as harder (requiring more effort) than one about which they have an understanding. People who are unfamiliar with a task will probably grossly over-estimate the actual effort. To complicate the situation, as task complexity increases, accurate judgment of expected effort decreases, regardless

Box 8.

Fine print or all caps print

The design technique of putting blocks of text in either fine print or all capital letters strives to take advantage of perceived effort. Reading text written in either one is more difficult than reading normal-sized, mixed-case text. As a result, the writer can count on people either to skip or to skim that text. This amounts to hiding information in plain sight by using formatting that discourages people from reading it, which is an ethical issue. The basic logic informing perceived effort needs to be considered in any design.

---

of people's experience. The findings of Fennema and Kleinmuntz (1995) of low correlation between anticipated and actual effort reinforce the notion that estimates of the difficulty of the HII necessary for a task are often nearly independent of actual task difficulty.

Improving the correlation of perceived effort to actual effort requires that the design address those factors which can increase the accuracy of the estimate. Some factors influencing the accuracy of perceived effort are:

- The accuracy of a mental estimate of perceived effort depends on how well the task fits into people's overall mental model.
- When the design does not effectively assist in resolving the question of effort, people make effort estimates and strategy decisions based on simple heuristic rules or just using what they already know (Fu & Gray, 2004). Unfortunately, the use of simple heuristic rules often leads to non-optimal or incorrect solutions.
- High perceived effort estimates lead people to suffice (Simon, 1979) and to be content with lesser amounts or poorer-quality information.
- Different display designs can also affect the perceived effort (and the actual effort) for finding and using information. The display format can actually change the way people view the information. Based on the amount of effort they judge it will take to understand the information, they change how they view the information. Slovic (1972) found that people tend to change their assessment strategy to fit the presentation method.
- Rather than mentally scheduling tasks in proportion to their significance and cognitive demands, people tend to use equal-scheduling, which assigns each task the same amount of mental effort (Langholtz, Gettys, & Foote, 1995).

Box 9.

Perceived effort of Word styles
I know Word very well and can handle making changes to styles at essentially an automatic level. On the other hand, even after teaching students how to use styles and requiring it in assignments, some will ignore them as too confusing or not worth the effort.

Defining the styles, which does require a rather unwieldy sequence of clicks and dialog boxes, can easily be perceived as more effort than the potential gain. The productivity loss does not occur until later in the project when changes, which could be accomplished quickly with some style updates, require going through the entire document and making the same format alterations repeatedly.

Of course, students are rarely faced with the need for the large-scale changes which make styles worth using, which greatly reduces styles perceived relevance and their perceived need to learn the material. All of the paragraphs in this book have styles applied since I can see their advantage.

- Perceived effort is very much based on short-term gains, rather than long-term improvements. In many situations, this short-term gain comes at the expense of learning, which would result in better longer-term performance (Payne, Howes, & Reader, 2001). This can be seen with people who have the attitude of "I just need to get this job done; I don't have time to learn a different way, even if it might be faster."

Physical Effort

Physical effort is the amount of physical work required to accomplish a task. This could range from walking down the hall to visiting a library to drilling down through a list of links because the required information is spread across multiple pages. In informational situations where people know what they want and know how to get it, the physical effort can be the major factor in judging overall effort. For instance, people know a web page contains the information they want, but they have to decide whether they need the information enough to open a web browser and go to that URL. Or, if they have the web page open, they have to decide whether it is worth making several mouse clicks and waiting during slow page downloads. Or, to make it more extreme, they might have to decide whether the information is worth their turning on a computer.

In many situations, a tradeoff exists between minimizing physical and cognitive efforts. Any choice that decreases one increases the other. How people handle this tradeoff depends on the situation, but the question is very sensitive to the amount of physical effort. Wickens (1992) reports that small differences in the amount of physical effort affect people's problem-solving strategy and performance. In order to save physical effort, people would engage in inefficient strategies or would accept slower task times.

Duggan and Payne (2001) explored different reading strategies in the design of written procedural instructions (for a simulated VCR). When people were forced to read several instruction steps in a chunk before executing those steps, they learned the procedures better. The extra physical cost of accomplishing the task forced the people into finding a more efficient method. Furthermore, when people were allowed to read and accomplish the procedure as they chose, they produced a spontaneous chunking strategy which improved procedure retention (Payne, Howes, & Reader, 2001). In both cases, people worked to minimize physical effort at the expense of some extra cognitive effort.

Gray and Fu (2004) found that performance differences can be attributed to individual differences in willingness to either memorize or access information. People seem willing to trade spending some cognitive resources in exchange for physical effort and waiting. When people had to access information on a covered screen, even in a well-known location, the effort and trade-off between clicking on the window and using information they already knew depended on the speed of response. "Milliseconds matter in that differences in effort measured in milliseconds suffice to induce users to ignore perfect knowledge in-the-world

for imperfect knowledge in-the-head." (Gray & Fu, 2004, p. 163). Studies which manipulated system response time by varying the delay time after clicking on a link show that as the response time increases, people take more time to analyze the situation and make a choice (Gray, Schoelles, & Sims, 2005). When clicking a link brings an almost immediate response, there is no time-price to pay for making the click, and people are willing to do more searching and to follow questionable paths. But with a higher delay, only paths which are judged as high-quality are followed. The physical effort of obtaining the information was considered not worth it. Of course, this strategy depends on people's ability to judge link quality, which itself is suspect.

Design teams need to include usability testing which considers the physical/cognitive tradeoff and how to minimize it. A common situation is when multiple windows are open on a computer desktop, or a browser window has multiple tabs. Systems that use multiple tabs, such as electronic medical records (Gray & Fu, 2004), are especially affected. From a design perspective, all of the information people need is available. But, from the perspective of people needing that information, physical actions are required. Windows may have to be moved to allow for comparing different sets of data. Or, as with browser tabs, some values need to be memorized before they can be compared to values on a different tab. The effort people will exert to view this information depends on its value to them. If the information crosses a low-value threshold, people will not expend the physical effort to view it.

Minimizing the physical effort typically requires some up-front planning before engaging in a task. O'Hara and Payne (1998) argued that planning actions continue until the estimated benefits are outweighed by the costs of the cognitive effort involved. They performed a study which had people copying information between files. Typically, people want to complete each destination document before going onto the next; however,

Box 10.

Effort of using external aids

Studies that look at the performance of student designers found they performed significantly better when their design process included a knowledge-based system (Antony, Batra, & Santhanam, 2005). However, there is an effort trade-off that depends on the ease of obtaining useful information from the knowledge-based system.

Deadlines were very important in forcing a team of engineering students engaged in a design project to think critically about what information was most important and to focus the information they sought to support their design efforts. One interesting result was that they tended to look for information in topics on which they felt knowledgeable and avoided looking up topics unfamiliar to them. For example, they looked up information on performing the mathematical analyses required for the design (such as stress and torque), but they avoided searching for information related to developing the project's budget. This can be attributed to the difficulty of determining how much effort would be required since, not understanding budgeting, they were faced with estimating efforts of unknown magnitude for an unknown benefit (Hayes & Akhavi, 2008).

---

in the study design, this was the most inefficient way. When slow time response was added to the operation (it took several seconds to copy each piece of information), people were much faster at finding more efficient ways of performing the task. In other words, with fast responses, little effort went into planning; with slow responses, it was worth the time to plan a better method. Since people don't know how fast a system may respond or how quickly information may be found, they will often continue to modify the effort they put into a task. How people work to minimize physical effort can change during a task, even when the task performed is routine, such as making photocopies of a book chapter (Gray, Schoelles, & Sims, 2005). A slow copier or one which makes it hard to position the book will cause people to skip pages, minimizing the overall physical effort of making the copies.

Cognitive Effort

Chapter 3: *What People Bring with Them* discussed how people have very limited available cognitive resources to allocate to all mental tasks in which

they are engaged. Each mental task consumes some of those cognitive resources. Once the resources are exhausted, people suffer from cognitive overload, which leads to a high number of errors, or to skipped information. As a result, people strive to minimize the amount of cognitive effort (amount of cognitive resources) used for a task.

The best design method to reduce cognitive effort is to ensure that the system design maps directly onto people's view or mental model of a specific task (Benbasat, Dexter, & Todd, 1986). If this fails, people tend to use incremental approaches that off-load the cognitive effort and use general procedures that start with interactive actions. When given a choice of different paths to a solution, people tend to choose the one which is composed of a sequence of interactions. They preferred working in an incremental fashion so that they can receive incremental feedback to ensure they are making progress. One possible explanation is that incremental performance requires less cognitive effort as people can depend on the displayed information rather than having to remember information while making greater leaps toward accomplishing the task (Fu & Gray, 2004). Likewise, in a study of note-taking, Cary and Carlson (2001) found that people tried to minimize cognitive effort and load in working memory by distributing the information between internal (mental) and external (the display) resources.

In a study about people looking for information on their computer (email or files), even when it was possible to jump straight to the desired information, people tended to use various navigation methods (Alvarado, Jeevan, Ackerman, & Karger, 2003). This was explained as a result of minimizing cognitive effort since going directly to the file required people to mentally process up-front all of the metadata about the file. By navigating to it, they only had to deal with that metadata in small pieces and could offload much of the effort to the display.

Design teams should not make procedural information too easy. Some level of cognitive effort is required to learn new tasks since the material must be encoded in long-term memory. Step-by-step training methods, with each action carefully described in the training manual, are problematical since they don't force the reader to do any evaluation or to exert any mental effort before performing the step. Each step is fully presented and only needs to be followed exactly. People can easily minimize cognitive effort by reading the step and remembering it only long enough to complete it. However, learning a procedure requires that people mentally encode both the individual steps and their relationships to the entire process and to store this information in long-term memory (Einstein et al., 2000). By failing to build relationships, people can perform well in a course but be unable to apply the material in a real-world situation.

SATISFICING

Another way of viewing how people minimize cognitive effort is to consider it as only doing enough work to get a result which is "good enough," an action which Simon (1979) defined as *satisfice*. In information search and interaction, people stop when they feel they have enough information to make a decision. With satisficing, rather than looking for the optimal choice, as in classical decision models, people make choices that are good enough (Klein, 1999, 1993; Orasanu & Connolly, 1993). Most rational models of thought assume that people collect all relevant information and then make a decision. However, for a non-trivial problem, there is no way of knowing in advance what all of the information is, and in addition, the time required to collect the information is typically excessive. Thus, people satisfice by accepting the first answer which is deemed close enough or good enough.

Satisficing also appears in the persistence of inefficient strategies for interacting with information (Rosson, 1983; Bhavnani & John, 2000). As

Krug (2000, p. 28) puts it, "Once we find something that works—no matter how badly—we tend not to look for a better way." In an information search, people accept the first information which they deem good enough for their needs. For example, in one study, when using a site map, subjects focused on one or two hierarchies and quickly developed a search strategy. Despite being sub-optimal, these search strategies showed little or no improvement over time, possibly because they were adequate to the task and required no further elaboration (Nilsson & Mayer, 2002). People may admit a search is incomplete, or even somewhat inaccurate, but as long as they consider it close enough, then it's accepted as an adequate answer.

In fact, people are often highly resistant to being shown better or easier ways of performing actions after they find a way that works. Many times, along with essentially admitting they are satisficing, people refuse to consider learning a new way and respond along the lines of, "I know this way. I don't have time to learn a better way." Rather than looking for an optimal path, people satisfice and settle for less-than optimal performance; instead of maximizing output, they minimize cognitive effort and attempt to produce satisfactory output with minimal exertion. For an infrequent task, this attitude is acceptable, but people will also exhibit it for tasks they perform several times daily.

A potential HII problem with satisficing is that people often do not know whether they have enough knowledge to evaluate an answer's quality, but although this does affect the quality of the decision, it does not factor into their decision. When searching for information in areas with which most people are not familiar, such as health care, inherently poor judgment in deciding what is "close enough" can impair overall knowledge acquisition. In these cases, where people lack adequate background knowledge, sufficing can be dangerous because they can't make good judgments on when to stop or on the quality of the information they have found.

Sufficing is also apparent in how most people learn to use software programs; people stop learning at whatever level allows them to get by. Once people figure out how to perform a task, they continue to always use that same method, often even while admitting that they know there is an easier or quicker way. If that means they only know a few functions, then that is acceptable if it meets their information needs, even if their operation of the software is highly inefficient. Carroll and Rossons (1987) call this the "paradox of the active user." Users of computer systems are so consumed with immediate goals that they are not motivated to take time out to learn better ways of accomplishing their tasks. Grayling (2002) uses sufficing as a potential explanation as to why many self-identified experts do not perform better in usability tests than novices. Since their methods were sub-optimal, they did not perform any better than people having to figure out the problem. Of course, a self-identified experts may not be as expert on the system as they think. Instead, they may understand only a subset of functions which they routinely use and may even have sub-optimal use of those.

When people engage in satisficing with procedural tasks, there are some predictable elements design teams can look for. Fu and Gray (2004, p. 901) found that the procedures which people followed bore two characteristics:

- "The preferred procedure is a well-practiced, generic procedure that is applicable either within the same task environment in different contexts or across different task environments,
- The preferred procedure is composed of interactive components that bring fast, incremental feedback on the external problem states."

Fu and Gray argue that the preference for a general, generic procedure privileges the global data in the situation and is used because it works most of the time. People only shift to a different procedure when the local data of the specific situation forces them to. Part of this issue can be addressed by providing information which allows people to understand and build relationships in the layers of context between the specific tool and the situation, an area in which most people are very weak. They understand very well either the situational context or the tool, but not both (Bhavnani & John, 2000). For example, designers might be very good with creating CAD drawings or with understanding the engineering situation being designed, but they rarely can do both at an expert level.

Superstitious Behavior

Closely related to sufficing is the superstitious behavior people display with software interfaces. This does not refer to the many long-standing social superstitions such as warnings against walking under a ladder, but to consistent (although highly inefficient) ways people have of interacting with software. Superstitious behavior is a confusion of correlation and causality; people tend to repeat actions that are reinforced.

In figuring out how to perform actions with software, people overwhelmingly use trial and error (Spool 1996, 1997). In the process, they find something that works and continue to use that sequence. Thus, they have performed an action and have received reinforcement. In many situations, the method found by trial and error works, but is highly inefficient, as Zimmermann and Vanderheiden (2005) explain:

By superstitious behavior, we mean that a person continues to do something in a certain way that does not correlate with necessity -- just because it worked that way before. For example, a phone user might always turn off his phone at the end of a call because his previous telephone required him to turn off the phone in order to hang up. Or, certain computer users might always fully delete and reenter information into a new record rather than just editing the old record -- a vestigial behavior associated with older technology. Or, someone who does page layouts might always use a certain format because she received it as a rule of thumb from another designer—not because she understood the basis for that designer's decisions. In other words, people engage in superstitious behavior when they continue to do what they used to do without questioning or understanding why—even if the action is no longer necessary or sufficient within the current context (Note 10).

After finding something that works, people continue to perform the action in the same manner and refuse to consider a different approach. Raskin (2003/2004) points out that the real problem follows after they have found an answer. Since people don't understand how they made the system work, all they can do is repeat the sequence they discovered without any variance.

No wonder we tend to act as if computers are run by magic. Many of us (including me) use the exact sequence of operations for a task because it worked once and we don't dare to vary it (even when somebody suggests a different method) (p. 12).

As with sufficing, people have found something that works and see no reason to change. Or they may have tried performing the task differently and found it didn't work, thus reinforcing the superstitious behavior. Typically, they do not understand why the known sequence works, so they cannot figure out what can be changed or modified without breaking it.

This can lead to sub-optimal performance, even on well-designed systems that support very efficient methods of accomplishing the task. This type of behavior also shows why design teams need to understand the whys behind usability test results, rather than just the actions themselves. When people are engaged in superstitious be-havior, modifications to the design that usability tests show increase interface efficiency will not improve performance since they will not be used. It can also prevent communicating the content since people will not work to manipulate the information, but will accept the one presentation they know how to produce.

MULTITASKING AND TASK SWITCHING

Consider this sequence of events:

A professor sits at a computer, attempting to write a paper. The phone rings; he answers. It's an administrator, demanding a completed "module review form." The professor sighs, thinks for a moment, scans the desk for the form, locates it, picks it up and walks down the hall to the ad-ministrator's office, exchanging greetings with a colleague on the way. Each cognitive task in this quotidian sequence—sentence-composing, phone-answering, conversation, episodic retrieval, visual search, reaching and grasping, navigation, social exchange—requires an appropriate configuration of mental resources, a procedural "schema" [men-tal model] or "task-set" (Monsell, 2003, p. 134).

Each of the tasks described in the quotation has a separate mental model which the professor must switch to before performing the task and then switching back to a previous one. In this example, each event happened in a long, linear series, but typically multitasking involves per-forming multiple tasks at once with rapid switches between them. Multitasking can be compared to the vaudeville act of balancing spinning plates. The performer must run from pole to pole to keep the plates spinning and to avert disaster. A good performer can keep many plates spinning; a poor one can spin only a few. And if any plate proves difficult to keep spinning and requires extra time, then they all crash.

Multitasking involves performing several different tasks at the same time. When people multitask, they have to constantly shift cognitive resources around (Figure 3). But limited resources do not allow people simultaneously to keep all of the tasks in working memory. Instead, a substantial time penalty is incurred as task information is moved in and out of long-term memory. It will take longer to multitask than to perform the tasks individually. The balance of cognitive resources between the tasks has strong influence in how effectively and efficiently the multitasking is performed.

Burgess et al. (2000) list three major skills required for multitasking:

- The ability to create and mentally schedule future intentions.
- The facility to remember those intentions and to prioritize them.
- The ability to switch from one intention to another.

Computer-based operations always force people into two tasks: reading content and manipulating the interface to show that content. The acts of reading or evaluating contextual information and interacting with a computer interface (such as,

clicking on links or manipulating windows) are two independent tasks, which must be performed simultaneously. Additional tasks are typically required because of the reason why people are reading the information. For example, using a help system forces multitasking on several levels since, besides working with the original interface and its information, people must also contend with manipulating the help interface and understanding the help information. In addition, factors such as the help window blocking part of the original application, forcing people to remember information, add to the cognitive load and multitasking difficulty.

Although it may appear that people are performing multiple tasks simultaneously, one task is receiving the central focus, while the other tasks are rapidly cycled into that central focus. It requires cognitive resources to perform that mental shift, resources in addition o those required for the task itself. As a result, operations which force people to multitask are not as efficient as they would be when performed alone. It typically can take 20-40 percent longer to accomplish a task via multitasking than by doing the separate tasks singularly because of the overhead of mentally switching between tasks (Rubinstein, Meyer, D. & Evans, 2001).

Figure 3. Multitasking involves moving task information rapidly between working and long-term memory. In this example, a person is working on tasks 1-4. Since task 2 has the current focus, it is in working memory while the other three tasks have been shifted to long-term memory. When the focus shifts to task 3, then task 2 is moved to long-term memory and task 3 moves to working memory. Lack of cognitive resources in working memory prevents keeping all four tasks in working memory at once.

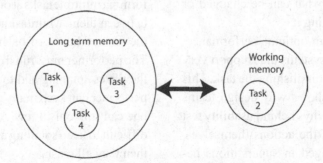

Each task requires attention to different information elements (such as content or interface widgets), or retrieval from memory of prior knowledge, to integrate into the current task. How well people can handle these three factors and the mental switching requirements determines how well they can multitask. People show a wide range in their abilities, from being very efficient and able to truly multitask, down to handling the multiple tasks in a linear fashion (Zhang, Gonetilleke, Plocher, & Lang, 2005).

Cognitive resources are limited and how efficiently people use them is a major determinant of multitasking ability (Baddeley, 1986). Efficient multitasking performance in complex task environments is dependent on skillful allocation of resources (Vu et al., 2000). For example, Schneider and Fisk (1982) had people perform two visual search tasks concurrently: one for which processing should be automatic and the other requiring attention. They found performance in the task requiring attention suffered because people devoted excess resources to the automatic task. When the people were instructed to strongly emphasize the attention-requiring task, they performed much better with no decrease in performance of the automatic task. The sidebar discussing the problems of laptops for the San Jose police force illustrates an example of this type of dual task. Driving is learned to automaticity, but working with a laptop requires attention. In this case, it required too much attention and diverted needed resources from the driving task.

Unfortunately, design commonly focuses on helping people accomplish one task at a time, providing little help in arranging the tasks into effective work orders, or supporting switching between multiple tasks (Cypher, 1986). Virtually every study that looked at switching between tasks (from task A to task B to task A) found a significant increase in time and errors as compared to performing the same tasks sequentially. People cannot just switch between tasks with no cost in either mental effort or time. The analysis of switching-time costs, in both the physical and cognitive sense, has been done for various types of tasks (Kieras, Meyer, Ballas, & Lauber, 2000). There is a switch cost, which increased the response time relative to non-switched tasks; individual steps of the task can be performed faster with a single task than a multitask. Task times are slower and error rates higher immediately after a switch, but these effects are seen long-term, probably because of issues of shifting mental models (Monsell, 2003) and knowing another shift will be occurring. A preparation effect has been seen where knowing the task switch was coming and having time to prepare will decrease (but not eliminate) the switch cost effects. Of course, in most multitasking situations of interest it HII, there is minimal preparation time available.

The switch costs vary based on how complex and familiar the tasks are. As would be expected, it is harder to switch from one complex task to another complex task. The level of familiarity with the task also affects switch cost; it also takes more time to switch from a familiar to an unfamiliar task than from an unfamiliar to a familiar task (Kushleyeva, Salvucci & Lee, 2005; Rubinstein, Meyer, D. & Evans, 2001).

A potentially serious impairment to multitasking is that it requires people to balance their limited cognitive resources between the tasks. However, rather than mentally scheduling cognitive tasks in proportion to their significance and cognitive demands, people use an equal-scheduling method, assigning each task the same amount of cognitive effort (Figure 4). The result is a mismatch of cognitive resources to demand. Some tasks receive insufficient cognitive resources while others get too many (Langholtz, Gettys, & Foote, 1995).

Deciding When to Switch between Tasks

When people are multitasking, a simplistic view is that they are performing several tasks simultaneously. However, the human mind cannot really

Figure 4. Mental scheduling of cognitive resources. The circle size corresponds to the amount of cognitive resources the task has allocated. People tend to use equal-scheduling, rather than optimal scheduling. In equal-scheduling example all three tasks receive the same resources so task 3 receives too many resources and task 2 receives too few.

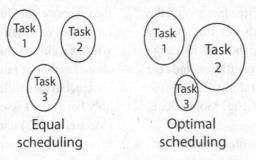

Equal scheduling

Optimal scheduling

Box 11.

Teenagers and multitasking

Many parents are amazed at how their teenagers can multitask, such as being able to text-message multiple friends, listen to music, and study at the same time. However, the research into this ability shows that these teens suffer the same decreased performance as seen in older people; they are, however, able to shift between tasks better. The overall comprehension and learning of new material (the textbook they are studying) shows a marked decrease compared to single-task performance. Also, most of the tasks they perform do not require a long-term memory component. Texting with multiple friends, watching a movie, and listening to music produce little information which must be commented to memory. On the other hand, if they are also studying history, then they will show comprehension of the material.

---

focus on multiple tasks at once. Instead, people rapidly shift between tasks, with each task receiving the bulk of attention for a short time. The previous section considered the time and error costs of making that switch; this section looks at what makes people decide to switch between tasks. The switch between tasks does not happen automatically. Something in the situation cues people to expend the cognitive resources to make a switch. Design teams need to recognize those factors and ensure that the design provides cues.

The motivation for a time-to-switch signal, especially for information web sites, is internal, not driven by external factors (Burgess et al., 2000). Emerson and Miyake (2003) found that people are silently telling themselves what task to

perform next and when. They describe this internal monitoring in terms of an increasing "pressure" over time that people working on one task feel as the need to switch to another task increases.

The internal pressure arises because in any sequence of tasks, some are more important than others to achieving the overall goal. People want to stay on the tasks they perceive as most important. In many tasks, such as assembling a bicycle or completing an online form, the desire to complete the task overrides the need to find information about properly completing it, which provides one clue for why people don't read documentation. Reading the document and assembling the bike requires people to switch between tasks: read step, do action, read step and relate to previous action, do action. If the effort to figure out the step and relate it to a previous step is too difficult, then they tend to minimize cognitive effort by ignoring the instructions and focusing on figuring out (guessing at) the actions. Difficulties in refinding the proper point in the instructions caused by poor design can also make people not want to use them.

Design teams must understand what tasks people are performing and how simple or complex they view them to be. The design may have to signal that a change is needed (that something on the second task requires attention).

Task Interweaving

Normal task analysis and most designs assume people accomplish one task at a time in a linear manner: they start a task, finish it, and then move on to the next task. Although people may describe their task performance in this linear sequence, research shows that they tend to use an opportunistic organization and interweave tasks (Visser & Morals, 1991). Cypher (1986) found that while people say they perform tasks in simple sequences, in reality they interweave multiple tasks. Often they stop one task and perform another simply because it is convenient to perform it right now.

People interweave tasks in a "while I'm at it" manner (while I'm going to the grocery store, I'll stop for gas on the way). This can range from working with another file because that folder happens to be open to doing a task because they will be in a room down the hall. Information search and analysis is often filled with many "while-I'm-at-it" kinds of activities. These can range from the normal "guess I'll do this now" to task shifts that relate to the information itself, such as when people stop to look up a definition or decide to get more information about a sub-topic to help understand the current topic.

Cypher (1986) claims that user dissatisfaction results from a failure of the system to support opportunistic work of interweaving tasks. Although the system supports the task, the task is not performed in the same manner people want. Unfortunately, current design methodologies give little emphasis to helping arrange the tasks into effective work orders or supporting multiple tasks at once. Cypher puts the problem squarely on the designer:

Program designers put a great deal of effort into allowing users to perform single activities well, but considerably less effort goes into allowing users to arrange those activities. If computer systems are designed so that they actively support and

facilitate multiple activities, they will be more comfortable for the user (p. 244).

Part of the problem can be traced to divorcing design requirements from their situational context. The requirements call for a task and the system performs it, but it fails to fit into the flow of related tasks. People typically have multiple information needs which do not necessarily appear in any fixed or linear sequence. The design needs to consider how to support multiple undefined (at design time) paths for information acquisition.

Task Interruptions

In addition to considering multitasking situations where people voluntarily take on tasks and switch between them until they are complete, task interruptions must also be considered. Task interruptions break the task switching cycle and force people to consider a completely different task. Task interruptions include phone calls, pop-up chat boxes, and pinging sounds of emails. A phone must be attended to, while the email ping can be ignored (McFarlane & Latorella, 2002). Storch (1992) found that pop-up windows were highly disruptive and led to increased errors. In general, their effect on decreased performance lasts much longer than the interruption itself.

In a business-based study, each employee only spent 11 minutes on any given project before being interrupted and took an average of 25 minutes to return to the original task and often performed more than just the task causing the interruption before returning to the original task (Gloria Mark, Gonzalez, & Harris, 2005). Then, upon returning to the main task, they had to mentally return to their location at the point of the interruption and resume the task. With highly complex tasks, this proves difficult.

This was clearly brought out in the work by Czerwinski, Horvitz, and Wilhite (2004).

The findings suggest that methods for capturing and remembering representations of tasks may be valuable in both reminding users about suspended tasks, and in assisting users to switch among the tasks. Examples of such methods include time-centric visualizations and tools that can record, and reconfigure upon demand, the layout of multiple windows of content and applications that comprise a task (p. 7).

Interruptions have three phases: before switch, during, and after. Design teams need to acknowledge that interruptions occur frequently and ensure that a design supports them. System design should support making a smooth switch to and from. Having the ability to easily save and return to the current work is vital. It should also help to allow people to switch when it is convenient, rather than forcing an interruption.

Interruptions are going to occur as people interact with information. The system design needs to allow for those interruptions and minimize their impact.

SALIENT INFORMATION

Information salience is defined as the prominence given to an information element. The most important information should have the highest salience.

Any information system has an overabundance of information that can quickly lead to cognitive overload (Thuring, Hannemann, & Haake, 1995). The raw information about a the situation is often at salience levels which may not match its importance. Design teams need to transform those salience levels into what people require based on their information needs. Design teams must ensure that all of the information the reader sees has proper salience to maximize communication and to minimize the risk of information overload.

The importance of the design team having clearly defined a hierarchy of information salience comes from the limited amount of attention people

can give to the overall text. The fundamental problem is that since attention is driven by limited cognitive resources, when people improve their knowledge of one aspect of a situation, it often occurs at the cost of not gaining information about another aspect (Endsley, 1995; Wickens & Hollands, 2000). In other words, people cannot and do not view and interpret everything on a display or page. Instead, they select the items which seem to have the highest salience and focus their cognitive processing on just those items. When a mismatch occurs between the most salient information, the most important information for the situation, and their desired information, they have to work harder to decipher which information is of current interest, creating a risk that the focus will go on the wrong information.

A typical misplaced salience problem occurs when the display contains lots of easy to collect/display information which is not highly relevant to understanding the situation. To comprehend the situation properly, people have to know what information they need and pull it from the noisy background of irrelevant information. With low prior knowledge, the person lacks the ability to sort relevant from irrelevant noise. Another example of misplaced salience is the use of bold text to make a word or phrase more salient. People's eyes are drawn to a bold word immediately upon looking at a page. However, if the word does not deserve to be bold, then that eye movement is distracting and interferes with comprehension. At the extreme, the overuse of bold text causes the non-highlighted text on the page to gain salience because the eye is drawn to the text which looks different. With too much bold, the non-bold text now looks different from the general page. Likewise, information at the top of a page receives a higher salience value than one lower on the page. The information placed at the top must deserve its higher salience.

Information salience plays a major factor in people's missing information or forming incorrect conclusions. People gain an understanding of the situation by following "a long and recursive process with backtracking and erratic switching among the following activities: thinking about ideas, production, reorganization, modification, and evaluation" (Nanard & Nanard, 1995, p. 50). Thus, supporting erratic methods of understanding requires providing salient information when people need it, and in the proper form. The important information must be clear enough so that they do not overlook it. Incorrect conclusions can be caused by focusing on some information while ignoring other information which would disconfirm the assumption. It could also be caused by improper information salience, which causes partial or irrelevant information to dominate people's view, causing them to reach an incorrect conclusion. Plus, as they gain an understanding of a situation or the situation evolves, the information which deserves the most salient presentation can change.

People think they use more information than they actually do. They tend to underestimate the weight placed on important cues and overestimate the weight placed on unimportant cues. The salient information that grabs attention can unduly influence a decision. Experts are just as susceptible to this as novices (Andriole & Adelman, 1995). Thus, in a retrospective interview during a usability test, it is hard to get clear answers from people about the salient information and how they used it.

If most people are asked what type of information they consider most salient, they answer something along the lines of "information to show I'm making the right choice." Contrary to that information want, the information people need is *not* that which shows they made the right choice, but rather is the information which might reveal that they made the wrong choice. In other words, too much confirming information is actually noise, although people think they want it. The design importance for disconfirming information comes from the way people make choices. As the amount of information increases, people increasingly ignore information incompatible with the

decision they want to make (Ganzach & Schul, 1995). In most cases, all of the factors will not be viewed. Rather, they have a solution in mind and will only look for confirming information. Because people look for confirming information, not disconfirming information, specific elements that can provide disconfirming information must be uncovered in the analysis and given a high salience level.

Expectancy bias leads people to see the expected answer (Klein, 1999) even when it is not really there. As a result, they find it easier to extract confirming information while ignoring disconfirming information. In addition, people tend to change their assessment strategy to fit to the presentation method, rather than transform the information to fit a better assessment strategy (Johnson, Payne, & Bettman, 1988). In other words, people will not mentally highlight the important information they know should have a high salience to give it the salience it requires if the presentation makes it difficult to do so.

Unfortunately, many designs fail to follow good practice for presenting salient information and end up with one of the following problems:

- All information receives equal salience. When the design team does not understand the information, they cannot determine effective salience, so everything is presented equally. Essentially, they take the view of "the user knows what they want, so they can figure it out."

- Overuse of salience indicators, such as bold fonts or colored text. Overuse results in the non-salient information becoming more prominent.

- Minor but easy-to-present information occupies an excessive amount of the display area and consequently diminishes the salience of important but harder-to-present information. Providing large sets of easy-to-obtain numbers or images can overpower the presentation of smaller sets of more

Box 12.

Information salience of tag clouds
Tag clouds provide information salience by varying the size of the text, with the largest size being the most important. Using www.tagcrowd.com, the following tag cloud was created for this section on information salience. The word size is based on word frequency. On a webpage, links could be created to connect the cloud text to relevant text. The actual usefulness of tag clouds is still being debated.

amount aspect attention **bold** causes cognitive comprehension conclusion decisions deserve design differ distract driven element endsley eye factor fixed forming gain higher highest important **information** interest issue items limited **needs** noise **page** **person** problem providing receive requires resources result **salience** salient simply situation teams **text** value view wide work wrong

---

relevant numbers. The screen becomes full of information that is easy to capture and display, but has no bearing on the current user goal (Hsee, 1995). For example, the long tables giving the technical specifications for a product when most people do not need or understand that information.

- Design decisions become driven by corporate politics, such as increasing the salience of features or upgrade options, which distract people from the information they really want.

Signal to Noise Ratio

The signal to noise (SNR) ratio is a common concept in radio communications and electronic communication in general. For a radio, the static is the noise. Too much static and a storm report gets drowned out, or at least you must listen closely to understand the announcer. Electrical engineers working on a voice circuit can easily define what are the signal and noise elements. The original voice spoken into the transmitter is a known quantity and anything else that comes out the speaker is noise that should be eliminated.

In an information system, "signal" consists of anything that people need to know but don't, and "noise" is anything that they don't need because it is irrelevant or already known and is just cluttering up the page or screen to the detriment of the signal. Tufte (1983) was referring to essentially the same concept when he discussed data/ink ratio and chart junk. Basically, noise consists of all the stuff that interferes with communicating what people need. Any time noise receives salience, the comprehension of information is impaired. In the hindsight provided by investigations of bad decisions (the type that led to millions of dollars of losses or damage), the excesses and irrelevancies of information are obvious, but they are never obvious to the person while making the decisions. The difficulties people have finding or comprehending information appear repeatedly in these studies. In many cases, they come down to low SNR with high levels of extra information blocking the communication of the information which was really needed.

A huge number of documents on corporate intranets were placed there "in case someone wants to read it." McGovern (2006a) points out that a couple of studies of web sites removed over 30% of the pages and no one noticed. Pages that no one looks at waste both the author's time and system resources, but as long as no one looks at them, they do not interfere with interpreting relevant information. On the other hand, a communication problem occurs when excessive or irrelevant information is provided. Unfortunately, people often cannot easily see that they either have too much or irrelevant information. Instead, they try to process all of it, which leads to problems. The useful information—the signal—is swamped by the non-useful information—the noise.

Unfortunately, design teams do not possess a clear-cut set of techniques, such as a radio circuit band-pass filter, available to electrical engineers. For information systems, taking the raw data in a system and deciding what is signal and what is noise is extremely difficult. A major problem is that each person has different needs, which means that different people perceive a different noise level in the same text. For example, many documents carefully define their terms; yet, if people already know those definitions, then they become noise. Of course, for a more novice reader, the definitions are essential to understanding the document. Because of the different goals and information needs each person brings to the system, there will never be a clean method of resolving the signal to noise ratio. Rather, task and audience analysis need to refine the understanding of what is signal, what is noise, and most importantly, what contextual situations cause noise to become signal and vice versa for each of the audience groups or personas.

An excess of noise can occur from either too much or too little information. Too much information causes information to be ignored since it takes too much effort to extract it. Too much information can result when the design strives for completeness over clarity, gives information that is not salient to the current situation, or gives information people consider irrelevant (or perhaps doesn't understand that it is important). On the other hand, the problem of not enough information can arise when the initial analysis didn't identify the needed information. It can also arise in a "one-size-fits-all" design. The information is constrained so it is appropriate for a subset of the potential readers, such as low-literacy readers. While an important design criterion for the low-literacy group, it fails to provide adequate information to other groups that want or need more information.

People often have a difficult time sifting out relevant from irrelevant information. Low signal to noise ratio makes it hard to distinguish and mentally rank the appropriate information (Albers, 2004b). People are very good at pulling information out of a noisy environment if they know what

information they need, but they have difficulty if they do not know what they need or whether the information even exists. Factors contributing to a low signal to noise ratio include:

- Lots of information exists online (especially in corporate intranets) which was placed there "because someone might want it." The result is lots of information of minimal relevance to anything. The trend has been to make more knowledge, such as best practices, success stories, policy books, and training manuals available online. However, successfully using that information also means that people must have access to the relevant knowledge in the context in which they need it (Schwartz & Tefieni, 2000). "Contextualized access means access to relevant task knowledge is immediate and within the problem-solving context rather than via searching in a separate context. Thus, there is no need to break the continuity of task performance to seek relevant domain knowledge" (Mao, & Benbasat, 2001, p. 788).
- Graphics tend to out-compete text for people's attention. The eye is naturally drawn to graphical images and graphics tend to be remembered better. Of course, that does not mean they are more important.
- Many computer systems present lots of easy-to-obtain/display information which hides the much smaller amount of important but hard-to-display information.
- Poor design can give high salience to irrelevant information or give all information the same salience, which forces people to work harder to identify what they need.

The real HII difficulties in communicating information do not fall within the technical realm. Rather, they fall within the people realm, which revolves around the contextual aspects of the information. The technical realm solves individual problems by placing widgets on the interface and developing algorithms for an efficient back end. In the people realm, the goals and information needs must fit within people's cognitive capabilities and social environment. They have goals they want to address and problems they want to solve; helping to achieve those goals and solve those problems requires systems that provide salient information appropriate to the situation. In other words, they need a strong signal with minimal noise.

Maximizing the signal means understanding both people's terminology (versus system terminology) and their situation. Quite simply, anything written in unfamiliar terms will be considered ignored, regardless of its importance. But more than just the proper terminology, the text must fit within the situation. For example, medical information and business balance sheets have formats fixed by long tradition. Changing the format could actually cause someone to ignore the entire page with a logic of "this doesn't look like the XX report, so it doesn't have the information I want." The change renders the entire page as noise.

The difficulty of resolving the SNR occurs at many different levels. For example, it is reflected in the basic ideas of the differences in writing for novice and experts or writing for high and low literacy levels. The extra explanation required for the novice becomes noise for the expert, which impairs communication. Interestingly, readers with a high knowledge level in the general subject tend to have poor comprehension of text written for a low-knowledge reader (McNamara & Kintsch, 1996). The extra detail bogs them down and results in less focused reading, resulting in missed information. The reverse also occurs: without more detail, a written-for-an-expert text degenerates into noise since it can't be understood by a non-expert. A similar situation also occurs in the fundamental information requirements for a job. A technician needs specific details about a task while a supervisor wants a higher-level, less detailed view. As a result, signal for the technician becomes noise for the supervisor and proper signal for the supervisor is inadequate for the technician.

SNR in Interface Design

System interface design provides a striking example of decreasing SNR as viewed over time. Each new release of a product contains more functionality but this functionality often comes at the price of lower usability. Norman (2002) calls this phenomenon creeping featurism and suggests that the complexity of use increases as the square of the increase in functionality. In other words, twice the functionality means a product is four times as hard to use. Shneiderman (1997) considered the issue of screen density and how the amount of information displayed relates to how easily people can use it. It is not a straightforward issue of low density equaling ease of use, but rather that all of the information must be relevant. People like very dense screens if the content is relevant and well organized. In other words, screens with a high SNR can be very dense and screen with a low SNR fail regardless of density.

The inherent problem in screen density is that any use of an interface distracts readers from ac-

Box 13.

Customer information screen
I once worked for a film processing company where we were building new customer service software. The system had a customer information screen. For this company, the customers were the retail stores where people dropped off a roll of film for processing. The customer information screen contained all of the information pertaining to the customer and was 3-4 full screens long. However, the first part of the screen was basic customer information such as address, phone number, etc.

The design problem was that all of this information was noise. The customer called the customer service representatives with questions. The customer knew their address and the customer service representative didn't normally care. Instead, they had to scroll down multiple screens to get to the invoice information relevant to a typical call.

From a data entry view and setting up a new customer, the overall screen design made sense, but from a customer service view, the important information was hidden.

---

complishing their goals. People don't want to use the interface; they are forced to use it as a means of reaching their goal. In reality, they are willing to work with an interface since that is the simplest path to obtaining information. Thus, they should be given a high SNR to support their information interactions.

Designing for Information Salience

A single salience value cannot be assigned to an information element. Information salience is not "one-size-fits-all." The amount of salience it deserves depends on a wide set of factors. Improper information salience can cause partial or irrelevant information to dominate people's view, causing them to make the wrong conclusion. Besides the obvious point of audience needs, information salience also varies over time. As a situation changes, information importance increases or decreases. Usability and comprehension problems occur when information salience remains fixed. For best comprehension, information needs to be provided only when people need it. Presenting it too early or too late is a distraction: what could have been valuable information simply reduces the signal to noise ratio by adding to the noise.

Information salience plays a major factor in people's missing information or forming incorrect conclusions. The important information must be clear enough so that people do not overlook it when it is crucial. An issue with good design for effective information salience is that design teams' and readers' definitions of important information can differ greatly. As a result, their expectations differ about which information should receive the highest salience. In addition, design decisions driven by corporate requirements, such as emphasizing features, upgrade options, or legal issues, shift the emphasis away from people's information needs and may actually distract them from the information that they do need. The result is that they have to work harder to decipher which information is

of current interest, increasing the risk that they will focus on the wrong information.

Essentially any formatting which makes text different from the surrounding text will increase its salience. The use of colored text in reports to direct manager's eyes to high or low values is one example (Table 1). Skimming the table and figuring out which values are high or low and may require further investigation can be difficult since the values are different for each product. Flagging the text in some manner increases the salience of the values of interest.

Complex sets of information can offer many different types of information of interest, which a design team may attempt to flag with different indicators. Readers must figure out on the fly, from context, the specific meaning of the emphasized text (bold, italics, square brackets, or other typography) and how to relate the flagging to its salience level. However, people cannot mentally figure out and keep track of more than two to three formatting methods without extensive training. Overuse of many methods of signaling salience levels causes all of them to be ignored. Having many different types of emphasis on the page imposes too high a cognitive load to be worth the effort to figure out the meaning of each. In general, if people don't understand why text is typographically different, that difference will be ignored. In contrast, dense information displays which people use all day long can have many different types of indicators, such as fonts or colors, which help increase the information salience in specific conditions. But in this instance, the people are very familiar with the display, have time and training to get past the learning curve, and are motivated to learn the different meanings. However, for people engaged in occasional system use, these same indicators become noise and will be ignored since they do not understand their meaning.

For the complex information relevant of many HII situations, simple signaling of information does not is not fully address people's needs. The

Table 1. Report with out-of-spec values flagged. Typically, the values would be printed in color. But other flagging for salience can be used for black and white printing, as done with this example with * and ** for high and high-high values and < and << for low and low-low values.

Monthly Sales Volume				
	Broadman	Mathison	Smith	Wagner
Product A (180-220)	203	225	190	173<
Product B (170-210)	193	168<	194	253**
Product C (30-37)	34	22<<	39*	35
Product D (850-950)	903	860	920	884

use of color or bold for single numbers or words does not highlight the information relationships which are vital for understanding the information. Design teams need to ensure that they place the salience at the proper level and highlight information and information relationships rather than data.

The proximity of two information elements to each other also strongly impacts their relative salience. Pomerantz and Schwaitzberg (1975) demonstrated that relating or comparing information requires both information elements to be close together and increasing the distance between elements decreases the information salience. Thus, information which needs to be processed together, must be positioned as a single unit. Wickens & Carswell (1995) have defined this need for proximity of information as grouping "like with like," essentially matching Gestalt theory. However, exactly what is meant by "like with like" depends upon the mental model and the information needs of the reader. What is considered the most salient information can vary immensely with different mental models. For example, a programmer may want to group all items from a particular database table. A decision maker, on the other hand, may want items which should fluctuate together, or which influence each other, to be grouped together. Furthermore, as people interact with a situation and conditions evolve, information salience and the information which should be grouped together changes. In all of these cases, only some readers would consider any

Box 14.

> **Over-signaling for design conventions in a manual**
> Many software manuals have a table in the front matter which describes the conventions used in the manual, such as:
>
> **Bold** type Word or characters you type
>
> *italic* type Specialized terms. Placeholders for information you supply, such as filenames. So you may see **cd** *filename.doc*
>
> `monospaced` font Examples of field syntax
>
> SMALL CAPS All key names are in SMALL CAPS.
>
> The problem with using too many of these conventions (I've seen more than these four in some manuals) is that people can't figure them out or easily remember them. People don't read the front matter; instead, they have to determine the coding on the fly. Having too many conventions creates a ransom note effect in the text. Instead of figuring them out, people just ignore all of them.

single design as meeting a "like with like" grouping requirement. Current trends toward adaptive and dynamic information may help, but design teams still need to understand audience needs from the beginning of the project.

Here are some design considerations for helping ensure information receives proper salience:

- Highly salient cues get more attention unless people are forced to learn to ignore them. Bright colors or flashing text draws the eye and makes those elements more salient. However, the overuse of these elements for advertising on web pages has resulted in banner blindness, with people mentally tuning them out. Attempts to draw attention to highly salient information using these methods will often backfire, with people purposely refusing to look at them. Nielsen's (2007) study found that people didn't see the large red numbers for the US population on the US Census Bureau's website (Figure 6-13).

- Top locations and larger presentations are more salient and over-weighted, especially for people under time pressure (Wallsten & Barton, 1982).

- Repetition of information increases its salience. If information is repeated in multiple places, people will give it a higher priority.

- Images, especially those of people, have a higher salience than text. Readers tend to always look at pictures of people first, with the gaze going directly to the eyes. The importance of the text then gets judged based on the image. Irrelevant images or eye-candy images can cause a reader to regard the text as irrelevant or less than credible.

- Information which is not visible has a lower salience (Hallgren, 1997). Thus, any information not currently being displayed receives a lower priority than what people are currently looking at, regardless of whether the unseen information has scrolled off the screen or is on another page (print or online). People find it difficult to remember or form goal-oriented *relationships* between information being displayed and relevant information not being displayed (Rubens & Rubens, 1988). Screen size limitations, especially with mobile displays, are problematical since all relevant information cannot be displayed simultaneously. The human trait of minimizing cognitive effort often causes people to go by memory for non-visible information and to over-emphasize the vis-

ible information in decision-making (Fu & Gray, 2004).

- People evaluate information based on the order in which they receive it (Klein, 1999). Changing the order of presentation can change the relative salience of information viewed later. Note that the desired order can vary depending on the situation, reader knowledge, or point of time within a dynamic situation. Systems that strive to always provide complete information often violate ordering because completeness can come at the expense of providing a subset of information in the proper order for the current situation.

- Complex displays or visual presentations with many elements competing for attention cause all of the elements to have a lower salience (Janiszewski, 1998). Visual complexity could distract viewers from the intended messages.

- The information requires good visual momentum (Woods, 1984).

Timing of Presentation and Information Salience

As the proceeding discussion makes clear, a single design that will maximize salience cannot be defined. The amount of salience an information element deserves depends on a wide set of factors which change, both between situations and within a situation. Information salience is not "one-size-fits-all." Only a thorough situational analysis can define when and how information salience needs change for various audience groups.

Besides the obvious differences between people's information needs, salience also varies with time. As a situation changes, the informational importance for any particular element increases or decreases (Klein, 1999). For best comprehension, information needs to be provided only when people need it, and as a result, usability and comprehension problems occur when information salience remains fixed (which occurs with most web information and with printed text). Information must not be presented until people need it, and then only the information they need should be presented. If it is presented too early or too late is a distraction, and what could have been valuable information is reduced to noise and lowers the signal to noise ratio of the overall communication.

Another complication in the timing of information salience is that many people refuse to look for information until they feel they are in trouble or have exhausted other options. As a result, they often receive information too late to effectively help them understand the situation. In this case, information salience becomes of minimal use. For example, in a study of how information affects prostate cancer screening, most men received information focused on helping them make a screening choice after they had already made a screening decision and, thus, it was of little value in their decision (Sheridan et al., 2004). On the other hand, the same information, given earlier, may have been extremely helpful and driven the decision process. In this type of situation, the proper information may appear to receive appropriate salience from a simple usability perspective, but the overall situation does not reflect it since the information was provided too late for any noticeable effect.

INFORMATION QUALITY

Any information must meet a certain level of quality before people will trust it. People must trust a source before they will be believe it, as Salvador, Barile, and Sherry (2004) point out in their study of e-commerce systems. Development of that trust depends strongly on people's perception of the quality of the information. Unfortunately for design teams, the level of perceived quality varies among people. Extensive research into information credibility and perception of information quality

has been performed by Stanford's Persuasive Technology Lab, (http://credibility.stanford.edu/).

In an interview discussed in Paiva (2000), Rosalind Picard reports on an empirical evaluation where people were asked to rate trustworthiness of an interface in relation to its design. In particular, she cites one participant's statement: "If it looks pleasant, I just trust it!" Research has consistently found that attractive designs and presentations work better (Müller, 2007; Norman, 2004). As would be expected, the use of appropriate color has a significant effect on the quality ratings people assign to websites (Cyr, Head, & Larios, 2010). In a study of healthcare information, people separately rated the visual design and information credibility, and the correlation between these two factors was statistically significant (Robins, Holmes, & Stansbury, 2010). In other words, people strongly judge the quality of information based on its appearance, rather than on its content.

Moving beyond appearance, a study by Stvilia, Mon, and Yi (2009) found five factors that people use to judge information quality as well as some of criteria which go into making those judgments (Table 2). The relationships among these five factors depend on the type of webpage; how people judge information quality varies based on the general type of information and does not remain the same across all web pages.

Accuracy: Accuracy means having correct information. More content influences lower-knowledge readers into believing the information is more accurate.

Completeness: Completeness means the quantity of information. The contributing criterion of clarity plays a role here since overly complete information leads to information overload and distracts from overall clarity. An excess of irrelevant information, with respect to a person's current situation, distracts from comprehension. Design can also contribute to a perception of completeness. The appearance of content such as statistics and quotes

Table 2. Information quality factors. The criteria on the right hand side use the common definition with all of them summed up to form the quality factor. (adapted from Stvilia, Mon, & Yi, 2009, p. 1786)

Quality Factor	Contributing Criteria
Accuracy	Accuracy, credibility, reliability
Completeness	Completeness, clarity
Authority	Authority
Usefulness	Ease of use, objectivity, utility
Accessibility	Accessibility, cohesiveness, consistency, volatility

increases people's perception of credibility (Rains & Donnerstein Karmikel, 2009).

Authority: Authority reflects the quality of the information source. Most guidelines say that web pages must state who is writing the information. As knowledge level on a topic increases, the quality evaluation depends more strongly on the credibility of the information source (Stanford et al., 2002). Sites with known brands (in health care) were also highly rated for both credibility and visual design (Robins, Holmes, & Stansbury, 2010). These studies are more or less in agreement that the general population, not knowing the credibility of most information sources (thus, not being able to make judgments), does assign authority when they have heard of the source.

Usefulness: Usefulness describes how the information relates to people's immediate situation. They tend to perceive information as higher quality when it fits their needs—specifically, when it fits their short-term, immediate needs rather than longer-term, epistemic needs. The more practical the information for the current situation, the more it will be perceived as high-quality (Jung Lee, Park, & Widdows, 2009). Information design factors had much stronger effects on consumer evaluation than on expert evaluation (Stanford et al., 2002).

Accessibility: Accessibility deals with how easily information can be obtained from the overall content. Overall text coherence and writing quality are factors here. Obviously, high-quality information would fit this factor; however, poor, but well-written information can have a high surface-level accessibility but lack real information value. In a study of diabetes sites, Bedell, Agrawal, and Petersen (2004) found a wide range of accessibility and quality issues which could lead patients to assign a better accessibility rating to an information-poor site than it deserved.

AGE ISSUES

Age is a significant factor in how people approach information, but HII-age interactions are much more complex than typically presented in most articles. The age range of the people using the information can have a strong influence on the overall information usability and effectiveness of the communication. Age-related differences do appear and must be considered, such as poorer working memory and reasoning ability (Freudenthal, 2001). A problem arises in many design situations where the user characteristics are over-generalized. For instance, one significant problem is that "older adults" are much too complex as a group and too highly differentiated to be considered a single entity. Too many projects try to consider the "older population" as a single unit, while they would not accept "25 to 40 years old" as a sufficiently descriptive audience characterization.

Regarding the moderating effects of user age, the findings show clearly, that it is definitively not sufficient to examine only young users' technical acceptance and performance and to generalize the results to the whole user population. The found age-specific pattern of relationships indicates that it is highly important to integrate the older user group in studies about user attitudes and behavior (Arning & Ziefle, 2007, p. 2922).

Compared to other factors that affect how people interact with information, age must be considered, but is not the dominate factor. Older people are often motivated to use computers because they perceive such use as an important element for inclusion in contemporary society, and as a method of fighting isolation. The increasing penetration of email and social networking into the older population stems from this motivation. For example, people age 40–59 make up over 50% health information seekers, with 15% over age 60.

The American Association of Retired Persons (AARP) uses a four-dimension model to describe people's abilities:

Age: Physical age is the least important element in the model. Age by itself has little influence on how people interact with information. For example, in a study of a portable multimedia player, the people's trial-and-error interactions and frustration levels were more strongly influenced by background knowledge than by age (Kang & Yoon, 2008).

Ability/disability: Ability is people's capacity to perform the physical actions. Ability considers areas such as vision, which degenerates with age, and motor coordination, which affects mouse control. People with impaired ability will have trouble interacting with information. A wide range of sources discuss how to design to overcome these problems, with the baseline coming from American Disabilities Act, section 508.

Aptitude: Aptitude is about expertise and experience with information situations. Obviously, people who are familiar working with information sets will be able to manipulate them more easily than those who are less familiar (Freudenthal, 2001; Kang & Yoon, 2008).

Attitude: Attitude is about the type of approach taken toward situations. It considers differences ranging from people who are risk-takers to those who are risk-averse.

Design teams must take into account all of these four dimensions when considering age as a component of the design. In addition, social and cultural issues are just as important, if not more important than just age.

Age is shown to be a factor in a number of usability issues with Internet interaction, even in studies that control for experience level. On the other hand, it seems that usability problems simply have a stronger effect on older people than on the young. When design changes were made to fix usability issues, overall performance improved in both older and younger groups (Chadwick-Dias, McNulty & Tullis, 2003). Poor usability is a significant factor on many websites failing to conform to guidelines of the National Institute on Aging (Becker, 2004, 2005). Problems can range from fonts and link targets that are too small to poorly written content. Many of these usability problems affect everyone using the site and need to be addressed in a global manner, not piecemeal. For example, most design guidelines say to increase the font size for older audiences (NIH, 2002). Although this is valid advice, simply increasing the font size does not begin to address all of the differences design teams need to consider and how changes ripple through the design. Larger fonts make the overall page longer, which increases the amount of scrolling; yet the same guidelines say to avoid scrolling.

Long-term experience with poor usability gives rise to the perception that many older adults have a mistrust of computer systems. However, such negative attitudes are more closely correlated with computer experience than with age. Marquie, Jourdan-Boddaert, and Huet (2002) consider the low confidence of many older people in their own computer ability and believe it is the main reason they have trouble with computers. In general, people who do not believe they are capable of performing a task will not make the required effort to succeed and have lower perseverance. Older adults show less confidence in their interaction, and consequently, tend to rate systems as harder to use. Lower confidence also plays out in error recovery: low-confidence users are less likely to try to solve a problem without outside help.

The ease-of-use issue, while important to effective communication, also helps to show how usability tests must cover all audience groups. When asked about the ease of use of menu navigation, younger and older adults used different criteria for rating performance. "Younger adults refer to their efficiency, i.e. how easy and effort-free they experienced the interaction with the device. For older adults, the determining factor in the evaluation of the perceived ease of use is effectiveness, i.e. the success when using a technical device" (Arning & Ziefle, 2007, p. 2921).

Age and Information Interaction

Older people do not process information differently, but do show a lower ability to cope with poor usability issues (van der Meij & Gellevij, 2002). As people age, their general cognitive processing speed decreases (Cerella 1985), with most of the slow-down attributed to a slowing of how the mind handles basic operations (Salthouse & Babcock, 1991). A direct side effect of this slow-down is tasks consume a higher percentage of available cognitive resources which can result in cognitive overload (Sayago & Blat, 2010). Older people do not understand poorly designed manuals as well as younger people (van Hees 1996). On the other hand, older people are more likely to use written documentation rather than asking other people

(Birdi & Zapf, 1997). They also make more syntax errors, which leads to higher frustration rates.

However, the cognitive slowdown does not mean that older readers will always respond more slowly; it only affects the information interaction when the cognitive requirements exceed the task requirements. For example, text size on a web page did not significantly affect performance across age groups until the font is too small for easy reading (Chadwick-Dias, McNulty & Tullis, 2003).

Designs need to work to minimize the overall cognitive load. Making procedural or navigational paths easier to remember and making functions easier to perform can reap major gains in overall communication effectiveness. The same task performance of Fitt's law applies, but older adults will tend to suffer cognitive overload at a lower task level.

One area where age differences can be important is in motor (hand motion) skills (Cerella 1985), with major implications for the use of a mouse (Walker, Millians, & Worden, 1996). Older people move the mouse slower and with less accuracy. They also have a higher level of perceived exertion during click-and-drag tasks, which means that designs should minimize mouse use if they are to be friendly to older adults (Chaparro et al., 1999). But instead of minimal use of the mouse, Becker (2004, 2005) found older users performed extensive use of movements which require precise mouse pointing ability, such mouseovers. Movement time in most HII situations is often trivial compared to the cognitive processing time of reading and interpreting the content.

Many usability tests focus on task completion time. However, in many HII situations, speed of task completion is not a significant factor, because people are more focused on understanding a set of information and reaching decisions based on it. For simple timed-retrieval tasks, older adults will be slower. Likewise, for tasks with high cognitive load, such as navigating deep into a hierarchical structure, pronounced age-dependent time differences will be found. Freudenthal (2001) points out that deep menu structures impose a high cognitive load and are less suited for older adults. As people move deeper into a menu structure, the choice of the next move is increasingly slowed as memory resources are consumed, making it harder to mentally handle the complex structures required to interact with the information. This supports claims of a breadth versus depth in menus and navigation structures.

Older audiences do present challenges for design teams seeking to maximize information search and comprehension. Because of increased vision problems, older people have a harder time reading a screen. This either forces them to use glasses or to set their monitors at a lower resolution, which reduces the amount of text displayed. A larger font also pushes more material below the fold, increasing the difficulty of integrating an entire information set. Still, older people tend to reject, for as long as possible, measures such as larger font sizes, lower screen resolution, or alternative input devices (Sayago & Blat, 2010).

NOVICE TO EXPERT CONTINUUM

Design teams often talk about people as ranging from novice to expert. However, people don't actually think of themselves in such terms. Their focus is not on a skill level, but on accomplishing a task or performing their job. As such, they think of themselves in terms of:

- Job
- Job role
- What they know about the task
- What they know about the tools
- Motivational differences

Notice how none of these views explicitly contains a placement within the novice-expert continuum. The design team needs to make that translation in order to fit people's information

needs with the HII required for information comprehension.

Each of the roles people play varies, even within a single task, and they can bring different levels of expertise to each. All of these views affect how people define themselves with respect to the novice–expert continuum. When interacting with computer-based information systems, these types of differences can be easily confused (Valero & Sanmartin, 1999).

- A new hire can be an expert at a tool, but not understand the current business rules or how to apply them to the job. They know how to do the task, but now the business does it. For example, an accountant knows how to enter account payable records, but does not know the coding used.
- People faced with a new software system may be expert at the task and with the old tool, with many years of experience at the company, but they are a novices with the new tool. They know what they need to accomplish, but don't know how to do it with this tool. For example, an accountant knows how to code the account payable charge, but don't know how to enter it using the new software system.
- People may have many years of experience with the system, but only know how to perform the tasks required for their own day-to-day work and have minimal knowledge of other functions. For instance, they may operate as an expert with the accounts receivable part of an accounting system, but have minimal knowledge of the accounts payable or human resources sections. Also, they may not have any understanding of creating reports beyond selecting report names off a menu.

Although it is easy to form stereotypes of either novice or expert, in reality, most people fall somewhere in the middle (Santhanam &

Figure 6. Movement from novice to expert. People start at novice, where they remain for a short time. They then follow the path toward expert, but will probably stop at some point when they know what their job requires (adapted from Hackos & Redish, 1998, p. 88).

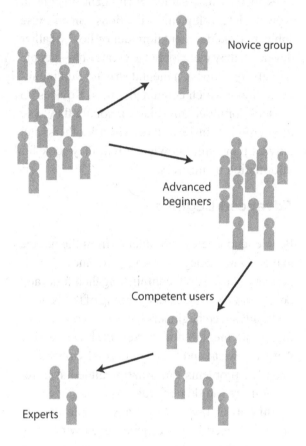

Wiedenbeck, 1993). Hackos & Redish (1998) define the novice-expert continuum as a four-tier structure (Figure 6). Each of the levels contains its own HII challenges.

Novice: A new user. Often a short-lived status. Prior knowledge does not prevent novice actions, but can reduce the duration of novice behavior. Novices tend to be very goal-oriented, and want to do, not learn. They transition quickly to advanced beginner.

Advanced Beginner: Focused "simply and exclusively on getting a job done as painlessly and quickly as possible" (Hackos & Redish, 1998, p. 82). Advanced beginners are content to know a few tasks that allow them to get their job done. Their use of information, or of the system, is incidental and infrequent. They have a poor mental model which often lacks a basis in knowledge and contains significant errors.

Competent Performer: Knows a significant number of the tasks and possesses a sufficient mental model to support their informational needs. Can perform more complex tasks and is sometimes willing to learn more efficient ways. Santhanam and Wiedenbeck (1993) found that people in the middle (those who do not fit as either a novice or an expert), show expert traits in the areas they consistently use and novice traits in other areas. Thus, even within the same information system, people's abilities can vary dramatically. For example, a person may show expert skill in the graphing part of Microsoft Excel, but novice skill in page formatting.

Expert: Commands a mental model that is comprehensive and consistent. Understands how to diagnose and correct a wide variety of problems. Highly motivated to learn more and to help others. Tends to experiment to learn more.

The early audience analysis helps define all the groups who may be receiving the information and provides an understanding of the people's prior knowledge, attitudes, and needs, allowing the design of appropriate content. Each group's needs are different and, unless they are understood in detail, providing usable content that addresses all levels is difficult (Rosenbaum & Walters, 1986). In a review of expertise in HCI, Mayer (1997) concluded, "The results of the expert–novice difference studies of computer users are remarkably consistent with corresponding research in other problem-solving domains" (p. 792).

Novice

By definition, a novice does not possess knowledge or skill. People may start as a novice, but remain so for a very short time before moving into the advanced beginner stage. Much of the technical information design literature tends to focus on designs for either novice- or expert-level performance. Or, perhaps worse, design teams seem to assume that a design will only be used by one those groups. Unfortunately, an over-focus on designing information for novices can degrade comprehension and performance of more knowledgeable people. Thus, most information should not be focused on the novice, but on the intermediate levels where most people fall. Information designed for a novice often fails to provide the proper level of cohesiveness for effective comprehension by intermediate and expert level people. Surprisingly, more knowledgeable people work better with less cohesive text (McNamara & Kintsch, 1996).

Carroll and Rosson (1987) point out that novices are not novices on everything, but are often experts in the basic area for which they are performing the task. Consider these examples:

- Secretaries are novices on the new software system, but experts in the tasks the system is asking them to perform.
- A car mechanic using a new automotive diagnostic system may be a novice with respect to using the system (interacting with the system to understand the car's problem) but is an expert at understanding and using the information to fix the car.
- A master cabinet maker with a new computer-controlled planer would show novice-level skills operating the planer, but expert-level skills at knowing what he wants to produce with it.

A major deficiency in novices is the lack of a mental model that allows them to comprehend the higher-level structure of the information (Cuevas et al., 2004). Novices find it almost impossible to make or justify predictions and inferences since they lack knowledge. For example, Lowe (2002) found that novices incorrectly ascribe cause-effect relationships to weather phenomena visible in typical meteorological animations. Since these subjects lacked a mental model of how weather develops, they were forced to create one—people will always impose a mental structure on the information—which contained errors. Novices do not look for much information, nor are they able to interpret it. Instead, they will ask others, and only as they gain knowledge will they look for information themselves.

Advanced Beginner

People tend to progress quickly from the novice to the advanced beginner stage. Advanced beginners are focused on accomplishing their tasks and possess a very basic understanding of the system. Since advanced beginners have an incomplete or inaccurate mental model, their problem-solving skills are weak and they are normally unable to diagnose problems. Information aimed at infrequent users should be focused on this stage.

Infrequent use makes many people operate at an advanced beginner level, even when they interact with the system at regular, but intermittent intervals. If sufficient time has elapsed between uses of the information, they will have forgotten nuances of interacting with it. An example are the problems encountered with actions such as forms or reports that are only done on a quarterly, semi-annual, or annual basis. The events occur so infrequently that most people do not remember how to complete them efficiently.

Advanced beginner errors arise from inappropriate actions because their mental view of how to approach the situation is incorrect. More than just being incomplete, it often contains erroneous concepts and ideas which will be replaced with better concepts as they gain in overall knowledge. As their mental model improves, they better interpret situations and react accordingly (Fu, Salvendy, & Turley, 2002). As such, domain knowledge is a powerful predictor of cognitive performance with that domain. Design teams need to explicitly ask about domain knowledge, rather than allowing people to self-identify since they typically over-rate their knowledge level.

Competent Performer

Competent performers know how to perform a significant number of tasks and have a sound mental model on which to base their information interaction. They are also able to diagnose and correct unexpected results of their actions within the limited areas where they work. The biggest differences between competent performer and expert people are gaps in knowledge, forgetting information, and commission of errors. Santhanam and Wiedenbeck (1993) found that the knowledge and performance levels of competent performers on any specific system are very similar, although their fields of expertise vary. For example, users of a desktop publishing program have similar performance although their actual uses of the program (marketing department versus legal secretary) can be very different. This consistent knowledge level allows a design team to assume comparable mental models of the various audience groups.

Competent performers can perform more complex interaction tasks and are willing to learn more efficient ways. Competent performers have some task knowledge and will search for information about things that they have forgotten (Brinkman et al., 2001). However, they are not interested in learning new features that are not directly relevant to their goals.

Grayling (2002) points out that once people reach some intermediate point (which can be any point within advanced beginner or competent performer), they stop increasing their knowledge; they are happy at that level, can accomplish their goals, and don't feel a need to know more. The

Box 15.

> **Infrequent use turns experts into competent performers**
> Technical improvements in the quality of machine parts have resulted in machines that last longer and need less mainte-nance. As a result, maintenance people have less experience with repairing the machine. This causes the maintenance people, who once had expert-level repair skills, to become competent performers. Lack of use causes the repair people to forget many of the low-level interaction details, and to require that the information be supplied each time. They have become people who interact with a system at irregular intervals rather than at the frequency of use assumed for experts (Brinkman et al., 2001).

current knowledge is sufficient for their needs and learning more requires expending effort with a low payback. While they are highly motivated to do their task, paradoxically, they are unwilling to learn methods that would enable them to do their task more effectively and efficiently. Once people know a process that works, they lose interest in finding a more efficient way (Krug, 2000).

Experts

Experts bring a wider repertoire of methods and techniques for achieving goals than do people who know a single procedure to accomplish a task (Johnson, 1992). Experts have a com-prehensive and consistent mental model of the system, allowing them to resolve ambiguities in information and to spot inconsistencies. Studies of differences between people operating at the novice and expert level demonstrate that experts go beyond merely acquiring knowledge; they are able to retrieve and apply knowledge within different contexts (Bransford & Schwartz, 1999). "Expert behavior requires an exquisite sensitivity to context and an ability to know what to commit to" (Weigand, 2006, p. 45). Some of the character-istics of expert interaction include efficient time allocation, sophisticated problem representation and assessment, and a selection of appropriate strategies matching task difficulties (Davidson, Deuser, & Sternberg, 1994).

Unlike the people at other levels, experts are highly motivated to learn more tasks and to help others. Experts also tend to experiment with a system to learn more about it; their mental model allows them to make accurate predictions of the system response to these experiments. Competent performers are happy with knowing just enough to perform their job, but experts will try to learn the entire system even if many parts of it are not relevant to their day-to-day needs.

An expert has two types of knowledge: declarative and procedural. Declarative knowledge is composed of facts and their meanings for specific contexts. Procedural knowledge consists of the strategies and sequences of operations used in understanding a situation or solving a problem. Declarative knowledge makes up the expert's background knowledge (Chao, Salvendy, & Lightner, 1999). Many information systems provide declarative knowledge, and people feel they have learned something. But without the procedural knowledge, they do not know how to apply declarative knowledge. Experts understand both types of knowledge and can combine them in order to comprehend a situation.

Characteristics of People in the Novice-Expert Continuum

People do not fall exactly into a category of novice or expert. Instead, they will show characteristics of both, depending on the specific context. However, their knowledge in one area may transfer to other areas. Table 3 shows a summary of various characteristics on the novice–expert continuum. Most people would not be placed in either column, but at some transitional area between them, indicated by the large arrow.

HII Approaches along the Novice-Expert Continuum

The HII differences between the novices/advanced beginners and the experts can be highly com-

plex, since it much more is at play than simple assumptions that experts know more. As people move toward the expert level, their fundamental approach to understanding a situation changes.

An important aspect of audience and content analysis is determining where on the continuum audience groups exist and how widely they are spread along it. Many methods in audience and task analysis depend on people self-reporting their knowledge level. However, this can be problematical. Competent performers users are often confused about their own knowledge levels, thinking they know more than they actually do. Grayling (2002) noted that most self-identified "experts" fared no better than novices in a set of usability tests. The self-identified "experts" had sufficient but inefficient methods to support how they normally worked, or they possessed a narrow range of expertise and showed novice-level skills once the usability tests moved them beyond their expertise.

An advanced beginner has a surface-level understanding of how to approach a situation. An expert is able to perceive the deeper-level structure of the program and considers it from that view. A very obvious difference in how advanced beginners and experts approach a situation is how quickly they arrive at a workable solution. Although the experts arrive at a solution first, there is an interesting difference, as well as a similarity, in their approaches.

- *Difference.* An advanced beginner tends to start solving the problem right away, immediately leaping in and trying to find a solution. An expert, on the other hand, tends to take time to evaluate the situation before interacting with it.
- *Similarity.* Both use about the same depth of search and thought processes evaluating possible solutions. Research comparing typical chess players to grandmasters found that both evaluate about the same number of possible moves and look ahead

Table 3. Characteristics of the novice-expert continuum. The middle area with the arrows combines the characteristics of Hackos and Redish's advanced beginner and competent performer as people's experience moves them from novice to expert.

Novice characteristics		Expert characteristics
Novices jump into the problem and immediately start working toward a solution (Sutcliffe & Maiden, 1992).		Experts spend more time examining a problem and structuring the problem space.
Novices do not try to reformulate the problem (Brand-Gurwel, Wopereis, & Vermetten, 2005).	⇔	Experts first try to reformulate the problem into a form they understand.
Novices focus on the problem at the surface level and do not construct any large meaningful patterns (Glaser & Chi, 1988).		Experts represent, articulate, and solve problems at a deep level and use abstract concepts to describe them. They also work to construct large-scale patterns within the problem.
Novices tend to describe and explain problems at a basic and superficial level and use bottom-up organization in which they try to find solutions using step-by-step procedures (Anderson, 1990; Vu et al., 2000).		Experts are able to use top-down organization in which they approach a problem by identifying the final and intermediate goals before developing a solution plan.
Novices focus more attention on finding a solution to a problem than understanding the problem.		Experts spend more time examining, familiarizing, and trying to understand the problem before trying to find a solution.
Novices view the entire problem as a single entity (Doane et al., 1990).	⇔	Experts show more detailed and conceptual organization than novices and decompose problems into more subparts.
Novices rely on the first plan they generate (Jeffries, Turner, Polson, & Atwood, 1981).		Experts tend to consider more alternative solutions to solving problems.
Novices are more likely to request information which corresponds to learning more about an overall concept. They deal more with general knowledge than with information specific to the situation (Kolodner, 1983; Mao & Benbasat, 2001).		Experts make fewer requests for information but they place it in the context of the problem.
Novice errors arise from erroneous concepts and ideas caused by poor mental models. They also have a hard time seeing that they made an error (Glaser & Chi, 1988; Fu, Salvendy, & Turley, 2002; Vu et al., 2000).		Experts make fewer errors, and the errors they do make tend to be errors in execution of a proper action, rather than performing the wrong action. Experts can rapidly access the situation and realize an error occurred.
Novices have a poor mental model which may cause them to reject or ignore relevant information as irrelevant (Duin, 1989).	⇔	Experts understand which information is relevant and seek it out.
Novices consider a problem space as a linear structure.		Experts break the problem space into hierarchical structures.

the same 2-3 moves (Chase & Simon, 1973). The difference is that the grandmasters only evaluate good solutions while typical players spend time evaluating poor solutions.

Two examples which show how the approaches are different:

- New and experienced programmers were asked to categorize problems. The new programmers divided them based on the external topic—an inventory problem, an accounting problem—while the experts divided them based on the type of algorithm which would be used to solve them. From the programming view, a sorting algorithm orders items, whether they are plane arrival times, widgets, or budget reports. Experts could see this and categorized the problem based on the deeper structure, not on the surface level of what is being done—something new programmers could not do.

- In a web study, when asked to draw a graphical presentation of a website, novice web users created labels that were more descriptive and precise than an expert's. However, their labels only described the surface-level issues of what the link contained. The expert's labels described the generic stereotype of the various links and what information should be contained behind the link.

Experts think differently about topics in their area of expertise and build knowledge into large, meaningful patterns (Glaser & Chi, 1988). To illustrate, as compared with novices, experts have better memory for domain-relevant material, such as chess positions (Chase & Simon, 1973) or bridge hands (Engle & Bukstel, 1978). Experiments with chess players, and other related studies, show that experts have a large mental collection of stereotypical solutions which they can apply. Experts can almost immediately sort through those solutions and select the best ones. The advanced beginner has not developed these solutions and thus has nothing to draw on. In support of this idea, Antony, Batra, and Santhanam (2005) found that novice designers did better with the help of a knowledge-based system that gave them design advice. The computer system essentially was fulfilling the part of the expert's learned collection of solutions. Hayes and Akhavi (2008) found similar results when providing computer-based support to student engineers engaged in a complex design project.

The comparison between the experts and the novices indicates some interesting differences between the two groups. First, experts spend more time than novices do on the whole information problem-solving task. Also, experts can accurately monitor their performance and progress (Glaser & Chi, 1988; Vu et al., 2000). Experts are able to mentally track progress toward a solution, and they know if the situation is progressing properly. Advanced beginners cannot do this. Competent performers are able to do this in a limited area, but if the situation moves outside of their narrow range of expertise, then they revert to advanced

Box 16.

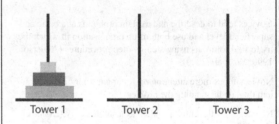

Characterizing the Tower of Hanoi problem
Many psychology experiments on problem-solving methods use variations of the Tower of Hanoi problem. Some studies have presented people with variations of the same problem, but couched in different terms (Kotovsky, Hayes, & Simon, 1985). Rather than realizing they are the same problem, most people jump right in and try to address and solve each problem from scratch. An expert performer, on the other hand, examines the deeper-level issues of the problem before trying to solve it, realizes that the problems are the same and uses the same strategy to solve each one.

The Tower of Hanoi. The object is to move all three disks, one at a time, so that they are stacked on tower 3. You can only put a small disk onto a larger disk, never the other way. Hint: the opening move is to put the smallest disk on tower 2.

beginner performance. People will sometimes need both feedback on a situation's progress and help interpreting that feedback: it depends on their knowledge level.

EXAMPLES

Astronomical Information

Issues of active versus passive approaches to information must be addressed by the design team. Students and the general public will tend to have a very passive approach: they will expect the site to provide them with fully integrated and synthesized information. They will also not be willing to exert much effort to either reading or understanding the text. Poor page design will make them quickly leave.

Gaining an understanding of the astronomical information requires the readers to comprehend the information and to build relationships within it. Otherwise, they risk learning a collection of disjoint facts (being able to quote the text, but not understanding it). One issue the design needs to address is how people ignore information they don't understand. Content written at a too complex or technical level will be skipped, which will cause later information to not be understood. The information relationships convert the text from a mass of data about astronomy to an interrelated and understandable collection of information. A table of the specifications for a star might make sense to the knowledgeable amateur, but that's because she has deep background knowledge to call on to internally form the relationships. Most people, however, lack that background knowledge and would only see a table of meaningless random numbers.

Building information relationships is one place were science writing departs from science journalism. In a newspaper article on astronomy, there is almost always a focus on the "why study this" and "how does this affect me, as a person on the street," both of which are not really relationships, but part of the journalistic requirements to build interest and draw the reader in. This information should be contained within any astronomy information system, but it should not be the focus. Most people with a strong interest in astronomy either already know this information or they consider it secondary. Instead, they want to see how this piece of information connects to other pieces of astronomical information. They want to build a more complete understanding of the topic being researched.

Business Reports

Think of these basic design problems when supporting report analysis (the list can easily be extended):

- Each person works in a different way when analyzing reports.

- The information of interest/concern to people differs depending on their management style.
- The researching and handling of problem situations is different from checking that everything is ok.

Work with a broad base of managers to determine what they consider the major goals to be, goals that must be better articulated than "ensure my department is running ok." What is most important: budget, productivity, employee retention or satisfaction? There will be along collection of goals, with each goal only applying to a subset of managers. However, as they will all be using the resulting system, it must support each person.

For any situation, there can be a large number of possible goals. Yet an effective, experienced person quickly eliminates them, normally so quickly that Klein (1999) found they would say they didn't consider them. Define what makes the goals the business analysts thought were important and relevant to the situation and what makes other goals irrelevant. Irrelevant goals that at first glance can appear to be relevant or might be relevant to a related situation should be specifically addressed. What information provides clues to distinguishing and differentiating them? Design teams, not readers, should be doing the work of distinguishing the relevant information.

The number of reports and amount of information which a business analyst must process often leads to satisficing. They will look at a section of a report and see the that the values are good enough. Rather than digging deeper and uncovering potential problems which may become critical in a few reporting periods, they accept them as-is and move on to other information. Good design of salient information and placing information into context can help the analyst judge if the values are good enough or if they deserve more inspection.

A business report has a huge amount of information behind it. Without a proper information needs analysis, the design team can create reports

Table 4. Regional sales figurse

Product	Total	Year over year change	East		West		South		North	
			Total	Year over year change	Total	Year over year change	Total	Year over year change	Total	Year over year change
1/8" adapter	101	11%	34	3%	23	-5%	20	5%	24	8%
1/4" adapter	161	6%	36	7%	46	12%	63	-7%	16	-6%
1/2" adapter	119	31%	27	23%	35	-8%	34	12%	23	4%
3/4" adapter	168	-16%	68	-3%	27	-4%	27	-11%	46	2%
1" adapter	119	0%	34	-5%	23	4%	37	5%	25	-4%
Total	700	32%	199	25%	154	-1%	181	4%	134	4%

with improper salience. Many business analysts have to extract information such as Table 4 to create a view that fits their needs. The low level information about each regions total sales dominates the table. If that is what the required information, then it is ok, but often it is higher summary data that is needed. The last row has the totals, but that row is lost in all of the other data. This table only shows one product category; if the analyst needs to compare multiple product categories, then the amount of non-salient information which is receiving a high salience because of volume increases even more.

Tables can be easy for design teams to construct based on queries into the database. But design teams must ensure the information has been integrated to fit the reader's needs and is not simply a data dump of easy-to-query or easy-to-display information.

SUMMARY

These chapters considered some of the factors influencing the ways people approach and interpret information. Information interaction and interpretation will vary dependent on people's goals and information needs. These differing goals and information needs shape what information is actually deemed important, and how hard people will work to understand it.

Approaching Information

Understanding what information is desired and audience expectations are essential to meeting their information needs and communication goals. Information is useful only when it fits within the contextual constraints of the current situation and the reader can understand how it fits. How people approach information can range from a very active to a very passive approach to interpreting it. Some people question all the information and some people prefer to avoid the information altogether. Design teams need to ensure that the information source conforms to both the situational context and the way people approach the information.

Effort

When people engage in a task or read information, they engage in an effort trade-off between obtaining the desired information and expending the least acceptable effort. People stop looking for information when they feel the information they have adequately addresses a question, with factors such as prior knowledge and desired level of knowledge influencing when they stop looking. As long as they know some way of accomplishing a task, they see no reason to expend effort finding a better way, assuming they even know that a better way might exist. People use strategies based on a trade-off between time and the amount of effort required to gain accurate and sufficient information and design teams need to account for this trade-off early in the design.

Sufficing

People stop looking for and interpreting information when they are happy with the answer because it fits their information needs or understanding of the situation. They only expend enough effort to obtain an answer that is "good enough," rather than working to obtain an optimal answer. Although the selected answer is not always sufficient, people have a hard time judging sufficiency and know how sub-optimal their solution is.

Multitasking

Multiple tasks pull people in different directions and they can rarely give full attention to interacting with information. Multitasking involves mentally switching between tasks and their related mental models in constantly changing sequence. Although it allows people to work on multiple things at once, they all suffer a performance decrease and comprehension of information is seriously impacted. Design commonly ignores multitasking and focuses on people accomplishing one task at a time. However, multitasking is a part of the typical HII and design teams must allow for it.

Salience

Not all information carries the same level of importance. The most important information should have the highest salience. Any information system has an overabundance of information that can quickly lead to cognitive overload. However, information salience is not "one-size-fits-all." The amount of salience it deserves depends on a wide set of factors. Design teams need to resolve what information people need to understand a situation and ensure that information receives proper salience.

Information Quality

Information must meet a certain level of quality before people will trust it and people must trust it before they will use it. People judge quality based on their perception of its accuracy, completeness, authority, usefulness, and accessibility.

Age

Age and its associated changes in cognitive ability change how people interact with information, but HII-age interactions are much more complex than simply being age-based. Older people do not process information differently, but do show a lower ability to cope with poor usability issues. Design teams must allow for age-related factors such as poorer working memory and reasoning ability, but must also avoid over-generalizing the audience purely on age.

Novice to Expert

Level of experience and background knowledge change how people interact with information. People interact with information in many different roles, even within a single task, and they bring different levels of expertise to each role. All of these views affect how people define themselves with respect to the novice–expert continuum and the skill levels they exhibit. It can be easy for design teams to form stereotypes of the system users as either novice or expert, in reality, people remain at novice for a very short time and most people exhibit skill levels that are somewhere in the middle between novice and expert.

REFERENCES

Albers, M. (2004a). *Communication of complex information: User goals and information needs for dynamic Web information*. Mahwah, NJ: Erlbaum.

Albers, M. (2004b). Signal to noise ratio of information in documentation. *Proceedings of 22nd Annual International Conference on Computer Documentation* (pp. 41–44). New York, NY: ACM.

Albers, M. (2009). Information relationships: The source of useful and usable content. *Proceedings of 29th Annual International Conference on Computer Documentation.* (pp. 171–178). New York, NY: ACM.

Albers, M. (2010). Usability and information relationships: Considering content relationships when testing complex information. In Albers, M., & Still, B. (Eds.), *Usability of complex Information Systems: Evaluation of user interaction* (pp. 109–131). Boca Raton, FL: CRC Press. doi:10.1201/EBK1439828946-9

Alvarado, C., Jeevan, J., Ackerman, M., & Karger, D. (2003). *Surviving the information explosion: How people find their electronic information* (pp. 1–9). MIT AI Memo AIM-2003-006. Retrieved from http://www.csail.mit.edu/~teevan/work/publications/papers/aim03.pdf

Anderson, J. R. (1990). *Cognitive psychology and its implications.* New York, NY: Freeman.

Andriole, S., & Adelman, L. (1995). *Cognitive System Engineering for User–Computer Interface Design, Prototyping, and Evaluation.* Mahwah, NJ: Erlbaum.

Antony, S., Batra, D., & Santhanam, R. (2005). The use of a knowledge-based system in conceptual data modeling. *Decision Support Systems, 41,* 176–188. doi:10.1016/j.dss.2004.05.011

Arning, K., & Ziefle, M. (2007). Understanding age differences in PDA acceptance and performance. *Computers in Human Behavior, 23,* 2904–2927. doi:10.1016/j.chb.2006.06.005

Baddeley, A. (1986). *Working memory.* Oxford, England: Oxford UP.

Bechky, B. (2003). Sharing meaning across occupational communities: The transformation of understanding on a production floor. *Organization Science, 14*(3), 312–330. doi:10.1287/orsc.14.3.312.15162

Becker, S. (2004). A study of web usability for older adults seeking online health resources. *ACM Transactions on Computer-Human Interaction, 11*(4), 387–406. doi:10.1145/1035575.1035578

Becker, S. (2005). E-government usability for older adults. *Communications of the ACM, 48*(2), 102–104. doi:10.1145/1042091.1042127

Bedell, S., Agrawal, A., & Petersen, L. (2004). A systematic critique of diabetes on the World Wide Web for patients and their physicians. *International Journal of Medical Informatics, 73,* 687–694. doi:10.1016/j.ijmedinf.2004.04.011

Belkin, N. (1980). Anomalous states of knowledge as a basic for information retrieval. *The Canadian. Journal of Information Science, 5,* 133–143.

Benbasat, I., Dexter, A., & Todd, P. (1986a). An experimental program investigating color-enhanced. and graphical information presentation: An integration of findings. *Communications of the ACM, 29*(11), 1094–1105. doi:10.1145/7538.7545

Bernhardt, S. (2002). *Technical writing for adults.* ATTW discussion list Sept 26, 2002.

Bhavnani, S., & John, B. (2000). The strategic use of complex computer systems. *Human-Computer Interaction, 15,* 107–137. doi:10.1207/S15327051HCI1523_3

Birdi, K., & Zapf, D. (1997). Age differences in reactions to errors in computer-based work. *Behaviour & Information Technology, 16*(6), 309–319. doi:10.1080/014492997119716

Brand-Gurwel, S., Wopereis, I., & Vermetten, Y. (2005). Information problem solving by experts and novices: Analysis of a complex cognitive skill. *Computers in Human Behavior, 21*, 487–508. doi:10.1016/j.chb.2004.10.005

Bransford, J. D., & Schwartz, D. L. (1999). Rethinking transfer: A simple proposal with multiple implications. In Iran-Nejad, A., & Pearson, P. D. (Eds.), *Review of research in education* (*Vol. 24*, pp. 61–101). Washington, DC: American Educational Research Association. doi:10.2307/1167267

Brinkman, W., Buil, V., Cullen, R., Gobits, R., & Van Nes, F. (2001). Design and evaluation of online multimedia maintenance manuals. *Behaviour & Information Technology, 20*(1), 47–52. doi:10.1080/01449290010020639

Burgess, P. W., Veitch, E., De Lacy Costello, A., & Shallice, T. (2000). The cognitive and neuroanatomical correlates of human multitasking. *Neuropsychologia, 38*, 848–863. doi:10.1016/S0028-3932(99)00134-7

Carroll, J., & Rosson, M. (1987). The paradox of the active user. In Carroll, J. (Ed.), *Interfacing thought: Cognitive aspects of human-computer interaction* (pp. 80–111). Cambridge, MA: MIT Press.

Cary, M., & Carlson, R. (2001). Distributing working memory resources in problem solving. *Journal of Experimental Psychology. Learning, Memory, and Cognition, 27*, 836–848. doi:10.1037/0278-7393.27.3.836

Casaday, G. (1991). Balance. In Karat, J. (Ed.), *Taking software design seriously: Practical Techniques for HCI design* (pp. 45–62). New York, NY: Academic Press.

Casner, S. (1994). Understanding the determinants of problem-solving behavior in a complex environment. *Human Factors, 34*(4), 580–596.

Cerella, J. (1985). Information processing rates in the elderly. *Psychological Bulletin, 98*, 67–83. doi:10.1037/0033-2909.98.1.67

Chadwick-Dias, A., McNulty, M., & Tullis, T. (2003). Web usability and age: How design changes can improve performance. *Proceedings of the 2003 Conference on Universal usability*, (pp. 30–37). New York, NY: ACM

Chadwick-Dias, A., McNulty, M., & Tullis, T. (2003). Web usability and age: How design changes can improve performance. *Proceedings of the 2003 Conference on Universal usability*, (pp. 30–37). New York, NY: ACM.

Chao, C., Salvendy, G., & Lightner, N. (1999). Development of a methodology for optimizing elicited knowledge. *Behaviour & Information Technology, 18*(6), 413–430. doi:10.1080/014492999118841

Chaparro, A., Bohan, M., Fernandez, J., Choi, S., & Kattel, B. (1999). The impact of age on computer input device use: Psychophysical and physiological measures. *International Journal of Industrial Ergonomics, 24*, 503–513. doi:10.1016/S0169-8141(98)00077-8

Chase, W., & Simon, H. (1973). The mind's eye in chess. In Chase, W. (Ed.), *Visual information processing* (pp. 215–281). New York, NY: Academic Press.

Cuevas, H., Fiore, S., Bowers, C., & Salas, E. (2004). Fostering constructive cognitive and metacognitive activity in computer-based complex task training environments. *Computers in Human Behavior, 20*, 225–241. doi:10.1016/j.chb.2003.10.016

Cypher, A. (1986). The structure of users' activities. In Norman, D., & Draper, S. (Eds.), *User centered system design: New perspectives on human-computer interaction* (pp. 243–264). Mahwah, NJ: Erlbaum.

Cyr, D., Head, M., & Larios, H. (2010). Colour appeal in website design within and across cultures: A multi-method evaluation. *International Journal of Human-Computer Studies*, *68*(1-2), 1–21. doi:10.1016/j.ijhcs.2009.08.005

Czerwinski, M., Horvitz, E., & Wilhite, S. (2004). A diary study of task switching and interruptions. Retrieved December 10, 2008, from http://research.microsoft.com/users/marycz/chi2004diarystudyfinal.pdf

Davidson, J., Deuser, R., & Sternberg, R. (1994). The role of metacognition in problem solving. In Metcalfe, J., & Shimamura, A. (Eds.), *Metacognition: Knowing about knowing* (pp. 207–226). Cambridge, MA: MIT Press.

Doane, S., Pellegrino, J., & Klatzky, R. (1990). Expertise in a computer operating system: Conceptualization and performance. *Human-Computer Interaction*, *5*, 267–304. doi:10.1207/s15327051hci0502&3_5

Duggan, G., & Payne, S. (2001). Interleaving reading and acting while following procedural instructions. *Journal of Experimental Psychology. Applied*, *7*(4), 297–307. doi:10.1037/1076-898X.7.4.297

Duin, A. (1989). Factors that influence how readers learn from test: Guidelines for structuring technical documents. *Technical Communication*, *36*(2), 97–101.

Dye, K. (1988). When is document accurate and complete. *Professional Communication Conference, 1988* (pp. 269–272). Seattle, WA. October 5–7, 1988.

Einstein, G., McDaniel, M., Owen, P., & Cote, N. (1990). Encoding and recall of texts: The importance of material appropriate processing. *Journal of Memory and Language*, *29*, 566–581. doi:10.1016/0749-596X(90)90052-2

Emerson, M., & Miyake, A. (2003). The role of inner speech in task switching: A dual-task investigation. *Journal of Memory and Language*, *48*, 148–168. doi:10.1016/S0749-596X(02)00511-9

Endsley, M. (1995). Toward a theory of situation awareness in dynamic systems. *Human Factors*, *37*(1), 32–64. doi:10.1518/001872095779049543

Engle, R., & Bukstel, L. (1978). Memory processes among bridge players of differing expertise. *The American Journal of Psychology*, *91*, 673–689. doi:10.2307/1421515

Fennema, M., & Kleinmuntz, D. (1995). Anticipation of effort and accuracy in multi-attribute choice. *Organizational Behavior and Human Decision Processes*, *63*(1), 21–32. doi:10.1006/obhd.1995.1058

Freudenthal, D. (2001). The role of age, foreknowledge and complexity in learning to operate a complex device. *Behaviour & Information Technology*, *20*(1), 23–35. doi:10.1080/01449290010020666

Fu, L., Salvendy, G., & Turley, L. (2002). Effectiveness of user testing and heuristic evaluation as a function of performance classification. *Behaviour & Information Technology*, *21*(2), 137–143. doi:10.1080/02699050110113688

Fu, W., & Gray, W. (2004). Resolving the paradox of the active user: Stable suboptimal performance in interactive tasks. *Cognitive Science*, *28*, 901–935. doi:10.1207/s15516709cog2806_2

Ganzach, Y., & Schul, Y. (1995). The influence of quantity of information and goal framing on decisions. *Acta Psychologica*, *89*, 23–36. doi:10.1016/0001-6918(94)00004-Z

Glaser, R., & Chi, M. (1988). Overview. In Chi, M. T. H., Glaser, R., & Farr, M. J. (Eds.), *The nature of expertise* (pp. xv–xxviii). Hillsdale, NJ: Erlbaum.

Gloria Mark, G., Gonzalez, V., & Harris, J. (2005). No task left behind? Examining the nature of fragmented work. *Proceedings of the SIGCHI Conference on Human Factors in Computing Systems,* April 2–7, 2005. Portland, Oregon.

Gorry, G. (2005). As simple as possible, but not simpler. *Communications of the ACM, 48*(9), 119–122. doi:10.1145/1081992.1082026

Gray, W., & Fu, W. (2004). Soft constraints in interactive behavior: The case of ignoring perfect knowledge in-the-world for imperfect knowledge in-the-head. *Cognitive Science, 28,* 359–382.

Gray, W., Schoelles, M., & Sims, C. (2005). Adapting to the task environment: Explorations in expected value. *Cognitive Systems Research, 6,* 27–40. doi:10.1016/j.cogsys.2004.09.004

Grayling, T. (2002). If we build it, will they come? A usability test of two browser-based embedded help systems. *Technical Communication, 49*(2), 193–209.

Hackos, J., & Redish, J. (1998). *User and task analysis for interface design.* New York, NY: Wiley.

Hallgren, C. (1997). Using a problem focus to quickly aid users in trouble. *Proceedings of the 1997 STC Annual Conference.* Washington, DC: STC.

Hayes, C., & Akhavi, F. (2008). Creating effective decision aids for complex tasks. *Journal of Usability Studies, 3*(4), 152–172.

Herbig, P., & Kramer, H. (1992). The phenomenon of innovation overload. *Technology in Society, 14,* 441–461. doi:10.1016/0160-791X(92)90038-C

Hsee, C. (1995). Elastic justification: How tempting but task irrelevant factors influence decisions. *Organizational Behavior and Human Decision Processes, 62*(3), 330–337. doi:10.1006/obhd.1995.1054

Janiszewski, C. (1998). The influence of display characteristics on visual exploratory search behavior. *The Journal of Consumer Research, 25,* 290–301. doi:10.1086/209540

Jeffries, R., Turner, A., Polson, P., & Atwood, M. (1981). *The processes involved in designing software.* Hillsdale, NJ: Erlbaum.

Jenkins, V., Fallowfield, L., & Saul, J. (2001). Information needs of patients with cancer: Results from a large study of UK cancer centres. *British Journal of Cancer, 84,* 48–51. doi:10.1054/bjoc.2000.1573

Johnson, E., Payne, J., & Bettman, J. (1988). Information displays and preference reversals. *Organizational Behavior and Human Decision Processes, 42,* 1–21. doi:10.1016/0749-5978(88)90017-9

Johnson, J., Andrews, J., & Allard, S. (2001). A model for understanding and affecting genetics information seeking. *Library & Information Science Research, 23*(4), 335–349. doi:10.1016/S0740-8188(01)00094-9

Johnson, P. (1992). *Human computer interaction: Psychology, task analysis and software engineering.* London, UK: McGraw-Hill.

Jung Lee, Y., Park, J., & Widdows, R. (2009). Exploring antecedents of consumer satisfaction and repeated search behavior on e-health information. *Journal of Health Communication, 14,* 160–173. doi:10.1080/10810730802659830

Kang, N., & Yoon, W. (2008). Age- and experience-related user behavior differences in the use of complicated electronic devices. *International Journal of Human-Computer Studies, 66,* 425–437. doi:10.1016/j.ijhcs.2007.12.003

Kieras, D., Meyer, D., Ballas, J., & Lauber, E. (2000). Modern computational perspectives on executive mental processes and cognitive control: Where to from here? In Monsell, S., & Driver, J. (Eds.), *Control of cognitive processes: Attention and performance XVIII* (pp. 681–712). Cambridge, MA: MIT Press.

Kieras, D., & Polson, P. (1985). An approach to the formal analysis of user complexity. *International Journal of Man-Machine Studies*, *22*, 365–394. doi:10.1016/S0020-7373(85)80045-6

Klein, G. (1988). Do decision biases explain too much? *Human Factors Society Bulletin*, *32*(5), 1–3.

Klein, G. (1993). A recognition-primed decision (RPD) model of rapid decision making. In Klein, G., Orasanu, J., Calderwood, R., & Zsambok, C. (Eds.), *Decision making in action: Models and methods* (pp. 138–147). Norwood, NJ: Ablex.

Klein, G. (1999). *Sources of power: How people make decisions*. Cambridge, MA: MIT.

Kolodner, J. (1983). Towards an understanding of the role of experience in the evolution from novice to expert. *International Journal of Man-Machine Studies*, *19*, 497–518. doi:10.1016/S0020-7373(83)80068-6

Kotovsky, K., Hayes, J., & Simon, H. (1985). Why are some problems hard? Evidence from Tower of Hanoi. *Cognitive Psychology*, *17*, 248–294. doi:10.1016/0010-0285(85)90009-X

Krug, S. (2000). *Don't make me think! A common sense approach to Web usability*. Berkeley, CA: New Riders.

Kushleyeva, Y., Salvucci, D., & Lee, F. (2005). Deciding when to switch tasks in time-critical multitasking. *Cognitive Systems Research*, *6*, 41–49. doi:10.1016/j.cogsys.2004.09.005

Kwan, M., & Balasubramanian, P. (2003). KnowledgeScope: Managing knowledge in context. *Decision Support Services*, *35*, 467–486. doi:10.1016/S0167-9236(02)00126-4

Langholtz, H., Gettys, C., & Foote, B. (1995). Are resource fluctuations anticipated. in resource allocation tasks? *Organizational Behavior and Human Decision Processes*, *64*(3), 274–282. doi:10.1006/obhd.1995.1105

Lefevre, J., & Dixon, P. (1986). Do written instructions need examples? *Cognition and Instruction*, *3*(1), 1–30. doi:10.1207/s1532690xci0301_1

Lowe, R. (2002). Animation and learning: Selective processing of information in dynamic graphics. *Learning and Instruction*, *13*(2), 157–176. doi:10.1016/S0959-4752(02)00018-X

Mao, J., & Benbasat, I. (2001). The effects of contextualized access to knowledge on judgment. *International Journal of Human-Computer Studies*, *55*, 787–814. doi:10.1006/ijhc.2001.0507

Marquie, J., Jourdan-Boddaert, L., & Huet, N. (2002). Do older adults underestimate their actual computer knowledge? *Behaviour & Information Technology*, *21*(4), 273–280. doi:10.1080/0144929021000020998

Mayer, R. (1976). Comprehension as affected by structure of problem representation. *Memory & Cognition*, *4*, 249–265. doi:10.3758/BF03213171

McFarlane, D., & Latorella, K. (2002). The scope and importance of human interruption in human-computer interaction design. *Human-Computer Interaction*, *17*, 1–61. doi:10.1207/S15327051HCI1701_1

McGovern, G. (2006a). *Making the customer CEO*. Retrieved from http://www.gerrymcgovern.com/nt/ 2006/nt-2006-06-12-customer-ceo.htm

McKenzie, P. (2002). Communication barriers and information-seeking counterstrategies in accounts of practitioner-patient encounters. *Library and Information Science, 24,* 31–47. doi:10.1016/S0740-8188(01)00103-7

McNamara, D., & Kintsch, W. (1996). Learning from text: Effects of prior knowledge and text coherence. *Discourse Processes, 22,* 247–287. doi:10.1080/01638539609544975

Mirel, B. (1988). Cognitive processing, text linguistics and documentation writing. *Journal of Technical Writing and Communication, 18*(2), 111–133. doi:10.2190/20JV-5N1E-6LNR-443U

Mirel, B. (1992). Analyzing audiences for software manuals: A survey of instructional needs for real world tasks. *Technical Communication Quarterly, 1*(1), 15–35. doi:10.1080/10572259209359489

Mirel, B. (2003). *Interaction design for complex problem solving: Developing useful and usable software.* San Francisco, CA: Morgan Kaufmann.

Mirel, B., Feinberg, S., & Allmendinger, L. (1991). Designing manuals for active learning styles. *Technical Communication, 38*(1), 75–87.

Monsell, S. (1993). Task switching. *Trends in Cognitive Sciences, 7*(3), 134–140. doi:10.1016/S1364-6613(03)00028-7

Müller, M. (2007). Being aware: Where we think the action is. *Cognition Technology and Work, 9*(2), 109–126. doi:10.1007/s10111-006-0047-7

Nanard, J., & Nanard, M. (1995). Hypertext design environments and the hypertext design process. *Communications of the ACM, 38*(8), 49–56. doi:10.1145/208344.208347

National Institute of Health. (2002). *Making your web site senior friendly.* Retrieved January 13, 2010, from http://www.nlm.nih.gov/pubs/staffpubs/ od/ocpl/agingchecklist.html

Navarro-Prieto, R., Scaife, M., & Rogers, Y. (1999). Cognitive strategies in Web searching. *Proceeding of the fifth Conference on Human Factors and the Web,* (pp. 43–56). Gaithersburg, MD.

Nielsen, J. (2001). *The 3Cs of critical Web use: Collect, compare, choose.* Retrieved December 3, 2008, from http://www.useit.com/ alertbox/20010415.html

Nielsen, J. (2007b). *Banner blindness: Old and new findings.* Retrieved November 11, 2007, from http://www.useit.com/alertbox/ banner-blindness.html

Nilsson, R., & Mayer, R. (2002). The effects of graphic organizers giving cues to the structure of a hypertext document on users' navigation strategies and performance. *International Journal of Human-Computer Studies, 57,* 1–26. doi:10.1006/ijhc.2002.1011

Norman, D. (2004). *Emotional design.* New York, NY: Basic Books.

Norman, D. A. (2002). *The design of everyday things.* New York, NY: Basic Books.

O'Hara, K., & Payne, S. (1998). The effects of operator implementation cost on planfulness of problem solving and learning. *Cognitive Psychology, 35,* 34–70. doi:10.1006/cogp.1997.0676

Orasanu, J., & Connolly, T. (1993). The reinvention of decision making. In Klein, G., Orasanu, J., Calderwood, R., & Zsambok, C. (Eds.), *Decision making in action: Models and methods* (pp. 3–20). Norwood, NJ: Ablex.

Paiva, A. (Ed.). (2000). *Affective interactions: Toward a new generation of computer interfaces.* New York, NY: Springer.

Payne, J., Bettman, J., & Johnson, E. (1988). Adaptive strategy selection in decision making. *Journal of Experimental Psychology. Learning, Memory, and Cognition, 14,* 534–552. doi:10.1037/0278-7393.14.3.534

Payne, S. (1991). Display-based action at the user interface. *International Journal of Man-Machine Studies*, *35*, 275–289. doi:10.1016/S0020-7373(05)80129-4

Payne, S. (2002). Balancing information needs: Dilemmas in producing patient information leaflets. *Health Informatics Journal*, *8*, 174–179. doi:10.1177/146045820200800402

Payne, S., Howes, A., & Reader, W. (2001). Adaptively distributing cognition: A decision making perspective on human-computer interaction. *Behaviour & Information Technology*, *20*(5), 339–346. doi:10.1080/01449290110078680

Penrose, J., & Seiford, L. (1988). Microcomputer users' preferences for software documentation: An analysis. *Journal of Technical Writing and Communication*, *18*(4), 355–366.

Pomerantz, J., & Schwaitzberg, S. (1975). Grouping by proximity: Selective attention measures. *Perception & Psychophysics*, *18*, 355–361. doi:10.3758/BF03211212

Rains, S., & Karmikel, C. (2009). Health information-seeking and perceptions of website credibility: Examining Web-use orientation, message characteristics, and structural features of websites. *Computers in Human Behavior*, *25*, 544–553. doi:10.1016/j.chb.2008.11.005

Raskin, J. (2003/2004). Silicon superstitions. *ACM Queue; Tomorrow's Computing Today*, *1*(9).

Redish, J. (2007). Expanding usability testing to evaluate complex systems. *Journal of Usability Studies*, *2*(3), 102–111.

Redish, J., & Schell, D. (1989). Writing and testing instructions for usability. In Fearing, B., & Sparrow, K. (Eds.), *Technical writing: Theory and practice* (pp. 63–71). New York, NY: Modern Language Association of America.

Robins, D., Holmes, J., & Stansbury, M. (2010). Consumer health information on the Web: The relationship of visual design and perceptions of credibility. *Journal of the American Society for Information Science and Technology*, *61*(1), 13–29.

Rosenbaum, S., & Walters, D. (1986). Audience diversity: A major challenge in computer documentation. *IEEE Transactions on Professional Communication*, *29*(4).

Rosson, M. (1983). Patterns of experience in text editing. *Proceedings of the CHI'83 Human Factors in Computing Systems* (pp. 171–175). New York, NY: ACM.

Rouet, J. (2003). What was I looking for? The influence of task specificity and prior knowledge on students' search strategies in hypertext. *Interacting with Computers*, *15*, 409–428. doi:10.1016/S0953-5438(02)00064-4

Rubens, P., & Rubens, B. (1988). Usability and format design. In Doheny-Farina, S. (Ed.), *Effective documentation: What we have learned from research* (pp. 213–234). Cambridge, MA: MIT.

Rubinstein, J., Meyer, D., & Evans, J. (2001). Executive control of cognitive processes in task switching. *Journal of Experimental Psychology. Human Perception and Performance*, *27*(4), 763–797. doi:10.1037/0096-1523.27.4.763

Russell, M. (2005). Using eye-tracking data to understand first impressions of a website. *Usability News*, *7*(1). Retrieved from http://psychology.wichita.edu/surl/usabilitynews/71/eye_tracking.html

Salthouse, T., & Babcock, R. (1991). Decomposing adult age differences in working memory. *Developmental Psychology*, *72*, 763–776. doi:10.1037/0012-1649.27.5.763

Salvador, T., Barile, S., & Sherry, J. (2004). Ubiquitous computing design principles: Supporting human-human and human-computer transaction. *Proceedings of the SIGCHI Conference on Human Factors in Computing Systems* (pp. 1497–1500). New York, NY: ACM.

Santhanam, R., & Wiedenbeck, S. (1993). Neither novice nor expert: The discretionary user of software. *International Journal of Man-Machine Studies, 38,* 201–229. doi:10.1006/imms.1993.1010

Sayago, S., & Blat, J. (2010). Telling the story of older people e-mailing: An ethnographical study. *International Journal of Human-Computer Studies, 68,* 105–120. doi:10.1016/j.ijhcs.2009.10.004

Scanlon, T. (1996). *Making online information usable.* Retrieved from http://www.uie.com/articles/online_information/

Schneider, W., & Fisk, A. (1982). Concurrent automatic and controlled visual search: Can processing occur without resource cost? *Journal of Experimental Psychology. Learning, Memory, and Cognition, 8,* 261–278. doi:10.1037/0278-7393.8.4.261

Schwartz, D., & Teleni, D. (2000). Tying knowledge to action with kMail. *IEEE Intelligent Systems and Their Applications, 15,* 33–39. doi:10.1109/5254.846283

Sheridan, S., Felix, K., Pignone, M., & Lewis, C. (2004). Information needs of men regarding prostate cancer screening and the effect of a brief decision aid. *Patient Education and Counseling, 54,* 345–351. doi:10.1016/j.pec.2003.12.003

Shneiderman, B. (1997). *Designing the user interface: Strategies for effective human-computer interaction.* Reading, MA: Addison-Wesley.

Simon, H. (1979). *Models of thought.* New Haven, CT: Yale UP.

Slovic, P. (1972). From Shakespeare to Simon: Speculations—and some evidence—about man's ability to process information. *Oregon Research Institute Research Bulletin, 12,* 1–29.

Spool, J. (1997). *Why on-site searching stinks.* Retrieved December 28, 2005, from http://www.uie.com/articles/search_stinks/

Stanford, J., Tauber, E., Fogg, B., & Marable, L. (2002). Experts vs. online consumers: A comparative credibility study of health and finance Web sites. *Consumer WebWatch Research Report.* Retrieved from http://www.consumerwebwatch.org/dynamic/web-credibility-reports-experts-vs-online-abstract.cfm

Storch, N. (1992). Does the user interface make interruptions disruptive? A study of interface style and form of interruption. *Proceedings of the SIGCHI Conference on Human Factors in Computing Systems,* (pp. 14–14). New York, NY: ACM.

Stvilia, B., Mon, L., & Yi, Y. (2009). A model for online consumer health information quality. *Journal of the American Society for Information Science and Technology, 60*(9), 1781–1791. doi:10.1002/asi.21115

Sutcliffe, A., & Maiden, N. (1992). Analyzing the novice analyst: Cognitive models in software engineering. *International Journal of Man-Machine Studies, 36,* 719–740. doi:10.1016/0020-7373(92)90038-M

Szulanski, G. (1996). Exploring internal stickiness: Impediments to the transfer of best practice within the firm. *Strategic Management Journal, 17,* 27–43.

Thuring, M., Hannemann, J., & Haake, J. (1995). Hypermedia and cognition: Designing for comprehension. *Communications of the ACM, 38,* 57–66. doi:10.1145/208344.208348

Tufte, E. (1983). *The visual display of quantitative information.* Cheshire, CT: Graphics Press.

Tyre, M. J., & von Hippel, E. (1997). The situated nature of adaptive learning in organizations. *Organization Science*, *8*(1), 71–83. doi:10.1287/orsc.8.1.71

Valero, P., & Sanmartiân, J. (1999). Methods for defining user groups and user adjusted information structures. *Behaviour & Information Technology*, *18*(4), 245–259. doi:10.1080/014492999119002

van der Meij, H., & Gellevij, M. (2002). Effects of pictures, age, and experience on learning to use a computer program. *Technical Communication*, *49*(3), 330–339.

van Hees, M. (1996). User instructions for the elderly: What the literature tells us. *Journal of Technical Writing and Communication*, *26*(4), 521–536.

Visser, W., & Morals, A. (1991). Concurrent use of different expertise elicitation methods applied to the study of the programming activity. In Ackermann, D., & Tauber, M. J. (Eds.), *Mental models and human-computer interactions* (pp. 97–114). Amsterdam, The Netherlands: North Holland.

Vu, K., Hanley, G., Strybel, T., & Proctor, R. (2000). Metacognitive processes in human-computer interaction: Self-assessments of knowledge as predictors of computer expertise. *International Journal of Human-Computer Interaction*, *12*(1), 43–71. doi:10.1207/S15327590IJHC1201_2

Walker, N., Millians, J., & Worden, A. (1996). Mouse accelerations and performance of older computer users. *Proceedings of the Human Factors and Ergonomics Society 40th Annual Meeting*, (pp.151–154). Santa Monica, CA: HFES.

Wallsten, T., & Barton, C. (1982). Processing probabilistic multidimensional information for decisions. *Journal of Experimental Psychology. Learning, Memory, and Cognition*, *8*, 361–384. doi:10.1037/0278-7393.8.5.361

Webster, D., & Kruglanski, A. (1994). Individual differences in need. for cognitive closure. *Journal of Personality and Social Psychology*, *67*(6), 1049–1672. doi:10.1037/0022-3514.67.6.1049

Weigand, H. (2006). Two decades of the language-action perspective. *Communications of the ACM*, *49*(5), 45–26.

Wickens, C. (1992). *Engineering psychology and human performance*. New York, NY: HarperCollins.

Wickens, C., & Carswell, C. (1995). The proximity compatibility principle: Its psychological foundations and its relevance to display design. *Human Factors*, *37*, 473–494. doi:10.1518/001872095779049408

Wickens, C., & Hollands, J. (2000). *Engineering psychology and human performance*. Upper Saddle River, NJ: Prentice Hall.

Woods, D. (1984). Visual momentum: A concept to improve the cognitive coupling of person and computer. *International Journal of Man-Machine Studies*, *21*, 229–244. doi:10.1016/S0020-7373(84)80043-7

Woods, D., Patterson, E., & Roth, E. (2002). Can we ever escape from data overload? A cognitive systems diagnosis. *Cognition Technology and Work*, *4*, 22–36. doi:10.1007/s101110200002

Zeng, Q., Kogan, S., Plovnick, R., Crowell, J., Lacroix, E., & Greenes, R. (2004). Positive attitudes and failed queries: An exploration of the conundrums of consumer health information retrieval. *International Journal of Medical Informatics*, *73*(1), 45–55. doi:10.1016/j.ijmedinf.2003.12.015

Zhang, Y., Goonetilleke, R., Plocher, T., & Liang, S. (2005). Time-related behaviour in multitasking situations. *International Journal of Human-Computer Studies*, *62*, 425–455. doi:10.1016/j.ijhcs.2005.01.002

Zimmermann, G., & Vanderheiden, G. (2005). *Creating accessible applications with RUP.* Retrieved April 28, 2006, from http://www.128. ibm.com/developerworks/rational/ library/jul05/ zimmerman/index.html#notes

ADDITIONAL READING

Albers, M. (2004). *Communication of complex information: User goals and information needs for dynamic Web information.* Mahwah, NJ: Erlbaum.

Hackos, J., & Redish, J. (1998). *User and task analysis for interface design.* New York, NY: Wiley.

Krug, S. (2000). *Don't make me think! A common sense approach to Web usability.* Berkeley, CA: New Riders.

Mirel, B. (2003). *Interaction design for complex problem solving: Developing useful and usable software.* San Francisco, CA: Morgan Kaufmann.

Norman, D. (2004). *Emotional design.* New York, NY: Basic Books.

Redish, J. (2007). Expanding usability testing to evaluate complex systems. *Journal of Usability Studies, 2*(3), 102–111.

Wickens, C., & Hollands, J. (2000). *Engineering psychology and human performance.* Upper Saddle River, NJ: Prentice Hall.

Chapter 5
How People Approach Technology–Based Interactions

ABSTRACT

Design teams should not consider a person's computer interface as just a set of hardware and software that make upcompose the computer (Grudin, 1990). Instead, from the person's point of view, the interface includes all of the elements which compose its context of use. From this perspective, one can view the interface of a computer as more than the screens, buttons, and knobs, and also include any documentation, other people present, and past knowledge directly relevant to the situation. In these situations, HII needs to consider more than just the button-pushing or system response, but how people and information interact with the situation in building comprehension.

BACKGROUND

If a screen displays precise and highly actionable information and the HCI is so poor nobody can figure out how to comprehend it, does it have any content?

This part of the book considers how people approach and interact with technology. HII in the modern world, and as viewed within this book, almost always consists of a computer-based interaction. The computer itself influences how people interact with the information. Design teams need to consider how technology often drives the HII. This chapter examines some of the major ways technology exerts its influence. The white area in Figure 1 shows the area of the HII model relevant to this chapter.

This chapter looks at:

Models of how people accept technology: Models work to address how people react to technology, how that reaction shapes their intentions to use it, and how it shapes their actual use.

Respond to system speed: Factors such as time and perceived time have a profound effect on how satisfied people are with technology interactions.

DOI: 10.4018/978-1-4666-0152-9.ch005

Figure 1. How people approach technology.

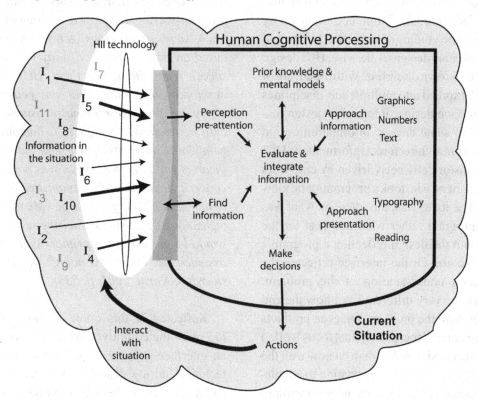

People-display interaction: People interact with the system based on the information the display provides them. This section considers the factors of good feedback and feedforward which allow the design team to maximize the HII of a system.

Technology factors driving user satisfaction: A wide range of factors influence people's satisfaction with an interface and the technology behind it. This section examines some of major factors.

Motor control and HII: Motor control and its influence on interactions via mouse and keyboard strongly affect how easily people can interact with technology.

INTRODUCTION

Many designs fail because they assume that technology can adequately address a problem, a view that Norman (1998) has dedicated a book to criticizing (*The Invisible Computer*). As he points out:

The proposals are always technical solutions, whereas the problems reside within the person; cognitive tools are needed to aid in the programming task, social and organizational tools are needed for the group problems. And these human problems are harder to solve than mere technical ones (p. 95).

Good HII is not and never will be a solution based in technology; it must be based in how people respond to and are influenced by both the information and the technology.

Questions about how people interact with machine interfaces predate computers, as shown by early ergonomic studies of aircraft cockpits and plant control panel designs. Likewise, HCI design has long been its own discipline. With the advent of the web, HCI spread into multiple sub-disciplines such as interface design, interaction design, usability, and to some degree, information design and information architecture. Unfortunately, HCI design has historically been driven by engineers and programmers, who took a programmatic view of design. The focus was, too often, on what was easiest to program rather what was best for the end user, with the design reflecting a program's internal structure. Or the interface reflected the programmer's understanding of the problem, which might be very different from how the end users understand the problem. Or, even products with a user-centered focus, the actual focus is often on the product design rather than on how well the product communicates its information to people. Typically, usability tests try to measure something; with the complex situations relevant to HII, the ability to measure what truly matters is difficult. Luckily, progress has been made to resolve this problem in recent years; although there is still a long way to go. But the fundamental problem still exists: people must use a computer interface to gain information from a computer.

The history of HCI is one in which we have experienced a gradual shift from attempts by different parts of the community to focus on their own narrow view of the field to a more cooperative effort to understand what it means to build systems that people value. When the first author of this paper first came to IBM Research, there was a "theory" group working to extend behavioral science theory to describe human interaction with a particular type of technology (mostly desktop computers). The group focused on the kind of behavioral theories that were largely individual and cognitive; that is, they looked mostly at the computer as a tool for individual use and were primarily interested in how cognitive activities such as learning and problem-solving developed in computer users. There were also various technology groups focused on issues such as display resolution and speech recognition. For them, HCI was about developing technology that was better without worrying specifically about measuring empirically how valuable it might be to humans. For the behavioral scientists, how useful the behavioral theories would be for design was not a primary concern. It was simply, optimistically perhaps, assumed that theory would be valuable. For the technologist, the uses to which the new technology would be put was not a primary concern. It was assumed that better technology would find uses (Karat & Karat, 2003, p. 533).

Reflected in this quote is the attitude that too often the cognitive aspects of working with an interface get ignored or subordinated to the technical during design and development. The technical aspects tend to dominate the design since they can be more easily measured and allowed for, and, of course, it's the technical aspects which make up the physical aspects. In addition, programmers and engineers have traditionally dominated development teams and the technical aspect is where their knowledge and interests lie. On the other hand, the cognitive aspects have a strong effect on how people view the design and the interaction. Often, systems which are technically adequate, or even superior to another, fail because people perceive them as cognitively demanding. The clean clockwork mechanism of a program's internal structure fails in the messy psychology-driven world of people interacting with information. "They are thus more akin to the noumenal cloud activity of humans than the comfortable stability of an epigram on stone" (Marchionini, 2008, p. 171).

Russo (1977) claims that better decision making depends upon displays providing information in an easy-to-process manner. While Russo's claim is hardly earth-shattering or unexpected, it still seems to be ignored in many hard-to-use interfaces. And many of those hard-to-use interfaces were intended to be easy to use. Design teams don't intentionally ignore Russo's advice, but can fail to have a clear grasp of what "easy to process" means and how to apply it. Although the advice is simple, the human performance issues relevant to applying it to HII and communicating information are more complex. A VCR's interface is technically correct and accomplishes the goals and requirements given to the design team, but proves so unwieldy that programming VCRs became fodder for late-night comedians.

With the increasing amount of information and the increasing complexity of information available online, design teams involved in information presentation must consider how information is displayed to fully accommodate the dynamic, interactive nature of information (Heba, 1997). As interaction shifts from performing specific, defined tasks to open-ended information collecting, the need for HII has entered into how people approach interacting with a computer. The interface is the first interaction people have when they begin to acquire information on a subject. The strong and weak points of a display's design have profound effects on the ease with which people can manipulate information, influencing their overall comprehension and attitude. If the interface obstructs accurate comprehension, then decisions will be flawed (Lightner, 2001). Both the HCI and IR communities are extending their traditional models of human-machine and query-document interactions to include social components that models how the relationships between information objects are based on people's interactions with those objects. Design teams must ensure content design is based on how people will interact with it. This chapter describes the factors specific to computer display that affect how people interact with information and how those factors can influence comprehension.

HOW PEOPLE ACCEPT TECHNOLOGY

When people first encounter any new technology (whether new hardware or software) they need to make a decision about whether or not they are willing to use it. Various models have been proposed for showing the factors that go into making that decision. The models work to address how people react to technology, how that reaction shapes their intentions to use it, and how it shapes their actual use.

Of the various models reviewed by Venkatesh et al., the Technology Acceptance Model (TAM) (Davis, 1989; Davis, Bagozzi & Warshaw, 1989) and a recent update to the model called TAM2 (Venkatesh & Davis, 2000) have come to dominate the others (Figure 2). The most significant change with TAM2 was the addition of social influences. In general, all of the models have similar characteristics, with the major differences being either the addition/subtraction of a few factors or changes to the relative weighting of the factors. Venkatesh et al. (2003) review eight different technology acceptance models and compare their strengths and weaknesses. Bagozzi (2007) also presents an analysis and critique of TAM models.

According to TAM, perceived ease of use and usefulness are assumed to be strong determinants of the actual and successful utilization of technology. Various studies have found that TAM accounts for 30–40% of IT acceptance (Bagozzi, 2007; King & He, 2006). Various studies into how TAM can be used include:

- For corporate Internet users, the relevance of information dominates perceptions of usefulness and ease of use, much more so than for home-based users (Shih, 2004).
- The model predicts the use of e-learning within the corporate environment (Hsia, 2007).
- With some additions, TAM has been modified for healthcare situations with great

Figure 2. TAM and TAM 2 models

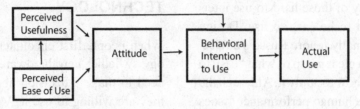

Technology Acceptance Model (TAM)

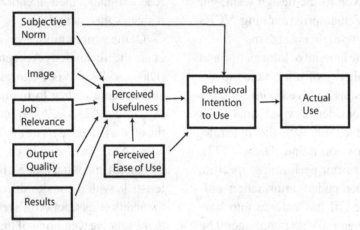

Technology Acceptance Model 2 (TAM2)

success (Holden & Karsh, 2010). Aggelidis and Chatzoglou (2009) found the model that included social influence, attitude, and facilitating conditions and self-efficacy explained 87% of the variance in behavior intentions. For a healthcare setting, with its strict hierarchical structure, it is not surprising to find social influence and attitude being more significant factors than would be found in a typical home or office setting.

TIME AND HII

Time plays a significant factor in how people interact with information systems. Design teams, as they work to maintain high-quality HII, must consider both perceived time of the interaction and actual response times.

Perceived Time of Information Interaction

Understanding how people deal with system response times or user input delays requires understanding how people perceive the passage of time while they interact with a system. Most quantitative studies look at how quickly a system responds to an action or how long people will wait for system response. The basic HII design problem is that time is not a fixed property of either the individual or the interactive system. Instead, people's response depends, not on actual time, but on perceived time, and these can be very different. It is too simplistic to rely on guidelines for how long people should wait. Moreover, Antonides, Verhoef, and Van Aalst (2002) found that perceived and actual waiting time show a non-linear relationship, so the effects of minor increases/decreases in actual time can have a substantial influence on overall time perception.

People have a tendency to overestimate passive durations, such as waiting for system response or for a webpage to download; and they underestimate active durations, as when they are actively interacting with information (Hornik, 1984). Thus, perceived time can be either under- or over-estimated, depending on how engaged people are in the situation. In one study, adolescents were given tasks of either playing Tetris or reading. When the task lasted 8 minutes, they overestimated both 8 minute times (but estimated the reading time as longer). When they played Tetris for 24 minutes, they underestimated the playing time. However, they accurately estimated the time of the entire study session (Tobin & Grondin, 2009). Antonides et al. (2002) found that information about the expected waiting time significantly reduced the overestimation of waiting time.

Poynter (1989) argues that since there are no physiological receptors for perceiving time; people have no internal, measurable clock that they use to perceive and measure time. Instead, the perception of time happens as an emergent feature of the situation (Fabre, Howard, & Smith, 2000). Block et al. (2000), in a meta-analysis of time estimation studies, found very few sex differences related to time estimation.

To reduce people's estimates of interaction times, the number of simple user actions should be minimized (Fabre, Howard, & Smith, 2000), a consideration that is often at odds with design conventions. A deep and clearly laid-out information architecture helps to guide people to the information they need. However, this type of structure also requires several clicks. Ignoring the ongoing debate about whether all information should be within three clicks, or whether people will follow information as long as they are making

progress (Porter, 2003), more clicks will contribute to increasing both actual and perceived time. In other words, more navigation clicks can make it seem to take longer to find information than it actually required (Tractinsky & Meyer, 2001).

Brown (1985) found that people were better at estimating time when they were told to do so during a task. He had people perform tasks and estimate the time it took. However, some of the subjects did not know that they would be asked for a time estimate. These people performed very poorly on the estimates and tended to underestimate if they were engaged in a cognitively demanding task. In most HII situations, people have no reason to prepare themselves beforehand to mentally estimate the time they spend on a task. However, they will experience a perceived time, and it will influence their level of satisfaction and their willingness to continue to interact with the system.

Response to System Speed

Research into how people respond to delays of obtaining information has found consistent patterns based on the length of the delay.

- Payne, Howes, & Reader (2001) looked at how people respond to different delays in help. They found that as the time delay increased people avoided using the help and relied on their memory, resulting in more errors. They interpreted this finding in terms of cost: people balance the costs and benefits of using the help with its time delay versus relying on knowledge-in-the-head, which might be incorrect or incomplete but is immediately available. Long delays made the cost of using potentially incorrect information acceptable.
- People need indications that something is happening. Unless they have prior knowledge about the expected time (this task always takes at least 30 seconds), people assume nothing is happening unless there

is some progress indication. The use of spinning balls and progress boxes provide an indication that the process is working and to provide an estimate of its expected time. Of course, the use of dialog boxes that count down to 1 second remaining and then sit there for several seconds are a constant source of irritation.

The general rules of thumb for handling system delays are based on old research (Card et al. 1991; Miller 1968), but nothing in modern design has changed the basic psychology of how people respond to delays (Nielsen, 1993). Overall, the view is that the system must respond within 2 seconds to maintain acceptable performance (Shneiderman, 1984).

- Second or less delay is required to give the feel of a system reacting instantaneously. The button depresses and immediately people the mouse cursor change or the browser window blank as it loads another page.
- Second is the upper limit on where people will feel they are directly interacting with the information. Beyond 1 second, the delay becomes noticeable enough that people are very conscious of it. Martin and Corl (1986) found that time delays of less than 1 second had little effect on overall productivity, but also that productivity showed a linear decrease as delays increased from 1 to 5 seconds.
- 10 seconds is the upper limit for expecting people to wait and to stay focused. Beyond the 10 second mark, people will try to multitask to avoid sitting, doing nothing. These longer wait times also demand feedback so that people know the system is working; progress indicators become vital for communicating between people and the system (Myers, 1985). Otherwise, they may stop the task or generally interfere with it on

Box 1.

> **Changing view of system response**
> Modern software products on relatively fast computers give very rapid response. People no longer expect to wait for a system to respond. In the late 1980's, I was writing documents on a terminal connected to an IBM mainframe. When I pressed the ENTER key, depending on the system load, I waited anywhere from sub-second to several seconds for the screen to refresh. This was the expected response and something to live with. If the word processor I'm using now gets that sluggish, I worry that the system is going to lock up, and I'd probably restart my computer. Or I would check to see if a background process such as a spyware scan had started.

the assumption that something is wrong. Feedback is especially important if the total delay time is highly variable, since people will not be able to form expectations about when a process should end. Likewise, for infrequent tasks, people need feedback since there is no opportunity to form expectations about the time delay.

While most of the research has focused on how people respond to delays, interestingly, the lack of a delay can also be a problem. Screen updates (especially tables or text screens, where one screen looks basically like another) which occur very fast, where people cannot see the screen flash or refresh, hindering interaction with the information. Since they did not see the information change, they must mentally compare what is currently displayed with what was displayed previously, look for the differences, and reach a decision that the screen *has* changed before they focus on determining *what* changed.

For people to accept delays, they must consciously initiate the cause of the delay and expect it. If people inadvertently perform an action that causes a lengthy delay, they will become frustrated. For example, most of the current HTML-based help systems take several seconds to load a browser and open the help file; the problem is that during this load time, the system is unresponsive and the process can't be stopped. If a person has requested the help, the load time may be irritating, but it is expected. On the other hand, if the F1 key was accidentally pressed, then the load time is highly frustrating. Some of the problems with slow system response are:

- Slow system response breaks people's workflow or at least imposes an unnatural pace to it. System delays as short as 1.6 seconds reduce reaction time and increase error rates (Szameitat et al., 2009).
- Slow response during Internet searches causes people to exhibit stress responses, such as evaluated heart rate. Their anxiety increases with slower real response (Guynes, 1988), which can lead to longer perceived time as well as increased error rates. The stress response does not decrease with expertise, but remains constant between novice and expert computer users (Trimmel, Meixner-Pendleton, & Haring, 2003).
- Slow system response times, besides slowing down the total interaction, also increases the perceived time it takes to perform a task and decreases user satisfaction with the system.

With modern networked computer systems, inconsistent delays in system response are unavoidable. Web pages have a highly variable response time, depending on the server being accessed and the network load between the server and the web browser. Early research revealed that people are impatient and will click again, which restarts the process and introduces additional delay. Even worse, as will be discussed in the next section, delays are inherent in network design and vary based on factors beyond either the design team's or the user's control. Because of the complexity of Internet data transfer and database searching, the length of system delays can hardly be controlled or predicted. System delays cause people to follow fewer links and to consider more carefully whether a link will provide useful information. In other

Box 2.

Delays in saving and opening files
I started writing this text on two computers: my desktop unit, which had Word 2007, and my laptop, with Word 2000. Although the laptop had a file converter and could handle the *.docx format ok, it was time consuming, taking about 10-20 seconds to save. Thus, I mostly worked with *.doc files so that they would rapidly save on both computers. When I created a new file in Word 2007 and forget to convert it to .doc, it was frustrating. But it gave me time to drink more coffee in this nice coffee shop.

---

words, when they know there will be a substantial delay, they only click on links which have a high perceived probability of providing useful information. On the other hand, these people have fewer total page views and tend to find answers to their questions more than people using a system with a faster response time (Payne, Howes, & Reader, 2001). They probably have better results because the slower speed forces them to read the text to consider its applicability, rather than essentially clicking every link and lightly skimming a page.

WWW Download Time

Webpage download times are affected by a wide range of technology: the load on the server, the speed of the Internet connection, the local network/computer, the performance of the browser, and the format of the webpage. What matters to HII is not any of these individual items, but how they all combine to impose some irregular delay on webpage downloads, which may lead people to decide the delay is unacceptable.

Generally, web guidelines say to keep the page size as small as possible to minimize download time. Nielson reported popular sites had average load times of 8 seconds while less popular ones took 19 seconds. Not surprisingly, he concluded that slower load times lead to frustrated people who would leave a page if the load time was too long (Nielsen, 1997). Although Nielsen's research was done when most people connected to the Internet via dialup, with the increased use of high-bandwidth access, many design teams are using more and larger graphics, which can still result in noticeable download delays.

Ramsay et al. (1998) varied download times from 2 seconds to 2 minutes and found that downloading delays exerted a strong effect on people's perceptions of websites, with fast downloading sites being perceived as more interesting. Likewise, Hoxmeier and DiCesare (2000) found that people's satisfaction with a site decreased after a 12-second delay. Nah (2004) reviews several of the studies and concludes that, besides affecting just satisfaction, wait times of over about four seconds affect people's performance and intentions more than their attitudes. From an HII viewpoint, changes in intentions can strongly affect how people interact with information and what they try to draw from it. If the response is too slow, people will stop trying to verify information and go with what they already believe. They will also decrease the number of comparisons and accept an answer as good enough.

Bouch, Kuchinsky, & Bhatti (2000) found that incremental download progress, with parts of a page displaying before download completion, made people much more tolerant of long download times and more willing to wait longer before they would rate download speed as unacceptable. This research is consistent with other research on page load times showing that it is not the actual time, but the perceived time which causes frustration. Rather than a simple measure of download time, the time until people can interact with the system has been found to strongly determine how quickly they think the screen loads. The sooner people can interact, the faster the website is perceived to download, even if overall load time is longer. Perfetti and Landesman (2001) found a strong correlation between perceived download time and successful task completion, but no correlation between actual download time and task completion. They concluded that people perceive sites as faster if they can accomplish their task faster.

Box 3.

Time until interaction happens

Older versions of Netscape would only display a table after the browser had processed the entire table. When a page design was based on tables, the site would initially load, and then the computer would sit, apparently doing nothing for several seconds, and suddenly the entire page would display. Or perhaps the banner or other top images would display and then nothing further would happen until the rest of the page (a single, large table) would appear. In reality, Netscape was downloading all images and processing the text before displaying any of it. But people using the browser didn't know that.

When the page was designed using nested tables (this was before CSS), people found the wait times difficult to handle, even people who knew what was happening "under the hood." They would see the browser go blank and then were faced with no visible indication that anything was happening. As a result, they might click off the site without waiting for the download to finish. Or they would click back to the original page and restart the page download, an action which accomplished nothing with respect to displaying the page.

This type of processing makes sense in terms of data efficiency and the system-engineering view, but it fails miserably from an HII view. When design teams realized how people were responding to this type of processing, browser rendering engines were changed to display partially rendered pages so people could see that something was happening.

When we looked at the actual download speeds of the sites we tested, we found that there was no correlation between these and the perceived speeds reported by our users. About.com, rated slowest by our users, was actually the fastest site (average: 8 seconds). Amazon.com, rated as one of the fastest sites by users, was really the slowest (average: 36 seconds).

PEOPLE-DISPLAY INTERACTION

People tend to interact with a system based on the display. They do not plan out the entire interaction, but rather engage in a display-based, trial-and-error interaction (O'Hara & Payne, 1998). In support of this idea, Zhang (1996) claims that the more information shifts to the interface—and consequently, the less it has to be retained in memory—the easier a task should become. (This display-based interaction will be discussed in more

Box 4.

> **Feedback and interface changes**
> People's interaction with electronic medical records (EMR) systems can bring strong improvements to medical practice, specifically screening and prevention tests.
>
> When a patient comes into an emergency department with a cardiac condition, there are seven things that should be done immediately. Some are very simple (give them aspirin), and some are tests that should be run. Every emergency department healthcare provider can easily recite the list. But an analysis of people's medical records found that compliance with ALL seven actions was low. As a result, the EMR interface was redesigned to automatically present the seven items as a checklist, and also to generate reports of overall compliance. Within a few months, both compliance and medical care levels had improved.
>
> This raises many issues, but the interesting one here is that an interaction change led to improvement in people's following procedures which they already knew. The presentation changed the context of the interaction and gave feedback into accomplishing the task.

detail in chapter 10: *How people interact with information presentation.*) For example, studies in puzzle solving have found that people make a few moves and then pause to evaluate before making more moves (Kotovsky, Hayes, & Simon, 1985; O'Hara & Payne, 1998). To support that interaction, people require feedback and feedforward from the system.

The various characteristics of a situation all interact and cause feedback within the situation that causes a response and resulting change of the situation. The HII for understanding and monitoring a situation requires that people receive feedback from the situation and be able to anticipate changes.

Feedback

People need to monitor and interact with a situation to ensure that they are achieving their goals. This requires receiving information about the current state of the situation. Feedback provides information on how the situation is responding to decisions. Without feedback, people don't know if the situation is changing as desired. Of course, defining time scales for automatic and rapid feedback depends on the situation. The internal feedback built into a system controls the performance of any system, at least any system that has regulatory properties.

Two types of feedback can occur: positive and negative.

Negative Feedback: Negative feedback acts to resist or stop the action. This is the more common version and is designed into many mechanical systems. The toilet float valve gives negative feedback that shuts off the water at the proper time. Lack of feedback, such as when the float valve breaks, results in the water never shutting off. Many systems manifest a cyclic pattern. Negative feedback inherent in the situation causes point-to-point values to increase and decrease around an average value. In this case, as long as the system is within the normal oscillation range, there is no need to make any adjustments. In fact, if people try to adjust the system to move the values back toward the average, the system is likely to over-react and the adjustment will cause the system to move further out of balance. As they interact with information about a situation, feedback between the reader, information creators, and design teams must occur to enhance the information's support for situational understanding.

Positive Feedback: Positive feedback reinforces the current action. It takes the current value and builds on it. In many cases, positive feedback can be harmful, such as the squealing of a speaker when a microphone gets too close. The sound from the speaker is picked up by the microphone, which goes through the speaker, and the sound becomes louder and louder in a loop. Major stock market corrections start with positive feedback as a first wave of selling induces more people to sell. (Of course, negative feedback eventually prevents a complete market crash.) If a toilet had positive feedback, the flow rate of water would increase as the tank level increases—most definitely not a desired response.

Feedback occurs at different rates under different conditions. What is slow in one situation may be normal for another. When driving a car, people expect immediate feedback when they turn the steering wheel. But when people come home to a cold house, they don't expect the house to be warm in immediately after they adjust the thermostat. Design teams must build in more than one kind of feedback: short-term immediate, action-related feedback; and longer-term information/situation feedback. Short-term feedback is the immediate response people expect when they click the radio button on a webpage or move a file. They expect the button to activate in synch with their mouse button, not several seconds later. Longer-term feedback is the result of information changes in the situation which result from evolving conditions. These changes follow from a decision, but they will not occur immediately. Depending on the situation, feedback may require updating information on time scales ranging the gamut of seconds to hours to days.

The problem with slow feedback is that people have trouble understanding how the system is responding. In systems with no or slow feedback, people are unable to make mid-course corrections because they don't know the current system's status and don't know if it is responding as they expect.

With slow feedback, poor decisions can have major effects before people even realize a change in course is necessary (Jagacinski, 1977; Wickens & Hollands, 2000). Consider driving a car in which, after pressing the accelerator, there is a 15-second delay before the speed change begins. In similar fashion, changing the water temperature in a shower involves a delay of a few seconds and changing the air temperature in a room has a several-minute delay. Turning a thermostat to 120 degrees will not warm up a room any faster than setting it to 79 degrees, the desired temperature. With room temperature, people expect delays, and will wait several minutes before noticing a faulty furnace is not producing warm air. The need for feedback also shows up on business reports, as a percentage difference between expected and actual values. Poor HII report feedback occurs when a person has to look at two different reports and make manual calculations to see those percentage differences. Looking at two reports imposes cognitive overhead and complexity which could be easily avoided with better design.

A system should be designed to provide *inherent feedback* which couples the natural consequence of the action and the feedback. For example, a pair of scissors gives visual, auditory and haptic feedback during cutting, which is a direct consequence of the cutting action. Software tends to lack this full range of feedback and often seems to have a random sound added late in development. "For electronic products to offer inherent feedback they have to be designed from the ground up with appearance, actions and feedback in mind. Inherent feedback cannot be added as an afterthought" (Djajadiningrat, Overbeeke, & Wensveen, 2002, p. 289).

Quality HII allows people to track the evolving situation. In other words, the information system must provide data so that the HII becomes an essential part of the feedback control. Some of the major reasons high-quality and timely feedback are required are:

- Some choices are risky with unknown outcomes. Feedback allows people to track the situation and know if it is performing as intended.
- Frequently decision outcomes can be both risky and delayed. Not only is the result uncertain, but the final outcome may not occur for a lengthy time interval (Weber & Chapman, 2005). People know what is go-

ing to happen, but must wait for the final result. Although a time delay is necessary, people should be given feedback as soon as possible so they know the situation is moving in the correct direction.

- Part of expert performance is knowing which factors will vary, in what order, and when to intervene. However, human activity in a familiar environment will not be goal-controlled; rather, it will be oriented toward the goal and be controlled by a set of rules that have previously proved successful (Rasmussen, 1986). Good feedback allows people to see that their expectations are correct and that the rules they invoked are moving the situation toward the goal.
- People often get distracted by the lack of predictability in complex situations. They need feedback to stay focused on salient information (Andriole & Adelman, 1995). Improper or confusing feedback can lead people to interact with the wrong data.
- Complex situations often contain unfamiliar or unintended feedback loops (Reason, 1990), which only occur in specific, difficult to predict, situations. When an unexpected feedback loop starts to exert a major effect on a situation, people need to know events are not tracking as expected.
- Feedback proves most beneficial for performance of simple tasks, not complex tasks or tasks that demand high cognitive ability. Feedback works well or for well-practiced tasks, but not novel ones since people lack experience interpreting the feedback in novel situations (Gonzalez, 2005).
- People's anxiety levels increase with poor or inconsistent system response Guynes (1988). Slow or inconsistent feedback can make a system appear non-responsive when it may actually be working fine.

Some sort of feedback is essential since a computer interface itself has no tactile feedback, although haptic devices with tactile feedback are appearing. When pushing a physical button, a person can feel it depress and stop. The typical interface gives some sort of visual feedback that the action has occurred. Examples include the visual depression of a button. Sound can also accompany the action, although many people consider it distracting and undesired in most office environments. Also, Zakay and Hornik (1991) found good feedback can affect people's perception of perceived time and make them willing to tolerate longer delays.

Feedforward

Feedforward is using predictable disturbances or variations of a system to make adjustments or to take action before an actual event happens. A restaurant manager is using feedforward when she schedules extra staff on the nights when big events are scheduled at the convention center two blocks away. She predicts that business will be well above average on those nights and schedules to handle the expected number of customers. In HII, feedforward means communication of the purpose of an action (Djajadiningrat, Overbeeke, & Wensveen, 2002).

Making use of feedforward requires both a solid baseline of how a situation responds and also prior knowledge of how various events can affect the stereotypical event. Having good system models allows the use of feedforward. Using the past and current state, the display can show projections of future conditions. Based on the difference between this predicted condition and the desired condition, people can make adjustments to the situation.

Feedforward in the context of the web means giving people clues about what the results of a link will be before that click is made. Use of descriptive links is one way of providing feedforward for web navigation. Another way is indicating file size next to links for large download files.

Box 5.

> **Feedforward and building temperature**
> The ambient temperature of a building is reduced from 72 degrees F to 55 degrees F at 6 p.m. every night. Starting at 6 pm each night, the temperature in a vat goes down because the ambient temperature of the room is going down. A thermostat on the vat will use feedback to increase the temperature after it has decreased by some value. However, since the temperature will decrease predictably at 6 pm, the design can preemptively begin adding extra heat to the vat at 6 pm so that the temperature never leaves the desired value. By using feedforward control to predict the temperature drop, it can be prevented from occurring.

Box 6.

> **Fitting information needs to the interaction**
> Clinicians seem to work from just a small portion of the traditional paper-based record (Jaspers et al., 2004). Thus, an electronic medical record that provides them with a properly detailed summary, matching that small, needed portion would suffice for their information needs. It would also simplify their interaction since irrelevant information would not interfere with their comprehension. The communication challenge is defining what "properly detailed summary" actually means for each clinician. Each medical specialty and, to a smaller extent, each physician, brings a unique definition of the proper summary. Plus, the "properly detailed summary" changes as the patient recovers.
>
> Issues of fitting the information needs rather simply providing all the information are not unique to health care. It applies to anyone needing information. This model fits most situations where people use a consistent body of information. For instance, with both medical records and business reports, although the actual values change, the report format and content presentation remains static.

People evaluate the potential content before clicking a link, especially on slow systems where a less-than-useful link incurs a significant time delay. Older adults often require more feedforward to reassure them that they are following the proper path to the information they want.

For web design, people get irritated when overloaded servers or networks cause intermittent slow responses. This has a bigger impact than simply forcing people to take more time to complete the task; they will adjust how they search and interact to compensate for the slow response (Payne, Howes, & Reader, 2001). Less information will be looked at and the chance increases they will reach faulty conclusions based on insufficient information increases. In either case, feedback and feedforward must be designed to short-circuit cognitive inertia and to keep people following or examining relevant data, rather than rationalizing all results as fitting with desired outcomes (Marchionini, 1995).

HII AND USABILITY

International Standards Organization (ISO) defines usability as the "effectiveness, efficiency and satisfaction with which a specified set of users can achieve a specified set of tasks in a particular environment." Unfortunately, ISO has left effectiveness, efficiency, and satisfaction undefined and open to interpretation as to what achieving

them means. Quesenbery (2003) operationalized the issues when she defined the usability of a system as how well people can use the system to accomplish their tasks. She describes the 5Es of usability as effective, efficient, engaging, error tolerant, and easy to learn. This section examines the research into user satisfaction and how Quesenbery's factors, along with the ideas of other researchers, feed into satisfaction.

User Satisfaction

Ensuring people like and use any interface requires some level of user satisfaction. The actual level can vary depending on how compelled they are. Obviously, in a corporate environment many people must use the internal software whether they like it or not. But for products where people have a choice, high user satisfaction is a must. In order to survive, web sites must offer high user satisfaction as reflected in both ease of use and usefulness since there are too many other sites with the same information. On the other hand, user satisfaction is a self-reported value which can be highly influenced by many personal factors outside

Figure 3. Factors affecting end-user satisfaction (adapted from Mahmood et al., 2000, p. 758)

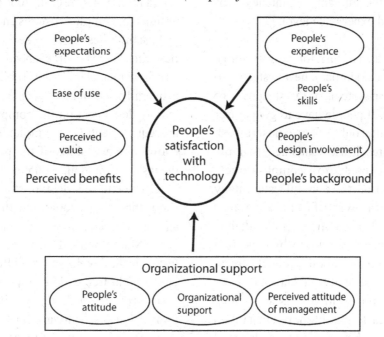

of the system or the HII aspects themselves. Factors such as prior knowledge, having a bad day, and good/bad interaction with the testing people can all influence user satisfaction rankings, but are outside the scope of a design team's work.

In somewhat of a contradiction, user satisfaction is not entirely based on being able to complete a task. Spool (1997) found people who could not complete a product purchase, but were satisfied with a site. Zeng et al. (2004) found similar results when subjects could not locate medical information. Howard (2007) found that students using a handbook for formatting citations used the wrong section (and go the wrong answer), but thought they completed the task properly and gave the design a satisfactory rating. These types of findings show that results of user satisfaction surveys, such as SUS (Brooke, 1996), need to be interpreted with respect to the overall situation in which the testing occurred and balanced against actual performance. Although these surveys provide useful information, the potential exists for high user satisfaction ratings with an unusable system.

Mahmood et al. (2000) looked at the factors which drive user satisfaction. While their research has specifically focused on software development, most information products fit into the model they developed (Figure 3). The two side boxes are the most important from people's points of view: perceived benefits and user background. They must perceive that it will be worth their while to read and interpret the information. Also, they must feel the material is written at a level which fits their needs. Failing to meet any of these criteria reduces user satisfaction. Information, design, and interface must work together to provide an integrated package if HII-dependent products are to deliver a high level of satisfaction. The design should:

- Support the information goals.
- Support finding the needed information.
- Present the information in a manner that is clearly comprehensible.
- Ensure that people trust the information to be accurate and sufficient for their needs.

- Ensure that the interaction matches people's skill and experience level.

User satisfaction, at least for new systems, often depends on how similar a new system is to a previous, familiar system, or the steepness of the learning curve. If people have to give a user satisfaction rating after only a short exposure, both of these factors can result in low satisfaction simply because they will not be able to accomplish much. After their first exposure to Adobe InDesign, many people would give it a low satisfaction rating since it works so differently from Microsoft Word; they suffer from some negative transfer by expecting it to work like Word since both products create documents. In the case of my students, they have probably never been in writing situations which require the additional formatting power that InDesign has over Word. Thus, they can't understand what they gain by performing any extra steps or doing something differently. Low user satisfaction based on first impressions relates to sufficing: people prefer a short-term optimization (get the task done quickly) rather than investment in time and effort for future productivity increases. The problem is that quite often people will define an interaction as "useful" based on their previous experience and what they are familiar with. If they do not know how to accomplish a task with a new system, it is by definition *not* useful, even if the system can accomplish the task much faster/better once it is learned.

Task Complexity and Usability

Focusing on usability of individual components makes it relatively simple to construct quantitative measures. The time to complete a component task, or a total number of clicks, can provide straightforward measures of usability for that component at some level. However, quantitative evaluation of a complex design is suspect since it often privileges one aspect over others without any solid theoretical foundation on which to base the

privileging (Sutcliffe et al., 2006). Instead, product designs for complex systems embrace flexibility; and usability testing must seek to ensure that the flexibility meets people's needs (Shearer, 2010). At a fundamental level, the usability issues connect to overall performance needs and "performance is mainly dependent on the compatibility between the requirements (i.e., complexity) of the task and knowledge and skills of the person performing the task" (Topi et al., 2005, p. 375).

User-centered design studies consistently show that both people and their tasks exert a strong impact on how information systems get used (Marchionini, 1995). The rise of usability testing in the development of information systems has brought tremendous improvements to those systems (Norman, 2002) by shifting design focus away from just software internals and meeting system requirements and more toward HII, ensuring that systems work the way people work. Mirel (2003) contends that although user-centered design methods do work in context, they all assume that a bigger task is a sum of individual components, which leads to a design focus on supporting discrete tasks. She strongly questions the validity of this assumption in complex problem solving. Usability testing focused on people's tasks rather than system tasks highlights the work and the interaction styles that are key to overall usability (Albers, 2010; Nielsen, 1989).

The ideal HII design will differ according to interaction style and task. Designs must be flexible enough to support multiple interactions, and not one-size-fits-all approach. In support of this flexibility, what appear to be nuances in design can make the difference between success and failure (Bates et al., 2003). Two very similar designs which accomplish the same thing may require different interactions or interaction styles which, as a result, turn one of the designs from effective to ineffective HII. For example, the micro-strategies involved in making choices of how to use the mouse to interact with a system can exert a strong force on the overall HII performance (Gray & Boehm-Davis,

Box 7.

Interaction and user satisfaction of software manuals

Although user manuals have improved in recent years, vendor-supplied documentation is still viewed as much poorer than third-party manuals (the ones from a book store).

Low user satisfaction of vendor-supplied software manuals, and user preference for third-party manuals, is frequently noted because vendor manuals privilege completeness over ease of use. The vendor manual explains each feature in detail, but fails to explain how features interrelate, or how people can accomplish real-world tasks. Third-party manuals, on the other hand, concentrate more on putting system features in a real-world context. They give more emphasis to how to use the common features and minimize time spend on rarely used features. In other words, they have content designed to address people's goals and information needs.

2000). Accordingly, design teams must rethink how they test; they must entertain new ideas and employ new methods for developing complex HII systems (Redish, 2007; Scholtz, 2006).

Expectations

A simple method of enhancing user satisfaction—one often lost in requirement definition and design—is simply to meet users' expectations.

For example, people consider response time an important factor in computer applications (Bates et al., 2003). A problem affecting user satisfaction with web applications is the high variability of response times (Nielsen, 1999; Guynes, 1988). Negative user responses are particularly likely when delays exceed people's expectations (Shneiderman, 1998). People have come to expect most computer systems to respond almost instantly. Any delays, especially inconsistent delays, lower their level of satisfaction.

The three click rule (everything on a website must be within three clicks of the home page) has been generally disproved. People will not just give up after three clicks. It is more accurate to say that they will give up when they feel they are not making progress. If they have low expectations of finding the desired information on a website, then they will stop at three clicks. On the other

hand, if they expect the information exists and can be found, they will keep clicking to find it. Issues of information scent and foraging play a major factor (Pirolli, 2007).

Attitude toward an Interface and Usability

The attitude people have toward an interface has a strong influence on both their expectations and their overall perceptions of an interaction. Attitude among a group of people has a strong social component. Interactions and mutual experiences within a group influence group members' attitudes by affirming or contradicting their ideas and thoughts. In many cases, attitude is more influential than the technology in getting people to accept a new information technology (Yang & Yoo, 2004). For example, although a new technology may be better, if it is forced on people without proper training they will rebel against it.

People's attitudes can be captured if usability test have people select words from a list reflecting their view of a system. Product reaction cards allow people to pick relevant words that reflect their experience with the system (Benedeck & Miner, 2002). Barnum and Palmer (2010) have extended this work to complex systems and found that it provides valuable feedback for focusing on the problematical sections of the interface. The cards help capture how people feel about the system's HII. After the interaction, they select cards, from deck of about 100 cards, that reflect how they felt about their experience.

One factor that can improve people's attitude is to have them involved in initial design and development. This gives people a feeling of buy-in with the design and also helps ensure the design will actually meet their needs (Hartwick & Barki, 1994). Guimaraes, Igbaria and Lu (1992) found increased user satisfaction among people who were involved early and helped define their requirements. On the other hand, the satisfaction level depends on how important the end-users view the need for their participation (McKeen & Guimaraes, 1997). End-user involvement is more critical where task and/or system complexity are high (Mahmood et al., 2000). Systems that provide people with information, and don't just work as a data entry point, have a high level of complexity because of the wide range of information they supply. Providing that information in a format which meets people's needs requires input throughout the design process (Albers, 2004).

Ease of Use

Ease of use constantly comes up in connection with web design and with software design in general. However, it's often confused or conflated with two other issues: easy to learn and perceived ease of use, both of which are addressed in sections which follow. As an intuitive definition, ease of use means how easily people can work within the system to find their required information (Quesenbery, 2003). Recording time to find information, or mapping out the path a person took to find the information, can be used to measure ease of use for a simple system. For complex systems, overall performance and error rates make better measures.

Products with excessive features or too many bells & whistles fail because they are harder to use, which impairs their HII and communication ability. Electronic products are falling prey to feature-creep as companies keep adding new features so that they can sell new versions. As a result, many products which were once easy to use are becoming increasingly difficult to use with each new feature adding a layer of complexity. Norman (2002) claims that the usability decreases or complexity increases exponential with the additional of features. It is an interesting contradiction that, while people buy the products with the most features, they rarely use more features than they did on older versions.

Several confounds exist that complicate measuring ease of use.

- People will want to work with a system differently, depending on their own skill level. While a methodical point-and-click hierarchical interface works well for novices or occasional users, experts or people who constantly use the system want faster access. The multiple clicks become time-consuming.

- Familiarity with another system causes negative transfer issues as people try to apply their knowledge of the old system to the new one with less-than-optimal results. Moving to a new system often brings with it complaints of how hard it is to use, even when usability tests show faster completion times. Likewise, systems with closed designs (such as the Apple Mac interface) cause interference which impedes ease of use of the less familiar system.

- Task complexity influences the interaction style which gives best performance. Speier and Morris (2003) found that a text-based query interface gave better decision-making performance when task complexity was low, while a visual query interface gave better decision-making performance when task complexity was high.

- Design workflow has to be fitted to actual workflow. Task analysis and system design assume tasks are accomplished in a linear manner, but people actually interweave tasks or want to be able to stop one task to accomplish another (Visser & Morals, 1991; Cypher, 1986). Failing to match people's expectations or needs results in lowering how easy a product is to use.

- Some people are unable to accomplish a task, but still say the system is easy to use (Spool, 1997). One potential explanation for these findings is that people's information needs are even harder to address through other methods, such as obtaining medical information by talking to clinicians, that they will struggle with the system as the lesser evil (Zeng et al., 2004). Or because of lack of feedback, they don't know the task was completed improperly.

Easy to use should not be confused with easy to learn. Many products are rather hard to learn, but easy to use. Commercial jet cockpits are easy to use, but difficult to learn. Boeing and Airbus spend millions of dollars making them easy to use. Once a pilot learns how to fly the plane, the design supports fast and efficient operation. Likewise, some software has a steep learning curve,

but provides power and efficient operation once it is learned.

Easy to Learn

Easy to learn defines how easy a system supports novice or infrequent users learning how to accomplish their tasks. It differs from ease of use because it only really applies to new or infrequent users. Once people understand how to use a system, an easy to learn system may become hard to use because it still forces all work to be done in a methodical manner. If they use an application

Box 8.

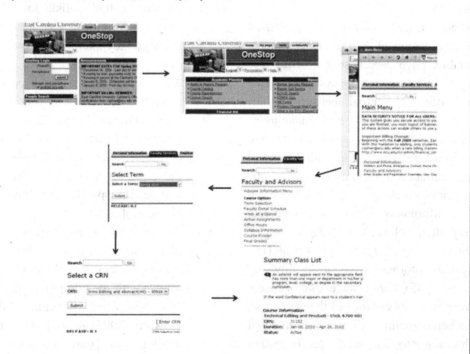

Easy to learn versus easy to use
The illustration below shows the steps needed for me to get a class roster. Each arrow involves at least a click to move to a new screen and may include interacting with dropdown lists. The path is very methodical and can be done with minimal training. Basically, the only training needed is knowing how to log on to the system and which option to select on the initial screen. However, if I worked in the registrar's office and had to produce class rosters many times a day, this type of interaction would become excruciatingly painful. It would soon seem very slow and clunky because it is not easy to use, but merely easy to learn.

Obtaining a class roster. Seven procedural steps are required to get a class roster. It is easy to learn and minimizes errors, but in a high-usage situation, it would prove hard to use because it is slow and causes a high frustration factor with need to constantly repeat the seven steps.

constantly, easy to learn may be less important in comparison to the need for it to be highly effective and efficient.

Perceived Ease of Use and Usefulness

Perceived ease of use refers to "the degree to which a person believes that using a particular system would be free of effort." Perceived usefulness is defined as "the degree to which a person believes that using a particular system would enhance his or her job performance" (Yang & Yoo, 2004, p. 19). Davis, Bagozzi, and Warshaw (1989) concluded that the main predictors of whether people will want to use an information system are their beliefs about the system: perceived usefulness and perceived ease of use. Likewise, Van Schaik (1999) concluded that perceived usefulness appeared to be a more important factor in the model than perceived ease of use; people will use a difficult system if they believe they will obtain what they need.

Unlike ease of use, which can be quantified and measured, perceived ease of use is a qualitative variable. Each person sees it differently and each person's value for the system design's ease of use differs. The actual, measured values are inconsequential to them. People make judgments about ease of use and usefulness that are inferential in nature. These judgments are based on the total amount of information accessed immediately prior to making the judgment, not on whether the information is correct or incorrect (which they often lack the knowledge to judge). In other words, people judge the quantity and not the quality of the information (Dunlosky, Rawson, & Middleton, 2005). For instance, Internet users do not assess the quality of the health information they find when searching online, but assume that a site with lots of information is better (Bernstam et al., 2005). Thus, sites with large quantities of poor-quality information may have a high perceived usefulness.

Multiple studies have discovered highly contradictory findings for perceived ease of use versus actually accomplished goals.

- Screen load times, combined with how quickly people can interact (stop waiting and do something), influence the perceived load time. If they can interact with a system quickly then it is perceived as faster, even if overall load time is longer. Perfetti and Landesman (2001) report little correlation between actual and perceived download time for a website. They did, however, find a strong correlation between perceived download time and successful task completion.
- Several studies have found that people are highly satisfied with the Internet as a health-information resource. However, other studies (Zeng et al., 2004) report that consumers often are unsuccessful in searching for health information. Although unable to find satisfactory information when performing a specific query, people reported they liked the Internet as a health-information source.
- Spool (1997) has asked people to buy products on various ecommerce sites. They were unable to complete the transaction either because of not finding the item or because they were unable to complete the checkout procedure. Yet, afterwards, people still gave the site a favorable rating for ease of use.
- A physician order entry was viewed by physicians as an efficient way to write prescriptions, but it took them significantly longer with the computer than with paper (Lee et al., 1996; Shu et al., 2001).
- Howard (2007) looked at using different writing style guides for properly formatting citations. He found that students had difficulty successfully completing the task, and preferred the style guide which gave

them the lowest completion rate. People reported high levels of satisfaction with the product and believed they had successfully completed tasks which they judged as easy when, in reality, they exhibited failure rates as high as 100%.

COMPUTER DISPLAY INFLUENCES ON INTERACTING WITH INFORMATION

The type, size, and resolution of a computer display exert a strong influence on how people interact with information. Design teams usually have no ability to control this aspect, but must design to handle a broad range of displays.

Menu Interaction

Menu selection has become the expected method of interacting with software, with the exception of the ribbon Microsoft introduced in Office 2010. The use of a mouse quickly moved menu-based interaction to the expected norm. At the same time, a large body of research quickly developed dealing with either trying innovative menu design or grappling with the issue of depth versus breadth. The innovative menu design seemed never to move beyond the individual conference and journal papers which presented them, and so they will not be discussed further.

The menu depth versus breadth issue concerns whether to have only a few menu items with many options on each or many menu items with few options on each. Related studies explored the question of how many levels of submenus people could effectively interact with. Overall, the research found a performance and preference advantage for shallow, broad menus (Kiger, 1984). When people search menus, they use both systematic top-to-bottom and random visual search strategies. They also seem to be able to mentally process menu items in parallel as long as

the spacing puts the items within the eye's fovea area (Hornof & Kieras, 1997). Fastest selection times occurred when three menu items could be focused on at once.

Other research looked at how to group menu items. A study by McDonald, Dayton, and McDonald (1988) looked at a multiple selection menu (in their case it simulated fast food ordering) based on either item similarity (like items together) or frequency (most common items together). The results showed that the frequency layout gave the fastest times and most accurate interaction.

Research in menu search mostly applies directly to web information architecture interaction since that entails a specialized menu structure. A medium structure that is neither broad/shallow nor narrow/deep gives the best search results. Also, three link depths give many more problems than do two levels, regardless of breadth (Larson & Czerwinski, 1998). In other words, link pages leading to link pages leading to link pages should be avoided in a design.

Screen Size/Resolution

The size of the display and size of the window have significant effects on how people approach information. With the current shift to Internet access via small, cell phone-based displays, design teams must plan for small screens. But it is more than just a small screen versus desktop issue. Small screens are coming in relatively few size variations, while desktop units offer a wide range of monitor sizes and resolutions. Design teams need to consider that entire range. And many business users are starting to have 2 or more monitors, which also affects how they view and interact with information.

Watters, Duffy & Duffy (2003) compared table search on PDA and larger tablet screens. For both the simple and complex tasks, and for both screen sizes, using some of the limited screen space for context information improves efficiency and effectiveness. The search function, however, improves efficiency for the complex task but reduces effectiveness. The inclusion of the search function, somewhat counter-intuitively, had a negative impact on the correctness of answers in search tasks. It was concluded that the search box takes up too much of the already minimal screen real estate. Kim & Albers (2003) found that people could handle a table two screens wide on a PDA with the need for a horizontal scroll, but that browsing times increased significantly when the table was three screens wide.

Halvey, Keane, and Smyth (2006) looked at how people surf websites with mobile interfaces such as cell phones and found that the resulting patterns (depth of links followed, etc.) closely match earlier findings on desktop systems (Huberman, Pirolli, Pitkow & Lukose, 1998), leading them to conclude that people tend to surf and browse in essentially the same way regardless of interaction device. Although at one level this conclusion sounds intuitive, many people have jumped to an unsupported claim that small-screen interaction is fundamentally different, mostly because it is smaller. In general, while the relative importance of the factors to a designer do differ, people's goals are essentially the same; it is the interaction which changes. With the technical aspects of small display changing so rapidly, this book is ignoring a more detailed analysis of this area, since it will be probably be outdated before it reaches print.

Monitor Resolution versus Size

The resolution of a monitor is the size of the entire screen expressed in pixels. The resolution of a monitor, measured in pixels, is independent of the monitor size, although this distinction is often ignored in design decisions and not understood by non-technical users. Two monitors, one 15-inch and other 24-inch, will show the same image if both are set at the same resolution, such as 1280 x 800 (Figure 4). Of course, images on the 24-inch monitor will be larger. On the 24-inch monitor,

they may be large enough that size becomes distracting. (Think of a screen with huge icons.) Or if the resolution is set high, then the images on the 15 inch monitor will be too small. The discussion on Fitts' law in this chapter describes the problem with clicking on targets which are too small, as well as reading difficulties because of tiny fonts.

Many web-design guidelines say to always design for a 800x600 or 1024x760 screen. Since the resolution of available monitors keeps continually increasing, the design guideline numbers also keep slowly increasing. A primary reason for the guideline is to ensure that the web page will display properly on the majority of monitors. The problem with the guideline is that it assumes the browser is maximized to fill the entire monitor. (Personally, I almost never use maximized windows.) In addition, although monitor resolution is adjustable, many people do not understand how to adjust their monitor's resolution, so it remains at the initial default setting. Or, for visual accessibility reasons, some people have their monitor set for very low resolution.

Rather than monitor size, designs should consider viewports, which is the actual window size on the screen. One set of unpublished data (McCrory, 2006) on viewport size for visitors to a website for government and non-profit users reveals that:

- 95% of visitors had viewports set wider than 732 pixels.
- 75% of visitors had viewports set wider than 778 pixels.
- 50% of visitors had viewports set wider than 991 pixels.
- 95% of visitors had viewports set taller than 380 pixels.
- 75% of visitors had viewports set taller than 433 pixels.
- 50% of visitors had viewports set taller than 571 pixels.

Figure 4. Monitor images at different resolutions. The browser window was not changed; only the monitor resolution was changed. Regardless of monitor size, a monitor set for the indicated resolution will show the same image.

800x600

1024x786

1280x800

McCrory estimates that about half of the people visiting his web site have a maximized browser. But with design that works to keep salient information visible without horizontal scrolling, designs that will accommodate 95% of the users requires designing for a 730x380 pixel window. If a webpage is designed to take advantage of the entire 1024 pixel width, then people not using a maximized window, or people with lower-resolution monitors, risk having horizontal scroll issues—something that web-design guidelines consistently consider as very bad. On the other hand, the prevalence in CSS-based designs rather than table-based designs has helped to reduce the horizontal scroll issues with the movement toward fluid design.

Paper versus Screen Resolution

Paper is printed at a minimum resolution of over 300 dots per inch and professional typesetting exceeds 4800 dots per inch. On the other hand, most monitors show about 96 dots per inch, with older monitors showing only 72 dots per inch. This difference in image quality is often considered a primary factor in differences noted in reading speeds (Gould et al., 1987). In addition, CRT monitors have an electron beam which scans the entire screen 60+ times per second. This can result in a potentially noticeable flicker to the image, and eye fatigue. LCD monitors present images using a different display method and have no flicker.

Early research (Dillon, 1992) showed that people read about 25% slower from a CRT monitor than from paper. (Reading is discussed in more detail in chapter 11: *How people read*.) This 25% factor is constantly quoted in the web-design literature. Unfortunately, this research was almost all done with old-style, monochrome monitors, which makes the findings questionable with respect to a modern GUI interface and LCD monitor. Other research with high-resolution monitors (specially designed for 300 dpi) showed that people can read as fast on a monitor as on paper (Nielsen, 1998).

In addition, the computer's type rendering can exert a substantial difference on reading speed because of improved image quality. For instance, Dillon, Kleinman, Choi, and Bias (2006) found that Microsoft's Clear Type resulted in substantially faster reading times (5.1%), but no change in comprehension. Too often the focus of computer-screen reading gets shifted to easy-to-measure factors, such as reading speed, without considering the more relevant but harder to measure factors, such as information comprehension. Design teams must focus on comprehension to maximize efficient HII.

Although there are claims that a modern monitor with a GUI interface (at 96 dpi) gives essentially the same reading speed as paper, other research continues to find slower reading speeds (Zaphiris & Kurniawan, 2001). Either way, with the improving monitor image quality, reading speed differences between paper and online should soon be minimal.

Paper versus Screen Size

A more significant problem than the slower reading speed is the lower amount of information which can be displayed on a screen versus what can be displayed on paper (Figure 5). With paper, the reader can see more of the information at once and can easily hold pages side-by-side (the equivalent of about 3-4 screens of information). With a standard monitor, people see less than half a printed page. For general reading, this does not pose a problem, but it does pose a problem if they

need to compare information. Since non-visible information mentally receives a lower salience and priority than visible information, the smaller amount of information being presented can negatively impact decision making.

Using a 2 column PDF online strongly reveals the differences between HII of paper and online. The 2 column layout provides a good line length for 10 pt fonts. However, when displayed online, people have to engage in too much interface manipulation (scrolling up and down and horizontally) when trying to read the text.

A longstanding web myth is that people don't scroll; however, this comes from early web days when people were accustomed to information presented via a paged interface with no scrolling. That mental model has changed. Spool (1998) found that people said one thing, "I don't scroll," but that they actually behaved quite differently. They do scroll if they find the content relevant and compelling. Nielsen's (2010) research found that people spend most of their time above the fold. While agreeing with Spool about scrolling, he frames the issue in terms of people having limited attention spans, and only scrolling if they think it is worthwhile and that they will find what they are looking for.

Personalization and Customization

Personalization and customization of a system interface are often implemented as part of a design.

Personalization: Settings which are dynamically set by the computer in response to user actions but are not directly set or chosen by the user.

Customization: Unique settings which are set by people to match their desired display appearance or system response to input.

While these seem like a good idea, in practice they have proved less than useful. They are often criticized as being surface-level changes (such as

Figure 5. Comparison of screen versus paper. The boxed section of text on the paper is the amount displayed on the computer monitor. In this example, the monitor was set at 1024x768. With lower settings, even less of the page would display.

How people approach   12/3/2008   page 30

CRT monitors have an electron beam which scanned the entire screen 60+ times per second. This resulted in a potentially noticeable flicker to the image and eye fatigue. Flat screen LCD monitors present their image using different methods and have no flicker.

Paper versus screen size

A more significant problem that the slower reading speed because of screen resolution is the lower amount of information which can be displayed on a screen versus what can be displayed on paper (figure xx). With paper, the reader can see more of the information at once and can easily hold pages side by side (the equivalent of about 3-4 screens of information). With a standard monitor, a person sees less than half a printed page. For general reading, this does not pose a problem, but if is does pose a problem if the person needs to compare information. Since not visible information mentally receives a lower salience (xxx) and priority than the visible information, the smaller amount of information being presented can negatively impact decision making.

FIGURE xx. Comparison of screen versus paper. The boxed section of text on the paper is the amount displayed on the computer monitor.

Using a 2 column PDF online strongly reveals the differences between HII of paper and online. The 2 column layout provides a good line length for 10 points fonts. However, when displayed online, the person has to engage in too much interface manipulation (scrolling up and down and horizontal) when trying to read the text.

Personalization and customization

Personalization and customization of a system interface are often implemented as part a design.

Personalization   A set of settings which are dynamically set by the computer based on user actions but are not directly set or chosen by the user.

Customization   A set of unique setting which are set by the user to match their desired appearance or system response.

While they seem like a good idea, in practice they have proved less than useful. Also, they are often criticized as being surface level changes (such as colors, background images, or menu ordering) rather than features directly related to the applications function (xxx).

Consider personalized menus. They seek to personalize the person's system based on what they do regularly and hide the options they rarely perform. Possible problems:

- People expect to find menu options in the same place each time. If they unexpectedly move, they get confused.
- People have trouble finding or learning more features because, since they are hidden, the person doesn't know they exist to look for them.

Customization seems to overcome the problems of personalization since a person must make the changes themselves. However, it turns out very few people actually use any customization features (xxx).

colors, background images, or menu ordering) rather than features directly related to system functionality.

Both personalization and customization change either the appearance or apparent functionality of a system. This proves confusing to many people who may be capable of doing the basics on a computer but who are not comfortable enough with the system to figure everything out when something is different. In addition, people are under time pressure or stress, they will revert to what they know. Having to work with a differently arranged interface increases stress levels and associated error rates.

Consider personalized menus. They seek to personalize a person's system based on tasks performed regularly, and to hide options that are rarely performed. Possible problems:

- People expect to find menu options in the same place each time. If those options unexpectedly move, they get confused.
- People have trouble finding or learning more features because, since they are hidden, they don't know they exist or how to look for them.

Customization seems to overcome the problems of personalization since people must make the changes themselves. However, it turns out that very few people actually use any customization features. People are rarely willing to customize an interface, or may not know how to, even if it might lead to large productivity gains. A potential design approach in this case is to apply machine learning techniques that make the customizations for people (Karger & Quan, 2004).

Box 9.

Problem with personalized menus
Some early Windows software allowed people to customize the entire menu. So, if people didn't like File at the beginning of the menu list, they could move it to wherever they desired. At first, programmers loved the flexibility, but they soon found it to be more trouble than it was worth. One problem was that it made it impossible them to switch to a different computer without getting confused. Each person had learned a menu structure which was different causing a serious slowdown in their interactions on any computer other than their own. Another issue is that this provided minimal customization: it simply reordered the menu structure, but did not provide any strong support for more efficient interaction (McGovern, 2006b).

MOTOR CONTROL

Interaction with a computer typically occurs via a mouse or keyboard. The speed and effectiveness of these interactions depend on how rapidly and accurately people can control the device. For a discussion of motor behaviors and using them to create models for use in HCI, see MacKenzie (2003).

This section highlights some of major research into device interactions with a computer as they relate to HII design considerations.

Fitts' Law

Fitts' law (1954) provides a model of human movement, which predicts the time required to rapidly move from a starting position (ballistic movement) to a final target area (non-ballistic movement), as a function of the distance traveled and target size. Fitts' law is one of the most lawful and robust relations in HCI and human-information interaction research, linking the time required to complete a pointing movement to the difficulty of the task as determined by the precision required. With the introduction of graphical interfaces, Fitts' law has proven to be useful in designing basic layout and understanding people's response times during usability tests.

The equation which describes Fitts' law is:

- $M_T = a + b \log_2 (D/W)$
- M_T is movement time
- a is an empirically determined constant
- b is an empirically determined constant
- D is distance from starting point to the center of the target
- W is the width of the target along the direction of motion

The equation states that a smaller target takes longer than a bigger target to select. While an obvious sounding finding, it provides an empirical basis for calculating the effects of reducing button size. When screen real estate is at a premium, buttons often must be made small. Fitts' law allows a calculation of the extra time required to click on smaller buttons versus larger ones, thus allowing a clearer decision about how small the buttons can realistically be and still meet design objectives.

Design techniques such as using a color picker that requires people to click on a tiny square to select a color need to consider Fitts' law. The smaller the squares, the longer people require to select each one (and obviously, with close-set squares, the chance of a mis-click increases). This needs to be balanced against the larger size of the palette if bigger squares are used. The same issue arises when building a toolbar. Some applications support both large and small toolbar icons which lets people make the choice of how much screen real estate to devote to the toolbar. Of course, the audience groups that most need the larger icons are also the ones with the smallest percentage of doing any interface customization.

Although Fitts' law gives a good estimate of how quickly a target can be selected, the actual time still varies among people. While different people will show the same relative response to changing target sizes, the absolute time will vary. It also will vary based on task difficulty since "movement time is (but) an emergent property of the underlying kinematics, and the kinematics patterns change in a very systematic fashion with task difficulty" (Bootsmaa, Fernandeza, & Mottet, 2004, p. 820).

Fitts' law has an age-related element. As people age, they both move a mouse more slowly and with less accuracy, especially for distant targets (Chaparro et al., 1999; Walker, Millians, & Worden, 1996). When applying the curves of Fitts' law to different age groups, the curve is shifted for younger audiences. In other words, if the goal is for a target to be clicked within x seconds, the target must be larger for older adults or children than for young or middle age adults. In mathematical terms, the a and b parameters have changed in value.

Box 10.

Size of the buttons at the edge of a screen

Placement of buttons along the edge of a screen helps to reveal the deeper intricateness that Fitts' law can expose in design decisions. The edge of a screen either stops the cursor or it wraps to appear on the opposite side. In both Windows and Mac operating systems, it stops forming an impenetrable edge. This gives the edge of the screen an infinite depth since a mouse cursor can hit it at any speed and will stop on the target. Walker and Smelcer (1990) found that menus could be selected faster if they were placed against the edge of the screen. Jones, Farris, and Johnson (2005) found that people would use this impenetrable edge to their advantage once they were aware of it, but would rarely discover it on their own.

Unfortunately for PC design, what occupies this edge space is the window border rather than a useful screen element. The Mac tool bar on the top of the screen, on the other hand, does extend to the edge and gives menu selection area an infinite height. As a specific example, in Windows XP and Vista, the Start button is clickable from the far-most corner even though the pixels in that corner are visually not inside the button area. However, the clock is not clickable at the screen border. The mouse cursor can be tossed to the lower left corner and clicked to select the Start button, which essentially eliminates the non-ballistic movement portion of the mouse motion and greatly decreases selection time. However, the same action will not open the clock in the lower right corner.

Young children have less mouse control. Fitts' law only models their actions until they are close to the target and then their lack of fine motor control makes it harder for them to position the cursor and click. They tend to overshoot and move the cursor across the target multiple times (Hourcade et al., 2004).

Decreasing the target size has a detrimental effect on the efficiency of both the motor and cognitive processes involved in the task, especially for the elderly (Fezzani et al, 2010). Besides the slowdown in time to click the target, the shift in concentration from the main task to controlling the mouse impairs performance.

Tasks which can be defined as input via a single finger or stylus (including mouse pointer) conform to Fitts' law. On the other hand, Fitts' law is not an appropriate model for predicting complex tasks using either both hands or multiple fingers of one hand, such as calculating typing speed, since these tasks involve parallel and/or

Figure 6. The time to search through and find an item on the Select menu is consistently shorter than for the Edit menu.

 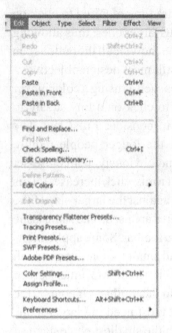

overlapping movements by both hands. Likewise, for multi-touch cell phones, Fitts' law may be of limited use. This limitation is not overly constricting for a webpage design team since most of the interaction on a web page is by a mouse, which fits the requirement for input by a single action. Design changes required to make content accessible by other devices may have to consider the consequences (or non-applicability) of Fitts's law.

Hick-Hyman Law

The Hick-Hyman law for choice reaction time (Hick, 1952; Hyman, 1953) gives an equation for predicting the reaction time for people to make a choice between several options. It shows a logarithmic increase with the number of items, so doubling the number of items would increase average response time by four (Figure 6). The Hick-Hyman law helps explain why it takes a person longer to make a selection from a longer list than a shorter one. Obviously, people will

take longer to read the entire list of choices, but those choices must also be mentally compared so that the selection will be the proper one. More choices impose a higher cognitive load on making that comparison. An interesting, but not surprising, outcome of Hyman's research was that he found stimuli which conveyed little information produced faster reaction times than unexpected or novel stimuli. From an HII perspective, this can be seen when people have an interaction with multiple dialog boxes. They will be rapidly clicking on each one until a dialog poses a question that is unexpected. Depending on how automatic their responses have become through repeated practice, they may even click on the dialog box before fully comprehending the novel situation.

Given a set of n stimuli, associated one-for-one with n responses, the time to react (RT) to the onset of a stimulus and to make the appropriate response is given by:

- $RT = a + b \log_2(n)$

- **RT** is the reaction time
- **n** is the number of choices
- **a** and **b** are empirically determined constants. **a** comes from factors that are outside the choice itself, such as environmental constraints. **b** comes from factors inherent in the design of the choices, such as font and spacing.

One aspect of this equation is that reaction time increases by a constant amount each time the number of choices doubles.

The Hick-Hyman equation assumes that people know which selection to make and is searching a random selection. An example would be when a person uses a menu from a software application (Landauer & Nachbar, 1985). They know which pull down menu contains the desired selection, but do not know where it is located on the list of items. When searching menus, people seem to be able to process multiple items in parallel; a study found fastest selection times when three menu items could fit at once into the fovea area of the eye (Hornof & Kieras, 1997). However, the law only applies when people know the sequencing of the items (such as alphabetical). In a random list, they must perform a linear search starting at the top, so the Hick-Hyman law will not apply.

Making it easier for people to make a choice leads to a faster overall time; however, a consistent design has a strong effect on how quickly people can respond. If they have to make several consecutive choices, the designs for each choice need to be similar and should be describable with a simple rule (Payne, 1995). (The design requirement cannot say "identical" because the choices themselves might be different.) Having different designs will result in a slower response to the second choice than if it was displayed alone. Designs for simulation controls and dialog boxes often show this problem. It seems obvious how to best design a single control, but the design is not consistent with the rest of the system. Many designers also say that a strict adherence to con-

sistency is bad, since that consideration begins to trump other design issues. The Hick-Hyman law's consistent design rule would seem to tell us that degree of consistency should depend on how close together the actions are. Controls which will frequently be used together must be consistent, while those which are never used together can violate consistency if this results in better performance or a more optimized presentation (Duncan, 1984).

Right and Left Handedness

People are not only two-handed, they use their hands differently, with the dominate hand receiving more resources and having different control ability (Guiard, 1987). The rise of multi-touch interfaces which support two-hand operation brings the issues of different hand operations back into consideration for some HII designs.

Studies of how people perform two-hand tasks has found that most tasks are asymmetric; each hand performs distinctly different tasks. For example:

- The non-preferred hand leads and sets a frame of reference in which the preferred hand works (Guiard, 1987).
- Without being instructed, if the system supports it, people will change to a two-handed interaction style (Buxton & Myers, 1986).
- Peters (1981) showed that when independent, asymmetric tasks are assigned to each hand, the dominant hand had more cognitive resources devoted to it.
- Balakrishnan and Hinckley (2002) showed that for right-handed people, the left hand has an 8% higher error rate (although not statistically significant) than the right hand when dealing with two-handed symmetric tracking tasks.
- Buxton and Myers (1986) found in a zooming and position task on a CAD system that people shifted to a two-hand strat-

Figure 7. Mouse cursor overshoot for a right-handed person. The cursor traveled too far and has to back-track to click on the gray target. For an undershoot, the cursor would pause before reaching the target.

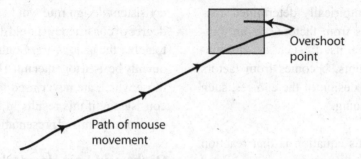

egy, which was faster than just using their dominate hand.

A keyboard has a strong right-side bias, favoring right-handed people. Interestingly, this design proves somewhat problematical to right-handers when the mouse is added. Most right-handers manipulate the mouse with the right hand, overloading it. To keep a hand on the mouse, many power-key sequences are performed with the left hand, which over-stretches to reach keys typically typed by the right hand while still pressing the CTRL or ALT keys (MacKenzie, 2003).

Mouse Movement

A mouse is the standard interaction device for web information on desktop computers. Using the touchpad on a laptop, the person's finger essentially substitutes for a mouse. Although a wide variety of other pointing devices exist (notably trackballs and pens) they tend to be used in either niche applications or because of various physical disabilities. Card et al. (1978) empirically established the superiority of the mouse over a joystick and it still continues to be the easiest pointing device to use (Epps, 1986).

The type of movements for any pointing device can be described as ballistic and non-ballistic (Phillips, Meehan, & Triggs, 2003).

Ballistic: Ballistic movements describe the large-scale movements of a mouse cursor across the screen. People are only focused on getting the cursor in the general area of the target.

Non-ballistic: Non-ballistic movements are the feedback-controlled movements as people move the mouse cursor from the end of the ballistic movement phase to the final target point.

The ballistic movement quickly moves the mouse pointer to the general area of interest. However, during the non-ballistic phase, cursor positioning is inefficient requiring many small adjustments (Phillips, Meehan, & Triggs, 2003). People make a series of increasingly smaller adjustments to the cursor location as the target is approached and accounts for an undershoot or overshoot following each movement. Murata (1999) found that the distribution of horizontal and vertical coordinates of response points fits a normal distribution centered on the target.

Fitts' law comes into play with defining how long the non-ballistic phase lasts since, in general, the ballistic phase is a small part of the total time. On the other hand, the actual mouse movement only occurs after the person has made a choice; people decide what they are going to click on before they move the mouse (Ojakaar, 2001). In usability tests, tracking the time between options being presented and the start of cursor movement can help to create designs which minimize the response time. It can also help to emphasize the choice aspects of the situation, rather than confounding target selection with the movement required.

While moving the mouse, in general, right-handed people overshoot when moving to the right and undershoot when moving to the left (Figure 7). Also, for right-handed people, rightward movements were slower and less accurate (Phillips, Meehan, & Triggs, 2003). There has been minimal research on left-handed people, but the expectation is that overshoot and undershoot will be reversed (Murata, 1999).

People judge distance between objects based on their visual center of mass. For mouse cursers, this leads to over or underestimates when moving because the cursor shape affects the selection ability with cursors pointing in the direction of movement overshooting the target. Essentially, people are trying to align the center of mass of the mouse arrow with the center of mass of the target. Thus, although the choice of cursor design has become very standard, the slightly left facing arrow used in a browser can contribute to positioning problems. Arrowhead cursors incompatible with direction of motion led to slower cursor movements and less efficient cursor trajectories (Phillips, Meehan, & Triggs, 2003).

People tend to move the mouse to where their eyes are located on a screen. There are strong correlations between eye gaze and mouse cursor position (Chen, Anderson, & Sohn, 2001). Also, as people read past the top part of a page of search results, the mouse may be used to help process the contents by either following the eye or by marking a specific result for later review (Rodden et al., 2008). These findings can be exploited in usability testing when eye tracking is not available.

Speed-Accuracy Trade Off

In many interface interactions, people want to complete the sequence as quickly as possible. A strong correlation exists between the speed of

performance and the number of errors, which slows overall time since errors must be corrected. This is called the speed-accuracy trade-off. Or worse, an error may not be noticed until later, when correction may be complicated by the events which occurred between the time of the error and the time it was noticed.

It seems that the processing power of the human mind is the fundamental limit, not speed of interaction; people can click faster than they can decide what to click on. When given sequences of choices, people respond fastest to a smaller number of more difficult choices than to a longer sequence of easier choices (Wickens & Hollands, 2000). A wizard seems to violate this research, but then a wizard is designed to lead people through a task for which they are unfamiliar and which rarely has a significant speed element. Since design considerations for efficient and effective interfaces are a trade-off dependent on audience, the fundamental design question becomes one of easy to learn versus easy to use.

Most people, if allowed to set their own pace, will soon work at a level of interaction which achieves a maximum performance: fastest speed while minimizing errors (Rabbitt, 1989; Seibel, 1972). In most informational computer work, people rarely have forced timed operations, except in games. The errors which occur at the higher levels of Tetris are an example of speed-accuracy trade-off, shifting toward speed and losing accuracy. On the other hand, if people have to operate an interface quickly, such as in emergency response or other real-time interactions, they will be under pressure to work faster than their optimal rate and will show increased error rates. For example, people in call centers or data entry tasks have production levels which they must be meet. The initial design considerations for these types of systems need to allow for errors caused by speed/time pressure. Likewise, usability tests for systems which will be used under time pressure need to include tests which require people to operate as fast as possible.

Box 11.

Scrolling a text window
When mouse-based windowing systems first appeared, people had to move the mouse to the small slider on the right side of the window to scroll the text. By Fitts' law, the small box is relatively difficult to move the mouse curser onto. It also splits their attention by shifting it from comprehending the text to finding and manipulating the scroll slider.

The introduction of the scroll wheel on a mouse transformed this task. It removed the need to shift attention or to move the mouse. Instead, minimal break in text reading is required to scroll the text.

Reaction Times

There has been extensive human factors research into how quickly people can respond to stimuli. While highly useful to human factors and ergonomic design of equipment and control rooms, much of it is only minimally applicable directly to HII because of the experimental design or the underlying purpose. The lack of applicability to HII stems from the fact that there are few situations which require rapid response to a single stimulus, especially in situations where people are interacting with information on a web page. Speed of single step interaction is rarely a design factor. Game design would be one instance where such studies are applicable, but game design is outside the scope of most communication situations. On the other hand, having an understanding of reaction times can help design teams avoid designs which violate basic principles.

People's reaction time varies depending on the number of choices required to perform the desired action. In general, it is divided into two different types.

Simple Reaction Time: There is no uncertainty on the action based on the stimulus. A simple example is that a sprinter starts running when the gun goes off. There is no other option and the sprinter can practice to minimize the reaction time. In a simple situation, reaction time could be measured with an experimental protocol of "push this button

when a light blinks," or "push the button below whichever of these four lights go out." Minimum response time for visual stimuli is roughly 130–170 milliseconds and for auditory stimuli, 30–50 milliseconds (Wickens & Hollands, 2000).

Choice Reaction Time: There is uncertainty on which of several different actions need to be performed. An action is required but, depending on the situation, only one is correct. An example is steering while suddenly applying the brakes in a car because the car in front has stopped. The options are to go straight, swerve right or left. Based on how the position of the stopped car and any surrounding cars, the proper direction to steer varies. Another example would be have four buttons and press A for a red light, B for a green light, C for a purple light, and D for a yellow light.

In web design or HII, this could correspond to moving through a sequence of dialog boxes or menu options, especially where the selected options change with the current situation. (As opposed to a poorly designed interaction which requires a sequence of identical moves which people can perform without considering any of the choices.)

Many control situations involve reacting to stimuli and immediately making changes. Experiments studying this type of control typically have people using a mouse or joystick to track an object moving around the screen. For instance, using a joy stick to control flow through a pipe. First-person shooter games are one example of complex control as the player moves through the field and must respond to monsters, etc.

Reaction time research can be invaluable when calculating the best times for complex sequences of actions which involve interactions between people and the computer. There is a minimum time in which people can complete a set of actions based on the time they need to respond to any prompts or dialog boxes and to actually perform the action. Some specific methods of performing this analysis are discussed with the Keystroke-Level Model (KLM) and Goal-Operators-Methods- Selection rules (GOMS) (Card, Moran, & Newell,1983) models. Reaction time research can give a clear estimate of the motor-mechanical aspects of the task sequence (seeing the prompt appear and mentally processing it, moving the mouse, typing information, etc.), leaving as the main uncertainty the cognitive processing needed to decide about the next action.

A significant factor in reaction time is the tool used for performing the selection. In terms of the Hick-Hyman equation, the "a" parameter will be varied. A mouse or other pointing device is typically faster than tabs or cursor keys, although the use of shortcut keys is faster for single actions. On the other hand, shortcut key speed depends on people having learned the shortcut key to automaticity. Other pointing devices such as track balls or touch pads, will have their own reaction times.

Most real-world reaction times, including those required for interaction with information, fall under the choice reaction times. Even a confirmation dialog box typically gives two choices of "ok" and "cancel." Training provides one of the best ways to minimize people's reaction time. They are given practice in multiple situations and learn how to respond in each. A quality design with any consistency will be easier to learn and will produce the fastest reaction times. However, training will never be able to overcome poor design. Performance and reaction times will be slower on inconsistent designs regardless of the amount of training, especially if people are under stress. Problem designs cannot be fixed by calling them training issues.

Reaction time research can also help to define the types of hand-eye actions which are easier for people to perform and those which can impede an action. In like manner, reaction time research helps to provide a basis for design decisions for physically challenged users, who will have (often substantially) different reaction times from non-physically challenged users.

Automaticity

Automaticity is the ability to complete tasks without conscious thought given to the step-by-step process. The value of automaticity is that it reduces the load on working memory by up to 90% (Schneider & Chein, 2003) and allows for higher-order processing of information.

When the brain recognizes tasks, it processes the information and applies the correct rules to complete the action. This action might be either a physical action (such as throwing as baseball in Figure 8) or cognitive processing (looking at a set of indicators and knowing system status) or a combination. Because people learn to drive to the point of automaticity, they can drive, talk, and listen to the radio all at the same time, even in heavy traffic. On the other hand, when they drive in an unfamiliar city in heavy traffic while looking for an addresses, most of the automaticity has been removed (except the very basic car operation itself).

The value of automaticity can be seen in the fast reaction times of people who know a software product's sequence of menus; they can click through them rapidly. People know the sequence of operations and the location of the function on the menu drop-down, often moving the mouse toward the dialog box before it appears. Interestingly, the use of dynamic menus, which automatically shuffle frequently used functions to the top or only show most recently used functions will slow people down since locations change. (At one time Microsoft Office operated this way by default, but this was dropped because people were confused by the changing menu order.)

When an action is first learned, it is procedure-based and each step must be mentally checked off as it's completed. Obviously, this process makes heavy use of working memory. However, rep-

Figure 8. Automaticity in baseball. In Figure 8.A the baseball player is learning to throw a ball. As a result, the player has to consciously think about each movement before making it. In Figure 8.B, the baseball player can throw the ball accurately without thinking about it. Instead, the player can concentrate on the best strategy with respect to the game (Collett, 2004).

etition leads to the development of automaticity (overlearned) and then the task can be performed with minimal cognitive effort. The task can be performed from beginning to end without consciously thinking about the individual steps. Basic web browsing has become automatic for most people. They do not consciously think about the need to move the mouse over a link and click or consider what the system response will be when they click. They may stop and ponder whether or not they *want* to click, but the action sequence itself is automatic. Likewise, a skilled typist does not think about the key positions. Many people can touch type, but still have to look at the numbers and special character keys since they have not been learned them to automaticity.

Automaticity and Incorrect Actions

While automaticity is normally a good thing, it can also cause problems when the automatic action isn't correct. If people learn one action to the point of automaticity and then must perform a closely related action, they will often perform the best known action. Problems such as this occur when they are least wanted, such as under conditions of time pressure. Automatic response often occurs if people are using divided attention and cannot give the action adequate attention, but rather assumes that the normal response will work. For example, people who primarily work on Windows may perform some incorrect actions if they have to shift to a Mac. If they were under time pressure to accomplish a task on the Mac, the error rate would greatly increase as they do actions which are automatic and correct for Windows, but incorrect on a Mac. Of course, the same occurs if a Mac user has to use a Windows computer.

It is automaticity which minimizes the effectiveness of warning messaging for frequently performed actions. For example, a warning dialog box is displayed to prevent accidental file deletion, but people fall victim to automaticity. Every time a file gets deleted, a dialog box pops up to say "are you sure?" They quickly learn to automaticity that deleting a file requires two keystrokes: DEL and Y. Both keys are pressed in sequence as a single action, without reading or considering the message. In most instances, this is response is acceptable. But if the wrong file is highlighted, it will get deleted by mistake before they are even conscious of the action.

CALCULATION OF TASK EXECUTION TIME

This section examines two related models of how to calculate the time required to perform an action. Both essentially work at counting all of the actions and adding up the times. Although multiple studies have shown them to be highly accurate (especially the GOMS model), most real-world interactions are too complex for keystroke modeling. The time required to capture the highly branched interaction tree prevents its use in all but the most safety-critical systems.

Although these models are too time-consuming to completely describe a system, some specific usability issues can be resolved through their use. The keystroke level interaction required for frequent or highly important tasks (such as check-out for ecommerce) can be tracked and different potential designs compared. The GOMS model is especially useful for identifying bottlenecks in a data entry process. For time-sensitive or system-critical designs, the use of a GOMS analysis can provide assurance that people are physically capable of accomplishing the task within the required time frame.

Keystroke-Level Model

An early and comprehensive model of reaction times for graphical user interfaces is the keystroke-level model (KLM) by Card, Moran, & Newell (1983). The KLM was developed to allow a designer to predict the time to accomplish a task on a computer system. The keystroke-level models are worthwhile for systems where usage by power-users or fast completion times is essential. But for most information interaction situations, the time required to capture the data for a full keystroke model (and they are very time-intensive) does not provide adequate return in enhancing people's ability to function better with the resulting information design. On the other hand, since its introduction, the KLM model has been found to be applicable to many different HCI situations: predicting usage patterns in editors (Toleman & Welsh, 1996), setting power key assignments (Nicols & Ritter, 1995), predicting performance with hierarchical menus (Lane, Napier, Batsell, & Naman, 1993), and predicting text entry performance for physically challenged users (Koester & Levine, 1994).

The initial research and development of the model establishes the basic times for people to perform the various individual actions. The total time to perform an action is considered the sum of the times of the individual actions. The result is the best possible time for completing the task. Depending on the amount of decision making which goes into the task, this best possible time value may or may not have any basis in reality since there is no component in the model for cognitive actions. When people need to choose between multiple actions at each step (Hick-Hyman Law), the cognitive processing time can dominate the total interaction time and thus render the time element of the key stroke level model less than useful. The keystroke-level modeling works well for simple repetitive tasks, but not as well for the complex HII situations.

KLM modeling uses the following input parameters:

- A task or series of sub-tasks
- Method used
- Command language of the system
- Motor skill parameters of the user
- Response time parameters of the system

A time to complete prediction is the sum of the sub-task times and the required actions. The model includes four motor-control operators (K = key stroking, P = pointing, H = homing, D = drawing), one mental operator (M), and one system response operator (R):

$$T_{EXECUTE} = tK + tP + tH + tD + tM + tR$$

Box 12.

Estimate of times to perform a computer action
In order to determine how long a task will take, a representative set of users was tested to determine their average reaction times for individual actions:

> **Action Times (in seconds)**
> click mouse button 0.1
> click and release mouse button 0.2
> move hands between mouse and keyboard 0.4
> single key click at 55 wpm 0.2
> point with mouse 1.1

The time for complex actions is the sum of these values. Notice that while a simple description of the actions might say "click at desired spot and type," the time required to move between the mouse and the keyboard must be allowed for. Moving the hand to the mouse and then selecting something from a pull-down menu and then going back to the keyboard involves two hand movements, two points, and a click and release (3.2 seconds). Typing "Karen" (without the quotes) would be 1.2 seconds (the Shift key counts as an additional click).

This estimate only has user-based actions. A better model would include factors for system response, especially if the system has a slight delay on actions, such as drop-down menus responding to a click or a dialog box displaying. The calculations give a best possible time based on physical interactions, but make no allowance for cognitive issues involved in determining which action to perform.

Some of the operations above are omitted or repeated, depending on the task. For example, if a task requires n keystrokes, tK becomes n × tK. Each tK operation is assigned a value according to the skill of the user, with values ranging from tK = 0.08 s for highly skilled typists to tK = 1.20 s for a typist working with an unfamiliar keyboard. The pointing operator, tP, is based on Fitts' law (MacKensie, 2003, p. 28).

One limitation of most KLM models is that they assume an optimal error-free sequence of key strokes, since that is the basis for calculating the time-to-complete the sequence. Unfortunately, people's actions rarely match the error-free sequence. Also, it contains an assumption of automaticity since it provides no time to analyze the next action.

GOMS Model

GOMS is a keystroke level model devised by Card, Moran, and Newell (1983) as an expansion of the KLM model. The GOMS model goes beyond the KLM model because it brings in the concepts of user goals. A GOMS model's value is that it can be used both to predict the time to complete a task and to identify any bottlenecks in the task sequence. It also provides a tool for analyzing different interface designs to help determine which should result in the best performance. However, like the KLM models, building a GOMS model is a very tedious task for a system of greater than trivial complexity.

GOMS is an acronym for:

Goals: The goals people want to accomplish. Goals typically come in a hierarchy with sub-goals required to achieve an overarching goal.

Operators: The low-level actions which must be taken to achieve the method (e.g., move mouse over button, click button). Obviously, these are highly hardware- and software-dependent. For example, people using a Mac or a PC will have the same goals and methods, but the operators required to achieve the method may be different.

Methods: The sequence of steps required to achieve the goal.

Selection rules: The rules which determine which of multiple methods people should choose in order to accomplish the goal.

A GOMS model can be created on the basis of design specifications and before the interface itself has been created. One useful purpose is that it allows a study of the potential slowdowns and a cost-benefit analysis of the expected effort to both use the interface and to create/maintain it versus the expected improvements. The result would be more efficient use of development time and better designs (Gray, John, & Atwood, 1993).

Box 13.

GOMS model example
This models the task of moving text in a word processor. Adding up the total individual times would give the best possible time to complete the action (Card, Moran, & Newell,1983; John & Kieras, 1996).
GOAL: EDIT-MANUSCRIPT
. GOAL: EDIT-UNIT-TASK…repeat until no more unit tasks
.. GOAL: ACQUIRE UNIT-TASK
… GOAL: GET-NEXT-PAGE…if at end of manuscript page
… GOAL: GET-FROM-MANUSCRIPT
.. GOAL: EXECUTE-UNIT-TASK…if a unit task was found
… GOAL: MODIFY-TEXT
… . [select: GOAL: MOVE-TEXT*…if text is to be moved
… . GOAL: DELETE-PHRASE…if a phrase is to be deleted
… . GOAL: INSERT-WORD]…if a word is to be inserted
… . VERIFY-EDIT
The MOVE-TEXT goal can be expanded to give actual times. (This is only a partial expansion.)
GOAL: MOVE-TEXT
. GOAL: HIGHLIGHT-ARBITRARY-TEXT
. MOVE-CURSOR-TO-BEGINNING 1.10
. CLICK-MOUSE-BUTTON 0.20
. MOVE-CURSOR-TO-END 1.10
. SHIFT-CLICK-MOUSE-BUTTON 0.48
. VERIFY-HIGHLIGHT] 1.35

In a study (Gray, John, & Atwood, 1993) which looked at telephone operator software interfaces, the conversation time (something basically outside of any design team's scope) is the major factor in task time. Both keystroke time and screen reading times would at best (for an extreme evaluation they were calculated as eliminated altogether) only improved interaction time by 5% each. System response time was found to have a bigger impact. They caution that traditional usability testing may ignore these two factors and can identify areas of significant improvements in either data entry or reading, but system response time and cognitive decision time dominated the interaction, then any improvement in data entry would do little to improve overall interaction time in an operational environment.

A GOMS model is a procedural representation of the knowledge that people must have in order to carry out tasks on a system. As a procedural representation, it contains the "how to do it" knowledge that is required by a system in order to get the intended tasks done. And, as "how to do it" knowledge, it carries an assumption that they know how to perform the task efficiently.

Thus, GOMS is designed for situations in which they have already mastered the task. It's not for a learning situation. Some specific applications include:

- User-paced, passive systems, such as typical single-user computer applications wherein people tell the system what to do, then the system does it. This includes programs such as word processors and web browsers.
- Single-user, active systems, wherein the system changes in unexpected ways such as found with single-player video games. GOMS analysis does allow design teams to make reasonable predictions of how long people will take to respond.

EXAMPLES

Astronomical Information

People go to the Web to read about astronomical information because it is the fastest method.

Figure 9. Electronic medical record screen. Each different test or report is placed under its applicable tab. Switching between tabs can be a slow process.

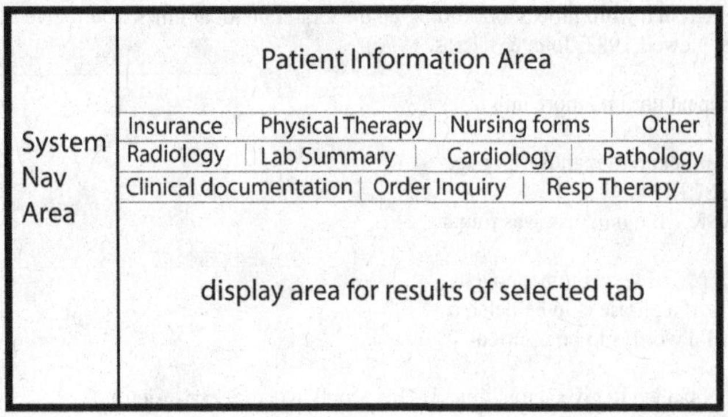

System Nav Area	Patient Information Area			
	Insurance	Physical Therapy	Nursing forms	Other
	Radiology	Lab Summary	Cardiology	Pathology
	Clinical documentation	Order Inquiry	Resp Therapy	
	display area for results of selected tab			

Most astronomy web pages take an encyclopedic approach to presenting information. The reader is presented with a list of topic arranged in a hierarchy. The text under each topic is static and rarely relates to other topics.

A system with good HII should be dynamic and make use of the technology. The design can go beyond a hierarchical listing of topics with static text. Instead of a collection of short definitions of the parts of a molecular cloud, the information can be presented as a hypertext article about the topic. The reader should be able interact with the text so that the text on a molecular cloud gets varied based on the prior knowledge and desired detail level. So, two readers with different knowledge levels can receive the same information, but presented with different text that corresponds to their current astronomy knowledge level. This could include one reader receiving different examples or more examples, more explanatory text to clarify terms or phrases, and different terms to replace astronomy jargon with more common terms.

Business Reports

System response must be considered fro online reports and is driven by whether or not the report is generated on demand. Reports which are created when a person clicks on it will incur time penalties. The audience analysis needs to consider how much time the users will tolerate. If they have to compare reports and click back and forth, this requires faster response than if the report is only created one time. Many medical electronic record systems require 5-10 seconds to retrieve the information after clicking on a tab (mock up shown in Figure 9). To properly evaluate the patient's status, a physician needs to click a tab, read the values, click a different tab, read the values, and then return to the first tab. A process that contains long pauses, leading to forgetting or using remembered information because it takes too long to verify it.

Fitts' law needs to be considered in the design of reports. Web-based reports allow drill-down, which is often implemented by requiring people to click on the tiny symbol: either the boxed plus sign or an arrow. Either way, these are small symbols and slow people down as they maneuver the mouse over them. The common practice of using them in almost every application has resulted in design teams not considering the interaction-speed impact, but it does exist. Related designs often involve lists, such as a list of report names, where the person has to click on a checkbox or a small box in front of the name. Fitts' law shows it is faster to click on the entire name since that is a larger target.

SUMMARY

From the user's point of view, the interface includes all of the elements which compose its context of use. From this perspective, one can view the interface of a computer as more than the screens, buttons and knobs, and also include any documentation, other people present, and past knowledge directly relevant to the situation. The design teams needs to consider all these factors as they design the system. Good HII is not and never will be a solution based in technology; it must be based in how people respond to and are influenced by both the information and the technology.

Models of how People Accept Technology

Various models have been proposed for showing the factors that go into making that decision. The Technology Acceptance Model (TAM) is currently the dominate model used to describe how people learn to work with and accept technology changes.

Respond to System Speed

Factors such as time and perceived time have a profound effect on how satisfied people are with technology interactions. However, a basic HII design problem is that time is not a fixed property of either the individual or the interactive system. Instead, it is an emergent property of the interaction. People need indications that something is happening and if they see something happening, they tend to estimate a faster perceived time.

People-Display Interaction

People interact with the system based on the information the display provides them. They need both good feedback and feedforward to maximize the HII of a system. Feedback provides information on how the situation is responding to decisions and feedforward provides predictions about the future development of the situation.

Technology Factors Driving User Satisfaction

A wide range of factors influence people's satisfaction with an interface and the technology behind it. Ensuring people like and use any interface requires some level of user satisfaction. Direct support for people's goals and information needs results in high user satisfaction.

Motor Control and HII

Motor control and its influence on interactions via mouse and keyboard strongly affect how easily people can interact with technology. Fitts' law relates to the performance of a mouse with various size of targets.

REFERENCES

Aggelidis, V., & Chatzoglou, P. (2009). Using a modified technology acceptance model in hospitals. *International Journal of Medical Informatics*, *78*(2), 115–126. doi:10.1016/j.ijmedinf.2008.06.006

Albers, M. (2004). *Communication of complex information: User goals and information needs for dynamic Web information*. Mahwah, NJ: Erlbaum.

Albers, M. (2010). Usability of complex Information Systems. In Albers, M., & Still, B. (Eds.), *Usability of complex Information Systems: Evaluation of user interaction* (pp. 3–16). Boca Raton, FL: CRC Press. doi:10.1201/EBK1439828946-3

Andriole, S., & Adelman, L. (1995). *Cognitive system engineering for user–computer interface design, prototyping, and evaluation*. Mahwah, NJ: Erlbaum.

Antonides, G., Verhoef, P., & Van Aalst, M. (2002). Consumer perception and evaluation of waiting time: A field experiment. *Journal of Consumer Psychology, 12*(3), 193–202. doi:10.1207/S15327663JCP1203_02

Bagozzi, R. (2007). The legacy of the technology acceptance model and a proposal for a paradigm shift. *Journal of the Association for Information Systems, 8*, 244–254.

Balakrishnan, R., & Hinckley, K. (2002). Symmetric bimanual interaction. *ACM CHI2002 Conference, CHI Letters, 2*(1), (pp. 33–40). New York, NY: ACM

Barnum, C., & Palmer, L. (2010). Tapping into desirability in user experience. In Albers, M., & Still, B. (Eds.), *Usability of complex Information Systems: Evaluation of user interaction* (pp. 253–280). Boca Raton, FL: CRC Press. doi:10.1201/EBK1439828946-17

Bates, D. (2003). Ten commandments for effective clinical decision support: Making the practice of evidence-based medicine a reality. *Journal of the American Medical Informatics Association, 10*(6), 523–530. doi:10.1197/jamia.M1370

Benedek, J., & Miner, T. (2002). *Measuring desirability: New methods for measuring desirability in the usability lab setting.* Retrieved from http://www.microsoft.com/usability/UEPostings/DesirabilityToolkit.doc

Bernstam, E., Sagaram, S., Walji, M., Johnson, C., & Meric-Bernstam, F. (2005). Usability of quality measures for online health information: Can commonly used technical quality criteria be reliably assessed? *International Journal of Medical Informatics, 74*, 675–683. doi:10.1016/j.ijmedinf.2005.02.002

Block, R., Hancock, P., & Zakay, D. (2000). Sex differences in duration judgments: A meta-analytic review. *Memory & Cognition, 28*(8), 1333–1346. doi:10.3758/BF03211834

Bootsmaa, R., Fernandeza, L., & Mottet, D. (2004). Behind Fitts' law: Kinematic patterns in goal-directed movements. *International Journal of Human-Computer Studies, 61*, 811–821. doi:10.1016/j.ijhcs.2004.09.004

Bouch, A., Kuchinsky, A., & Bhatti, N. (2000). Quality is in the eye of the beholder: Meeting users' requirements for Internet quality of service. *Proceedings of the SIGCHI Conference on Human Factors in Computing Systems* (pp. 297–304). New York, NY: ACM.

Brooke, J. (1996). SUS: A "quick and dirty" usability scale. In Jordan, P., Thomas, B., Weerdmeester, B., & McClelland, A. (Eds.), *Usability evaluation in industry* (pp. 189–194). London, UK: Taylor and Francis.

Brown, S. (1985). Time perception and attention: The effect of prospective and retrospective paradigms and task demands on perceived duration. *Perception & Psychophysics, 38*, 115–124. doi:10.3758/BF03198848

Buxton, W., & Myers, B. (1987). A study in two-handed input. *Proceedings of the ACM Conference on Human Factors in Computing Systems,* (pp. 321–326). New York, NY: ACM.

Card, S., English, W., & Burr, B. (1978). Evaluation of mouse, rate-controlled isometric joystick, step keys, and text keys for text selection on a CRT. *Ergonomics, 21*, 601–613. doi:10.1080/00140137808931762

Card, S., Moran, T., & Newell, A. (1983). *The psychology of human-computer interaction.* Hillsdale, NJ: Erlbaum.

Card, S., Robertson, G., & Mackinlay, J. (1991). The information visualizer: An information workspace. *Proceedings of the SIGCHI Conference on Human Factors in Computing Systems,* (pp. 181–188). New York, NY: ACM.

Chaparro, A., Bohan, M., Fernandez, J. E., Choi, S. D., & Kattel, B. (1999). The impact of age on computer input device use: Psychophysical and physiological measures. *International Journal of Industrial Ergonomics, 24*, 503–513. doi:10.1016/S0169-8141(98)00077-8

Chen, M., Anderson, J., & Sohn, M. (2001). What can a mouse cursor tell us more? Correlation of eye/mouse movements on Web browsing. *Conference on Human Factors in Computing Systems,* (pp. 281–282). Seattle, WA.

Collett, J. (2004). Automaticity. *The encyclopedia of educational technology.* Retrieved September 6, 2010, from http://edweb.sdsu.edu/eet/ articles/autoskills/index.htm

Cypher, A. (1986). The structure of users' activities. In Norman, D., & Draper, S. (Eds.), *User centered system design: New perspectives on human-computer interaction* (pp. 243–264). Mahwah, NJ: Erlbaum.

Davis, F. (1989). Perceived usefulness, perceived ease of use, and user acceptance of Information Technology. *Management Information Systems Quarterly, 13*(3), 319–339. doi:10.2307/249008

Davis, F., Bagozzi, R., & Warshaw, P. (1989). User acceptance of computer technology: A comparison of 2 theoretical models. *Management Science, 35*, 982–1003. doi:10.1287/mnsc.35.8.982

Dillon, A. (1992). Reading from paper versus screens: A critical review of the empirical literature. *Ergonomics, 35*, 1297–1326. doi:10.1080/00140139208967394

Dillon, A., Kleinman, L., Choi, G., & Bias, R. (2006). Visual search and reading tasks using ClearType and regular displays: Two experiments. *Proceedings of the SIGCHI Conference on Human Factors in Computing Systems,* April 22–27, 2006, Montréal, Québec, Canada.

Djajadiningrat, T., Overbeeke, K., & Wensveen, S. (2002). But how, Donald, tell us how? On the creation of meaning in interaction design through feedforward and inherent feedback. [London, England.]. *Proceedings of, DIS2002,* 285–291.

Duncan, J. (1984). Selective attention and the organization of visual information. *Journal of Experimental Psychology. General, 113*(4), 501–517. doi:10.1037/0096-3445.113.4.501

Dunlosky, J., Rawson, K., & Middleton, E. (2005). What constrains the accuracy of metacomprehension judgments? Testing the transfer-appropriate-monitoring and accessibility hypotheses. *Journal of Memory and Language, 52*, 551–565. doi:10.1016/j.jml.2005.01.011

Epps, B. (1986). Comparison of six cursor control devices based on Fitts' law models. *Proceedings of the Human Factors Society 30th Annual Meeting,* (pp. 327–331). Santa Monica, CA: Human Factors Society.

Fabre, J., Howard, S., & Smith, R. (2000). Designing time at the user interface. *Behaviour & Information Technology, 19*(6), 451–463. doi:10.1080/014492900750052705

Fezzani, K., Albinet, C., Thon, B., & Marquie, J. (2010). The effect of motor difficulty on the acquisition of a computer task: A comparison between young and older adults. *Behaviour & Information Technology, 29*(2), 115–124. doi:10.1080/01449290701825139

Fitts, P. (1954). The information capacity of the human motor system in controlling the amplitude of movement. *Journal of Experimental Psychology, 47*(6), 381–391. doi:10.1037/h0055392

Gonzalez, C. (2005). Decision support for real-time, dynamic decision-making tasks. *Organizational Behavior and Human Decision Processes, 96*, 142–154. doi:10.1016/j.obhdp.2004.11.002

Gould, J., Alfaro, L., Finn, R., Haupt, B., & Minuto, A. (1987). Reading from CRT displays can be as fast as reading from paper. *Human Factors, 29*(5), 497–517.

Gray, W., & Boehm-Davis, D. (2000). Milliseconds matter: An introduction to microstrategies and to their use in describing and predicting interactive behavior. *Journal of Experimental Psychology. Applied, 6*(4), 322–335. doi:10.1037/1076-898X.6.4.322

Gray, W., John, B., & Atwood, M. (1993). Project Ernestine: Validating a GOMS analysis for predicting and explaining real-world performance. *Human-Computer Interaction, 8*(3), 237–309. doi:10.1207/s15327051hci0803_3

Grudin, J. (1990). Interface. *Proceedings of Conference on Computer-Supported Cooperative Work 90,* (pp. 269–278). New York, NY: ACM.

Guiard, Y. (1987). Asymmetric division of labor in human skilled bimanual action: The kinematic chain as a model. *Journal of Motor Behavior, 19,* 486–517.

Guimaraes, T., Igbaria, M., & Lu, M. (1992). The determinants of DSS success: An integrated model. *Decision Sciences, 23,* 409–429. doi:10.1111/j.1540-5915.1992.tb00397.x

Guynes, J. (1988). Impact of system response time on state anxiety. *Communications of the ACM, 31*(3), 342–347. doi:10.1145/42392.42402

Halvey, M., Keane, M., & Smyth, B. (2006). Mobile web surfing is the same as Web surfing. *Communications of the ACM, 49*(3), 76–81. doi:10.1145/1118178.1118179

Hartwick, J., & Barki, H. (1994). Explaining the role of user participation in Information System use. *Management Science, 40,* 440–465. doi:10.1287/mnsc.40.4.440

Heba, G. (1997). Digital architectures: A rhetoric of electronic document structures. *IEEE Transactions on Professional Communication, 40*(4), 275–283. doi:10.1109/47.650005

Hick, W. (1952). On the rate of gain of information. *The Quarterly Journal of Experimental Psychology, 4,* 11–26. doi:10.1080/17470215208416600

Holden, R., & Karsh, B. (2010). The technology acceptance model: Its past and its future in health care. *Journal of Biomedical Informatics, 43,* 159–172. doi:10.1016/j.jbi.2009.07.002

Hornik, J. (1984). Subjective vs. objective time measures: A note on the perception of time in consumer behavior. *The Journal of Consumer Research, 11,* 615–618. doi:10.1086/208998

Hornof, A., & Kieras, D. E. (1997). Cognitive modeling reveals menu search is both random and systematic. *Proceedings of the SIGCHI Conference on Human Factors in Computing Systems,* (pp. 107–114), New York, NY: ACM.

Hourcade, J., Bederson, B., Druin, A., & Guimbretière, F. (2004). Differences in pointing task performance between preschool children and adults using mice. *ACM Transactions on Computer-Human Interaction, 11*(4), 357–386. doi:10.1145/1035575.1035577

Howard, T. (2007). Unexpected complexity in a traditional usability study. *Journal of Usability Studies, 3*(4), 189–205.

Hoxmeier, J., & Dicesare, C. (2000). System response time and user satisfaction: An experimental study of browser based applications. *Proceedings of the Americas Conference on Information Systems,* (pp. 140–145). August 10–13, 2000. Long Beach, CA: Association for Information Systems.

Hsia, J. (2007). An enhanced technology acceptance model for e-learning systems in high-tech companies. *Proceedings of the 7th WSEAS International Conference on Distance Learning and Web Engineering* (pp. 338–343). Beijing, China. New York, NY: ACM Press.

Huberman, B., Pirolli, P., Pitkow, J., & Lukose, R. (1998). Strong regularities in World Wide Web surfing. *Science, 280,* 95–97. doi:10.1126/science.280.5360.95

Hyman, R. (1953). Stimulus information as a determinant of reaction time. *Journal of Experimental Psychology, 45,* 188–196. doi:10.1037/h0056940

Jagacinski, R. (1977). A qualitative look at feedback control theory as a style of describing behavior. *Human Factors, 19,* 331–347.

Jaspers, M., Steen, T., Bos, C., & Geenen, M. (2004). The think aloud method: A guide to user interface design. *International Journal of Medical Informatics, 73,* 781–795. doi:10.1016/j.ijmedinf.2004.08.003

John, B., & Kieras, D. (1996). The GOMS Family of user interface analysis techniques: Comparison and contrast. *ACM Transactions on Computer-Human Interaction, 3*(4), 320–351. doi:10.1145/235833.236054

Jones, K., Farris, J., & Johnson, B. (2005). GUI Objects with impenetrable borders: Instructions (not practice) makes perfect. *International Journal of Human-Computer Studies, 62*(6), 687–712. doi:10.1016/j.ijhcs.2005.02.002

Karat, J., & Karat, C. (2003). The evolution of user-centered focus in the human-computer interaction field. *IBM Systems Journal, 42*(4), 532–541. doi:10.1147/sj.424.0532

Karger, D., & Quan, D. (2004). Prerequisites for a personalizable user interface. *Proceedings. of Intelligent User Interface 2004 Conference,* Ukita, 2004.

Kiger, J. (1984). The depth/breadth trade-off in the design of menu-driven user interfaces. *International Journal of Man-Machine Studies, 20,* 201–213. doi:10.1016/S0020-7373(84)80018-8

Kim, L., & Albers, M. (2003). Presenting information on the small-screen interface: Effects of table formatting. *IEEE Transactions on Professional Communication, 46*(2), 94–103. doi:10.1109/TPC.2003.813165

King, W., & He, J. (2006). A meta-analysis of the technology acceptance model. *Information & Management, 43,* 740–755. doi:10.1016/j.im.2006.05.003

Koester, H., & Levine, S. (1994). Validation of a keystroke-level model for a text entry system used by people with disabilities. *Proceedings of the First ACM Conference on Assistive Technologies,* (pp. 115–122). New York, NY: ACM.

Kotovsky, K., Hayes, J., & Simon, H. (1985). Why are some problems hard? Evidence from Tower of Hanoi. *Cognitive Psychology, 17,* 248–294. doi:10.1016/0010-0285(85)90009-X

Landauer, T., & Nachbar, D. (1985). Selection from alphabetic and numeric menu trees using a touch screen: Breadth, depth, and width. *Proceedings of the SIGCHI conference on Human factors in computing systems,* (pp.73–78), New York, NY: ACM.

Lane, D., Napier, H., Batsell, R., & Naman, J. (1993). Predicting the skilled use of hierarchical menus with the keystroke-level model. *Human-Computer Interaction, 8,* 185–192. doi:10.1207/s15327051hci0802_4

Larson, K., & Czerwinski, M. (1998). Web page design: Implications of memory, structure and scent for information retrieval. *Proceedings of the SIGCHI Conference on Human Factors in Computing Systems,* (pp. 25–32). New York, NY: ACM.

Lee, F., Teich, J., Spurr, D., & Bates, D. (1996). Implementation of physician order entry: User satisfaction and self-reported usage patterns. *Journal of the American Medical Informatics Association, 3*, 42–55. doi:10.1136/jamia.1996.96342648

Lightner, N. (2001). Model testing of users' comprehension in graphical animation: The effect of speed and focus areas. *International Journal of Human-Computer Interaction, 13*(1), 53–73. doi:10.1207/S15327590IJHC1301_4

MacKenzie, I. (2003). Motor behaviour models for human-computer interaction. In Carroll, J. (Ed.), *HCI Models, theories, and frameworks: Toward a multidisciplinary science* (pp. 27–54). San Francisco, CA: Morgan Kaufmann.

Mahmood, A., Burn, J., Gemoets, L., & Jacquez, C. (2000). Variables affecting Information Technology end-user satisfaction: A meta-analysis of the empirical literature. *International Journal of Human-Computer Studies, 52*, 751–771. doi:10.1006/ijhc.1999.0353

Marchionini, G. (1995). *Information Seeking in Electronic Environments*. New York, NY: Cambridge UP. doi:10.1017/CBO9780511626388

Marchionini, G. (2008). Human–information interaction research and development. *Library & Information Science Research, 30*, 165–174. doi:10.1016/j.lisr.2008.07.001

Martin, G., & Corl, K. (1986). System response time effects on user productivity. *Behaviour & Information Technology, 5*(1), 3–13. doi:10.1080/01449298608914494

McCrory, J. (2006). 800 or 1024 - Which min. display resolution to build for? *Sigia-l discussion list* (May 2, 2006).

McDonald, J., Dayton, T., & McDonald, D. (1988). Adapting menu layout to tasks. *International Journal of Man-Machine Studies, 28*, 417–435. doi:10.1016/S0020-7373(88)80020-8

McGovern, G. (2006a). *Making the customer CEO*. Retrieved from http://www.gerrymcgovern.com/nt/ 2006/nt-2006-06-12-customer-ceo.htm

Mckeen, J., & Guimaraes, T. (1997). Successful strategies for user participation in systems development. *Journal of Management Information Systems, 14*, 133–150.

Miller, R. (1968). Response time in man-computer conversational transactions. *Proceedings of the. AFIPS Fall Joint Computer Conference*, (Vol. 33, pp. 267–277).

Mirel, B. (2003). *Interaction design for complex problem solving: Developing useful and usable software*. San Francisco, CA: Morgan Kaufmann.

Murata, A. (1999). Extending effective target width in Fitts' law to a two-dimensional pointing task. *International Journal of Human-Computer Interaction, 11*(2), 137–152. doi:10.1207/S153275901102_4

Myers, B. A. (1985). The importance of percent-done progress indicators for computer-human interfaces. *Proceedings of the SIGCHI Conference on Human Factors in Computing Systems*, (pp. 11–17). New York, NY: ACM.

Nah, F. (2004). A study on tolerable waiting time: How long are Web users willing to wait? *Behaviour & Information Technology, 23*(3), 153–163. doi:10.1080/01449290410001669914

Nicols, S., & Ritter, F. (1995). A theoretically motivated tool for automatically generating command aliases. *Proceedings of the SIGCHI Conference on Human Factors in Computing Systems*, (pp. 393–400). New York, NY: ACM.

Nielsen, J. (1989). The matters that really matter for hypertext usability. *Proceedings of the ACM Hypertext Conference*, (pp. 239–248). New York, NY: ACM

Nielsen, J. (1993). *Usability engineering*. San Diego, CA: Academic Press.

Nielsen, J. (1997). *The need for speed.* Retrieved November 17, 2007, from http://www.useit.com/alertbox/9703a.html

Nielsen, J. (1998). *Electronic books—A bad idea.* Retrieved November 11, 2007, from http://www.useit.com/alertbox/980726.html

Nielsen, J. (1999). *The top ten new mistakes of Web design.* Retrieved from http://www.useit.com/alertbox/990530.html

Nielsen, J. (2010). *Website response times.* Retrieved August 8, 2010, from http://www.useit.com/alertbox//response-times.html

Norman, D. (1998). *The invisible computer.* Cambridge, MA: MIT Press.

Norman, D. A. (2002). *The design of everyday things.* New York, NY: Basic Books.

O'Hara, K., & Payne, S. (1998). The effects of operator implementation cost on planfulness of problem solving and learning. *Cognitive Psychology, 35,* 34–70. doi:10.1006/cogp.1997.0676

Ojakaar, E. (2001). *Users decide first; move second.* Retrieved May 16, 2006, from http://www.uie.com/ articles/users_decide_first/

Payne, S. (1995). Naive judgments of stimulus-response compatibility. *Human Factors, 37*(3), 495–506. doi:10.1518/001872095779049309

Payne, S., Howes, A., & Reader, W. (2001). Adaptively distributing cognition: A decision making perspective on human-computer interaction. *Behaviour & Information Technology, 20*(5), 339–346. doi:10.1080/01449290110078680

Perfetti, C., & Landesman, L. (2001). *The truth about download times.* Retrieved December 2, 2008, from http://www.uie.com/articles/download_time/

Peters, M. (1981). Attentional asymmetries during concurrent bimanual performance. *Quarterly Journal of Experimental Psychology, 33A,* 95–103.

Phillips, J., Meehan, J., & Triggs, T. (2003). Effects of cursor orientation and required precision on positioning movements on computer screens. *International Journal of Human-Computer Interaction, 15*(3), 379–389. doi:10.1207/S15327590IJHC1503_04

Pirolli, P. (2007). *Information foraging theory: Adaptive interaction with information.* Oxford, UK: Oxford UP. doi:10.1093/acprof:oso/9780195173321.001.0001

Porter, J. (2003). *Testing the three-click rule.* Retrieved May 16, 2010, from http://www.uie.com/articles/three_click_rule/

Poynter, D. (1989). Judging the duration of time intervals: A process of remembering segments of experience. In Levin, I., & Zakay, D. (Eds.), *Time and human cognition: A life-span perspective* (pp. 305–331). Amsterdam, The Netherlands: North-Holland. doi:10.1016/S0166-4115(08)61045-6

Quesenbery, W. (2003). Dimensions of usability. In Albers, M., & Mazur, B. (Eds.), *Content and complexity: Information design in software development and documentation* (pp. 81–102). Mahwah, NJ: Erlbaum.

Rabbitt, P. (1989). Sequential reactions. In Holding, D. (Ed.), *Human skills* (2nd ed.). New York, NY: Wiley.

Ramsay, J., Barbesi, A., & Preece, J. (1998). A psychological investigation of long retrieval times on the World Wide Web. *Interacting with Computers, 10,* 77–86. doi:10.1016/S0953-5438(97)00019-2

Rasmussen, J. (1986). *Information processing and human-machine interaction: An approach to cognitive engineering.* New York, NY: North-Holland.

Reason, J. (1990). *Human error*. Cambridge, UK: Cambridge UP.

Redish, J. (2007). Expanding usability testing to evaluate complex systems. *Journal of Usability Studies, 2*(3), 102–111.

Rodden, K. Fu, X., Aula, A., & Spiro, I. (2008). Eye-mouse coordination patterns on Web search results pages. *CHI '08 Extended Abstracts on Human factors in Computing Systems* (pp. 2997–3002). April 5–10, 2008. Florence, Italy.

Russo, J. (1977). The value of unit price information. *JMR, Journal of Marketing Research, 14*, 193–201. doi:10.2307/3150469

Schneider, W., & Chein, J. (2003). Controlled & automatic processing: Behavior, theory, and biological mechanisms. *Cognitive Science, 27*, 525–559.

Scholtz, J. (2006). Metrics for evaluating human information interaction systems. *Interacting with Computers, 18*, 507–527. doi:10.1016/j.intcom.2005.10.004

Seibel, R. (1972). Data entry devices and procedures. In Van Cott, H., & Kinkade, R. (Eds.), *Human engineering guide to equipment design*. Washington, DC: US Government Printing.

Shearer, H. (2010). An activity-theoretical approach to the usability testing of information products meant to support complex use. In Albers, M., & Still, B. (Eds.), *Usability of complex Information Systems: Evaluation of user interaction* (pp. 181–206). Boca Raton, FL: CRC Press. doi:10.1201/EBK1439828946-13

Shih, H. (2004). Extended technology acceptance model of internet utilization behavior. *Information & Management, 41*(6), 719–729. doi:10.1016/j.im.2003.08.009

Shneiderman, B. (1984). Response time and display rate in human performance with computers. *Computing Surveys, 16*, 265–285. doi:10.1145/2514.2517

Shneiderman, B. (1998). *Designing the user interface*. Boston, MA: Addison-Wesley.

Shu, K., Boyle, D., Spurr, C., Horsky, J., Heiman, H., & O'Connor, P. (2001). Comparison of time spent writing orders on paper with computerized physician order entry. *Studies in Health Technology and Informatics, 84*(2), 1207–1121.

Speier, C., & Morris, M. (2003). The influence of query interface design on decision-making performance. *Management Information Systems Quarterly, 27*(3), 397–423.

Spool, J. (1997). *Why on-site searching stinks*. Retrieved December 28, 2005, from http://www.uie.com/articles/ search_stinks/

Spool, J. (1998). *As the page scrolls*. Retrieved May 25, 2010, from http://www.uie.com/articles/ page_scrolling/

Sutcliffe, A., Karat, J., Bodker, S., & Gaver, B. (2006). Can we measure quality in design and do we need to? *Proceedings of Designing Interactive Systems: Processes, Practices, Methods, &* [New York, NY: ACM.]. *Techniques, 2006*, 119–121.

Szameitat, A., Rummel, J., Szameitat, D., & Ster, A. (2009). Behavioral and emotional consequences of brief delays in human-computer interaction. *International Journal of Human-Computer Studies, 67*, 561–570. doi:10.1016/j.ijhcs.2009.02.004

Tobin, S., & Grondin, S. (2009). Video games and the perception of very long durations by adolescents. *Computers in Human Behavior, 25*, 554–559. doi:10.1016/j.chb.2008.12.002

Toleman, M., & Welsh, J. (1996). Can design choices for language-based editors be analysed with keystroke-level models? *Proceedings of the HCI '96 Conference on People and Computers,* (pp. 97–112). Surrey, UK: Springer-Verlag.

Topi, H., Valacich, J., & Hoffer, J. (2005). The effects of task complexity and time availability limitations on human performance in database query tasks. *International Journal of Human-Computer Studies, 62,* 349–379. doi:10.1016/j.ijhcs.2004.10.003

Tractinsky, N., & Meyer, J. (2001). Task structure and the apparent duration of hierarchical search. *International Journal of Human-Computer Studies, 55,* 845–860. doi:10.1006/ijhc.2001.0506

Trimmel, M., Meixner-Pendleton, M., & Haring, S. (2003). Stress response caused by system response time when searching for information on the Internet. *Human Factors, 45*(4), 615–621. doi:10.1518/hfes.45.4.615.27084

Van Schaik, P. (1999). Involving users in the specification of functionality using scenarios and model-based evaluation. *Behaviour & Information Technology, 18*(6), 455–466. doi:10.1080/014492999118878

Venkatesh, V., & Davis, F. (2000). A theoretical extension of the technology acceptance model: Four longitudinal field studies. *Management Science, 46,* 186–204. doi:10.1287/mnsc.46.2.186.11926

Venkatesh, V., Morris, M., Davis, G., & Davis, F. (2003). User acceptance of Information Technology: Toward a unified view. *Management Information Systems Quarterly, 27*(3), 425–478.

Visser, W., & Morals, A. (1991). Concurrent use of different expertise elicitation methods applied to the study of the programming activity. In Ackermann, D., & Tauber, M. J. (Eds.), *Mental models and human-computer interactions* (pp. 97–114). Amsterdam, The Netherlands: North Holland.

Walker, N. Millians, J., & Worden, A. (1996). Mouse accelerations and performance of older computer users. *Proceedings of the Human Factors and Ergonomics Society 40th Annual Meeting,* (pp. 151–154). Santa Monica, CA: HFES.

Walker, N., & Smelcer, J. (1990). A comparison of selection time from walking and bar menus. *Proceedings of the SIGCHI Conference on Human Factors in Computing Systems,* (pp. 221-225). New York, NY: ACM.

Watters, C., Duffy, J., & Duffy, K. (2003). Using large tables on small display devices. *International Journal of Human-Computer Studies, 58,* 21–37. doi:10.1016/S1071-5819(02)00124-6

Weber, B., & Chapman, G. (2005). The combined effects of risk and time on choice: Does uncertainty eliminate the immediacy effect? Does delay eliminate the certainty effect? *Organizational Behavior and Human Decision Processes, 96*(2), 104–118. doi:10.1016/j.obhdp.2005.01.001

Wickens, C., & Hollands, J. (2000). *Engineering psychology and human performance.* Upper Saddle River, NJ: Prentice Hall.

Yang, H., & Yoo, Y. (2004). It's all about attitude: Revisiting the technology acceptance model. *Decision Support Systems, 38,* 19–31. doi:10.1016/S0167-9236(03)00062-9

Zakay, D., & Hornik, J. (1991). How much time did you wait in line? A time perception perspective. In Chebat, J. C., & Venkatesan, V. (Eds.), *Time and consumer behaviour* (pp. 1–18). Montreal, Canada: University of Quebec at Montreal.

Zaphiris, P., & Kurniawan, S. (2001). Effects of information layout on reading speed: Differences between paper and monitor presentation. *Proceedings of the Human Factors and Ergonomics Society 45th Annual Meeting,* (pp. 1210–1214). Santa Monica, CA: HFES.

Zeng, Q., Kogan, S., Plovnick, R., Crowell, J., La-croix, E., & Greenes, R. (2004). Positive attitudes and failed queries: An exploration of the conundrums of consumer health information retrieval. *International Journal of Medical Informatics*, *73*(1), 45–55. doi:10.1016/j.ijmedinf.2003.12.015

Zhang, J. (1996). A representational analysis of relational information displays. *Journal of Human-Computer Studies*, *45*(1), 59–74. doi:10.1006/ijhc.1996.0042

ADDITIONAL READING

Bagozzi, R. (2007). The legacy of the technology acceptance model and a proposal for a paradigm shift. *Journal of the Association for Information Systems*, *8*, 244–254.

Card, S., Moran, T., & Newell, A. (1983). *The psychology of human-computer interaction*. Hillsdale, NJ: Erlbaum.

Marchionini, G. (2008). Human–information interaction research and development. *Library & Information Science Research*, *30*, 165–174. doi:10.1016/j.lisr.2008.07.001

Mirel, B. (2003). *Interaction design for complex problem solving: Developing useful and usable software*. San Francisco, CA: Morgan Kaufmann.

Norman, D. (1998). *The invisible computer*. Cambridge, MA: MIT Press.

Pirolli, P. (2007). *Information foraging theory: Adaptive interaction with information*. Oxford, UK: Oxford UP. doi:10.1093/acprof:oso/9780195173321.001.0001

Shneiderman, B. (1998). *Designing the user interface*. Boston, MA: Addison-Wesley.

Section 2
People and Information Presentation

Chapter 6
How People Perform a First Glance Evaluation

ABSTRACT

This chapter looks at some of the factors that drive how people form their first impression of a text and how design teams can ensure their material leaves a good impression within the first 2 seconds of people looking at a page, the time during which people evaluate the appearance and begin to read and comprehend the text. People's initial perception of text happens within a few seconds, long before they actually read any text; some research has found initial impressions can form within 50 milliseconds (Lindgaard, Fernandes, Dudek, & Brown, 2006). That first glance evaluation depends on their initial perception of the font choices, text design, and graphics. The first few seconds of viewing a text can be critical to the HII by activating a mental model and setting up how the text will be interpreted. Or if it creates a poor first impression, people may flag the text as unreadable and ignore it.

BACKGROUND

This report, by its very length, defends itself against the risk of being read.—Winston Churchill

This chapter considers the information as it moves from the situation to the person. The white area in Figure 1 shows the area of the HII model relevant to this chapter. It deals with how a person perceives the information and decides what information will receive further consideration. The gray shape in the drawing plays a gatekeeper since any situation contains a huge amount of information from which people must select what is relevant and funnel it down to manageable amounts as they work on comprehending it and applying it to their situation.

The main areas covered in this chapter are:

Perception and Pre-Attentive Processing: Discussion of the underlying psychological theories about how people perceive information and sort it out without consciously thinking about it.

Salience Issues at First Glance: The first few seconds are critical for ensuring the reader

DOI: 10.4018/978-1-4666-0152-9.ch006

Figure 1. First glance evaluation of the information

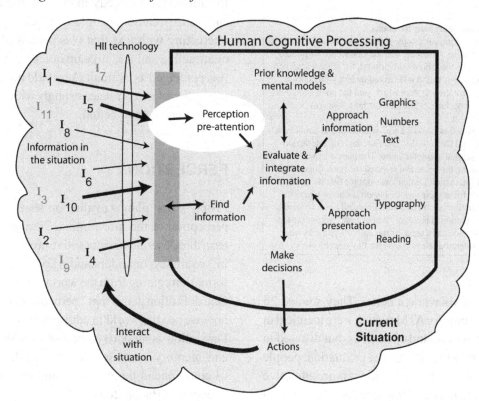

perceives the document correctly. This section looks a the factors that influence those first few seconds.

Gestalt Theory: Discussion of the main points of Gestalt theory and how it influences initial impressions of a page.

Cue-Conflicts: Discussion of the factors which can lead to conflicts between what a page presents to people and what it is suppose to present.

Change Blindness: Discussion of how people completely ignore some aspects of a design and how that can impact communication.

INTRODUCTION

The first glance evaluation of an information display sets people's expectations; if they believe it will be highly usable, they will tend to continue

to believe that. Factors driving evaluation of the first glance at a text depend on people's initial perception of the font choices, text design, and graphics. The first few seconds of viewing a text can be critical to the HII by activating a mental model and forming a first impression of both the information quality and contents. If the wrong mental model is activated, people may misinterpret the text. Or if it leaves a poor first impression, people may not examine the page further.

With any written communication, whether on the web, a long printed report, or a one-page brochure, a significant factor of how deeply people will read the material—or read it at all—happens with the first glance at the page. Kurosu and Kashimura (1995) demonstrated that based on a first glance evaluation, people who determined an interface looked more attractive also rated it as easier to use. They demonstrated this when they found that people consistently said that the

Box 1.

First glance and searching for books

A person was looking for a copy of the book *About Face 2.0* in a large bookstore. Assuming that the title would be printed along the spine as most books are printed, the person searched for a while but never found it. He asked a clerk who checked the bookstore inventory system which said the book should be there. Several days later, while looking for a different book, the person found it.

The problem was that "About Face" was printed in small type across the top and the subtitle "The Essentials of Interaction Design" was printed along the spine. The person expected the full title along the spine and rejected the book titled "The Essentials of Interaction Design" was not the title he was looking for. People focus their vision only on the areas where the desired information is expected and ignore all other areas and available information. The small "About Face" across the top occupied space normally used for the author's name as was, thus, not considered a relevant area for this search.

---

attractive ATMs worked better. They studied 26 different layouts for ATMs which were identical in number of buttons and operations, but differed in layout. During the first glance evaluation, people who determine the interface looks more attractive will also rate it as easier to use.

Of course, the opposite is true, if the first glance sets an expectation that it will be difficult, then people will find the interaction difficult. Lindgaard et al. (2006) found that people can form a first impression of a web page with only a 50 millisecond exposure. That impression activates a reader's mental model and can either excite or turn off the reader to a text. A vibrant exciting looking text will make them want to read more, while a dense gray text block may make them look elsewhere for information.

People very quickly formulate an estimate of the perceived effort required to read a text and base their decision on whether or not it is worth reading on that estimate; however, people are notoriously poor at in their estimate accuracy. Thus, the first glance evaluation sets the expectations about both content quality and usability; an evaluation that directly affects measurements of effectiveness and user satisfaction. One element of effectiveness is the number of people who give up without finding an answer. The amount of time spent searching

for information directly maps onto the estimate and the expectation: people will spend more time interacting with text that was perceived as easy or attractive and will give up quickly on text that was perceived as difficult. As would be expected, user satisfaction correlates strongly with difficulty, both perceived and actual.

PERCEPTION

People's first glance evaluation starts with their perception of the information. Perception is the term that describes the cognitive process of attaining awareness or understanding of the sensory information coming from the world around a person. One definition states that "perception determines how we see the world in addition to what we see. Perception is an active process in which vision and memory work seamlessly together to help us comprehend the world around us" (Johnson-Sheehan & Baehr, 2001, p. 23).

Raw data constantly hits the senses. Perception can be considered the mind's initial processing for decoding that raw data. To prevent overload, people have the inherent ability to screen out most of those sensory inputs and only respond to relevant or unique ones.

Both visual search studies and reading comprehension studies show that people are highly skilled at directing attention to aspects of the perceptual field that are of high potential relevance given the properties of the data field and the expectations and interests of the observer (Woods, Patterson, & Roth, 2002, p. 26).

Perception is fast while most cognitive processes are slow. The initial response to an alarm is perception while figuring out the actual error requires cognitive effort. Perception may make people immediately focus on a dip in a graphical display, but understanding why that dip occurs is not perception. One possible point of confusion is that typical English word usage would be that people finally perceived the problem after spending 10 minutes reading/examining data, but this is not perception, it is the result of cognitive effort. Perception is only the fast, initial screening of sensory inputs which resulted in focusing on the dip and not on other aspects of the display.

In-depth understanding of perception and how it affects people's reactions is required for many human factors areas which require read-time control (such as plant operations) or detecting changes (such as pilots or radar operators). HII, with its longer time frames, does not require as deep a knowledge of human perception, but design teams should still concern themselves with verifying that information supports efficient and effective perception. If the information design does not support good perception, the communication process is compromised and people may ignore information or be misdirected to the wrong information.

The psychology literature contains two competing views of perception:

- *Constructivist* theorists believe that seeing is an active process in which our view is constructed from both information in the environment and from previously stored knowledge. Perception involves the intervention of representations and memories. What we see is not a replica or copy; rather a model that is constructed by the visual system through transforming, enhancing, distorting, and discarding information. Gestalt theory is a constructivist theory.
- *Ecological* theorists believe that perception is a process of "picking up" information from the environment, with no construction or elaboration needed. Users intentionally engage in activities that cause the necessary information to become apparent. We explore objects in the environment. Norman's (2002) and Gibson's (1977)

theories of affordances are both ecological theories.

Most of HCI and HII work within an ecological theory view, but, in general, the differences in the competing views are far enough removed from the practical design needs as to not be highly relevant. Instead, it is a matter of taking the useful points of each and using them in communicating information.

As a fast, automatic mental process, perception operates with few cognitive resources and minimal conscious control. For example, perception leads to banner blindness with flashing areas of a website being classified as ads and ignored without any eye gaze directed to them. How the information gets perceived can be described as driven from the data (bottom-up) or from expectations (top-down). In most situations, a combination of the two applies.

Top-down: Used when minimal external stimulus is received and people have to fill-in substantial amounts of what is occurring in the situation. Although this is very efficient at forming an understanding with minimal information, if perception is wrong, then follow-on information will be misinterpreted. For example, in a haunted house, every creak is interpreted as the monster getting closer.

Perception interacts with human bias so that the perceived information is strongly affected by any expectations or preconceived ideas about the content. People will believe they saw something they wanted/expected to see regardless of whether or not it actually was present. Mentally, they fill-in any missing but expected information. Likewise, when objects or information are viewed without understanding, people's minds will impose on that information some structure that is already recognized, in order to process what it is viewing. Even when given random data, people will see patterns because they expect to the data to contain patterns.

Bottom-up: Based on an analysis of the information arriving from the environment. Bottom-up perception takes the actual text being read and any other visual or aural cues and forms them into an integrated first glance understanding of the situation. Bottom-up processing would typically only be used if there is a basic understanding of the situation and top-down processing couldn't be applied.

Recent studies on visual perception emphasize the role of attention in the perception of information in computer displays (Resnick et al., 1997; Simons & Levin, 1997). People do not passively receive information, but must internally process the light, sound, touch, etc. before it can be considered as perceived. From an HII perspective, this means that communicating information requires people to be actively giving the information their attention. It requires about half a second after a stimulus occurs before people are fully conscious of it. (People can detect a stimulus in less than half a second, but that is pre-attentive processing. If a weak stimulus lasts less than half a second, it is unlikely to be perceived. This plays a significant factor in multitasking and people claiming they can give full attention to a presentation while texting or listening to music. Human factors accident reports consistently find people missing a short warning tone or visual indicator (not perceiving it) while engaged in a separate task that required full cognitive resources.

Pre-Attentive Processing

Pre-attention is the rapid unconscious mental processing done before a person knows there is a stimulus. Pre-attentive processing is carried out automatically in the mind and organizes the visual image into groups of related objects (Kahneman, 1973). After this initial organization, a person consciously begins to examine the various groups of objects.

Research into eye movements has found that it takes about 200 milliseconds to comprehend a single object and 230 milliseconds to move between objects. From this, the minimum time to see multiple areas of a scene within a large text, a presentation slide or multiple slides can be calculated by:

$$Y = n[200 + 230(a-1)]$$

n = number of frames, a = areas of interest per screen.

Thus, 3 areas over 15 frames requires 9.9 seconds minimum. This would also apply to graph animation and how quickly any changes can be perceived. Of course, these are minimum times and any delay on the part of the viewer would result in lowered perception. These are the minimum perception times; comprehension requires additional time.

Although it takes 200 milliseconds to visually process an image and 230 msec to move between objects, people can process overall images and detect a small set of features more quickly (figure 2). The ability to process these features is called pre-attentive because they occur faster than focused attention can mentally process them (Treisman, 1985; Wolfe, 1994). Typically, visual tasks that can be performed in less than 200 to 250 msec are considered pre-attentive.

Pre-attentive processing tends to be measured in two different ways: speed of detection and accuracy (Treisman, 1991; Treisman, & Gelade, 1980). For example, an image, such as Figure 3, is displayed for a very brief time (200 to 250 milliseconds) which prevents eye movement and a person has to state whether or not a target (the circle) was in the image. An accuracy test would display the image until the person said 'yes' or 'no' to the target being present. On the other hand, while people can detect the existence of the target,

Figure 2. Pre-attentive attributes applicable to visual information displays. A person can detect the differences shown in each of the boxes very quickly, faster than the 200 msec required to fully perceive the scene. For example, in the first box, with a very short exposure a person would be able to state one of lines was not vertical but would not may be able to say which one or how it deviated from vertical (adapted from Few, 2009).

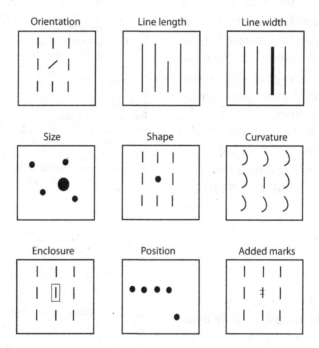

Figure 3. Visual search in a field with distracters. In A, pre-attentive processing allows a person to quickly identify that a solid dot exists in the image. In B, rather than being able to use pre-attentive processing, a person must scan the entire image to determine if a solid black dot is present. The black squares prevent pre-attentive processing because of their similarity to a black circle (Healey, 2007).

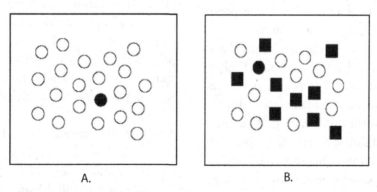

more details, such as location, spatial arrangement, etc., are not clearly distinguished. Pre-attentive processing allows people to accurately state if the image contained the dark circle, but they could not consistently properly place it on the image. Person who saw field 6-3A for a very short exposure and then had to darken in the black circle on a sheet with all of circles, would have a high error rate. They would know one of the circles was black, but not which one.

With pre-attentive processing, people can easily detect some features. Interestingly, with pre-attentive processing, the number of distracters on the screen is not a factor. On the other hand, without pre-attentive processing, people have to do a serial scan of all of the objects, a very time-consuming and error-prone process as the number of distracters increase. Also, some of pre-attentive feature detections are asymmetric. For example, a sloped line in a sea of vertical lines can be detected pre-attentively. However, a vertical line in a sea of sloped lines cannot (Healey, Booth, & Enns, 1996; Treisman & Gormican, 1988).

SALIENCE ISSUES AT FIRST GLANCE

A text has only a few seconds to draw people in; long before they begin to actually read for comprehension, they have read enough to decide if it is relevant information and if they should continue to read. In addition to the 50 millisecond initial impression a page leaves with a reader, the HII depends on how quickly readers can decide if the page probably contains information relevant to their current needs. In other words, does the page design support answering the question "is it worth my time to read this?" Information salience plays a major part in answering that question. Which information is prominent and its location on a page contribute to its salience and to the reader deciding if the text is worthwhile reading. Whatever information is most salient drives the decision. If irrelevant information has high salience, the reader may ignore the page thinking it is all irrelevant. In the first few seconds, the design must ensure a reader sees enough relevant information to judge the page worthwhile. Design teams must remember that people base their evaluation on estimates of perceived effort (Fennema & Kleinmuntz, 1995)—which are poorly correlated with actual

Box 2.

Browsing in a bookstore
One of my students told this story during a discussion on how people respond to texts.

On each trip to the bookstore, my boyfriend keeps picking up the same nonfiction (biography) book. He'll browse the racks, pull out the book, do a check of its weight, flip the pages, and comment on the density of the paragraphs. I can tell he is interested in the topic and the book, but he mumbles "I'll never read this book," and returns it to the shelf.

The boyfriend knows the type of book he reads and this particular book fails to fit those criteria during his few seconds looking at it. In the end, he decides he isn't willing to make the commitment to read the book, which fails in some way to be what he looks for in a book. He hadn't read any of the text and is interested in the topic, thus only the overall impression of the book can be driving him away.

---

effort required—and people try to avoid tasks which require high mental effort. If the page does not appear to contain relevant information or it looks like it will be hard to extract, people will try to avoid reading it. Pages with small type, little white space, or large tables can give the impression of being too hard to read.

Bold text, headings, graphics, and overall page design drive the page salience and help people quickly reach a conclusion about the text's relevance. Poor information salience or miscuing information can make people either reject a relevant page or spend time reading an irrelevant page. Writing textbooks stress creating an inviting page design, but seldom dwell on the rapid response a reader makes about either accepting or rejecting the page's overall design.

Bold text: The intensity of bold text makes it very salient and draws the eye to it immediately. People see the bold words on a page, out of context with the surrounding text. Thus, the bold text must be relevant to the reader without being in context.

Headings: The larger font, bold text, and white space surrounding a heading make them highly salient. They also drive activation

Box 3.

Pre-attentive process and ad-like images

Some groups, as a way of trying to overcome poor information design, used ad-like images to draw their employee's attention to information in the image. During one test of a potential page redesign, a person pointed to one of those ad-like images and commented that if the new page contained that link, then he would be able to find most of the information he needed.

The usability problem was that the image had been on the current page in the same location for over six months. The test subject interacted with the web page everyday and never saw it. Pre-attentive processing for avoiding information that looks like ads is so strong that even on internal corporate pages, which don't contain ads, people ignore anything which looks like them.

---

of the reader's mental model (Duin, 1989). If their wording activates an inappropriate mental model, the text will be deemed irrelevant. Use of generic headings, such as introduction, or analysis, also fail to activate a mental model and can result in the material being ignored.

Graphics: Graphics, especially images of people, are highly salient and are typically the first areas people look at when initially viewing a page. Quality graphics which seem to contain highly readable information draw people to the page. On the other hand, eye candy images, such as clipart or pictures for the sake of having pictures, distract the reader from the relevant information needed to judge the text's relevance.

Page design: Overall page design with the margins, white space around headings, use of bullet lists, etc. all make the page appear easier to read and comprehend. Dense gray pages turn off a potential reader. Good layout results in higher satisfaction and less mental fatigue than poor designs (Chaparro, Shaikh, & Baker, 2005).

Affordances

Throughout the HCI literature, there are continual references to ensuring that the design offers affordances. An affordance is simply that the basic design visually signals it affords doing something: a button looks like it can be pushed; a slider looks like can slide; a door handle looks like it should be pulled. An example of a poor affordance is doors with handles on both sides. People's natural inclination is to pull on a handle, yet on one side, a push is required to open the door. Likewise, the smooth toolbar designs of some software which only display as a button when the mouse rolls over it hides the affordance of a clickable spot.

People perceive the affordance at first glance and make assumptions about the interaction based on that interpretation. Usability tests find some users clicking on images since sometime they are linked and other times they are not. From users' perspectives, the image has no affordance that it is clickable, so they either waste time trying to click it or misses links by never clicking on images. Likewise, not using blue underline for in-text web links hides the affordance that the link exists. Some designers want to remove the blue underline because it breaks the single text block they desire. But, from a reader's view, the links must be flagged with some affordance so they are clearly and immediately visible (Bailey, 2000).

The definition of affordance in the previous paragraphs follows Norman (2002), which is the definition typically followed in HCI, usability, communication, and information architecture. There is, however, no fully accepted definition; when various authors write about an affordance, although they use similar definitions to Norman, they do vary from it, often at the subtle levels critical to clear communication. The psychology of perception researchers often work with a different definition which was advanced by Gibson (1977) and is much more general than Norman's. Gibson defined an affordance as the possibilities for action that existed in the environment and that are perceived directly with no sensory processing. He also considered affordances as measurable and independent of the observer.

The difference in the definitions can be summed up as: Gibson sees an affordance as the action possibility itself, independent of whether or not a person can perceive the possibility, and Norman sees it as a design that suggests both the action possibility and the way that that action possibility is conveyed or made visible (McGrenere & Ho, 2000). In Norman's view, if the person cannot perceive the possibility (perhaps by poor design or lack of prior knowledge), then there is no affordance.

GESTALT THEORY

Gestalt is a general description for the psychological concepts that make unity and variety possible in design. It is a German word that roughly translates as "whole" or "form." Gestalt theory is involved with visual perception and the psychology of art among other things. It is concerned with the relationship between the parts and the whole of a composition. Gestalt principles build on the idea that people perceive information at the global level first and that, depending on the presentation, the holistic view is made up of more than the individual components.

The visual world is so complex that the mind has developed strategies for coping with the confusion. Gestalt principles build a unified view of those strategies. When faced with visual complexity and multiple options, the mind tries to find the simplest solution to a problem. One of the ways it does this is to form groups of items that have certain characteristics in common. When people look at a grouping of lines and circles, they do not look at each line and circle individually; instead, they mentally structure them in some coherent, integrated way.

The basic Gestalt ideas and some examples follow.

Figure to Ground: The image changes based on whether or not the light or dark area is seen as the figure or the background. This leads to optical illusions such as the face or vase. In more practical examples, too tight kerning can introduce extra figures. In Figure 4, it could be the two letters or an arrow, depending on what is seen as the figure. In the word Bob, the first B is reversed out shifting the use of black and white as figure or background.

Proximity: Grouping based on the relative placement of objects (Figure 5).

Because of the different space between the lines, the image appears to be two double rows of dots. Likewise, the small circles or squares appear to be grouped with the large circles or squares they are close to. However, in neither case is anything in the image actually driving this view.

Proximity violation: A student said her mother saw this headline for a concert ad and wanted to know who Elton Billy was. Most people know the singer's names and were able to essentially immediately parse them. But normal reading is left to right, and so a

Figure 4. Figure to ground

Figure 5. Gestalt proximity

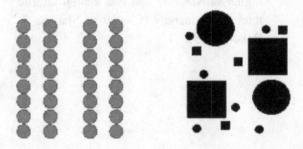

Figure 6. Elton-Billy

Elton Billy
John Joel

reader not familiar with the singers would expect the names to go across the page and not vertically (Figure 6).

Closure: Objects are completed to form the simplest possible figures (Figure 7).

The image consists of three circles with a triangle cut out, but because of their relative placement, the eye also sees a triangle. Moving the circles to a different place destroys the gestalt aspects of the image and turns them into three random Pac-man characters.

Most people read the following text as 'the cat,' yet the symbol for 'H' and the 'A' are the same (Figure 8). The simplist interpretation is to see 'the cat' and, thus, that is what people perceive.

Symmetry: Objects are grouped so they form symmetrical shapes around their center (Figure 9). The image is seen as two overlap-

Figure 7. Gestalt closure

Figure 8. Gestalt- the cat

Figure 9. Gestalt symmetry

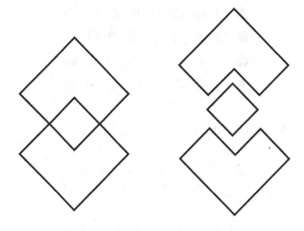

ping squares since that is the simplest interpretation, rather than as a small square and two squares with cutouts.

Similarity: Grouping objects that share visual characteristics or grouping by how things look more alike than the other objects in the set (Figure 10). The basic circle pattern is the same, but with similarity, the eye groups these in rows of black and white circles or into groups of four objects forming squares. For control gauges, designing the system so the normal position is the same on all of the gauges makes it easier to spot any deviation (Figure 11). Assume only the third gauge in each row has an abnormal reading. In the first row, each gauge would need to be examined individually, but the third gauge in the second row breaks the pattern of the other three and is easily visible.

Continuance: Grouping by how people will follow a path seeking a conclusion or resolution from clues that point in a particular direction (Figure 12).

The eye sees three lines going behind a dark area, since it is simpler to see three rather than 6 separate objects. In the other image, the finger points to the small ball and the eye is drawn to it, rather than to the larger

Figure 10. Gestalt similarity

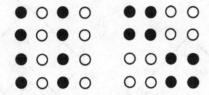

Figure 11. Gestalt gauges

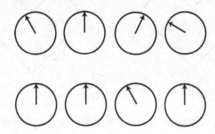

Figure 12. Gestalt continuance

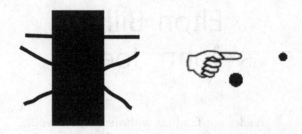

HII by pulling together information relationships, relevance, and salience. Although this idea may appear self-evident, many systems violate it, especially systems based around dumping information on the reader or systems developed without a clear understanding of the HII requirements.

ball. Without the pointing finger, the eye would go to the large ball.

Gestalt ideas are important because people always impose structure on information regardless of how unstructured it might be (Kwasnik, 1992; Witkin, 1978). It is up to the design team to ensure the overall design matches the HII needs. Gestalt concepts help the design team to focus on the overall presentation and not get too focused on the individual elements. Likewise, people can identify website layouts with 'greeked' text (Tullis, 1993) purely based on the overall appearance.

Wickens and Carswell (1995) developed the idea of the proximity compatibility principle (PCP), which is similar to gestalt proximity concepts. PCP states that the perceptual characteristics of the information should be designed so that its arrangement fits the cognitive demands of the task. In other words, information which is used together should appear close together. If the task requires two sets of information to be integrated, the system performs the integration and displays the results. Conversely, information that is not used together should not appear together. Notice how this principle helps the design team build good

CUE-CONFLICTS

Cue-conflicts occur when the diagram can be interpreted in multiple ways and typically the strongest perceived image conflicts with the way people would typically interpret the design. Information has multiple dimensions and people process that information in parallel; essentially all of the dimensions are processed at once (MacLeod, 1991). If a conflict exists between the information, then a cue-conflict exists which both slows up mental processing and increases errors.

In Figure 13, people's initial mental ordering of the balls can conflict with the intended design. People see single balls at the end and two pairs in the middle. The oval frames change that pairing. Use of framing to group objects is a common HCI and human factors design technique; the problem arises when lines or frames inadvertently connect objects that are not related or allow two different groupings of objects.

Most optical illusions suffer from cue-conflicts as do drawings by M.C. Escher (Figure 14). Use of an overall design scheme which clashes with

Figure 13. Cue-conflicts in object relationships. The balls which are close together are typically assumed to be related. In the top row, without any other indicators, the balls which are close together are assumed to be related. In the bottom row, the ovals form the groupings, connecting the balls and overriding the closeness assumptions of the top row.

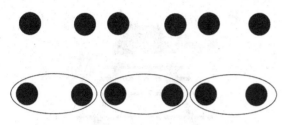

Figure 14. M.C. Escher drawing. A cue-conflict results in a reader seeing a three dimensional image of a triangle which cannot be composed in a real 3D model.

the text or purpose of the website can also create a cue-conflict and disorient the reader.

Some examples of cue-conflicts relevant for information displays are:

- Speed of making judgments of an arrow's direction as up or down depends on its location on a display: up arrows in the upper half are faster to judge than up arrows in the lower half (Clark & Brownell, 1975).
- Speed of deciding if a word was 'left' or 'right' was faster if the word matched its location in the display ('left' on the left side was faster than 'left' on the right side (Rogers, 1979).

It can be difficult for a design team to spot a cue-conflict because they already understand the intended result. Regardless of the balls grouping or framing in Figure 13, because the design team knows how it should be portrayed, they will see it the way they expect the reader to see it. When analyzing usability test results of potential designs, considering cue-conflicts as a source of potential slowdowns or errors can help with the analysis.

Stroop Effect

Poor text design can create reader difficulties by creating cue-conflicts that reflect the Stroop effect (MacLeod, 1991). In a standard Stroop test, a person views a word (for example, tree) printed in a color (for example, red) and must name the color (Stroop, 1935). With a word such as 'tree,' the test is not too difficult. But if the word is changed to a color, such as a person sees the word 'purple' printed in red ink, response time is slowed down and a response of the word rather than the color is not uncommon.

The basic problem a cue-conflict situation creates for readers is that there are conflicting cues (the word purple and the color red) that they must mentally analyze. In addition, people read words faster than they can see/identify a color, resulting in them naming the first task (the word) rather than the color. Dealing with designs that have cue-conflict situations imposes a high mental workload and causes mental fatigue (Kaplan, 1995).

Although a Stroop test is obviously a psychology laboratory exercise and a typical web page would not ask anyone to name the word or color, web pages could contain a mismatch of color words and color ink would fatigue a reader. The basic premise of cue-conflicts applies to any design which provides visual cues in conflict either with itself or with its text.

Optical Illusions

Optical illusions are visual images which contain cues that force the mind to interpret them incorrectly. Even when people know they are looking at an optical illusion, they continue to see the illusion. The Mueller-Lyer illusion (Figure 15) is a common example. Even though people know the lines are the same length, they still look different. As a result, inadvertently introducing them into a design can cause problems. On the other hand, interface design depends on optical illusions to give the appearance of 3D buttons and texture to the interface.

The problem of optical illusions arises when fancy designs are used without consideration of how they may be perceived. Typically, this happens with 3D graphics. The Ponzo illusion (Figure 16) shows how the mind can see lines or objects as different sizes when they are actually the same. Since people tend to interpret graphics quickly and without careful analysis of the scales, they can be misled by the relative sizes of surrounding objects.

A 3D version of an illusion, which depends purely on viewing angle is illustrated in Figure 17. The image looks like a cube floating in space, but viewed from a different angle, the illusion is broken. Design teams need to consider how im-

Figure 15. Mueller-Lyer illusion

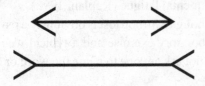

Figure 16. Ponzo illusion. The white lines are the same length. The length or height of the objects appear different and can lead to misinterpreting a graph. Since the illusion is caused by the ties of the railroad track appearance, it helps to follow Tufte's (1983) advice of avoiding chart junk; any ink not directly important to communicating the information should be removed from the graph.

ages will be viewed and ensure misleading illusions are not present.

Another potential optical illusion which graphics may suffer from is called *multistable perception*, which is when there are two possible interpretations of a figure (Figure 18). Some of Esher's drawings of impossible staircases were caused by this perception illusion. When multiple different perceptions exist, a person can flip between them, but design teams cannot ensure people are seeing what was intended. Also, flipping between them requires people to realize there is more than one possible way of viewing the image, a condition which rarely exists. Of course, design teams would rarely intentionally create a multistable graphic, but designs with lots of lines and little shading, such as a multiple line graph, risks having the illusion.

Figure 17. Illusion of a cube based on viewing angle (a video version is available at: http://www.you-tube.com/watch?v=skotd6g7etU)

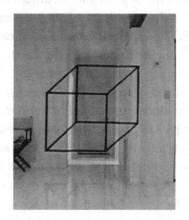 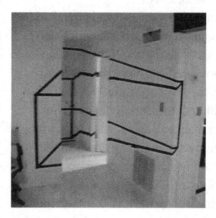

Figure 18. Multistable perception and the Necker cube. The basic Necker cube can be viewed in two different ways, as indicated by the dotted lines in B and C.

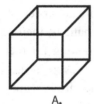 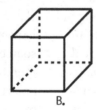 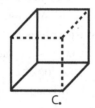

Use of multiple colored or gradated backgrounds can also cause illusions by making the foreground colors appear as different shades. If Figure 19, the foreground gray looks lighter or darker depending on the background (with colors, the effect is more pronounced).

CHANGE BLINDNESS

The term "change blindness" refers to the surprising difficulty observers have in noticing large changes to visual scenes or data displays (Simons & Rensink, 2005). For example, previous studies have shown that observers often fail to notice the displacement of a target dot or the change in shape of a line-drawn object if the change occurs during an eye movement. Change blindness is strongly associated with cognitive load and

Figure 19. Illusion of different foreground colors. The gray squares or the gray bar are the same color. Based on the background, they appear as different shades of gray.

people's working memory capacity (Richards, Hannon, & Derakshan, 2010).

Change blindness is especially problematical for changes that can occur to information which updates without user interaction; if the person is looking away or not specifically looking at that section of the screen, they will not notice the change. This can occur either during rapid changes which happen during an eye saccade or when working with multiple windows or monitors. For example, stock analysts often use multiple monitors with different applications tracking changes in the stock market. The problem they have is if something changes in application A's window while they are looking at application B, they may not realize it or may take several seconds to notice. Of course, a stock analyst's screens are dense with the changes being numbers and minimal change in overall appearance. Consider how changes to values in a table can be very critical to contextual awareness, but since the table looks essentially the same, the change may be missed. As a result, they will continue to use the old information as part of their contextual awareness of the situation. The same effect has been found in areas such as military command and control monitoring where there are many contacts; a new contact or one disappearing may be missed if the operator was not watching when the change occurred (DiVita, Obermayer, Nugent, & Linville, 2004).

To draw attention to the change, the changed information needs to have a higher salience; however, only truly salient information should be flagged. Otherwise, if every change is flagged, the reader will begin to consider all change notices as noise since the majority will not be immediately relevant. One common design technique is to use colored text (perhaps changes appear in red) with an aging algorithm fading the text from red to black over some time period.

Taken together, the research on change blindness shows that people must be paying attention to notice changes. Change blindness results

whenever the resulting change fails to properly signal that something is different.

Most of the psychology research for change blindness has revolved around experiments with explicit changes occurring, such as a colored dot changing position (Figure 20). The problem is much more pronounced if the change had occurred to numbers in a table. For web design, information which updates when a page refreshes or when the information changes on the server, the change would likely be missed unless it is flagged.

All changes to a display are not the same. Changes to items in the center, where people tend to focus their attention, are detected faster (Rensink, O'Regan, & Clark, 1997) than in non-focus areas, but even then their detection is not assured. Change blindness is even stronger when the changes are unexpected; if people are not expecting any changes, they do not expend mental resources looking for them. Triesch et al. (2003) found that even as people were manipulating objects in a virtual reality environment (including manipulating them both before and after the change), they often didn't notice a change. They concluded that people only pay attention to the

Figure 20. Change blindness. Unless the person was specifically looking at the dark gray dot, when it changes position from A to B, they may not notice the change. If the change occurred while they were looking at another window or talking to another person, they may be hard-pressed or require several seconds of thought to decide if the dot has moved.

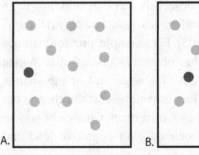

features of the object relevant for achieving the immediate task and disregard any others. In another extreme example, when an actor in a scene was replaced by another person during a shift in camera position, most people did not notice (Levin & Simons, 1997).

One interesting factor about change blindness is that people tend to deny it happens to them. If asked before hand, most people would say they would notice the changes discussed in the previous paragraph, but the research consistently shows the opposite (Levin et al., 2002). These counterintuitive findings of change blindness under naturalistic conditions strongly support the view that it occurs because of a general failure to retain and/or compare information from moment to moment (Simons & Rensink, 2005). Performing these types of comparisons imposes a high cognitive load, which is only rarely rewarded with finding a change; thus, people minimize cognitive effort by not doing it.

Another factor strongly influencing change blindness and very relevant to web design is that change blindness varies with task difficulty. The harder the task, the higher the chance of missing a change because of the higher cognitive load. With high task loads, people are already devoting significant cognitive resources to working on their current task, leaving few resources to allocate to comparing moment-to-moment changes on a page.

Banner Blindness

Banner blindness is a term used to describe the learned inattention people give to many areas of a webpage. It could be considered a special form of change blindness with specific areas of the screen mentally eliminated from any mental processing. A major online reservation site wanted to stress their loyalty program. So the designers tried to pin that information at top of the page; when people scrolled down, the loyalty program information remained fixed. Usability testing found nobody

noticed that information, much less responded to it (WebTorque, 2011).

Banner blindness operates as a learned response that arises from the pre-attentive processing of the page; anything that looks like an ad gets ignored; areas containing flashing text or animation tend to be ads and, thus not relevant to the content (Figure 21). The flip side of the learned behavior to ignore ads is that people have a clear mental image of what they expect web content to look like and don't waste time looking at anything which violates that image. Some studies (Spool, Scanlon, Schroeder, Snyder & DeAngelo, 1997) have found people ignore relevant content if it looks like an ad. Norman (1999) attributes the effect to violating people's schema expectations in the basic design assumptions. People look for specific information and they have an expectation that it will be displayed as normal text within the content area of the page. Everything that fails to meet this expectation (such as a large box with brightly colored or flashing text) is ignored. Unfortunately, this effect can carry over to web sites which don't have banners (or other forms of advertising). For example, if a corporate intranet added a red flashing box at the top of the page telling people they must go to HR and sign a form before they can get paid, many people will literally not see it since they would subconsciously associate it with an ad and never mentally process it.

From the designer's view, banner blindness is a warning against continual attempts at giving irrelevant information (from the reader's viewpoint) high salience. People don't like looking at ads and quickly learned to ignore anything which looked like one. Discussions of banner blindness date from the mid-1990s, matching when banner ads started appearing on web pages.

Banner blindness provides an interesting reversal of attention-grabbing techniques between web and print: with paper-based printing, large highly salient fonts and color draw attention, while web page content formatted with those same large fonts and color is likely to be ignored.

Figure 21. People don't view text which looks like an ad. These are image of heatmaps created from eye tracking studies. The longer a person looked at one area, the more it shows up on the heatmap. The original heatmaps used color. The gray areas with the white outlines were red (most viewed). Notice how the eye spent all of the time in the content area and not in the banner areas (Nielsen, 2007). Image copyright Jakob Nielsen. Reprinted from http://www.useit.com/alertbox/banner-blindness.html

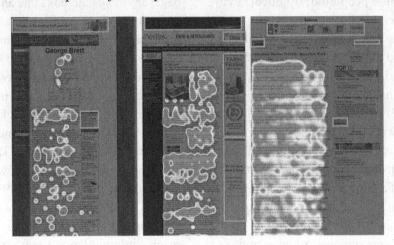

Banner blindness is highest when people are actively seeking information. When people were either given specific facts to find or told to browse a website for general information, those browsing aimlessly had a much higher recall of banner ads (Pagendarm & Schaumburg, 2001). When given specific facts to find, people ignored the banner ads, but during general unspecified browsing, the high salience of the banner drew people's eye. In a different study, total time to select the proper link also increased if the proper link was large but looked like an ad (Benway & Lane, 1998). Nielsen (2007) found that even with the U.S. population in large red letters, (Figure 22) many people had trouble answering the question "What is the US population?" Eye tracking studies showed that people even looked at it, but didn't register the number, probably because it looked too much like an ad. People know government websites never have advertising, but banner blindness has become a deeply ingrained response.

EXAMPLES

Astronomical Information

A person wants information matching a goal. If the goal is to find out about giant molecular clouds, then any page which at first glance doesn't seem to contain that information will be ignored. Design teams need to ensure the most salient information visible at first glance fits a webpage's contents. Adding pretty astronomical images at random may make the page look very nice, but if they don't match the contents then they distract from it. Giant molecular clouds make very nice images—the Orion nebula is one example—, but if the person wants information on the Hertzsprung–Russell diagram on stellar evolution, then an image of Orion will make them think they are on the wrong page.

Different audiences need different presentations and the same page will create a different first glance impression. The first glance information presentation can make people reject a page. If a page contains mathematical equations, a general reader may ignore the page assuming it is too dif-

Figure 22. Inability to find the U.S. population. The value in the upper right corner appears red on the webpage. Obviously, it was designed to stand out, yet many people had trouble finding it. (Image captured from http://www.census.gov/ November 24, 2008).

ficult. On the other hand, the knowledge amateur may not fully understand the math, but will read it for the content they can acquire. Unfortunately for a design team, they cannot simply reject all equations in a design. Instead, they need to figure out how to adjust the presentation for the reader's needs.

Business Reports

Business recommendation reports and proposals must compete with many other reports for the reader's attention. Design teams that fail to provide for a high quality first glance impression risk a reader rejecting the report unread. If the page is poorly designed with dense type and small margins, it will appear to take too much effort to read. If information not directly relevant to the reader's core business interests have the highest salience, then the report will also not seem worth reading. The first few seconds, before a person starts to read the text, creates an impression which the design team must ensure is highly favorable. Many business decisions get made based on which report was easiest to process; rather than carefully read four competing reports, the best looking one is selected almost immediately.

The most salient information must fit the reader's goals, not the design team's agenda. That information must be tuned to be clearly and directly relevant to those goals. A design team should consider how their readers consider the information and what context makes it important to them. That information should receive the highest salience and be clearly in context. They should consider:

• What goals drive each major area (budget, productivity, sales) of the report?
• What questions need to be answered to understand if a problem exists?
• What questions need to be answered to ensure the situation is normal or corresponds to the current business strategy?

A major advantage of graphics is that they support pre-attentive processing and allow a rapid grasp of trends. However, that same speed of mental processing can also lead to misinterpretation if they are designed poorly. Figure 23 shows graphs that may easily be placed side by side in a report since they show the US and non-US sales for a time period. An initial glance makes it appear as if the non-US sales were substantially better than US

Figure 23. Graphs with different scales. Graphs of the same topic (in this case total sales) that are placed side by side will be compared against each other. The scales must be adjusted to support that comparison.

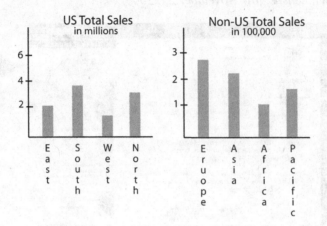

sales. The problem is that the graphs look similar, but have very different scales. The information is correct, but can be misinterpreted at first glance because of poor design.

SUMMARY

People's initial perception of text happens within a few seconds, long before they actually read any text. Many factors influence how people form that first impression of a text and how design teams can ensure their material creates a good initial impression. Factors driving evaluation of the first glance evaluation depend on people's initial perception of the font choices, text design, and graphics. The first few seconds of viewing a text can be critical to the HII by activating a mental model and forming a first impression of both the information quality and contents. The first glance evaluation of the information sets people's expectations; if they believe it will be highly usable, they will tend to continue to believe it is usable.

Perception and Pre-Attentive Processing

Perception is the term that describes the cognitive process of attaining awareness or understanding of the sensory information coming from the world around a person. People constantly receive raw data which they must sort out and determine which is worth further evaluation. To prevent cognitive overload, most incoming information is disregarded as part of pre-attentive processing; the person is never conscious of having received the stimulus. Pre-attention is the rapid and unconscious mental processing performed on incoming information.

Salience Issues at First Glance

The first few seconds are critical for ensuring the reader perceives the document correctly. In the first few seconds, the design must ensure a reader sees enough relevant information to judge the page worthwhile.

Whatever information is most salient drives the decision. The information's prominence and its location on a page contribute to its salience and to the reader deciding if the text is worth reading. If irrelevant information has high salience, the reader may ignore the page thinking it is all irrelevant.

Gestalt Theory

Gestalt principles build a unified view of the complexities of real-world images. When faced with visual complexity and multiple options, the mind tries to find the simplest solution to a problem. One of the ways it does this is to form groups of items that have certain characteristics in common. Gestalt theory works to understand those grouping methods.

Cue-Conflicts

Cue-conflicts occur when the diagram can be interpreted in multiple ways and typically the strongest perceived image conflicts with the way people would typically interpret the design. Optical illusions arise when designs present conflicting interpretations. Information has multiple dimensions and people process that information in parallel. If a conflict exists between the information elements, then a cue-conflict exists which both slows up mental processing and increases errors of interpretation.

Change Blindness

"Change blindness" refers to the difficulty people have in noticing large changes to visual scenes or data displays. They are problematical when the changes occur to information which updates without user interaction; if the person is looking away or not specifically looking at that section of the screen, they will not notice the change. Research on change blindness reveals that people must be paying attention to notice changes. Design teams can help avoid change blindness by ensuring any change gets properly signal to the reader.

REFERENCES

Bailey, R. (2000). *Link affordance.* Retrieved April 27, 2009, from http://webusability.com/article_link_affordance_11_2000.htm

Benway, J., & Lane, D. (1998). Banner blindness: Web searchers often miss "obvious" links. *Internetworking, 1*(3). Retrieved May 4, 2006, from http://www.internettg.org/newsletter/dec98/banner_blindness.html

Chaparro, B., Shaikh, A., & Baker, J. (2005). Reading online text with a poor layout: Is performance worse? *Usability News, 7*(1). Retrieved from http://psychology.wichita.edu/surl/ usabilitynews/71/page_setting.html

Clark, H., & Brownell, H. (1975). Judging up and down. *Journal of Experimental Psychology. Human Perception and Performance, 1,* 339–352. doi:10.1037/0096-1523.1.4.339

DiVita, J., Obermayer, R., Nugent, W., & Linville, J. (2004). Verification of the change blindness phenomenon while managing critical events on a combat information display. *Human Factors, 46*(2), 205–218. doi:10.1518/hfes.46.2.205.37340

Duin, A. (1989). Factors that influence how readers learn from test: Guidelines for structuring technical documents. *Technical Communication, 36*(2), 97–101.

Fennema, M., & Kleinmuntz, D. (1995). Anticipation of effort and accuracy in multi-attribute choice. *Organizational Behavior and Human Decision Processes, 63*(1), 21–32. doi:10.1006/obhd.1995.1058

Few, S. (2009). *Data presentation: Tapping the power of visual perception.* Retrieved May 1, 2009, from http://www.intelligententerprise.com/showArticle.jhtml?articleID=31400009

Gibson, J. (1977). The theory of affordances. In Shaw, R., & Bransford, J. (Eds.), *Perceiving, acting and knowing* (pp. 67–82). Hillsdale, NJ: Erlbaum.

Healey, C. (2007). *Perception in visualization.* Retrieved May 1, 2009, from http://www.csc.ncsu.edu/faculty/healey/PP/index.html

Healey, C., Booth, K., & Enns, J. (1996). High-speed visual estimation using preattentive processing. *ACM Transactions on Human Computer Interaction, 3*(2), 107–135. doi:10.1145/230562.230563

Johnson-Sheehan, R., & Baehr, C. (2001). Visual-spatial thinking in hypertexts. *Technical Communication, 48*(1), 22–30.

Kahneman, D. (1973). *Attention and effort.* Englewood Cliffs, NJ: Prentice-Hall.

Kaplan, S. (1995). The restorative benefits of nature: Toward an integrative framework. *Journal of Environmental Psychology, 15*, 169–182. doi:10.1016/0272-4944(95)90001-2

Kurosu, M., & Kashimura, K. (1995). Apparent usability vs. inherent usability. *CHI '95 Conference Companion*, (pp. 292–293). New York, NY: ACM.

Kwasnik, B. (1992). A descriptive study of the functional components of browsing. In J. Larson & C. Unger (Eds.), *Engineering for Human-Computer Interaction: Proceedings of the IFIP TC2/WG2.7 Working Conference on Engineering for Human-Computer Interaction*, (pp. 191–203). Amsterdam, The Netherlands: North-Holland.

Levin, D., Drivdahl, S., Momen, N., & Beck, M. (2002). False predictions about the detectability of unexpected visual changes: The role of beliefs about attention, memory, and the continuity of attended objects in causing change blindness blindness. *Consciousness and Cognition, 11*(4), 507–527. doi:10.1016/S1053-8100(02)00020-X

Levin, D., & Simons, D. (1997). Failure to detect changes to attended objects in motion pictures. *Psychonomic Bulletin & Review, 4*, 501–506. doi:10.3758/BF03214339

Lindgaard, F., Fernandes, G., Dudek, C., & Brown, J. (2006). Attention Web designers: You have 50 milliseconds to make a good first impression. *Behaviour & Information Technology, 25*(3), 115–126. doi:10.1080/01449290500330448

MacLeod, C. (1991). Half a century of research on the Stroop effect: An integrative review. *Psychological Bulletin, 109*, 163–203. doi:10.1037/0033-2909.109.2.163

McGrenere, J., & Ho, W. (2000). Affordances: Clarifying and evolving a concept. [Montreal, Canada.]. *Proceedings of Graphic Interface, 2000*, 179–186.

Nielsen, J. (2007). *Banner blindness: Old and new findings.* Retrieved November 11, 2007, from http://www.useit.com/alertbox/ banner-blindness.html

Norman, D. (1999). Commentary: Banner blindness, human cognition and Web design. *Internetworking.* Retrieved May 6, 2009, from http://www.internettg.org/newsletter/ mar99/commentary.html

Norman, D. A. (2002). *The design of everyday things.* New York, NY: Basic Books.

Pagendarm, M., & Schaumburg, H. (2001). Why are users banner-blind? The impact of navigation style on the perception of web banners. *Journal of Digital Information, 2*(1). Retrieved May 6, 2006, from http://jodi.tamu.edu/Articles/ v02/i01/Pagendarm/

Rensink, R., O'Regan, J., & Clark, J. (1997). To see or not to see: The need for attention to perceive changes in scenes. *Psychological Science, 8*, 368–373. doi:10.1111/j.1467-9280.1997.tb00427.x

Richards, A., Hannon, E., & Kerakshan, N. (2010). Predicting and manipulating the incidence of inattentional blindness. *Psychological Research, 74*, 513–523. doi:10.1007/s00426-009-0273-8

Rogers, B. (2003). Measuring online experience: It's about more than time! *Usability News, 5*(2). Retrieved from http://psychology.wichita.edu/surl/usabilitynews/52/experience.htm

Simons, D., & Levin, D. (1997). Change blindness. *Trends in Cognitive Sciences, 1*, 261–267. doi:10.1016/S1364-6613(97)01080-2

Simons, D., & Rensink, R. (2005). Change blindness: Past, present, and future. *Trends in Cognitive Sciences, 9*(1), 16–89. doi:10.1016/j.tics.2004.11.006

Spool, J., Scanlon, T., Schroeder, W., Snyder, C., & DeAngelo, T. (1997). *Web site usability: A designer's guide*. Andover, MA: User Interface Engineering.

Stroop, J. (1935). Studies of interference in serial verbal reactions. *Journal of Experimental Psychology, 18*, 643–662. doi:10.1037/h0054651

Treisman, A. (1985). Preattentive processing in vision. *Computer Vision Graphics and Image Processing, 31*, 156–177. doi:10.1016/S0734-189X(85)80004-9

Treisman, A. (1991). Search, similarity, and integration of features between and within dimensions. *Journal of Experimental Psychology. Human Perception and Performance, 1*(3), 652–676. doi:10.1037/0096-1523.17.3.652

Treisman, A., & Gelade, G. (1980). A feature-integration theory of attention. *Cognitive Psychology, 12*, 97–136. doi:10.1016/0010-0285(80)90005-5

Treisman, A., & Gormican, S. (1988). Feature analysis in early vision: Evidence from search asymmetries. *Psychological Review, 95*(1), 15–48. doi:10.1037/0033-295X.95.1.15

Triesch, J., Ballard, D., Hayhoe, M., & Sullivan, B. (2003). What you see is what you need. *Journal of Vision (Charlottesville, Va.), 3*, 86–94. doi:10.1167/3.1.9

Tufte, E. (1983). *The visual display of quantitative information*. Cheshire, CT: Graphics Press.

Tullis, T. (1993). Is user interface design just common sense? In G. Salvendy & M. Smith, (Eds.), *Proceedings of the 5th International Conference on Human-Computer Interaction,* (Vol. 2, pp. 9–14). New York, NY: Elsevier.

WebTorque. (2011). *Movement and change in user interfaces*. Retrieved from http://webtorque.org/?p=1141

Wickens, C., & Carswell, C. (1995). The proximity compatibility principle: Its psychological foundations and its relevance to display design. *Human Factors, 37*, 473–494. doi:10.1518/001872095779049408

Witkin, H. (1978). *Cognitive styles in personal and cultural adaptation*. Washington, DC: Clark UP.

Wolfe, J. (1994). Guided search 2.0: A revised model of visual search. *Psychonomic Bulletin & Review, 1*(2), 202–238. doi:10.3758/BF03200774

Woods, D., Patterson, E., & Roth, E. (2002). Can we ever escape from data overload? A cognitive systems diagnosis. *Cognition Technology and Work, 4*, 22–36. doi:10.1007/s101110200002

ADDITIONAL READING

Gibson, J. (1977). The theory of affordances. In Shaw, R., & Bransford, J. (Eds.), *Perceiving, acting and knowing* (pp. 67–82). Hillsdale, NJ: Erlbaum.

Kurosu, M., & Kashimura, K. (1995). Apparent usability vs. inherent usability. *CHI '95 Conference Companion,* (pp. 292–293). New York, NY: ACM.

Simons, D., & Rensink, R. (2005). Change blindness: Past, present, and future. *Trends in Cognitive Sciences, 9*(1), 16–89. doi:10.1016/j.tics.2004.11.006

Spool, J., Scanlon, T., Schroeder, W., Snyder, C., & DeAngelo, T. (1997). *Web site usability: A designer's guide*. Andover, MA: User Interface Engineering.

Stroop, J. (1935). Studies of interference in serial verbal reactions. *Journal of Experimental Psychology, 18*, 643–662. doi:10.1037/h0054651

Chapter 7
How People Approach Typography

ABSTRACT

This chapter considers how the typography used for presenting information exerts a profound effect on the effectiveness of the communication. The white area in figure 1 shows the area of the HII model relevant to this chapter. The design goal is to ensure that the typography gives proper salience to the important information and does not distract the reader with poor readability. In many failed designs, the typography itself gets in the way of communicating information.

BACKGROUND

Design is not just what it looks like and feels like. Design is how it works. —Steve Jobs

This chapter looks at:

Legibility: Describes the research into what make fonts legible and what factors impair it.

Readability: Describes the research into what make fonts readable and what factors impair it.

Font Elements: Describes the basic structure and terminology for fonts.

Paragraph Layout Elements: Describes the basic terminology of paragraph layout with respect to fonts, such as leading, and type alignment.

Typeface and Emotion: Describes how fonts evoke emotions in people and how design teams need to match the perception of the font to the information.

INTRODUCTION

Typography forms the base of all communication. Any written message must appear in some font. However, with an appropriate choice, the font recedes into the background rather than calling attention to itself (Benson, Olewiler, & Broden, 2005). It is one of the interesting contradictions of design: when properly done, it is invisible to the reader.

DOI: 10.4018/978-1-4666-0152-9.ch007

Figure 1. Information and typography

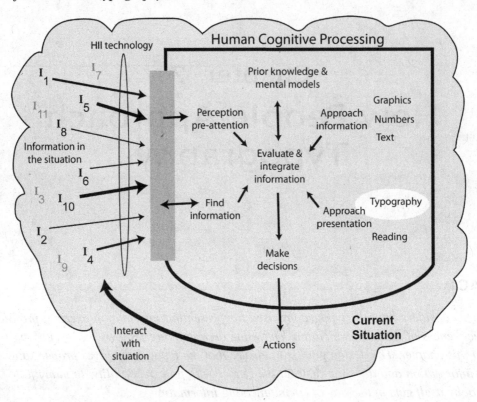

Schriver (1997) discusses the role of typeface mood, personality, and tone, and emphasizes the importance of connecting these to a document's genre, purpose, and context. As she argues:

... . designing legible documents is not enough. A second important characteristic of well-chosen typography is rhetorical appropriateness—the relationship between the typeface, the purpose of the document, its genre, the situation, and the audience's needs, desires, and purposes. (p. 283)

She continues by pointing out the main reason driving typeface choices.

Designers select typography that will make it easier for readers to see the relationships among the parts of the document. Good typography can enhance the reader's ability to infer the purpose and organization of the document (p. 284).

Box 1.

> **Fonts as invisible servants**
> I watched a period movie set in the Gilded Age in a British lord's house. It was interesting how his servants had become essentially invisible to him. He sat down to eat and food simply appeared before him. He walked toward a door and it opened. The people serving the food or opening the door didn't exist as far as he was concerned. The only time he noticed them was when something happened which drew his attention, such as the clang of a dropped plate.
>
> Likewise, fonts should be invisible to the reader. They carry the text to people's eyes and evoke the proper emotional response for the text. The only time they get noticed are when they are inappropriate (wrong font choice, too small/too large). If a font is noticed, then a design team needs to reconsider the font choice.

Two measures of how people can read fonts are their legibility and their readability. Legibility measures how easily people can resolve single characters, while readability measures how easily people can actually read the text. Legibility has a strong influence on both initial impressions of a text and, if the font has legibility problems, a strong influence on the readability.

Beyond legibility and readability, fonts bring a personality to a document, a personality which must be allowed for and matched to the text content.

LEGIBILITY

Legibility measures how well people can resolve individual characters. Typical measurement tests involve actions such as decreasing the lighting or making the fonts smaller until people are not able to distinguish the letters anymore or the reverse with increasing the lighting until the letters can be read. Eye doctors essentially perform a legibility test when they display smaller and smaller letters and ask a patient to say when the letters cannot be read anymore. How people actually identify a letter is a deeper question than it seems on the surface and has been the subject of a substantial amount of research (Grainger, Rey, & Dufau, 2008), but is outside the scope of the HII.

Legibility of Fonts

The overall design of a typeface determines its legibility. A poorly designed font has letter shapes that closely resemble each other, which makes it difficult to distinguish the letter. A highly legible typeface contains features such as large, open counters, ample lowercase x-heights, and character shapes that are obvious and easy to recognize. The most legible typefaces are not excessively light or bold.

Lower case letters are more legible than capital letters because of their higher variation in shape and contrasting heights of ascenders and descenders (Tinker, 1963).

An ongoing debate revolves around the legibility of serf versus sans serif fonts. Reading speed has been shown to be the same. Legibility

of serif fonts seems to be higher, unless the font is very small. Then the serifs interfere with the legibility (Arditi & Cho, 2005).

Legibility values will differ when the measurements are made going light to dark and dark to light. Once people know the letters, they can be pulled from a low contrast background much easier than they can initially be detected. One example is the poorly designed web pages, such as those found on MySpace, that use black text on dark blue background. Since the designer knows what it says, she can read it and believes everyone can. Granted, the letters can be read, but only with difficulty.

Same sized black fonts on a white background are more legible than white fonts on a black background (reversed type) because the large black area visually bleeds into the white area (Taylor, 1934; Scharff & Ahumada, 2003) (Figure 2). Use of serif fonts makes for a more pronounced visual bleeding of the black background into the serifs. Thus, most design guidelines call for sans serif fonts for reversed text.

People have strong perceptions of font legibility based on font size and type. A study by Bernard et al., (2002) found that Arial, Courier, and Georgia were considered the most legible fonts (table 1). However, reading efficiency and reading time differences were not significant between all of the fonts and sizes. Thus, design teams can give readers' preferences strong consideration when choosing a font.

Font legibility depends strongly on four features of the typeface:

Large X-Height: The x-height is the height of the lower case letters. Larger lower case letter makes its shape easier to see. Many fonts designed for compact text have small x-heights (figure 3), which reduces legibility. The FDA ruled that drug information should be printed at a minimum of 6 pt font so it would be legible, but Bix et al. (2003) argue that x-height should be the defining factor

Figure 2. Legibility of different font sizes and background contrast. The gray background remains constant while the fonts (Times New Roman and Arial) get progressively smaller. Notice how the text remains readable at a smaller font size on the white background and the small Arial is easier to read.

12 pt line of text	12 pt line of text
10 pt line of text	10 pt line of text
8 pt line of text	8 pt line of text
6 pt line of text	6 pt line of text
4 pt line of text	4 pt line of text

12 pt line of text	12 pt line of text
10 pt line of text	10 pt line of text
8 pt line of text	8 pt line of text
6 pt line of text	6 pt line of text
4 pt line of text	4 pt line of text

Table 1. Font legibility by font size and type (Bernard et al., 2002)

Finding	Font sample (at test size)	
14-point Arial was perceived as being more legible than 14-point Comic.	Arial	Comic Sans
12-point Verdana and Courier were perceived as being more legible than 10-point Comic, Schoolbook and Verdana.	Verdana Courier	Comic Sans Century Schoolbook Verdana
10-point Tahoma was perceived as more legible than 12-point schoolbook.	Tahoma	Century Schoolbook
10-point Georgia was perceived as more legible than 12-point Tahoma and Schoolbook.	Georgia	Tahoma Century Schoolbook
10-point Arial was perceived as more legible than 12-point Tahoma.	Arial	Tahoma

rather than overall font size. Fonts with small x-heights become illegible at a larger font size than fonts with large x-heights since the lower case letters quickly become too small to read.

Large Counters: The counter is the white space within a font. For example, the o of some fonts is round and in others it is very oval. The more round and higher amounts of white space, the more legible the font.

Stroke Weight: The variation of the strokes making up a letter. Very thin strokes can cause the stroke to almost disappear and leads to confusing the letter with a similar one. For example, if e and c can be confused if

the horizontal stroke is too light to be seen (Tinker, 1963). The mono-weight design of common san serif fonts eliminates this factor and increases their legibility.

Simple Letterforms: The simpler the design of the letter, the more legible it is. Old English and cursive fonts, with the excess curlicues have a low legibility. San serif fonts generally have a higher legibility than serif fonts, since they do not have the serifs. San serif fonts tend to not be as readable in print, but with screen distortion, are more legible on computer displays. Bernard et al. (2001) tested 12 fonts for participants' perception of font legibility and found perceived font leg-

Figure 3. x-height variation. The top row is all lowercase x of different fonts set at 60 points. Although they are same font size, their x-height varies. The bottom example shows how the lowercase letters can become too small to read. All three lines are the same font size.

XXxXXXXxX

Skunks Are Cute Animals -- Arial
Skunks Are Cute Animals -- Century Schoolbook
Skunks Are Cute Animals -- Palace Script

ibility showed significant differences across the 12 fonts with sans serif fonts being more legible than the ornate fonts. Heavy serifs on a font, such as on courier, also decrease its readability (Tinker, 1963)

Legibility of Words

Words are recognized as a single unit, with the ease of recognition depending on the legibility of both the individual letters and the overall shape of the word (Reicher, 1969). The mix of letter sizes of lower cases letters makes a word more recognizable. One reason all caps reads slower is that people have to build up most of the words from individual letters rather than recognize the word at a glance. These ideas will be discussed further in the chapter 11: *How people read*, "Word recognition."

The transition from the legibility of individual letters to legibility of words is not a simple relationship that simply depends on letter/background contrast. Other factors such as the font choice and kerning create a nonlinear relationship (Scharff & Ahumada, 2003).

The shape of individual letters within a word can cause word legibility problems, but only when examined out of context. For example, a subject being shown 'put' and 'pat' or 'draw' and 'drew'

in a low legibility situation can confuse some letters and misrecognize the word. However, placing the words in context within a normal text all but eliminates this confusion (Tinker, 1963). The main exception is text being read by people with very low reading levels. In this case, they are essentially reading each word individually and not seeing them in the context of the sentence. Then a font choice with highly distinctive letter forms works best. Current recommendations are to use fonts, such as Myriad Pro, which were designed for these situations.

Distorting Text

Ornamental typefaces, such as Old English, distort the text with their use of decorative features. Along with the distortion comes a low legibility since many letters start to resemble another or the ornaments hide or distort the basic letter shape. For special purposes or short headings, these typefaces work well. However, they work very poorly as body fonts.

Captchas (an acronym for Completely Automated Public Turing test to tell Computers and Humans Apart) are the distorted words (Figure 4) on various websites which prevent automated systems from using those sites. They exploit how distorted a set of letters can be recognizable to

Figure 4. Captchas B and C have a potential of being too distorted for a person to easily read. Captchas also demonstrate that although people can read the words, they would not want to read a block of text with this distortion.

Figure 5. Distortion caused by text rotation. Interestingly, the legibility of the text is minimally affected by the rotation. People encounter this distortion is a normal day occurrence as they read signs from various angles. For example, driving down a street or walking in a mall (adapted from Larson et al., 2000, p. 145).

a person, but unrecognizable to a computer. On the other hand, some captchas can result in such extreme distortion or distraction that it makes them hard to solve.

Many computer-generated 3D environments display text on what appear to be sidewalls. As a result, the text appears rotated (Figure 5). However, the text legibility does not appear to be impacted by the rotation. Small font sizes showed a small decrease in reading performance, but large font sizes were unaffected (Larson et al., 2000).

READABILITY

Readability refers to the ease with which people can read lines of type. While legibility is basically a feature on the typeface design, readability arises by the choices made in laying out the line of type. Along with font type and size, factors such the kerning and leading play a major role in the readability of a font. This section considers what makes a text readable; chapter 11: *How people read* discusses the details of the reading comprehension and making sense out of a text.

Readability is typically measured by either the reading rate for the text (measure of speed) or reading efficiency (reading time/accuracy) based on a comprehension test. However, studies have generally found no significant font size or type

effects that make measuring both of these variables worthwhile (Bernard & Mills, 2000; Boyarsk, et al.,1998). That is, fonts that were read faster were generally read less accurately, and thus had comparable reading efficiency scores. This, of course, brings up the question of how fast is too fast and can the choice of a very easy to read font actually decrease comprehension by allowing the text to be read too fast? Thus far, no research seems to address this question.

There have been a wide range of recent studies looking at the readability of online fonts. The general conclusion from these studies is that for design situations with only a page or so of text, the reading time differences caused by a font will be overshadowed by other design features.

• A study of online fonts compared four sans serif fonts (Arial, Comic, Tahoma and Verdana), and four serif fonts (Courier New, Georgia, Century School Book and Times New Roman). (Bernard, et al., 2002). They found no difference in reading efficiency between serif and sans serif. However, significant differences were found for reading times of the fonts with the serif fonts producing quicker reading times. Times and Arial were read faster than Courier, Schoolbook, and Georgia. However, while the reading time difference was statistically significant, the actual

Figure 6. Reading time in seconds for approximately two pages of text (adapted from Atwood, 2005). Notice how most of the standard fonts tend to cluster at about same reading time.

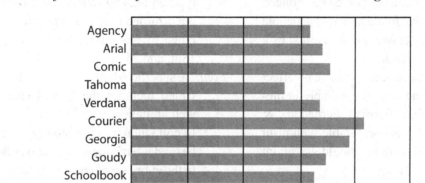

time differences were small. Fonts at the 12-point size were read faster than fonts at the 10-point size.

• Georgia was easier to read online than Times Roman (Boyarsk et al., 1998). Georgia was specifically designed for on-line reading.

• Verdana and Georgia comparisons give mixed results (Boyarsk et al., 1998). Both were designed for online reading, but are sans serif and serif fonts, respectively.

A study of print reading time (Atwood, 2005) gave a relatively wide range of times based on the font (Figure 6). Corsiva is a semi-script font and the slow reading time would be expected. The surprising finding is that Courier has the second worst time, behind Corsiva.

A highly legible font can be made unreadable by poor typographic design. Many other factors affecting readability and font choice, while significant, can be overshadowed by poor decisions on how to present the text. Some of the other factors to consider are:

Contrast: People read light text on a dark background slower and less accurately (Scharff & Ahumada, 2005). They hypothesize that since people have more experience reading dark text, they have developed full letter templates, while light letters are recognized based on component features.

Leading: The leading has no significant effect on reading online, but does affect people's perception of the text (Chaparro et al., 2004).

Kerning: There was no difference in reading speed between the serif and sans serif typefaces used in a study that looked at the effect of close-set type (Moriarty & Scheiner, 1984).

Italics: Reading speed for italics is about 5% slower and the people did not like reading large blocks of italics (Tinker, 1963).

Bold: Reading speed for bold shows little difference from regular type (Tinker, 1963). Any substantial effect probably would require using some extra heavy fonts that which have small counters, such as Arial Black, because the width of the stoke leaves little extra space.

All Caps: Reading speed for all caps is about 15% slower (Tinker, 1963). In addition, all caps takes about 30% more space because of the wider letters. Fisher (1975) reproduced Tinker's work, but found a result that people read reliably faster with lowercase text by a 5-10% speed difference.

Line Length: Line length seems to have no effect on online reading, but people do prefer medium length lines (Bernard, Fernandez, & Hull, 2002). This is comparable with print research showing lines should be about 50–60 characters long,

One font choice issue which is clear, is that the font choices should come from a standard set. The use of uncommon fonts slows reading speed and may also impact comprehension. But the font choice needs to be balanced against the typeface personality needs. Fonts are not rhetorically neutral (Brumberger, 2003a, 2003b). Font choices cause an emotional response which gives a text a specific feel and which design teams must take into account.

FONT ELEMENTS

The choice of a typeface can have a substantial affect on the HII. The wide range of typefaces available present design teams with the challenge of both picking an appropriate font and not making their documents seem too boring by overuse of standard fonts.

This section first reviews some basic type definitions and then looks at the research into how typeface choices affect how people read it. See Boag (1996) for a history of typography measurement.

Typeface: A design for a set of characters for printing or display, such as Times Roman or Arial. It contains the entire design, including roman, bold, italics, small caps, etc., as well as all sizes. (Some sources use font family for the entire set and typeface for a specific

style, such as bold.) With computer-based typesetting, any size is now easy to obtain, but with lead type, a typeface comes in a range of fixed sizes, such as 8 pt, 12 pt, 18pt, and 24 pt.

Font: A specific implementation of a typeface which includes the factors such as size, weight, italics, etc.

In colloquial use, font and typeface tend to be used interchangeably, but typeface refers to the entire set of characters and font refers to a particular implementation. Arial is a typeface and Arial 12 pt bold is a font.

Proportional Font: A font where each of the characters is allocated different widths based on the size of the letter. Most of the common fonts used on a computer, such as Times Roman and Arial, are proportional.

Monospaced Font: A font where each of the characters is allocated the same space. Courier is a monospaced font.

Typefaces can be classified into five main groups (Figure 7):

Old Style: Serif fonts used for newspapers and books. Old style fonts tend to be the most legible.

Modern: Serif fonts that are less legible than old style fonts. Their major difference from old style is they have more extreme contrast in their line weights. Typically, they have very thin serifs and very heavy vertical lines.

Square Serif: Serif font which have squared-off or block-shaped serifs. Also called a slab serif. The serif may be the same weight as the line weights. Typically used as a display font.

Sans Serif: Font without serifs. Used primarily as headings. Lacking serifs, the font can be printed in large sizes without the serifs becoming distracting.

Ornamental: Fancy fonts such as Old English, script fonts, or decorative fonts. They have special uses, but rarely are appropriate for

Figure 7. Examples of the four type groups. Each of the font's names is set in that font.

Old style Garamond Baskerville

Modern Times New Roman

Square serif Stymie

Sans serif **Arial**

technical documentation. This book will not consider them further.

Typography is an old art, starting with Gutenberg, and has developed a very rich nomenclature. This list only presents some of the main points which are relevant to modern design teams. Figure 8 provides a visual description of these terms

Ascenders: Vertical extension above the body of a letter, as in "b"

Baseline: The imaginary line on which the letters sit. Decenders go below the baseline.

Cap-height: Height of capital letters measured from the baseline. The capital height can be less than highest letters. Note in Figure 8, that the capital T is smaller than the lowercase f.

Counters: Enclosed space found within some letters, as in "e" or "o"

Descenders: Vertical extension below the body of a letter, as in "p"

Point size: The size of font measured from the top of the highest ascender to the bottom of the lowest descender.

Stroke weight: Width of the lines which make up the font. Many serif fonts use different weight strokes, such as the right half of the Times Roman letter "U" being thinner than the left half. Most modern sans serif fonts are mono-weight, meaning the lines forming the letter are all the same weight, such as with Arial.

X-Height: Height of lowercase letters measured from the baseline, excluding ascenders and descenders, as in "x."

Serif versus San Serif

The two main categories of font types are serif (with the little tails on the letters) and sans serif (without the little tails). The serifs are supposed to help guide the eye along the row of text and enhance reading.

U.S. readers typically see serif body fonts, while European readers often see san serif body fonts. The reading speed and comprehension research finds little differences between the two as long as reasonable font choices are made. Researchers do consistently find a preference among U.S. readers for serif, but attribute it to familiarity with the typeface. In a interesting contradiction,—but one that is rather common in the usability literature—Bernard et al., (2002) found that Verdana was the most preferred font, while Times was the least preferred for online reading. However, they also found that Georgia and Times serif fonts are considered more attractive. In other words, people thought Times was more attractive, but wanted to read text formatted with Verdana. Contradictions such as these reveal the importance of usability testing with real users and not basing

Figure 8. Typography terms

designs on either design rule-of-thumb or asking people which they prefer. People's preferred choice may not be the best choice for comprehension. Likewise, Brumberger, (2004) found typefaces have persona which they impart on the text, but that persona does not have a significant impact on either comprehension or reading time.

For print (at least in the US), there is general agreement to use serif for body fonts and sans serif for headings. However, there is an ongoing debate about whether or not to use serif or sans serif fonts for online text since computer monitors have trouble properly displaying the serifs on a serif font because of their relatively low resolution (compared to print). The lower resolution of a monitor causes the serifs to display poorly. "One reason for this could be that at smaller font sizes on computer screens, the serifs stop acting as distinguishers and start becoming visual 'noise'" (Bernard & Mills, 2000). The argument is the width of a serif cannot be less than one pixel and must always be in full pixel increments, however, the strokes of the font may also only be one pixel. Thus, the serif width is the same size as the stroke widths. While some specialty fonts may have this as part of their letter design, common fonts such as Times Roman and Garamond do not. Their serifs are designed to be much smaller and narrower than the stroke widths. This same argument applies to display of unequal stroke widths common in serif fonts, where the monitor has a difficult time properly displaying the varying line width. Modern LCD monitors have improved ability to display serifs and the serif/sans serif debate for online information may soon be passé.

While designers continue to debate the serif/sans serif online issue, research on reading speed and individual preferences is mixed. Although reading speed may be slower on a monitor than paper, the serif and sans serif reading speeds on a monitor tend to be about the same. In an online study, reading efficiency is the same for serif and sans serif fonts, but serif fonts read faster (Bernard, Lida, Riley, Hackler & Janzen, 2002).

On the other hand, with printed close-set type, there was no different in reading speed between serif and sans serif (Moriarity & Scheiner,1984). Studies have found serif fonts promote greater reading comprehension than sans serif fonts. For example, a study by Boyarski, et al., (1998) found small but significantly higher levels of comprehension for a serif font (Georgia) over a sans serif font (Verdana).

For small type or text with lots of numbers, sans serif fonts are the most readable.

Font Size

Not surprisingly, larger text sizes are perceived to be more readable than smaller sizes (Mills & Weldon, 1987; Rudnicky & Kolers, 1984). Any actual readability differences are often not significant until the size difference becomes larger than would normally be considered in font choices (Tinker, 1963). For example, finding a readability difference may require comparing a 12 pt and 24 pt font, but design teams essentially never have to pick between 12 pt or 24 pt fonts. Bernard et al., (2002) believe these results should also be true for online reading; this conclusion is in agreement with Chadwick-Dias, McNulty & Tullis (2003) who found text size on a web page did not significantly affect performance in any age group

Word legibility seems to moderately increase up to a 12 pt type size. Although reading speed does not seem to be significantly impaired by smaller sizes, readers do suffer visual fatigue if forced to read long passages in small type (Tinker, 1963). Tinker claims that for body font text in print, 9–12 pt fonts with 2 pts of leading will all have essentially the same reading speed. For online text 12 pt was read faster than fonts at the 10 pt (Bernard, et al., 2002).

Eye tracking studies show larger font sizes are read slower than 10–12 point type. The area seen by the eye does not change, but the amount of type seen at a glance decreases (see Figure 3-5). This increases the amount of cognitive effort

Figure 9. Variation in actual height of fonts sizes. All fonts shown are 40 points, but each E is from a different font. Notice how the height of the letter varies.

EEEEEEEE

required to put the words together. The font size also influences how long people focus on the text. Smaller fonts extend the focus and larger fonts lead to lighter skimming (Chu, Paul, & Ruel, 2009).

Guidelines for choice the font size.

- For most general audiences, font size at 10–12 pts is good.
- For a predominantly older readership of 65 and over or for audiences with known visual handicaps, use a body text font at 14–18 pts. Consider how many greeting card companies and Reader's Digest offer large print versions.
- For young children or beginning readers of any age, a type size around 14 pts in san serif is best (Bernard et al, 2001).

Although these guidelines give rules in point, the actual and apparent size of the letters in a font can vary greatly. Figure 9 shows fonts that are the same size, but display very different actual heights. Font choices need to be tested with the intended readers.

Kerning and Tracking

Kerning is the adjustment of space between pairs of letters. Tracking is the adjustment of space for groups of letters and entire blocks of text. Excessively tight or loose tracking causes readability problems since it makes the words harder to distinguish (Figure 10). Very tight kerning is useful for special effects, such as logos where the letters are touching. For example, in the FedEx and IBM logos, the letters all but touch.

People read faster with close set type than with regular set type. Reading speed was the same with serif and sans serif (Moriarty & Scheiner, 1984). The justification is that with close set type, more letters can be seen within the fixation area. However, this study was only of reading speed over a short time period and did not attempt to measure comprehension.

The proper use of tracking lets the text fit on the page with minimal hyphenation and orphans. The tracking is used to adjust text to prevent widows and orphans, but at times the change is excessive. Design teams need to ensure text adjustments

Figure 10. Example of different font tracking. Settings here are expanded or condensed 1.1 pts versus Microsoft Word's default of 1.0.

close set	The proper use of tracking lets the text fit properly onto the page with minimal hyphenation and orphans.
normal	The proper use of tracking lets the text fit properly onto the page with minimal hyphenation and orphans.
loose set	The proper use of tracking lets the text fit properly onto the page with minimal hyphenation and orphans.

made for a paragraph's appearance do not reduce the overall readability.

PARAGRAPH LAYOUT ELEMENTS

The previous section looked at various aspects of a typeface itself. This section looks at the typographic factors that affect how a typeface is set in longer blocks of text. Good layout results in higher satisfaction and less mental fatigue than poor designs (Chaparro, Shaikh, & Baker, 2005).

Leading

Leading is the space between the lines of text (also called line spacing). The guideline for normal body text is to have leading equal to 20% of the font size. Long lines of text need more leading.

Vertical spacing effects how people perceive online text. They seem to prefer a larger amount of vertical space than is standard for web browsers (Holleran & Bauersfeld, 1993), but reading speed and comprehension seem to be relatively unaffected unless taken to an extreme (Chaparro, Shaikh, & Baker, 2005).

Line Lengths

The line of text should be about two alphabets (52 characters) long for best reading. Research into the relative legibility of different line lengths in print has led to recommendations that line lengths should not exceed about 70 characters per line.

Most articles tend to claim longer or shorter lines will slow down reading speed. For longer lines, the eye often gets lost during the return to the next line. If the lines are too short, readers cannot make use of much information in each fixation, and there is significant time lost as the eye is constantly having to return to the next line (Rayner & Pollatsek, 1989).

Line length has also been found to affect reading rates online. Dyson and Haselgrove (2001) found the length for best compromise between reading speed and comprehension was 55 characters, comparable to that for print. Longer line lengths do seem to be read faster (Dyson & Kipping, 1998; Shaikh, 2005). Shaikh found lines with 95 characters read the fastest, but the readers preferred shorter lines. On the other hand, 95 characters was the longest line, but reading on paper could easily have a longer line. A portrait-formatted page with .5 inch margins contains 90–95 characters; pages formatted landscape would greatly exceed that length and cause reading trouble.

Type Alignment

The most readable alignment is left justified, ragged right. It provides a distinct visual appearance to each page based on the line breaks. Fully justified text, although used by many book and magazine publishers, does not provide that visual distinction. Left justified, ragged right text also provides the most consistent word and character spacing. Fully justified text often has to use overly tight or loose tracking to align the text.

Centered texts or ragged left–justified right texts are difficult to read since they do not provide a consistent left margin for the eye flyback to return to. They should be used only as special formatting and not for body text or any blocks of text more than a few lines long.

Background Contrast

The eye distinguishes the text based on the relative contrast between the foreground and background. Reducing that contrast makes the eye work harder, which lowers reading speed and comprehension.

The color used for the background also has a significant effect on the legibility. A study of slides displayed on a computer screen found reading speeds were highest for color combinations with high contrast between the letters and backgrounds (Garcia & Caldera, 1996). Black-on-white, yellow-on-blue, black-on-gray, and

Figure 11. Legibility with different font/background contrasts. Text is 12 pt Time Roman with the background shading increasing by 20% per step from 0-100%.

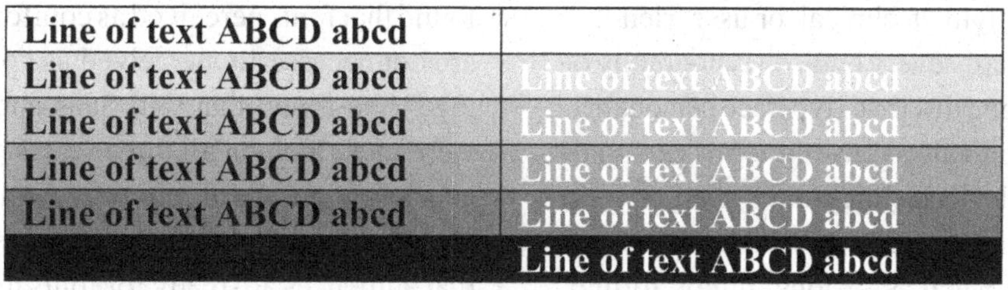

Line of text ABCD abcd	
Line of text ABCD abcd	Line of text ABCD abcd
Line of text ABCD abcd	Line of text ABCD abcd
Line of text ABCD abcd	Line of text ABCD abcd
Line of text ABCD abcd	Line of text ABCD abcd
	Line of text ABCD abcd

yellow-on-black were read significantly faster than other combinations.

Based on the lighting, the legibility of the text can change. With lower light levels, the font must be larger for people to distinguish it. The background contrast also plays a major role in legibility, with smaller fonts being more legible on a high contrast background (Figure 11).

Reversed out Text

Reversed type is a lighter typeface on a darker background (Figure 12). The large dark area easily draws the eye to it. Reversed type works well for a headline, but not large blocks of text. Black fonts on a light background are more legible than white fonts on a black background (Taylor, 1934; Scharff & Ahumada, 2003). Text with large reversed areas are rated as less visually appealing and as harder to read.

Reversed type is read about 10% slower and requires more eye fixations (Tinker, 1963). Reversed type can be harder to read since the ink

can spread into the white areas of the reversed type. With normal black on white printing, the ink spreads out and makes the letter wider; with reversed text, the ink spreads in and makes the letter smaller. The ink spread is most pronounced with serif type since narrow serifs can handle very little spreading before looking jagged or broken. The broken appearance makes the page look bad. The large dark area slows down reading. In general, reversed text should be done with larger sans serif fonts and the lines should have increased leading.

TYPEFACE AND EMOTION

The typeface in a presentation carries with it an emotional element that affects how the audience responds to a text and what they learn from it (Larson, 2004). High quality HII ensures that any emotional elements within the text fit the information being communicated. Kostelnick (1990) points out that the typography carries a

Figure 12. Reversed type. Notice how the 10 pt lines of serif (Times Roman) and sans serif (Arial) read differently as the black visually bleeds into the serifs. Use of modern serif fonts, with their small serifs would exacerbate the bleed problem.

"visual texture, tone, and mood," that "suggests a rhetorical stance: serious, conversational, low key, energetic, highly technical, or user friendly" (p. 199). Essentially every book on typography or desktop publishing discusses typeface personality, although they don't always use the term "personality." For example, Kostelnick and Roberts (1998) claim that typefaces are perceived as having an emotional state, such as serious, funny, formal, friendly, personable, or technical. Likewise, Parker (1997) and Shushan and Wright (1994) discuss how a typeface conveys mood, communicates attitude, and sets tone.

Typeface personality comes from both the typeface anatomy and its context, since long use of certain typefaces in certain contexts has connected them in people's minds (Mackiewicz, 2005), such as use of cursive or Old English fonts for invitations. The full typeface personality is not an instant or pre-defined attribute, but rather an emergent one which arises from reading a text with a particular typeface within the overall context of the document, as Brumberger (2004) explains:

The data emphasizes that typefaces and texts interact during the reading process, countering the notion that a typeface with a particular persona will lend that persona to any document. Although a group of readers may consistently assign particular personality attributes to a particular typeface, that typeface may not consistently color every text they read in the same way. Thus, the project reinforces the notion of technical communication as rhetorical problem solving (Flower 1989), in which context is crucial and each communication situation requires a carefully considered and appropriately tailored solution (p. 22).

In general, each typeface has a distinct persona and the design team must match that persona with the text. In an ongoing design battle, some designers want to pick fonts based on their appearance to add interest, while others argue for using standards such as Arial or Times Roman to privilege

easy-to-read even if the font is considered boring. Working against the latter idea, Mackiewicz (2005) found that fonts perceived as comfortable-to-read are not necessarily perceived as "plain" or "boring." She found that Gill Sans and Souvenir Lt were rated high on all three scales she tested for: comfortable to-read, attractive, and interesting. Her findings on the interesting variable suggest that audiences are ready for fonts that break from default settings and old standards. Design teams need to test their font choices, but other fonts besides the basic standards of Times Roman and Arial can be effectively used (Mackiewicz, 2007a).

Brumberger (2003a, 2003b, 2004) has performed the most extensive examination of how a typeface carries with it an emotional element and how people react to it. Figure 13 shows some of the typefaces she examined and how they were perceived. Concluding her review of past research into typeface appropriateness, Brumberger (2003a) states "each of these studies demonstrates readers' awareness of typeface appropriateness and their ability to make judgments regarding the appropriateness of typefaces for a specific purpose or text" (p. 225). Of note, she found readers expect the emotional element to match the tone of the text and any mismatch causes some level of cognitive dissidence.

There seems to be little correlation between typographic considerations, personality, people's preferences, and objective measures of readability. The fonts that people say they prefer to read do not increase speed or comprehension and likewise, fonts that they say they don't like to read may have higher reading speed or comprehension. Preferred choice of typeface often does not translate the faster completion times (Garcia & Caldera, 1996). On the other hand, many of the studies looking at completion time are based on short readings. Longer interaction times may show a closer correlation between preference and task times, as real usage factors have a chance to overcome initial perception. Participants in the above study were also asked to identify their most

Figure 13. Typeface persona. The fonts in group 2 are the typical fonts used is business communication. (adapted from Brumberger, 2003b, p. 214)

Group 1 Elegance	Group 2 Directness	Group 3 Friendliness
Black Chancery	Arial	Bauhaus
Harrington	Garamond	Comic Sans
Adler	Times New Roman	VanDijk
	Courier New	Lucida Sans Italic

"preferred format." Interestingly, for over half of the 36 participants, their preferred format was not the format they were most accurate at processing, at either the gross-level or more detailed task level (Feldman-Stewart, & Brundage, 2004).

Perception of Fonts

Brumberger (2004) found emotional perception in specific fonts. These results can be extended to suggest that personality traits can be attributed to fonts on the basis of their design family and, as a result, define their appropriate use (Shaikh, Chaparro, & Fox, 2006).

While Brumberger dealt with a wide range of typefaces, even research of common typefaces and staying within a serif or sans serif font style, Tantillo, DiLorenzo-Aiss, and Mathisen (1995) found significant differences in how people perceived a font. When students were asked to evaluate six typefaces (Avant Garde, Century Schoolbook, Goudy Old Style, Helvetica, Times New Roman, and Univers) using 28 variables, the three sans-serif typefaces were rated as significantly different from the three serif typefaces on many of the variables. Serif fonts were rated as more elegant, charming, emotional, distinct, beautiful, interesting, extraordinary, rich, happy, valuable, new, gentle, young, calm, and less traditional than the sans serif type styles. They summed up the

findings by concluding that sans serif styles were perceived as more readable and less legible than the serif styles. This research used common typefaces which readers should see and read with some regularity, yet there were significant differences in how they were perceived. Design teams need to carefully consider the impact of their font choices on the text and not pick a designer's favorite font or simply falling back on Times Roman or Arial. In one piece of helpful research, Mackiewicz (2005) found that examining only five of the letters within a font—uppercase J and lowercase a, g, e, and n letterforms—gives enough information for a design team to make decisions about the font's emotional attributes and to determine if it is appropriate for the document.

Stopke and Staley (1994) related specific letter characteristics to people's perception of a typeface.

- **Contemporary.** Sans serif fonts with large x-height. Helvetica.
- **Traditional.** Serif fonts with small x-height and tall ascenders and descenders. Goudy.
- **Trendy.** Strongly condensed or extended counters and high ascenders. Futura Condensed.
- **Elegant.** Angled counters, hairline accents, small x-height, and tall ascenders and descenders. Palatino Italic and Bodoni.

- **Friendly.** Rounded letterforms. New Century Schoolbook.
- **Serious.** Squeezed counters and vertical. Times Roman.

Research has compared the perception of various fonts and found that:

- Ornate sans serif fonts, Bradley and Corsiva, are perceived as having a great deal of personality and being elegant, whereas Times New Roman is perceived as being "business-like" (Bernard et al., 2002).
- Serif fonts were rated as more elegant, beautiful, and less traditional than the sans serif fonts (Tantillo, DiLorenzo-Aiss, & Mathisen, 1995).
- Georgia is perceived as being significantly more attractive than Arial, Courier, and Comic Sans (Bernard et al., 2002).

For the technical documents of interest to HII, it appears that fonts that display overall moderation in their letter characteristics and use less open letter spacing are perceived as readable, professional, and attractive (Mackiewicz, 2007a).

Typeface Clashes

Brumberger (2003a) found that readers are aware of dissonance between typeface and text personas. In her study, people clearly perceived typefaces with particular personas to be more appropriate for texts with matching personas. Not surprisingly, a typeface whose persona matched closely that of the text was seen as more appropriate for that text. When typeface imparts an emotional or perceptual quality that is not consistent with the text, the response to the words tends to be slower (Lewis & Walker, 1989) and comprehension risks being impaired.

Choice of typeface can cause a clash when the typeface fails to fit the purpose of the content and reader expectations. A typeface clashing with the tone or mood of the content often does not directly affect simple typography measures such as legibility or reading speed. As long as the font itself doesn't hinder reading speed, people will read the text at the same speed, but will still feel the cognitive dissonance of the clash, although they often cannot articulate what is wrong. However, the overall response of readers to the text can be impaired. It may lower subjective ratings such as trustworthiness or professional quality. Detecting such a mismatch requires usability testing which asks readers for their impressions; quantitative readability or usability measurements will not detect it.

Haskins (1958) investigated whether there were "all purpose" typefaces that could be used in a variety of contexts. Although he didn't find any all-purpose typeface, he did suggest that matching personas of typeface to the text is more of an issue for texts involving "some kind of conflict or tension" (p. 191) and was less important for entertainment. Because most text that is relevant to HII is focused on communicating information rather than on entertainment, design teams need to carefully consider the choice of typeface with respect to the content and not to simply select standard fonts such as Calibri, Arial or Times Roman. Most documents, including business reports, have some level of tension and design teams must match the font choice against that tension.

EXAMPLES

Astronomical Information

Creators of web-based information need to create a revenue stream to pay for the content. Unfortunately, this means many sites overload the page with ads. The result is a visual mismatch of images and text. The reader has a hard time figuring out what is valid site content and what is advertising. When it is difficult to read, the casual readers of

Figure 14. Inviting page design. These two pages show the initial page of the same report and contain the same information. However, because of the more inviting page layout of the left hand page, people will be more inclined to read it. The right hand page appears dense and gives the impression that it will be hard to read.

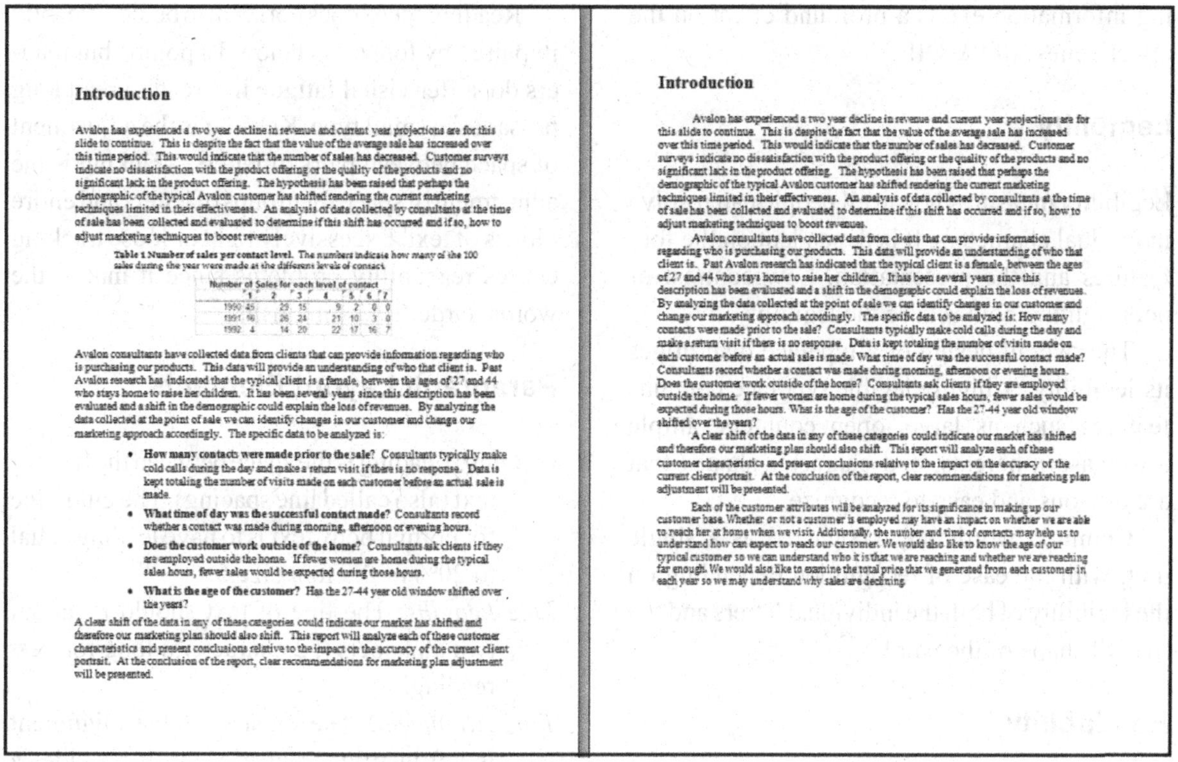

Introduction

Avalon has experienced a two year decline in revenue and current year projections are for this slide to continue. This is despite the fact that the value of the average sale has increased over this time period. This would indicate that the number of sales has decreased. Customer surveys indicate no dissatisfaction with the product offering or the quality of the products and no significant lack in the product offering. The hypothesis has been raised that perhaps the demographic of the typical Avalon customer has shifted rendering the current marketing techniques limited in their effectiveness. An analysis of data collected by consultants at the time of sale has been collected and evaluated to determine if this shift has occurred and if so, how to adjust marketing techniques to boost revenues.

Table 1 Number of sales per contact level. The numbers indicate how many of the 100 sales during the year were made at the different levels of contact

	Number of Sales for each level of contact						
	1	2	3	4	5	6	7
1990	45	29	15	9	2	0	0
1991	16	26	24	21	10	3	0
1992	4	14	20	22	17	16	7

Avalon consultants have collected data from clients that can provide information regarding who is purchasing our products. This data will provide an understanding of who that client is. Past Avalon research has indicated that the typical client is a female, between the ages of 27 and 44 who stays home to raise her children. It has been several years since this description has been evaluated and a shift in the demographic could explain the loss of revenues. By analyzing the data collected at the point of sale we can identify changes in our customer and change our marketing approach accordingly. The specific data to be analyzed is:

- **How many contacts were made prior to the sale?** Consultants typically make cold calls during the day and make a return visit if there is no response. Data is kept totaling the number of visits made on each customer before an actual sale is made.
- **What time of day was the successful contact made?** Consultants record whether a contact was made during morning, afternoon or evening hours.
- **Does the customer work outside of the home?** Consultants ask clients if they are employed outside the home. If fewer women are home during the typical sales hours, fewer sales would be expected during those hours.
- **What is the age of the customer?** Has the 27-44 year old window shifted over the years?

A clear shift of the data in any of these categories could indicate our market has shifted and therefore our marketing plan should also shift. This report will analyze each of these customer characteristics and present conclusions relative to the impact on the accuracy of the current client portrait. At the conclusion of the report, clear recommendations for marketing plan adjustment will be presented.

Introduction

Avalon has experienced a two year decline in revenue and current year projections are for this slide to continue. This is despite the fact that the value of the average sale has increased over this time period. This would indicate that the number of sales has decreased. Customer surveys indicate no dissatisfaction with the product offering or the quality of the products and no significant lack in the product offering. The hypothesis has been raised that perhaps the demographic of the typical Avalon customer has shifted rendering the current marketing techniques limited in their effectiveness. An analysis of data collected by consultants at the time of sale has been collected and evaluated to determine if this shift has occurred and if so, how to adjust marketing techniques to boost revenues.

Avalon consultants have collected data from clients that can provide information regarding who is purchasing our products. This data will provide an understanding of who that client is. Past Avalon research has indicated that the typical client is a female, between the ages of 27 and 44 who stays home to raise her children. It has been several years since this description has been evaluated and a shift in the demographic could explain the loss of revenues. By analyzing the data collected at the point of sale we can identify changes in our customer and change our marketing approach accordingly. The specific data to be analyzed is: How many contacts were made prior to the sale? Consultants typically make cold calls during the day and make a return visit if there is no response. Data is kept totaling the number of visits made on each customer before an actual sale is made. What time of day was the successful contact made? Consultants record whether a contact was made during morning, afternoon or evening hours. Does the customer work outside of the home? Consultants ask clients if they are employed outside the home. If fewer women are home during the typical sales hours, fewer sales would be expected during those hours. What is the age of the customer? Has the 27-44 year old window shifted over the years?

A clear shift of the data in any of these categories could indicate our market has shifted and therefore our marketing plan should also shift. This report will analyze each of these customer characteristics and present conclusions relative to the impact on the accuracy of the current client portrait. At the conclusion of the report, clear recommendations for marketing plan adjustment will be presented.

Each of the customer attributes will be analyzed for its significance in making up our customer base. Whether or not a customer is employed may have an impact on whether we are able to reach her at home when we visit. Additionally, the number and time of contacts may help us to understand how can expect to reach our customer. We would also like to know the age of our typical customer so we can understand who it is that we are reaching and whether we are reaching far enough. We would also like to examine the total price that we generated from each customer in each year so we may understand why sales are declining.

an astronomical site will search for information elsewhere.

Business Reports

Font choices are business reports rarely depart from basic serif or sans serif choices and are often dictated by corporate style guides. However, the page layout does not fall under the style guide or, if it does, the style guide uses overly general terms that do not provide a clear way to design a page.

The problem with poor page design is that it can turn a reader off by making the page look too dense. People do not like pages that have a high overall grayness. It creates a high perceived effort for extracting information. Figure 14 shows two example pages with the same information. The left hand one has more white space through the use of tables and lists. This makes the page appear to require less effort to read.

Business readers have too many choices of text to read. If a report looks like it will be difficult, there is a high chance it will not be read unless the reader is forced to read it. A report that is an unsolicited proposal, which may contain excellent benefits for the company, will not be read if it looks like the right-hand example in Figure 14. The reader has little motivation to wade through dense text. Some design teams assume if the content is good then the report will be read, but the reality is that first the report must look readable. If not, it's not read rendering the content is irrelevant.

SUMMARY

Typography forms the base of all communication. As such, the typography used for presenting information exerts a profound effect on the effectiveness of the HII.

Legibility

Legibility measures how well people can resolve individual characters. It is dependent on the font features and the presentation. Low contrast or poor lighting both reduce the legibility.

The overall design of a typeface determines its legibility. A highly legible typeface contains features such as large, open counters, ample lowercase x-heights, and character shapes that are obvious and easy to recognize.

Common words are recognized as a single unit, with the ease of recognition depending on the legibility of both the individual letters and the overall shape of the word.

Readability

Readability refers to how easily people can read lines of type. Readability arises by the choices made in page layout, with factors such as font type and size, kerning, and leading playing a major role in the overall readability. Readability is typically measured by either the reading rate for the text (measure of speed) or reading efficiency (reading time/accuracy) based on a comprehension test.

Font Elements

Typefaces can be classified into five main groups: old style, modern, square serif, sans serif, and ornamental.

The two main categories of font types are serif (with the little tails on the letters) and sans serif (without the little tails). For print (at least in the US), body fonts typically use serif and headings use sans serif. There is an ongoing debate about whether or not to use serif or sans serif fonts for online text since computer monitors have trouble properly displaying the serifs on a serif font because of their relatively low resolution.

Reading speed does not seem to be significantly impaired by font sizes below 12 points, but readers do suffer visual fatigue if forced to read long passages in small type. Kerning is the adjustment of space between pairs of letters. Tracking is the adjustment of space for groups of letters and entire blocks of text. Excessively tight or loose tracking causes readability problems since it makes the words harder to distinguish.

Paragraph Layout Elements

Leading: Leading is the space between the lines of text (also called line spacing). The guideline for normal body text is to have leading equal to 20% of the font size.

Line Lengths: The line of text should be about two alphabets (52 characters) long for best reading.

Type Alignment: The most readable alignment is left justified, ragged right. It provides a distinct visual appearance to each page based on the line breaks.

Background: The eye distinguishes the text based on the relative contrast between the foreground and background. Reducing that contrast makes the eye work harder, which lowers reading speed and comprehension. Same sized black fonts on a white background are more legible than white fonts on a black background

Reversed Text: Reversed type is a lighter typeface on a darker background. Reversed type works well for a headline, but not large blocks of text.

Typeface and Emotion

The typeface in a presentation carries with it an emotional element that affects how the audience responds to a text. Typeface personality comes from both the typeface anatomy and its context, since the use of certain typefaces in certain contexts has connected them in people's minds. High quality HII ensures that any emotional elements within the text fit the information being communicated.

Readers expect the typeface and text to match. If they don't, they are aware of emotional dissonance between a typeface and text context. This impedes comprehension.

REFERENCES

Arditi, A., & Cho, J. (2005). Serifs and font legibility. *Vision Research, 45*, 2926–2933. doi:10.1016/j.visres.2005.06.013

Atwood, J. (2005). Comparing font legibility. *Coding Horror.* Retrieved from http://www.codinghorror.com/blog/2005/11/comparing-font-legibility.html

Benson, J., Olewiler, K., & Broden, N. (2005). *Typography for mobile phone devices: The design of the Qualcomm sans font family.* Retrieved April 9, 2010, from http://www.aiga.org/resources/content/2/0/9/3/documents/typography_for_mobile_phone_devices.pdf

Bernard, M., Lida, B., Riley, S., Hackler, T., & Janzen, K. (2002). A comparison of popular online fonts: which size and type is best? *Usability News, 4*(1). Retrieved from http://www.surl.org/usabilitynews/41/onlinetext.asp

Bernard, M., & Mills, M. (2000). So, what size and type of font should I use on my website? *Usability News, 2*(2). Retrieved from http://psychology.wichita.edu/surl/usabilitynews/22/font.asp

Bix, L., Lockhart, H., Selke, S., Cardoso, F., & Olejnik, M. (2003). Is x-height a better indicator of legibility than type size for drug labels? *Packaging Technology and Science, 16*(5), 199–207. doi:10.1002/pts.625

Boag, A. (1996). Typographic measurement: A chronology. [Department of Typography and Graphic Communication: University of Reading.]. *Typography Papers, 1*, 105–121.

Boyarsk, D., Neuwirth, C., Forlizzi, J., & Regli, S. H. (1998). A study of fonts designed for screen display. *Proceedings of the SIGCHI Conference on Human Factors in Computing Systems* (pp. 87–94). New York, NY: ACM.

Brumberger, E. (2003a). The rhetoric of typography: The awareness and impact of typeface appropriateness. *Technical Communication, 50*(2), 224–231.

Brumberger, E. (2003b). The rhetoric of typography: The persona of typeface and text. *Technical Communication, 50*(2), 206–223.

Brumberger, E. (2004). The rhetoric of typography: Effects on reading time, reading comprehension, and perceptions of ethos. *Technical Communication, 51*(1), 13–24.

Chadwick-Dias, A., McNulty, M., & Tullis, T. (2003). Web usability and age: How design changes can improve performance. *Proceedings of the 2003 Conference on Universal usability,* (pp. 30–37). New York, NY: ACM.

Chaparro, B. Baker, J., Shaikh, A., Hull, S., & Brady, L. (2004). Reading online text: A comparison of four white space layouts. *Usability News, 6*(2). Retrieved April 14, 2010, from http://www.surl.org/usabilitynews/62/whitespace.asp

Chaparro, B., Shaikh, A., & Baker, J. (2005). Reading online text with a poor layout: Is Performance worse? *Usability News, 7*(1). Retrieved from http://psychology.wichita.edu/surl/usabilitynews/71/page_setting.html

Chu, S., Paul, N., & Ruel, L. (2009). Using eye tracking technology to examine the effectiveness of design elements on news websites. *Information Design Journal, 17*(1), 31–43. doi:10.1075/idj.17.1.04chu

Dyson, M., & Haselgrove, M. (2001). The influence of reading speed and line length on the effectiveness of reading from screen. *International Journal of Human-Computer Studies, 54*, 585–612. doi:10.1006/ijhc.2001.0458

Dyson, M., & Kipping, G. (1998). The effects of line length and method of movement on patterns of reading from screen. *Visible Language, 32*, 150–181.

Feldman-Stewart, D., & Brundage, M. (2004). Challenges for designing and implementing decision aids. *Patient Education and Counseling, 54*, 265–273. doi:10.1016/j.pec.2003.09.007

Fisher, D. (1975). Reading and visual search. *Memory & Cognition, 3*, 188–196. doi:10.3758/BF03212897

Garcia, M., & Caldera, C. (1996). The effect of color and typeface on the readability of on-line text. *Computers & Industrial Engineering, 31*(1-2), 519–524. doi:10.1016/0360-8352(96)00189-1

Grainger, J., Rey, A., & Dufau, S. (2008). Letter perception: From pixels to pandemonium. *Trends in Cognitive Sciences, 12*(10), 381–387. doi:10.1016/j.tics.2008.06.006

Haskins, J. (1958). Testing suitability of typefaces for editorial subject matter. *The Journalism Quarterly, 35*, 186–194. doi:10.1177/107769905803500205

Holleran, P., & Bauersfeld, K. (1993). Vertical spacing of computer-presented text. *INTERCHI Adjunct Proceedings,* 179–180.

Kostelnick, C. (1990). The rhetoric of text design in professional communication. *The Technical Writing Teacher, 17*(3), 189–202.

Larson, K. (2004). *The science of word recognition.* Retrieved May 28, 2009, from http://www.microsoft.com/typography/ctfonts/WordRecognition.aspx

Larson, K., van Dantzich, M., Czerwinski, M., & Robertson, G. (2000). Text in 3D: Some legibility results. In *Extended Abstracts of CHI '2000, Human Factors in Computing Systems* (pp. 145–146). New York, NY: ACM. doi:10.1145/633292.633374

Lewis, C., & Walker, P. (1989). Typographic influences on reading. *The British Journal of Psychology, 80*, 241–257. doi:10.1111/j.2044-8295.1989.tb02317.x

Mackiewicz, J. (2005). How to use five letterforms to gauge a typeface's personality: A research-driven method. *Journal of Technical Writing and Communication, 35*, 291–315. doi:10.2190/LQVL-EJ9Y-1LRX-7C95

Mackiewicz, J. (2007a). Audience perceptions of fonts in projected PowerPoint text slides. *Technical Communication, 54*(3), 295–307.

Moriarty, S., & Scheiner, E. (1984). A study of close-set type. *The Journal of Applied Psychology, 69*(4), 700–702. doi:10.1037/0021-9010.69.4.700

Parker, R. (1997). *Looking good in print.* Research Triangle Park, NC: Ventana Communications Group, Inc.

Rayner, K., & Pollatsek, A. (1989). *The psychology of reading.* New York, NY: Prentice-Hall.

Reicher, G. (1969). Perceptual recognition as a function of meaningfulness of stimulus material. *Journal of Experimental Psychology, 81*, 275–280. doi:10.1037/h0027768

Rudnicky, A., & Kolers, P. (1984). Size and case of type as stimuli in reading. *Journal of Experimental Psychology. Human Perception and Performance, 10*, 231–249. doi:10.1037/0096-1523.10.2.231

Scharff, L., & Ahumada, A. (2003). Contrast measures for predicting text readability. In Rogowitz, B., & Pappas, T. (Eds.), *Human Vision and Electronic Imaging VIII* (pp. 463–472). Santa Clara, CA: SPIE.

Schriver, K. (1997). *Dynamics in document design: Creating texts for readers*. New York, NY: Wiley.

Shaikh, D. (2005). The effects of line length on reading online news. *Usability News, 7*(2). Retrieved April 13, 2010, from http://www.surl.org/usabilitynews/ 72/LineLength.asp

Shushan, R., & Wright, D. (1994). *Desktop publishing by design*. Redmond, WA: Microsoft Press.

Stopke, J., & Staley, C. (1994). *An eye for type*. Ann Arbor, MI: Promotional Perspectives.

Tantillo, J., Di Lorenzo-Aiss, J., & Mathisen, R. E. (1995). Quantifying perceived differences in type styles: An exploratory study. *Psychology and Marketing, 12*, 447–457. doi:10.1002/mar.4220120508

Taylor, C. (1934). The relative legibility of black and white print. *Journal of Educational Psychology, 25*(8), 561–578. doi:10.1037/h0074746

Tinker, M. (1963). *Legibility of print*. Ames, IA: Iowa State University Press.

ADDITIONAL READING

Brumberger, E. (2003). The rhetoric of typography: The persona of typeface and text. *Technical Communication, 50*(2), 206–223.

Brumberger, E. (2003). The rhetoric of typography: The awareness and impact of typeface appropriateness. *Technical Communication, 50*(2), 224–231.

Brumberger, E. (2004). The rhetoric of typography: Effects on reading time, reading comprehension, and perceptions of ethos. *Technical Communication, 51*(1), 13–24.

Schriver, K. (1997). *Dynamics in document design: Creating texts for readers*. New York, NY: Wiley.

Usability News. (n.d.). Retrieved from http://www.surl.org/usabilitynews/

Chapter 8
How People Approach Graphical Information

ABSTRACT

The previous chapter dealt with how people typography affected how people interpret documents. This chapter continues in the same vein by looking at how people interpret graphics' influence on how they interpret the overall document (Figure 1). As considered in this chapter, graphics are any visual element placed in a text, such as: tables, diagrams, graphs, and photographs. Use of graphics helps a person interpret a situation more quickly. However, even if people find information which is accurate and reliable, that information is essentially useless to those people unless they are able to interpret it and apply it to their current situation. "The power of a graph is its ability to enable one to take in the quantitative information, organize it, and see patterns and structure not readily revealed by other means of studying the data" (Cleveland & McGill, 1984, p. 535). Of course, the design teams must ensure the information presentation fits the people's information needs.

BACKGROUND

I think it is important for software to avoiding imposing a cognitive style on workers and their work —Edward Tufte

Graphics in technical material rarely exist without text, and material with integrated text and graphics improves comprehension (Betrancourt & Bisseret, 1998). In a majority of HII situations, text and graphics appear within the same document; an assumption which will be explicitly covered in this chapter. Since graphics do not stand alone, it is important to consider how people interpret graphics, how text and graphics interact, and how together they affect communication.

This chapter looks at:

Approaches to texts with graphical elements: Texts contain both text and graphics which people have to read and integrate together. However, images and text are mentally processed differently.

Types of graphics in technical documents: Reviews the major types of graphics and discusses the

DOI: 10.4018/978-1-4666-0152-9.ch008

Figure 1. HII model – Approaching graphical information

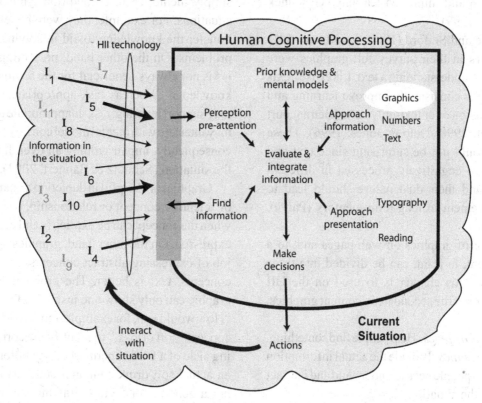

research finding on what makes that graphic type effective.

How people comprehend a graphic: Reviews what makes graphics work within a specific context and what factors interfere with interpreting the graphic.

INTRODUCTION

Reading text is essentially a linear task of word recognition and then the word recognition builds to text comprehension via the construction-integration model described in Chapter 11: *How people read*. Reading text is fundamentally an unnatural communication method, while visuals evolved with humans interacting with their environment. Thus, since graphical communication is basically entirely visual, graphics have played an important role as user-interfaces changed from

command-line to a GUI. Many people expected that "purely visual communication, without the use of words, could become an international auxiliary language…however, a purely graphic presentation does not usually catch the meaning of the information" (Garcia & Tissiani, 2003, p. 51). In the end, for communicating complex technical information and supporting HII, the use of graphics is extremely important, but much of the concrete information can only be communicated by text. Design teams need to be conscious of the best uses of both and how to merge them effectively.

Unlike text, comprehending graphics is multidimensional with the entire image being interpreted simultaneously. Multiple theories have been advanced about how graphics improve text comprehension and their rhetorical effect (Brasseur, 2003). Material gets presented twice (text and graphic) which leads to repetition of presentation and improved learning (Gyselinck & Tardieu, 1999).

Penrose and Seiford (1988) found over 50% of the users in their survey felt graphics were important to understanding a text. Likewise, texts with pictures consistently improve learning and comprehension over text-only texts (Betrancourt & Bisseret, 1998; Delp & Jones, 1996). These finding should not be surprising since text and graphics are cognitively processed in different channels and their dual nature should lead to better placement in long-term memory (Paivio, 1971; 1986).

The use of graphics on web pages and, to a lesser extent, in print, can be divided into three categories. This chapter is focused on the HII implications of the second item, content graphics.

Navigation Graphics: Help people find something.
Content Graphics: Provide the actual information which people need to understand and interact with the situation.
Ornamental Graphics: Eye candy with no useful content or navigation support, such as pictures of people shaking hands on a site for a customer-relations company, scrollwork on a page edge, or a picture of a corporate team. Design teams use them to break up the text, but the value of eye candy is questionable (Spool, 2009). In one study, people looked for information in brochures that either contained no graphics, content graphics, or ornamental graphics. The older participants had more trouble with the ones containing ornamental graphics and younger participants performed the same across all three (Griffin & Wright, 2009).

Integrated presentation of text and graphics improves learning material over putting the image in text in separate screen areas or using user-activated pop-ups (Betrancourt & Bisseret, 1998). This finding was strongest when the people had to mentally integrate the material, rather than simply memorize it; a condition typical of HII situations. For example, they were better able to transfer the knowledge to aid in solving related problems. On the other hand, presenting graphics is not always beneficial for the acquisition of knowledge. Whereas task-appropriate graphics may support learning, task-inappropriate graphics may interfere with mental model construction and, consequently, impair gaining an overall view of the situation (Schnotz & Bannert, 2003).

Graphics are helpful in depicting a quantitative or scientific concept or relationship, particularly when the concept can be explicitly and concretely expressed. On the other hand, graphics do a poor job of expressing abstract concepts; for abstract concepts, text is better. The problem is that a graphic can only show one instance of a concept. "How would you, for example, render visually the concept "soft drinks," to identify the corresponding aisle of a food supermarket? A photograph of an actual soft drink container suggests a brand, not a generic concept. A drawing can be more generic, but nevertheless suggests specific types of container (cans, bottles,. . .) rather than a specific type of beverage" (Doumont, 2002, p. 221).

Any graphic must match with readers' goals and information needs. If those information needs do not require graphics, either because of prior knowledge or the concepts are too abstract, the graphics are not appropriate (Benbast, Dexter, & Todd, 1986b). It must be remembered that graphics "are not drawn to store (or, worse, decorate) data, but to answer questions, either for oneself or for an audience" (Doumont, 2002, p. 2).

As with text, the goal is to create graphics which clearly communicate the most salient information about a situation. Even if people believe the information is accurate and reliable, that same information is essentially useless unless they are able to interpret and apply it to their current situation. Graphics need to support the communication about the situation and not be either eye candy (pretty images with minimal connection to the text) or unfamiliar graphic formats which are difficult to interpret. Both the task and the audience must be considered when deciding if a graphic is appropriate (Weiss, 1985). In a study which compared graphs versus tables on performance, response times, and learning, the graphics group performed better but the table group showed stronger evidence of learning (Atkins, Wood, & Rutgers, 2002). When deciding on graphic choices in cases such this one, the design team needs to consider if the best presentation needs to support learning, simply support completing an infrequent task quickly, or persuading an audience.

How to best create a mix of text and graphics to answer those questions remains an open question. An open question which is confounded by much of the existing research. Although it is easy to find research that evaluates the effectiveness of graphics (for example, Benbasat, Dexter, & Todd, 1986; DeSanctis, 1984), that research often compares several variables at a time. As a result, although it can give advice for a specific graphic type for a specific task, there is a lack of ability to make a priori predictions about how a graphic will work in specific situation (Lohse, 1993).

APPROACHES TO TEXT WITH GRAPHICAL ELEMENTS

A majority of technical communication documents contain text and graphics which work together to communicate the texts' message. Although text can stand alone, graphics typically do not, and thus it is important to consider both how people approach graphics and how they approach text and graphics together.

Graphics are used in technical documentation since they help people comprehend the material more quickly. Use of integrated text and graphics improves comprehension and people interpret information within an HII situation more quickly (Betrancourt & Bisseret, 1998). Depending on the nature of the material to communicate, the flow of information may require a highly graphical

design. Graphics become invaluable if there are many branch points that depend on either previous actions or decision points. Although the ideas of using graphics may seem trivial, actually deciding on the proper choice is not. Instead, people tend to use only a few familiar formats without considering the impact or appropriateness.

Our own training and consulting experience reveals a poor graph literacy on the part of engineers, scientists, and managers. These professionals and others typically use the same few graph types for all their data sets, regardless of the amount and nature of their data. When asked how else they could graph the same data, they usually do not have a clue. Yet when shown a different graphical representation (new to them or not) of the same data, they recognize it as insightful; they just "didn't think of graphing it that way." (Doumont, 2002, p. 2)

Even more than words, graphics overwhelmingly influence people's first impression of a text, since they mentally process the layout before any reading occurs. Consequently, effective graphics have long been recognized as an important factor in receiving a favorable perception of a text (Rubens, 1986). The most effective graphic depends on the goal; people use different graphics when their goal is to lead to an optimal solution versus persuade the audience (Tractinsky & Meyer, 1999).

Once people read the text, graphics provide a second chance to grasp the message it contains. People remember pictures better than words and have lower false recognition rates in tests where they must identify if a word/picture was previously seen. For example, they falsely recognize a word/image of a chair because it is associated with a list of previously studied words/images (table, desk, sofa). People also rate such picture-based tests as easier than word-based tests (Gallo, Weiss, & Schacter, 2004).

Spool (2009) discusses the issue of trying to buy a suitcase online if the website didn't show any pictures of suitcases. A verbal description may be adequate for a suitcase expert, but most people could not recognize the industry name which describes the type of suitcase they want. Instead, they must have an image.

A wide body of research consistently found that display format influences both people's spontaneous interpretations and how that information gets integrated with the textual information. A notable research finding is that the amount of integrative (global) content was highest for bar graphs and lowest for tables (Carswell & Ramzy, 1997). An even more interesting research result shows the disconnect between people's preferred graphical format and the one which gives the most accurate results. Lusk and Kersnick (1979) claim the most familiar format will be perceived as the easiest to comprehend. But, when Feldman-Stewart and Brundage (2004) asked people to use various graphics to solve problems, they are often more accurate on other formats rather than ones they preferred. People may prefer a 3D graph and give compelling reasons, but if asked to use a graph, they'll be faster and more accurate with a 2D graph of the same information. This finding calls into question whether or not people should be allowed to choose the graphical format they wish to use to view data. In addition, there is also a danger of people sufficing (Simon, 1979) by only looking at the graphics and not reading the text, thus missing important information by not mentally processing all of the information. A responsibility of design teams is to strongly connect both the graphics and text so the reader grasps the significance of both in gaining a clear understanding of the situation.

People approach instructions and other procedural material with expectations of a strong graphical focus. In many cases, they use graphics as the primary information source with minimal text reading, whether or not this was the design team's intention. On the other hand, a document can have too many graphics; a common error is assuming each section or each procedural step needs a visual. As with all writing, both the task and the audience must be considered when deciding if a graphic is appropriate (Weiss, 1985). Research into using graphics in procedural material has found:

- Well-designed graphics can be understood and used for procedures quicker than the same information in a mixed text and diagram format. However, this finding was qualified as only applying to one-time manipulation where no learning or long-term retention of the material is required. Issues of longer-term retention of the material was not studied (Rodriguez, 2002).

- People often claim they want more examples and give "it has lots of examples" as a reason they like a particular text. However, they often only use the graphics and ignore the text; when there was information intentionally missing from the graphics people had problems but that same information missing from the text was not noticed (Lefevre and Dixon, 1986).

- In software manuals, example syntax must remain specific and realistic; abstract syntax or generic examples do not aid learning or performing the action. (Carroll et al, 1988; Foss, Smith-Kerker, & Rosson, 1987).

- The graphics are used more for verification of an action and reassurance that the procedure is proceeding properly than as part of the how-to aspects (Horton, 1993).

- Software manuals use screen captures liberally which both decrease task completion time and reduce errors (van der Meij & Gellevij, 1998, 2002). Nowaczyk and James (1993) found that learning was better when the example only consisted of the relevant part of the screen.

Kosslyn (1994) looked at how people perceive information and concludes that the eye is not a camera. Design teams who use such a camera-based model can impede the communication.

Cameras are passive recording devices, while people are active information processors. The difference explains a problem people have when taking photographs: the pole extending from a person's head, which is obvious in the photo was never noticed through the viewfinder. People merge the individual parts into an image they want/expect to see and ignore the rest. The camera records everything and then, when people view the photo, they see the entire scene with all the flaws exposed.

Interpreting Graphics

Communication and writing guidelines typically say to use graphs to show information since people find them easier to interpret. In the broad case, this is true. However, reading graphics, graphs, and charts and drawing inferences may not be as intuitive as it seems. At a basic level, the reorganization and interpretation of a graphic depends on the limitations of working memory. People first construct a visual description of the graphic which is constrained by several factors, including Gestalt laws of grouping and prior experience. Next, people must construct propositions about the information encoded in the graph and merge those propositions with the preceding text and prior knowledge (Pinker, 1990).

Graphic design which forces people into serial scanning of the image imposes a high working memory load and causes previously viewed information to decay. This problem is most severe for complex information tasks (Lohse, 1993). Consider how corporate annual reports are graph-heavy, but they typically fail to follow research guidelines for good graphs. Frownfelter-Lohrke and Fulkerson (2001) found they had a high number of graphs designed in ways which easily mislead readers, such as non-zero scales and choice of graph style.

To a skilled reader, graphics can quickly present the entire picture and connect many factors through their ability to display patterns which would not be easily apparent in text. A study examining people's eye fixations as they interpreted graphs showed they continuously reexamined the labels to refresh their memory (Carpenter & Shah, 1998). Although graphics aid in comprehension, interpreting them efficiently and effectively requires practice. For example, consider the use of graphs: most people only know to look at the shape of the graph. It is easy to look at a graph and gain a surface-level understanding (the trend is up), but moving beyond that superficial level to gain a deeper knowledge of what the up trend means involves looking past the shape of the graph and applying situational knowledge. The difficulty is drawing the inferences. Reading a graph and stating a trend is easy, but making a statement about what that trend means is difficult. Comprehending a situation requires that people understand how that trend fits into other relevant information and the trends relationship with other information. Understanding comes from connecting the graph's shape to its ideal/desired shape, and knowing what is happening in the situation to cause that shape and how to make adjustments to the situation to change the graph shape. HII helps to ensure people can properly interpret the graph at a deeper level.

Feldman-Stewart and Brundage (2004) point out that graphic formats which best support obtaining a high-level view are different from those which support a low-level, more accurate view. They found people typically ask for a format which supports how they like to interpret content (either high or low level) even though the actual problem required them to use the other. Relating each graphic to the corresponding text statement involved an analytic processing of the details of the picture. Conversely, relating several statements to several graphics draws attention to the global configuration of elements in the pictures (Betrancourt & Bisseret, 1998). The design team needs to figure out at which level the material will be used and provide for graphical interactions which support that level. This may simply require the

Figure 2. Different graphical presentation of North and South populations. People found B easier to interpret than A. With A, they compared all four bars in a single time and did not distinguish the trends across time (Shah & Hoeffner, 2002, p. 49). Reprinted from Educational Psychology Review, 14.1, with permission from Elsevier.

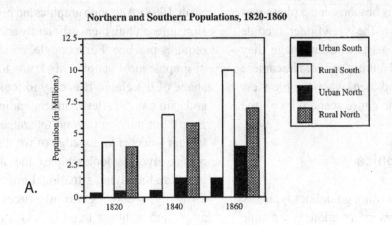

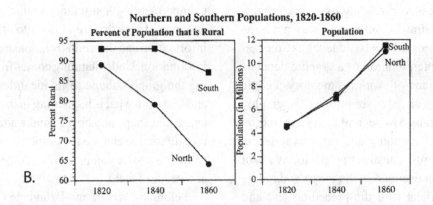

ability to change the graphical presentation, but it may also require some controls that assist people by focusing them on better presentation formats.

Information structure and prior knowledge about the nature of that structure are important factors in whether or not graphs or tables are better at extracting that structure and making predictions, with graphs typically favoring the more experienced person in most situations. In others, a bias can occur. In a comparison of tables and graphs, people made better predictions for trended series but not for untrended ones. To a large extent, this was because the trends were underestimated to a much greater extent with

a table than with a graph. With untrended data, there was no distinctive up/down slope on which to base decisions (Harvey & Bolger, 1996). Only when the information's structure matches people's information needs will the table/graph presentation show a significant gain over the other one (Meyer, Shamo, & Gopher, 1999).

People make systematic errors when they interpret graphs, a problem which is highly problematical when the relevant quantitative information is not explicit (Shah & Hoeffner, 2002). One problem is that given unstructured information, either in graphs or tables, most people claim to see structure and use that as a basis for their answers.

This shows once more how people will always try to impart a pattern on a collection of data (Meyer, Shamo, & Gopher, 1999). Likewise, how the graphics are designed can cause people to view the information differently. Gestalt principles apply to interpreting graphics and visual closeness, same shades or colors, or connecting lines will encourage people to mentally group those items and focus on their relationship.

In a study by Shah and Hoeffner (2002) the accompanying text explained that graph (Figure 2) showed that in the decades preceding the Civil War the North was urbanizing but the South was still rural. But they found people were unable to easily interpret the graph to show that. Instead, they compared the relative populations in each of the four categories across time (they focused on comparing all four bars of a single shade). When the people viewed the same information with a different graph (Figure 2.B), they easily comprehended the goal of the graph.

Redundancy and Equivalence of Text and Graphical Information

Text and graphics must support each other and also support people's goals and information needs for good HII (Carney & Levin, 2002) and not simply provide equivalent or redundant information. Both are better at providing certain types of information and a design team must work to achieve the proper balance (Table 1). Effectively integrating text and graphics requires they work together and not simply repeat each other. Both should provide unique information which is not explicitly available in the other. Typically, because of the different way texts and graphics are mentally processed, information that is explicit in one often has to be inferred from the other (Betrancourt. & Bisseret, 1998).

If texts and graphics should not be equivalent, than that brings up the question of when a graphic and the text can be considered equivalent. A graphic may be informationally equivalent to a

Table 1. Graphic and text communication abilities. Graphics and tables have different strengths and weaknesses.

	Graphics	Text
Trends	good	poor
Abstract concepts	poor	good
Concrete concepts	good	ok
Showing relationships	good	ok

text description, but in an HII sense, it can be distinct because how a person mentally processes it (i.e. search, recognition, and inference) can be very different (Hicks et al., 2003). The ability to grasp the entire graphic all at once simplifies the interpretation and also reduces the chance of misunderstanding. A slight misinterpretation of text early in a document can cause later text to be interpreted differently than the author intended, but a graphic reduces that type of misinterpretation. The design of the graphic provides a secondary method to focus readers on the salient or global aspects of the overall message. Larkin and Simon (1987) summarized the idea as:

Two representations are considered to be 'informationally equivalent' if all of the information is also inferable from the other, and vice versa. Two representations are 'computationally equivalent' if they are informationally equivalent and, in addition, any inference that can be drawn easily and quickly from the information given explicitly in one, can also be drawn easily and quickly from the information given explicitly in the other, and vice versa (Larkin & Simon, 1987, quoted in Hicks et al., 2003, p. 186).

The goal of a balanced presentation requires design teams to work to achieve a balance between having text and graphics that do not repeat or overlap in their content. Effectively integrating text and graphics requires they work together.

Both provide unique information which is not explicitly available in the other. The best design requires integration of the two with enough overlap to tightly connect them while still allowing each to communicate the type of information they communicate best.

TYPES OF GRAPHICS IN TECHNICAL DOCUMENTS

Technical documents contain a wide range of different types of graphics, with graphs (typically line or bar graphs), tables, diagrams, or images making up the majority of the graphics. Each of these different types is highly effective at communicating certain types of information and poor at communicating other types. A problem with many documents is that the designer selected the inappropriate type, often based on availability or ease of creation rather than quality of communication. Most sources on graphics give guidelines on how to design them; this book will not repeat those but will concentrate on the research findings of how different designs affect how people interact with and interpret graphics. The four types of graphics covered in this section include:

Graphs: Graphs in technical documents are typically line or bar graphs, but a huge variety of different formats have been developed for special purposes. For an extensive selection (many more than appear in Microsoft Excel) see Harris (1996).

Tables: Tables are columnar arrangements, typically of numbers but have many other uses such as listing computer commands and the associated switches. They work best when exact values are needed.

Diagrams: Diagrams are line art or schematics which do not attempt to portray a realistic image of the object or system.

Images: Images are photographs or drawings which attempt to portray a realistic image.

The choice of graphic affects how people make judgments and interact with the information. In user-centered design, part of the audience analysis is to understand how the readers want graphs presented. Using standard ethnography techniques, they would be asked what they preferred, their answers would be evaluated against the information needs, and the design would provide graphics for the best comprehension. However, that design still requires usability testing since people's preferred methods do not always give the best performance (Feldman-Stewart & Brundage, 2004; Wills & Holmes-Rovner, 2003). Meeting audience desires must be balanced against task demands for both accuracy and speed.

Interestingly, although design of effective graphs has been an area of research, there is still little experimental research testing how people's perception of information and understanding vary across different graphical formats. Both of which are vital factors for good HII. The lack of this research directly ties to difficulties in creating clear guidelines on how to better design graphics which improve comprehension and forming information relationships.

Graphs

Graphs, by their basic design, are made to be perceived and interpreted at an all encompassing level. This ease of global interpretation proves to be both their strength and their weakness, depending on whether or not the global perception is correct for the situation. They provide a fast way to obtain good, but not optimal, solutions to problems, particularly when the optimal solution requires reacting to very small changes in the numbers. Tables, on the other hand, provide specific values.

Graphs can display four different types of scales, each of which requires the information to be interpreted differently.

Nominal: Different values, but no magnitude comparison. For example, a graph that shows values by department.

Ordinal: Different value by relative size, but no magnitude comparison. For example, a graph that shows temperature values of cold, warm, and hot.

Interval: Different value that allow relative magnitude comparisons. For example, a graph with temperatures in degree can show two temperatures differ by 34 degrees.

Ratio: Different value that allow magnitude comparisons and absolute comparisons. For example, a graph showing temperatures with a scale starting at absolute zero. The relative difference between temperatures can be calculated as well as the ratio change with respect to absolute zero.

Graphs provide a way to display patterns in numbers which cannot be easily seen in the numbers themselves. One of their strongest points is they provide a way of visually displaying the relationships of two or more elements. How well a person is able to accurately judge those relationships and receive the intended message depends on the design of the graphs and how it relates to how people perceive graphs. It is possible for a designer to manipulate a graph so it shows correct information, but will be perceived as showing different information, such as when explaining risks and the designer attempts to either mitigate or highlight risk factors.

By acting within the visual areas of working memory, graphs reduce cognitive load by replacing a verbal (reading text) mental analysis with perceptual inferences (Lohse, 1993). Of course, such a shift is only useful if the perceptual inference is relevant to the situation. People can judge a line slope using perceptual inference, but have a difficult time picking individual values off it.

The following three criteria that can usefully guide the choice of graph type (Doumont, 2002):

- The intended message. Why does the graph exist and what is the take-away message the reader should obtain? In the end, the intended message drives the proper graph choice. Also, the format can strongly influence how the message is perceived: pie graphs rank as least trustworthy and scientific, and tables as the most effective, trustworthy and scientific (Hawley et al., 2008).

- The intended use of the graph. The graph can be designed to support a range of messages from raw data analysis to summary evaluation, with any one graph falling someplace on this continuum. Failure to match the design to the purpose risks the graph actually interfering or detracting from understanding the material (Wills & Holmes-Rovner, 2003).

- Graphs that allow a rich analysis may not excel at conveying a message effectively and vice versa. High level and low level information needs are different and require different types of graphs. Graphs are not good when the task is to show values with a maximum number of decimal points. For that task, a table is needed. (Benbasat, Dexter, & Todd, 1986b; Cleveland & McGill, 1984). One study found vertical bars resulted in the most accurate and fastest responses to gross-level comparisons while tables were most accurate for the detailed-level comparisons (Feldman-Stewart, & Brundage, 2004). In the end, no single graph design works for all situations and typically a combination is required. Powers et al. (1984) found a combination of graphs and tables produce slower but more accurate performance.

- The structure of the data. How many variables and what type: continuous or discrete? What type of relationship is being displayed? A 1:1 relationship displays easily on a 2D graph, but 1:many relationships are much harder to display and comprehend.

What Graph Type is Better?

This section provides a brief summary of some of the studies which compared graph types with respect to accuracy and task time.

As in any HII situation, how a graph gets interpreted depends on the prior knowledge of the people viewing the graph.

Interpreting graphs is to a large extent, dependent upon a background theory as to how knowledge has been encoded within the graph. In the absence of such a theory, graphs can prove an ambiguous form of representation. Ambiguous representations can hinder the sharing of knowledge both between systems and between people. (Cheng, Cupit, & Shadbold, 2001. p. 460)

All forms of graphical presentation are not equal. Depending on graph format, people will interpret it differently with the most familiar form of graph presentation being perceived as the easiest to comprehend (Lusk & Kersnick (1979). Systematic variation of graphic format changed perceptions of the data trends (Schapira, Nattinger, & McAuliffe, 2006). Interestingly, people adopt a wider range of interpretation strategies when working with a small set of data points than with a larger set. People did not increase the time needed to interpret graphs as the number of data points increased. A result that suggests efficient parallel processing of the graph information (Carswell & Ramzy, 1997).

One ongoing debate is when to use a bar chart and when to use a line chart. In many cases, they are equivalent, though the purists insist on line graphs for continuous variables and bar graphs for discrete variables. By contrast, people typically use bars and lines according to a different principle. The bars on a graph are seen as containers which hold one kind of thing. Lines, on the other hand, are seen as paths between data points. "Since bars contain and separate, it seems natural for them to convey discrete relationships. And since lines form paths and connect separate entities, it seems natural for them to convey trends" (Tversky et al., 2000. p. 224).

Research into various types of graphs has found:

- People are more accurate making discrete comparisons from bar graphs than from pie graphs, while the opposite was true for proportion-of-the-whole judgments (Simkin & Hastie, 1987).
- Pie charts, the default graphic format for many graphing programs, are rarely the best formats to convey either gross- or detail-level information. (Feldman-Stewart, & Brundage, 2004).
- People read the data in line graphs as continuous, even it makes for absurd conclusions. Consider that a reader may interpret a line that connects two data points representing male and female height as saying, "The more male a person is, the taller he/she is" (Zacks & Tversky, 1999).
- People make faster discrete comparisons from bar graphs than from line graphs (Zacks & Tversky, 1999).
- People make more accurate discrete comparisons from bar graphs than from pie graphs (Simkin & Hastie, 1987).
- Adults prefer bar graphs for conveying detailed information about individual data points and lines for conveying trends (Levy et al., 1996; Tversky et al., 2000).
- For changes over time, line and bar charts are more effective than divided bar graphs and pie charts (Hollands & Spence, 1992).
- For complicated judgments, a pie chart is slightly better than a bar chart; for simpler judgments they are equivalent (Spence & Lewandowsky, 1991).
- Bar graphs showing multiple variables appear to have less biasing than similar line graphs. (Shah & Hoeffner, 2002).

- People are more accurate in retrieving *x–y* trends from line graphs than from bar graphs (Carswell & Wickens, 1987).
- In general, pie charts are more accurate for making part/whole judgments than divided bar graphs are because divided bar graphs often require adding up information from different parts of the bar (Simkin & Hastie, 1987). However, divided bar charts are better when absolute values as well as proportions are important (Kosslyn, 1994).
- In scatterplots, people underestimate correlations with a wide scatter of points and overestimate those with a tight scatter of points (Meyer, Taieb, & Flascher, 1997).
- When asked to estimate the variance of a set of data, people are strongly influenced by the mean of the overall set (Lathrop, 1967). Information with a large mean is seen as having less variance than information with a small mean (Figure 3).

Tables

Tables lack the mapping of symbols to data which occurs in a graph and, consequently, impart a lower cognitive load. Unfortunately, the lower cognitive load comment only applies to simple lookups (finding individual values in the table) which are rarely how tables get used in technical

Figure 3. Estimating variance of information. Both of these sets of lines have the same mean and variance. However, most people will estimate that B has more variation; people are highly influenced by the ordering. (adapted from Wickens & Hollands, 2000, p. 300).

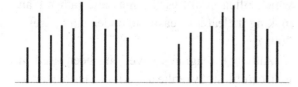

documents. For more complex analysis, a table requires people to look up several values and then perform some sort of comparison between them. For example, if the analysis is to find trends, reading from a table requires holding several numbers in working memory and mentally imagining their change, while a graph gives the trend in a single glance (Lohse, 1993).

A common design question is whether to use a table or a graph. Interestingly, while personal preferences many indicate one or the other, the research shows little support for choosing one over the other. DeSanctis (1984) reviewed 20 studies which compared user preference and performance with tables and graphs and found no overall advantage for either format. In the end, it depends on what type of information needs to be communicated. Trends and relationships are easier to interpret with a graph, but values are easier with a table. Dickson, DeSanctis, and McBride (1986) found that graphs may be most effective in situations where the amount of data is large.

- People who viewed tables had better verbatim knowledge versus graphs, but a lower overall gist knowledge (Hawley et al., 2008). They knew the individual facts better, but lacked a clear global picture of the situation.
- The tables, unlike graphs formats, showed little systematic content change with increasing complexity (Carswell & Ramzy, 1997). By their two dimensional nature, tables tend to simply get longer/wider rather than adding visual complexity, such multiple lines on a graph.
- Spence and Lewandowsky (1991) found that the advantage of graphs over tables increased with task complexity rather than with the number of data values. Design teams often focus on the amount of data, but instead they should focus on how complex the information needs are to gain an understanding of the situation.

- Coury & Boulette (1992) found that graphs were more useful than tables when subjects were under time stress.

The overall result is that the task demands must be used to determine whether to use a table or a graph. The choice often must be based what determines acceptable performance. For example, should the graphic support speed or accuracy? Graphs support faster lookups, but tables give more accuracy. Providing both clutters up a document.

Diagrams

The use of diagrams in technical instruction has a long history, dating back to at least the 15th century (Ferguson, 1977). Diagrams are not meant to provide a realistic description of a physical action or situation. Rather they depict a conceptual reality. Figure 4 shows a schematic of a steam-driven electrical generator. It is helpful to learn how the plant works in an abstract way, but would be less helpful if trying to identify parts while standing in the building looking at the real components. Diagrams work to portray the parts of a system and display the interrelationships between those parts and provide an easy way of describing relationships that are difficult to describe in words or other graphics (Tversky, 2002). Figure 5 shows a reproduction of Snow's map of the cholera deaths in the 1854 London epidemic. By matching death locations with the water sources, he was able to trace the cause to a specific pump. Presenting the same information in table or text form would not provide such a concise view of how the problem centered on one point. Yet, the fact that that the cholera cases center around a water pump is obvious in the diagram.

As with a graph, diagrams work within the visual/spatial component of working memory; people can look at a diagram and grasp the entire object at once rather than building it up via a linear text. Of course, only when the diagram fits the rhetorical aspects of the information will it be

Figure 4. Schematic of a steam driven electrical generator

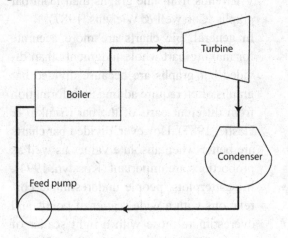

Figure 5. Snow's map of the 1854 London cholera epidemic. Each of the black bars is for one death in the building. (http://www.ph.ucla.edu/epi/snow/mapsbroadstreet.html)

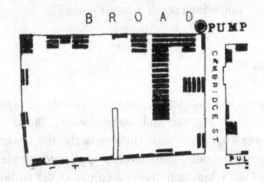

able to effectively communicate. Like most other graphics, people tend to go directly to the diagram and ignore the text, thus diagrams which cannot carry communication loads can distract from the message. Many web pages violate this idea. Although the web is a highly graphical medium, many writers seem to believe that more graphics are better and each block of text needs a diagram, which often confuses the message rather than making it clearer or easier to understand (Kress, 2005).

Although diagrams have long been used in text, careful study of the use is much more recent.

For extensive literature reviews on diagrams, see Fillippatou and Pumfrey (1996) and Carney and Levin (2002).

Texts with or without Diagrams

Diagrams work with text to help develop a better overall understanding of complex information, but the strength of the affect depends on the nature of the task. They improve HII when the person has to integrate information, but have little effect on tasks which principally require recognition or declarative knowledge (Fiore, Cuevas, & Oser, 2003; Mayer & Gallini, 1990).

Research which has looked at texts with or without diagrams has found:

- In procedural instructions, text and diagrams together were understood better and the tasks were completed faster than with diagram-only instructions. This finding was qualified by noting these were one-time tasks with no learning component (Rodriguez, 2002) .
- Diagrams are most helpful with complex text and that people with low prior knowledge are especially likely to be helped by diagrams (Carney & Levin, 2002; Fillippatou & Pumfrey,1996; Levie & Lentz, 1982). However, people with poor reading ability will not be helped since they have to focus on individual elements and don't form a clear overall picture of the task (Fillippatou & Pumfrey, 1996).
- Diagrams help people form correlations and relationships which improved their ability to make predictions about the future development of a situation (Cuevas et al 2004).
- When patients were given medical brochures with diagrams at discharge, they had a higher rate of being read and higher recall several days later than brochures with just text (Houts et al., 2006; Delp &

Jones, 1996) and they also showed higher comprehension (Austin et al. 1995; Michielutte et al. 1992). Interestingly, the diagrams Delp and Jones used in their brochure were cartoony and could be considered an ornamental graphic, rather than a content graphic. In these studies, recall was differentiated from comprehension, with recall involving stating what was in a document and comprehension requiring people to explain or do something with the information.

- In a study which compared the text recall of college students and people over 50 years old after they read texts with and without diagrams, both groups had better recall of texts with the diagrams. The college student group had better recall in both cases (Winograd, Smith, & Simon, 1982).

Comprehension of Diagrams

Diagrams improve comprehension when they show relationships among ideas or when they show spatial relationships (Houts et al., 2006). They make it easier to activate or populate the proper mental model or, in learning material, develop a mental model (Fiore, Cuevas & Oser, 2003). Typically, diagrams cause the greatest performance gains when the task requires the integration of information, but have minimal effect on declarative knowledge tasks (learning facts) (Mayer & Gallini, 1990).

Simple drawings are often the most effective in supporting text comprehension. Moll (1986) found reader comprehension was highest, in order of: cartoon drawings, stick figures, and photographs. Likewise Readance and Moore (1981) found line drawings resulted in higher comprehension than shaded drawings or photographs. On the other hand, expert audiences often have a collection of diagrams which they use constantly and effectively, but which are almost unintelligible outside of the specific field. For example, engineers and

Figure 6. Arrows imply function. People saw figures that were identical except for the arrows, but that small change resulted in people interpreting the drawing differently. Without arrows, people described the system components and with arrows they described how the system operated.

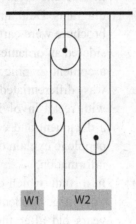 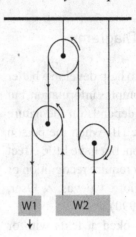

architects use projective and isometric drawings, both of which are hard to understand without training. In this case, their prior knowledge allows them to use the diagrams effectively, but acquiring that knowledge has a learning curve which must be considered when deciding the type of diagrams to include in a text.

Although diagrams are usually helpful, there are situations where they can interfere with comprehension, especially among very poor readers. Fillippatou and Pumfrey (1996) point out that diagrams typically allow readers to more easily integrate information from the text, but very poor readers ignore the text and only focus on the diagrams. The comprehension problem is that when readers cannot read and understand the basic information, they cannot understand the diagram. Instead, they may use only the diagram to guess at the meaning and confuse their guess with actually understanding the material. Fillippatou and Pumfrey's overall conclusion is that diagrams that represent concepts that are beyond the reader's ability to understand will interfere with overall comprehension.

Diagrams are ideal for conveying structural information, but functional information is more difficult since the diagram is static and function implies dynamic action. Design conventions

such as arrows often help overcome this limitation (Heiser & Tversky, 2006). For example, two forms of Figure 6, with or without arrows, were given to people, who were then asked to write a description (Levin & Mayer, 1993; Tversky et al., 2000). The people who saw the diagram without arrows wrote a structural description (described each part) and those with arrows wrote a functional description (how the object operated). The arrows function to show the action sequence of events in the operation of the system. Without the arrows, the diagrams primarily illustrate the structure of the system; that is, what the parts are and how they are connected together. With the arrows, how an object operates is more apparent.

Students who observed diagrams with arrows included nearly twice as much functional information as students who saw diagrams without arrows. Conversely, students who saw diagrams without arrows included more than twice the structural information as students who saw diagrams with arrows. For example, one participant who saw a diagram of the bicycle pump without arrows wrote a primarily structural description: "I see a picture of some type of machine or tool that has many different parts which are called handle, piston, inlet valve, outlet valve, and hose. Also the diagram shows a similar tool or machine but the parts are not labeled and are in different positions than the machine on the left." ... Or this description of the bicycle pump, by a participant who saw a diagram with arrows: "Pushing down on the handle pushes the piston down on the inlet valve which compresses the air in the pump, causing it to rush through the hose." (Tversky et al., 2000, p. 228).

Images

Images are defined here as both photographs and realistic drawings that are intended to mimic a photograph.

Moll (1986) found reader comprehension of a medical brochure was highest with cartoon drawings, then stick figures, and finally photographs. Contrasting with the comprehension findings, people preferred cartoon images in booklets but overall, they preferred photographs for most material. Color photographs have a greater effect than black and white photographs (Readance & Moore, 1981). With the added expense of color printing, design teams need to consider the cost trade-off between color and black and white photographs.

Most software documentation makes extensive use of screen captures as a way to provide images to accompany the step-by-step directions.

The screen captures sped up the subjects' task completion considerably. There was a significant time gain of about 35% for the processing of procedures fully supported by screen captures. In addition, the screen captures helped subjects make 21% fewer mistakes and reduced correction time by 24% (van der Meij & Gellevij, 1998, p. 539).

However, if the task requires long sequences of actions, extensive use of screen captures decrease people's performance (Kehoe et al., 2009). Likewise, van der Meij and Gellevij (2002) found no learning benefit to lots of images in training material. A potential reason for this somewhat

Figure 7. Car window buttons. Although this shows the exact image, the poor quality distracts the reader. A line drawing would show the components more cleanly.

counter-intuitive finding is that too many images leads to a superficial processing and surface-level understanding of the steps, rather than committing them to long-term memory. Although this is acceptable in single-time procedures, if people are expected to perform them frequently, design teams need to consider the effect of the number of screen captures and their affect on learning.

Irrelevant visual detail can be a nuisance in reasoning and can impede the process (Knauff & Johnson-Laird, 2002). While photos can be very useful in documents, they are often too detailed. Figure 7 shows a photographs the button for a car window. Some of the problems are:

- Lines and shadows on the background are distracting.
- Text is hard to read.
- Low contrast makes the image looks muddy.
- Excess material in the image is distracting.
- Model specific. Each car's controls look different.
- Difficult to get a good photograph. Managers want to use photographs since diagrams require hiring graphic artists

and they assume anyone can take a photograph. But good images requires a skilled photographer.

HOW PEOPLE COMPREHEND A GRAPHIC

How people comprehend a graphic has received a large amount of research in cognitive psychology, but it still remains an open problem with each situation containing its own twists and confounds. See Shah and Hoeffner (2002) for an overview of graph comprehension. There is a poor understanding of how graphics actually work cognitively and the area is rife with unresearched assumptions and fallacies (Scaife & Rogers, 1996). Design teams have only weak principles to guide the design and integration of graphs into system interfaces. It is not so much the failure of any specific type of graphics, but overgeneralizations between different types and audience needs. Diagrams are different from graphics which are different from images. Cheng, Cupit, and Shadbold (2001) state that too much of the research has focused on the cognition of graph reading and has ignored how to use those findings or their relevance in complex situations. And, of course, most HII situations fall within the realm of complex situations (Albers, 2004).

Interpreting and comprehending a graphic requires practice. Most people only know to look at the shape of the graph. It is easy to look at a graph and gain a surface-level understanding (the trend is up), but moving beyond the superficial to gain a deeper knowledge means looking past the shape of the graph and applying situational knowledge to understand both how the graph shape relates to the desired shape and what adjustments to the situation are required to change the graph from its current shape to the desired shape.

Brasseur (2003) points out that graphs fall into two different groups: analytical and presentational. Each of these two has different goals and the audience expects to take away different information from each, as a result, they are interpreted differently. Confusing them at the design level can result in poor communication.

Writers like Tufte who focus on presentation graphs will spend a good deal of textual space writing about issues of audience. How does the audience perceive this? What is the best way to communicate my message? Alternatively, writers like Tukey who focus on analysis graphs will spend their textual space concentrating on the ways in which particular graph types can reveal information that will help the computer user think about the data and situation (p. 21).

Graph comprehension requires people to mentally encode the information and identify major features (such as the line shape) and then they must connect those features to the relevant elements in the situation. Eye tracking studies have shown the cyclic nature of graph comprehension (Carpenter & Shaw, 1998; Peebles & Cheng, 2003) with the person's eyes jumping around the graph as it is mentally processed. When a visual feature does not automatically evoke a particular fact or relationship, then that information is more difficult to comprehend (Shah & Hoeffner, 2002).

One way to aid in graph comprehension is to use different presentations of the same information (Larkin & Simon, 1987; Cheng & Simon, 1995). Rather than using a single graph, the various needs of the reader must be addressed. Different displays make different information salient, so plotting the same data in multiple formats may be beneficial if there are multiple quantitative facts to be communicated, especially when the data are complex (e.g., a table to make exact quantities readable and a line graph to communicate a trend). (Shah & Hoeffner, 2002). A combination of graphical and tabular data gives the best comprehension over either just graphs or just tables (Powers et al., 1984). However, the combination resulted in slower performance, so if speed of interpretation is an issue, only one format should be presented.

Poor graph design is a constant problem, with the design teams producing graphics to intentionally mislead or hide information from readers or unintentionally, through ignorance of good design principles. Huff and Geis (1993) show many examples of how to distort information. Tufte (1983, 1990, 1997) gives multiple examples of what he calls 'chartjunk,' essentially everything on a graphic that does not directly support the main message. Kosslyn (1994) points out how the rapid mental processing of a graph is also its shortcoming. People form an initial impression very rapidly and then have a hard time shifting from that impression; generally, they do not unless forced to do so by the situation. As a result, it is easy to design graphics which give a desired initial impression which leave out or distort information, but which will not stand up to deeper scrutiny. However, the cynical design team can feel comfortable most of the readers will not engage in that deeper, more detailed look.

Scaling

Graph scaling has a strong influence on both how people interpret and comprehend its information. Scaling is also often the major issue in discussion of graphs distortions and ethically presenting information (Allen, 1996).

Honest graphs require the x and y scales to start at zero, so as to not over-amplify the relative relationships between the graph points. Figure 8 shows how the quick glance appearance of the graph is very different even though they both present identical information. Figure 8.B. looks like there have been dramatic changes in writer productivity over the past few years. But when viewed with a zero scale, the change rate has been minimal.

The scale interval can also interfere with interpreting a graph. Figure 9 shows two identical graphs, but the spacing of the x-axis is doubled.

This results in the line slope appearing to be less than its actual value. In Figure 10, the y-axis scales of the two graphs are different. Yet, they are presented side by side and contain similar information, leading a reader to compare them and potentially draw the wrong conclusion.

People are very poor at judging changes in area. But even worse is when that poor judgment is exploited to give an indication of more change than really occurred. In Figure 11, the tree on the right is three times higher than the left one, but it has nine times the area. The eye responds to the increase in area more than just the height change, giving the impression that the change is greater than 3 times.

Unless the presentation is aimed at an experienced science or engineering audience, the x and y axis should have a linear scale and not a log scale (Figure 12). Although use of log scales is typical in the sciences, they pose a substantial comprehension problem for anyone not trained in reading them. Few people without extensive exposure to scientific graphics would understand why the axis intervals are changing (or probably even notice it is changing), much less be able to read the graph. In particular, they would not realize that a straight line with a log scale will be an exponential curve on a linear scale. Of course, some graphs because of the nature of their contents do require log scaling, but the use of such an interval needs to be explained in the figure captions.

Trends

A fundamental object of graphing information is to be able to see a trend in the data. The advantage of graphs over tables is that they make the trend explicit and available for pre-attentive processing. A primary reason to include graphs in a document is that people are very poor at transforming numbers into rates or trends. People can look at a table or a list of numbers and see the values are increasing, but can't mentally calculate the shape of the

Figure 8. Change of y axis scale. The graphs display the same information, but the use of a different y axis scaling makes the information look very different. B gives a misleading portrayal of the data because of the choice of scale.

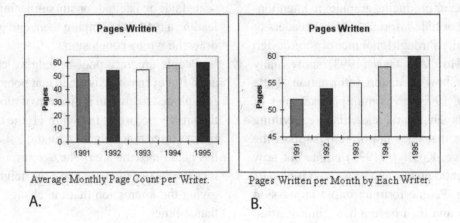

A. Average Monthly Page Count per Writer.

B. Pages Written per Month by Each Writer.

Figure 9. Change of scale. Changing the x and y scales from an equal distance to an unequal distance distorts the visual appearance of the line. Readers of the right hand graph will tend to interpret the increase as less rapid than with the left hand graph.

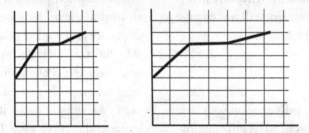

Figure 10. Side by side comparison with different scales. The two graphs appear to present relatively similar sales figures; however, the y scales are substantially different. The problem is that many readers only visually compare the two without actually reading the scales. If they should be compared, they should both use the same y scaling.

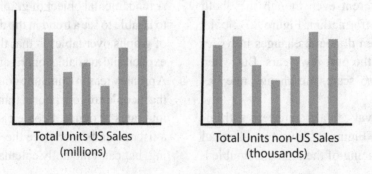

Total Units US Sales (millions)

Total Units non-US Sales (thousands)

Figure 11. Large areas distort linear changes. People will perceive a much greater increase than really occurred. The area increases by a square while the height increase is linear. Thus, the change from 2005 to 2009 was only 3 times, but the area of the 2009 tree is 9 times the area of the 2005 tree.

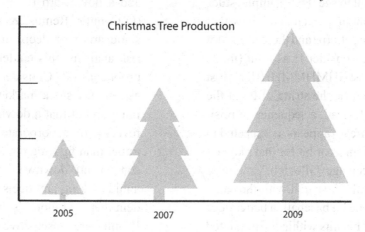

Figure 12. Log-log scale graph. Both axis in the graph use a log scale since they must present data that varies over a wide range. However, many people will assume a linear scale and not properly interpret the information.

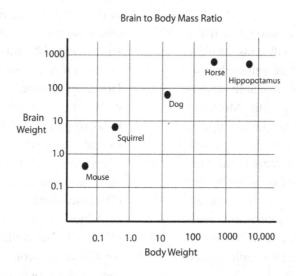

curve or the relative size of the bars. And often the primary message is the shape of the curve and not the actual values themselves. Also, it takes time for a person to analyze a set of numbers and extract any trends while a graph allows the trends to be seen at a glance. Although, as discussed in the previous section, a person can still misinterpret the trend lines because poor choice of scales fails to accurately reflect reality.

People expect to see trends in data; most graphs which they see contain some sort of trend (Remus, O'Connor, & Griggs, 1995). However, the human visual system is so focused on seeing trends that it will find trends in random data. Or will find trends about the specific item they want even if the data does not reflect it. Superstitious behavior (needing a lucky pen for an exam or wearing a specific jacket for big presentations) arises from the same innate desire to see trends in random data. When combined with confirmation and expectancy biases, a person will see trends that fit what they want to see. For example, studies of basketball shooting percentages show that they follow statistical patterns and there is no "hot streak" for a player. Consider H as a hit (made basket) and M as a miss: HHMHMMMHHHH. Most players and fans interpret the string of Hs at the end as a hot streak. Instead, a sequence of positive values (the hot streak) appears as expected in random sequences of miss or hit for that player's overall shooting percentage (Gilovich, Vallone, & Tversky, 1985). Similar research with the same findings has been done on baseball; a batter does not have a hot streak but hits within the predicted sequence of hits and outs for his batting percentage (Albright, 1993).

Some of the other problems people have with trends are:

- People assume a linear relationship. If the data is non-linear this will cause widely wrong predictions of future values. In particular, it can result in significantly underestimating exponential growth. Mosteller et al. (1981) found that people are able to draw lines of best fit that are reasonably close to a least-squares regression. This indicates that people can assess trends reasonably well. However, Collyer, Stanley, and Bowater (1990) questioned the quality of the people's ability to draw best fit lines when they found that people tended to merely bisect scatter plots.

- People assume the trend has no discontinuities. Graphical information with discontinuities proves especially difficult for people to make estimates about (O'Connor, Remus & Griggs, 1993).

- People overestimate downward trends and underestimate upward trends and they are poorer at estimating downward trends than upward trends (Remus, O'Connor, & Griggs, 1995). Upward and downward

trends get interpreted differently. People assume an upward trend will continue and a downward trend will reverse itself (O'Connor, Remus, & Griggs, 1997). In some areas of decision making, such as risk analysis, this tendency can be highly problematical. Consider how people will assume the stock market will always continue up but that a down market will soon reverse. In a corporate business setting, rather than figuring out the underlying reason for any downward trend, people may avoid making any decision and feel confident that next month's data will be better.

- People are insensitive to sample size. Small or large samples make no difference. A small sample which has one outlier will cause the interpretation to be skewed.

- Exponential data series are very common in the sciences and in business, especially when the business environment is turbulent. Being able to make judgments based on exponential data is thus important. However, people consistently under-estimate when they extrapolate exponential data (Wagenaar & Sagaria, 1975). The bias to under-estimate is so strong that it even occurs when people know the data shows an exponential curve. Also, there is no difference between working with graphs or tables (Wagenaar & Timmers, 1977, 1979). In what could be considered a contradiction, as people are given more data, they make worse estimates (Wagenaa & Timmer, 1978). Remus (1984) claims the bias occurs because people use the differences between data points rather than the ratio change when they extrapolate data. One way to mathematically change an exponential curve to a linear curve is to use logarithmic scales. However, Arnott and O'Donnell (2008) found this transformation made little difference in the quality of people's estimates.

- People are sensitive to biases from recent effects or past experience. Recent experiences exert an undue bias. If a problem occurred the last time something happened, people assume that it will happen again, even while admitting it was a freak event.

Contextual information has been found to play an important role in determining trends. People, especially when analyzing unfamiliar information, may improperly apply trend analysis. A significant portion of information falls into categorical or ordinal data rather than numeric data. In these cases, trend analysis does not apply. Yet, when presented with graphical representations, people will establish trends. For example, Zacks and Tversky (1999) found that 3 out of 25 participants used trend analysis when viewing graphs relating gender to height and drew conclusions such as "The more male a person is, the taller he/she is."

2D versus 3D Graphs

Modern graphing software can easily produce 3D graphs. However, in most cases the graph contents are two dimensional and the depth dimension is essentially ornamentation which does not contribute to the message. Often the graph choice, especially by non-designers or non-communication professionals, is to pick a graph style with a high coolness factor without regard for the overall readability of the graph or its ability to communicate the information. Consider how Microsoft PowerPoint's default is 3D graphs, which many designers suggest should be changed to 2D to enable better communication (Mackiewicz, 2007b).

Different graph formats have a significant effect on the amount of cognitive effort required to interpret the graph (Hicks et al., 2003). Mentally processing the extraneous information impairs comprehending the information. Research into 2D versus 3D graphs has found:

- The accuracy of reading point values or making comparisons between points on 3D graphs are lower than for equivalent 2D graphs (Zacks *et al.*, 1998).
- Size changes were judged more quickly with 3D objects than 2D, but the accuracy of the judgment was less (Carswell, Frankenberger, & Bernhard, 1991; Spence, 2004). However, the more rapid judgment was limited to cases were only one dimension changed, such as 3D bar charts with same width bars of varying heights. When multiple dimensions changed, 3D estimates were slower and less accurate.
- Estimates of changes between simple 3D objects (boxes) are more accurate than estimates of changes between more complex 3D objects (pyramids, truncated pyramids). In addition, the accuracy differences increased at non-linear pace for complex objects (Spence, 2004).
- People may say they prefer 3D graphs, but they read 2D graphs more accurately (Feldman-Stewart & Brundage, 2004).
- People rate 2D graphs as better at conveying information than 3D (Mackiewicz, 2007b). In HII relevant situations, the need for rapid judgment of graph changes is low while the need for accuracy is high, which supports using 2D graphics.
- Information presented in 2D format is remembered better than with 3D formats (Carswell, Frankenberger, & Bernhard, 1991).

Salience of Graph Information

The power of a graph comes from its ability to translate existing data structure into a visible salient representation (Meyer, Shamo, & Gopher, 1999). The design team's task is to ensure the salient information in the graph is relevant to the situation. For a discussion on information salience in general, chapter 4: *How people approach information*, "Salient information."

Information salience influences how people perceive the graph and combine its information with the rest of the text. Interestingly, when people evaluate information they think they use more information than they actually do. They also tend to underestimate the weight placed on important cues and overestimate weight placed on unimportant cues (Andriole & Adelman, 1995). As a result, the relative salience of the information can result in important information not being properly weighted with respect to the remainder of the information. Overly prominent, but of lesser importance, graphical information can skew people's decision making. Consider how in Figure 13, the words 'million' and 'thousand' are in small type under the number. With their decreased salience of the words under the numbers, the readers will only remember the numbers 5 and 100 rather than that the 100 represents a number many times smaller than the 5.

Text and graphics need to be positioned together as a single unit. Standard writing guidelines say to put a graphic immediately after it is referenced in the text. Relating or comparison information requires both information elements to be close together. Pomerantz and Schwaitzberg (1975) demonstrated that increasing the distance between two elements decreases information salience.

Janiszewski (1998) showed diagrams of varying complexity to students and found the ones placed in visually competitive environments tended to receive less attention. Therefore, visual complexity could distract viewers from the intended message. Excess use of graphics can rapidly make for a visually noisy environment which makes it difficult to read a single graph or compare multiple ones. In either case, the overall design has impacted the salience of the information.

Elementary Graphical Tasks

Cleveland and McGill (1984) defined a set of elementary graphical tasks (Figure 14) which a person performs to comprehend the graph. They acknowledge that the tasks are not independent of each other but that each task is cognitively complex and shares substantial overlap with other tasks. Graphic comprehension is improved if the graph design uses the elementary graphical tasks which people are most accurate at. In this work, Cleveland and McGill defined accuracy as being human estimates closest to the actual quantities depicted. For example, people were more accurate at judging relative values of the length of two lines than they were at judging the relative values of the area of two quadrilaterals.

The six tasks they found, in order of accuracy, are described here. Some of the tasks are grouped because their study was unable to clearly define the order of the items within the group.

Position along a common scale: Detecting the order or value of two points when they are both measured with respect to a single scale.
Positions along non-aligned scales: Detecting the order or value of two points when they are measured along different scales. The basic perceptual problem here is that the point visually higher or lower may not have the

Figure 13. Numbers with small text or explanation. With the words 'million' and 'thousand' printed so much smaller than the numbers 5 and 100, a reader will remember the number and its text, but not the relation between them.

5 million Number of refurbished units shipped last year

100 thousand Number of new units shipped last year

Figure 14. Elementary perceptual tasks. The tasks are shown in their relative order for accuracy and comprehension reading across the images (adapted from Cleveland & McGill, 1984).

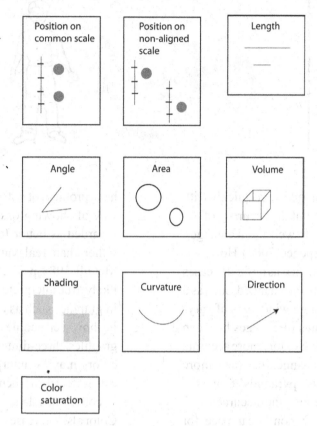

higher or lower value, a condition which causes cognitive dissidence and slows down the mental analysis.

Length, direction, angle: Comparing the length of two lines. The easiest way is to have parallel lines with an end aligned. However, most length comparisons are not arranged that way. Direction is comparing two or more lines and determining if they point in different directions and how much they differ. Angle is comparing the angles made by two different angles.

Area: Comparing the areas of two objects. Shape and area are processed serially, so it is slow. (Lohse, 1993). The strength and weakness of many graphics are their ability to display comparison information. While people are very good when the comparison is linear,

when forced to address the 2-dimensional aspects of comparing areas people perform much more poorly (Figure 15). When multiple dimensions change, estimates become even slower and less accurate (Spence, 2004).

While the relationships in Figure 16 were all essentially linear, but designed with questionable choice of images, sometimes the graphic requires a person to judge area. Area increases as the square of the linear dimensions, but people find it hard to make accurate judgments in non-linear relationships (Spence, 2004).

Volume, curvature: Curvature is the relative change in between two arcs. Volume is the space enclosed by a 3-dimensional object.

Figure 15. All of the images pairs are twice as tall, but they can be perceived as different.

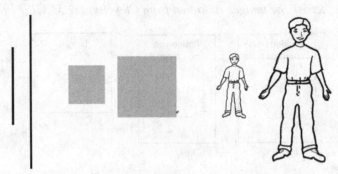

Size changes were judged more quickly with 3D objects than 2D, but the accuracy of the judgment was less (Carswell, Frankenberger, & Bernhard, 1991; Spence, 2004). However, the more rapid judgment was limited to cases were only one dimension changed, such as a 3D bar chart with same width bars of varying heights. Estimates of changes between simple 3D objects (boxes) are more accurate than estimates of changes between more complex 3D objects (pyramids, truncated pyramids). In addition, the accuracy differences increased at non-linear pace for complex objects (Spence, 2004).

Shading, color saturation: Color saturation is the visible color. Shading is the grayscale equivalent of color.

One major use of color can be to group elements in a display. For example, color can help viewers group data in scatterplots. Color

has a problem of not having an unambiguous way of showing order and "thus might be regarded as better for encoding categories rather than real variables" (Cleveland & McGill, 1984, p. 532). Some colors are more likely to be interpreted as "higher" or "lower" in graphics such as contour plots, influencing how well people mentally interpret these graphics three-dimensionally. In addition, colors may be interpreted as representing categorical data when they represent changes in continuous data.

Color also decreases the number of iterations people require to go through graphics to make a decision (Benbasat, Dexter, Todd, 1986). Color is processed in parallel, so it is fast, but the speed is more valuable in situations where a fast response is needed (such as, when this indicator turns red, do X) as opposed to an analysis-based situation where people have

Figure 16. Twice the size has two meanings. B is twice the area of A and C is twice as high/wide as A, which gives it four times the area. Most people will estimate B is less than twice the area of A.

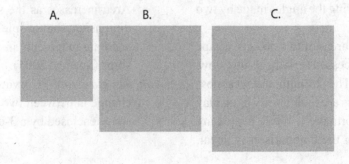

A.   B.   C.

more time and have to cognitively process the information rather than simply react (Lohse, 1993).

EXAMPLES

Astronomical Information

Reports of various interplanetary space probes often have an illustration of the path they will take to get from Earth to the planet. Various TV shows and movies give people the incorrect impression that the travel path should be a direct line, when the reality is a long, highly elliptical path. Many missions also use close planet flybys to give them a gravity assist. The only way to effectively communicate this concept is with an illustration. Figure 17 shows the gravity assist for Voyager 2. Flight paths such as for the Messenger probe to Mercury with flybys of multiple planets can only be clearly visualized with an illustration. A textual description would not adequately capture the complexities of the flight path.

Business Reports

Choice of scales can cause people to misinterpret the information on a graph. At first glance, Figure 18A shows an increasing trend for sales. Looking closer, the years are in reverse order with the latest year on the left. The upward trend is the most salient element of the graph, but is an illusion of the data plotting. Of course, the ethics of presenting information in this manner is questionable. Figure 18B shows what appear to be widely different sales by region. Yet, the y-axis has a very narrow span; if the data was plotted with a zero scale, the four regions would appear to all have essentially equal sales. The high salience of the different bar heights can override the y-axis values and make people perceive that the south region has about 1/3 the sales of the east region.

Figure 17. Messenger flight path. The Messenger probe required multiple flybys of Earth, Venus, and Mercury before it could be in position to orbit Mercury (adapted from http://solarsystem.nasa.gov/ multimedia/display.cfm?IM_ID=2143).

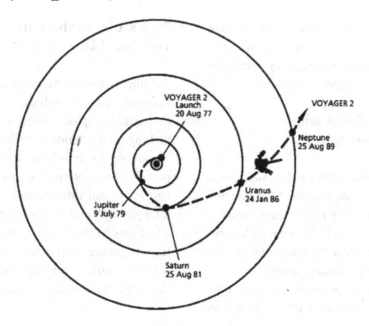

Figure 18. Improper salience misrepresents data. A has reversed years which shows an upward trend when the reality is a downward trend. B has four bar that are almost the same, but the choice of y-axis exaggerates the differences.

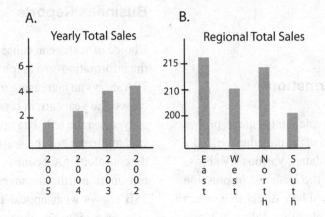

SUMMARY

Use of graphics helps a person interpret a situation more quickly. Unlike text, comprehending graphics is multidimensional with the entire image being interpreted simultaneously. Graphics are particularly helpful in depicting a quantitative or scientific concept or relationship, especially when the concept can be explicitly and concretely expressed. On the other hand, graphics do a poor job of expressing abstract concepts; for abstract concepts, text is better.

Graphics in technical material rarely exist without text, and material with integrated text and graphics improves comprehension over either text-alone or graphics-alone documents.

Approaches to Texts with Graphical Elements

Texts contain both text and graphics which people have to read and integrate together. However, images and text are mentally processed differently. Graphics overwhelmingly influence people's first impression of a text, since they mentally process the layout before any reading occurs.

Communication and writing guidelines typically say to use graphs to show information since people find them easier to interpret then. In the broad case, this is true. However, reading graphics, graphs, and charts and drawing inferences may not be as intuitive as it seems. At a basic level, the reorganization and interpretation of a graphic depends on the limitations of working memory. Also, information structure and prior knowledge about the situation are important factors in whether or not graphs or tables are better, with graphs typically favoring the more experienced person in most situations.

Types of Graphics in Technical Documents

Technical documents contain a wide range of different types of graphics, with graphs (typically line or bar graphs), tables, diagrams, or images making up the majority of the graphics.

Graphs, by their basic design, are made to be perceived and interpreted as a single entitiy. This ease of global interpretation proves to be both their strength and their weakness. They provide a fast way to obtain good, but not optimal, solutions to problems, particularly when the optimal solution requires reacting to very small changes in the numbers. Trends and relationships are easier to interpret with a graph, but values are easier with a table.

Diagrams depict a conceptual reality, rather than a realistic description of a physical action or situation. They work to portray the parts of a system and display the interrelationships between those parts and provide an easy way of describing relationships that are difficult to describe in words. Diagrams best improve comprehension when they show relationships among ideas or when they show spatial relationships.

Images are photographs or realistic drawings. While photos can be very useful in documents, they are often too detailed. Irrelevant visual detail can be a nuisance in reasoning and can impede the process. They work well for emotional material or giving a high-level description.

How People Comprehend a Graphic

Interpreting and comprehending a graphic requires practice. Most people only know to look at the shape of the graph and gain a surface-level understanding (the trend is up). But moving beyond the superficial understanding to gain a deeper knowledge means looking past the shape of the graph and understanding the relationships it portrays.

Graph comprehension requires people to mentally encode the information and identify major features (such as the line shape) and then they must connect those features to the relevant elements in the situation.

There is a poor understanding of how graphics actually work cognitively and the area is rife with assumptions and fallacies. Design teams have only weak principles to guide the design and integration of graphs documents. It is not so much the failure of any specific type of graphics, but overgeneralizations between different types and audience needs which lead to the problem.

REFERENCES

Albers, M. (2004). *Communication of complex information: User goals and information needs for dynamic Web information.* Mahwah, NJ: Erlbaum.

Albright, S. (1993). A statistical analysis of hitting streaks in baseball. *Journal of the American Statistical Association, 88*(424), 1175–1183. doi:10.2307/2291254

Allen, P. (1996). User attitudes toward corporate style guides: A survey. *Technical Communication, 43*(3), 237–243.

Andriole, S., & Adelman, L. (1995). *Cognitive system engineering for user–computer interface design, prototyping, and evaluation.* Mahwah, NJ: Erlbaum.

Arnott, D., & O'Donnell, P. (2008). A note on an experimental study of DSS and forecasting exponential growth. *Decision Support Systems, 45*, 180–186. doi:10.1016/j.dss.2007.11.006

Atkins, P., Wood, R., & Rutgers, P. (2002). The effects of feedback format on dynamic decision making. *Organizational Behavior and Human Decision Processes, 88*, 587–604. doi:10.1016/S0749-5978(02)00002-X

Austin, P., Matlack, R., Dunn, K., Kosler, C., & Brown, C. (1995). Discharge instructions: Do illustrations help our patients understand them? *Annals of Emergency Medicine, 25*, 317–320. doi:10.1016/S0196-0644(95)70286-5

Benbasat, I., Dexter, A., & Todd, P. (1986b). The influence of color and graphical information presentation in a managerial decision simulation. *Human-Computer Interaction, 2*, 65–92. doi:10.1207/s15327051hci0201_3

Betrancourt, M., & Bisseret, A. (1998). Integrating textual and pictorial information via pop-up windows: An experimental study. *Behaviour & Information Technology, 17*(5), 263–273. doi:10.1080/014492998119337

Brasseur, L. (2003). *Visualizing technical information: A cultural critique*. Amityville, NY: Baywood.

Carney, R., & Levin, J. (2002). Pictorial illustrations still improve students' learning from text. *Educational Psychology Review, 14*(1), 5–26. doi:10.1023/A:1013176309260

Carpenter, P., & Shah, P. (1998). A model of the perceptual and conceptual processes in graph comprehension. *Journal of Experimental Psychology. Applied, 4*, 75–100. doi:10.1037/1076-898X.4.2.75

Carroll, J., Smith-Kerker, P., Ford, J., & Mazur-Rimetz, S. (1988). The minimal manual. *Human-Computer Interaction, 3*, 123–153. doi:10.1207/s15327051hci0302_2

Carswell, C., Frankenberger, S., & Bernhard, D. (1991). Graphing in depth: Perspectives on the use of three dimensional graphs to represent lower-dimensional data. *Behaviour & Information Technology, 10*(6), 459–474. doi:10.1080/01449299108924304

Carswell, C., & Ramzy, C. (1997). Graphing small data sets: Should we bother? *Behaviour & Information Technology, 16*(2), 61–71. doi:10.1080/014492997119905

Carswell, C., & Wickens, C. (1987). Information integration and the object display: An interaction of task demands and display superiority. *Ergonomics, 30*, 511–527. doi:10.1080/00140138708969741

Cheng, P., Cupit, J., & Shadbold, N. (2001). Supporting diagrammatic knowledge acquisition: An ontological analysis of Cartesian graphs. *International Journal of Human-Computer Studies, 54*, 457–494. doi:10.1006/ijhc.2000.0455

Cheng, P., & Simon, H. (1995). Scientific discovery and creative reasoning with diagrams. In Smith, S., Ward, T., & Finke, R. (Eds.), *The creative cognition approach* (pp. 205–228). Cambridge, MA: MIT Press.

Cleveland, W., & McGill, R. (1984). Graphical perception: Theory, experimentation, and application to the development of graphical methods. *Journal of the American Statistical Association, 79*, 531–554. doi:10.2307/2288400

Collyer, C., Stanley, K., & Bowater, C. (1990). Perceiving scattergrams: Is visual line fitting related to estimation of the correlation co-efficient. *Perceptual and Motor Skills, 71*, 371–378.

Coury, B., & Boulette, M. (1992). Time stress and the processing of visual displays. *Human Factors, 34*, 707–726.

Cuevas, H., Fiore, S., Bowers, C., & Salas, E. (2004). Fostering constructive cognitive and metacognitive activity in computer-based complex task training environments. *Computers in Human Behavior, 20*, 225–241. doi:10.1016/j.chb.2003.10.016

Delp, C., & Jones, J. (1996). Communicating information to patients: The use of cartoon illustrations to improve comprehension of instructions. *Academic Emergency Medicine, 3*, 264–270. doi:10.1111/j.1553-2712.1996.tb03431.x

DeSanctis, G. (1984). Computer graphics as decision aids: Directions for research. *Decision Sciences, 15*, 463–487. doi:10.1111/j.1540-5915.1984.tb01236.x

Dickson, G., DeSanctis, G., & McBride, D. (1986). Understanding the effectiveness of computer graphics for decision support: A cumulative experimental approach. *Communications of the ACM, 29*, 40–47. doi:10.1145/5465.5469

Doumont, J. (2002). Choosing the right graph. *IEEE Transactions on Professional Communication*, *45*(1), 1–6. doi:10.1109/47.988358

Feldman-Stewart, D., & Brundage, M. (2004). Challenges for designing and implementing decision aids. *Patient Education and Counseling, 54*, 265–273. doi:10.1016/j.pec.2003.09.007

Ferguson, E. (1977). The mind's eye: Nonverbal thought in technology. *Science, 197*, 827–836. doi:10.1126/science.197.4306.827

Fillippatou, D., & Pumfrey, P. (1996). Pictures, titles, reading accuracy and reading comprehension: A research review (1973–95). *Educational Research, 38*, 259–291. doi:10.1080/0013188960380302

Fiore, S., Cuevas, H., & Oser, R. (2003). A picture is worth a thousand connections: The facilitative effects of diagrams on mental model development and task performance. *Computers in Human Behavior, 19*(2), 185–199. doi:10.1016/S0747-5632(02)00054-7

Foss, D., Smith-Kerker, P., & Rosson, M. (1987). On comprehending a computer manual: Analysis of variables affecting performance. *International Journal of Man-Machine Studies, 26*(3), 277–300. doi:10.1016/S0020-7373(87)80064-0

Frownfelter-Lohrke, C., & Fulkerson, C. (2001). The incident and quality of graphics in annual reports: An international comparison. *Journal of Business Communication, 38*(3), 337–368. doi:10.1177/002194360103800308

Gallo, D., Weiss, J., & Schacter, D. (2004). Reducing false recognition with criterial recollection tests: Distinctiveness heuristic versus criterion shifts. *Journal of Memory and Language, 51*, 473–493. doi:10.1016/j.jml.2004.06.002

Garcia, F., & Tissiani, G. (2003). Guideline for adaptive graphical user interfaces using universal networking language. *Journal of Digital Contents*, *1*(1), 51–55.

Gilovich, T., Vallone, R., & Tversky, A. (1985). The hot hand in basketball: On the misperception of random sequences. *Cognitive Psychology, 17*, 295–314. doi:10.1016/0010-0285(85)90010-6

Griffin, J., & Wright, P. (2009). Older readers can be distracted by embellishing graphics in text. *The European Journal of Cognitive Psychology, 21*(5), 740–757. doi:10.1080/09541440802155627

Gyselinck, V., & Tardieu, H. (1999). The role of illustrations in text comprehension: What, when, for whom, and why? In van Oostenddorp, H., & Goldman, S. (Eds.), *The construction of mental representations during reading* (pp. 195–218). Mahwah, NJ: LEA.

Harris, R. (1996). *Information graphics: A comprehensive reference*. Atlanta, GA: Management Graphics.

Harvey, N., & Bolger, F. (1996). Graphs versus tables: Effects of data presentation format on judgmental forecasting. *International Journal of Forecasting, 12*, 119–137. doi:10.1016/0169-2070(95)00634-6

Hawley, S., & Zkmund-Fisher, B., Ubel, Pl, Jancovic, A., Lucas, T., & Fagerlin, A. (2008). The impact of the format of graphical presentation on health-related knowledge and treatment choices. *Patient Education and Counseling, 73*, 448–455. doi:10.1016/j.pec.2008.07.023

Heiser, J., & Tversky, B. (2006). Arrows in comprehending and producing mechanical diagrams. *Cognitive Science, 30*(3), 581–592. doi:10.1207/s15516709cog0000_70

Hicks, M., O'Malley, C., Nichols, S., & Anderson, B. (2003). Comparison of 2D and 3D representations for visualising telecommunication usage. *Behaviour & Information Technology, 22*(3), 185–201. doi:10.1080/0144929031000117080

Hollands, J., & Spence, I. (1992). Perception of graphical displays: The stacking model. In *Proceedings of the 25th Annual Conference of the Human Factors Association of Canada* (pp. 187–192). Mississauga, Canada: Human Factors Association of Canada.

Horton, W. (1993). Dump the dumb screen dumps. *Technical Communication, 40*, 146–148.

Houts, P., Doak, C., Doak, L., & Loscalzo, M. (2006). The role of pictures in improving health communication: A review of research on attention, comprehension, recall, and adherence. *Patient Education and Counseling, 61*, 173–190. doi:10.1016/j.pec.2005.05.004

Huff, D., & Geis, I. (1993). *How to lie with statistics*. New York, NY: Norton.

Janiszewski, C. (1998). The influence of display characteristics on visual exploratory search behavior. *The Journal of Consumer Research, 25*, 290–301. doi:10.1086/209540

Kehoe, E., Bednall, T., Yin, L., Olsen, K., Pitts, C., Henry, J., & Bail, P. (2009). Training adult novices to use computers: Effects of different types of illustrations. *Computers in Human Behavior, 25*, 275–283. doi:10.1016/j.chb.2008.12.005

Knauff, M., & Johnson-Laird, P. (2002). Visual imagery can impede reasoning. *Memory & Cognition, 30*, 363–371. doi:10.3758/BF03194937

Kosslyn, S. (1994). *Elements of graph design*. New York, NY: Freeman.

Kress, G. (2005). Gains and losses: New forms of texts, knowledge, and learning. *Computers and Composition, 22*, 5–22. doi:10.1016/j.compcom.2004.12.004

Larkin, J., & Simon, H. (1987). Why a diagram is (sometimes) worth ten thousand words. *Cognitive Science, 11*, 65–99. doi:10.1111/j.1551-6708.1987.tb00863.x

Lathrop, G. (1967). Perceived variability. *Journal of Experimental Psychology, 73*, 498–502. doi:10.1037/h0024344

Lefevre, J., & Dixon, P. (1986). Do written instructions need examples? *Cognition and Instruction, 3*(1), 1–30. doi:10.1207/s1532690xci0301_1

Levie, W., & Lentz, R. (1982). Effects of text illustrations: A review of research. *Educational Communication and Technology Journal, 30*, 195–232.

Levin, J., & Mayer, R. (1993). Understanding illustrations in text. In Britton, B., Woodward, A., & Brinkley, M. (Eds.), *Learning from textbooks* (pp. 95–13). Hillsdale, NJ: Erlbaum.

Levy, E., Zacks, J., Tversky, B., & Schiano, D. (1996). Gratuitous graphics? Putting preferences in perspective. In *Proceedings of the SIGCHI Conference on Human Factors in Computing Systems* (pp. 42–49). New York, NY: ACM Press.

Lohse, G. (1993). A cognitive model for understanding graphical perception. *Human-Computer Interaction, 8*, 352–388. doi:10.1207/s15327051hci0804_3

Lusk, E., & Kersnick, M. (1979). The effect of cognitive style and report format on task performance: The MIS design consequences. *Management Science, 25*, 787–798. doi:10.1287/mnsc.25.8.787

Mackiewicz, J. (2007). Perceptions of clarity and attractiveness in PowerPoint graph slides. *Technical Communication, 54*(2), 145–156.

Mayer, R., & Gallini, J. (1990). When is an illustration worth ten thousand words? *Journal of Educational Psychology, 82*, 715–726. doi:10.1037/0022-0663.82.4.715

Meyer, J., Shamo, M., & Gopher, D. (1999). Information structure and the relative efficacy of tables and graphs. *Human Factors, 41*(4), 570–587. doi:10.1518/001872099779656707

Meyer, J., Taieb, M., & Flascher, I. (1997). Correlation estimates of perceptual judgments. *Journal of Experimental Psychology. Applied, 3*(1), 3–20. doi:10.1037/1076-898X.3.1.3

Michielutte, R., Bahnson, J., Digman, M., & Schroeder, E. (1992). The use of illustrations and narrative text style to improve readability of a health education brochure. *Journal of Cancer Education, 7*, 251–260. doi:10.1080/08858199209528176

Moll, J. (1986). Doctor–patient communication in rheumatology: Studies of visual and verbal perception using educational booklets and other graphic material. *Annals of the Rheumatic Diseases, 45*, 198–209. doi:10.1136/ard.45.3.198

Mosteller, F., Siegel, A., Trapido, E., & Youtz, C. (1981). Eye fitting straight lines. *The American Statistician, 35*(3), 150–152. doi:10.2307/2683983

Nowaczyk, R., & James, E. (1993). Applying minimal manual principles for documentation of graphical user interfaces. *Journal of Technical Writing and Communication, 23*(4), 379–388.

O'Connor, M., Remus, W., & Griggs, K. (1993). Judgmental forecasting in times of change. *International Journal of Forecasting, 9*, 163–172. doi:10.1016/0169-2070(93)90002-5

O'Connor, M., Remus, W., & Griggs, K. (1997). Going up–going down: How good are people at forecasting trends and changes in trends? *Journal of Forecasting, 16*, 165–176. doi:10.1002/(SICI)1099-131X(199705)16:3<165::AID-FOR653>3.0.CO;2-Y

Paivio, A. (1971). *Imagery and verbal processes*. New York, NY: Holt, Rinehart, and Winston.

Paivio, A. (1986). *Mental representations: A dual coding approach*. Oxford, England: Oxford UP.

Peebles, D., & Cheng, P. (2003). Modeling the effect of task and graphical representation on response latency in a graph reading task. *Human Factors, 45*(1), 28–46. doi:10.1518/hfes.45.1.28.27225

Penrose, J., & Seiford, L. (1988). Microcomputer users' preferences for software documentation: An analysis. *Journal of Technical Writing and Communication, 18*(4), 355–366.

Pinker, S. (1990). A theory of graph comprehension. In Freedle, R. (Ed.), *Artificial intelligence and the future of testing* (pp. 73–126). Hillsdale, NJ: Erlbaum.

Pomerantz, J., & Schwaitzberg, S. (1975). Grouping by proximity: Selective attention measures. *Perception & Psychophysics, 18*, 355–361. doi:10.3758/BF03211212

Powers, M., Lashley, C., Sanchez, P., & Shneiderman, B. (1984). An experimental comparison of tabular and graphic data presentation. *International Journal of Man-Machine Studies, 20*, 545–566. doi:10.1016/S0020-7373(84)80029-2

Readance, J., & Moore, D. (1981). A meta-analytic review of the effect of adjunct pictures on reading comprehension. *Psychology in the Schools, 18*, 218–224. doi:10.1002/1520-6807(198104)18:2<218::AID-PITS2310180219>3.0.CO;2-1

Remus, W. (1984). An empirical investigation of the impact of graphical and tabular data presentations on decision making. *Management Science, 30*(5), 533–542. doi:10.1287/mnsc.30.5.533

Remus, W. E., O'Connor, M. J., & Griggs, K. (1995). Does reliable information improve the accuracy of judgmental forecasting? *International Journal of Forecasting, 11*, 285–293. doi:10.1016/0169-2070(94)00578-Z

Rodriguez, M. (2002). Development of diagrammatic procedural instructions for performing complex one-time tasks. *International Journal of Human-Computer Interaction, 14*(3&4), 405–422.

Rubens, P. (1986). A reader's view of text and graphics: Implications for transactional text. *Journal of Technical Writing and Communication, 16*(1/2), 73–86.

Scaife, M., & Rogers, Y. (1996). External cognition: How do graphical representations work? *International Journal of Human-Computer Studies, 45*, 185–213. doi:10.1006/ijhc.1996.0048

Schapira, M., Nattinger, A., & McAuliffe, T. (2006). The influence of graphic format on breast cancer risk communication. *Journal of Health Communication, 11*, 569–582. doi:10.1080/10810730600829916

Schnotz, W., & Bannert, M. (2003). Construction and interference in learning from multiple representation. *Learning and Instruction, 13*(2), 141–156. doi:10.1016/S0959-4752(02)00017-8

Shah, P., & Hoeffner, J. (2002). Review of graph comprehension research: Implications for instruction. *Educational Psychology Review, 14*(1), 47–69. doi:10.1023/A:1013180410169

Simkin, D., & Hastie, R. (1987). An information processing analysis of graph perception. *Journal of the American Statistical Association, 82*, 454–465. doi:10.2307/2289447

Simon, H. (1979). *Models of thought*. New Haven, CT: Yale UP.

Spence, I. (2004). The apparent and effective dimensionality of representations of objects. *Human Factors, 46*(4), 738–747. doi:10.1518/hfes.46.4.738.56809

Spence, I., & Lewandowsky, S. (1991). Displaying proportions and percentages. *Applied Cognitive Psychology, 5*, 61–77. doi:10.1002/acp.2350050106

Spool, J. (2009). Deciding when graphics will help (and when they won't). *UIEtips*. Retrieved April 30, 2010, from http://www.uie.com/articles/deciding_when_graphics_help/

Tractinsky, N., & Meyer, J. (1999). Chartjunk or goldgraph? Effects of presentation objectives and content desirability on information presentation. *Management Information Systems Quarterly, 23*(3), 397–420. doi:10.2307/249469

Tufte, E. (1983). *The visual display of quantitative information*. Cheshire, CT: Graphics Press.

Tufte, E. (1990). *Envisioning information*. Cheshire, CT: Graphics Press.

Tufte, E. (1997). *Visual explanations: Images and quantities, evidence and narrative*. Cheshire, CT: Graphics Press.

Tversky, B. (2002). Some ways that graphics communicate. In Allen, N. (Ed.), *Words and images: New steps in an old dance* (pp. 57–74). Westport, CT: Ablex.

Tversky, B., Zacks, J. M., Lee, P. U., & Heiser, J. (2000). Lines, blobs, crosses and arrows. In Anderson, M., Cheng, P., & Haarslev, V. (Eds.), *Theory and application of diagrams* (pp. 221–230). Edinburgh, UK: Springer. doi:10.1007/3-540-44590-0_21

van der Meij, H., & Gellevij, M. (1998). Screen captures in software documentation. *Technical Communication, 45*, 529–543.

van der Meij, H., & Gellevij, M. (2002). Effects of pictures, age, and experience on learning to use a computer program. *Technical Communication, 49*(3), 330–339.

Wagenaar, W., & Sagaria, S. (1975). Misperception of exponential growth. *Perception & Psychophysics, 18*(6), 416–422. doi:10.3758/BF03204114

Wagenaar, W., & Timmers, H. (1977). Inverse statistics and misperception of exponential growth. *Perception & Psychophysics, 21*(6), 558–562. doi:10.3758/BF03198737

Wagenaar, W., & Timmers, H. (1978). Extrapolation of exponential time series is not enhanced by having more data points. *Perception & Psychophysics, 24*(2), 182–184. doi:10.3758/BF03199548

Wagenaar, W., & Timmers, H. (1979). The pond-and-duckweed problem: Three experiments on the misperception of exponential growth. *Acta Psychologica, 43*(3), 239–251. doi:10.1016/0001-6918(79)90028-3

Weiss, E. (1985). *Writing a Usable User Manual*. Philadelphia, PA: ISI Press.

Wills, C., & Holmes-Rovner, M. (2003). Patient comprehension of information for shared treatment decision making: State of the art and future directions. *Patient Education and Counseling, 50*, 285–290. doi:10.1016/S0738-3991(03)00051-X

Winograd, E., Smith, A., & Simon, E. (1982). Aging and the picture superiority effect in recall. *Journal of Gerontology, 37*, 70–75.

Zacks, J., Levy, E., Tversky, B., & Schiano, D. (1998). Reading bar graphs: Effects of depth cues and graphical context. *Journal of Experimental Psychology. Applied, 4*, 119–138. doi:10.1037/1076-898X.4.2.119

Zacks, J., & Tversky, B. (1999). Bars and lines: A study of graphic communication. *Memory & Cognition, 27*, 1073–1079. doi:10.3758/BF03201236

ADDITIONAL READING

Anderson, M., Meyer, B., & Olivier, P. (2002). (Eds.), *Diagrammatic representation and reasonin.* London, UK: Springer-Verlag.

Cleveland, W., & McGill, R. (1984). Graphical perception: Theory, experimentation, and application to the development of graphical methods. *Journal of the American Statistical Association, 79*, 531–554. doi:10.2307/2288400

Harris, R. (1996). *Information graphics: A comprehensive reference*. Atlanta, GA: Management Graphics.

Heiser, J., & Tversky, B. (2006). Arrows in comprehending and producing mechanical diagrams. *Cognitive Science, 30*(3), 581–592. doi:10.1207/s15516709cog0000_70

Huff, D., & Geis, I. (1993). *How to lie with statistics*. New York, NY: Norton.

Mayer, R., & Gallini, J. (1990). When is an illustration worth ten thousand words? *Journal of Educational Psychology, 82*, 715–726. doi:10.1037/0022-0663.82.4.715

Shah, P., & Hoeffner, J. (2002). Review of graph comprehension research: Implications for instruction. *Educational Psychology Review, 14*(1), 47–69. doi:10.1023/A:1013180410169

Simon, H. (1979). *Models of thought*. New Haven, CT: Yale UP.

Tufte, E. (1983). *The visual display of quantitative information*. Cheshire, CT: Graphics Press.

Tufte, E. (1990). *Envisioning information*. Cheshire, CT: Graphics Press.

Tufte, E. (1997). *Visual explanations: Images and quantities, evidence and narrative*. Cheshire, CT: Graphics Press.

Chapter 9
How People Approach Numbers, Statistics, and Risks

ABSTRACT

The previous chapter dealt with how people interpret graphics. This chapter examines how people interpret numbers, typically given as probabilities or risks (Figure 1). In a majority of HII situations, numbers are essential for gaining a full understanding of the situation. This chapter covers how people react to numbers. Since many people have a high literacy level but a low numeracy (number literacy), design teams must understand how people interact with and interpret numbers as it is essential to understanding how it affects the communication process.

BACKGROUND

Numerical quantities focus on expected values, graphical summaries on unexpected values. —John Tukey

This chapter looks at:

Numeracy and Literacy: Explains the definitions of numeracy and literacy and how they affect understanding numerical data.

Interpretation of Numbers: Discusses the basic issues involved in interpreting quantitative data.

Causes of Misinterpreting Numbers: Most quantitative data is presented in the form of statistical data, but most people have trouble understanding it. Discusses how people interpret and misinterpret statistics.

Risk Perception: Risk information can be presented in different ways and people's interpretation of each way can change their perception of the risk.

INTRODUCTION

A significant portion of technical material relevant to HII contains numbers which must be effectively communicated to people. Without some level of experience or training, people are quite poor at

DOI: 10.4018/978-1-4666-0152-9.ch009

Figure 1. HII model – Approaching numbers and statistics

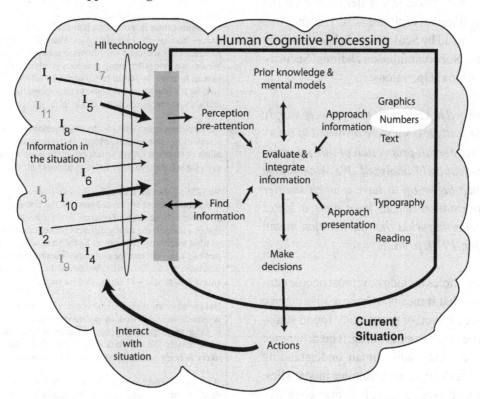

comprehending how the numbers apply to their situation. Numbers typically get presented as an abstraction (3 of 10 drivers will have a major accident within 5 years), and people are not good at cognitively handling abstraction. Likewise, they are not good at dealing with big numbers (a 10 billion dollar government program) or in comprehending probabilities (a drug has a 15% chance of a side effect). In addition, people tend to see causal relationships within data where a relationship does not exist, leading to actions such as wearing lucky hats.

A large quantity of HII information contains data which describes statistics, probabilities, or risks. Examples include healthcare information containing effectiveness of treatment options, financial investment information, results of a study for constructing a new building in a city, or proposals for hiring new employees. Unfortunately, people have a difficult time fully comprehending

information presented as a probability. Healthcare research has found that patients find it difficult to adequately comprehend risk information (Evans et al, 1994; Lerman, Kash, & Stefanek, 1994). For example, given a range of risks for heart disease, people consistently place themselves at the low end, but believe other people are at high risk. However, making informed decisions about lifestyle and treatment options requires that they understand and effectively use that risk information. An HII goal is to effectively communicate that numerical information.

Statistics and probability theory are mathematical models that describe the uncertainties in the world. Many risk experts promote quantitative probabilities because they believe that numbers are more precise and convey more information to the public than qualitative risk statements (Monahan & Steadman, 1996; Murphy & Winkler, 1971). How people perceive the results and interpret the uncertainties frequently differ from what the mathematical model itself predicts. This fact was vividly portrayed by Schlesinger in his testimony to the Senate Subcommittee on National Security and International Operations:

What happened in Vietnam is that we were simply drowned in statistics; we were drowned in information. A very small proportion of this information was adequately analyzed. We would have been " much better off to have a much smaller take of information and to have done a better job of interpreting what that information meant (Schlesinger, 1970, p. 482).

Other examples include how most people cannot explain what it means to have a 30% chance of a drug side effect, or that a study found statistical significance for a new drug. The difference between the theory and human understanding arises from lack of formal training in statistics, but also from biases inherent in human cognitive processing. Biases, as this chapter will discuss, extend to experts and are not just an untrained or layperson problem. It is important for a design team to understand how people interpret (and misinterpret) numbers and statistical information to create designs which minimize the chance of misinterpretation (Meyer, Taieb, & Flascher,1997).

Across the research literature, there is substantial support showing that people have trouble grasping the intended meaning of probability statements. However, the opinions vary on how and why this problem exists. Although often considered a lack of training or a layman issue, Garfield and Ahlgren (1988) found evidence that both novices and experts encounter difficulties with respect to understanding probabilistic concepts or estimating probabilities. For example, while typically expected in laymen analysis, Slovic et al. (1982) found experts were often overconfident in the exactness of their estimates and put too much confidence in statistics done on small samples.

Box 1.

Communication is more than just the words

Except from an interview with Alice Huang (president of the American Association for the Advancement of Science).

We are at a time when many decisions involving science will have to be made by lawmakers — or even voters at the ballot box. So it's important for people to understand the issues. And that's where we, as scientists, can help.

Unfortunately, there isn't much consideration given to training scientists to communicate, except with other scientists. And much of that is in jargon, which can make what we say hard even for scientists in other fields to understand.

We held a National Science Foundation–supported program one summer where we invited some of the best communicators from various fields of science. And what was amazing is that physicists had a totally different concept than biologists of what a cell was. We were using the same words but in ways that had very different meanings. So imagine how nonscientists must get confused when we throw these terms out and expect that people will know what we mean.

But probably the most difficult concept to get across to nonscientists is that we look at data and then use probabilities to judge those data. The public wants an absolute black-and-white answer. We may look at something that is 80 percent likely as being good enough to base decisions on.

We'd like absolute answers, but we realize that sometimes decisions must be made with partial data or some uncertainties. And…as we collect more data, what we thought of as truth might change.

If we can be patient and explain this to nonscientists—how we are seeking truth with the best tools available—they are less likely to be negative or skeptical of our conclusions. (Huang, 2009, p. 32)

A significant factor in misjudging numbers comes from not clearly understanding the basic question being addressed and how the numbers apply to it. People may know the numbers but don't understand the relationships which connect them to comprehending the situation. Garfield and Ahlgren (1988) provide this example:

When asked what the probability is that a particular attractive, well-dressed woman is a fashion model (Beyth- Marom & Dekel, 1983), students typically give an answer of about 70%, and they give about that same value for the probability that she is an actress or the probability that she is a cosmetics distributor. Instead of answering with a probability about the woman's profession, the students apparently are estimating the probability that a fashion model (or actress or cosmetics distributor) would be attractive and well dressed. (p. 55)

Design teams need to switch this idea around and make sure that the information they are presenting does not lend itself to this type of misinterpretation. They need to consider how people can misperceive or misinterpret the numbers and allow for that in the content. When interpreting usability test results, it is important to consider why a person had the problem, rather than just noting they didn't seem to understand the numbers.

NUMERACY AND LITERACY

Understanding numbers requires a degree of numeracy. Rothman et al. (2006) defines numeracy simply as the ability to understand and use numbers in daily life. Most other definitions go somewhat further or at least clarify what "use numbers" means. In general, they all consider that numeracy encompasses a range of skills, which includes the ability to perform basic math functions (calculations, fractions, algebra, geometry), to understand time, money, measurement, graphs, probability, and to perform multi-step math. Health communication is currently the major research area for studying numeracy-related communication issues (Golbeck et al., 2005; Peters et al., 2007; Schapira, Nattinger, & McAuliffe, 2006) and most of the examples of this chapter will be health related.

Golbeck et al., (2005) defines numeracy as consisting of four main skills:

- Basic skills of identifying and relating numbers.
- Computational skills of basic mathematical operations of addition, subtraction, multiplication and division.

- Analytical skills of being able to use numbers to form inferences, make estimates based on numbers, and determine proportions. Analytical skills also allow a person to take numbers from various sources and mentally integrate them.
- Statistical skills of evaluating and understanding probability and risk, and how they apply to the current situation.

Data from the National Literacy Survey indicates about half of Americans lack the minimal mathematical skills needed to use numbers embedded in printed materials (Kirsch et al., 2002). Most researchers accept a correlation between print literacy and numeracy; however, studies have also found that people with adequate print literacy are still unable to use appropriate numeracy skills (Rothman et al., 2006). Golbeck et al. (2005) point out that although many studies consider numeracy a subset of literacy, it should be considered as an equal-level complementary set of skills. More than just being able to read a number, numeracy also includes the ability to interact with, evaluate, and comprehend those numbers in a manner applicable to a situation. It means being able to build the relationships between the numbers and textual information.

Developing a clear situation model, being able to draw inferences about the information, and making informed decisions between potential choices requires understanding what the numbers mean. In many audiences, a significant percentage of the readers do not have sufficient numeracy skills: Estrada et al.(2004) found about half of their subjects correctly answered fewer than two of six numeracy questions. These readers are literate and can comprehend the text, but they still have trouble dealing with its numerical aspects. High numeracy people tend to draw stronger and more precise meanings from numbers and numerical comparisons and want numeric risk information (Peters et al., 2006). On the other hand, Gurmankin, Baron, and Armstrong (2004) found that less numerate individuals wanted verbal risk information rather than numeric risk information: They preferred hearing a low chance of rain rather than a 20% chance of rain. People with high numeracy are more likely to retrieve and use appropriate numerical principles and also tend to avoid framing effects. People with lower numeracy are more influenced by irrelevant information, probably because they draw less meaning from the relevant numbers (Peters et al., 2006).

Part of the communication difficulty is that the communication of risks and probabilities is a complex matter that has a strong dependence on both prior subject knowledge and prior experience with evaluating similarly presented information. For instance, people who evaluate financial graphical presentations as part of their work will have an easier time evaluating health risk graphs. Of course, people who routinely evaluate financial graphs also have a high numeracy level.

A basic problem when HII involves interacting with numbers isn't communicating a textual-level understanding (which means the reader can recall the values). Rather, the problem is communicating a deeper understanding so that they can develop information relationships between the numbers and the situation. It is very easy for people to remember actual numbers and say they made a choice because it was 40% better. However, they often lack a clear understanding of what 40% better actually means and how 40% better pragmatically applies to the situation. Rather than assuming people understand what 40% means, the design team needs to ensure the overall content clearly lays out the meaning and helps build the relationships (Albers, 2010).

INTERPRETATION OF NUMBERS

People try to use common sense when considering statistics, but they often lack enough experience to have developed the proper common sense. Consider these different examples.

Box 2.

Video card review numbers

While researching a new computer, I was reading the reviews of various video cards. The reviews had long lists of numbers comparing them. What was more interesting was reading the comments people posted about the reviews. It was very clear that some of those people only looked at one or two numbers which defined the raw speed of the card and unilaterally declared that "fastest is best, period."

Depending on the use of the card, that may not be true. For a gamer, 3D rendering speed is vital. I mostly do word processing and use Adobe drawing tools. I need dual monitor support, but fast 3D rendering will not improve my performance. Making sense of the numbers in the review requires connecting them to the situation.

- A person is in a club with 40 members which has a big birthday party for each member. With 40 people, what is the chance of two members having the same birthday? The actual chance is more than 90% that two will share a birthday. The misinterpretation is that many people think of it in terms of sharing their birthday: any person they meet has a 1/365 chance of that. The real question is for any pair of people in the club.

- Most people regard an average as the typical value. For example, when asked how they could use the average temperature for a city, a common response was that it can tell you want to wear during a visit (Garfield & Ahlgren, 1988). In reality, knowing the average yearly temperature of Chicago would be useless in deciding what type of clothes to bring.

One communication issue with statistics is that most explanations are in terms of events or sampling. An event could mean that there is a 30% chance of a part being damaged or a 74% chance a person likes pizza. Then, these events or samples are combined, such as the chance of two parts being damaged or all three people in a group liking pizza. The move from the abstract event to clearly specified examples makes many statistical

Box 3.

Group probabilities and individual probability perceptions differ

Assessments of people's understanding of probabilistic information have frequently concluded that people do not understand probabilistic information, but typically ignores that how a person interprets the chance of an event happening to a group and to that individual differ.

After completing cancer training, cancer patients were asked to estimate how many patients treated with each of the two possible treatments would be live 3 years after treatment. In addition, they were asked to estimate their own chances of being alive at 3 years. The patient's interpretations for cancer patients in general and their personal probability interpretation were widely different. Eighty percent reported the population outcomes correctly. However, comparing personal outcomes to the group with the two different treatment options,

- With radiotherapy, 25% thought their personal outcomes were the same as the population,
- With combined-modality treatment, only 5% thought their personal outcomes were the same as the population. (Feldman-Stewart, & Brundage, 2004). The rest thought they had a better chance than the group.

In both of these example, people thought their own response to treatment would be better (more favorable results) than the general population. Yet, there is nothing which actually supports that decision. Instead, it's a natural bias for people to see themselves as better than average.

---

situations easier to understand (Pollatsek, Lima, & Well, 1981).

People view themselves as different from the group—usually as better—when asked to make estimates of where they stand within the group. A substantial part of that mental difference may exist because favorable and unfavorable outcomes are weighed differently when people consider a situation (Dahlbäck, 1990) and are reflected in how people interpret the information. If 60% of businesses have a problem getting good return on investment with a product, most businesses will invest with a feeling that they are clearly in the 40% which will have no problems because they are better than a typical business. When presenting statistical information to people within a group, design teams need to consider how it will be interpreted.

When writing content, probabilities can be described as either a percentage (20%) or a fre-

quency (2 out of 10). Although these numbers are identical mathematically, people tend to respond to them differently. In an interesting display of the potential contradictions, Slovic, Monahan, and MacGregor (2000) asked social workers about the chance of violent criminals repeating a violent crime within six months. They found:

- Frequency scales led to a lower estimate that a person would commit a violent crime than percentages.
- Frequency scales led to a higher estimate the person posed a higher risk than percentages.
- Frequency scales led to a person being judged as more dangerous than percentages.

The second and third bullets contradict the first one, although the values given to the social workers making the estimates were the same. Slovic, Monahan, and MacGregor suggest that both formats be used when communicating information. "Of every 100 patients similar to Mr. Jones, 20 are expected to be violent to others. In other words, Mr. Jones is estimated to have a 20% likelihood of violence." (p. 285). In addition, understanding the audience's numerical literacy is essential and, depending on their numeracy, may require explaining how to evaluate the material. The design team must take responsibility for clearly communicating the information and not assume the reader will properly interpret statistical information. If the presentation will contain numbers, the audience analysis must measure the numerical literacy of the audience.

Since probabilities can be expressed either verbally or numerically, it is important to know how people interpret the words and what sort of probabilities they apply to them. If told there is a low chance of X, how do people mentally translate 'low' into a probability? Mazur and Hickam (1991) looked at how patients translate the verbal expressions for the chance of side effects for

Table 1. Verbal probability expressions and their numerical equivalents (adapted from Mazur & Hickam, 1991, p. 239)

Word	Mean probability	Word	Mean probability
Almost certain	86%	Possible	49%
Very likely	77%	Not unreasonable	47%
Likely	64%	Improbable	31%
Frequent	64%	Unlikely	31%
Probable	60%	Almost never	15%

a medical procedure (Table 1). Although they found a spread of actual numerical values for each term, the verbal term order was very consistent. So, although people may have different mental values for "likely," they consistently put "likely" as higher than "frequent."

Data Distribution

Data does not exist a single value. It is often condenses into a single value, such as the average or the median, but the data actually covers a range of values. How it is spread across that range has a significant effect on how the data should be interpreted.

The two most common measures of distribution are the mean and the median. The mean is the mathematical average and the medium is the middle number (half of the values are lower and half are higher). With a normal distribution, the mean and the median are equal, but with a skewed distribution, the two are not. In most cases with a skewed distribution, the median gives a better representation of the data. A few outlier values can pull the mean significantly away from the median value. However, if people know about the outliers, they do not weigh them too heavily. They recognize the outliers as rare occurrences and thus not more important than the more frequently occurring occurrences (Peterson & Beach, 1967)

Consider the values of {10, 15, 20, 24, 74}. The mean is 28.6, larger than all but one value, while the median is 20. A news report showed that the median sales price of new homes fell significantly, to $195,200, from a revised $215,600 in July. The mean price sank to $256,800 in August from $273,100. With house sales, the median is a better since the sales of multi-million dollar houses does not distort the results.

Standard deviation is a value which is reported in essentially all formal statistical reports which provide the mean (Figure 2.A). This gives an indication of the spread of data by showing the width of the data distribution curve that would contain 68% of the data. Large standard deviations show that the data has a wide spread and a small standard deviation show the data has a narrow spread. On the other hand, if the distribution has two peaks, the mean and standard deviation smooth across them and can give a very misrepresentation of the real data.

Most basic explanations of data distributions only give a normal curve (Figure 2.A), with the data equally distributed around the center. But most distributions are skewed, with more data to one side than the other. With skewed distributions, the median should be used for reporting, and for extremely skewed data, even that may not have much meaning. Consider how people's reaction time (and most timed activities are) is positively skewed. It will graph with a large peak to left and a long tail to the right (Figure 2.B). With a skewed distribution, people's estimate of the mean is closer to the median than it really is (Peterson & Miller, 1964).

Figure 2. Data distribution. The curves in A and B could have the same mean, but obviously represent very different types of data and should be interpreted very differently.

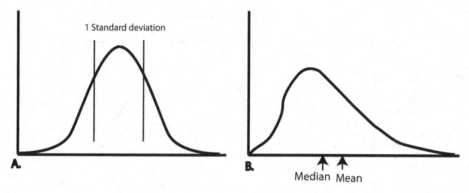

Box 4.

Comparing two sets of numbers

A common analysis problem is to compare two sets of numbers to determine if they came from different populations. For example, are the data entry times faster with the new interface than with the old one. This test is essentially looking at two bell curves and measuring if the offset between them is greater than chance.

Measuring this requires doing a statistical test, such as a t-test. Some people will try to simply calculate the average and pick the higher as better. But that does not show if they are different.

Ranges of Values

Researchers and statisticians understand that reported numbers have some level of uncertainty. The journal paper may report an event as occurring 30±4% of the time or every 45±6 days. As that information is transposed into laymen terms, the ±4 factor gets dropped. In addition, the ±4 needs to be defined: is it the standard deviation, 25%/75% variance levels, or the actual observed high/low. And, of course, there is the problem that a significant part of the audience may not understand what a term such as standard deviation means when applied to a value. On the other hand, although some writers believe giving a range confuses the reader, (occurs 26-34% of the time), a range does not decrease the perceived information quality (Lipkus, Klein, & Rimer, 2001).

A graph can be a visual representation of 30±4%, but the error bars impose communication issues (Figure 3). Error bars permit making inferences about the stability of information, but requires a trained reader. Timmermans et al. (2004) question if vertical error bars are a suitable method of graphically presenting information, especially risk information, since it projects a feeling of more complex information. The error bars should help facilitate readers perceiving detailed data patterns. In particular, they permit making inferences about the stability of reported data values. Of course, the error bar's meaning must be defined, but, in addition, many audiences require an explanation of how to interpret error bars. People who understand error bars mentally impose some segment of a bell curve on to the span of the bar. But people without experience in evaluating data with error bars tend to ignore the bars and only look at the center point. If the data is already mistrusted, they may see all points on the error bar as equal and decide the data is suspect. At one level, the mistrust of the data stems from being able to see how precise (or imprecise) the values actually are. People lack any experience with error bars and they are normally removed as science research information is transformed into layman terms. Zacks et al., (2002) found error bars used in about 10% of the journals they sampled, but not in newspapers. Without training

Figure 3. Graphics with error bars (arrow points to the error bars). Depending on the audience knowledge level, the meaning of the errors bars needs to be explained. (NASA/WMAP Science Team)

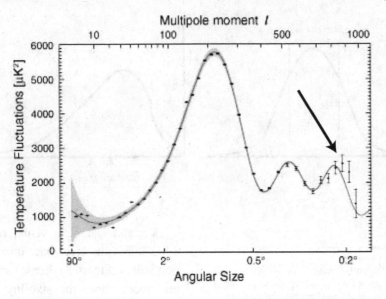

Box 5.

Presenting an allowable range of values

My dog's white blood cell count was 9.43 with a normal range of 5.5-16.0. (See figure 10.6 for a graphical display of the report.) In medicine, lab results are typically reported with the 5.5-16.0 listed as the normal range. In this case, as the owner, I see the value is within that range and I feel ok. On the other hand, it could be reported as a normal range of 10.75±5.25, which says the same thing. In that case, I'd see the value is actually somewhat below the mid-point and may be concerned that the value is low.

In addition, presenting information as 10.75±5.25 with no visual requires a person to perform a mental calculation to see if a value of 5.6 is within the normal range or is low. This risks a miscalculation which could either cause undue worry or missing a low/high value that should be addressed, depending on the direction of the math error.

in the sciences, most people do not realize that essentially all data has some level of uncertainty with it. When creating content for either experts or laymen, design teams need to obtain a solid understanding of the audience's knowledge about interpreting this presentation format and provide adequate information about how to interpret it.

The Law of Large Numbers

The law of large numbers describes the long-term expectations of the mean of a random variable. Simply stated, if you roll a die lots of times, your outcomes should on average be equal to the theoretical average. This is a very common sense statement (Well, Pollatsek & Boyce, 1990).

Consider rolling a die 600 times. How many times does it come up 2? An exact answer is not possible, but there should have been 100 times. If a 2 came up 300 times, the fairness of the die would be questionable. At the same time, if the die was rolled in sets of 600 many times, in any one set the number of 2s would not be exactly 100, some would be higher and some lower, but taken as a group, they would approach the 2 showing up 1 in 6 times.

The real misinterpretation problem stems not from large numbers (lots of tosses of the die), but in a belief that small numbers operate the same way. People expect that the results shown by a small sample are representative of the larger set. "They regard a sample randomly drawn from a population as highly representative, that is, similar

Box 6.

Misapplying small numbers

Consider a survey with the following question:

Would 10 tosses or 100 tosses of a fair coin was more likely to have exactly 70% heads?

People tend to correctly choose the small sample. People have trouble transferring the abstract coin toss questions to real world situations. When asked essentially the same question:

Would a large, urban hospital or a small, rural hospital be more likely to have 70% boys born on a particular day?

People answered that both hospitals were equally likely to have 70% boys born on that day. The large urban hospital will have lots of babies born on any particular day, which will drive its average closer to 50% boys. On the other hand, the rural hospital, like tossing a coin 10 times, will show large fluctuations in the boy/girl ratio on any one day since it will have only a few births each day. But over the course of a year, both hospitals will deliver essentially equal percentages of boys and girls (Garfield & delMas, 1991).

Box 7.

Course grades as weighted averages

A course has three exams and a final, with each exam worth 20% of the grade and the final worth 40%. Up until the final, it is easy to calculate the current grade in the course, since a simple average works. To calculate the final grade, each of the exams much be properly weighted.

Assume the first two exam scores were 84 and 80 which gives an average of 82. The third exam score is 76 and the course average is $(84 + 80 + 76)/3 = 80$. The final exam score is 93.

Calculated (incorrectly) as a simple average $(84 + 80 + 76 + 93)/4 = 83.25\%$.

Calculated (correctly) with the weighting: the 80 gets 60% and the 93 final score gets 40% which gives $(80 * 60\%) + (93 * 40\%) = 85.2\%$

With proper weighting, the overall score is 2 points higher.

---

to the population in all essential characteristics" (Tversky & Kahneman, 1971, p. 105). Small samples are generally believed to be more reliable representatives of a population than they should be. A preference for Brand X over Brand Y in four out of five people can be marketed as showing a preference—although the probability of getting four out of five by chance is 3/8. In the long run, the numbers will represent the population, but with a small sample, this does not apply. For example, a coin flipped 4 times has a reasonable chance of 4 heads or 4 tails, but a coin tossed 100 times has a minimal chance of 100 heads. Likewise, sampling just four people for their opinion on a political candidate (even if they were randomly selected) does not mean their views will reflect the election results.

Weighted Averages

Weighted averages are essential to combining and understanding averages when the numbers come from different sized groups.

Reports constantly contain information which must be interpreted as a weighted average, but many people ignore the weighting and perform a simple average. Pollatsek, Lima, and Well (1981) asked college students to combine two grade point averages that were based on different numbers of courses into a single average, but they were unable to do the task correctly. Rather than doing a weighted average, most did a simple average. But beyond not understanding how to do the calculation, it seemed that a simple average was all they knew. They did not understand the need to weight data in computing a mean. Interestingly, they also found that students realized that averaging a cumulative GPA with the current semester GPA would not be fair since it over-weights the current work, but didn't know how to solve the problem.

Interpreting Extreme Events or Outliers

Extreme events tend to bias an estimate of the average. Outlier events tend to be the ones people remember or try to adjust for. For example, after seeing the task correctly performed 99 times, the 1 time the event fails leaves a strong impression and will biases the person to estimate higher failure rate. This bias leads to overestimating the relative frequency of problem events in a hindsight estimate. Consider how a significant incident at a corporate event, even after years of hold the event with no problems, will make the management team question holding the event again. Or people's fear about flying after a recent plane crash.

When reading a report that recommends doing X, people will remember the one time (an outlier event) that X would not have been appropriate and question the report's conclusions. The logical problem here is that they ignore the large number of times that X was the proper conclusion and focus on the small number of times it was not.

The outlier may or may not actually be an outlier. Perhaps the data is just a small sample, so that the apparent outlier is really part of a normal distribution of data.

CAUSES OF MISINTERPRETING NUMBERS

People do not need an in-depth understanding of the probability theory to understand it when it appears in a text, but they do need a functional understanding. The real problem doesn't seem to be knowing what the numbers mean, but how to apply and relate them to a situation. For example, the actual term a 60% chance of rain does not pose a problem, but understanding what 60% chance of rain means with respect to when and where and for how long has many interpretations for a general reader and most of them are not what the Weather Service intended to communicate (Handmer & Proudley, 2007).

Biases in Interpretation

People perform as "intuitive statisticians" (Peterson & Beach, 1967) and use multiple information sources to build up their situation model. In the process, they show many biases that influence the quality of their interpretation and resulting model. However, many design teams assume the

readers will use the information with an unbiased approach, which is an unrealistic expectation.

A central premise of normative decision making is that choices should be made on the basis of unbiased assessments of relevant information. Depending on the context, such information may consist of product attributes, legal evidence, medical symptoms, or the behavior of others. Although these considerations do inform many decisions, inferences also operate in the opposite direction. Specifically, when one decision alternative is favored over another, information is often evaluated as being more consistent with the preferred alternative than is warranted. (DeKay et al, 2009, p. 79)

Previous research has suggested that the affect heuristic, an emotional response to perceived risk based on past experiences, also plays a role in risk perception and interpretation of risk communication messages (Slovic, Finucane, Peters, & MacGregor, 2004; Keller, Siegrist, & Gutscher, 2006). Risk perception can be further influenced by information available via the Internet, which often uses emotional appeals rather than number-based appeal to convey messages. For example, in a study of perceptions of the need to get a child vaccinated, there was clear influence from hearing news stories about a child with adverse effects and the emotional appeals found on anti-vaccination websites. They ignore the numerical aspects of the disease versus vaccination risks and focus on the emotional (Wolfe, Sharp, & Lipsky, 2002).

Another cognitive bias is the value-induced bias, in which the nature of an outcome influences judgments of its probability of occurring (Wallsten, 1981). For instance, people may have an inappropriately high perception of the risk of cancer because of their view of the seriousness of having cancer, or as a means of justifying having an unpleasant cancer screening test with unnecessary frequency. Value-induced bias violates a principle of decision theory, which holds that the probability of an outcome is independent of its value or importance (Levy & Hershey, 2006).

Cognitive dissonance is the discomfort experienced when there is inconsistency between multiple cognitions or behaviors. To reduce this discomfort, we adjust or distort one of the cognitions to justify the other or to make the cognitions consistent with each other....Smokers, for example, may try to align their knowledge of the harms of smoking with their smoking behavior to reduce or avoid dissonance. They may change the belief that smoking is harmful by convincing themselves that the data on the harms of smoking is inconclusive. Alternatively, they may try to add new cognitions to reduce the perceived threat, such as adopting the belief that the filter traps the truly harmful chemicals in the cigarette. It is clear that people will engage in extraordinary rationalizations or distortions to reduce the discomfort of cognitive dissonance. (Levy & Hershey, 2006, p. 52)

As described in chapter 3: *What people bring with them*, "Bias in information comprehension", people do not approach a text in a logical, analytical way. Instead, interpretation is biased, since they use heuristics that provide shortcuts which work most of the time, but can give highly inaccurate results at others. Unfortunately, when probabilities are involved heuristics often fall short for good decision making, but people use them to avoid dealing with the numbers. Some heuristics which play a major part in how people interpret numbers are (Kahneman & Tversky, 1979):

Availability Heuristic: Situations that can be most easily brought to mind or imagined are judged to be more likely than situations that could not easily be imagined. Numbers which contradict this heuristic tend to be ignored or distorted to fit.

Anchoring Heuristic: People will start with a known information element and then adjust it to create a risk estimate for an unknown

situation. Typically, the adjustment is not big enough.

Threshold Effects: People prefer to move from uncertainty to full certainty rather than making a similar percentage gain in certainty that does not lead to full certainty. For example, most people would choose a vaccine that reduces the incidence of disease A from 10% to 0% over one that reduces the incidence of disease B from 20% to 10%.

Certainty Effect: People place excess weight on some outcomes. For example, given the choice between $30 for sure and $45 with 80% probability, people will tend to choose $30 for sure. However, when choosing between $30 with 25% probability and $45 with 20% probability, most people select the $45 option, despite the fact that the second set of options is the same as the first with all probabilities reduced by a factor of 4.

People may distort the probability to fit their desired answer. Distorting probabilities simplifies the decision process by reducing cognitive effort. Levy and Hershey (2006, 2008) noted that the people in their study distorted the probability of treatment success when they explained the justification for a preference for or against a medical treatment. Even when they had been given the numerical probability, the people who wanted the treatment judged the probability of success to be higher than the number given, and those who did not want the treatment judged it to be lower. For example, people may decide to not have an advisable but unpleasant health care test (for example, a colonoscopy) by distorting to a very low number the probability the disease could affect them. When a choice seems to be supported by most of the available information, it is easier to distort the remaining data to fit rather than take the cognitively demanding route of resolving the differences of the remaining data. Basically, people make an easy choice rather than worrying about the best choice. In addition, people tend to make

Figure 4. Bar graph versus pictorial displays. All three show a 9% chance. However, B is perceived as truer than A. The bar graph was perceived as having a lower risk/value (adapted from Schapira, Nattinger, & McAuliffe, 2006, p. 571-572).

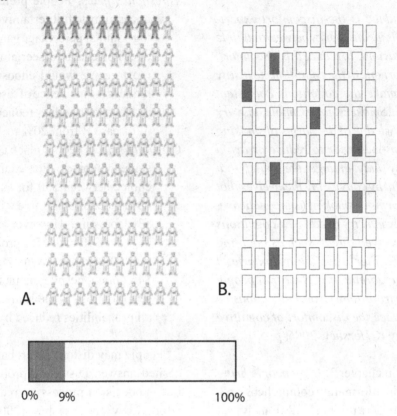

a choice very early in the decision making process and distort the data to fit that choice. Unfortunately, that choice can be influenced by unjustifiable or irrelevant information (Hsee, 1995) or factors such as order of presentation (Carlson et al., 2006). Interestingly, information distortion can lead to a decision which the people making the decision will judge to be an inferior, but preferred, decision (Russo et al., 2006).

The graphical presentation can also bias people. Figure 4 shows three ways of presenting 9% probability. Most design teams would probably pick A as the way to create a pictorial presentation of the probability. However, people consider B, with the random placement of shaded blocks, to be a truer presentation (Schapira et al., 2006). And if a bar graph is used instead, the perceived value will be

of lower magnitude as compared with a pictorial display (Schapira, Nattinger, & McAuliffe, 2006).

Cause-Effect versus Correlation Relationships

A basic purpose of many documents is to communicate information about cause-effect relationships. They need to explicitly connect the cause (when A happens) with the effect (then B happens). When a document's content includes cause and effect relationships,—a significant portion of the numbers in business reports work to identify cause-effect relationships—part of comprehension involves identifying the chains of events that give rise to that cause and effect. However, the difference between cause and effect and correlation is hard for people to distinguish and a correlation relationship is often mistaken for cause-effect relationship. The two terms are defined as:

Causation: Cause and effect relationship. The presence of A causes B. It may be deterministic (gravity always causes objects to fall), but in most cases it is statistical (A has a 70% chance of causing B). A statistical analysis of properly collected experimental data determines one thing causes another. For example, having high blood pressure causes an increased risk of stroke.

Correlation: A and B are both present, but do not cause the other to occur; they may both be caused by another factor C. Correlation relationship simply says that two things change in a synchronized manner and measures the strength of the relationship between the factors (Silvestri, 1989). If it's cloudy, it might rain (leading to an erroneous belief that clouds cause rain). But clouds do not cause it rain; instead, they are caused by the meteorological conditions that lead to rain.

Many people have a hard time clearly distinguishing between cause-effect relationships and correlation relationships (Devroop, 2000). In general, they assume cause-effect relationships, even when the relationship is correlational. For instance, there is a correlation between inflation and unemployment. When inflation is high, unemployment is also high. When inflation is low, unemployment is low. The two variables are correlated, but neither directly causes the other. In a less intuitive correlation, it is relatively easy to prove that a high school student's performance is related to the number of bathrooms in their house (more bathrooms corresponds to higher performance). This is not a cause-effect relationship, but instead reflects the underlying factor of parents' incomes. Higher income tends to mean a larger home with more bathrooms and children of higher income parents tend to do better in

school. In a more realistic situation, cause-effect and correlation relationships can be harder to distinguish, especially if one always lags the other. Poor management causes poor sales, but the sales drop lags behind the start of poor management. For the first four months after the new management team took over, sales were fine, but then they started to drop off. With longer term delays, it can be easy to believe the company went out of business because of low sales instead of of poor management which led to poor sales.

Cause-effect relationships may be deterministic (a big snowstorm causes lower sales for the week) or they may be statistical (28% of low income students will drop out of school) in nature. Deterministic cause-effect can be disproven with one counter example, such as a ball not falling when dropped. Statistical cause-effect relationships cannot be refuted by one counter example; they deal with the group as a whole, not individual members. However, many people try to reject a statistical cause-effect with anecdotic evidence about one situation they have experienced. But one specific example does not reject a statistical cause-effect relationship. Insurance companies know that people who drive red cars have more accidents. Comments about knowing a person who drives a red car and who has never had an accident does not refute the fact that red cars have more accidents. (Actually, it's not red cars that are accident prone. Red is a common sports car color and sports cars have more accidents. The cause-effect is sport cars–accidents, the correlation is red cars–accidents.) Likewise, low-income people who get accepted to Harvard do not disprove the cause-effect relationship of low income and low performance in high school; as a statistical relationship, it doesn't say anything about a particular student, just the group as a whole.

Previous studies have shown that people tend to infer events that occur in a sequence as causal propagation (Hegarty, 1992; Lowe, 1999); they think the previous event caused the current one. When people watched a computer simulation of

Figure 5. All cause and effect graphs are not straight lines. If people have always worked within the basically linear (descending) section of the graph, they would be unprepared for the change and would not be able to include it in their situation model.

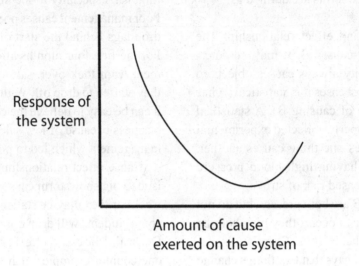

weather, they described cause-effect of events based solely on the sequence of them occurring and not on the underlying meteorological interactions. Also, people have a hard time connecting cause-effect relationships across systems. They may see the cause-effect of two separate systems, but fail to grasp how the two systems also have cause-effect relationships (Narayanan & Hegarty, 2002). For these systems, to grasp the relationships requires readers to also understand the time durations and ordering of events. This typically requires text, since the relationships do not lend themselves to simple graphical representations. Design teams need to consider the cause-effect relationships which must be apparent in the documents and how to best communicate that information.

A common communication problem when providing information about the cause-effect relationships inherent in complex systems is that people become aware of the cause-effect relationships, but are unable to cope with their complex interactions. For simple linear systems with minimal branching, it can be easy for a graphic to communicate the cause-effect relationships. However, complex systems (especially mechanical ones)

contain cyclical operations or complex branching that merge cause-effect interactions with positive or negative feedback. The feedback changes the strength of the cause-effect which makes it harder for a person to clearly see it.

Unfortunately, neither tabular nor graphical formats seemed to improve understanding (Atkins, Wood, & Rutger, 2002). Graphs can, in fact, lead to irrelevant conclusions, such as viewing graphs relating gender to height and drew conclusions such as "the more male a person is, the taller he/she is" (Zacks & Tversky, 1999). Many graphs that show cause and effect relationships tend to have straight lines. But many relationships are not linear; instead, the relationship can change substantially. The problem is that people tend to use linear extrapolation and are very poor at non-linear extrapolation (Wickens & Hollands, 2000). Any supporting text and the graphic itself should point out the non-linear nature of the relationship and explicitly state any cause-effect. With curves as seen in Figure 5, the cause of the lowest point (or other inflections points in the graph) should be explicitly explained.

Box 8.

> **Does drinking soda cause pancreatic cancer?**
> A news story (Yarett, 2010) reported a study by Mueller et al (2010) which linked sugar-sweetened soda to an increased rate of pancreatic cancer. They reported an increase rate of 87%, a number which was displayed in the story headline. However, looking closer at the real risk involved reveals less shocking result. Pancreatic cancer is rare (about 12 cases per 100,000 people), so a minimal increase in absolute risk can cause a drastic increase in relative risk. Thus, the soda drinkers should have a rate of about 20 cases per 100,000 people.
>
> In addition, the news stories portrayed the study as showing a cause-effect relationship, but the study itself only claimed to find a correlation. For instance, heavy soda drinkers tend to have poor eating and exercise habits, or other dietary issues may be the underlying cause.

Box 9.

> **Facebook users get lower grades**
> Karpinski (2009) found that Facebook users had lower grades than non-Facebook users. What she reported was a correlation and made no claim of causation. In fact, she suggested that the real cause is one of many variables that could be studied: perhaps people with higher GPAs are less social and study more, or Facebook users spend more time on non-studying activities. Any of these factors would affect GPA.
>
> A web search on the research found lots of sites with text such as "found a link between grades and Facebook usage." The comments made by the sites' authors and the readers reflect the same lack of understanding of correlation and causation. Readers made (paraphrased) comments such as:
>
> - "I have a 3.8 GPA and I use Facebook, therefore the survey is wrong."
> - "Facebook was designed by some Harvard students. What are their GPAs?"
> - "You can't put everyone in one box and say we'll fail if we use Facebook." (A true statement, but one which misses the statistical nature of the study's findings.)
>
> Karpinski points out a correlation and labels it as such. But notice how people either take it as a cause or try to discredit the research by pointing out one specific example (their own GPA and Facebook usage). Correlation and causation are both typically statistical. Given a large group of random students, the relations will hold, but it says nothing about any individual student within that random group. For correlations, the underlying cause can be any other factors the group shares.

People are not likely to spot a correlation unless they expect it, but if they do expect to find one, they tend to see it even if it is not there (Bracy, 1998; Kahneman & Tversky, 1982). Superstitious behavior is an example of incorrectly seeing a correlation. For example, a person believes his high school basketball team wins because he wears his lucky hat. In deciding the hat is a factor, the person ignores that the team has two all-state forwards. Also, since people tend to ignore disconfirming data, he also ignores that the team lost two games when he wore the hat and only remembers the fifteen wins. The all-state forwards are a cause of the team winning; the hat has no relationship at all other than being present.

Design teams need to consider how an audience will react to a statistical presentation and how to carefully present correlation findings so the audience will not read it as a cause-effect relationship. A significant problem with web-based information is that it is difficult to consider cause-effect relationships unless both sets of information are present. The limited display space on a computer monitor makes this a difficult problem for design teams to overcome. Short term memory limitations make it difficult to jump between different sets of data and effectively compare them (Casaday, 1991; Endsley, 1995). The mental and physical actions and information processing required to jump between data sets is noise and impair seeing the relationships.

Statistical and Practical Significance

To be publishable, quantitative research findings need to be statistically significant. Many people equate statistical significance to "significance" in the ordinary use of the word. However, many times, although the findings are statistically significant, the improvement is too little to be practically significant or useful. For example:

- A travel company was considering upgrading the agents' displays with new and expensive displays. A survey of the agents found they needed to enter reservations 10 seconds faster to make the new displays worthwhile. A usability test of the old and new displays found the new ones were 3 seconds faster. The results were statistically significant, but not practically significant since the 3 second increase was slower than what would justify the cost of new displays (Lane, 2007).

- A drug study finds a new drug lowers blood pressure from 140/90 to 138/88. Although the decrease is statistically significant, the decrease is not clinically significant enough to justify using the drug.

- Similarly, when studies claim that a chemical causes a "significantly increased risk of cancer," they often mean that it is just statistically significant. The total number cancer cases may have increased from a baseline of 10 per 10,000 to 13 per 10,000, possibly posing only a tiny absolute increase in risk.

When presenting information with claims of being statistically significant, the design team needs to consider if that significance is enough to be practically significant for the readers. Of course, the meaning of practically significant differs between audiences, which must also be considered.

In addition, most people do not know what statistically significant actually means. Statistical significant is expressed by the p-value of the statistical function. To be considered significant in most tests the p-value must be less than .05, which means there is only a five percent chance that the observed results would be seen if there was no real effect. However, this consistently gets switched around:

A recent popular book on issues involving science, for example, states a commonly held misperception about the meaning of statistical significance at the .05 level: "This means that it is 95 percent certain that the observed difference between groups, or sets of samples, is real and could not have arisen by chance." That interpretation com-

mits an egregious logical error (technical term: "transposed conditional"): confusing the odds of getting a result (if a hypothesis is true) with the odds favoring the hypothesis if you observe that result. A well-fed dog may seldom bark, but observing the rare bark does not imply that the dog is hungry. A dog may bark 5 percent of the time even if it is well-fed all of the time (Siegfried, 2010, p. 26).

An additional problem to handle when reporting statistical significance is the problem of testing many items, such as individually performing a t-test on each questions of a survey taken between two groups. If the survey had 20-30 questions, there is a high probability at least one will show a result of being statistical significance when it is not. A p-value of .05 means 1 in 20 tests will show an unjustified significance. In studies with large numbers of tests, such as genetics were hundreds or thousands of genes may be compared, the test design must address this issue. Design teams need to consider it as they create texts about the results.

Independence and Belief in the Recent Past Affects the Future

A fundamental assumption in statistics and probability is that events are independent of each other. Each toss of a coin has no connections with the previous tosses. People, on the other hand, often assume that past performance will predict the future. The standard example is to consider a fair coin that comes up heads 8 times in a row. The probability of heads on the ninth toss is still 50% since each toss is independent of the rest; people, on the other hand, will use the 8 heads in their prediction that the next toss must be tails. They are confusing the odds of a single toss being heads with the odds of 9 consecutive tosses being heads.

People expect to find that any string of events that is statistically high or low is likely to be followed by events that move toward the mean. In the process, they ignore the independence of the events. People see 8 heads and, knowing that 8 consecutive heads is a rare event, believe the odds of a tail on the next toss are greater than 50%. The same logic gets applied in gambling (the gambler's fallacy) by believing a slot machine is ready to payout big since it hasn't paid out recently, but each spin is independent of every other spin. The problem is that they use past events to predict future ones even though the events are independent (Konold, 1989).

People ignore event independence and interpret statistical information with a bias toward recent events, even though the event has nothing to do with their current situation.

- Many people are hesitant to fly during the weeks after a commercial airplane crash even though the actual risk is both very low and, in most cases, their flight does not have the actual factors which contributed to the crash.
- A business project recently had problems and was cancelled, so any proposal that sounds similar to the cancelled one will be rejected.
- Chance of a hit in baseball is independent of the previous at-bats (Albright, 1993). Likewise, a basketball player's chance of making a shot is independent of his previous shots (Gilovich, Vallone & Tversky, 1985). Sports players do not have a hot streak. The fans and players dispute this result, but the hot streaks do not last longer than predicted by a statistical analysis.

It can be hard to allow for effects of past events when communicating information since design teams have no knowledge of what recent events people will be considering.

Randomness

In typical data analysis, people see clusters of events (good or bad) and assume they cannot be random. People want to see a pattern and have a hard time recognizing random information. A string of numbers or a scatter plot may be random, but people will see patterns in it. If asked if a sequence is random, (for example, TTHTTH-HHHTTHTTHTH), people will often confuse random sequences and non-random sequences. Part of the problem is that random sequences will have strings of events which people see as non-random. In the example just shown, the four Hs might make some people declare it as nonrandom. Likewise, a baseball player batting .295 will have some random sets of four consecutive hits and four consecutive misses.

The clustering illusion refers to the tendency to erroneously perceive small samples from random distributions as having significant "streaks" or "clusters," caused by a human tendency to under-predict the amount of variability likely to appear in a small sample of random or semi-random data due to chance. Albright (1993) looked at baseball hitting and found there are no hot or cold streaks but that the hitting exhibited a pattern expected by a random model. In other words, although it may seem like a batter is on a hot streak (is batting .600 for the week), when compared to his normal batting average, a seven game average of .600 is expected on occasion. He will also hit .200 for a week at some time during the season. The hitting pattern fits a bell curve and at times some sequence of consecutive hits will be outside of one standard deviation. But whether the current performance places the player in the standard deviation above or below normal occurs essentially the same. Likewise, Gilovich, Vallone and Tversky (1985) contested the existence of a "hot hand" in basketball. They examined successive shots by NBA basketball players and found that the concept of a "hot hand," strings of successive shots made when a player is "hot" does not really exist. In both hitting in baseball and shots in basketball close examination of the data shows no hot or cold streaks, although players, coaches, and fans all believe a player can be hot or cold.

Box 10.

Patterns in multiple pendulum motion
A youtube video (https://www.youtube.com/watch?v=yVkdfJ9PkRQ) show several pendulums of slightly longer lengths swinging. Various sinusoidal shapes are very evident in the motion. However, each pendulum is swinging independent of the other with a different period. Any patterns seen are the eye imposing order on the overall group of pendulums and are not inherent in the pendulums. The snake pattern which appears (it is only one of many different patterns) is not inherent in the pendulums, but in how people impose order on the scene.

 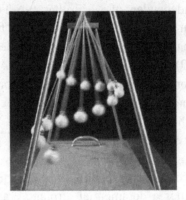

Pendulums of different lengths. If released together, these pendulums will appear to form various coordinated pattern which are constantly changing.

The sequence of successive hits or baskets made did not differ in length from sequences that would be expected by chance alone. Instead, the chance of a hit or a basket was a random probability based on the player's percentage. The hot streak appeared only by looking at a small sequence of the player's yearly or lifetime playing.

Randomness also does not work the other way; people cannot create a random set of numbers (Boland, P. & Pawitan, 1999). When asked to generate lottery number sequences, the sequences that people created were not random, even when they were told to create a random sequence.

Conditional and Joint Probability

People often have trouble with probabilities of multiple events. When talking about inherited disease trait, a text could say ""one out of four babies born to parents…" If this is the second child, most people use their knowledge of whether or not the first child had the trait as they interpret the statement. However, the one in four chance still applies to the second child, regardless of the first child. Likewise, if told a couple has four children and asked about the boy-girl mix, most people will say 2 boys and 2 girls. Actually, 1 and 3 is the most likely, because it includes 1 girl –3 boys and 1 boy–3 girls.

Understanding the statistics of multiple events requires understanding conditional probability and joint probabilities.

Conditional Probability: A second event is true if and only if the first event is true. Conditional probability is the probability of some event A, given the occurrence of some other event B and is read "the probability of A, given B". Toss a nickel and, if it comes up heads, toss a penny and it comes up heads. This is different from tossing both at once since the penny is only tossed if the nickel is heads.

Joint Probability: The probability of events A and B occurring together. Toss two coins and have both come up heads.

People tend to confuse conditional and joint probabilities. Pollatsek, Well, Konold and Hardiman (1987) found that the wording of the text and not people's reasoning was a major factor in misinterpreting the information. People were asked to give estimates about a health survey. The estimates were higher for the question "What percentage of the men surveyed are both over 55 years old and have had one or more heart attacks?" than for "What percentage of the men surveyed have had one or more heart attacks?" In any survey, more men will be over 55 than men over 55 who have had heart attacks, since the heart attack group is a subset of the over 55 group (Pollatsek, Well, Konold & Hardiman, 1987). Their answers showed how they misunderstand a situation which required a conditional probability.

RISK PERCEPTION

Risk, in a formal definition, can be represented by precise probabilities. However, the view of what risk means and how to consider it differs between situations, and between laymen and experts (Williams & Noyes, 2007). For HII purposes, it is not so much the formally defined risk, but the way people perceive the risks within a situation which design teams must consider. Based on those perceptions, people will make decisions and take actions which may or may not be appropriate.

With risk messages, trusting the accuracy of the message is an important component (Williams & Noyes, 2007) in clearly communicating the meaning. Interestingly, messages talking about risk are more trusted than messages that suggest an absence of risk (Slovic, 1993; Siegrist & Cvetkovich, 2001).

A major factor effecting the communication of risk information is that the actual risk and people's

Box 11.

> **Sledding injuries**
> I saw a television report on injuries that result from snow sledding. It said that 34% are head injuries and that 9% of those are traumatic brain injuries. In other words, 9% of the 34% (2.9% are traumatic brain injuries. However, what was displayed on the screen was "34% Head injuries 9% traumatic brain injuries." This leads the viewer to think that 9% (three times the actual value) are traumatic brain injuries.

perceived risk can be very different and viewed in inconsistent ways (Bohnenblust & Slovic, 1998). Perceived risk is what people feel the risk for an event is; a value influenced by many factors outside of the actual risk itself. For example, after a major airplane crash, people perceive the risk of flying as higher than before the crash, or after a relative or close associate dies from a disease, the perception of the risk of getting that disease is higher. In both of these instances, the actual risk has not changed. In general, perceived risk leads to small risks being overestimated and large risks being underestimated (Sjöberg, 2000). As would be expected, perceived risk most closely matches actual risk when people have some experience with the risk event (Thompson & Mingay, 1991). Unfortunately, that experience can also lead to risk avoidance and making decisions which are overly conservative to avoid a reoccurrence of a past event.

People have a difficult time imagining future consequences. This acts as a confounding factor when communicating risk or other statistical information. For example, in healthcare, patients may not fully appreciate the likelihood of medication side effects until they actually experience the side effects. The physician may have told them that although this is a faster acting drug, 10% of the recipients experience a particular side effect, such as severe nausea. People have trouble interpreting the meaning of a 10% chance of the side effect and how to apply it to their particular situation. Research into how people evaluate surgical options suggests they tend to over focus on avoiding short-term risks rather than longer-term risks (McNeil et al., 1982). This short-term avoidance can be problematical and leads to poor decision making. Consider how, after a major airplane crash, some people avoid flying because they fear another crash, but that fear soon abates and they fly again. The long term perceptions of lifetime risk are difficult to change. Lipkus, Klein, and Rimer (2001) studied women's perception of their breast cancer risks. They found that giving women lifetime risk based on the various risk factors in their life only caused a short-term modification to the perceived chance of getting breast cancer. After six months, their perception had returned to the value it was before the study, just like people will fly again a few months after a crash as their perception of flying returns to the baseline.

The framing, good or bad, of risk information has a strong influence on how people perceive the risk (Edwards & Elwyn 2001). Consider how risks can be described with either a range (there is a 3-6% chance) or as a point (there is a 4% chance). The point estimate works as an anchor from which people access their risk (Tversky & Kahneman, 1974). Using a range introduces a bias; people reveal a strong bias to see themselves at lower rather than higher risk when presented with the probabilities for their situation (Weinstein, 1980). For example, if people are told that with their risk factors they have a 4-10% risk for getting a disease, they assume their individual risk would be in the 4-5% range. On the other hand, they correctly place other people's risk in the middle of the range. In general, people reframe the issue and always tend to place themselves at the lower (most favorable) end of the continuum.

One factor in misunderstanding risks is that the 10% chance of an event typically gets presented without enough context for the person to place it into their situation. Weather forecasts say there is a 30% chance of rain tomorrow, but most people do not understand what that 30% actually means. To fully explain the situation, the rain forecast might explain what area could get rain

Box 12.

How people can interpret 'a 30-50% chance'

A psychiatrist who prescribed Prozac to depressed patients would inform them that they had a 30–50% chance of developing a sexual problem, such as impotence or loss of sexual interest. On hearing this, many patients became concerned and anxious. Eventually, the psychiatrist changed his method of communicating risks, telling patients that out of every 10 people to whom he prescribes Prozac, three to five experience sexual problems. This way of communicating the risk of side effects seemed to put patients more at ease.

The psychiatrist had never checked how his patients understood what "a 30–50% chance of developing a sexual problem" means. It turned out that many thought that a side effect would occur in 30–50% of their sexual encounters. The psychiatrist's original approach to risk communication left what the 30–50% was referring to unclear: Does the percentage refer to a people (patients who take Prozac), to events (a given person's sexual encounters), or to some other factor? Whereas the psychiatrist's understood he meant 30–50% of his total number of patients who take Prozac, his patients' understood it to mean their own sexual encounters (Gigerenzer et al., 2005).

---

and how a successful calculation is made. For a drug with a 10% chance of side effect, the physician needs to explain that 10% of the people taking the drug will get a side effect, and not that once for every 10 pills will a person will feel the side effect.

Some factors which strongly influence communicating risk are (Williams & Noyes, 2007):

Signal Word: Signal words both attract attention and communicate the degree of risk associated with the situation or product. The presence of a signal word in a warning is better than its absence (Wogalter et al. 1994). The American National Standards Institute (ANSI 1998), defines the four most commonly used signal words: 'Danger,' 'Warning,' 'Caution,' and 'Notice.' However, many researchers believe that just four signal words are too limited and fail to properly communicate. Wogalter and Silver (1990) did a study of 84 signal words and found they could be judged on a term they called 'arousal strength.' Design teams need to test the ability of the signal words used in their texts to ensure people perceive them properly.

Color: The color of the message, especially for signs or other small stand alone texts, draws the reader's eye in and gives an emphasis to its importance. The color must match the overall message importance. Wogalter and Silver (1990) found that the arousal strength of signal words varied based on their color.

Surround Shape: The overall shape of a risk or warning can communicate by itself. For example the octagonal shape of a stop sign.

Absolute versus Relative Risks

When choices are compared, choices can be described in either absolute or relative risk terms.

Absolute Risk: The actual statistical probability of the event occurring. The absolute risk of betting that a fair coin will be heads in 50%.

Relative Risk: The statistical probability of the event occurring as compared to another event. For example, a comparison that says smokers have an X% higher chance of developing a disease than non-smokers is a relative risk. X% might be a large number, such as 400%, but yet the absolute risk of the disease might be tiny, such as less than 1%. For instance, 1 out of 1000 nonsmokers will get a disease and 40 out of 1000 smokers will get a disease.

Understanding risks for decision making requires knowing the absolute risk in real numbers, such as 20 out of 1000, not percentages. For example drug X might lower the risk of a disease from 20% to 10%. This is a far more important reduction than if it reduced the risk from 0.002% to 0.001% but the relative reduction (50%) is the same. The first has a highly practical significance

while the second may be statistically significant, but not practically significant.

Absolute risk reduction can be thought of as the difference between risk of an event in a control group and risk of an event in a treatment group. In contrast, relative risk reduction is the ratio of risks of the treatment and control group. Thus, a risk reduction from 6% to 3%, for example, can be expressed as an absolute risk reduction of 3%, or as a relative risk reduction of 50%. (Berry, Knapp, & Raynor, 2005).

The 'biasing' effects of relative risk presentations are not always beneficial for health. The most classic demonstration of this is the 1995 'pill scare', in which the Committee on Safety of Medicines (CSM) issued a warning that third generation oral contraceptives were associated with "around twice the risk" compared with second generation preparations. This relatively simple risk communication was taken up by the media and resulted in a dramatic decrease in use of the pill and a steep rise in pregnancies and terminations. However, what was not stated was that the starting level of risk was actually very low (rising from around 15 cases per year per 100,000 users to around 25 cases) and that the risk in pregnancy was actually several times higher. (Berry, Knapp, & Raynor, 2005, p. 90)

Natter and Berry (2005) point out the importance of informing people about the baseline level of risk when presenting information about comparative risk. Without knowing the baseline, people have no way of judging the meaning of a 0.3% increase or a doubling of risk (Berry, Knapp, & Raynor, 2005).

People prefer choices presented as relative risk rather than absolute risk, but do not fully grasp the true differences in the absolute risk associated with their choices (Malenka et al., 2003). Studies in which relative and absolute risks were compared showed that risks were considered to be greater when information was expressed as relative risk than when it was presented as incidence rates (Halpern et al., 1989; Stone, Yates, & Parker, 1994). Clearly reading a 400% greater risk will get more of a reader response than reading the risk increases to a .03% chance, even if both are correct in terms of relative and absolute risk. An extreme example would be to compare the crash chances when flying in two different models of commercial jets. It is highly possible that one model has 3 times (or 300% greater) the chance of crashing; although in absolute terms, it might mean 1 versus 3 crashes out of the thousands of flights the jet has made over many years. If given a choice of two flights to a destination and type of plane, some people would pick the jet with the lower number of crashes. Of course, this ignores potential mitigating factors in the existing crashes such as a snow storm or a lightening strike. It also directly leads to the valid (although pragmatically useless) conclusion that a model of plane that has never crashed is infinitely safer than one which has one crash.

One compounding factor that affects how people interpret the presentation is that people have a hard time comprehending absolute risk when it pertains to a future event. If given a 33% chance of problems occurring, most people would attempt a task. If they encounter problems, they would justify it away by saying there was a 33% chance of the problem. Also, comprehending absolute risk is problematic when the absolute risk is very small. For instance, most people overestimate their risk of hereditary cancer, which has a risk of 5% and 10% (de Vries et al, 2005). Such estimates can be greatly skewed if a close relative has recently been diagnosed. In this case, both near-term effects of the relative's diagnosis and a person's natural fear of developing cancer will cause them to highly overestimate the chance they will develop it.

When developing a text, the design team must carefully consider how people perceive and react to both the absolute and relative numbers. More

Box 13.

Casino slots are 30% looser and relative risk
Casino ads like to claim that their slot machines have higher payouts than their competitors. One claimed its slots had a payout that was 30% more than the industry average. However, this number presents a change in relative risk. When viewed in terms of absolute risk, the actual change in people winning is quite small (since this is a section on risk, you have to interpret what 'quite small' means).

Typical slot machines have about a 96% payout. So for every $100 which goes into them, they payout $96. A casino with a payout that is 30% more, would be paying 30% more of $4, or $1.20. So, the slot machines at the casino with 30% looser slots pay out $97.20 for every $100, rather than the industry average of $96 for every $100.

patients typically agree to treatment based on relative risk than when the risks were presented as absolute differences (Slovic, 2000; Stone et al., 2003). For example, the likelihood of medical treatment choices has been found to differ based on absolute or relative risk formats. Malenka et al. (2003) find that, when presented with information about two equally effective medications for treating a hypothetical serious disease, more than 50% of patients selected the medication that was described in terms of relative benefit, but less than 15% selected the medication that was described in terms of absolute benefit (the remainder made no choice). When questioned about their choice, they said the one presented with relative risk was better. In reality, both were the same. Stone et al. (2003) point out that using only relative risks may result in generating reader action, but at the expense of the reader fully understanding the risks. In this case, design teams face the ethical issues of the reader response they desire and the amount of information they desire to communicate.

The strong effects seen for the differences between relative and absolute risk presentation bring up ethical issues for the design team since it strongly influences a reader's choice. The reason for the choice of presenting the information via relative or absolute values must be considered by the design team during content development.

Box 14.

Examples of relative versus absolute risk

Assume the absolute risk of developing a disease is 4 in 100 for non-smokers. Also, assume the relative risk of the disease is increased by 50% in smokers. The 50% relates to the '4,' so the absolute increase in the risk is 50% of 4, which equals 2 more cases. So, the absolute risk for a smoker developing the disease is 6 in 100.

A large reduction of relative risk for a rare event might not mean much reduction in the absolute risk. Assume an event has a 4 in a million chance of occurring. A 75% reduction in relative risk brings the absolute risk down to 1 in a million. Although the reduction may be 75%, the chance of the event happening for any specific individual is minimal in either case. In a report seeking funding, stating a change of 4 in a million to 1 in a million is likely to not get funded, but a 75% reduction sounds much bigger and may get funding. The readers perceive the number differently.

If there is an absolute risk of 10% for an event, and a change caused a risk reduction of 50%, then there would be a 5% absolute risk. If there is an absolute risk of 1%, and change caused a risk reduction of 50%, then there would be a .5% absolute risk. Even though both situations experienced a 50% reduction in risk, for the smaller one the risk decrease may be too small to be practical given any extra expense.

Graphical Risk Presentation

Risk information can be presented graphically or numerically, either in a table or in the text. Although the information is identical, from an HII view, graphs and numbers affect people differently. Unfortunately, how the different presentations affect people's understanding is not as well researched as it should be (Timmermans et al., 2004). The type of graph has a significant effect on how people perceive the risk. The research also shows a set of conflicting results, particularly in the use of pictographs.

- When presented with numbers, people were less risk averse, probably because it is harder to fully comprehend the numbers (Stone Yates, & Parker, 1997). The salience of a graphical format scared people (Timmermans et al., 2004), probably because the risk area on a graph is very salient versus reading numbers. In other

words, the numbers, by being harder to understand, impaired communication which resulted in people being more willing to make decisions without fully comprehending the risks. On the other hand, if queried about the absolute values rather than the relationships necessary for good decisions, people would probably know the numbers, although it would be a surface level understanding. This can be considered an issue of knowing the actual risk value versus understanding the information.

- Graphical presentations that focus on the number of people harmed at the expense of total people at risk result in the greatest risk avoidance behaviors (Stone et al., 2003).

- The effectiveness of a format not only depends on the characteristics of the information, such as the magnitude of the risk, but also on people's cognitive leaning styles (Lipkus & Holland, 1999).

- Schapira et al. (2006) recently showed that patients perceived lifetime breast cancer risk to be lower when risk information was communicated with a bar graph compared with a pictorial display of risk. The study used icons that were either human-shaped or rectangular boxes with the same results. Timmermans et al. (2004) found that using human-shaped icons resulted in less people making the optimal choice, yet they preferred that format. A suggested reason is that people focus on avoiding short-term risks (McNeil et al., 1982).

- Pictographs are the best format for communicating probability information to people in shared decision making environments, particularly among lower numeracy individuals (Hawley et al., 2008), who make up a significant portion of the population.

- Bars and icons are the most frequently used graphical formats for presenting risks in health care, and have been shown in a few studies to be superior to other graphical displays, especially for comparing risks (Timmermans et al., 2004)

- Vertical bars are perceived as "more complex and more threatening" (Timmermans et al., 2004, p. 260) than presentations that use either numbers or human-shaped icons.
- When people are asked to make predictions using either a graph or a table, they are more accurate with a graph. Interestingly, this finding holds even if they prefer data formatted in a table (Carey, & White, 1991). They also point out that the potential improvement in task effectiveness is highly sensitive to the individual task and, thus, sweeping generalizations about the study results cannot be made
- Cultural factors also play a major role. Current American culture places high emphasis on zero risk; the American public expects major initiatives such as space shuttle launches or nuclear power to be perfect. Yet, engineers know that any complex system contains a full set of risks. In an interesting cultural conflict, a group may demand zero risk before accepting nuclear power, but accepts a non-zero risk of accidents when driving a car. Attitude toward risk and what constitutes acceptable risk seems be a question of ideology (Sjöberg, 2000).

Small Risk Presentation

Communicating small risks presents a special problem to the design team. Presenting information as 1 in a million or 1 in 10,000 is, by itself, an abstract concept. In addition, many of the risks being discussed in these terms are also abstract, unfamiliar, or not visible, such as food contamination or product safety. There may also be controversy around the idea, such as toxic contaminants in food, with different sources giving wildly different risk information and often

ignoring the details the reader's want (Handmer & Proudley, 2007). The problem faced by design teams is trying to ensure people comprehend what a very low probability risk really means to them. For example, it is hard for a person to relate to what it means for an adverse drug reaction to be "very rare" or 1 in 10,000. Also, people either show a tendency to either reduce very small risks to zero risk (Kahneman & Tversky, 1979; Stone et al, 2003) or they overestimate the likelihood of a low probability event (Baron, 2000).

Low numbers can be hard to present in a way that makes sense. Consider a report that shows incidents of:

- 217 per 100,000 members
- 2.17 per 1000 members
- 0.217% of members

These values can cause a very different response in people. The percent value seems so small as to be disregarded and equated to zero. The 217 value has a seeming large absolute value until it is compared against the 100,000, but the value itself may exert an influence on people's perception or response.

Consider a report showing the chances for developing stomach cancer are still very low in young adults, but the incidence among 25 to 39 year-old-white males nonetheless climbed by almost 70 percent in the past three decades. In absolute value, it may have changed from 6 per 100,000 to 10 per 100,000. If asked to estimate their own chance of developing stomach cancer, most people will put themselves at the low end and essentially say it is zero. However, if a person had a relative or friend diagnosed with stomach cancer, they would overestimate their own chance by a substantial amount.

Small absolute value changes can make for large percentage changes. A report on a fast-growing type of cosmetic surgery said the surgery rate had increased 30% between 2005 and 2006. In absolute terms, the procedure went from 793 to

1,030, a very small number of total surgical procedures. Likewise, each year there are lists of the fastest growing companies. A company that goes from 50 to 200 employees shows 400% growth while a company that goes from 1,000 to 1,150 employees shows 15% growth, but both hired the same number of employees. Design teams need to ensure they are not overhyping or misleading readers by stressing large percentage gains which are caused by small starting numbers.

Risk Denial

Risk denial is defined as instances where people's personal perceived risk is less than the risk to the general population.

Because of risk denial, people do not make the same estimate when they rate the risk to themselves, to their family, or to people in general. For example, a study asked for estimates of risk to self, family, and general population for 15 hazards (Weinstein, 1987). The study presented the risks to each group such that they should have been the same; any differences between risks in each group were from risk denial. Risk denial was strongly evident and each of the three groups had clearly different estimated risk levels. Because of people's propensity to see themselves at lower rather than at higher risk, they tend to place themselves at the lower end of the continuum (Weinstein, 1980). In other words, when given a range of risk for a situation, a 30–50% chance of the project failing, most people see their project as being at the 30% end of the range. For some probabilities, such as for a business project, where the numbers are very soft, this could be justified but is often unsupported rationalization. In areas such as healthcare, where the probabilities come from long term studies, people still ignore or rationalize their mitigating factors and assume they are at the most favorable position in the range.

Effectively communicating risk information and getting compliance with the risk message often requires considering risk denial and ensuring people's view of their perceived risk matches the actual risk. Perceived relevance and risk denial act together as a strong deterrent to people fully accepting a risk message. One suggestion from Williams and Noyes (2007) is that by "making the warning more specific to the individual, they are more likely to identify with, and accept the level of risk indicated in the message, and comply with the behaviours outlined in the message or, behave in a way befitting the situation" (p. 21).

EXAMPLES

Astronomical Information

Any content about astronomy will contain large numbers that deal with time and distance. For example:

- Average distance of the Earth from the Sun: 149,597,900 kg
- Mass of the Sun: 1,989,000,000,000,000,0 00,000,000,000,000 kg
- Age of the Earth: 4,550,000,000 years (4.55 Billion years)
- The Moon: 384,000 km
- The Sun: 149,600,000 km (1 AU)
- Alpha Centauri (nearest star): 4.2 light years (266,000 AU)
- Center of the Milky Way Galaxy: 26,000 light years (1.65×10^9 AU)

Typically, the values are expressed in scientific notation, such as the 1.65×10^9 AU in the last bullet. Scientific notation presents a problem because, depending on the numeracy of the readers, that expression may be meaningless and providing a two sentence explanation of scientific notation will probably not help much. Also, the units within the solar system change to *astronomical units (AU)* which is a value most readers are not familiar with. People understand distance by mentally comparing it to what they know. When measurements are in multiples of an unknown unit—one that is too big to get a clear concept of—they will tend to ignore it.

As a result, although astronomical content contains numbers, the design teams need to consider how important they really are to understanding the text. Many general reader texts do little more than present numbers. What people want are the concepts put into terms they can understand. Numbers are basic data, not information.

Business Reports

Cause-Effect and Correlation

Reports on production issues have three different factors which often get conflated in the final report. Factors of cause-effect, correlation, and random events. Since they all have to be figured out from a post-event analysis (why did production drop 10% in the last quarter versus the previous year?), it can be hard to not assign cause-effect to either correlation or random events.

Actually, a random event might be the cause, but it is not one that a business can control for. If a major electrical transformer blew up causing a two day power outage, the expense of preventing a reoccurrence combined with the risk of a reoccurrence make it a poor business decision to do anything about it. The cost of installing and maintaining backup generators may exceed the loss of the two day power outage. The report needs to consider both the loss and the risks of that event happening again.

Minimizing Risk

Business executive want to minimize risk. This leads to them expecting a risk assessment for any major project and for the project team to strive to present any risk in the best possible way. Unfortunately, for a design team, the numbers which go into a risk assessment are very soft with the final risk value often varying widely based on the initial

assumptions. Fully explaining those calculations provide too much detail for the audience who only want to see the conclusions.

The risk assessment needs to consider various reasonable scenarios and should present them. Adding alternatives makes decision makers feel more confident in their choices. It also gives them a base on which to interpret future decisions which may negatively impact the current project.

SUMMARY

A significant portion of technical material relevant to HII contains numbers (statistics, probabilities, or risks) which must be effectively communicated to people. Without some level of experience or training, people are quite poor at comprehending how the numbers apply to their situation. Design teams need to allow for the audience's numerical knowledge and ensure that the information they are presenting does not lend itself to misinterpretation. They need to consider how people can misperceive or misinterpret the numbers and allow for that in the presentation.

Numeracy and Literacy

Understanding numbers and placing them into context requires a degree of numeracy. Numeracy can be defined as the ability to understand and use numbers in daily life. In general, numeracy encompasses a range of skills, which includes the ability to perform basic math functions (calculations, fractions, algebra, geometry), to understand time, money, measurement, graphs, probability, and to perform multi-step math. Data from the National Literacy Survey indicates about half of Americans lack the minimal mathematical skills needed to use numbers embedded in printed materials.

HII involves interacting with numerical information which requires working above a textual-level understanding (which means the reader can only recall the values). Rather, HII requires communicating a deeper understanding so that people can develop information relationships between the numbers and the situation.

Interpretation of Numbers

Across the research literature, there is substantial support showing that people have trouble grasping the intended meaning of numerical presentations. Consider how probabilities can be described as either a percentage (20%) or a frequency (2 out of 10). Although these numbers are identical mathematically, people tend to interpret and respond to them differently.

Data does not exist a single value but is part of a distribution of value. This distribution is often condensed into a single value, such as the average or the median. The mean is the mathematical average and the medium is the middle number (half of the values are lower and half are higher). With a normal distribution, the mean and the median are equal, but with a skewed distribution, the two are not. In most cases with a skewed distribution, the median gives a better representation of the data. However, people often have difficulties with both medians and skewed distributions.

People ignore the size of a data set and consider large and small samples as equivalent. The real misinterpretation stems not from large numbers, but in a belief that small numbers operate the same way. In the long run, the numbers will represent the population, but with a small sample, chance can significantly skew the values.

Causes of Misinterpreting Numbers

When people misinterpret numbers, the real problem doesn't seem to be knowing what the numbers mean, but how to apply and relate them to a situation.

People exhibit many biases with interpreting numbers where they distort the values to better reflect the outcome they desire. They also confuse cause-effect and correlation relationships by assuming most relationships are cause-effect. In addition, they are influences by the recent past when interpreting probabilities rather than considering them as independent events.

Risk Perception

Risk can be formal defined by precise probabilities. For HII purposes, it is not so much the formally defined risk, but the way people perceive the risks within a situation which design teams must consider. Based on those perceptions, people will make decisions and take actions which may or may not be appropriate. How the information is presented text versus graphical and the form of the graphic can influence interpretation.

People need to know, but frequently confuse absolute risk and relative risk. Absolute risk is the actual statistical probability of the event occurring and the relative risk is the statistical probability of the event occurring as compared to another event.

For small risks, people typically exhibit risk denial and do not believe the risk probabilities apply to them.

REFERENCES

Albers, M. (2010). Usability and information relationships: Considering content relationships when testing complex information. In Albers, M., & Still, B. (Eds.), *Usability of complex Information Systems: Evaluation of user interaction* (pp. 109–132). Boca Raton, FL: CRC Press. doi:10.1201/EBK1439828946-9

Albright, S. (1993). A statistical analysis of hitting streaks in baseball. *Journal of the American Statistical Association*, *88*(424), 1175–1183. doi:10.2307/2291254

American National Standards Institute. (1998). *Warning signs, labels, tags, colours and symbol standards Z535* (pp. 1–5). Arlington, VA: National Electrical Manufacturers Association.

Atkins, P., Wood, R., & Rutgers, P. (2002). The effects of feedback format on dynamic decision making. *Organizational Behavior and Human Decision Processes, 88*, 587–604. doi:10.1016/S0749-5978(02)00002-X

Baron, J. (2000). *Thinking and deciding (Vol. 3)*. Cambridge, UK: Cambridge UP.

Berry, D., Knapp, P., & Raynor, T. (2005). Expressing medicine side effects: Assessing the effectiveness of absolute risk, relative risk, and number needed to harm, and the provision of baseline risk information. *Patient Education and Counseling, 63*, 89–96. doi:10.1016/j.pec.2005.09.003

Beyth-Marom, R., & Dekel, S. (1983). A curriculum to improve thinking under uncertainty. *Instructional Science, 12*, 67–82. doi:10.1007/BF00120902

Bohnenblust, H., & Slovic, P. (1998). Integrating technical analysis and public values in risk-based decision-making. *Reliability Engineering & System Safety, 59*, 151–159. doi:10.1016/S0951-8320(97)00136-1

Boland, P., & Pawitan, Y. (1999). Trying to be random in selecting numbers for Lotto. *Journal of Statistics Education, 7*(3). Retrieved May 10, 2009, from http://www.amstat.org/publications/jse/secure/v7n3/boland.cfm

Bracy, G. (1998). Tips for readers of research—No causation from correlation. *Phi Delta Kappan, 79*(9), 711–712.

Carey, J., & White, E. (1991). The effects of graphical versus numerical response on the accuracy of graph-based forecasts. *Journal of Management, 17*(1), 77–96. doi:10.1177/014920639101700106

Carlson, K., Meloy, M., & Russo, J. (2006). Leader-driven primacy: Using attribute order to affect consumer choice. *The Journal of Consumer Research, 32*, 513–518. doi:10.1086/500481

Casaday, G. (1991). Balance. In Karat, J. (Ed.), *Taking software design seriously: Practical techniques for HCI design* (pp. 45–62). New York, NY: Academic Press.

Dahlbäck, O. (1990). An experimental analysis of risk taking. *Theory and Decision, 20*(3), 183–202. doi:10.1007/BF00126801

de Vries, H., Mesters, I., van de Steeg, H., & Honing, C. (2005). The general public's information needs and perceptions regarding hereditary cancer: An application of the integrated change model. *Patient Education and Counseling, 56*, 154–165. doi:10.1016/j.pec.2004.01.002

DeKay, M., Patiño-Echeverri, D., & Fischbeck, P. (2009). Distortion of probability and outcome information in risky decisions. *Organizational Behavior and Human Decision Processes, 109*, 79–92. doi:10.1016/j.obhdp.2008.12.001

Devroop, K. (2000). *Correlation versus causation: Another look at a common misinterpretation.* ED 445 078.

Edwards, A., & Elwyn, G. (2001). Understanding risk and lessons for clinical risk communication about treatment preferences. *Quality in Health Care, 10*, 9–13. doi:10.1136/qhc.0100009

Endsley, M. (1995). Toward a theory of situation awareness in dynamic systems. *Human Factors, 37*(1), 32–64. doi:10.1518/001872095779049543

Estrada, C., Martin-Hryniewicz, M., Peek, B., Collins, C., & Byrd, J. (2004). Literacy and numeracy skills and anticoagulation control. *The American Journal of the Medical Sciences, 328*, 88–93. doi:10.1097/00000441-200408000-00004

Evans, D., Blair, V., Greenhalgh, R., Hopwood, R., & Howell, A. (1994). The impact of genetic counselling on risk perception in women with a family history of breast cancer. *British Journal of Cancer, 70*, 934–938. doi:10.1038/bjc.1994.423

Feldman-Stewart, D., & Brundage, M. (2004). Challenges for designing and implementing decision aids. *Patient Education and Counseling, 54*, 265–273. doi:10.1016/j.pec.2003.09.007

Garfield, J., & Ahlgren, A. (1988). Difficulties in learning basic concepts in probability and statistics: Implications for research. *Journal for Research in Mathematics Education, 19*, 46–63. doi:10.2307/749110

Garfield, J., & del Mas, R. (1991). Students' conceptions of probability. In D. Vere-Jones (Ed.). *Proceedings of the Third International Conference on Teaching Statistics*, (Vol. 1, pp. 340–349). Voorburg, The Netherlands: International Statistical Institute.

Gigerenzer, G., Hertwig, R., van den Broek, E., Fasolo, B., & Katsikopoulos, K. (2005). A 30% chance of rain tomorrow: How does the public understand probabilistic weather forecasts? *Risk Analysis, 25*(3), 623–629. doi:10.1111/j.1539-6924.2005.00608.x

Gilovich, T., Vallone, R., & Tversky, A. (1985). The hot hand in basketball: On the misperception of random sequences. *Cognitive Psychology, 17*, 295–314. doi:10.1016/0010-0285(85)90010-6

Golbeck, A. L., Ahlers-Schmidt, C. R., Paschal, A. M., & Dismuke, S. E. (2005). A definition and operational framework for health numeracy. *American Journal of Preventive Medicine, 29*, 375–376. doi:10.1016/j.amepre.2005.06.012

Gurmankin, A. D., Baron, J., & Armstrong, K. (2004). The effect of numerical statements of risk on trust and comfort with hypothetical physician risk communication. *Medical Decision Making, 24*, 265–271. doi:10.1177/0272989X04265482

Halpern, D., Blackman, S., & Salzman, B. (1989). Using statistical risk information to assess oral contraceptive safety. *Applied Cognitive Psychology, 3*, 251–260. doi:10.1002/acp.2350030305

Handmer, J., & Proudley, B. (2007). Communicating uncertainty via probabilities: The case of weather forecasts. *Environmental Hazards, 7*, 79–87. doi:10.1016/j.envhaz.2007.05.002

Hawley, S., Zkmund-Fisher, B., Ubel, P., Jancovic, A., Lucas, T., & Fagerlin, A. (2008). The impact of the format of graphical presentation on health-related knowledge and treatment choices. *Patient Education and Counseling, 73*, 448–455. doi:10.1016/j.pec.2008.07.023

Hegarty, M. (1992). Mental animation: Inferring motion from static diagrams of mechanical systems. *Journal of Experimental Psychology. Learning, Memory, and Cognition, 18*, 1084–1102. doi:10.1037/0278-7393.18.5.1084

Hsee, C. (1995). Elastic justification: How tempting but task irrelevant factors influence decisions. *Organizational Behavior and Human Decision Processes, 62*(3), 330–337. doi:10.1006/obhd.1995.1054

Huang, A. (2009). Science needs ace communicators and politicians. *Science News, 175*(9), 32. doi:10.1002/scin.2009.5591750922

Kahneman, D., & Tversky, A. (1979). Prospect theory: An analysis of decision under risk. *Econometrica: Journal of the Econometric Society, 47*, 263–291. doi:10.2307/1914185

Kahneman, D., & Tversky, A. (1982). The psychology of preferences. *Scientific American, 246*, 160–173. doi:10.1038/scientificamerican0182-160

Karpinski, A. (2009). *Facebook users get worse grades in college.* Retrieved from http://www.livescience.com/culture/ 090413-facebook-grades.html

Keller, C., Siegrist, M., & Gutscher, H. (2006). The role of the affect and availability heuristics in risk communication. *Risk Analysis, 26*, 631–639. doi:10.1111/j.1539-6924.2006.00773.x

Kirsch, I. S., Jungeblut, A., Jenkins, L., & Kolstad, A. (2002). *Adult literacy in America: A first look at the findings of the national adult literacy survey* (3rd ed., NCES 1993-275). Washington, DC: U.S. Department of Education, Office of Educational Research and Improvement, National Center for Education Statistics.

Konold, C. (1989). An outbreak of belief in independence? In C. Maher, G. Goldin & B. Davis (Eds.), *Proceedings of the 11th Annual Meeting of the North American Chapter of the International Group for the Psychology of Mathematics Education* (Vol. 2, pp. 203-209), Rutgers, NJ: Rutgers.

Lane, D. (2007). Statistical and practical significance. In *HyperStat online statistics textbook*. Retrieved May 12, 2009, from http://davidmlane.com/ hyperstat/B35955.html

Lerman, C., Kash, K., & Stefanek, M. (1994). Younger women at increased risk for breast cancer: Perceived risk, psychological well-being and surveillance behavior. *Journal of the National Cancer Institute. Monographs, 16*, 171–176.

Levy, A., & Hershey, J. (2006). Distorting the probability of treatment success to justify treatment decisions. *Organizational Behavior and Human Decision Processes, 101*, 52–58. doi:10.1016/j.obhdp.2006.04.003

Levy, A., & Hershey, J. (2008). Value-induced bias in medical decision making. *Medical Decision Making, 28*, 269–276. doi:10.1177/0272989X07311754

Lipkus, I., & Holland, J. (1999). The visual communication of risk. *Journal of the National Cancer Institute. Monographs, 25*, 149–163.

Lipkus, I., Klein, W., & Rimer, B. (2001). Communicating breast cancer risks to women using different formats. *Cancer Epidemiology, Biomarkers & Prevention, 10*, 895–898.

Lowe, R. (2002). Animation and learning: Selective processing of information in dynamic graphics. *Learning and Instruction, 13*(2), 157–176. doi:10.1016/S0959-4752(02)00018-X

Malenka, D., Baron, J., Johansen, S., & Ross, J. (1993). The framing effect of relative and absolute risk. *Journal of General Internal Medicine, 8*, 543–548. doi:10.1007/BF02599636

Mazur, D., & Hickam, D. (1991). Patients' interpretations of probability terms. *Journal of General Internal Medicine, 6*, 237–240. doi:10.1007/BF02598968

McNeil, B., Pauker, S., Sox, H., & Tversky, A. (1982). On the elicitation of preferences for alternative therapies. *The New England Journal of Medicine, 306*, 1259–1262. doi:10.1056/NEJM198205273062103

Meyer, J., Taieb, M., & Flascher, I. (1997). Correlation estimates of perceptual judgments. *Journal of Experimental Psychology. Applied, 3*(1), 3–20. doi:10.1037/1076-898X.3.1.3

Monahan, J., & Steadman, H. (1996). Violent storms and violent people. *The American Psychologist, 51*, 931–938. doi:10.1037/0003-066X.51.9.931

Mueller, N., Odegaard, A., Anderson, K., Yuan, J., Gross, M., Koh, K., & Pereira, M. (2010). Soft drink and juice consumption and risk of pancreatic cancer: The Singapore Chinese health study. *Cancer Epidemiology, Biomarkers & Prevention, 19*, 447–455. doi:10.1158/1055-9965.EPI-09-0862

Murphy, A. H., & Winkler, R. L. (1971). Forecasters and probability forecasts: Some current problems. *Bulletin of the American Meteorological Society, 52*, 239–247. doi:10.1175/1520-0477(1971)052<0239:FAPFSC>2.0.CO;2

Narayanan, N., & Hegarty, M. (2002). Multimedia design for communication of dynamic information. *International Journal of Human-Computer Studies, 57*, 279–315. doi:10.1006/ijhc.2002.1019

Natter, H., & Berry, D. (2005). Effects of presenting baseline risk when comparing absolute and relative risk presentations. *Psychology Health and Medicine, 10*, 326–334. doi:10.1080/13548500500093407

Peters, E., Hibbard, J., Slovic, P., & Dieckmann, N. (2007). Numeracy skill and the communication, comprehension, and use of risk-benefit information. *Health Affairs, 26*, 741–748. doi:10.1377/hlthaff.26.3.741

Peters, E., Västfjäll, D., Slovic, P., Mertz, C., Mazzocco, K., & Dickert, S. (2006). Numeracy and decision making. *Psychological Science, 17*(5), 407–413. doi:10.1111/j.1467-9280.2006.01720.x

Peterson, C., & Beach, L. (1967). Man as an intuitive statistician. *Psychological Bulletin, 68*, 29–46. doi:10.1037/h0024722

Peterson, C., & Miller, A. (1964). Mode, median and mean as optimal strategies. *Journal of Experimental Psychology, 68*, 363–367. doi:10.1037/h0040387

Pollatsek, A., Lima, S., & Well, A. (1981). Concept or computation: Students' understanding of the mean. *Educational Studies in Mathematics, 12*, 191–204. doi:10.1007/BF00305621

Pollatsek, A., Well, A., Konold, C., & Hardiman, P. (1987). Understanding conditional probabilities. *Organizational Behavior and Human Decision Processes, 40*, 255–269. doi:10.1016/0749-5978(87)90015-X

Rothman, R. L., Housam, R., Weiss, H., Davis, D., Gregory, R., & Gebretsadik, T. (2006). Patient understanding of food labels: The role of literacy and numeracy. *American Journal of Preventive Medicine, 31*, 391–398. doi:10.1016/j.amepre.2006.07.025

Russo, J., Carlson, K., & Meloy, M. (2006). Choosing an inferior alternative. *Psychological Science, 17*, 899–904. doi:10.1111/j.1467-9280.2006.01800.x

Schapira, M., Nattinger, A., & McAuliffe, T. (2006). The influence of graphic format on breast cancer risk communication. *Journal of Health Communication, 11*, 569–582. doi:10.1080/10810730600829916

Schlesinger, J. (1970). *Planning, programming, budgeting.* Inquiry of the subcommittee on national security and international operations for the Senate Committee on Government Operations, 91 Cong. 1 Sess., 482.

Siegfried, T. (2010). Odds are, it's wrong: Science fails to face the shortcomings of statistics. *Science News, 177*(7), 26. doi:10.1002/scin.5591770721

Siegrist, M., & Cvetkovich, G. (2001). Better negative than positive? Evidence of a bias for negative information about possible health hazards. *Risk Analysis, 21*(2), 199–206. doi:10.1111/0272-4332.211102

Silvestri, P. (1989). A note on cause and correlation. *Psychological Reports, 64*(2), 445–446. doi:10.2466/pr0.1989.64.2.445

Sjöberg, L. (2000). Factors in risk perception. *Risk Analysis, 20*(1), 1–12. doi:10.1111/0272-4332.00001

Slovic, P. (1993). Perceived risk, trust, and democracy: A systems perspective. *Risk Analysis, 13*, 675–682. doi:10.1111/j.1539-6924.1993.tb01329.x

Slovic, P. (2000). *The perception of risk*. London, UK: Earthscan.

Slovic, P., Finucane, M., Peters, E., & MacGregor, D. (2004). Risk as analysis and risk as feelings: Some thoughts about affect, reason, risk, and rationality. *Risk Analysis, 24*, 311–322. doi:10.1111/j.0272-4332.2004.00433.x

Slovic, P., Monahan, J., & MacGregor, D. (2000). Violence risk assessment and risk communication: The effects of using actual cases, providing instruction and employing probability versus frequency formats. *Law and Human Behavior, 24*, 271–296. doi:10.1023/A:1005595519944

Stone, E., Sieck, W., Bull, B., Yates, J., Parks, S., & Rush, C. (2003). Foreground:background salience: Explaining the effects of graphical displays on risk avoidance. *Organizational Behavior and Human Decision Processes, 90*, 19–36. doi:10.1016/S0749-5978(03)00003-7

Stone, E., Yates, J., & Parker, A. (1994). Risk communication: Absolute versus relative expressions of low probability risks. *Organizational Behavior and Human Decision Processes, 60*, 387–408. doi:10.1006/obhd.1994.1091

Stone, E., Yates, J., & Parker, A. (1997). Effects of numerical and graphical displays on professed risk-taking behavior. *Journal of Experimental Psychology. Applied, 3*, 243–256. doi:10.1037/1076-898X.3.4.243

Thompson, C., & Mingay, D. (1991). Estimating the frequency of everyday events. *Applied Cognitive Psychology, 5*, 497–510. doi:10.1002/acp.2350050605

Timmermans, D., Molewijk, B., Stiggelbout, A., & Kievit, J. (2004). Different formats for communicating surgical risks to patients and the effect on choice of treatment. *Patient Education and Counseling, 54*, 255–263. doi:10.1016/S0738-3991(03)00238-6

Tversky, A., & Kahneman, D. (1971). The belief in the law of small numbers. *Psychological Bulletin, 76*, 105–110. doi:10.1037/h0031322

Tversky, A., & Kahneman, D. (1974). Judgment under uncertainty: Heuristics and biases. *Science, 185*, 1124–1130. doi:10.1126/science.185.4157.1124

Wallsten, T. (1981). Physician and medical student bias in evaluating diagnostic information. *Medical Decision Making, 1*(2), 145–164. doi:10.1177/0272989X8100100205

Weinstein, N. (1980). Unrealistic optimism about future life events. *Journal of Personality and Social Psychology, 39*, 806–820. doi:10.1037/0022-3514.39.5.806

Weinstein, N. (1987). Unrealistic optimism about illness susceptibility: Conclusions from a community wide sample. *Journal of Behavioral Medicine, 10*, 481–500. doi:10.1007/BF00846146

Well, A., Pollatsek, A., & Boyce, S. (1990). Understanding the effects of sample size in the mean. *Organizational Behavior and Human Decision Processes, 47*, 289–312. doi:10.1016/0749-5978(90)90040-G

Wickens, C., & Hollands, J. (2000). *Engineering psychology and human performance*. Upper Saddle River, NJ: Prentice Hall.

Williams, D., & Noyes, J. (2007). How does our perception of risk influence decision-making? Implications for the design of risk information. *Theoretical Issues in Ergonomics Science, 8*(1), 1–35. doi:10.1080/14639220500484419

Wogalter, M., Jarrard, S., & Simpson, S. (1994). Influence of warning label signal words on perceived hazard level. *Human Factors, 36*(3), 547–556.

Wogalter, M., & Silver, N. (1990). Arousal strength of signal words. *Forensic Reports, 3*, 407–420.

Wolfe, R. M., Sharp, L. K., & Lipsky, M. S. (2002). Content and design attributes of antivaccination websites. *Journal of the American Medical Association, 287*, 3245–3248. doi:10.1001/jama.287.24.3245

Yarett, I. (2010). *Does soda cause pancreatic cancer? What the latest study really says.* Retrieved May 13, 2010, from http://blog.newsweek.com/blogs/ thehumancondition/archive/2010/02/18/does-soda-cause-pancreatic-cancer-what-the-latest-study-really-says.aspx

Zacks, J., & Tversky, B. (1999). Bars and lines: A study of graphic communication. *Memory & Cognition, 27*, 1073–1079. doi:10.3758/BF03201236

Zacks, J. M., Levy, E., Tversky, B., & Schiano, D. (2002). Graphs in print. In Anderson, M., Meyer, B., & Olivier, P. (Eds.), *Diagrammatic representation and reasoning* (pp. 187–206). London, UK: Springer-Verlag. doi:10.1007/978-1-4471-0109-3_11

ADDITIONAL READING

Gilovich, T., Vallone, R., & Tversky, A. (1985). The hot hand in basketball: On the misperception of random sequences. *Cognitive Psychology, 17*, 295–314. doi:10.1016/0010-0285(85)90010-6

Gurmankin, A. D., Baron, J., & Armstrong, K. (2004). The effect of numerical statements of risk on trust and comfort with hypothetical physician risk communication. *Medical Decision Making, 24*, 265–271. doi:10.1177/0272989X04265482

Kahneman, D., & Tversky, A. (1979). Prospect theory: An analysis of decision under risk. *Econometrica: Journal of the Econometric Society, 47*, 263–291. doi:10.2307/1914185

Stone, E., Sieck, W., Bull, B., Yates, J., Parks, S., & Rush, C. (2003). Foreground: background salience: Explaining the effects of graphical displays on risk avoidance. *Organizational Behavior and Human Decision Processes, 90*, 19–36. doi:10.1016/S0749-5978(03)00003-7

Chapter 10
How People Interact with Information Presentation

ABSTRACT

This chapter considers how the presentation of information on a display affects the HII. The type and order of the presentation exerts a strong influence on how people perceive and interpret information. The white area in figure 1 shows the area of the HII model relevant to this chapter. The design team's goal must be to ensure the presentation provides only relevant information, presents it in a salient manner, and in a way that corresponds to people's expectations and needs. It must make information relationships salient. In many failed designs, these simple concepts fail to hold true.

BACKGROUND

People's first assumptions about meaning are derived from the presentation, before they engage with the content—Peter Merholz

This chapter looks at:

Adapting to displayed information: Examines how people change how they view information based on how it gets presented.

Amount of information: Describes how the ability of people to integrate information depends on the amount they have to handle. Large amounts of information often result in in-

formation overload and dumping of information. While consistency of presentation is important, the consistency choices must first fit the information needs for a proper presentation.

Framing effects: How the information gets framed has a strong effect on the type of decision people reach. Framing takes one or more aspects of a situation and increases their relative salience, even when they don't necessarily deserve that increase.

Presentation order: Information gets its relative priority based on the order in which it was viewed. The first information read is viewed as more important and effects how later information gets interpreted.

Integration of visual and verbal information: HII information almost always consists

DOI: 10.4018/978-1-4666-0152-9.ch010

Figure 1. How people approach information presentation

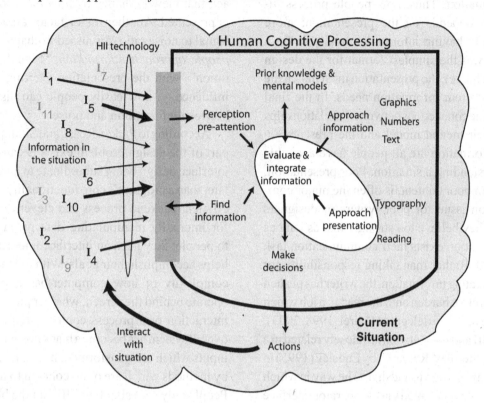

of a combination of textual and graphical information. Effective integration requires the two forms work together.

INTRODUCTION

The idea of properly presenting information can be described with a cooking analogy. The raw data is like providing restaurant diners with the flour, eggs, shortening, baking powder, and milk and expecting them to mix and bake biscuits. People deserve to be served biscuits, not the ingredients to make biscuits. Even worse is not providing them with shortening because it tends to make a greasy mess (i.e., this data is hard to collect or display). But obviously without it, the biscuits are less than appetizing and may not even be biscuits.

Unfortunately, after long-term exposure to consistently poor presentations and content, many people either expect to make their own biscuits or simply go without because the end result is always so bad. People can easily tell when biscuits are uneatable, but with information, the poor quality is not as obvious. Missing information (not providing shortening), poor quality information, or providing easy-to-obtain information (we have lots of baking powder, so let's use lots of that) all compromise the HII. People expect biscuits to be served a nice golden brown and flaky. Burned or undercooked gooey biscuits cause them to turn away. Likewise, the information needs to be properly presented, but creating golden-brown and flaky information is much harder than baking golden-brown and flaky biscuits.

In the end, the information presentation to a plant operator, a physician, a business executive, or a general reader strongly influences how they build the mental picture of a situation and, consequently, how they respond to or act upon the information. Thus, how people process information depends on the presentation; more than simply having information available (in a way that was the simplest format for the design team to achieve), the presentation must match the person's current information needs. In the final analysis, the connections between the relationships within their mental model and the presentation of the information are all people have available for understanding a situation. Poor presentation, rather than poor content, is often the major communication issue for poor writers or designers because they believe too strongly that as long as the information exists their communication task is finished. Rather than taking responsibility for communicating information, the writer has pushed the interpretive burden onto the reader, a job which should never be so delegated (Mirel, 1998, 2003).

The HII and presentation are closely related in a dynamic interplay. Research by Endsley (1995) in situation awareness found that "The way in which information is presented via the operator interface will largely influence SA [situation awareness] by determining how much information can be acquired, how accurately it can be acquired, and to what degree it is compatible with the operator's SA needs" (p. 50). People perceive information and develop situational models via active and recursive interactions with the information. The information presentation provides access to and drives those interactions. Thus, the presentation format is a major influence on how people perceive information relationships (Johnson, Payne, & Bettman, 1988). Presentation format is also a crucial factor in maintaining the flow of information, which enables people to achieve their goals and form a valid situation model within their context (Laplante & Flaxman, 1995). The presentation contains more than just the information; it exerts a strong influence on how people responsed to information as they gain an understanding of the situation (Robertson, Card, & Mackinlay, 1993). Hollnagel (1988) points out that since people's mental models define how they interpret, plan, and

act, that view is shaped by how the information is presented. Another major factor affecting the signal to noise ratio (discussed in chapter 4: *How people approach information*, "Signal to noise ration") with the presentation exerting a strong influence on how easily people can distinguish between information and noise.

According to Parker, Roast, and Siddiqi (1997), part of the design problem exists because of the interface design being subordinate to and defined later than a program's core functionality. A highly efficient backend process and clever algorithms for internally manipulating data mean nothing to people; they need an interface interaction that helps accomplish their goals. With the increasing complexity of how computer-based processes operate behind the screen, whether pure software interaction or a process-control interaction, the overall system has become a black box with visible inputs which are transformed into visible outputs by methods which are of no concern to the users. People only care about the HII, not the black box or background operations.

Norman (2002) and other researchers (such as Wilson & Rutherford, 1989) have observed that for computer users, their view of the display essentially constitutes the entire process. No matter how or why people interact with and read information content, the quality of the presentation strongly affects both user satisfaction and performance (Mirani & King, 1994). For typical computer users, the presentation becomes the basis for their active mental model, how they interpret the presented information, and how they instantiate their situation model.

A higher quality presentation contains information which fits the information needs required to gain a full understanding of the situation (Robertson, Card, & Mackinlay, 1993). Placing information online to provide easier access and achieve lower maintenance costs has been advocated for many years. Various research has examined pre-web online report development within corporate environments (Doheny-Farina,

1988; Paradis, Dobrin, & Miller, 1985). There has also been research into the effective presentation of online documentation (Horton, 1990). However, online help research has generally focused on the learning-to-do format that supports data entry or short procedural tasks with software, not on how the presentation affected how people acquired and comprehended information, especially complex information. As information moved onto the web, both Nielsen and Spool, along with many others, have led the discussion on how to present information. Unfortunately, web research is often sidetracked by navigation issues or the relationship of text versus graphics, or it confuses ease-of-finding data with the comprehension of meaningful and useful information. In the end, many of the issues discussed in this section, such as how presentation directly affects design, salience, and comprehension require more detailed research.

An ongoing problem faced by design teams is that people's information needs vary both between and within situations, but methods of dynamically changing the presentation format in real-time has proven difficult (and has not benefited from enough research). The different ways of organizing the problem representation influence the amount of information that can be processed during problem solving (Mayer, 1976). One interesting and consistent research finding is that information is processed in ways that fit the presentation format without restructuring it (Bettman & Zins, 1979; Johnson, Payne, & Bettman, 1988; Slovic, 1972). In addition, people tend to adjust the time spent on choice tasks to maintain high accuracy, but time pressure can cause problems with maintaining this trade-off at an effective level. As a result, formats that give acceptable accuracy with no time pressure may result in unacceptable accuracy rates under time pressure. Since high quality presentation works as a general aid and provides faster access to information in working memory, well-structured problem representations should result in better HII performance (Mayer, 1976).

Box 1.

Dealer information screen

One customer relations system I worked with dumped everything about the dealer onto the Dealer Information screen. This was the screen the customer support people would pull up when a dealer called (it was almost always a dealer and not an end-customer who called). A significant presentation problem was that the first screen-and-half of data contained the dealer's address, phone numbers, etc. useful information,—and the first information to enter when creating a new account—but noise for a phone call from an existing dealer. Dealers know their address and phone number and the customer service reps didn't have an immediate need for that information. What they needed was account status and invoicing information, which required scrolling down.

The best presentation for data entry of new accounts or account maintenance is different from the best presentation for using the account information. The customer relations system used the same entry screen for both. Account clerks and customer reps have different information needs and require different presentation formats. The presentation design should fit both situations.

ADAPTING TO DISPLAYED INFORMATION

People need support from an interface to make problem solving easier. Interfaces often display relevant information, making recall unnecessary and relieving working memory. Zhang (1996) claims that the more information a design shifts to an interface and, consequently, the less information people must retain in memory, the easier a task. However, (and counter-intuitively) shifting information to the interface can be detrimental in many instances, especially when task learning is required or when the task is prone to interruptions. Information that is available on-screen is not mentally processed and moved to long term memory, which impairs learning. This is problematic when interruptions occur because people do not remember where they are in the task; task planning is not typically done. Information on the interface encourages display-based trial and error problem-solving rather than planning (O'Hara & Payne, 1998). It's easier to read it off the interface than to remember it. People seem to ignore even explicit directions to plan ahead when they know the information will be available on the interface (Van Nimwegen, Van Oostendorp, & Tabachneck-Schijf, 2005).

Even people operating at the expert level seem to lack a deep knowledge of system operation and often cannot recall commonly used procedures without depending on the interface (Mayes, Draper, McGregor, & Oatley, 1988). Likewise, people may not know the precise results of mouse operations, such as the location of the cursor after a command. Instead, they depend on obtaining this information from the display (Payne, 1991). But all action is not purely displayed-based. In many situations of more complex problem-solving, people seem to use a combination of both display-based and cognitive actions. For example, when asked to solve puzzles, people often make a few rapid moves, pause to examine the overall display, and then make another sequence of moves. Rather than examining the display after each move, the problem gets broken into what Card, Moran, and Newell (1983) called "unit tasks," short series of semi-independent tasks. With tasks that require planning, not providing everything on the interface, but forcing people to mentally plan ahead and maintain a mental image, results in better performance (Van Nimwegen, Van Oostendorp, & Tabachneck-Schijf, 2005). Design teams need to consider the sequences people construct for these unit tasks and support them in the display.

Presentation of Warnings and Errors

Software systems contain a large number of warnings and error messages, but often seem to present them in a manner inconsistent with good HII. In TV and radio, any new information seems to receive attention; however, this does not carry over to computers. Instead, warning information needs to fall either into a new category (at least with respect to the current situation) or a signal category (learned response to a signal that de-

notes relevant information). (Lang et al. 2002). For example, warnings fail if they are located in areas already blacked out by banner blindness.

A typical problem is that a system provides too many warnings, most of which are irrelevant to the situation. People learn to ignore warnings if the invalid rate is high (cry wolf effect). How quickly they adjust depends on the attention demands of the situation. In low-demand situations, they respond to non-valid warnings for a long time, but in high-demand situations, they rapidly begin to ignore non-valid warnings or low-value warnings. Instead, they adjust their response to depend on salient cues (such as red text) to flag high value warnings (Maltz & Meyer 2001). Without salient cueing, most warnings are ignored since people have no easy way of mentally classifying a warning's importance.

In a medical prescription system which gave warnings, a one year study found that physicians were only slightly more likely to change the prescription based on a warning. However, the warnings were not universally disregarded, but strongly depended on the type of drug. Warnings for warfarin or central nervous system drugs tended to be acted upon and the prescription or dosage adjusted (Judge et al., 2006). Thus, long-term interactions with warnings can change behavior, if the people see a reason to change.

Although people often complain about warnings interfering with work flow, they also show a riskier behavior in systems with warnings than without. They seem to depend on the system warnings to avoid poor interaction rather than closely monitoring the system themselves (Maltz & Meyer 2001). They assume the system will give them a warning before anything bad happens.

AMOUNT OF INFORMATION

In response to the ability to provide large amounts of information to customers at low cost, many companies are placing huge amounts of information on their websites. Interestingly, this may not be the best approach. Although the web has provided people with large amounts of information of varying quality, people typically rate the quality of a website's information on the basis of quantity, rather actually evaluating information quality, which is something they may not have the knowledge to do. This, in turn, leads to problems when mentally dealing with the large amounts of available information.

Design teams want to provide readers with the information they need. The problem is that meeting the information needs of multiple audience groups can result in a large amount of information irrelevant to any single group. Meeting the design goals of clear, usable, and complete information requires the proper information with the proper presentation. The important element is that information be accessible, not merely stuck in front of people. Information dumps lead to cognitive overload which makes information less usable. The amount of information people need out of the total available, versus the HII of that information, follows an inverted U-graph (Figure 2).

People need the proper amount of information and have a hard time selecting and choosing when given too much. A relatively narrow range, which varies among individuals, determines when they have the proper amount of information. Contradicting many design team's intuition, providing more information may actually reduce the amount of information people use. Research finds that when provided with increasing amounts of information:

- People increasingly ignore information which does not confirm their preferred decision (Ganzach & Schul, 1995).

Figure 2. Amount of information versus usable HII of the information. The optimal information presentation happens at the top point of the curve. Presenting too little or too much lowers the overall quality of the HII (adapted from Albers, 2004, p. 112).

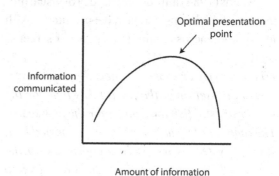

- People try to avoid having to integrate multiple sources; instead, they make choices based on methods that are error-prone, but easy to use. It seems as if people "will not be able to correctly anticipate the simultaneous influence of more than one task feature" (Fennema & Kleinmuntz, 1995, p. 23).
- Under time pressure, performance deteriorates when more information rather than less is provided (Wright, 1974).

In the end, people respond to too much information by shedding tasks to avoid information overload and to simplify mentally processing the information. The problem is that this can seriously degrade how well they comprehend the information.

Visual Momentum

Human factors research, especially in plant control, has found that people are highly influenced by how the system gets presented in the interface. If a person has to interact with displays that show schematics of various interconnected systems, those schematics must contain the information required to allow the person to integrate them into a single mental image and develop a deep knowledge of the situation. The presentation complexity arises from screen size, forcing people to view multiple screens to assess the entire situation.

Woods (1984) introduced the idea of visual momentum, which considers how people interact with information across multiple displays or screens.

When the viewer looks to a new display there is a mental reset time; that is, it takes time for the viewer to establish the context for the new scene. The amount of visual momentum supported by a display system is inversely proportional to the mental effort required to place a new display into the context of the total data base and the user's information needs. When visual momentum is high, there is an impetus or continuity across successive views which support the rapid comprehension of data following the transition to a new display. It is analogous to a good cut from one scene or view to another in film editing. Low visual momentum is like a bad cut in film editing—one that confuses the viewer or delays comprehension. Each transition to a new display then becomes an act of total replacement (i.e. discontinuous); both display content and structure are independent of previous "glances" into the data base. The user's mental task when operating with discontinuous display transitions is much like assembling a puzzle when there is no picture of the final product as a reference and when there are no relationships between the data represented on each piece. (p. 231)

The concept of visual momentum has become very important with the large amounts of information available on the web. The information architecture and the sheer volume of information require it to be broken into multiple pages. Good visual momentum lets the reader to move smoothly between pages and to maintain a coherent view of the information. Woods conceptualized visual momentum as dealing with multiple displays in a plant control environment, but it applies just as strongly to the multiple pages of a web site and for building the relationships between information elements on a single page.

Even with large monitors, understanding most significant problems require more information than can be displayed at once. As a result, the information must be designed to support interacting with and comprehending information across multiple screens. Unfortunately, it is easier to optimize for presentation of individual screens than design for a sequence of screens. The problem is not new, but was recognized early in HCI design (Hollnagel & Woods, 1983). Yet, it still exists as a significant design issue.

Woods identifies many problems of information with low visual momentum, including:

- Cognitive tunnel vision. A person locks into a single chain of information or reasoning and ignores everything else.
- Failure to know what to look at next. Too many links on a page with nothing to indicate order or relevance can cause a person to ignore all of them.
- Short term memory problems because of cognitive overload. A person has to remember the important points on previous web pages; designs which impart a high cognitive load make the already difficult task of remembering the information almost impossible. Unfortunately, people tend to go with poorly remembered information in the head rather than looking at previous pages (Fennema & Kleinmuntz, 1995).
- Decreased problem-solving and decision-making ability. The HII goal is to fulfill an information need to address a problem, typically requiring some type of decision. Confused information resulting from low visual momentum tends to force a person into a heuristic problem-solving mode. Or they may simply go with first inten-

tions, rather than fully understanding the situation.

Designs with high visual momentum provide strong connections across screens and information elements. How this is best accomplished depends on the specific interaction. It may require repeating some information, or a zoom design where a person moves between a full system view and narrower views. When people mentally synthesize multiple screens of information, they need perceptual landmarks to maintain an awareness of where they are within the stream of information. And these landmarks must be designed to minimize the cognitive resources they consume.

Displayed and Not Displayed Information

People working with information need to build relationships between the various information elements in order to understand the situation (Albers, 2010). However, it is difficult to remember or form goal-oriented *relationships* between information that is being displayed and relevant information not being displayed (Rubens & Rubens, 1988).

Information that people do not see or in some way is not present is disregarded more than information that can be seen. Information which is not seen receives a lower salience than information which can be seen. While this does not seem surprising, it has ongoing consequences for presenting information, especially online. Because of the limitations of browser and screen size, people looking at more than a trivial amount of information will be forced either to scroll or to link to a new page (for example, see Figure 5-6: Comparison of screen versus paper). When this happens, information on previous web pages receives less salience and less consideration than information currently being viewed. If the information is arranged in a structured hierarchy, as people move down through an information hierarchy, lower level information can be given more importance

Box 2.

Medical test selection
A hospital was concerned with the number and type of tests physicians were ordering. They were not complying with hospital policy or best-practices as defined the various medical organizations. An analysis of the situation placed part of the blame on the system that was used to order tests. It had too many options and was difficult to use, so physicians were always ordering the same tests since it allowed them to minimize their system interaction.

Changes were made to a laboratory test order form used by physicians to attempt to improve the rate of ordering appropriate tests. As part of the form redesign, the number of tests that could be ordered via check boxes was reduced from 51 to 26, with 27 tests deleted and 2 added. The tests added to the form showed an increase of in usage of 60.7% in the first year. The deleted tests showed a decrease usage of 27% the first year (Shalev, Chodick, & Heymann, 2009). The display or non-display of the tests strongly influenced the physician's choices when ordering tests.

---

than it deserves simply because it is being viewed when they finally make a decision. There is also the risk that the order of presentation will cause a preference reversal, discussed later in this chapter.

The displayed/not displayed information problem is especially acute when the person needs to consider subtle cause-and-effect relationships between visible and non-visible information. Subtle differences can be lost since people tend to use the less accurate information in their head, rather than going back to verify information, which, of course, then requires them to remember the information currently being viewed. Failure to go back to verify previous information is strongly associated with the effort required to obtain the information and the accuracy required by the situation (Payne et al., 1993). People seem willing to risk errors to save on effort. Lengthy navigation paths up and down a hierarchy can easily impose a higher effort than the perceived value. Likewise, having to manipulate multiple reports and windows (e.g., having multiple tabs open in a web browser or multiple PDF files opens) also imposes greater effort to figure out which window contains the needed information. An additional complication is that confirmation and expectancy biases lead people to see the expected answer and accept displayed information as verifying the choice instead of searching for disproving information (Klein, 1999).

People with lower knowledge levels cannot develop the needed relationships because, although they can see the data, they lack the background knowledge to make the necessary connections to form meaningful relationships. In addition, currently presented information can act as a distraction if it contains information not directly relevant to the situation, but is presented in a highly salient manner (Hsee, 1995). Design teams need to determine both the information relevant for a situation and the audience's ability to distinguish the relevant from the irrelevant. Information's relevance depends on context and the relationships among various pieces of information and the situation. Overcoming some of the problems imposed by visible and non-visible information requires a design that fosters good visual momentum (Woods, 1984) to help the reader maintain clear connections across the information.

Presentation and Cognitive Overload

Knowledge results when people form relationships among information elements. Remembering relationships among all of the relevant factors and then translating those factors into causal relationships can impose a high cognitive workload (for an explanation of cognitive load, see chapter 3: *What people bring with them,* "Cognitive load"). Thus, information presentation is highly influential in determining the cognitive resources required to comprehend the text and transform it into knowledge. Hix and Hartson (1993) discuss the concept of cognitive directness which involves designs focused on minimizing the mental transformations that people must form. They make the point that even small cognitive transformations take effort away from people's intended task and increase cognitive load. This section considers how cognitive load relates to presentation of information

and how reducing the load levels can increase comprehension.

Although there is general agreement that cognitive load is a major factor for determining how efficiently people comprehend information, there has been minimal research into how to reduce cognitive load while reading or using technical material. As a result, this section discusses the effects of cognitive load, but presents little in how to reduce it. Further research in this area is urgently needed. On the other hand, cognitive load research has looked at educational material and consistently demonstrates that lower loads cause higher learning (Sweller et al, 1990), although too low of a cognitive load can also be a problem (McNamara et al, 1996). Unfortunately, the transfer from educational material to technical material is difficult since that research tends to address entire classroom design and interaction, rather than just the material itself. In addition, the technical material relevant to HII tends to be focused on reading-to-do rather than the reading-to-learn discussed by Redish (1988).

Presentation changes that make it easier to process information also increase the information's impact upon people and their comprehension of that information. And vice-versa, presentation changes that make it harder to process information can result in lower comprehension, with information being ignored or incorrectly interpreted.

- Cognitive load research in hypertext found that nonlinear information presentation of narrative text increases cognitive load and decreases knowledge acquisition. However, for encyclopedia text, participants' knowledge acquisition was not affected by linear or non-linear presentation format (Zumbach & Mohraz, 2008).
- Dual coding theory leads to a conclusion that reading and hearing text at the same time should lead to better retention. For example, many multimedia presentations use this technique when they announce the

text presented on the screen. However, a non-concurrent presentation may work better since it reduces the cognitive load (Kalyuga, Chandler, & Sweller, 2004). They found simply reading the screen, a common design method, did not improve comprehension. Likewise, they found identical auditory and auditory-visual technical text was not as efficient as auditory only.

- Invariant displays lower cognitive load and improve information recall. When displays contain both changing and non-changing information, the best performance is obtained when the information that must be remembered across time maintains a constant location on the display (Hess, Detweler, & Eliss, 1999).

- People find it difficult to effectively search for and integrate multiple sources of information (Lansdale & Ormerod, 1994).

- If the information is too hard to cognitively process, people will disregard it, and thus will risk missing important information.

- Graphs reduce cognitive processing load by shifting the load to visual perception (Wickens & Carswell, 1995). Lohse (1997) agrees but claims that graphs will only cause a noticeable comprehension or performance effect for complex tasks which are normally constrained by cognitive resources.

- Illustrations improve comprehension when they contain or summarize the major points of a text, effectively reducing the cognitive load required to integrate it with prior knowledge (Larkin & Simon, 1987).

The amount of perceived cognitive effort seems to drive how different displays affect assessment strategies. People show a tendency toward sufficing minimizing cognitive effort (Simon, 1979) and these effects come into play when people interact with information presentation. "Since different display formats affect the effort required by various

strategies, decision-makers may react to changes in display format by adapting strategies which minimize effort" (Johnson, Payne, & Bettman, 1988, p. 2). The problem with ineffective information presentation is that, from a psychological standpoint, people suffer from poor information dissemination. Mentally processing and reshaping a collection of data is highly inefficient with high cognitive workload. In poor design, extracting relevant pieces of data, converting them into information, and building relationships get pushed onto the reader, rather than being performed by the system (Albers, 1996). Unfortunately, people perform very poorly at achieving this conversion, are very error-prone, and often don't do it.

One issue with how people minimize cognitive effort is that they tend to over-minimize unless they have sufficient prior knowledge to know the proper level of effort to expend. In addition, display format can actually change the way users view information. People change strategies rather than change data for better processing (Slovic, 1972). Essentially, rather than expend the cognitive resources to mentally transform the available information to fit a better assessment strategy, people simply take what is provided and change their method of interpreting it. However, this change in interpretation can cause information to be ignored or given inappropriate salience, which results in improper interpretation or comprehension.

In one study, the subjects evaluated graphs primarily using the shape of the graph (limiting their cognitive effort to looking at a trend line) to make their decisions, and ignored external information; but when presented with the same information in tabular form, they considered more of the content before making a decision (Atkins, Wood, & Rutger, 2002). Bettman and Zins (1979) also found that tabular formats were more conducive to information processing than other formats. One explanation was that tables both supported decision-making and made people actually analyze the information. These studies reveal how people minimized cognitive effort and used the fast visual processing of the graph to make decisions while ignoring other relevant information which would have uncovered problems with a table-based decision.

Solicited versus Unsolicited Information

Solicited information is information which a person has requested, and unsolicited is information which was not requested. Effective presentation of unsolicited information requires addressing the when/what/how of the information's relevance to the situation (Owen, 1986). Of course, just because the information was not solicited does not mean it is not important. The information people want and need makes up two different information spaces—ideally, spaces with significant overlap. Design teams need to understand the differences and to ensure that needed information has more salience than less relevant, but wanted information (see chapter 2: *Information in the situation*, "Information needs versus information wants").

Many poor decisions are made because the decision-maker refuses to consider any information not asked for explicitly. In many instances, unsolicited information is more important because it may contain the contradictory information people need to properly form a situation model. Unsolicited information has a higher chance of being ignored, thus it must receive a higher salience. Basically, people want to confirm their hypothesis and ignore or downplay information that may disprove it (Einhorn & Hogarth, 1981). If the unsolicited information contains that contradictory information, then it must be made more salient so people have to respond to it in a way the draws the current situation model into question.

Of course, it must first be determined that the unsolicited information is really needed to understand the situation. The amount of mail thrown away unopened shows the normal response to unsolicited information. Most people respond by ignoring any new information unless they can see how it fits into the current situation model. If people don't understand it, then it gets discarded as irrelevant. With unsolicited information, people are not going to work hard to see the relevancy; it requires less cognitive effort to ignore it. In general, it makes sense to ignore most new information. People are given too much information all day long, and the majority gets ignored. New information must be heavily filtered to avoid information overload. Thus, people are essentially programmed to ignore most information. Trying to mentally process more than a tiny amount of total information received would lead to cognitive and sensory overload.

Post-accident reports often reveal that the person had the information available to avoid the accident, and ignored it. At times, another person involved in the situation may even comment on it, but the comment is brushed aside. It is not that the person didn't want a good situation model, but rather that the piece of information was not relevant in the (incorrect) situation model being used. Likewise, much unsolicited information will be perceived as irrelevant to a decision-maker's situation model. Presentation salience and timing of presentation must fit people's needs and, done properly, increases their response to the information.

Importance and Problems of Consistent Presentation

Consistency is a reoccurring theme in many web-design and writing articles about information presentation. For example, Ozok and Salvendy (2004) give 20 guidelines on how to create webpages with consistent language, and *Research Based Web Design* (Koyani, Balley, &Nall, 2006) also has a section devoted to it. While consistency of presentation is important, that consistency must first be borne out in proper presentation. "The best presentation for a specific communication depends on the situation—on the answers to the planning questions that the broader definition [of information design] makes us think through" (Redish, 2000, p. 164). Some examples include:

- In a clinic setting, a touch screen system and a printed leaflet were compared for presenting information to help women make decisions about prenatal testing. In the end, neither was superior to the other at conveying information. But the touch screen group did show reduced anxiety levels (Graham et al, 2000). Anxiety levels are not normally measured or considered a component of communicating information, but different presentation methods can result in different levels of secondary factors which do influence comprehension.
- A study which compared web versus paper surveys found that college students responded faster and with higher completion rate for sensitive health items using web than with paper (Pealer et al, 2003). How information is presented and how people perceive it has a major effect on how they answer questions, especially uncomfortable questions.
- Matrix formats are faster than other non-graphical layouts and more conducive to information processing (Bettman & Zins, 1979).
- Most systems have a presentation which supports data entry, not retrieval. They use the same screen for data entry and retrieval of the same information, although the audiences may be totally separate, with different needs (Wyatt & Wright, 1998). The screen design is highly consistent, but its communication is impaired.

In general, HII and communicating information does not lend itself to simplistic, one-size-fits-all solutions in which a strict adherence to consistency overrules contextual factors (Wyatt & Wright, 1998). As such, consistency is a double-edged sword. An extreme focus on consistency often pro-

Box 3.

Too much consistency in the shape of aircraft controls
During World War II, a common cause of P-47, B-17, and B-25 airplane crashes was a "pilot error" associated with retracting the wheels instead of the flaps during landing. The wheels and flaps used identical toggle switches or levers that were placed side-by-side. The pilots were inadvertently selecting the wrong switch when they wanted to adjust the flaps and, as a result, retracted the landing gear. In the C-47 airplane, these two switches were not close together and the problem never occurred.

The overly consistent design of using identical switches, which makes for faster/easier construction, was the root cause of the crashes, not pilot error. The solution was to put shape-coded rubber fittings over the controls, with a wheel shape for the wheels and a wedge shape for the flaps, a coding strategy that has persisted with modern aircraft (Roscoe, 1968).

In many modern designs, design teams want a clean control panel which uses identical buttons. Although this makes sense from a pure engineering viewpoint (consistent appearance and fewer different parts required), people often benefit from distinct button shapes and colors.

---

duces consistently poor interfaces or information presentation. Over-emphasis on consistency can make a system fail to connect a design to people's needs, neglecting rhetorical aspects that maximize communication (Grudin, 1989). For example, web navigation elements should be consistent enough so that a reader recognizes them as a navigation elements and knows where to find them, but different enough so that distinctions in meaning are easily understood (Lynch & Horton, 2002). The required level of consistency is strongly situation dependent (Bennett & Flacch, 2011).

FRAMING EFFECT

Theories of decision-making have tended to postulate that people use analytic processes to guide their choices (see chapter 13: *How people make decisions and take action*). However, a large body of psychological research tends to disagree (see Klein, 1999). In particular, it has been found that the way information gets framed has a strong effect on the type of decision people reach. Framing takes one or more aspects of a situation and increases their relative salience, even when they don't necessarily deserve that increase. Framing can also be considered a filter for viewing a situation (Druckman, 2001). Thus, framing affects the factors people consider when analyzing a situation and making decisions. For example, Levin and Gaeth (1988) found that perceptions of the quality of ground beef depended on whether the beef was labeled as "75% lean" or "25% fat." The beef was rated as better tasting and less greasy when described as 75% lean.

Framing effects occur when the same information is evaluated differently in terms of gain or loss frames, and such framing effects are strong. Essentially any information situation can be framed in either a positive or a negative light: you have a 70% chance of winning a teddy bear, or a 30% chance of losing. Although these two phrases say the same thing, expressing the information in positive or negative terms affects how a person responds to it. A medical treatment can be described as "60% effective" (positive frame) or as "40% ineffective" (negative frame). When given a choice between these, people prefer that information be presented in positive terms, even though results would be the same. If asked to justify their choice, most people do not consider these to be equivalent; they would say that the "60% effective" choice is better because 60% is better than 40% (Malenka et al., 1993). Because people respond so differently to positive or negative framing, design teams must consider that frames within the information presentation—negative or positive—have a strong influence on how people will interpret the information. *"Choices involving gains are often risk averse and choices involving losses are often risk taking" (Tversky & Kahneman, 1981, p. 453).*

In many situations, people have to evaluate multiple information elements. Besides the framing effects imposed by any positive or negative presentation formats, those multiple pieces of information must be presented in the same format.

Box 4.

Framing and financial decision-making
In one study, participants were told they had received $50. They were then told they could not keep the entire amount, but had to make a choice. They could either:

A) Keep $20 or gamble with a chance of keeping the entire $50 or losing it all (gain frame).
B) Lose $30 or gamble with a chance of keeping the entire $50 or losing it all (lose frame).

Notice how the framing is whether or not the person 'keeps' $20 or 'loses' $30. Either way, the same amount of money is kept, but the presentation differs. The results reveal that people were risk-averse in the gain frame, tending to choose the sure option (keeping $20) and were risk-seeking in the loss frame, preferring the gamble option that gives a chance of keeping the entire $50 (De Martino et al, 2006). This result of positive frame = risk-adverse and negative frame = risk-seeking is a consistent finding in framing research.

People have a hard time mentally comparing factors when some are presented as a positive and some as a negative. The comparison requires that the information be mentally transformed so that it is either all positive or all negative. A substantial part of the HII problem with communicating multiple sets of numbers is that when information is presented in both positive and negative frames, rather than transform one into the other, people tend to simply read them both as positive frames. Obviously, this means the negative framed information gets misinterpreted. Reading both in a positive frame reduces cognitive effort, but causes problems with decision-making. Design teams must ensure that all information is presented in either a positive frame (the preferred way) or a negative frame.

- Patients showed different preferences for chemotherapy depending on whether survival was represented in the 1-year or in the median survival format (Feldman-Stewart, & Brundage, 2004).
- When making choices between surgery and radiation therapy for lung cancer, people choose surgery when the outcome of treatment is framed as the probability

Box 5.

Framing and the Asian Disease problem

A dramatic example of the framing effect comes from the seminal work by. In their Asian Disease problem, participants were told to: Imagine that the US is preparing for the outbreak of an unusual Asian disease, which is expected to kill 600 people. Two alternative programs to combat the disease have been proposed. Assume that the exact scientific estimates of the consequences of the programs are as follows.
They were then given two options, either in a positive frame:

If Program A is adopted, 200 people will be saved (certain).
If Program B is adopted, there is 1/3 probability that 600 people will be saved and 2/3 probability that no people will be saved (risky).

or in a negative frame:

If Program C is adopted, 400 people will die (certain).
If Program D is adopted, there is a 1/3 probability that nobody will die, and 2/3 probability that 600 people will die (risky).

Despite all options being logically equivalent (but not transparently equivalent), with only the degree of risk inherent in the option differing, it was found that in the positive domain, participants displayed a risk-aversion bias (72% choosing the certain option over the risky option). In contrast, in the negative frame participants showed a risk-seeking bias (78% choosing the risky option over the certain option) (Tversky & Kahneman, 1981).

---

of surviving rather than as the probability of dying (McNeil et al., 1982). A similar effect can be found in business when presenting potential choices and casting their effects as a probability of project success versus failure.

Framing is not dependent upon prior knowledge. Tversky and Kahneman (1981) found framing effects across various scenarios both among knowledgeable experts and the general public. The most widely researched area seems to be health care, where both physicians and patients show similar framing effects. Therefore, design teams need to be conscious of how they frame information since it will exert a strong effect regardless of audience expertise.

Framing when Comparing Positive/Negative Features

When people are comparing different items, any comparison tends to become one of either negative or positive features. Positive features could be factors such as larger computer hard drive or more miles per gallon, while negative features could be factors such as potential for cost overrun or poor service rating.

People's framing of goals affects decisions by influencing the extent of processing of positive vs. negative information. If the decision is framed as an acceptance decision, people are likely to test hypotheses concerning the acceptance of alternatives, and therefore they tend to attend to, and rely on, positive information more than on negative information. On the other hand, when the decision is framed as a rejection decision, the reverse is likely to occur and they focus on negative information. Thus, how people weight positive and negative features varies depending on whether they are accepting or rejecting an item, with the higher weight given to features that fit their overall goal (Houston, Sherman, & Baker, 1989). For example, a person reviewing a large quantity of resumes is looking to reject most of them. In this case, negative features of the resume (misspelling, poor layout) have a high weight. Later, when the hiring manager is reviewing a few resumes, she must make an acceptance decision and puts more weight on positive features (good layout, proper buzzwords). Ganzach and Schul (1995) consider this an example of goal framing, where the person's overall goal (reject resumes or call a person for an interview) causes a confirmation bias toward the features which support the goal. So poor layout, which confirms that a resume should be rejected, has a high weight in the reject scenario. In another study, Snyder and Campbell (1980) asked people to determine whether a target person was an extrovert. They found that their subjects asked questions associated with extroversion. Likewise, when asked to determine whether the person was an introvert, the questions were associated with introversion. The subjects showed a strong confirmation bias to prove the question as it was framed.

Design teams must also consider overall social issues that can lead people to focus only on the negative or positive parts of the information. Russo et al. (1986) reported that consumers are more likely to be affected by nutrition labels that relate information regarding negative dietary components, defined as nutrients such as fat and cholesterol, of which most people need to consume less, compared to positive dietary components, defined as nutrients such as vitamins and minerals, of which most people need to consume more. People have become very conscious of negative dietary components, so they frame the situation as trying to avoid anything containing them. The positive components are downplayed since they do not fit within the negative frame people have mentally set up. They could reject a product which contains lots of vitamins and minerals because it also contains some reported amount of cholesterol unacceptable to them, even if that amount is actually low.

Framing when Comparing Unique Features

Besides comparing based on positive or negative features, many items have unique features. A unique feature is one that only one of the items possesses, such when one laptop has a firewire port and the other one does not. Or one job applicant has experience with a specific software package and the other does not. Obviously, in some situations, a firewire port (or specific software experience) is a must-have requirement, but typically it is not. When people compare items with unique features sequentially, they give the unique features of the visible item more weight than the non-visible item. In other words, people focus on the unique features of the visible item and ignore the non-visible item. The unique fea-

tures of the item being compared tend to drive people's preferences. Thus, the first item would be preferred when negative features were unique, and the second when positive features were unique. Of particular significance to design teams is that order of presentation could cause a preference reversal (discussed later in this chapter) (Bruine de Bruin & Keren, 2003; Houston, Sherman, & Baker, 1989).

One way to overcome some of the comparison problems is to provide a side-by-side comparison. When the choices can be compared side-by-side rather than sequentially, over-focus on either the negative or positive features is significantly reduced (Houston & Sherman, 1995). It seems obvious to present comparisons side-by-side if at all possible, but many complex items do not lend themselves to such a simple presentation. For example, while the potential pros and cons of a new office building can be reduced to a table, large amounts of detailed information that decision-makers need to consider will be hidden within each cell.

Another method to overcome the sequential comparison problem is to provide overall evaluations first. When overall evaluations toward the choice are available (reading about the stuff before seeing the specific choices), people are less likely to show an order bias and also are less likely to lose focus on the unique features of an visible item when making a choice (Sanbonmatsu, Kardes, & Gibson, 1991).

PRESENTATION ORDER

One of the assumed rules of web design is that information can be read in any order. Although this is true for a website (and for most printed technical material), it is not always in the best interest of readers to be able to pick and choose the order. Often, organic designs (such as websites which had grown by adding links for each new topic without fitting them into a clear information architecture) impede information comprehension because people receive their information in too random an order. Not all presentation orders have the same affect on the readers and lead to the same decisions. Design teams need to consider potential reading orders and attempt to structure the overall design to guide readers along logical reading paths.

Information receives its relative priority on the basis of the order in which it is viewed (Klein, 1999), and ordering exerts a strong influence on the interpretation of information which follows. In other words, the first information read is viewed as more important, affecting how later information is interpreted. Thus, the order in which people read information has a deep effect on how they remember information and form relationships between information elements.

The higher priority assigned to the first information viewed means information presented at the top of a display receives a higher priority than information at other places in the display. As a result, any following information, including links deeper into a website, is evaluated on the basis of that first information. Design teams must ensure that the first information activates the proper mental model and does not interfere with other information.

Order of presentation effects play a major factor in typical HII because of the lack of time to devote to information analysis. Time pressure increases the tendency to select the first information (Wallsten & Barton, 1982). Since people tend to search for confirming information, if the first information supports their desired goal, they accept it and stop looking for more information (Klein, 1999).

People have trouble recognizing what information is relevant to their situation and separating it out from irrelevant information, especially if the presentation fails to fit their mental model (Larkin & Simon, 1987). As a result, if the presentation order initially gives low-quality or low-content information, the attention and cognitive

Box 6.

Comparing products between showrooms
When you are shopping for a big-ticket item, the kind that a salesman helps you pick out, consider your thought processes. The first salesman goes on about a feature on his model and stresses how important it is. Before you walked onto the sales floor, you didn't realize that some of those features even existed. When you go to the next store, you find yourself comparing and ranking all of the products against the one described by the first salesman and, more importantly, how they compare to the features he stressed.

The interesting idea here is that if you had visited the showrooms in reverse order, you would still be comparing and ranking the products against the first product you saw. But it would be a different model from a different store (whichever store was visited first) with different features being considered important.

---

resources people will devote to comprehending the remaining information are reduced (assuming they continue reading).

Order of Information Integration

Order of interpretation issues are a major problem with much of the information people encounter. Design teams have provided what they consider complete, correct, and concise information (and it typically is), but because the order fails to match reader needs, communication is impaired. The early design analysis must go beyond defining the information needed and also determine the order in which information should be presented for maximum communication in various situations. Since different situations have different ordering requirements, design teams must determine how to handle needs of multiple audiences and multiple situations against the time and budget of the project.

Information presentation must be in the order that best gives a clear understanding (Klein, 1999) since people evaluate information based on the order in which they receive it. New information is interpreted on the basis of previous information. The first information viewed activates a mental model and all of the information that follows gets interpreted in view of that mental model. Problems arise when the wrong mental model is activated.

The mental model carries with it some of the biases that affect information interpretation and integration. An anchoring bias based on the first information viewed leads people to compare everything that follows to the first item they saw, regardless of whether it actually fits their goals. The anchoring bias also sets the reader's expectations and contributes to the expectancy bias. In an e-commerce situation or other shopping-type situation, people set expectations about a product based on the first one, and evaluates others based on it. When a product has better, but different, features than the first one, it may be mentally rated lower because of it lacks some of the first product's features. The relative relevance of those features tends to be disregarded. In other words, the second product may have fewer but more important features, but since it lacks some found on the first product, it is rated lower.

In many situations, design teams have little control over the order in which people receive information. People often use multiple sources in essentially a random order, which poses a major challenge regarding order of interpretation. Design teams have no control over the quality or content of other sources, nor the order in which they are viewed. When engaged in answering open-ended questions, people typically evaluate information from multiple sources to address the questions inherent in a situation. Unfortunately, as situational complexity increases, the ability of design teams to define a "right way" to achieve the goal or present information dissipates. Instead of following a predefined, fixed path, users continually adjust their mental paths as new information is presented (Albers, 2004; Mirel, 1998). How that information gets interpreted depends on what has already been observed.

Prior knowledge can partially overcome information-ordering problems. The effect does decrease with training (Wang, Johnson, & Zhang, 2006). Scheiter and Gerjets (2002) found that high prior-knowledge people would rearrange a sequence of problems to improve their problem solving ability while low prior-knowledge people did not. They attributed this to the lack of knowledge on which to base any rearrangement. However, they also noted that even the high-prior knowledge people tended not to rearrange the sequence unless given hints about how a rearrangement could help solve the problem. Time pressure or a high-stress environment also reduce any mental rearrangements.

Priming

A text often can imply several different interpretations, or there can be many different potential actions/decisions arising from those interpretations. Any interpretation depends on prior knowledge and people "perform generative cognitive tasks by bringing to mind potentially relevant information about the task at hand" (Marsh, Bink, & Hicks, 1999, p. 355). More influential than people's general prior knowledge is specific guidance given just before reading the text. If people are given some guidance before they interpret the text, the interpretation or decision tends to reflect the guidance. This is called priming. Priming means that being exposed to a certain stimulus influences the response to a second stimulus.

Positive Priming: Positive priming results in a faster response. If people are told what to expect or have recently experienced a situation, positive priming allows them to react faster. Before reading a document, if people are told it contains the reasons for a project failure (the priming), they will notice the negative issues more than the positive issues of the project. The reverse would be true if they were told the document contained the project success story.

Negative Priming: Negative priming results in a slower response. If people are told of negative consequences about a decision, they take longer to make that decision because of the negative priming. Engle et al. (1995) found that the negative priming effect diminished as cognitive load increased. Negative priming is mentally effortful and resource-demanding, and therefore, when the cognitive load is high, inhibition is no longer possible (Conway et al., 1999).

In priming research, people are intentionally given a specific priming event. In reality, the priming may be intentional or unintentional. Both can strongly influence comprehension of a text. Headings form a major way of priming in documents. Through the mental models they activate, they influence what people expect to find in the section and how they interpret the information. Design teams can lead readers by priming in the introduction with statements of what a document contains. They also can inadvertently introduce priming effects by poor design, irrelevant elements, or poor information order. Likewise, many jokes depend on priming for their humor: the set up line uses priming which causes people to interpret innocent statements differently (often sexually) than if they heard the sentence without the priming.

Priming works as an anchor for a person's focus. When priming occurs, it activates a specific mental representation and the information is judged from that view. As a result, people tend to become fixated on confirmatory information compatible with the priming and ignore alternative interpretations, even though they might be equally visible (Saariluoma & Kalakoski, 1998). Consider these three examples of priming and how priming influences people's interpretation of the information. In all of these studies, priming caused people to view the problem in a manner consistent with the priming rather than alternative approaches or answers.

- When people were given the problem of weighing an elephant (a standard problem

in problem-solving research since it presents obvious scale issues) and were cued about either placing the elephant in a water-filled container and measuring the water displacement or using a hanging scale, almost everyone devised methods which reflected the priming cue (Helfenstein & Saariluoma, 2007).
- People were asked to devise novel space creatures with the priming emphasizing hostility (large fangs, weapons, etc.). The resulting designs contained multiple features which were consistent with hostility (Marsh, Bink, & Hicks, 1999).
- Engineering students were asked to create designs based on some examples. Their final designs incorporated design flaws that were present in the examples (Jansson & Smith, 1991).

Priming also happens in the interpretation of numbers, but its strength reflects the experience level of the analyst. When professional investment counselors and students were presented information sets about investments, the professionals' decisions were more influenced by the priming than students' decisions, probably because the professionals used a more intuitive approach rather than the analytic approach of the students. Lack of expertise forced the students to ignore the priming and focus on performing the analysis with the rule-based procedures they had been taught. With increasing experience, people shift to using more heuristics in decision-making, and thus become more susceptible to priming effects (Gilad & Kliger, 2008). This somewhat counterintuitive result shows how design teams must consider what other information is being presented, especially the information immediately before a section of text. Chapter 13: *How people make decisions and take action*, "Decision-making influences and biases" will examine this issue in more detail.

Preference Reversals

The previous few sections have shown some examples of how display format can change the way users view information. Different information presentations change both how the problem is framed and which mental model is activated. As Endsley (1995) points out, "there is considerable evidence that a person's manner of characterizing a situation will determine the decision process chosen to solve a problem" (p. 39). Based on the framing of the problem, any priming, and the activated mental model, people mentally prioritize information as they use it to create their situation model. As a result, improperly framing the current situation can cause information to be ignored or incorrectly interpreted. But even if people do frame the information properly, their choices may be colored by preference reversals caused by presentation format.

Preference reversal has been a subject of extensive study in psychology (Tversky, Slovic, & Kahneman, 1990; Tversky & Kahneman, 1981). In a preference reversal, the interesting point is not just that people consistently choose A over B, but that depending on how the information is presented, that choice can vary (Figure 3). With one presentation they will consistently choose A and with another, consistently choose B; and in both cases they will believe they made the best choice (Johnson, Payne, & Bettman, 1988). The preference reversal effect is strong enough that it has been observed in a Las Vegas casino with real gamblers playing with real money (Lichtenstein & Slovic, 1973).

Although preference reversal research has found it to be very robust, longer-term interactions can reduce them. Chu & Chu (1990) found that preference reversals reduced as people gain experience within an environment which gives them both losses and gains across time (a typical market-like environment). However, this was a laboratory study which leaves open the question of whether or not these findings would carry

Figure 3. Preference reversal. Depending how the information is presented, the best choice can switch. However, people will believe they made the best choice in both cases.

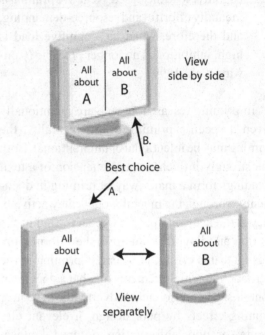

forward to future experiences, especially if information was presented in different formats. Other research finds that if comparisons are explicitly discouraged, choices are less likely to show either an order effect or a preference reversal (Sanbonmatsu et al, 1991).

Preference reversals are highly relevant to effective HII since presentation design choices risk leading people to different conclusions with the same information. If the same information presented differently can lead to different conclusions, the importance of understanding people's information needs and expectations, and the relationships inherent in the situation model, cannot be over-emphasized. Luckily for design teams, preference reversals seem to be consistent depending on presentation, so user testing should be able to reveal designs which tend to cause it.

Some examples of preference reversals:

- People were given three ways of comparing products: a data table formatted by brand, and by attribute; by product with all the information on that product tighter; and by attribute (such as price) for each product. In the product and attribute formats, there was one page for each product/attribute. The product people selected as the best varied depending on the presentation (Johnson, Payne, & Bettman, 1988).

- When given options, an attribute was more favored when surrounded by small numbers than by large numbers (Wong & Kwong, 2005).

- Novice stock traders were more willing to invest in stocks which they had moderate familiarity after viewing unfamiliar stocks than after viewing familiar stocks. Thus, "an opportunity to invest in the domestic stock market and an opportunity to invest in an emerging market index may both seem more attractive when presented to potential investors in order of increasing familiarity (emerging. ... domestic) than when presented in order of decreasing familiarity (domestic. .. emerging)" (Fox & Weber, 2002. p. 496).

Reversals with Serial versus Concurrent Evaluation

Evaluating two options jointly can lead to a different preference order than evaluating each option separately. People show a tendency to pick different alternatives depending on whether they make the comparisons together or separately (Hsee, 1996; González-Vallejo, & Moran, 2001). This is the situation displayed in figure 10.3.

When compared together, the preference is primarily driven by the most important attribute, irrespective of how hard or easy to evaluate that attribute is. "Reversals occur because one of the attributes involved in the options is hard to evaluate independently and another attribute is relatively

Box 7.

> **Potential preference reversals in e-commerce**
> Consider an online store that sells sweaters. There are typically two different ways of comparing the sweaters being offered. The site may only support a basic tree structure which requires the user to click on each sweater image to view the details. The comparison requires repeated moving up and down a tree structure. Or there may be checkboxes by the sweaters, allowing the user to select three or four, click a compare button, and see a page with a table containing a side-by-side attribute listing of the selected sweaters.
>
> At first glance, these two methods of evaluation seem to be the same. However, because of preference reversals, the side-by-side style of comparison might lead to a different decision than an evaluation of each product separately.

easy to evaluate independently" (Hsee, 1996, p. 247). As part of the study, Hsee found that difficult-to-evaluate attributes are given more weight in joint evaluation and easy-to-evaluate attributes had more weight in sequential evaluation. For example, price is easy to compare, but attributes such as "projected increase in user satisfaction" or "impact on ship date" are much more difficult. As a result, if comparing the two numbers side-by-side, people will go with the better number and tend to downplay the comparison in sequential evaluation. Direct comparisons tend to use highly qualitative measures (such as price or speed execution), but in separate comparisons, quantitative measures (such as the number of features or available accessories) would be the main decision factors of comparison. Since realistic evaluations involve multiple attributes of highly varying weights, design teams must recognize and consider how the interactions between the attributes and presentation will influence the reader's decision-making process (Weber & Chapman, 2005).

INTEGRATION OF VISUAL AND VERBAL INFORMATION

The use of illustrations or diagrams to supplement text-based instruction has a long history, dating back at least to the 15th century (Ferguson, 1977).

Larkin and Simon (1987) consider a major effect of illustrations to be their selection ability, bringing out the important points and relieving the reader of having to mentally separate the important and non-important aspects. Of course, this implies that the illustration does contain the major points. Poor illustrations impair HII by forcing the reader to do extra work. The effect of poor illustrations connects back to the findings of Carney and Levin (2002) regarding the negative effect of decorational images. Rather than highlighting important points, they force the reader to mentally evaluate and reject them as not relevant.

Part of the allure of graphics owes to the multi-dimensional view they give of a situation, versus the linear, one-dimensional view of text. People can look at a graphic and see in a single glance the entire object rather than having to mentally build it up piece-by-piece from a linear progression of text. Effective HII presentation often depends on the integration of both textual and visual information, with the visual working within the area Kostelnick (1988, 1996) defined as the "extra-textual" part of his visual rhetoric matrix. Carney and Levin (2002) performed an extensive review of the literature on learning and graphics. As expected, they found that graphics did enhance learning. Mayer (1976) found that the quality of the diagram and text strongly influenced whether a diagram or text is better.

The present results indicate that (1) diagrams produce better performance if they replace particularly complicated verbal representation presumably due to faster accessing of information, and (2) diagrams result in poor performance if they are substituted for well-structured verbal representation, presumably due to distraction. There was, however, no consistent evidence that diagrams resulted in a different kind of internal processing style in working memory (Mayer, 1976, p. 253).

To be effective, the graphic must fit the information and convey knowledge appropriately. Simply choosing to represent information with a graph, chart, picture, or video does not solve the communication problem, and improper graphics choices can severely hinder the HII. Only when a graphic properly captures the rhetorical aspects of the information being conveyed will it have a chance of communicating the information in a manner which meets people's need (Laplante & Flaxman, 1995; Tufte, 1983).

At the very least, then, these results ask us to approach the document design process as a problem-solving task in which decisions regarding visual language are made as carefully as are decisions about verbal language. At a more global level, the results of this project suggest the potential importance of visual rhetoric. If readers perceive a document to carry distinct verbal and visual messages, then how may conflicts between those messages shape readers' interactions with a document? (Brumberger, 2003b, p. 221).

The focus of designing visual presentations, especially graphs, can be fall into one of four types:

- **Conventional:** emphasis on imitating generic forms that meet readers' expectations.
- **Perceptual:** emphasis on optimizing reader behavior in accessing data visually.
- **Informational:** emphasis on transferring information clearly and concisely from designer to reader.
- **Aesthetic:** emphasis on taste, cultural values, and expressive elements.

While each of these areas has merit, and some overlap occurs among them, they often conflict with one another, forcing design teams to decide which to follow (Kostelnick, 1988). In user-centered design, a significant part of audience analysis needs focus on understanding how the readers want visuals presented and how visuals work/get interpreted within readers' mental models (Kostelnick, 1993). Using standard ethnography techniques, readers could be asked for their preferences and the design matched to those answers. However, the results still require usability testing to determine the most accurate and efficient presentation. Meeting audience desires must be balanced against the task demands of both accuracy and speed. In addition, many audience members may pick a more glitzy graph, such as 3D, since most audience-preference surveys do not require people to actually interact with the information, but rather to simply look at it. And people consistently state preferences for designs that do not produce the best performance.

Often, it seems, design teams decide that a block of text is complicated and needs a visual to help communicate the information, thus a visual is found and inserted. The problem is that the graphic may or may not clearly connect to the text content and clearly support it. Of course, any visual is only useful if people understand how to use it. It may support highly efficient mental processing, but design teams must understand what makes a good visual with respect to the situation. For example, Larkin and Simon (1987) point out that physics professors complain that their students both refuse to draw diagrams of physics problems and fail to understand the value of using a diagram. They attribute it to a lack of background knowledge to see how the diagram fits into the problem being solved. When people do not see the relevance, they see no reason to exert the effort to create or use a graphic.

Marketing brochures and magazines in which a cutting-edge or trendy impression is attempted are filled with graphics which are only loosely connected to the text. The glitz of the image takes precedence over the content value. Although this practice may have good marketing logic, it should not be applied to the use of technical visuals relevant to HII. Likewise, the web is a highly graphical medium, and many design teams seem to believe that more graphics are better, which often

Box 8.

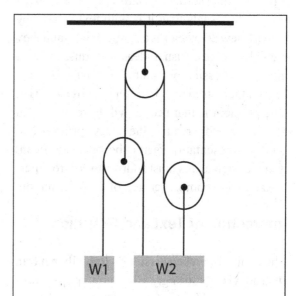

Consider a problem given in the following natural language statements. We have three pulleys, two weights, and some ropes, arranged as follows:

1. The first weight is suspended from the left end of a rope over Pulley 'A. The right end of this rope is attached to, and partially supports, the second weight.
2. Pulley A is suspended from the left end of a rope that runs over Pulley B, and under Pulley C. Pulley B is suspended from the ceiling. The right end of the rope that runs under Pulley C is attached to the ceiling.
3. Pulley C is attached to the second weight, supporting it jointly with the right end of the first rope.

(Larkin & Simon, 1987, pp. 72–73).

confuses the message rather than making it clearer or easier to understand (Kress, 2005). Interestingly, many websites which appear highly graphical at first glance have no or minimal content-related graphics. Instead, all of the graphics are either navigation elements, decoration, or ads—all of which distract from comprehension of the content (Levin & Simon, 1987).

A difficulty with graphics supporting content effectively is that the graphic has to be designed *for* the content. Graphs are easy to create with modern software, although creating a effective graph still requires understanding the rhetorical situation; but other visuals are still difficult and expensive to create since they require a graphic artist. It is also harder to control people's interactions with visuals than it is with text since they tend to view the visual as a single object, and they mentally process visual ideas very quickly. Fast mental processing proves to be visuals' best asset and their strongest detriment to effective HII. One problem is that people will have processed the image before reading the text, so priming and order-of-presentation factors become significant issues design teams must address to control interpretation and comprehension of the information.

Interaction of Text and Graphics

The choice of a visual is not rhetorically neutral. Instead, visuals strongly affect how people make judgments and interact with information. Readers use their prior experiences and knowledge to evaluate a visual, just like they do to evaluate text (Kostelnick, 1988). Also, to maximize comprehension, the visuals must remain specific and realistic (Foss et al, 1987). Representing information with a graph, chart, picture, or video never truly solves the design problem; only when it properly captures the rhetorical aspects of the information being conveyed will it have a chance of addressing the user's problem. The visualization mechanism must fit both the information and the readers' experiences and expectations to convey the knowledge appropriately (Laplante & Flaxman, 1995; Tufte, 1983).

A user manual normally includes examples. Although providing examples seems easy, presenting them in context requires careful thought and planning (van der Meij & Gellevij, 1998, 2002). Research into using examples reveals an interesting conflict on the use of visuals. People often claim they want more examples and give "has lots of examples" as a reason they like a particular manual. However, extensive examples with the step-by-step instructions can cause problems. People routinely ignore the written procedure and follow the example. They often ignore the text so strongly that text errors go unnoticed although

graphic errors cause errors from which people have trouble recovering (Lefevre & Dixon, 1986). If examples are used, example syntax must remain specific and realistic; abstract syntax does not aid learning or performing the action. (Foss et al, 1987). Generic examples fail since they lack a context (Carroll et al, 1988). Although many manuals use screen examples liberally, Nowaczyk and James (1993) found that learning was actually better when the example only consisted of the relevant part of the screen.

A wide body of research consistently finds that display format influences both the spontaneous interpretation of visuals (typically first glance before reading any content) and how the visual information gets integrated with the textual information. A notable research finding for graphs is that the amount of integrative (global) content was highest for bar graphs and lowest for tables (Carswell & Ramzy, 1997). An even more interesting research result comes from Feldman-Stewart and Brundage (2004), who found a disconnect between preferred graphical format and the one which gave the most accurate results. When they asked people to identify their preferred format for graphical information, over half of their subjects preferred a format that did not accurately aid processing of content in either gross-level tasks or detailed tasks. There is also the danger of people sufficing (Simon, 1979) by only looking at the graphics and not reading the text, thus missing important information by not mentally processing all of the information. Larkin and Simon (1987) explain that this type of result arises from the highly efficient mental processing that people can perform on graphics. Design teams are responsible to strongly connect the graphics and the text so that readers grasp the significance of both to gain a clear understanding of the situation.

Functions of Graphics in a Text

Textual and graphical information presentations are cognitively interdependent. Each must support the other in an integrated manner. A problem with many documents is that design teams selected an inappropriate type of graphic, often because of availability or ease of creation rather than quality of communication. How well each type of graphic communicates a specific type of information can vary widely; maximizing HII requires choosing the proper graphic and not just the most expedient graphic. In addition, graphing software such as Microsoft Excel provides a wide range of formats which are very easy to create, many of which look cool to the untrained designer but fail adequately to support communicating the information.

Manning and Amare (2006) discuss the importance of design teams' differentiating among decorative, indicative, and informative visuals. Levin (1981) proposed that graphics serve five functions:

- *Decorational:* They decorate the page with no relationship to the content. Many images on the web and in marketing material fit into this category. Manning and Amare (2006) consider the empty third dimension in 3D graphs to be decoration.
- *Representational:* An illustration which mirrors or repeats part of the text. For example, the drawings in a book of fiction, or a drawing of the equipment being discussed in the text.
- *Organizational:* Structural version of the text. For example, an organizational chart or an illustration showing procedural steps.
- *Interpretational:* Helps to clarify difficult parts of the text. Typically these use analogy, such as comparing a neurosystem to a roadway.
- *Transformational:* Contains mnemonic components that allow for improved infor-

Figure 5. Effect size by graphic function. The higher the bar, the more the image type contributes to the ability of the graphic to support communication. The negative value for decorative means it impaired the communication (adapted from Carney & Levin, 2002, p. 8).

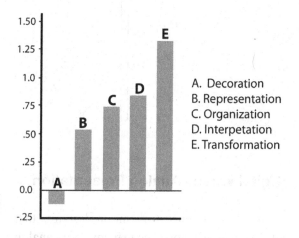

mation recall and for making the concept more concrete.

In follow-on work to Levin (1981), Carney and Levin (2002) reconsidered early findings on what type of effect graphics have on the reader's interpretation based on the five categories (Figure 5). They found that transformational showed by the far the strongest effect for creating effective HII. They also found that decorational images actually had a negative effect. Although they may add a "graphical flourish" (Levy, et al., 1996, p. 48), decorative graphics decrease the ability of a text to clearly communicate information.

The negative effect of decorational images is interesting considering the high incidence of clipart or non-informational photos on both webpages and presentation slides. Authors working under the false assumption that all webpages/presentations need graphics insert images without considering how they support (or fail to support) the content.

Figure 6. Digital & analog gauge & digital gauge with numbers. The analog display in A contains relationship information which the digital display in B does not. Even placing high/low limits next to a digital display does not overcome mental processing issues as people still must perform a mental math calculation. The center gauges in C is visually different from the other two and requires attention.

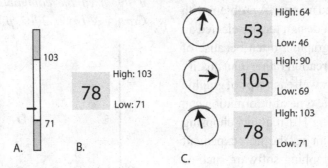

Digital versus Analog Presentation

A common and current theme in design is that all-digital is best; however, in many cases, analog provides for easier interpretation. (Think of the needle on a gauge versus a digital indicator with a number.) Displays with digital-only and no analog graphical configuration showed the poorest results when used for simulated plant system control and fault detection (Bennett & Walters, 2001).

Although not normally thought of as a digital-versus-analog issue, considerations of graphs versus tables follow similar design choices. The designs of many corporate performance dashboards show a mix of digital and analog presentation. An analog visual image is easier to process rapidly than is a number; one is mentally processed as an image and the other as text. Analog displays also take advantage of Gestalt principles that let a person see the location of the indicator within the entire allowed space. Numbers require mentally interpolating the location of the number within that same space. The basic rule is that a digital display works best when a value with high precision is required, while analog works best when rate-of-change or relationship to a limit is required (Sanders & McCormick, 1993).

An analog presentation is more information-rich than digital. The entire visual image of an analog gauge contains much more information about the explicit relationships between current values and acceptable ranges. Design decisions about using digital or analog presentation revolve around the problem that when presented with a number, people have to mentally perform a calculation to know how close it is to high or low limits, versus having it visually contained within an analog indicator (Figure 6). If people need the precision of absolute values, then a digital presentation is required, but if the premium is on comparison or rate-of-change information, then analog works better. The digital-to-analog, real-world transformation requires increased fixation times (longer mental processing time) and it increases error rate (Tole et al., 1982). Similar problems have been found with car speedometers which read digitally, giving a single number rather than showing a needle against a range.

Early research comparing analog to digital clocks revealed that digital formats were best for reading exact times and analog formats were best for rapid estimates of "time until" or "time remaining" (Zeff, 1965; Sinclair 1971). Work with control-panel operations yielded similar findings: people who had to read digital gauges had a harder time keeping a clear image of the overall situation. They knew the individual values, but had a much lower sense of how the overall system was performing, especially when it was operating close to the limits of the allowed range. For instance, the actual temperature of the coolant in your car is not as important as knowing that it's running hot or approaching the hot limit, thus an analog display works well. Mentally converting digital to analog information slows down decision-making and increases error rates (Wickens & Hollands, 2000).

In addition, comparison across multiple values is much easier with analog. The display design can use Gestalt principles to have everything centered for normal values. Any high or low value is apparent with a single glance. Notice in Figure 6 that the normal ranges of the values are all scaled so that the normal ranges are all the same width. Any bar to the left or right is visible with pre-attentive processing. Having a list of values and ranges next to them requires that people mentally compare each one.

Presentation design choice should strive to maximize the compatibility between the actual system, the display, and the mental model of the situation. A good design must minimize mental transformation or calculations, such as calculating how close a reading is to the high or low value. Posting high and low values by a digital gauge in Figure 6 still requires people to make a mental calculation. Especially critical for matching a mental model is that information for a process or flow be designed to match that flow. Roscoe's (1968) principle of pictorial realism states that features such as direction and shape should be matched along with values. In other words, if the information is the temperature and pressure at various places in a system, it should be displayed on a schematic of the system, not in two columns labeled "temperature" and "pressure."

Control panels often contain a schematic of the system with switches and gauges mapped onto the schematic. So a pump start/stop switch and the pump operation gauges are all clustered around the pump on the schematic. Although this same design would work well for solving many

informational problems, the presentation on a computer monitor imposes severe limitations. The entire presentation is typically too large to fit when displaying the level of detail needed. And drilling down or panning across the screen proves problematical since people often need to see multiple parts of the presentation at once. Remembering values and scrolling to other parts greatly increases errors and cognitive-load issues (Fennema & Kleinmuntz, 1995).

EXAMPLES

Astronomical Information

Astronomical information needs to have good organization that works to address people information needs. This can be more difficult that it first sounds since many general readers just expect to see pretty pictures while more advanced readers want to hear explanations of the pictures and of related studies. The results of most science experiments are not pictures, but are various sort of spectrographic diagrams. Figure 8 shows a generic version. These contain the raw information which must be translated into information for the readers. Most people lack the prior knowledge to interpret a graph like that shown in Figure 8 and even if they do, unless they are the researcher, they expect it to be done for them. In an interesting shift, when a site displays an image of a nebula or other astronomical image, there tends to be no interpretation. The image is presented without explaining why it has the shape it has. It should explain the forces that give the nebula its shape and variation in lighting and color.

Business Reports

Framing effects and order of presentation have a major effect on how the information in a busiess report gets interpreted. People will compare all alternatives against the first alternative. If it is

Box 9.

Digital and analog in veterinary tests

Many designs provide a combination of digital and analog. The mix of both graphical and exact values for a blood test can improve HII since it allows the veterinarian to scan the graph and note any values which are out of norm (outside the center third). To minimize cognitive effort, the vet can look at the graph to gain an overview and assurance that everything is ok. Then, if a value is high or low, she can look at the exact values. Without the graphical presentation, a quick scan of just the numbers might cause her to miss a high or low value. It also allows her to review the results quicker since she doesn't have to mentally compare each value to its normal range.

In addition, the graphical presentation can help with a diagnosis where multiple values take on distinctive patterns, such as for a specific disease in which five values will appear at the low end of normal. Individually, the values are within the normal range, but viewed as a unit, they may indicate a condition to be checked further.

MCV	*	66.4 fl.	(60.0 - 77.0)
RDW	*	15.6 %	(14.7 - 17.9)
MCHC	*	36.3 g/dL	(30.0 - 37.5)
MCH	*	24.10 pg	(18.50 - 30.00)
PLT	*	407 K/μL	(175 - 500)

Complete blood count test results. This is a partial printout of the results for my dog, showing the actual value, the normal range, and a graphical presentation with the normal range scaled to be the center third of the graph. Out-of-range values would appear in as yellow or red boxes.

very poor, the others may look too good. If it has unique, but not really needed features, it may result in the other options looking worse since they do not have those options.

All of the options need to receive the same presentation. They should be evaluated in the same order and at the same level of detail. Too often the non-preferred options are evaluated at a higher level and some may not be evaluated at all. Also, the design team should understand what options are preferred by the readers and consider if the report itself supports those preferences. Information receiving high salience may have to change to prevent people from reading the report with a strong expectancy bias and making their preferred decision when the report does not support it.

Consider a report to a power company that is making recommendations about their long-term strategy, such as how many new plants to build and how to update their transmission infrastructure. The various options of the number and types (coal, natural gas, alternative energy) of new plants need to be evaluated. The detail of each needs to be at the same level. For example, if the company is against investing in solar, the solar

power section still should match the others and not summarily dismiss it.

SUMMARY

People are highly influenced by how information gets presented in the interface. How they process it relates directly to the presentation; more than simply having information available, the presentation must match the current information needs. A high quality presentation contains information which fits the information needs required to gain a full understanding of the situation. A poor presentation, rather than poor content, fails to communicate clearly and is often the major communication issue.

HII and presentation are related in a dynamic interplay. With the increasing complexity of computer-based internal processes, the overall system becomes a black box with visible inputs which are transformed into visible outputs by methods which are of no concern to the users. People only care about the HII, not the transformations internal to the black box.

Figure 8. Spectrometry. The results of many astronomical science experiments create output like this. The design team must interpret these results for the readers.

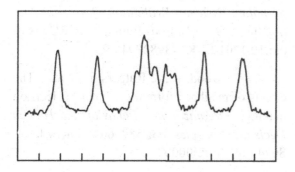

Adapting to Displayed Information

People need support from an interface to make problem solving easier. However, they are highly influenced by how the system gets presented in the interface. Interfaces often display relevant information, making recall unnecessary and relieving working memory. The more information a design shifts to an interface, the less information people must retain in memory, making for an easier task.

Amount of Information

Design teams want to provide readers with the information they need. The problem is that meeting the information needs of multiple audience groups can result in a large amount of information irrelevant to any single group. People need the proper amount of information and have a hard time selecting and choosing when given too much. Large amounts of information lead to information overload and ignoring information. A relatively narrow range, which varies between individuals, determines when they have the proper amount of information.

Visual momentum has become an important concept that considers the large amounts of information available on the web. The websites information architecture and the sheer volume of

information require it to be broken into multiple pages. Good visual momentum allows the reader to move smoothly between pages and to maintain a coherent view of the information.

Information presentation is highly influential in determining the cognitive resources required to comprehend the text and transform it into knowledge. Designs need to be focused on minimizing the mental transformations since even small cognitive transformations take effort away from people's intended task and increase cognitive load.

All information is not weighted equally. Information that people do not see is weighted less than information that can be seen. Information which is not seen receives a lower salience than information which can be seen. The displayed/not displayed information problem is especially acute when the person needs to consider subtle cause-and-effect relationships between visible and non-visible information across different screens.

Framing Effects

How the information gets framed has a strong effect on the type of decision people reach. Framing effects occur when the same information is evaluated differently in terms of gain or loss frames. Framing takes one or more aspects of a situation and increases their relative salience, even when they don't necessarily deserve that increase.

Presentation Order

Information gets its relative priority based on the order in which it was viewed. The first information read is viewed as more important and affects how later information gets interpreted. The early design analysis must go beyond defining the information needed and also determine the order in which information should be presented for maximum communication.

More influential than people's general prior knowledge is specific guidance given just before reading the text. If people are given some guidance before they interpret the text, the interpretation or decision tends to reflect the guidance. This is called priming which means that being exposed to a certain stimulus influences the response to a second stimulus.

In a preference reversal, people consistently choose A over B, but the choice depends on how the information is presented. With one presentation they consistently choose A and with another, they consistently choose B. In both cases, they will believe they made the best choice

Integration of Visual and Verbal Information

HII information normally consists of a combination of textual and graphical information. The choice of a visual is not rhetorically neutral. Instead, visuals strongly affect how people make judgments and interact with information. Readers use their prior experiences and knowledge to evaluate a visual, just as they do to evaluate text.

Textual and graphical information presentations are cognitively interdependent and each must support the other in an integrated manner. Visuals have an ability to highlight the important points and relieve the reader of having to mentally separate the important and non-important aspects. However, to be effective, a graphic must fit the information and convey knowledge appropriately.

REFERENCES

Albers, M. (1996). Decision-making: A missing facet of effective documentation. *Proceedings of the 14th Annual International Conference on Computer Documentation*, Raleigh, NC, October 21–22, 1996.

Albers, M. (2004). *Communication of complex information: User goals and information needs for dynamic Web information*. Mahwah, NJ: Erlbaum.

Albers, M. (2010). Usability and information relationships: Considering content relationships when testing complex information. In Albers, M., & Still, B. (Eds.), *Usability of complex Information Systems: Evaluation of user interaction* (pp. 109–132). Boca Raton, FL: CRC Press. doi:10.1201/EBK1439828946-9

Atkins, P., Wood, R., & Rutgers, P. (2002). The effects of feedback format on dynamic decision making. *Organizational Behavior and Human Decision Processes*, 88, 587–604. doi:10.1016/S0749-5978(02)00002-X

Bennett, K., & Flacch, (2011). *Display and interface design: Subtle science, exact art*. Boca Raton, FL: CRC Press.

Bennett, K., & Walters, B. (2001). Configural display design techniques considered at multiple levels of evaluation. *Human Factors*, 43(3), 415–434. doi:10.1518/001872001775898304

Bettman, J., & Zins, M. (1979). Information format and choice task effects in decision making. *The Journal of Consumer Research*, 6(2), 141–153. doi:10.1086/208757

Bruine de Bruin, W., & Keren, G. (2003). Order effects in sequentially judged options due to the direction of comparison. *Organizational Behavior and Human Decision Processes*, 92, 91–101. doi:10.1016/S0749-5978(03)00080-3

Brumberger, E. (2003b). The rhetoric of typography: The persona of typeface and text. *Technical Communication*, 50(2), 206–223.

Card, S., Moran, T., & Newell, A. (1983). *The psychology of human-computer interaction*. Hillsdale, NJ: Erlbaum.

Carney, R., & Levin, J. (2002). Pictorial illustrations still improve students' learning from text. *Educational Psychology Review*, 14(1), 5–26. doi:10.1023/A:1013176309260

Carroll, J., Smith-Kerker, P., Ford, J., & Mazur-Rimetz, S. (1988). The minimal manual. *Human-Computer Interaction, 3*, 123–153. doi:10.1207/s15327051hci0302_2

Carswell, C., & Ramzy, C. (1997). Graphing small data sets: Should we bother? *Behaviour & Information Technology, 16*(2), 61–71. doi:10.1080/014492997119905

Chu, Y., & Chu, R. (1990). The subsidence of preference reversals in simplified and market-like experimental settings: A note. *The American Economic Review, 80*, 902–911.

Conway, A., Tuholski, S., Shisler, R., & Engle, R. (1999). The effect of memory load on negative priming: An individual differences investigation. *Memory & Cognition, 27*, 1042–1050. doi:10.3758/BF03201233

De Martino, B., Kumaran, D., Seymour, B., & Dolan, R. (2006). Frames, biases, and rational decision-making in the human brain. *Science, 313*, 684–687. doi:10.1126/science.1128356

Doheny-Farina, S. (1998). *Effective documentation: What we have learned from research.* Cambridge, MA: MIT.

Druckman, J. (2001). On the limits of framing effects: Who can frame? *The Journal of Politics, 63*(4), 1041–1066. doi:10.1111/0022-3816.00100

Einhorn, H. J., & Hogarth, R. M. (1981). Behavioral decision theory: Processes of judgment and choice. *Annual Review of Psychology, 32*, 53–88. doi:10.1146/annurev.ps.32.020181.000413

Endsley, M. (1995). Toward a theory of situation awareness in dynamic systems. *Human Factors, 37*(1), 32–64. doi:10.1518/001872095779049543

Engle, R., Conway, A., Tuholski, S., & Shisler, R. (1995). A resource account of inhibition. *Psychological Science, 6*, 122–125. doi:10.1111/j.1467-9280.1995.tb00318.x

Feldman-Stewart, D., & Brundage, M. (2004). Challenges for designing and implementing decision aids. *Patient Education and Counseling, 54*, 265–273. doi:10.1016/j.pec.2003.09.007

Fennema, M., & Kleinmuntz, D. (1995). Anticipation of effort and accuracy in multi-attribute choice. *Organizational Behavior and Human Decision Processes, 63*(1), 21–32. doi:10.1006/obhd.1995.1058

Ferguson, E. (1977). The mind's eye: Nonverbal thought in technology. *Science, 197*, 827–836. doi:10.1126/science.197.4306.827

Foss, D., Smith-Kerker, P., & Rosson, M. (1987). On comprehending a computer manual: Analysis of variables affecting performance. *International Journal of Man-Machine Studies, 26*(3), 277–300. doi:10.1016/S0020-7373(87)80064-0

Fox, C., & Weber, M. (2002). Ambiguity aversion, comparative ignorance, and decision context. *Organizational Behavior and Human Decision Processes, 88*(1), 476–498. doi:10.1006/obhd.2001.2990

Ganzach, Y., & Schul, Y. (1995). The influence of quantity of information and goal framing on decisions. *Acta Psychologica, 89*, 23–36. doi:10.1016/0001-6918(94)00004-Z

Gilad, D., & Kliger, D. (2008). Priming the risk attitudes of professionals in financial decision making. *Review of Finance, 12*(3), 567–586. doi:10.1093/rof/rfm034

González-Vallejo, C., & Moran, E. (2001). The evaluability hypothesis revisited: Joint and separate evaluation preference reversal as a function of attribute importance. *Organizational Behavior and Human Decision Processes, 86*(2), 216–233. doi:10.1006/obhd.2001.2953

Graham, W., Smith, P., Kamal, A., Fitzmaurice, A., Smith, N., & Hamilton, N. (2000). Randomised controlled trial comparing effectiveness of touch screen system with leaflet for providing women with information on prenatal tests. *British Medical Journal*, *320*(7228), 155–160. doi:10.1136/bmj.320.7228.155

Grudin, J. (1989). The case against user interface consistency. *Communications of the ACM*, *32*, 1164–1173. doi:10.1145/67933.67934

Helfenstein, S., & Pertti Saariluoma, P. (2007). Apperception in primed problem solving. *Cognitive Processing*, *8*, 211–232. doi:10.1007/s10339-007-0189-4

Hess, S., Detweiler, M., & Ellis, R. (1999). The utility of display space in keeping-track of rapidly changing information. *Human Factors*, *41*(2), 257–281. doi:10.1518/001872099779591187

Hix, D., & Hartson, R. (1993). *Developing user interfaces: Ensuring usability through product and process*. New York, NY: Wiley.

Hollnagel, E. (1988). Mental models and model mentality. In L. P. Goodstein, H. B. Andersen & S. E. Olsen (Eds.), *Task errors and mental models* (pp. 261–268). Risẽ National Laboratory, Denmark: Taylor & Francis.

Hollnagel, E., & Woods, D. (1983). Cognitive systems engineering: New wine in new bottles. *International Journal of Man-Machine Studies*, *18*, 583–600. doi:10.1016/S0020-7373(83)80034-0

Horton, W. (1990). *Designing and writing online documentation*. New York, NY: Wiley.

Houston, D., & Sherman, S. (1995). Cancellation and focus: The role of shared and unique features in the choice process. *Journal of Experimental Social Psychology*, *31*(4), 357–378. doi:10.1006/jesp.1995.1016

Houston, D., Sherman, S., & Baker, S. (1989). The influence of unique features and direction of comparison on preferences. *Journal of Experimental Social Psychology*, *25*, 121–141. doi:10.1016/0022-1031(89)90008-5

Hsee, C. (1995). Elastic justification: How tempting but task irrelevant factors influence decisions. *Organizational Behavior and Human Decision Processes*, *62*(3), 330–337. doi:10.1006/obhd.1995.1054

Hsee, C. (1996). The evaluability hypothesis: An explanation of preference reversals between joint and separate evaluations of alternatives. *Organizational Behavior and Human Decision Processes*, *67*(3), 247–257. doi:10.1006/obhd.1996.0077

Jansson, D., & Smith, S. (1991). Design fixation. *Design Studies*, *12*, 3–11. doi:10.1016/0142-694X(91)90003-F

Johnson, E., Payne, J., & Bettman, J. (1988). Information displays and preference reversals. *Organizational Behavior and Human Decision Processes*, *42*, 1–21. doi:10.1016/0749-5978(88)90017-9

Judge, J., Field, T., DeFlorio, M., Laprino, J., Auger, J., & Rochon, P. (2006). Prescribers' responses to alerts during medication ordering in the long term care setting. *Journal of the American Medical Informatics Association*, *13*(4), 385–390. doi:10.1197/jamia.M1945

Kalyuga, S., Chandler, P., & Sweller, J. (2004). When redundant on-screen text in multimedia technical instruction can interfere with learning. *Human Factors*, *46*, 567–581. doi:10.1518/hfes.46.3.567.50405

Klein, G. (1999). *Sources of power: How people make decisions*. Cambridge, MA: MIT.

Kostelnick, C. (1988). Conflicting standards for designing data displays: Following, flouting, and reconciling them. *Technical Communication*, *45*(4), 473–482.

Kostelnick, C. (1993). Viewing functional pictures in context. In Blyler, N., & Thralls, C. (Eds.), *Professional communication: The social perspective* (pp. 243–256). Newbury Park, CA: Sage.

Kostelnick, C. (1996). Supra-textual design: The Visual rhetoric of whole documents. *Technical Communication Quarterly, 5*(1), 9–33. doi:10.1207/s15427625tcq0501_2

Koyani, S., Balley, R., & Nall, J. (2006). *Research based Web design*. Washington, DC: National Cancer Institute. Retrieved from http://www.usability.gov/guidelines/

Kress, G. (2005). Gains and losses: New forms of texts, knowledge, and learning. *Computers and Composition, 22*, 5–22. doi:10.1016/j.compcom.2004.12.004

Lang, A., Borse, J., Wise, K., & David, P. (2002). Captured by the World Wide Web: Orienting to structural and content features of computer presented information. *Communication Research, 29*(3), 215–245. doi:10.1177/0093650202029003001

Lansdale, M., & Ormerod, T. (1994). *Understanding interfaces: A handbook of human-computer dialogue*. London, UK: Academic Press.

Laplante, P., & Flaxman, H. (1995). The convergence of technology and creativity in the corporate environment. *IEEE Transactions on Professional Communication, 38*(1), 20–23. doi:10.1109/47.372389

Larkin, J., & Simon, H. (1987). Why a diagram is (sometimes) worth ten thousand words. *Cognitive Science, 11*, 65–99. doi:10.1111/j.1551-6708.1987.tb00863.x

Lefevre, J., & Dixon, P. (1986). Do written instructions need examples? *Cognition and Instruction, 3*(1), 1–30. doi:10.1207/s1532690xci0301_1

Levin, D., & Simons, D. (1997). Failure to detect changes to attended objects in motion pictures. *Psychonomic Bulletin & Review, 4*, 501–506. doi:10.3758/BF03214339

Levin, I., & Gaeth, G. (1988). How consumers are affected by the framing of attribute information before and after consuming the product. *The Journal of Consumer Research, 15*, 374–378. doi:10.1086/209174

Levin, J. (1981). On functions of pictures in prose. In Pirozzolo, F., & Wittrock, M. (Eds.), *Neuropsychological and cognitive processes in reading* (pp. 203–228). New York, NY: Academic Press.

Levy, E., Zacks, J., Tversky, B., & Schiano, D. (1996). Gratuitous graphics? Putting preferences in perspective. In *Proceedings of the SIGCHI conference on human factors in computing systems* (pp. 42–49). New York, NY: ACM Press.

Lichtenstein, S., & Slovic, P. (1973). Response-induced reversals of preference in gambling: An extended replication in Las Vegas. *Journal of Experimental Psychology, 101*, 16–20. doi:10.1037/h0035472

Lohse, G. (1997). The role of working memory on graphical information processing. *Behaviour & Information Technology, 16*(6), 297–308. doi:10.1080/014492997119707

Lynch, P., & Horton, S. (2002). *Web style guide* (2nd ed.). New Haven, CT: Yale UP.

Malenka, D., Baron, J., Johansen, S., & Ross, J. (1993). The framing effect of relative and absolute risk. *Journal of General Internal Medicine, 8*, 543–548. doi:10.1007/BF02599636

Maltz, M., & Meyer, J. (2001). Use of warnings in an attentionally demanding detection task. *Human Factors, 43*(2), 217–226. doi:10.1518/001872001775900931

Manning, A., & Amare, N. (2006). Visual-rhetoric ethics: Beyond accuracy and injury. *Technical Communication, 53,* 195–211.

Marsh, R., Bink, M., & Hicks, J. (1999). Conceptual priming in a generative problem-solving task. *Memory & Cognition, 27*(2), 355–363. doi:10.3758/BF03211419

Mayer, R. (1976). Comprehension as affected by structure of problem representation. *Memory & Cognition, 4,* 249–265. doi:10.3758/BF03213171

Mayes, J., Draper, S., McGregor, A., & Oatley, K. (1988). Information flow in a user interface: The effect of experience and context on the recall of MacWrite screens. In Jones, D. M., & Winder, R. (Eds.), *People and Computers IV* (pp. 275–289). New York, NY: Cambridge University Press.

McNamara, D., Kintsch, E., Songer, N., & Kintsch, W. (1996). Are good texts always better? Interactions of text coherence, background knowledge, and levels of understanding in learning from text. *Cognition and Instruction, 14,* 1–43. doi:10.1207/s1532690xci1401_1

McNeil, B., Pauker, S., Sox, H., & Tversky, A. (1982). On the elicitation of preferences for alternative therapies. *The New England Journal of Medicine, 306,* 1259–1262. doi:10.1056/NEJM198205273062103

Mirani, R., & King, W. (1994). Impacts of end-user and information center characteristics on end-user computing support. *Journal of Management Information Systems, 11*(1), 141–160.

Mirel, B. (1998). Applied constructivism for user documentation. *Journal of Business and Technical Communication, 12*(1), 7–49. doi:10.1177/1050651998012001002

Mirel, B. (2003). Dynamic usability: Designing usefulness into systems for complex tasks. In Albers, M., & Mazur, B. (Eds.), *Content and complexity: Information design in software development and documentation* (pp. 233–261). Mahwah, NJ: Erlbaum.

Norman, D. A. (2002). *The design of everyday things.* New York, NY: Basic Books.

Nowaczyk, R., & James, E. (1993). Applying minimal manual principles for documentation of graphical user interfaces. *Journal of Technical Writing and Communication, 23*(4), 379–388.

O'Hara, K., & Payne, S. (1998). The effects of operator implementation cost on planfulness of problem solving and learning. *Cognitive Psychology, 35,* 34–70. doi:10.1006/cogp.1997.0676

Owen, D. (1986). Answers first, then questions. In Norman, D., & Draper, S. (Eds.), *User centered system design: New perspectives on human-computer interaction* (pp. 362–375). Mahwah, NJ: Erlbaum.

Ozok, A., & Salvendy, G. (2004). Twenty guidelines for the design of Web-based interfaces with consistent language. *Computers in Human Behavior, 20*(2), 149–161. doi:10.1016/j.chb.2003.10.012

Paradis, J., Dobrin, D., & Miller, R. (1985). Writing at Exxon ITD. In Odell, L., & Goswami, D. (Eds.), *Writing in nonacademic settings* (pp. 281–307). New York, NY: Guidford.

Parker, H., Roast, C., & Siddiqi, J. (1997). HCI and requirements engineering: Towards a framework for investigating temporal properties in interaction. *SIGCHI Bulletin, 29*(1). http://www.acm.org/sigchi/bulletin/1997.1

Payne, J., Bettman, J., & Johnson, E. (1993). *The adaptive decision maker.* Cambridge, UK: Cambridge University Press.

Payne, S. (1991). Display-based action at the user interface. *International Journal of Man-Machine Studies, 35,* 275–289. doi:10.1016/S0020-7373(05)80129-4

Pealer, L., Weiler, R., Pigg, R., Miller, D., & Dorman, S. (2001). The feasibility of a Web-based surveillance system to collect health risk behavior data from college students. *Health Education & Behavior, 28*(5), 547–559. doi:10.1177/109019810102800503

Redish, J. (1988). Reading to learn to do. *The Technical Writing Teacher, 15*(3), 223–233.

Redish, J. (2000). Readability formulas have even more limitations than Klare discusses. *ACM Journal of Computer Documentation, 24*(3), 132–137. doi:10.1145/344599.344637

Robertson, G., Card, S., & Mackinlay, J. (1993). Information visualization: Using 3D interactive animation. *Communications of the ACM, 36*(4), 57–71. doi:10.1145/255950.153577

Roscoe, S. (1968). Airborne displays for flight and navigation. *Human Factors, 10,* 321–332.

Rubens, P., & Rubens, B. (1988). Usability and format design. In Doheny-Farina, S. (Ed.), *Effective documentation: What we have learned from research* (pp. 213–234). Cambridge, MA: MIT.

Russo, J., Staelin, R., Nolan, C., Russell, G., & Metcalf, B. (1986). Nutrition information in the supermarket. *The Journal of Consumer Research, 13,* 48–70. doi:10.1086/209047

Saariluoma, P., & Kalakoski, V. (1998). Apperception and imagery in blindfold chess. *Memory (Hove, England), 6,* 67–90. doi:10.1080/741941600

Sanbonmatsu, D., Kardes, F., & Gibson, B. (1991). The role of attribute knowledge and overall evaluations in comparative judgment. *Organizational Behavior and Human Decision Processes, 48*(1), 131–146. doi:10.1016/0749-5978(91)90009-I

Sanders, M., & McCormick, E. (1993). *Human factors in engineering and design.* New York, NY: McGraw-Hill.

Scheiter, K., & Gerjets, P. (2002). The impact of problem order: Sequencing problems as a strategy for improving one's performance. In W. D. Gray & C. D. Schunn (Eds.), *Proceedings of the 24th Annual Conference of the Cognitive Science Society* (pp. 798–803). Mahwah, NJ: Erlbaum.

Shalev, V., Chodick, G., & Heymann, A. (2009). Format change of a laboratory test order form affects physician behavior. *International Journal of Medical Informatics, 78,* 639–644. doi:10.1016/j.ijmedinf.2009.04.011

Simon, H. (1979). *Models of thought.* New Haven, CT: Yale UP.

Sinclair, H. (1971). Digital versus conventional clocks: A review. *Applied Ergonomics, 2,* 178–181. doi:10.1016/0003-6870(71)90044-5

Slovic, P. (1972). From Shakespeare to Simon: Speculations—and some evidence—about man's ability to process information. *Oregon Research Institute Research Bulletin, 12,* 1–29.

Snyder, M., & Campbell, B. (1980). Testing hypotheses about other people: The role of the hypothesis. *Personality and Social Psychology Bulletin, 6,* 421–426. doi:10.1177/014616728063015

Sweller, J., Chandler, P., Tierney, P., & Cooper, M. (1990). Cognitive load as a factor in the structuring of technical material. *Journal of Experimental Psychology. General, 119,* 176–192. doi:10.1037/0096-3445.119.2.176

Tole, J., Stephens, A., Harris, R., & Ephrath, A. (1982). Visual scanning behavior and mental workload in aircraft pilots. *Aviation, Space, and Environmental Medicine, 53,* 54–61.

Tufte, E. (1983). *The visual display of quantitative information.* Cheshire, CT: Graphics Press.

Tversky, A., & Kahneman, D. (1981). The framing of decisions and the psychology of choice. *Science*, *211*, 453–458. doi:10.1126/science.7455683

Tversky, A., Slovic, P., & Kahneman, D. (1990). The causes of preference reversals. *The American Economic Review*, *80*, 204–217.

van der Meij, H., & Gellevij, M. (1998). Screen captures in software documentation. *Technical Communication*, *45*, 529–543.

van der Meij, H., & Gellevij, M. (2002). Effects of pictures, age, and experience on learning to use a computer program. *Technical Communication*, *49*(3), 330–339.

Van Nimwegen, C., Van Oostendorp, H., & Tabachneck-Schijf, H. (2005). The role of interface style in planning during problem solving. In *Proceedings of the 27th Annual Cognitive Science Conference* (pp. 2771–2776). Mahwah, NJ: Erlbaum.

Wallsten, T., & Barton, C. (1982). Processing probabilistic multidimensional information for decisions. *Journal of Experimental Psychology. Learning, Memory, and Cognition*, *8*, 361–384. doi:10.1037/0278-7393.8.5.361

Wang, H., Johnson, T., & Zhang, J. (2006). The order effect in human abductive reasoning: An empirical and computational study. *Journal of Experimental & Theoretical Artificial Intelligence*, *18*(2), 215–247. doi:10.1080/09528130600558141

Weber, B., & Chapman, G. (2005). The combined effects of risk and time on choice: Does uncertainty eliminate the immediacy effect? Does delay eliminate the certainty effect? *Organizational Behavior and Human Decision Processes*, *96*(2), 104–118. doi:10.1016/j.obhdp.2005.01.001

Wickens, C., & Carswell, C. (1995). The proximity compatibility principle: Its psychological foundations and its relevance to display design. *Human Factors*, *37*, 473–494. doi:10.1518/001872095779049408

Wickens, C., & Hollands, J. (2000). *Engineering psychology and human performance*. Upper Saddle River, NJ: Prentice Hall.

Wilson, J., & Rutherford, A. (1989). Mental models: Theory and application in human factors. *Human Factors*, *31*, 617–634.

Wong, K., & Kwong, J. (2005). Comparing two tiny giants or two huge dwarfs? Preference reversals owing to number size framing. *Organizational Behavior and Human Decision Processes*, *98*, 54–65. doi:10.1016/j.obhdp.2005.04.002

Woods, D. (1984). Visual momentum: A concept to improve the cognitive coupling of person and computer. *International Journal of Man-Machine Studies*, *21*, 229–244. doi:10.1016/S0020-7373(84)80043-7

Wright, P. (1974). The harassed decision maker: Time pressure, distractions, and the use of evidence. *The Journal of Applied Psychology*, *59*(5), 555–561. doi:10.1037/h0037186

Wyatt, J., & Wright, P. (1998). Design should help use of patients' data. *Lancet*, *352*, 1375–1378. doi:10.1016/S0140-6736(97)08306-2

Zeff, C. (1965). Comparison of conventional and digital time displays. *Ergonomics*, *8*, 339–345. doi:10.1080/00140136508930811

Zhang, J. (1996). A representational analysis of relational information displays. *Journal of Human-Computer Studies*, *45*(1), 59–74. doi:10.1006/ijhc.1996.0042

Zumbach, J., & Mohraz, M. (2008). Cognitive load in hypermedia reading comprehension: Influence of text type and linearity. *Computers in Human Behavior, 24*(3), 875–887. doi:10.1016/j.chb.2007.02.015

ADDITIONAL READING

Bennett, K., & Flacch, J. M. (2011). *Display and interface design: Subtle science, exact art*. Boca Raton, FL: CRC Press.

Card, S., Moran, T., & Newell, A. (1983). *The psychology of human-computer interaction.* Hillsdale, NJ: Erlbaum.

Hix, D., & Hartson, R. (1993). *Developing user interfaces: Ensuring usability through product and process*. New York, NY: Wiley.

Kostelnick, C., & David, D. R. (1998). *Designing visual language: Strategies for professional communicators*. Needham Heights, MA: Allyn and Bacon.

Section 3
People and Information Use

Chapter 11
How People Read

ABSTRACT

When people try to read technical information, they try to assess the relevance of information as quickly as possible. They set their own reading goals in performing this task and skip the paragraphs or sections they do not consider relevant (Janssen & Neutelings, 2001). This idea is reflected in the Web reading mantra that if a website does not grab a person immediately, they will leave. While the full truth of this mantra can be debated, the rapid reading and evaluation of information must be considered as part of designing for HII to allow people to comprehend the information.

BACKGROUND

I can't write without a reader. It's precisely like a kiss–you can't do it alone.—John Cheever

This chapter considers how people read and comprehend information. The white area in Figure 1 shows the area of the HII model relevant to this chapter. More than just reading text, people must comprehend its message for communication to occur. The underlying psychological concepts of how people read can help design teams make clear content decisions and evaluate problematic usability test results of technical information. Often the problem is not the content itself, but that the writing fails to conform to how people read and comprehend information.

The main areas covered in this chapter are:

Reading Theory: How people recognize words, how they construct mental propositions, and the construction-integration model of reading.

Comprehension: How people comprehend information and the factors which influence it, such as reading speed, coherence, and cohesion.

Coherence and Cohesion: How people form connections within a text and the text factors which either support or impede the formation of those connections.

Inferences: How people mentally integrate information to make inferences which are not explicitly contained in the text.

DOI: 10.4018/978-1-4666-0152-9.ch011

Figure 1. How people read information

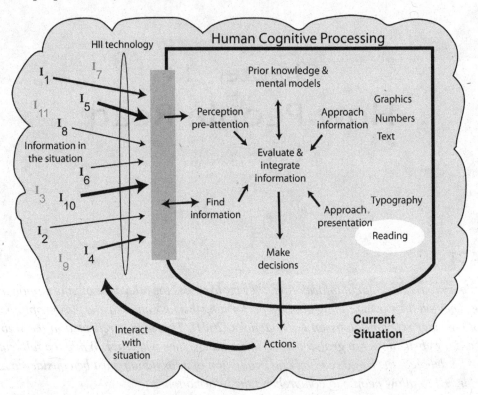

INTRODUCTION

When people read, they process information on three levels: readability, understandability, and comprehension.

Readability: Readability is how people identify and perceive individual words. It has been the focus of the majority of cognitive psychology's research into reading. But the other two levels, understandability and comprehension, carry the meaning of the information.

Understandability: Understandability is the ability to form the words into a coherent and logical sentence. In other words, the sentence makes logical sense even if it has lost its context. People may not actually know what the sentence means, but do know it is a logical English (or other language) sentence.

Comprehension: Comprehension is extracting the intended meaning from the text and being able to relate it to the world (Warren, 1993). As such, comprehension is a higher level than understandability since it requires the sentence information to be understood in a specific context and see the relationships with the information in surrounding sentences.

Current theories of text comprehension (such as Kintsch's (1988) construction-integration model discussed in this chapter) consider that comprehension is achieved through constructing a multilayered mental representation of the text (Potelle & Rouet, 2003). More specifically, a distinction is made between two levels of representation, which are called the textbase and the situation model.

Textbase: Textbase is the mental representation of the explicitly stated semantic information of the text.

The explicitly stated semantic information is derived directly from the text without applying prior knowledge. People rarely understand a text solely on the textbase, instead they need to combine it with their prior knowledge. On the other hand, people who know very little about a topic have to depend upon the textbase to provide their entire subject information. For example, Shah and Carpenter (1995) found people could redraw graph lines from memory, including the distances between the lines, but could not explain what the relationships between the lines meant within the situation. People reading about a new science discovery may only have the textbase to interpret the information. For example, people can read an article about gamma bursts, but cannot explain what gamma rays are or how they form beyond repeating the text. Likewise, people with minimal knowledge of a newly diagnosed disease reading about treatment options has nothing on which to base their decision other than the text contents.

Situation model: The situation model is a mental representation of the "state of affairs denoted in a text" (Zwaan & Singer, 2003, p. 85). It can be considered the textbase information combined with the reader's prior knowledge and past experience. It's an instantiated mental model (see chapter 3: *What people bring with them,* "Mental models.")

The situation model integrates the information provided by the text with prior knowledge, often reorganizing and restructuring it in terms of the reader's understanding of the knowledge domain as a whole rather than the particular text just read. The resulting mental representation allows for a deeper understanding of the text, which is linked to the reader's longterm memory and knowledge (Potelle & Rouet, 2003, p. 328).

Tapiero (2007) describes the situation model as the cognitive representation of the situation which the text describes. She also builds a description which describes the situation model as possessing a hierarchical tree structure which can be captured as part of the user analysis.

READING THEORY

Psychologists have proposed many different theories of how people read and what occurs in the mind as they make sense of a text. Early reading models tended to be top-down models where the mind used a set of rules to understand the text.

The "top-down" model viewed reading as following a rule-based structure that fit each new element into a whole. The problem with these top-down models is that the research findings show comprehension exists as a highly associative structure of information that does not fit a rule-based structure. Essentially, "the mind is not a well-structured, orderly system but is a little chaotic, being based on perception and experience rather than on logic, being Aristotelian rather than Cartesian" (Kintsch, 1998, p. 5). A long-term problem in artificial intelligence has been trying to develop the rules for understanding natural language, when, in fact, even fully parsing sentences, much less understanding them, fails to follow the logical, rule-based approach of a computer. Opposite to the "top-down" models are the "bottom-up" models.

The "bottom-up" model views reading as a linear process that progresses from parts to whole where the reader seeks a starting point from which to work through the content of a document. Then the reader is likely to read through the document from start to finish in a linear fashion. In general, they give little value to a reader's prior knowledge, but view reading as a process which starts with people decoding the smallest linguistic units of the text (letters to words to phrases to sentences) and building up meaning based on those units (Gough, 1972; Laberge & Samuels, 1974). Phonics methods of learning to read are one example of a bottom-up approach.

Contrary to early research on reading, we now know that we do not simply first identify words and word meanings, then combine word meanings to get the meanings of sentences, and then combine sentence meanings to get the gist of a larger text. Many of the early reading models took a computer-like view that saw people as passive decoders of symbols, regardless of whether they were top-down or bottom-up models. But reading theories have evolved to view reading as a much more complex and interactive activity. The view of reading as a decoding process leading to the passive acquisition of isolated facts and skills has been replaced with a more cognitively oriented view in which reading is an active, self-regulated meaning-construction process in which the reader interacts with text in a strategic way (Mannes & Kintsch, 1987).

When a reader reads a text, an "understanding" of the text is created in the reader's mind. The process of constructing a situation model is called the "comprehension process." Van Dijk and Kintsch (1983) claim that readers of a text build three different mental representations of the text:

- A verbatim representation of the text.
- A semantic representation that describes the meaning of the text.
- A situational representation of the situation to which the text refers.

Reading for comprehension involves maintaining semantic coherence by fitting new information into the existing mental model and knowledge structures. At one level, comprehension can be based on completing the mental model used for interpreting the text. Consider a mental model

as consisting of many empty slots, which need to be filled in order to transform it to a situation model. When people read new information, it not only must be compatible with the current mental model (incompatible information is deemed irrelevant and ignored), but it must be mentally placed into the proper slot before comprehension occurs (Nist & Mealey, 1991). Misperceptions cause wrong slots (or no slots) to exist for the information. Comprehending and learning from a text realigns the slots.

Readers merge new information with prior knowledge, or work to resolve any conflicts between new and prior knowledge (Johnson & Afflerback, 1985). Prior knowledge often takes precedence over any new information. Thus, it is important for information to challenge people's preconceived notions. This will improve both their comprehension and help to clear up any misperceptions. As an example, pamphlets for breast cancer do not explicitly challenge misconceptions women have and, thus, often fail to communicate their message (Powe et al, 2005).

Most recent work in how people read and comprehend text builds upon Kintsch's (1998) construction-integration model, which will be the model briefly described in this chapter. Current reading theories see reading and processing text as a multi-level cognitive process. Comprehension of information occurs when a reader connects the current text with prior knowledge and is able to relate it to the current situation. People constantly form inferences connecting various parts of a text together and connecting the text to prior knowledge and experiences. This skill of forming inferences, although important to reading at all levels, is actually a complex set of skills that never fully develop in many readers, leading to a wide range of reading abilities (Murray, 2003).

Because of the necessity of connecting to prior knowledge, design teams must consider the amount of and specifics of prior knowledge readers possess. Issues of how people handle conflicting information are discussed in Chapter

2: *Information in the situation*, "When all needed information is not available."

Word Recognition

Recognizing the individual words is the first step in reading. Although, obviously, understanding the words is essential to understanding a text, it is by no means the most important factor. "It is now acknowledged that understanding a source depends more on pragmatic knowledge than on the semantics of the words it contains" (Tapiero, 2007, p. 7.)

Psychology research has looked at whether people recognize words by first identifying individual letters or by identifying the entire word as a single object. How words are seen as a complete unit has undergone considerable debate and research. The overwhelming amount of evidence supports people recognizing the entire word as a single unit rather than working through the word one letter at a time (Reicher, 1969). The use of lower case letters gives each word a distinctive shape based on a pattern of the letters with ascending, descending, and neutral characters (Figure 2). Based on experience with the word, that pattern of letters becomes recognized as the word. Words in all uppercase letters (UPPER CASE) or mixed case (mIxED CaSe) letters become harder and slower to read since, rather than recognizing the

word as a unit, the mind has to parse the individual letters and mentally build up the word.

Recognition of the word as a unit, of course, depends on familiarity with a word. Unfamiliar words will be built up letter by letter, but common words get recognized as a unit. This allows people to read blurred or partially obscured words. In one study, where people were told to read for both comprehension and copyedit at the same time, errors in small words, such as *and, the*, and *for*, were detected at a much lower level than errors in more complex words (Haber & Schindler, 1981). In addition, they found the hardest errors were ones that did not change the shape of the word, such as *anl* instead of *and*. The people recognized and mentally processed the small words as a single unit, rather than using the letter-by-letter processing required for copyediting.

Current research on word recognition supports a parallel letter recognition model. This model says that the letters within a word are recognized simultaneously, and the letter information is used to recognize the words. Figure 3 shows the multiple levels of processing that occur when a word is first seen. The underlying details of the various levels and how the brain actually performs this processing is an area of current research, but operates at too low of a cognitive level to be of direct concern for HII. In Figure 3, the reader sees the word 'work'. The process of identifying the word can be considered as:

Each of the stimulus letters are processed simultaneously. The first step of processing is recognizing the features of the individual letters, such as horizontal lines, diagonal lines, and curves. These features are then sent to the letter detector level, where each of the letters in the stimulus word are recognized simultaneously. The letter level then sends activation to the word detector level. At this level, all similar words are initially considered. The W in the first letter position sends activation to all the words that have a W in the first position (WORD and WORK). The O in the second letter

Figure 2. Word shapes formed by letter patterns. The lower case letters create a unique shape for the word. Upper case letter only create rectangles. Violating case conventions creates a shape that has not been seen before, which slows up reading.

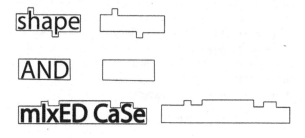

Figure 3. Parallel letter recognition model. (adapted from Larson, 2004 and Wickens & Holland, 2000)

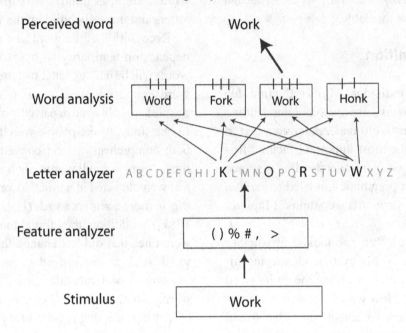

detector position sends activation to all the words that have an O in the second position (FORK, WORD, and WORK). While FORK and WORD have activation from three of the four letters, WORK has the most activation because it has all four letters activated, and is thus the recognized word. (Larson, 2004)

Propositional Representations

Each language has highly different syntax and structures. Consider how English, Italian, Arabic, and Chinese all have very different grammars and syntax structures for what makes a well-formed sentence. However, the mind does not store information in a form that corresponds to the language syntax. Instead, information is stored in the mind in the form of *propositions*, which are its semantic processing unit. Comprehension, at a very simplistic level, can be considered as translating written text into a set of propositions.

Comprehending information involves transforming a text into a set of propositions. A proposition has one predicate and one or more arguments. For example, the sentence:

The museum that contained a dinosaur overlooked a park.

parses into propositions shown in Figure 4.A. The main predicate *overlook* has two arguments (*museum* and *park*). The sentence also contains information about the museum itself, which parses into the predicate *contains* and its arguments (*museum* and *dinosaur*). If the sentence was more

Figure 4. Sentences parsed into propositions. The mind stores the sentence as a collections of propositions and not in the language syntactic form which the sentence was written.

A.
The museum that contained a dinosaur overlooked a park.

overlook [museum, park]
└───── contains [museum, dinosaur]

B.
Purplish blood tends to lack oxygen

Tend [purplish[blood], lack [purplish[blood], oxygen]]

complex (as in Figure 4.B), more propositions could be created from either museum, park, or dinosaur.

Recall studies find that using a cue word of *overlook* will typically recall *park*, rather than *dinosaur*, even though *dinosaur* and *park* are closer in the sentence structure. People tend to recall the information in propositional units and either recall the entire unit or forget it (Goetz, Anderson, & Schallert, 1981).

The propositional representation consists initially of a list of propositions that are derived from the text. After having read a complete sentence, this list of propositions is transformed into a network of propositions built up from preceding sentences. Comprehension and coherence is the result of a strongly interconnected web of propositions. Arguments appearing in one proposition are more strongly connected in memory to those appearing in other propositions. If the text is coherent, all nodes of the network connect to each other. An incoherent text has propositions which do not connect or only connect to a few other propositions.

Propositionally complex sentences impose significant problems on people's comprehension and use of the information. It takes longer to read sentences with multiple propositions (Kintsch & Keenan, 1973). Also, errors in understanding the information increase. Doubling propositions from two to four increased the error rate in instructions from 3% to 52% (Barshi, 1997). It is the number of propositions in a sentence and not the number of words which cause learning, recall, or memory problems. Sentences which contain only one proposition tend to be recalled in whole, while sentences with multiple propositions tend to be recalled in part. In the previous example with two propositions, recall might be 'a museum by a park' or 'museum with a dinosaur.'

The actual parsing of sentences into proposition form is too tedious and time consuming for design teams to perform when developing a document. However, on a smaller scale, it can help as an analysis tool when people are not understanding information. Thus, sentences which seem to be especially problematic for readers can be parsed into its propositions and potential rewrites based on simplifying that structure.

Construction-Integration Model

This section describes at a high level Kintsch's (1988) construction-integration model of text comprehension where he proposed a reading comprehension model where the concepts stated in a text and information from prior knowledge interact to produce a mental representation of the text. The model works to capture the complexity of how people actually move from reading the words on a page to comprehending the information and being able to use it to make decisions.

We comprehend a text, understand something, by building a mental model. To do so, we must form connections between things that were previously disparate: the ideas expressed in the text and relevant prior knowledge. Comprehension implies forming coherent wholes with Gestalt-like qualities out of elementary perceptual and conceptual features (Kintsch, 1998, p. 93)

Mental models, discussed in chapter 3: *What people bring with them,* "Mental models," provide a mental scaffold based on experience and prior knowledge on which people hang new information. Each new piece of information must have a place on that scaffold or it is considered as irrelevant. How that mental model gets populated and transformed into a situation model forms the basis of the construction-integration model.

The model consists of two phases: knowledge construction and knowledge integration (Wharton & Kintsch, 1991) (Figure 5).

The construction phase begins when a person first reads a text. A text is processed one chunk at a time (clause or a sentence) using a bottom-up approach, based on a set of very loose construction rules, that parses the text into its propositions. Word meaning is activated and inferences and elaborations are produced without regard for the

Figure 5. The construction-integration model (adapted from Wharton & Kintsch, 1991, p. 170)

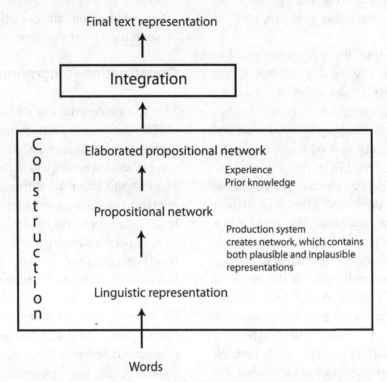

context. The initial construction of information is very crude and context-free. As a result, it contains approximations and potential solutions that contain irrelevant or redundant information which will be cleared up or rejected during the integration phase.

An interesting point here is that during the construction phrase erroneous propositions based on word meaning are formed, but will eventually be rejected. A sentence containing the word *plane* would result in retrieving the meanings of an aircraft, a hand tool, geometric object, and any other known definitions of *plane*. Likewise, any sentence containing *bug* will have propositions based on both insect and spy devices formed. The use of these loose construction rules differentiates Kintsch's model from most models, especially those used in AI research, where strong rules attempt to generate proper meaning from the beginning of text parsing.

When the construction phase ends, the mind has a network of propositions which must be integrated with prior knowledge. In the integration phase, the propositions are formed into an associative network which then undergoes multiple cycles of integration with both within the network and with prior knowledge. During this time, the associations which make sense are strengthened and those which do not decay. The cycle continues until it reaches a stabilization point where the person comprehends the sentence and connects it with the previously read text. As a trivial example, Kintsch points out that people never consider (actually he says they activate it during construction but then unconsciously reject it during integration) the idea of a chocolate mint in the sentence "The earthquake destroyed all the buildings in town except the mint." Constraints based on prior knowledge reject the potential meaning of mint as a food. Prior knowledge provides a filter through which people interpret

Table 1. Readability formulas. Calculations for three of the more common readability formulas.

Flesch-Kincaid Grade Level Most common. Number which corresponds to US school grade level.	$(.39 \times ASL) + (11.8 \times ASW) - 15.59$ ASL = average sentence length (the number of words divided by the number of sentences) ASW = average number of syllables per word (the number of syllables divided by the number of words.
Flesch reading ease Number from 0 to 100, with a higher score indicating easier reading. An average document has a score between 6-70.	$206.835 - (1.015 \times ASL) - (84.6 \times ASW)$ ASL = average sentence length (the number of words divided by the number of sentences) ASW = average number of syllables per word (the number of syllables divided by the number of words)
Gunnings's Fog Index Number which corresponds to US school grade level.	$(AWS + NW3) \times .4$ Based on a 100 word sample. ASW = average number of words per sentence NW3 = number of words of 3 syllables or more

information and controls how they comprehend text. "People understand correctly because they sort of know what is going to come." (Kintsch, 1988, p. 164)

During the integration phase, inferences develop based on the strong associations. McKoon and Ratcliff (1992) modify the previous example sentence to read "All of the buildings in the town except the mint collapsed." People still associate mint with a building, but the sentence itself does not give a reason for the collapsed buildings. However, earthquake as a potential reason will be weakly associated based on prior knowledge. Reading additional sentences strengthens the earthquake inference if they mention trembling or shaking. On the other hand, comments such as wind and rain would cause the earthquake inference to be rejected and would strengthen one for a hurricane or tornado as the cause.

At the end of the integration cycle the modified network of associations gets moved into long term memory (Kintsch & Welsch, 1991). At the same time, a small number of highly active associations remain in short term memory and become part of the next cycle. The associations left in short term memory provide the base for text coherence as they have a strong influence on how the interpretation of the information (strengthening/weakening of associations) proceeds in the new cycle.

Readability Formulas

Readability formulas provide a quick and quantitative method of judging how easy a text is to read. More than 40 readability formulas have been developed over the years (Klare, 2000); Table 1 lists the three most commonly used and describes how they are calculated.

Readability formulas are available in most of the major word processing programs. Multiple studies of healthcare material have found them consistently very difficult to read, with the text at a college level. Writing to maximum grade levels as defined by a formula has been adopted by many different organizations. Redish (2000) points out that "Insurance laws in several states define clear language as a score of 40 or 50 on the Flesch Reading Ease Scale. However, no research was ever done on the correlation between those scores and users ability to find what they need or understand what they find in insurance documents." (p. 133).

Both the Flesch Reading Ease and Flesch-Kincaid scores should use at least 200 words—a number which is typical for most readability formulas. However, those 200 words are assumed to fit a narrative format. Technical material, with its use of headings, lists, and graphics, fails to fit the basic text assumptions designed into the reading formulas.

Table 2. Low and high coherence sentences. The low cohesion sentences have a low readability score, but are harder to for inferences from. As a result, they lower comprehension.

		Flesch Reading Ease	Flesch-Kincaid Grade
low cohesion	The streets were wet. It had rained.	100	0.0
high cohesion	The streets were wet because it had rained.	100	0.8
low cohesion	One part of the cloud develops a downdraft. Rain begins to fall.	80.8	3.4
high cohesion	One part of the cloud develops a downdraft, which causes rain to fall.	83	4.9

A newer readability measurement which tries to overcome this difficulty is the Golub Syntactic Density Score (Golub & Kidder, 1974). Unlike the simplistic word or syllable counts of most formulas, this readability formula evaluates prose by descending deeply into sentence syntax, an approach which works better for technical material (Giles & Still, 2005). Other research has worked to replace simple readability formulas with analysis based on the cohesion of the text (Dufty et al., 2006; McNamara, 2007).

Readability formulas have been highly criticized as not adequately or reliably measuring the components of writing that make it easy to read or, more importantly, easy to understand. Redish and Selzer state "readability formulas are a simplistic answer to a very complex problem" (1985, p. 49). In addition, most of the readability formulas were developed for assessing reading materials for grade school children (Giles & Still, 2005). Yet, they are applied to all forms of material. There have also been arguments advanced that, while they may apply to children's material, they are not appropriate measures for texts written for adults (Stevens, Stevens, & Stevens, 1992).

A significant problem with readability formulas is that although there are many factors that affect how easy a given text is to read and understand—including sentence length, word choice, layout and formatting, overall organization of the content, and use of illustrations—most readability formulas consider only two factors: the number of syllables (or letters) in a word, and the number of words in a sentence. This poses problems since writing which strictly adheres to readability formulas often consists of short choppy sentences which impair comprehension as shown by the examples in Table 11-2. Readability formulas suffer from three other major flaws.

Measure surface characteristics: The word count and sentence length are surface characteristics of the text and do not adequately capture the text elements important for comprehension (Kintsch, Welsch, Schmalhofer & Zimny, 1990; McNamara et al., 1996). It's not the word count which affects comprehension but the number of propositions within a sentence (Barshi, 1997; Kintsch & Keenan, 1973).

Ignore reader's prior knowledge: How well people understand a text depends on their background knowledge and overall language skills rather than just knowing the words.

Ignore cohesion and coherence: The cohesion and coherence of a text has a much greater affect on how easy a text is to understand than the words themselves. (Cohesion and coherence are discussed later in the chapter.) Not surprisingly, readers have problems understanding low coherence texts (Graesser, Gernsbacher & Goldman, 2003; McNamara, 2001; McNamara & Kintsch, 1996; McNamara et al., 1996). In a contradiction to the goal of readability formulas, short choppy sentences have better readability scores, but lower coherence and are less understandable (Table 2).

COMPREHENSION

An outdated view of reading saw it as a passive process that consisted of collecting isolated facts. Kintsch's construction-integration model has replaced this passive process with an active comprehension process where the reader interacts with the text to build meaning. Text comprehension can be considered reading while trying to maintain semantic coherence—"fitting new information into existing knowledge structures" (Murray, 2003. p. 840).

Reading comprehension involves an interaction between the reader's prior knowledge and the message contained in the text. In a vague way, it can be considered how well people understand the text. Kintsch (1998) discusses how the terms *understanding* and *comprehension* are not scientifically defined terms, but are instead common sense terms with a large range of meaning in their use. Generally, they are used interchangeably. But that still leaves open the question of what is really meant when trying to determine how people understand or comprehend information and how to perform any testing to measure comprehension.

Although a basic understanding of comprehension is clear to most design teams, providing a clear definition has proven elusive.

Comprehension has traditionally been one of the elusive, controversial constructs in cognitive science (i.e., Kintsch, 1980; Winograd & Flores, 1986). It is perhaps impossible to propose a definition that is complete and that would be accepted by all researchers in all disciplines. Everyone agrees that comprehension consists of the construction of multi-level representations of texts. Everyone agrees that comprehension improves when the reader has adequate background knowledge to assimilate the text, but what else exists or occurs

when comprehension succeeds? (Graesser, Singer, & Trabass, 1994, p. 373).

An HII analysis often needs to reverse the last sentence of the above quote and ask "when comprehension fails, what prior knowledge or factors impaired the comprehension?" It must determine what needs to change. Random, arbitrary rewrites of difficult to comprehend text are a norm, with the writer not clearly understanding why it was misunderstood and, thus, being unable to know how to fix it.

Another term sometimes confused with comprehension is perception. The difference between comprehension and perception is that perception only uses inputs from the environment, while comprehension takes that perception and combines it with previous knowledge during the integration cycles (of the construction-integration model) so that it logically fits the situation. Perception only lets you know what the words or design on a page are (specific words, stars, boxes, etc.); comprehension puts them into a meaningful context and lets you know this is the weekly TV guide and lists what movies are on tonight.

Comprehension as the Interaction of Different Factors

Comprehension results from the interaction of multiple factors, all of which contribute to understanding the text. This section looks specifically at prior knowledge and reading ability.

The healthcare literature contains many studies revealing that patients cannot understand the information they are given. For example, Patel, Branch, & Arocha (2002) found that many people had trouble understanding and using the labels on over-the-counter medications: They were unable to correctly interpret the dosage amounts and time intervals for taking the drug. Excluding those with reading disabilities, readers know all of the individual words, but they still have trouble comprehending the information. Most people tend to have impoverished medical knowledge (poor prior knowledge) and the label design privileges fitting the text to the package design over creating a highly readable set of directions.

Prior knowledge, reading ability, and the text are not the only factors which affect how people comprehend a text. The medium exerts a strong, but less controllable, influence. Dillon (1992) found that speed, comprehension, and accuracy are greater on paper than on screen documents. Since his research was done in 1992, he was obviously using lower quality monitors than current computer systems. But the ongoing debate about accuracy levels online versus print editing shows that some of the differences remain.

Prior Knowledge

People's prior knowledge has a substantial affect on how well they acquire new information and how well they comprehend it (Bransford & Johnson, 1972). Readers with greater prior knowledge exhibit superior comprehension and thus enhanced learning compared to those with less prior knowledge (McNamara, 2001; McNamara & Kintsch, 1996; McNamara, Kintsch, Songer, & Kintsch, 1996). Prior knowledge provides people with a mental model with which to interpret the text. People with poor or non-existent prior knowledge must work with a very impoverished or non-existent mental model. With no mental model slots in which to place the text's information and ready-made relationships, comprehension is seriously impeded. For example, people with better baseball knowledge will remember more of a passage about baseball than people with low baseball knowledge, regardless of reading ability (Chiesi, Spilich, & Voss, 1979).

Prior knowledge helps people build the relationships between different pieces of information which are vital to comprehension by providing the knowledge to fill in gaps (Albers, 2010; McNamara, Kintsch, Songer, & Kintsch, 1996). Any text will not contain all of the information required to fully understand it; the more relevant prior knowledge the readers bring to the text, the easier time they have building the relationships. At the same time, since they can fill in the gaps, people with prior knowledge also use more effective reading strategies (O'Reilly & McNamara, 2006). Calisir, Eryazici, and Lehto (2008) looked at people reading hypertext documents with different structures. They found high knowledge people had similar comprehension regardless of presentation structure. Low knowledge people, on the other hand, performed better with a hierarchical presentation rather than a linear text. The hierarchy gave them a basic structure to use to for relationships.

Since no two people come to the text with the same experiences, design teams need to consider both the quantity and quality of prior knowledge brought to the text and how it will influence the comprehension. In general, the minor differences can be safely overlooked with the design teams focusing on various audience groups and their associated personas. But the end result will be that different people will have slightly different interpretations and comprehend the text slightly differently, an effect which arises from the variability of readers and not the psychological process of comprehending the text (Royer & Cunningham, 1981). Significant departures from the intended comprehension found during usability testing may indicate a missing persona or that the content assumed prior knowledge the readers lacked.

Reading Ability

Reading ability is a nebulous term which often ends up with a cyclic definition of how well people read. Measurement of reading ability is performed using various standard forms. Typically, the Nelson Denny adult reading comprehension test, which measures vocabulary development, reading rate, and comprehension is used.

People's reading ability have a significant effect on comprehending a text since it influences how well they can parse the sentences and build up a meaningful mental structure on which to integrate their prior knowledge. Reading ability has been shown to be a stronger predictor of text comprehension than prior knowledge (Cottrel & McNamara, 2002).

There is no doubt that better readers better comprehend text—because, of course, that is the underlying definition of reading skill. Skilled readers also tend to experience the reading process as more automatic and effortless than less skilled readers. Skilled readers tend to make reading process decisions below the level of consciousness, particularly when reading familiar material. Thus, skilled readers unconsciously, or with very little conscious effort, understand the thoughts communicated through the texts and are reminded of the knowledge they have regarding the topic covered within a text (Cottrel & McNamara, 2002, p. 244.)

Skilled readers monitor their comprehension and use active reading strategies while less skilled readers tend to read the text in a linear fashion and rarely relate various parts of a text to each other (O'Reilly & McNamara, 2006). As a result, poor readers have difficulty moving beyond a textbase understanding of a text.

Reading ability seems to be tightly connected to people's working memory, with larger working memory equating to better reading skills (McDaniel, Hines, & Guynn, 2002). People that have difficulty comprehending texts also perform poorly on tasks that tax their working memory. Working memory holds the information as it is first read and integrated into prior knowledge and information which was recently read. Poor working memory ability impairs that integration process since it impairs the ability of people to relate the current text to previous text (Palladino et al., 2001). However, this statement only tends to apply to verbal material. Text comprehension abilities do not correlate with visual-spatial tasks or simple memory tasks. Meta-analysis has revealed

a highly complex set of interrelationships between high and low ability readers and their ability to comprehend information (Carretti et al., 2009).

Design teams must consider the reading ability of their intended audiences. Consider that reading ability is a strong predictor of text comprehension, even more so than prior knowledge (Cottrel & McNamara, 2002). Recent studies found that online consumer oriented health information was often above the expected reading ability of a significant proportion of the U.S. population (Bernstam et al., 2005). Thus, governments and corporations are spending millions of dollars producing information for their consumers and customers, but may be wasting that money since those consumers and customers cannot comprehend the material.

Measuring Reading Comprehension

Comprehension can be measured to assess how well people understand either the textbase or situation model of a text. Testing for both are very different and the results from a test for one will not necessarily carry over to an analysis for the other.

Textbase measurements are the simplest to implement, but also only reveal a shallow understanding of a text. In general, they involve free recall or cued recall tests of what is remembered about a text (discussed in the next sectin). The drawback is that people may remember the words or phrases in a text (scoring high on a textbase measurement) but not understand what the words or phrases mean (comprehending the text at only a superficial level).

Situation model tests are more difficult to implement since they assume some level of shared prior knowledge. They often involve inferential reasoning, which requires people to move beyond what the text says and combine the text with prior knowledge to arrive at an answer. A difficulty here is that comprehension is independent of problem-solving skills, but inferential reasoning conflates the two (McNamara et al., 1996). Rover and Cunningham (1981) point out that if a reader and author/tester have very different backgrounds, the reader may have developed a substantially different, but consistent situation model. However, if in responding to questions which make sense in the author/tester's view, they would appear to have a very low comprehension.

People with high comprehension will give correct answers to questions but will not word their answer in similar terms to the text. On the other hand, people who remember but do not understand a concept will often repeat the text essentially verbatim. One test of deep comprehension is that people must answer in their own words, rather than repeating the text's words.

For simple reading tasks (tasks that focus on either recall or learning isolated information such as a list of words), the reading comprehension measurements of both people with poor and good comprehension are very similar. However, the differences increased as the need to integrate more and more prior knowledge increased (Carretti et al., 2009). This reveals that many comprehension tests are confounded by the need for prior knowledge to understand the text. Although for measuring people's reading ability, the interrelationship with prior knowledge is a major concern, in most HII situations, it's the overall communication of the text which is important and not a measurement of people's ability to read (Rover & Cunningham, 1981).

Studies into how people recall material divide recalls into three categories: recall of details, more general ideas, and higher order processes requiring inferences (Wagner & Sternberg, 1987). People remember what they consider to be the main concepts much better than the details and also better recall material they consider interesting (Wade, Schraw, Buxton & Hayes, 1993). In addition, depending upon the specific situation and mental model in use, people's ability to remember individual items and how they relate to other information will vary depending on how important they consider remembering the information (Einstein et al., 1990). Information they consider most salient to the situation will be remembered. If they remember unimportant information, but still seem to consider it important, design teams must ensure the text has not given undue salience to that information.

Recall and Recognition of Previously Read Material

While reading, all of the mental processing of information and connecting the new information with old information must occur in working memory. To understand a text, a reader is engaged not only in maintaining some piece of information in memory but also, for example, in merging that information with previous knowledge, therefore actively processing incoming information. Some reading studies and tests of document comprehension measure only textbase surface level detail. Textbase studies tend to focus on recognition, cued recall, or free recall.

Recognition: Recognition is to identify something, whether an object such as a bird, or text or images, and normally implies factual knowledge or identification.

Recognition depends on forming strong associations between cues and targets. The lack of the proper cue or an out of context cue can result in low recognition. Communication which depends on people recognizing information must provide the appropriate cues. The failure of some people to recognize the similarity between two situations arises from the different sets of cues and a lack of general knowledge connecting the situations.

Recognition can use a multiple choice test. It will show people can identify the information that was in the text, but does not measure understanding. Recognition tests tend to measure a surface level understanding of the text since recognizing an answer is easier than short answer; people can more easily identify an answer rather than retrieve it from memory.

Also recognition (have you seen this sentence?) and verification (is this statement true based on what you just read?) also provide a means of testing what people comprehend.

Cued recall: Cued recall is being able to remember specific information if given clues to the answer.

Cued recall uses prompts such as "tell me the four symptoms of the disease." Cued recall may also give one sentence in a text and people have to give the next one.

One problem with cued recall is that it does not reveal if people know the relationships within the information. In a test of disease symptoms, it can show that people have learned the symptoms, but does not provide a reliable measurement of whether, if presented with two of symptoms, would they be connected with the disease.

Free recall: Free recall is remembering something without specific prompting. Free recall is an important part of the reading comprehension process since it forms the basis of answering questions of the form "what happened…and then what happened?"

Free recall uses very general prompts such as "tell me what you remember about the text." There is a fine line between free recall and cued recall prompts; tests must ensure they do not inadvertently cue the reader.

Interestingly, people with a high understanding of a topic may also have relatively poor free recall of the specific information in a text. They have mentally combined the text information with their prior knowledge and give answers based on that combination. For example, regular users of a Macintosh exhibit very poor recall for menu headers and menu labels—even for those headers that are always on the screen. Yet, they have no trouble rapidly finding and interacting with those menus (Mayes *et al.*, 1988; Payne,

1991). They have learned the menus to automaticity and know where they are, but can no longer easily articulate it or draw a picture of it.

Tests of textbase comprehension can use all three types of recall since each one measures information comprehension in a different way. Comprehension tests which plan on using all three types should use them in order of free recall, cued recall, and recognition. This avoids priming the reader with earlier prompts.

Examples of the differences between the three tests are:

- *Free recall:*
  ○ What are the stops on the bus system blue route?
  ○ Explain all you can remember about the system commands.
- *Cued Recall:*
  ○ Where is the city library stop on the blue bus route?
  ○ What's the command for "delete a file from your system"?
  ○ Explain how the delete command works.
- *Recognition:*
  ○ Is Filmore Park the city library stop on the blue bus route?
  ○ Which is the command for "delete a file from your system"? (delete, erase, nuke).

Recognition, cued recall and free recall measure text recall and textbase level comprehension. Although situation model comprehension is typically correlated with recall, in many situations it is possible to have a high recall with incorrect or minimal understanding. Unfortunately, high recognition or free recall does not necessarily indicate people understand the topic. People can recognize an object or answer or memorize a response without understanding what the answer means. They know what the text contains, but does not understand what the text means or how it relates to their current situation. A basic example is a student who can answer a question by quoting the book but not examine in her own words what she just quoted or how to apply it to a problem situation. Measuring comprehension in an HII-relevant situation typically means measuring how well people have integrated the new information into their existing mental models and built a coherent picture which they can use to move forward.

While most people will say that recognition is easier than free recall, recall can be easier if it is cued. The GUI interface's major advantage over command lines comes from the visual cueing rather than requiring the user to memorize all the commands. Likewise, information architecture works to organize information and support interactions that match how people mentally encode the situation information. They can apply what they know about other sites by recalling that design and using that cued knowledge to navigate the new site.

An interesting set of research about free recall finds that the difficulty in mentally encoding the text has a significant influence on how well it is learned and remembered. Text which is either too easy or too hard will not be well learned. In the former case, people fail to process it since it seems trivial and in the latter it is not processed because the difficulty makes it impossible to connect into the current mental model (McDaniel, Hines, & Guynn, 2002; McNamara & Kintsch, 1996). In other words, some difficulty is required for effective learning and recall; the problem facing design teams is determining that level of difficulty for each audience group.

Comprehension and Reading Speed

A significant amount of reading is done at faster than normal speeds (Masson, 1982). Studies of web reading consistently find people skimming large amounts of information and only closely reading text which is considered of high interest.

The question then is how does fast reading affect comprehension.

Tinker's (1963) research in the 1930's and 1940's found that faster readers had higher comprehension. Regardless of speed, people recall general information better than specific details. On the other hand, Poulton (1958) found that text recall increased significantly when reported speed of reading decreased from about 300 words/min to about 150 words/min. The explanation for this apparent contradiction is that when people increase their reading rate, comprehension decreases. However, people who are naturally faster readers have a higher comprehension rate than naturally slower readers (Jackson & McClelland, 1979). Thus, it is not the actual reading rate which affects comprehension, but rather the increase over the natural reading speed.

In addition, reading faster increases the amount of material read, but at the expense of gaining a lower level of understanding. Studies of comprehension when people were told to skim text found that, as expected, comprehension decreased. One significant point is that as people skim, they skip information, with an equal chance of skipping both important and unimportant information (Masson, 1982). Other studies found that people can get the general gist of a text, but retain little of the detailed information (Just & Carpenter, 1980).

Reading from a computer screen has traditionally been slower, although with modern monitors that speed difference is decreasing. The often cited value of 25% slower reading was done with monochrome green text monitors. Early research also found lower comprehension (Belmore, 1985), however this is also no longer considered a serious factor (Dyson, & Haselgrove, 2001). In general, although the lower resolutions of a monitor may slow reading and affect comprehension, it seems to exert little significant effect on comprehension. A more significant factor affecting comprehension is that the online readers tend to skim, rather than read the text.

In most text of interest to HII, it is the details which matter. Thus, design teams need to consider how fast the text will be read and create designs which support acquiring the important material faster than with normal reading. Use of headings and bullet lists are two of the standard methods.

COHERENCE AND COHESION

When people read, they attempt to construct a mental representation of the text that addresses their goals and is coherent at both local and global levels (Campbell, 1994). That mental representation should explain the actions and events contained in the text and the overall situation. Clear communication of any text requires it to be both cohesive and coherent.

We know that some texts are more communicative than others. In some documents the words, phrases, and sentences fit the ideas better; the level of formality is appropriate to the audience; the groups of sentences fall together as if they were written for the readers' easy assimilation. We also know that in less communicative texts the ideas are obscured by the words or the arrangement of sentences; the language is either too formal, too informal, too technical, too general, or vacillates among these extremes; or there is no logical relationship among the sentences (Beene, 1988, p. 109).

Cohesion and coherence can be defined as:

Cohesion: The local connections in a text that are based primarily on linguistic and textual features that signal the relationships between the text's ideas. The use of connective such as and, because, or however, as well as the old/new form of sentences help to shape the cohesion level of a text. Likewise, the use of anaphoric references (references to or repetition of previous ideas) helps with cohesion. They connect the text ideas together and reduce the number of inferences people have

to make to understand the text. The lack of appropriate connectives impairs the formation inferences essential to understanding the text (Singer & O'Connell, 2003)

Coherence: The organization of local information elements into higher order chunks which shapes the text into an integrated whole and form the situation model. (Graesser, Singer, & Trabasso, 1994). Unlike cohesion, coherence is a global property of the text and may not be explicating encoded within in it (Beene, 1988) A text's coherence is an interaction between the reader's skill level, background knowledge, motivation, and the cohesion of the text which helps to form the situation model (Tapiero, 2007).

When people read a text, they try to form the most globally coherent mental representation possible. In the *coherence assumption* advanced by Graesser, Singer, and Trabasso (1994), people attempt to construct coherent meanings and connections among text constituents unless the text is very poorly composed, which causes them to quit trying to make connections. More importantly for HII, people can be assumed to make connections; the problem is that incoherent texts lead to the wrong connections, wrong situation models, and wrong decisions.

A globally coherent cognitive representation is successfully achieved when the following conditions are met: (a) the textual features support global coherence, (b) the reader has the prerequisite background knowledge, and (c) the reader does not have a specific goal that prevents understanding of the material (Graesser, Singer, & Trabasso, 1994, p. 378).

In a coherent text, people can easily see the relationships between different text elements (Zwaan & Singer, 2003) because comprehension depends on building those relationships and connecting them to the situation (Albers, 2009). Clearly, people who lack background knowledge will have trouble forming global coherence. Design teams need to ensure the audience analysis captures the expected range of prior knowledge. Also, people who strongly disagree with a text (for example, a text conflicting with their strongly held political or religious beliefs) would essentially refuse to see the text as a coherent whole.

Zwaan and Singer (2003) point out that coherence lets people track factors such as: time space, causation, and motivation. If the text violates these, it becomes harder to form into a coherent whole. Consider two sentences they used as an example:

A. Harry put the wallpaper on the table. Then he set a coffee mug on the paper.
B. Harry put the wallpaper on the wall. Then he set a coffee mug on the paper.

These two sentences linguistically parse exactly the same and only have one word different, but the second violates expectations since people know a coffee mug cannot be placed on a wall. If these sentences appeared in a longer test, comprehension and recall of the second sentence would be impaired. Eye tracking studies find people rereading sentences such as B to help resolve the logical conflict it contains.

As people read sentences they sometimes commit (or at least partially commit) to an analysis that later-arriving information reveals to be wrong. Forming a globally coherent model of a text requires constantly reevaluating the existing information with respect to what was just read. Tabor and Hutchins (2004) show reading times slow when people have to reanalyze how they parsed a sentence when the additional information sets up a clear conflict with the current interpretation. For instance, consider if the next statement in B mentions a suction cup on the coffee mug, an unexpected item, but one that explains the ability to put the mug on the wall.

Although people attempt to mentally shape a text into a globally coherent whole, if the text lacks sufficient cues, they will settle for local coherence. When this happens, people end up seeing the text as a collection of disconnected statements. Usability testing would reveal this by people having a good surface knowledge, but not being able to discuss the text ideas as a whole or not being able to relate different parts of the text to each other. Some of the difficulties people have reading healthcare information could be explained in this manner. Lacking adequate background knowledge to for a globally coherent view of the text, they form isolated locally coherent views which they are unable to connect.

As expected, research consistently finds relationships between a reader's comprehension and the coherence level of a text. However, counterintuitively, high coherence texts are not always best. Depending on prior knowledge and reading ability, they may improve textbase knowledge, but not knowledge of the situation model and inference making (Ozuru et al., 2005).

- Readers with low knowledge improve comprehension on high-cohesion texts (O'Reilly & McNamara, 2006). They require the connectives to properly parse the text since they have no prior knowledge to apply to the task.
- High knowledge readers with lower reading skills perform better on low-cohesion text, called the *reverse cohesion effect* (McNamara, 2001). The lack of connectives forces the reader to exert mental effort to understand the text, which results in better understanding.
- High knowledge readers with high reading skills perform better on high-cohesion texts. They are able to take their better reading skills and build strong inferences from a high-cohesive text.

An interesting result of recent research on coherent texts is that if a text is either too easy or too difficult, then any comprehension effects attributable to cohesion or reading ability disappear (Linderholm et al., 2000; McNamara et al 1996; Ozuru et al., 2005). If it is too easy, people begin to skim and miss information, and if it is too difficult, they simply can't mentally parse the sentences and build a coherent mental image.

DOCUMENT MACRO STRUCTURE AND READING

The document structure has a significant effect on overall comprehension of the text. The issue is severe enough that poor design and inability to mentally grasp the macrostructure shifts people's initial perception to the assumption that the information is wrong and inaccessible (Jordan, 1989).

A basic tenet of technical communication is to use headings and overviews to signal the document structure. Organization techniques such as chunking and labeling material with headings, topic sentences, and lead paragraphs help readers find the familiar knowledge and move onto any new information. The use of signaling within a text is also perceived as a more logical construction (Spyridakis & Wenger, 1992). A text activates readers' prior knowledge and mental models through the use of signals such as titles, headings, subheadings, and checklists or lists of key words or key concepts at the beginning of documents (Duin, 1989).

Headings and overviews facilitate the comprehension of texts, especially when the text is long, complex or unfamiliar. When consistent with the actual contents and organization of text, headings and overviews help the reader integrate text information into a globally coherent situation model, by facilitating thematic processes and the integration of new information with prior knowledge. (Potelle & Rouet, 2003, p. 330)

The use of organizers such as headings and textual elements which provide for global co-herence all contribute to the development of the reader's view of the text's macrostructure. Global coherence depends on forming connections among multiple paragraphs and sentences which are not adjacent to each other. Making these connections depends on more than the grammatical elements that give rise to local coherence, but also involves prior knowledge and shaping the understanding of the text so it has both an internal and external (fitting prior knowledge) consistency. Typically the information needed to develop the global coherence appears in different places within the text; people with a good textbase understanding but a poor prior knowledge fail to create a global coherence (Hayes-Roth & Thorndyke, 1979). They have trouble connecting concepts that are not sequential within the text. Prior knowledge and the proper mental model activation are essential to developing a globally coherent view of a text.

Kintsch (1989) explains that a good text macrostructure frees readers' memory capacities by providing a construct into which individual information units can be related during microprocessing. The result is a well-organized memory representation than can serve as the framework for further operations. In contrast, without a good macrostructure, readers focus primarily on local-level meanings. Thus, each new incoming fact is related only to the immediately preceding ones, and the resulting memory structure tends to be fragmented and poorly integrated (Baker, 1994, p. 457).

Kintsch was discussing printed text, but the same issues of working memory capacity apply to hypertext. Research results suggest that explicit structural information helps people become more efficient in their navigation of a hypertext document over time. Lowering the cognitive effort required to comprehend the structure of the website improved user navigation over time (Nilsson & Mayer, 2002)

Research into how people develop a document macrostructure has found many interesting, if conflicting, results.

- Loman and Mayer (1980) found that people had much better recall and comprehension of texts with an explicit structure than texts without. Likewise, Spyridakis (1989a, 1989b) found the explicit structure resulted in people developing hierarchical mental frameworks which made it easier to process unfamiliar information.
- In a study of web pages, a group either had or did not have a map of the web. The map group initially found information faster, but the no-map group soon surpassed them and also had more flexible search strategies. The no-map group had to develop their own macrostructure which took time, but then had more efficient search than the group provided one. This indicates design teams need to consider the tradeoffs between organizers that are initially useful and those which promote readers to develop their own structure (Nilsson & Mayer, 2002)
- Titles facilitate local and global representation of expository texts (Chung, 2000).
- Macrostructure signals in easy or familiar texts have minimal effect on comprehension (Spyridakis & Standal, 1987).
- Texts should contain an overview. With the overview, people recalled more information, especially information signaled as important (Lorch, Lorch, & Inman, 1993).
- People, especially those with high spatial ability, impose structure on information regardless of how unstructured it might be (Kwasnik, 1992; Witkin, 1978) and will develop a macrostructure for a text. The formation of the wrong or inefficient structure impedes communication. Nilsson and Mayer's (2002) work on how people develop macrostructures found that spatial

ability was a strong predictor in how effectively people both developed and used them.

HII requires design teams to move beyond consideration of single texts and consider how people form a macrostructure of multiple documents (an area with minimal research). When people read a web site, they are reading a collection of many texts. How well they comprehend the overall site's message depends on how they mentally structure that information.

INFERENCES

Understanding of a text comes when the reader interprets the information with the proper mental model and can use the deep structure of the text to make decisions. Within the context of that mental model, people use prior knowledge to build relationships between information elements and to make inferences to fill-in what the text does not explicitly say. Shears and Weiss (2005) describe forming inferences as "a process that draws from a reader's general knowledge to connect text ideas" (p. 195). Using prior knowledge, readers make inferences which bridge what they know and what the text says to what should come next, what should occur, or how the text is relevant to their situation. They also make inferences to build their view of the text's macrostructure which supports the development of their overall comprehension of the text.

It is usually the case that the reader must contribute information that was not stated explicitly in the text from his or her own store of knowledge about the domain in question. Furthermore, active inferencing may be required to link the text with the reader's prior knowledge. The result of such inferencing is the situation model. (Potelle & Rouet, 2003, p. 328)

Box 1.

> **Inferences about how to wash clothes**
> The following paragraph is a standard example of how people make sense of texts.
>
> *First you arrange items into different groups. Of course one pile might be sufficient depending on how much there is to do. If you have to go somewhere else due to lack of facilities, then that is the next step; otherwise you are pretty well set. It is important not to overdo things. That is, it is better to do too few things at once than too many. In the short run this may not seem important but complications can easily arise. A mistake can be expensive as well. At first the whole procedure seems complicated. Soon however, it will become just another facet of life. It is difficult to see any end to the necessity for this task in the immediate future but then one can never tell. After the procedure is completed, one arranges the material into different groups again. Then they can be put into their appropriate places. Eventually they will be used once more and the whole cycle will have to be repeated. However, that is part of life (Bransford & Johnson, 1972, p. 722).*
>
> Readers cannot form inferences since the text fails to activate a relevant mental model and lacks clues to a text macrostructure. When given a title of "Washing clothes," each of the sentences makes sense and the reader can build both inferences and a macrostructure. Of course, a title of "Doing taxes" also allows people to create a coherent macrostructure for this paragraph, although the last few sentences are incompatible for doing taxes. Design teams must ensure the text leads readers to the proper interpretation.

Consider the inferences required to answer the question in this example. The text never states the report was burned, but a reader will make an inference that it was.

1. The spy tossed the report in the fire. The ashes floated up the chimney.
2. The spy tossed the report in the fire. Then he called the airline.
Q: Did the spy burn the report? First line is answered faster (Zwaan & Singer, 2003).

Much of the work on inferences has used narrative, since narratives typically do not require special background knowledge to understand. A reader can easily relate to a novel's main characters and infer the reasons for their actions. However, in most HII contexts, the text is expository rather than narrative. With expository texts, readers may lack the background knowledge to easily form inferences, yet they are essential for comprehension. In general, most of the ideas about drawing inferences apply regardless of text type.

When making inferences, people prefer to move from more general to less general (deductive inference) rather than from less general to more general (inductive inference) (Collister & Tversky, 2005), a finding that reiterates the writing guideline of moving from general to specific. It also supports the writing guide of moving from given to new information (Clark & Haviland, 1977). In addition, in explanatory text, readers expect the sentences to contain some level of causal connectiveness and use that connectiveness to build inferences. The absence of appropriate connectives reduces the formation of inferences critical to comprehending a text (Singer & O'Connell, 2003).

Graesser, Singer, and Trabass (1994) discuss how reader's form inferences based on three assumptions:

Reader Goal Assumptions: Information gets interpreted and inferences are based on the goals a reader wants to achieve. In general, these are the deep-level goals of the text and how it relates to the reader's situation. Readers with goals engage in more and deeper inference making and have higher recall (van den Broek, Lorch, Linderholm, & Gustafson, 2001).

Coherence Assumptions: Readers try to build a mental image of the text that is coherent at both local and global levels with appropriate macrostructures to support their goals.

Explanation Assumptions: As readers build a coherent mental image, they try to explain the text contents in a meaningful way. One purpose of metaphor and analogy is to help support this assumption.

Along with these three assumptions, Graesser, Singer, and Trabass also point out that people abandon any attempt at forming inferences if they find the text incoherent, lack proper background knowledge, or lack a need to deeply understand the text. To draw correct inferences requires the reader to have some knowledge relevant to the text's content and context. Without that knowledge, people mentally process the text as a set of disjointed, isolated information elements and they often do not see how those information elements relate to each other (Einstein et al., 1990), a substantial problem with much information relevant to HII (consider the layperson reading science or health material). Without domain knowledge, they cannot generate the inferences required to mentally interpret the text without the text or other source providing assistance (Noordman, Vonk, & Kempff, 1992; Potelle & Rouet, 2003). A patient who trusts the surgeon and who doesn't really care about the details of an upcoming surgery will not form inferences when reading any required pre-operative material because they lack background knowledge and don't feel a need to understand it. On the other hand, people who want to understand the surgery will struggle with the text and form inferences. Of course, depending on their background knowledge, those inferences may or may not be correct. In these cases, they can have good textbase knowledge (they may be able to quote sections of the text), but cannot comprehend the full text or connect it to their situation. One study found that when searching for information on the Internet, people ignored relevant information because they lacked the knowledge to correctly identify relevant information written using a slightly different terminology (Pollock & Hockley, 1997).

The time people are given to read a text can have a substantial impact on their ability to make inferences. People were presented with information one sentence at time with a delay between sentences. Increasing the delay also increased the number of inferences formed (Calvo et al, 1999). Interestingly, changing the presentation rate of the words within individual sentences had no effect on understanding the sentence. In typical reading behavior, people pause after each sentence and the duration of that pause has a strong correlation with how well they comprehend the text. Skimming text suppresses between-sentence pauses and reduces comprehension.

Much of the prior knowledge needed to interpret the text come from domain knowledge, reinforcing the need for design teams to clearly understand the audience and audience knowledge levels. When the audience lacks the knowledge to make inferences, then the text must supply low-level details to the reader. Design teams can use the concept of building inferences to develop texts which properly match the readers' knowledge level. When developing expository text—the normal text for HII—design teams face significant challenges since the reader's knowledge level are much lower than for narrative text. Best et al. (2005) show that high school science textbooks fail on many levels. The texts have a low cohesion factor which requires students to make many inferences to comprehend them; yet, students lack both the prior knowledge and the reading strategies to make those essential inferences.

Inferences in Expository Text

When people read expository text, comprehension depends on them making inferences that elaborate on the text and connect it with their broader goals. In general, this will only happen if they have the required background knowledge or specific reading goals which cause people to work hard to understand the text (Noordman, Vonk, & Kempf, 1992; Wiley & Myers, 2003).

There has been some contradictory research on inferences in expository text. Noordman, Vonk, and Kempf (1992) found people did not form inferences in science texts, except when they were explicitly encouraged. On the other hand, other research has found people do form inferences in science texts (Millis & Graesser, 1994; Singer & Gagnon, 1999). An explanation for this difference is that Noordman, Vonk, and Kempf's texts were much more difficult than the texts used by other researchers. Although people will form inferences, with low background knowledge their ability is tenuous and even one or two extraneous sentences or filler information can break the flow and prevent inference formation (Wiley & Myers, 2003). The quality of the inferences and the ability of people to detect inconsistencies in the text depend strongly on the closeness of the information in the text. Inferences in narrative, on the other hand, can be made with gaps across several paragraphs. Likewise, when the information needed to support an inference appear in two different places, people with a good textbase understanding but a poor deeper text comprehension fail to connect the ideas (Hayes-Roth & Thorndyke, 1979).

In the end, it seems that people will try to form inferences if they can; design teams need to ensure the text content and presentation matches the reader's prior knowledge, reading ability, and information needs. Both too much and too little material will have strong negative effects on how people draw inferences and their subsequent comprehension of the text.

EXAMPLES

Astronomical Information

Cohesion and coherence are related and are essentially a textual version of visual momentum. The cohesion and coherence of a text are two topics stressed in writing courses, but the overall focus of those courses tend to make students focus on sentence level writing. As such, people learn to construct good sentences, but are less capable at putting those sentences together into longer paragraphs and sections. However, for a person to read information and fully comprehend it requires that all of the sentences and paragraphs exhibit a high level of cohesion and coherence. Achieving this requires the design teams to have a good technical editor who can edit each text for the factors leading to cohesion and coherence.

The goal of a text is not to have a person memorize its phrases, but to be able to connect it with prior knowledge (or build the base knowledge) and be able to draw inferences from it. A coherent text allows a reader to build a much better understanding of the text and, thus, more easily draw inferences.

Business Report Analysis

The overall structure of a document with the use of headings and lists contributes to how easily people can read it. A document needs meaningful headings which make sense in the context of the document rather than generic ones which can be used for any report. A person should be able skim the table of contents of a document and get an idea of the contents based on the headings. In Table 3, the first column has generic headings that could be used in many reports. As a result, the reader does not know what content will appear under it within the context of the current report. The second column lists meaningful headings for the same report. The heading also helps to activate

Table 3. Meaningful headings

Generic headings	Meaningful headings
Introduction	Introduction of the Problem
Authorization	Authorization for expansion into California
Purpose	Explanation of need to increase production
Sources	Sources for potential revenue increases
Locations	Regional locations to minimize transportation costs

the proper mental model so the person interprets the information properly.

Meaningful headings also support refinding information since it makes it easier for people to judge if they should skim that section. Use of bullet lists also makes refinding information easier since they isolate the important points, rather than burying them within a paragraph.

SUMMARY

When people read, they process information on three levels:

- *Readability.* How people identify and perceive individual words
- *Understandability.* Ability to form the words into a coherent and logical sentence.
- *Comprehension.* Ability to extract the intended meaning from the text and relate it to the world.

During reading they build up two different mental presentations of the text.

Textbase: Textbase is the mental representation of the explicitly stated semantic information of the text.

Situation model: The situation model is a mental representation information and relationships within the text. It is formed form the textbase combined with the reader's prior knowledge and past experience.

Reading Theory

Many different theories consider how people read and what occurs in the mind as they make sense of a text. Early reading models tended to be top-down models where the mind used a set of rules to understand the text. Newer research has invalidated the assumptions of those models since people do not simply first identify words and word meanings, then combine word meanings to get the meanings of sentences, and then combine sentence meanings to understand a text. Current eading theories view reading as a much more complex and interactive activity. Reading for comprehension requires building and maintaining a semantic coherence by fitting new information into the existing mental model and knowledge structures. Kintsch's (1988) construction-integration model of text comprehension is the currently accepted model. He proposed a that understanding requires mentally building a model of all the possible propositions of the concepts stated in a text that were then integrated with prior knowledge to produce a coherent understanding.

Comprehension

Text comprehension can be considered reading while trying to maintain semantic coherence. Kintsch's construction-integration model has replaced older passive processes with an active comprehension process where the reader interacts with the text to build meaning. Reading comprehension involves an interaction between the reader's prior knowledge and the message contained in the text.

People's reading ability has a significant effect on comprehending a text since it influences how well they can parse the sentences and build up a meaningful mental structure on which to integrate their prior knowledge. Reading ability has been shown to be a stronger predictor of text comprehension than prior knowledge.

People's prior knowledge has a substantial affect on how well they acquire new information and how well they comprehend it since it helps people build the relationships between different pieces of information which are vital to comprehension by providing the knowledge to fill in gaps. Readers with greater prior knowledge exhibit superior comprehension and thus enhanced learning compared to those with less prior knowledge.

Coherence and Cohesion

When people read, they attempt to construct a mental representation of the text that addresses their goals and is coherent at both local and global levels.

Cohesion: The local connections in a text that are based primarily on linguistic and textual features that signal the relationships between the text's ideas.

Coherence: The organization of local information elements into higher order chunks which shapes the text into an integrated whole and form the situation model.

In a coherent text, people can easily see the relationships between different text elements. Design teams need to ensure the audience analysis captures the expected range of reading ability and prior knowledge.

Inferences

Comprehension of a text comes when readers interpret information with the proper mental model and can use the deep structure of the text to make decisions. Within the context of that mental model, people make inferences to fill-in what a text does not explicitly say. To draw correct inferences requires the reader to have some knowledge relevant to the text's content and context. Without that knowledge, people mentally process the text as a set of disjoint, isolated information elements and they often do not see how those information elements relate to each other. When making inferences, people prefer to move from more general to less general (deductive inference) rather than from less general to more general (inductive inference).

Text coherence strongly affect forming inferences since people abandon any attempt at forming inferences if they find the text incoherent, lack proper background knowledge, or lack a need to deeply understand the text.

REFERENCES

Albers, M. (2010). Usability and information relationships: Considering content relationships when testing complex information. In Albers, M., & Still, B. (Eds.), *Usability of complex Information Systems: Evaluation of user interaction* (pp. 109–131). Boca Raton, FL: CRC Press. doi:10.1201/EBK1439828946-9

Baker, H., Uus, K., Bamford, J., & Marteau, T. (2004). Increasing knowledge about a screening test: preliminary evaluation of a structured, chart-based, screener presentation. *Patient Education and Counseling, 52,* 55–59. doi:10.1016/S0738-3991(02)00249-5

Barshi, I. (1997). *Effect of message length in ATC communication: Linguistic and cognitive aspects.* Paper presented at the Ninth International Symposium on Aviation Psychology, Columbus, OH.

Beene, L. (1988). How can technical writing be made more cohesive and coherent? In Beene, L., & White, P. (Eds.), *Solving problems in technical writing* (pp. 108–129). New York, NY: Oxford UP.

Belmore, S. (1985). Reading computer-presented text. *Bulletin of the Psychonomic Society, 23,* 12–14.

Bernstam, E., Sagaram, S., Walji, M., Johnson, C., & Meric-Bernstam, F. (2005). Usability of quality measures for online health information: Can commonly used technical quality criteria be reliably assessed? *International Journal of Medical Informatics, 74,* 675–683. doi:10.1016/j. ijmedinf.2005.02.002

Best, R., Rowe, M., Ozuru, Y., & McNamara, D. (2005). Deep-level comprehension of science texts: The role of the reader and the text. *Topics in Language Disorders*, *25*, 65–83. doi:10.1097/00011363-200501000-00007

Bransford, J., & Johnson, M. (1972). Contextual prerequisites for understanding: Some investigations of comprehension and recall. *Journal of Verbal Learning and Verbal Behavior*, *11*, 717–726. doi:10.1016/S0022-5371(72)80006-9

Calisir, F., Eryazici, M., & Lehto, M. (2008). The effects of text structure and prior knowledge of the learner on computer-based learning. *Computers in Human Behavior*, *24*, 439–450. doi:10.1016/j.chb.2007.01.032

Calvo, M., Castillo, M., & Estevez, A. (1999). On-line predictive inferences in reading: Processing time during versus after the priming context. *Memory & Cognition*, *27*, 834–843. doi:10.3758/BF03198536

Campbell, K. (1994). *Coherence, continuity, and cohesion*. Mahwah, NJ: Erlbaum.

Carretti, B., Borella, E., Cornoldi, C., & De Beni, R. (2009). Role of working memory in explaining the performance of individuals with specific reading comprehension difficulties: A meta-analysis. *Learning and Individual Differences*, *19*, 246–251. doi:10.1016/j.lindif.2008.10.002

Chiesi, H., Spilich, G., & Voss, J. (1979). Acquisition of domain-related information in relation to high and low domain knowledge. *Journal of Verbal Learning and Verbal Behavior*, *18*, 257–273. doi:10.1016/S0022-5371(79)90146-4

Chung, J. (2000). Signals and reading comprehension. Theory and practice. *System*, *28*, 247–259. doi:10.1016/S0346-251X(00)00010-5

Clark, H., & Haviland, S. (1977). Comprehension and the given-new contract. In Freedle, R. (Ed.), *Discourse production and comprehension* (pp. 1–40). Norwood, NJ: Ablex.

Collister, D., & Tversky, B. (2005). *Nonanalytic inference*. Retrieved April 24, 2010, from http://www-psych.stanford.edu/~bt/concepts_categories/papers/cogscidc01.doc.pdf

Cottrell, K., & McNamara, D. (2002). Cognitive precursors to science comprehension. In W. D. Gray & C. D. Schunn (Eds.), *Proceedings of the Twenty-fourth Annual Meeting of the Cognitive Science Society* (pp. 244–249). Mawah, NJ: Erlbaum.

Dillon, A. (1992). Reading from paper versus screens: A critical review of the empirical literature. *Ergonomics*, *35*, 1297–1326. doi:10.1080/00140139208967394

Dufty, D., Graesser, A., Louwerse, M., & McNamara, D. (2006). Is it just readability, or does cohesion play a role? In R. Sun & N. Miyake (Eds.), *Proceedings of the 28th Annual Conference of the Cognitive Science Society* (p. 1251). Mahwah, NJ: Erlbaum.

Duin, A. (1989). Factors that influence how readers learn from test: Guidelines for structuring technical documents. *Technical Communication*, *36*(2), 97–101.

Dyson, M., & Haselgrove, M. (2001). The influence of reading speed and line length on the effectiveness of reading from screen. *International Journal of Human-Computer Studies*, *54*, 585–612. doi:10.1006/ijhc.2001.0458

Einstein, G., McDaniel, M., Owen, P., & Cote, N. (1990). Encoding and recall of texts: The importance of material appropriate processing. *Journal of Memory and Language*, *29*, 566–581. doi:10.1016/0749-596X(90)90052-2

Giles, T., & Still, B. (2005). A syntactic approach to readability. *Journal of Technical Writing and Communication, 35*(1), 47–70. doi:10.2190/PHUC-GY8L-JRLE-VMNN

Goetz, E., Anderson, R., & Schallert, D. (1981). The representation of sentences in memory. *Journal of Verbal Learning and Verbal Behavior, 20,* 369–385. doi:10.1016/S0022-5371(81)90506-5

Golub, L., & Kidder, C. (1974). Syntactic density and the computer. *Elementary English, 51,* 1128–1131.

Gough, P. (1972). One second of reading. In Kavanagh, J. F., & Mattingley, I. G. (Eds.), *Language by ear and by eye* (pp. 331–358). Cambridge, MA: MIT Press.

Graesser, A., Gernsbacher, M., & Goldman, S. (2003). *Handbook of discourse processes.* Mahwah, NJ: Erlbaum.

Graesser, A. C., Singer, M., & Trabasso, T. (1994). Constructing inferences during narrative text comprehension. *Psychological Review, 101,* 371–395. doi:10.1037/0033-295X.101.3.371

Haber, R., & Schindler, R. (1981). Errors in proofreading: Evidence of syntactic control of letter processing? *Journal of Experimental Psychology. Human Perception and Performance, 7,* 573–579. doi:10.1037/0096-1523.7.3.573

Hayes-Roth, B., & Thorndyke, P. (1979). Integration of knowledge from text. *Journal of Verbal Learning and Verbal Behavior, 18,* 91–108. doi:10.1016/S0022-5371(79)90594-2

Jackson, M., & McClelland, J. (1979). Processing determinants of reading speed. *Journal of Experimental Psychology. General, 108,* 151–181. doi:10.1037/0096-3445.108.2.151

Janssen, D., & Neutelings, R. (2001). *Reading and writing public documents.* Amsterdam, The Netherlands: John Benjamins.

Johnson, P., & Afflerback, P. (1985). The process of constructing mean ideas from text. *Cognition and Instruction, 2*(3&4), 207–232. doi:10.1080/07370008.1985.9648917

Jordan, M. (1989). Beyond impression: Evaluating causal connections. In Fearing, B., & Sparrow, K. (Eds.), *Technical writing: Theory and practice* (pp. 102–114). New York, NY: MLA.

Just, M. A., & Carpenter, P. A. (1980). A theory of reading: From eye fixations to comprehension. *Psychological Review, 87,* 329–354. doi:10.1037/0033-295X.87.4.329

Kintsch, W. (1980). Learning from text, levels of comprehension, or: Why anyone would read a story anyway. *Poetics, 9,* 87–98. doi:10.1016/0304-422X(80)90013-3

Kintsch, W. (1988). The role of knowledge in discourse comprehension: A construction-integration model. *Psychological Review, 95,* 163–182. doi:10.1037/0033-295X.95.2.163

Kintsch, W. (1998). *Comprehension: A paradigm for cognition.* New York, NY: Cambridge University Press.

Kintsch, W., & Keenan, J. (1973). Reading rate and retention as a function of the number of propositions in the base structure of sentences. *Cognitive Psychology, 5,* 257–274. doi:10.1016/0010-0285(73)90036-4

Kintsch, W., & Welsch, D. (1991). The construction–integration model: A framework for studying memory for text. In Hockley, W. E., & Lewandowsky, S. (Eds.), *Relating theory and data: Essays on human memory in honor to Bennet B. Murdock* (pp. 367–385). Hillsdale, NJ: Erlbaum.

Klare, G. (2000). The measurement of readability: Useful information for communicators. *ACM Journal of Computer Documentation, 24*(3), 107–121. doi:10.1145/344599.344630

Kwasnik, B. (1992). A descriptive study of the functional components of browsing. In J. Larson & C. Unger (Eds.), *Engineering for Human-Computer Interaction: Proceedings of the IFIP TC2/WG2.7 Working Conference on Engineering for Human-Computer Interaction*, Ellivuori, Finland, 10–14 August 1992 (pp. 191–203). Amsterdam, The Netherlands: North-Holland.

Laberge, D., & Samuels, S. (1974). Towards a theory of automatic information processing in reading. *Cognitive Psychology*, *6*, 293–323. doi:10.1016/0010-0285(74)90015-2

Larson, K. (2004). *The science of word recognition*. Retrieved May 28, 2009, from http://www.microsoft.com/typography/ctfonts/WordRecognition.aspx

Linderholm, T., Everson, M. G., van den Broek, P., Mischinski, M., Crittenden, A., & Samuels, J. (2000). Effects of causal text revisions on more- and less-skilled readers' comprehension of easy and difficult texts. *Cognition and Instruction*, *18*, 525–556. doi:10.1207/S1532690XCI1804_4

Loman, N., & Mayer, R. (1980). Signaling techniques that increase the readability of expository prose. *Journal of Educational Psychology*, *75*(3), 402–412. doi:10.1037/0022-0663.75.3.402

Mannes, S., & Kintsch, W. (1987). Knowledge organization and text organization. *Cognition and Instruction*, *4*(2), 91–115. doi:10.1207/s1532690xci0402_2

Masson, M. (1982). Cognitive processes in skimming stories. *Journal of Experimental Psychology. Learning, Memory, and Cognition*, *8*, 400–417. doi:10.1037/0278-7393.8.5.400

Mayes, J., Draper, S., McGregor, A., & Oatley, K. (1988). Information flow in a user interface: The effect of experience and context on the recall of MacWrite screens. In Jones, D. M., & Winder, R. (Eds.), *People and Computers IV* (pp. 275–289). New York, NY: Cambridge University Press.

McDaniel, M., Hines, R., & Guynn, M. (2002). When text difficulty benefits less-skilled readers. *Journal of Memory and Language*, *46*, 544–561. doi:10.1006/jmla.2001.2819

McKoon, G., & Ratcliff, R. (1992). Inference during reading. *Psychological Review*, *99*(3), 440–466. doi:10.1037/0033-295X.99.3.440

McNamara, D. (2001). Reading both high and low coherence texts: Effects of text sequence and prior knowledge. *Canadian Journal of Experimental Psychology*, *55*, 51–62. doi:10.1037/h0087352

McNamara, D. (2007). (Ed.), *Reading comprehension strategies: Theories, interventions, and technologies*. Mahwah, NJ: Erlbaum.

McNamara, D., Kintsch, E., Songer, N., & Kintsch, W. (1996). Are good texts always better? Interactions of text coherence, background knowledge, and levels of understanding in learning from text. *Cognition and Instruction*, *14*, 1–43. doi:10.1207/s1532690xci1401_1

McNamara, D., & Kintsch, W. (1996). Learning from text: Effects of prior knowledge and text coherence. *Discourse Processes*, *22*, 247–287. doi:10.1080/01638539609544975

Millis, K., & Graesser, A. (1994). The time-course of constructing knowledge-based inferences for scientific texts. *Journal of Memory and Language*, *33*(5), 583–599. doi:10.1006/jmla.1994.1028

Murray, T. (2003). Applying text comprehension and active reading principles to adaptive hyperbooks. *Proceedings of Cognitive Science*, July, 2003, Boston, MA, (pp. 840–845).

Nilsson, R., & Mayer, R. (2002). The effects of graphic organizers giving cues to the structure of a hypertext document on users' navigation strategies and performance. *International Journal of Human-Computer Studies*, *57*, 1–26. doi:10.1006/ijhc.2002.1011

Nist, S., & Mealey, D. (1991). Teacher-directed comprehension strategies. In Flippo, R., & Caverly, D. (Eds.), *Teaching reading and study strategies at the college level*. Newark, DE: International Reading Association.

Noordman, L., Vonk, W., & Kempff, H. (1992). Causal inferences during the reading of expository texts. *Journal of Memory and Language, 31*, 573–590. doi:10.1016/0749-596X(92)90029-W

O'Reilly, T., & McNamara, D. (2006). Reversing the reverse cohesion effect: Good texts can be better for strategic, high-knowledge readers. *Discourse Processes, 43*, 121–152.

Ozuru, Y., Best, R., & McNamara, D. (2004). Contribution of reading skill to learning from expository texts. In K. Forbus, D. Gentner & T. Regier (Eds.), *Proceedings of the 26th Annual Cognitive Science Society* (pp. 1071–1076). Mahwah, NJ: Erlbaum.

Palladino, P., Cornoldi, C., De Beni, R., & Pazzaglia, F. (2001). Working memory and updating processes in reading comprehension. *Memory & Cognition, 29*(2), 344–354. doi:10.3758/BF03194929

Patel, V., Branch, T., & Arocha, J. (2002). Errors in interpreting quantities as procedures: The case of pharmaceutical labels. *International Journal of Medical Informatics, 65*, 193–211. doi:10.1016/S1386-5056(02)00045-X

Payne, S. (1991). Display-based action at the user interface. *International Journal of Man-Machine Studies, 35*, 275–289. doi:10.1016/S0020-7373(05)80129-4

Pollock, A., & Hockley, A. (1997). What's wrong with Internet searching? *D-Lib Magazine, 3*(3). Retrieved from http://www.dlib.org/dlib/march97/bt/03pollock.html doi:10.1045/march97-pollock

Potelle, H., & Rouet, J. (2003). Effects of content representation and readers' prior knowledge on the comprehension of hypertext. *International Journal of Human-Computer Studies, 58*(3), 327–345. doi:10.1016/S1071-5819(03)00016-8

Poulton, E. (1958). Time for reading and memory. *The British Journal of Psychology, 49*, 230–245. doi:10.1111/j.2044-8295.1958.tb00661.x

Powe, B., Daniels, E., Finnie, R., & Thompson, A. (2005). Perceptions about breast cancer among African American women: Do selected educational materials challenge them? *Patient Education and Counseling, 56*, 197–204. doi:10.1016/j.pec.2004.02.009

Redish, J. (2000). Readability formulas have even more limitations than Klare discusses. *ACM Journal of Computer Documentation, 24*(3), 132–137. doi:10.1145/344599.344637

Redish, J. C., & Selzer, J. (1985). The place of readability formulas in technical communication. *Technical Communication, 32*(4), 46–52.

Reicher, G. (1969). Perceptual recognition as a function of meaningfulness of stimulus material. *Journal of Experimental Psychology, 81*, 275–280. doi:10.1037/h0027768

Royer, J. M., & Cunningham, D. J. (1981). On the theory and measurement of reading comprehension. *Contemporary Educational Psychology, 6*, 187–216. doi:10.1016/0361-476X(81)90001-1

Shah, P., & Carpenter, P. (1995). Conceptual limitations in comprehending line graphs. *Journal of Experimental Psychology. General, 124*, 43–61. doi:10.1037/0096-3445.124.1.43

Shears, C., & Weiss, E. (2005). Inference vs control sentences: Are readers able to detect our intended differences? *Brain and Cognition, 57*, 195–197. doi:10.1016/j.bandc.2004.08.044

Singer, M., & O'Connell, G. (2003). Robust inference processes in expository text comprehension. *The European Journal of Cognitive Psychology, 15*, 607–631. doi:10.1080/095414400340000079

Spyradakis, J. (1989a). Signaling effects: A review of the research—Part I. *Journal of Technical Writing and Communication, 19*(3), 227–240.

Spyradakis, J. (1989b). Signaling effects: Increased content retention and new answers—Part II. *Journal of Technical Writing and Communication, 19*(4), 395–415.

Spyridakis, J., & Wenger, M. (1992). Writing for human performance: Relating reading research to document design. *Technical Communication, 39*(2), 202–215.

Stevens, K., Stevens, K., & Stevens, W. (1992). Measuring the readability of business writing: The Cloze procedure versus readability formulas. *Journal of Business Communication, 29*(4), 367–382. doi:10.1177/0021943692029004044

Tabor, W., & Hutchins, S. (2004). Evidence for self-organized sentence processing: Digging-in effects. *Journal of Experimental Psychology. Learning, Memory, and Cognition, 30*(2), 431–450. doi:10.1037/0278-7393.30.2.431

Tapiero, I. (2007). *Situation models and levels of coherence*. Mahwah, NJ: Erlbaum.

Tinker, M. (1963). *Legibility of print*. Ames, IA: Iowa State University Press.

van den Broek, P., Lorch, R., Linderholm, T., & Gustafson, M. (2001). The effects of readers' goals on inference generation and memory for texts. *Memory & Cognition, 29*(8), 1081–1087. doi:10.3758/BF03206376

Van Dijk, T., & Kintsch, W. (1983). *Strategies of discourse comprehension*. New York, NY: Academic Press.

Wade, S., Schraw, G., Buxton, W., & Hayes, M. (1993). Seduction of the strategic reader: Effects of interest on strategies and recall. *Reading Research Quarterly, 28*, 93–111. doi:10.2307/747885

Wagner, R., & Sternberg, R. (1987). Executive control in reading comprehension. In Britton, B. K., & Glynn, S. M. (Eds.), *Executive control processes in reading* (pp. 1–21). Hillsdale, NJ: Erlbaum.

Warren, T. (1993). Three approaches to reader analysis. *Technical Communication, 40*(1), 81–87.

Wharton, C., & Kintsch, W. (1991). An overview of construction-integration model: A theory of comprehension as a foundation for a new cognitive architecture. *ACM SIGART Bulletin, 2*(4), 169–173. doi:10.1145/122344.122379

Wickens, C., & Hollands, J. (2000). *Engineering psychology and human performance*. Upper Saddle River, NJ: Prentice Hall.

Wiley, J., & Myers, J. (2003). Availability and accessibility of information and causal inferences from scientific text. *Discourse Processes, 36*(2), 109–129. doi:10.1207/S15326950DP3602_2

Winograd, T., & Flores, F. (1986). *Understanding computers and cognition: A new foundation for design*. Norwood, NJ: Ablex.

Witkin, H. (1978). *Cognitive styles in personal and cultural adaptation*. Washington, DC: Clark UP.

Zwaan, R., & Singer, M. (2003). Text comprehension. In Graesser, A., Gernsbacher, M., & Goldman, S. (Eds.), *Handbook of discourse processes* (pp. 83–121). Mahwah, NJ: Erlbaum.

ADDITIONAL READING

Kintsch, W. (1998). *Comprehension: A paradigm for cognition*. New York, NY: Cambridge University Press.

McNamara, D. (Ed.). (2007). *Reading comprehension strategies: Theories, interventions, and technologies*. Mahwah, NJ: Erlbaum.

Winograd, T., & Flores, F. (1986). *Understanding computers and cognition: A new foundation for design*. Norwood, NJ: Ablex.

Zwaan, R., & Singer, M. (2003). Text comprehension. In Graesser, A., Gernsbacher, M., & Goldman, S. (Eds.), *Handbook of discourse processes* (pp. 83–121). Mahwah, NJ: Erlbaum.

Chapter 12
How People Approach
Finding Information

ABSTRACT

This chapter does not address the topics typically covered in articles on searching for Web information, such as search engine optimization or how to develop an information architecture (IA). At best it could only touch on those topics, and many more sources give better coverage. Instead, it considers the cognitive processes of how people go about searching for information, which is at the root of any effective IA. It considers the forces which drive people to search for information and what mental processes are involved as they evaluate search results as they work toward a stopping point. For an extensive review article on information search research, see Hsieh-Yee (2001).

BACKGROUND

He who would search for pearls must dive below.
—*John Dryden*

Rein, McDue, and Slein (1997) emphasize that the "reader is first a seeker of information. The search process identifies and locates relevant documents. The reader then uses document content for some purpose" (p. 85). The information search process of any text, whether printed page or web site, can be viewed as HII which combines visual perception of the information presentation, the processes of mentally manipulating the information in working memory and long-term memory, and the decision-making processes of defining relevant information and interpreting it with respect to the situation (Wickens, 1992).

Any information search could be considered as follows. People examine the various information elements on the page (Figure 1). There is a visual search coupled with the mental filtering discussed in Chapter 6: *How people perform a first glance evaluation*. If some information is relevant or interesting, it is read. If that information fits within their goals and information needs, it is mentally integrated into the current situation model. If they cannot find relevant or interesting information, a new search path is chosen. This process repeats until they are satisfied with the amount of information gathered. As part of an iterative search, a mental image of the overall

DOI: 10.4018/978-1-4666-0152-9.ch012

Figure 1. HII model – Approaching finding information

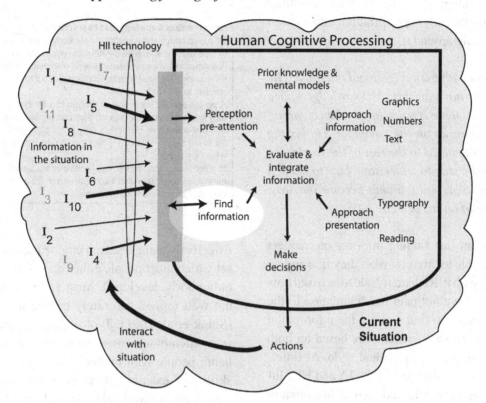

search space is built up which feeds back into mentally tracking the location of information and choosing new or modified search paths (Zhang & Salvendy, 2001).

It is easy for a design team to consider searching or browsing as an end to itself, but searching or browsing are only the first steps toward obtaining the information required to address the current goal. High quality HII means people must find the information, but they also must then be able to interpret it and use it. Simply ensuring people have the information in hand does not fulfill a design team's mandate or the user's goals.

This chapter looks at:

Models of how people search: Reviews the models that researchers have developed of how people search for information.

Factors of successful searches: Describes how people search information and how their goals directly influence the search strategies they use and the success or failure of those strategies.

Finding relevance information: Describes how people evaluate and assess the relevance of found information.

Searching graphical images: Considers the factors that are different in searching for information in graphical images from searching for information in text.

INTRODUCTION

The Web contains a vast amount of information relevant to a specific task or goal as well as a vast amount of irrelevant or downright wrong/ fraudulent information about a specific task or goal. Finding and interpreting this information requires working within a complex search environment. In many ways, for the web, searching is becoming the only way of finding information and navigating around it.

Search is becoming a navigational interface. The way we use to navigate this vast knowledge, space that exists out there is much larger than anything we could jump up on the computer. This is the computer connected to the rest of the world. We need to find a way to understand how to make a sense of all that, and searches become our way. (The future of online search, 2005).

More than just finding information, readers have to be able to interpret what they find and do something with it. Richards (2000) discussed how researchers have not paid much attention to the needs of people to find and use the information in a variety of ways, which vary based on both the situation and the individual style. At times, it seems a substantial part of the IA and HCI literature takes an unbalanced view of information with too much focus on effectively and efficiently finding it (supporting only the search process) and not enough on supporting interpretation once it is found. Yet, these issues strongly influence the ability of people to find information. The HII concerns of searching for information permeate the entire communication process since people constantly engage in multiple searches at some level as they read texts. High quality HII requires both presenting the information to people, helping them interpret it, and to integrate it into their situation model. For example, when they look back for clarifying information, when they work to refind information in previously read text, and when they compare information across multiple documents.

People constantly use the Web to search for information. Yet, in contrast to this high frequency of use, people possess a relatively low mastery of the metacognitive skills required to effectively and efficiently search the Web (Lazonder & Rouet, 2008). Web search is a highly complex operation.

Box 1.

> **Search means knowing what to search for**
> Effective search requires that people know what keywords to type into the search box. Although sounds like an obvious statement, a major difficulty with many sites is that the terminology for what people need is unknown to the person or specific to the site's company.
> A person needs a lag screw, so they go to a hardware store. If they know the term "lag screw" they can go directly to the section that sells them. But if they only know they need to a screw for wood, they will have a difficult time figuring out exactly what they need.
> In a hardware store, people can browse or ask a clerk. With most websites, if they don't know to search for a lag screw, they may never find what they need.

Effectively using a search engine requires a skill set which most people either don't have or have only poorly developed. Most search queries are not well formed and rarely exceed three words (Spink et al, 2001). Typically, terms are added in an attempt to narrow the results. On the other hand, people with higher metacognitive search skills will examine the existing terms to see if any of them should also be replaced. Consider how Zeng et al (2004) found people searched for information about MRIs by typing in "MRI" as the sole search term and, consequently, were unable to find information fitting their goal. People assume the answer to any question is "I'll just type it into Google," but it seems they are less successful at finding answers than they realize.

Healthcare information search has received a high focus in the research literature. Consistently, the results reflect the findings of Arora et al. (2008) who found that when people searched for cancer information, they found the results confusing and frustrating. More interesting, is the conflict found by Zeng et al (2004): people search for health information and hold a positive view toward it, but a high percentage of their searches are not successful. Likewise, Khan and Locatis (1998) found that experienced high school students could prioritize search tasks better than novices, but their searches were not necessarily more successful or more accurate.

To help ensure people are able to search information, design teams need to consider the preparation and presentation of information that matches the information which needs to be extracted and the methods people will use to retrieve the information (Proctor et al., 2002). Thus, an important element of HII is understanding how people search for information and to ensure both that they can find the information and that it is presented appropriately. Presentation has been covered in earlier chapters, now this chapter covers how people search for information.

Searching for information on a computer is not a trivial task. The search engine companies try to make it seem like they have a silver bullet to people's needs. Just type in text and all the sources magically appear on the screen. Of course, there are many problems with the list of search results that appear:

- The lists are long and people only tend to look at the first couple of screens.
- Poor use of keywords in the search query and simple keyword matching by the search engines produce many false hits. A search for "mustang" finds cars, horses, basketball teams, etc.
- It is hard for people to separate the good information from the questionable or bad. And some relevant information is completely missed. People often assess the value based on the quantity available rather than its quality (Shenton & Dixon, 2004a)
- It is hard for people to know that the information is sufficient for their needs. Information overload results as people try to process too much information, too detailed information, or irrelevant information.
- It assumes people know what to search for and how to interpret the information. In many instances when the search is for more than a simple answer, this is a questionable assumption. For instance, Stoop,

van't Riet, and Berg (2004) note people want online health information and most people have looked up health information. However, people lack the knowledge to make a diagnosis; they need a medical practitioner to tell them their problem, so they can look for information. And a text written in medical terminology is inaccessible to most people, even if it does contain exactly the information they need.

- None of the search results support letting people compare and integrate information elements, which is one of the most common web search tasks (Nielsen, 2001). When the information need moves beyond a simple answer, people need to be able to compare, contrast, and evaluate multiple sources.

Savolainen and Kari (2004) found that people look for information in order of preference, which they divided into three information horizons. The quality of information and ease of access were the major factors which influence the choice of zone. In Figure 2, zone 1 uses 31% human sources and 29% Internet or other networked sources. In zone 2, human sources were 28% followed by print media at 24%. In zone 3, the range of broadcast and print media dominated. Their work is in partial agreement with Sonnenwald and Wildemuth, (2001) who looked at students' information sources for course work, which placed the Internet first and faculty second. In both cases, people seem willing to seek information from other people. More importantly, they both show that either Web-based or print material is not viewed as the only source of information and that people draw on familiar information sources. The use of people as an information source is especially important to consider in the workplace, where people are available and often are known to have the desired information. Generally, people find it faster and easier to ask someone else rather than do the information search themselves (Penrose & Seiford, 1988). Many

Figure 2. Information source horizons. People search for information in zone 1 first and work their way outward. (Savolainen & Kari, 2004, p. 409). Reprinted from Library & Information Science Research, 26, "Placing the Internet in information source horizons," 415–433, 2004, with permission from Elsevier.

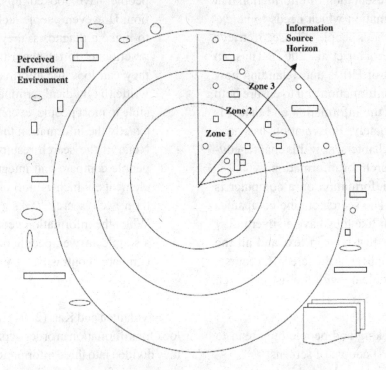

search articles seem to combine home and work searching, but they have very different information resources available. Likewise, design teams must not fall into the trap of considering their technological solution of providing information as the only source. People will use any and all sources based on the ease of obtaining the information.

MODELS OF HOW PEOPLE SEARCH

There have been many different models developed for how people seek information. Two different models are described here; other models are very similar. In general, the basic path described by the models is similar, with the major differences being how they define the stages. Rouet (2003) has a good literature review of cognitive models and task constraints which are applicable to searching for information.

Marchionini (1995) developed an eight-phase model of information seeking:

- Recognize and accept an information problem
- Define and understand the problem
- Choose a search system
- Formulate a query
- Execute search
- Examine results
- Extract information
- Reflect/iterate/stop

In contrast to Marchionini's eight-phase model, Shneiderman et al. (1998) proposed a four-phase framework for text search that can apply to the analysis of information retrieval tasks on the web:

- Formulation
- Action

- Review of results
- Refinement

Both models reflect the same basic pattern, although they describe them in a different number of steps. The first four steps of Marchionini's model correspond to the first step in Shneiderman et al.'s model. Design teams can use the models to their advantage since the various stages, especially a detailed model such as Marchionini's, gives solid checkpoints from which to examine the design. The choice of model for design teams to use depends on how people look for information, the detail level required, the stage of the search process, and people's thought processes with respect to the situation.

Both of the models start with phases where people search for and interpret information, before moving on to using that information to make decisions. Kim and Lee (2002), in a study of e-commerce systems, found those early phases

in the search process were the most important for a successful search.

While both models are given in a linear form, the information search process does not proceed linearly, but should be regarded as an iterative process (Figure 3) with people jumping between steps. People rarely find all of the desired information at once, instead they use an iterative process to build a full picture. People define a goal, select an information category, extract information and integrate it into previous information. This repeats until they are satisfied that the information is sufficient for their goal (Guthrie, 1988; Dreher, 1992; Armbruster & Armstrong, 1993). Instead of following the steps in a model exactly, people are adaptive in how they seek information (Payne et al. 1993). They mix the order and switch between phases frequently as new information presents itself or as a goal gets modified (Navarro-Prieto Scaife, & Rogers, 1999). Each new text brings in new information which must be integrated and

Figure 3. Iterative looping in the search process. The actual search process operates with constant backtracking, rather the clear linear process of most models. People find information which they believe fits with their goals and information needs. When they evaluate and integrate the information, it can either satisfy their need or be wrong/incomplete which requires looping back to obtain more information.

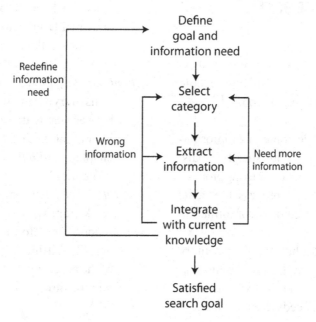

which changes the understanding of the situation. As a result, people have to reformulate the queries or reexamine previous results.

Within an iterative model, people search for information until they are satisfied. When a consistent pattern of no new information emerges, people stop looking as the cost-benefit of the search effort has crossed a threshold. With poor design, this threshold can be reached long before people obtain the needed information.

A significant shortcoming of these models is that although they explain how people search, they don't provide the design team with a basis for guidance in either how to help people succeed or evaluate why they failed in the search.

Rouet and Tricot (1996) developed a cognitive model that included factors such as the degree of precision of people's objective (vague vs. precise), how well they extracted unique points of information, and their experience. Rather than seeing searching for information as a simple "seek and find" operation, design teams must considers searching as an activity strongly influenced by text comprehension and decision-making, the main concepts of HII as presented in this book.

FACTORS OF SUCCESSFUL SEARCH

A model developed by Song and Salvendy (2003) addresses the cognitive aspects of how people interact with information on the Web.

Goals and Context: People come to an information-seeking situation with specific goals, which drive the information-seeking process. Of course, during that process the goals may be modified based on the information which is found.

Memory: Memory includes both working memory and long-term memory. Because the information processing capacity of working memory is limited, a design needs to ensure a maxi-

mum amount of cognitive resources can be focused on searching for and interpreting information rather than on navigating within the information space. Thus, design teams need to ensure navigational elements are designed in the ways that minimize the cognitive load they impose on people (Ketamo, Kiili & Haaparanta, 2003).

People have a very hard time searching for information, often working very close to information overload. They often don't know where to find the desired information—if it even exists—and are easily fatigued during the search. Often, rather than wanting new information, simply want to verify a decision they already have made. Even in the best case, when people generally knows the basic contents of all the documents (for instance, an executive reviewing a set of monthly reports), the task of mentally coordinating and relating the information contained within a large information space increases at a highly nonlinear rate with respect to the number of reports (Carlson, Wenger, & Sullivan, 1993; Mirel, 1998). In the end, searching for information has three major areas of difficulty: knowing where to look, information overload, and unavailable information (Kwasitsu, 2001). Of course, all three of these are interrelated with extensive overlap.

Attention: Attention covers the human limitations of trying to divide cognitive resources between navigation, searching, reading, and interacting with the overall situation. (see chapter 3: *What people bring with them,* "Attention")

Mental Model: Mental models provide the framework from which to build up the situation model. The information which people read gets filtered through the mental model as part of the process of determining if it is relevant and for fitting it into existing information.

There are multiple factors which must mesh for people to successfully find the information they need. These depend on both the users and the characteristics of the information space as defined by the design team. Obviously, if any of these factors are sub-optimal, then finding the required information takes longer and people risk missing critical information.

Problem Frame: A problem needs to be mentally framed in a way that lends itself to solving with the available information.

A potential issue with how people frame a problem is that they will change the problem to fit information presentation (Johnson, Payne, & Bettman, 1988). Rather than searching for information to fit their situation, they mentally redefine the situation to fit the information available. This is another way of saying that people change their work habits to fit the system and accept whatever it gives them. As a result, they may ignore information or may take action without proper support.

Strategy Selection: Strategy adopted to find the information. McEneaney (2001) found that the orienting strategy people adopt when faced with a complex cognitive task that required hypertext navigation was the most predictive factor for their success or failure.

Information Architecture: Arrangement of the information across the information space. The importance of having an effective IA which matches people's information needs cannot be overemphasized. For example, a common complaint of many corporate web sites is that they match the corporate organizational hierarchy rather than how customers mentally organize the information. As a result, people are forced to guess how their information needs map onto the corporate structure as the first step in finding information.

Many IA design failures are not a failure of developing the categories or even of having a navigation scheme that fits those categories. Instead, the IA fails because it fails to fit how the people look for information. The developed information categories may make sense in some situations—and often fit how the information is logically/physically related—but to the primary audience, they are the wrong categories. Or more precisely, people want information related with respect to the situation. Different situations may require different categories to effectively address them.

People interact with an IA, not with the global view of the design team, but with a narrow localized view. They navigate locally via multiple small steps driven by the contextual relevance of the information to their situation (Alvarado, Jeevan, Ackerman, & Karger, 2003). The design team's view includes the entire forest from a bird's eye perspective while people only see the area on the path before them.

These three factors lead into three factors that affect how people can interact with the information.

Knowing Where to Look: In any search, people must have an idea of how to get started. When people decide they need to find information, they must have a reasonable idea of where to look and how to look for it. When people select the wrong category on a web site, they don't know where to look and, consequently, probably will not find what they are looking for. Likewise, entering the wrong keywords into a search box is essentially the same as selecting the wrong category. A common help desk complaint is people calling with problems and questions that are documented; the problem may be the system organization prevents people from finding those answers.

Information Overload: Finding information is mentally taxing and working memory puts a limitation on information search performance (Zhang & Salvendy, 2001). Ackoff (1967) suggests that managers typically suffer from a shortage of decision-relevant information and a simultaneous overabundance of irrelevant information. To prevent information overload, the information must be filtered (Bowie, 1996). During a search, large amounts of information get evaluated and either integrated into the current situation model or rejected as irrelevant. More interestingly, it seems as if people have a hard time anticipating the interrelation of different information and how it will affect their situation (Fennema & Kleinmuntz, 1995).

Unavailable Information: At times people are looking for information which doesn't exist within the information space. Also, if they don't know where to look, they might conclude the information is unavailable. (Reflected in the user experience mantra of "if the user can't find it, it's not in the system.") Either way, they have to make a decision about whether to continue searching with a different strategy or stop. Lacking knowledge about whether or not the desired information exists makes making the continue/stop decision difficult.

McGovern (2010) claims that 70% of the people he watched started a search task by clicking on a link while only 30% started with the search box. His results fit well with Spool's (1997) results that although people are quick to use search facilities, they are 50% better at finding information when they use links. In related research, McEneaney (2001) found that, rather than a link versus browse issue, it's the strategy which people adopt when faced with a complex cognitive search task that is the most predictive factor of search success. People who were more aggressive at the search,

rather than taking a page-turning approach, had more success.

Search Strategies

The information search literature breaks down the type of searching people do, typically based on how they interact with the system. The search classifications pre-date web search (Canter, Rivers, & Storrs, 1985), but they have changed little in the web-based search literature.

The classification of search strategies tends to fall into six categories, with other models having more or fewer categories, depending on how the authors draw their dividing lines.

Searching: Searching is characterized by people trying to reach a defined goal. They are reading information to locate highly specific information and move on quickly if it does not meet their needs. Of the strategies, searching is the most systematic and has the most logical sequence of screens. Searching normally starts with looking for matches to specific words within the text.

Work-related information needs tend to be addressed by searching. People are highly knowledgeable in the subject, know what they are looking for, and have a good idea how to find it.

Note that this search definition is more constrained than simply defining search as using a search box on a web page. Even after searching for and finding an information source, people may browse within it to determine if it contains the desired information (Song & Salvendy, 2003). The length of the found text determines how people browse it, whether or not they read, skim, or just look at the headings. Any of these search strategies can be done using a web search box. The distinguishing factor is how people interact with the information, not how they obtain it.

Browsing: Browsing involves moving through the text to find the information of interest. Browsing is characterized by linear information access. People tend to read most of the material in a linear way, although text may still be skimmed and blocks of text skipped. Browsing tends to be used when they do not really understand what information is available or what information they need. It's not unlike clothes shopping where people keeps looking at racks until something catches their eye.

Scanning: Scanning is characterized by people trying to see a large amount of information but at a shallow level. It often occurs when people are trying to get a feel for what information is available. Retention of any specific information will be low.

Exploring: Exploring involves following many different paths through the information. When exploring people are seeking the extent and nature of the information available rather than looking for specific information.

Wandering: Wandering normally can be interpreted as a lack of a search strategy; instead, people visit a lot of pages with short visit times. Web surfing with no real goal would be classified as a wandering. People are not seeking specific information and have no real goal (Lawless & Kulikowich, 1998). From a usability test standpoint, if the environment is very familiar people may act like a wanderer, but are actually rapidly integrating information and jumping around to fill-in very specific information gaps (Ketamo, Kiili & Haaparanta, 2003).

Structured: Structured search strategy tries to offload the work to the computer. People expect to be led through a series of choices to help narrow the focus. As such, it relates more to the design and use of wizards, decision trees, or teaching scenarios; none of these will be directly addressed in this chapter.

Qiu (1993) found that the types of search tasks influenced the search strategies. The general task led to browsing, while a specific task led to search. For example, when asked to familiarize themselves with a site, people tend to browse using links and if asked specific questions, they will use a search box.

Active or Passive Search Strategies

People tend to approach information seeking using one of two approaches: active or passive engagement. Whether people adopt an active or a passive search strategy tends to depend upon individual personality (McEneaney, 2001).

Active: An active search strategy involves strongly interacting with the text and evaluating its meaning. In general, readers using an active strategy are more effective and adapt a more strategic approach to text. Mirel Feinberg, and Allmendinger's (1991) work on designing manuals for active learning styles reflects the needs of people actively seeking information.

An active information-seeking style correlates with higher levels of education and younger age. For healthcare information, the percentage of patients who reported they sought information passively increased with age (Eheman et al., 2009)

Passive: A passive search strategy requires little effort on the part of the reader, but also may not be relevant to the search task. In general, with a passive approach, people show little critical engagement with a text. Whatever the text provides is accepted without analyzing its relevance to the current situation. People using a wandering search tend to take a passive approach, as do people interacting with text written above their reading/comprehension level.

Mental Images of the Search Space

People bring their mental model to the search task, and the extent of that model depends on where they are in the search and information-gathering process. Good mental representations of the overall information space and having a clear understanding of the current situation problem space is very important when dealing with complex or open-ended questions because they lack a clear stopping point (Rouet, 2003). Factors such as prior knowledge and desired level of knowledge influencing when the stopping point occurs (Albers, 2004) all depend strongly on how people visualize the information space. The mental image contains both the structure and expected information which people expect to find.

When people search for information, their searches tend to break into two categories: "known-item search" and "subject search." Most research on finding information in paper documents or on the Web tends to be a variation on one of these two (Kim, 2001).

Known item: People have a good idea about the specific information that is desired. This can range from needing a specific value for setting a computer parameter to looking up prices of a specific camera to finding the details about a healthcare issue or a dance recital. But, in general, people recognize the information once it is found. Known-item searches often involve refinding information since this makes people more confident they are searching in the proper location.

Subject search: People generally know what information they want, but do not clearly know what they are looking for. In addition, the exact information they want will probably change as the search progresses and they learn more about the situation. A review of point & shoot cameras would be a subject search. The person knows the type of camera, but not the specific model or even the

features. A sufficient answer to the search has to be built up as part of the search.

Working memory and visualization ability play important roles in the information search process (Stanney & Salvendy, 1995). Spatial visualization ability (SVA) is important for searching which depends on hierarchical structures. People with low SVA take longer to complete tasks and have more errors as they attempt to find information (Downing, Moore, & Brown, 2005). As such, audience analysis methods may need to include determining visualization abilities. Design teams need to adjust for how effectively the audience groups can visualize the information space. A difficult task since different groups for the same information can have varying SVA ability.

Designs that display the web site structure can help people (especially those with poor SVA) to mentally visualize the site and mentally organize the information. The design helps shift the work from a mental image to a physical image (Zhang & Salvendy, 2001). On the other hand, it is possible to make the task of navigation too easy. A study that provided either a site map or no site map, found the map group did not spend time integrating the structure information while moving through the website. As a result, they never really formed a mental image of the site, and search performance did not improve over time. The no-map group had to build a clear site mental image to effectively navigate. When given a complex search task, the no map group had much better performance and used better search strategies (Nilsson & Mayer, 2002). Frequency of information access and how the site will be used are important elements in HII design.

Experience and Search Approach

It seems most people search the Internet in the same way, regardless of search experience or age group (Slone, 2003). Experience levels, even at the level of novices and experts, showed little difference in the search strategy for Internet information. Even when search style was broken down by type: goal-driven, data-driven, or opportunistic, experts and novices showed little difference in how they searched (Brand-Gurwel, Wopereis, & Vermetten, 2005). However, design teams seem unable to predict the search strategies of that the users would employ (Chevalier & Kicka, 2006).

The relationships of background knowledge and search strategies, as well as some of the differences between experienced and novice searchers, emphasize that usability tests need to carefully consider what they are testing. Although the search strategy is similar, people with more experience tend to be more analytical in their search (Campagnoni & Ehrlich, 1989) and are more successful (Barrick & Spilker, 2003; Hsieh-Yee, 1993). Experts use much more efficient search methods, such as: using multiple search terms, editing their search query, using multiple windows, and using the 'Find' functionality of the web browser (Aula & Käki, 2003).

Delays in the Search Process

The page load and system response times consistently appear as a major factor impeding the HII; slow system responses lead to frustration. Slow response during Internet search causes stress responses, such as elevated heart rates. Interestingly, this stress response remains constant across experience levels (Trimmel, Meixner-Pendleton, & Haring, 2003). Nielsen (2010b) points out that speeds of less than 1 second don't break people's trains of thought and they will accept delays of up to 10 seconds. Over 10 seconds and the interaction is compromised. Other researchers found delay times of around 8 seconds defining the line of "too slow" (Dennis & Taylor, 2006).

Nielsen sees the problem as people abandoning a website, but for many information searchers, especially on corporate sites, people must continue to use the site because it is the only source of information. When this happens, people's search

behavior changes. With fast response, they are likely to follow many links and quickly look at and reject pages. With slower response, however, people examine the information more closely. As long as the response time remained within the acceptable area, total pages views remained the same. With longer response times, as would be expected, total page views decrease (Dennis & Taylor, 2006).

An unconscious factor in picking a browsing strategy is minimizing effort and maximizing accuracy. With fast response times, there is minimal effort cost to viewing many pages, but as the response time increases, the effort becomes greater. However, people are poor judges of anticipated effort (Fennema & Kleinmuntz, 1995) and, depending on experience with the information set, they have minimal basis for judging the expected accuracy of the information. Thus, although people tend to look at fewer pages in a slow system, they don't do a good job of estimating how many they should look at.

In transitioning from one information source to another, the information forager incurs costs. Like its wildlife counterpart, the information forager will tend to engage in "within-patch" foraging until some point where the perceived benefits of foraging in a new patch outweighs the cost of moving between patches. In our case, the delay increased the costs of moving between information patches (Web pages). As a result, decision makers engaged in higher levels of within-patch (i.e., within-page) foraging resulting in a higher average number data points examined per page. (Dennis & Taylor, 2006, p. 819)

Goals and Information Needs Influencing Search

People situation goals and information needs guide the entire search process. Depending on the situation goals, people will have various levels of motivation and will use different search strategies (Slone, 2002). Research into the various search strategies people use to find information has found:

- Most people have problems with specifying search terms, judging search results, judging quality of both source and information, and regulating their search process (Walraven, Brand-gruwel, & Boshuizen, 2008)
- Search queries rarely exceed one or two words. Yet, the goals which people could clearly state were much more complex. It seems they couldn't easily translate their goals into search terms.
- People often have only vague ideas of the relevant query terms and, thus, must use an iterative process (Chli & Wilde, 2006). On the other hand, they often replace all of the search terms with new ones rather than using an iterative approach of only replacing some search terms.
- People navigate an information space more efficiently when its organization matches their cognitive model (Roske-Hofstrand & Paap, 1986). Thus, people who use shallow, hierarchical search strategies that match the IA are more successful in their search, than those who adopt a more linear path (McEneaney, 2001). In addition, people using a shallow search strategy made use of the structure of the information space through repeated use the high level navigation elements.
- In long, repetitive search tasks, such as thesis writing or healthcare, people change their search tactics and query term choices as they develop expertise and complete their mental model of the topic (Vakkari, 2001).
- Experienced searchers tend to limit the depth of their search before returning to a known point, while novice searchers

moved through more layers. As a results, novices frequently would get lost and were forced to return to the home page and restart the search (Kim, 2001).

- People often search using their established strategies. Even if the task demands the use of different multiple information resources, people remain reluctant to move beyond basic keyword searches, even when it fails to uncover adequate information. New methods for discovering and selecting information are adopted only when immediately relevant to the task at hand (Warwick et al, 2009).
- There is not a strong correlation between background knowledge and search strategy with respect to either time or accuracy (Rouet, 2003). However, experienced searchers can prioritize search tasks better than novices, although their searches are not necessarily more successful (Khan & Locatis, 1998).
- The relevance ratings displayed by search engines are ignored (Spink & Xu, 2000).
- People use the most accessible information sources first. Ease of access overrides searching for information in less accessible but known higher quality sources (Shenton & Dixon, 2004a). The ranked order for using a source of information is: accessibility, availability, technical quality, and relevance (Kwasitsu, 2001).
- Although almost every search engine and database tool provides for Boolean operations, very few people understand or use them (Shenton & Dixon, 2004a). A potential conflict occurs when the design team, which does understand Boolean search, considers it a major element in the design's search strategy.

Misses and False Alarms

When searching for information instead of correctly finding the desired information, people may either:

- Not find the information (a miss). In this case, people may waste time continuing to search until they find it or may stop searching, thinking the information does not exist. In many search situations, they do not know whether or not the information exists, so they are inclined to quit searching.
- May find the wrong information but believe it is correct (false alarm). In this case, tpeople risk making a decision based on incorrect information or wasting time determining that the information is incorrect. A potential problem is that many people lack the prior knowledge to determine the incorrectness of the information, so they will use it as part of their problem-solving process.

Most of the research into misses and false alarms focuses on detecting elements, such as with a military radar operator noticing a new contact and classifying it as a threat (see Wickens & Hollands (2000) for a detailed explanation). This type of miss or false alarm is not of much interest for HII, but the issue of missed information or misinterpretation does still exist. As shown in Table 1, only one of the four quadrants (upper left) contain useful information. The lower right also contains a good, but in this case, it may mean the person didn't notice irrelevant information. Although the person will not have to contend with irrelevant information, there are still the interactions issues of why it wasn't noticed.

Searching through large data tables provides a good example of misses or false alarms. The reader is presented with a large table of numbers (perhaps several pages) and must deal with long rows. Poor design could cause a miss or false

Table 1. Found and false alarms of finding information

	Found	Missed
Relevant information	Good	Miss
Irrelevant information	False alarm	Good

Box 2.

> **False alarms in medical tests**
> False positives can have profound effects. In the current debates on frequency and age to begin mammograms, the potential of false positives enters into the discussion.
>
> *Women need to be clear about their chance of developing breast cancer, how much mammography reduces that chance and what are its associated harms. Imagine 10,000 women age 40. Over the next 10 years, without mammogram screening, about 35 will die of breast cancer. With screening, 30 will die — five fewer. But of 10,000 getting screened, 600 to 2,000 will have at least one false positive leading to a biopsy, and 10 to 50 will be overdiagnosed. They will be told they have cancer, and they will undergo surgery, chemotherapy or radiation, which can only hurt them since their cancer was never destined to cause symptoms or death (Schwartz, 2010, p. 32).*
>
> A significant HII problem is that most non-medical people have trouble understanding both the statistics and the false positive issue. They see the test as an absolute yes/no value and they react and make decisions accordingly. As a result, they can make a good treatment decision based on the information they have, but are, in fact, making a bad treatment decision since they do not have cancer (Pauker & Pauker, 1999).

alarm by leading the reader to shift a row up or down as they move across the table. It could also cause problems if small fonts and similar cell contents make each cell look almost identical. Likewise, the formatting on a webpage can lead people to miss information. Long blocks of text are hard to skim, as opposed to design features such as short paragraphs or bullet lists.

Information salience plays a major factor in misses or false alarms. If poor design directs people to less important information, there is a false alarm risk as they incorrectly interpret the situation. The important information must be clear enough so they do not overlook it (miss), while not being so overpowering that other important information is ignored (false alarm). Giving one set of information too much salience can cause a miss of other relevant information. It could also cause partial or irrelevant information to dominate and thus activates the wrong mental model, causing people to misinterpret the information and make the wrong decisions. False alarms would be caused by focusing on some information and ignoring other information which would disconfirm the assumption. Misplaced high salience can cause false alarms by focusing the reader on irrelevant information or by providing inadvertent connections between relevant and irrelevant information. In either case, improper information salience causes people to mentally process irrelevant information.

FINDING RELEVANT INFORMATION

When people search for relevant information, at a simplistic level, they only need to find information to fill their information need. However, they also have the problem of needing to know what information is available and what information they really need to understand the situation.

Searching to Fill Information Gaps

The reason people search for information is to fill in information gaps between what they currently know about the situation and what they feel they should know. At times, it seems like some discussions on search see it as an end in itself, but information seeking and problem solving are goal directed (Newell & Simon, 1972) which means that success depends on both correctly identifying the problem and finding the proper information to address it.

Many designs seem focused on communicating *all* of the information about a topic. Such a design seems to arise from one of two underlying assumptions: (1) the design team has no idea what the readers will want, so everything is provided

without regard for context, or (2) the reader may want everything, so it is provided. Both cases lead to information overload and large amounts of irrelevant information. Although it may not necessarily be irrelevant information for everyone, it is not relevant for the situation faced by the current readers.

The underlying problem with trying to provide all possible information is that people rarely try to find everything. Instead, they continue searching for information until they acquire "sufficient information" about their understanding of the situation; in Simon's terms they "suffice" (Klein, 1999; Simon, 1979). In reaching what is considered sufficient, people mentally integrate the available information and the information relationships and evaluate how it corresponds to meeting their goals and information needs. Unfortunately for the design team, the definition of sufficient depends on the situation and user goals. Personas have developed as a standard method of trying to capture the different audience groups different information needs.

The search for sufficient information involves mentally balancing the trade-off between the time to find/analyze information and the amount of information available (Orasanu & Connolly, 1993). People know more information exists, what they do not know is how much, how high of quality, and how relevant. They lack an answer to the question "Is it worthwhile to find more information?" Lacking a clear answer, people quit searching when they feel they have enough to make a decision. The problem is that the feeling of sufficient information is often not grounded in reality since people doesn't know what they are missing. In addition, they may experience anchoring, exposure and order biases while searching for information, and these biases may influence the quality of decision making during and after the use of information retrieval systems. Prior beliefs (anchoring bias) exert a significant impact on post-search answers.

Another issue which can hinder information search is that searching for information takes effort. Both the physical acts of interacting with the computer or paper and mentally processing the text to integrate it into the current situation model are cognitively high-load actions. In general, people try to minimize the effort they put into searching for information. So, if they already posses some knowledge, they will be willing to use the imperfect information from memory rather than interact with a system to find it. Going with information in memory is more error-prone, but less time and cognitive resource intensive. Many web pages that contain lots of information almost actively discourage people from interacting with that information by making it too difficult to extract and integrate the needed information.

Known Information versus Need to Know Information

When people start to search for information, they typically have some idea of what type of information they want to find. Depending on their prior knowledge, the concept of the needed information can be well developed. For example, a business executive can ask very detailed questions about specific points on a monthly status report of an ongoing project. On the other hand, people searching for healthcare information about a newly diagnosed disease may have no real clue about what they need to know. But in both cases, there are two different areas that are concerns for HII.

Based on experience, people use their activated mental model to begin the search for information. The mental model provides the basic skeleton, which they fill in with information specific to the situation. The mental model provides the filter that allows them to sift through all of the information available and only focus on the relevant information.

Consider how Casner (1994) found that with most commercial jet pilots, a large propor-

tion of the processes used to fly a known route were environmental. With experience, the pilots learned what to look for and what to expect next. The commercial pilot knows what information is needed and knows when and where to look for specific information. Before looking at the specific information, the pilot will not be able to state its value, but will know it is needed and how it will fit into the current situation model. Most people search for information in the same way. People may know what information is needed and how to find it, and simply need to acquire it. For example, reading monthly reports or booking an airline flight. People new to the situation lack this ability because of lack of experience, but through interaction with a particular site (for instance, a corporate intranet) they build up a base of experiences which help them remain oriented and find information quickly. The faster and easier a design supports the building of this experience, the better the communication across time and multiple interactions. The experience helps people build a good mental representation of the overall site and, consequently, lets them easily find the information which fits into their mental model of the current problem situation. The specifics of the desired information and people's prior knowledge affect the coherence of the mental representation, which in turn, affects the quality of the final result (Rouet, 2003).

Wanting to Know Information and Needing to Know Information

Design teams must work to understand people's information needs: how they use and understand the information, and how they intend to manipulate the information. Notice that the previous sentences talk of *needs*, not *wants* (see chapter 2: *Information in the situation*, "Information needs versus information wants" for more detail). Unfortunately, people's needs and wants are often quite different, with people rarely knowing what they actually need. Because it is difficult to find out what information a user wants, it becomes even more important to understand what a user needs. The importance of a thorough audience analysis and a task analysis cannot be overemphasized.

Survey's often fail since they simply ask what information people want. But that approach is likely to reveal either the standard line or a view of what they honestly thinks they want. But the information people needs to make high quality decisions is often different from the information they want. They may not realize more information is available or that they are focusing on the wrong subset of the information. They often can't even ask for what they need because they may not realize that information exists or may not realize that alternate paths to finding the information are possible.

Refinding Information

A significant part of the research in areas such as information retrieval and information architecture that deals with finding information on web pages assumes that people are looking for new information; in other words, finding something for the first time. However, more important than finding information is *refinding information*. Most of the time, people are not looking for new information, they are refinding information which they previously have seen.

In many instances, people know they have previously found the information they currently need; rather than looking in new places, they try to refind it where they last saw it. This may range from needing a specific value on a chart they use regularly to the instructions on how to complete a quarterly financial report. They are not looking for something new, but something they will probably recognize when they see it. Tauscher and Greenberg (1997) found that 58% of the pages visited during a Web browsing session were revisits. Likewise, approximately 81% of all the web pages people visit have been previously visited by them (Cockburn and McKenzie, 2001).

Within a session of web use, we are likely to encounter much more information than we are able to analyze in the time we have available. We often look for ways to insure that we can return to a promising looking web site for further study later on. And, once we have determined that the information of a web page is useful, we want to be sure that we can retrieve this information, in some form and with reasonable speed and ease, when a need for this information arises some weeks or months later (Bruce, Jones, & Dumais, 2004).

People should be able to refind useful information without having to go through the initial process of constructing the query again from scratch. A well-designed online system should provide an efficient way of recording previously accessed information so it can be found again easily (O'Malley, 1986). Unfortunately, support for refinding is limited. Search engines force people to start the search from scratch which causes frustration as they try to remember on which web site it was located. Or, as Whittaker and Hirschberg (2001) found, people do not trust the Web as a repository for information, and instead keep paper copies of web documents for archival purposes despite the costs incurred.

People develop preferences for information sources to which they have previous exposure. Interestingly, this extends to when recognition of the previous exposure is very low (Kunst-Wilson & Zajonc, 1980). Consider how many times people look for specific information with a mental image of the page: they know the answer is on a page with a skunk in the upper half. When using references, familiarity often trumps better quality information. With a known source, people know where to look, which minimizes the effort of refinding the information.

While the Internet is often portrayed as an endless source of information on any topic, few people actually tap more than a trivial amount of that information. Rather than seeking information from new sources, people tend to draw on only a few source types that are familiar and easily accessible. The satisfaction of finding the needed information leads to the intention to repeatedly search for information in the one location (Jung Lee, Park, Widdows, 2009). Savolainen and Kari's (2004) findings on information search supports the idea that people exert minimal effort. Perhaps one reason for people returning to the same information time and again is that they have a mental image for what the information should look like (dense text, full page article, brief text, non-textual information, etc) and each time they look at the information they want to conform to that image (Slone, 2002). Obviously, that mental conception is formed by their previous exposure to the information. Thus, the easiest way to satisfy that mental image is to revisit old information. It also minimizes effort since they already know that what they want exists, rather than having to risk a source not containing what they need.

Some of the specific research findings on how people go about refinding information:

- When people revisit a web site, the first three methods they use are: directly entering the URL into the browser; searching with a search engine; or accessing it via another Web site. People are able to effectively return to a site 3 to 6 months later (Jones, Bruce, & Dumais, 2004).
- People show a strong preference for "location-based" finding. The preferred strategy is to guess where the information will be (Barreau & Nardi, 1995).
- People return to information using the same path they used to originally find it. Changes to the information structure which impair following the original path inhibit refinding information (Jeevan, 2004; Maglio & Barret, 1997).

Recently accessed web documents are more likely to be re-accessed in the near future. The strong emphasis on refinding information can be seen in how the web use patterns follow a Zipf's law distribution. While Zipf (1949) originally analyzed on words in spoken speech, the relationship fits many other situations. What he showed was the probability of occurrence of words or other items starts high and tapers off. For the web search it means a few web pages are retrieved very often while many others are retrieved very rarely. Zipf's law also applies to the use of search words in a search engine: a few keywords are constantly used and others are very infrequent. In formal terms:

$P_n = 1/n^a$, where P_n is the frequency of occurrence of the nth ranked item and a is close to 1.

Zipf's law can help a design team by providing a clear plot of which pages are most important or which search terms are used most often. The information must fit within the high use area of the graph as defined by the users.

Factors Hindering Search

On any page of text some of the information will be more relevant to the current situation than the rest of the information, assuming that any of the information is relevant. When people first skim the page, they must evaluate what information, if any, is relevant and worth reading further. The information which is first considered will be the information which is highly salient on that page. As a result, the highly salient information has a disproportionate effect on the use and interpretation of the overall information content. If the highly salient information is relevant, this effect can be good, but when it is not relevant, it can cause relevant information to be disregarded or skipped. In addition, people need to understand what they are searching for; it is easy to miss relevant information if they lack the proper terminology (Pollock and Hockley (1997). In one study, students were found to lack confidence in evaluating the relative usefulness of information resources because of their lower knowledge level (Warwick et al, 2009)

Before people have a chance to evaluate information on a page, navigation problems often require too much effort to make finding a solution worthwhile. When the IA fails to match their needs, they have trouble finding the information. Poor category names (or at least ones that don't map onto the person's mental model) impede navigating to the information (Englmeier & Mang, 1997). People access information based on: accessibility, availability, technical quality, and relevance (Kwasitsu, 2001). Having quality and relevance as the lowest rated aspects can be detrimental to good HII. These are the factors design teams rightly tend to focus on, but poor navigation or accessibility can cause readers to go to lower quality information which is easier to find.

Besides the text wording, its formatting also exerts a strong effect on search quality. Weller (2004) evaluated the effects of white space on visual search time. Participants searched for a target word on a web page with different levels of white space. Interestingly, only low contrast levels caused increased search times. He found no effect for use of graphics or borders, and although search times were longer, no significant differences for higher numbers of objects on the page. In addition he found:

Participants reported that locating the target was difficult in the contrast display when the target was both (1) not in a colored grouping, or, in other words had the appearance of being in a "white box," and (2) was located in the uppermost right hand corner. Participants noted that they would tend to see the word when located in the blue area but not as quickly when located in the white corner. These findings support the guideline that suggests color is a poor delineator of screen elements and a border should be used to set off adjacent areas of different colors (Weller, 2004).

Information search is highly correlated with factors forcing people to look at more information. People's motivation plays a significant factor in how deeply they search and how long they will search (Slone, 2002). Under time pressure, people tend to increase the rate of information search (Ben Zur & Breznitz 1981, Maule & Mackie 1990; Wright 1974). When time pressure is so great that simply accelerating the search fails to make it fast enough, people resort to heuristics-based decision rules. Payne et al. (1988) found that, under time pressure, intuitive strategies were adopted in place of more comprehensive evaluation strategies. Simplifying search strategies reflect how people rapidly filter information under time pressure. However, this simplification of search also leads to increased errors as people tend to be working with partial information, which leads to poor decisions (Lin & Su, 1998).

Avoiding Getting Lost

Many sources talk about "lost in hyperspace" and disorientation with computers during searching. Chalmers (2003), in a version of "getting lost in hyperspace," mentions the possible problems of links causing people to get lost or confused, rather than providing them expanded exploration ability. But much of this research seems to be older (pre-early 2000s). With a much higher percentage of the population familiar with hypertext, unless the main audience is truly novice, this issue should go away as a high percentage of the audience gains search experience. Also, in recent years, the design of web pages has become more consistent in both its use of links and in only linking relevant information.

As one method of keeping oriented, experienced searchers tend to only move down a hierarchy a couple of levels before returning to the start. Interestingly, lower ability searchers move through the hierarchy more and use embedded link frequently. In the process, they tend to return to the home page and restart their search more than an experienced searcher (Kim, 2001). At the same time, experience searchers move in a non-linear search pattern, while lower ability searchers move in a linear pattern (Qiu, 1993). It seems that the experience searchers use a seemingly shallower search strategy which keeps them mentally anchored and keeps them from getting lost—they are cognizant of this approach and list it as advice to improve searching (Kim, 2001). The lower ability searchers lack this mental anchoring and keep starting over from the home page.

Subjective lostness (the person felt lost, regardless of actually being lost) was best predicted by similarity to the optimal path and time on task. The best overall predictor of success on individual tasks was similarity to the optimal path (Gwizdka & Spence, 2007).

SEARCHING GRAPHICAL IMAGES

Searching for graphical objects is easier than searching for text. Lansdale, Jones and Jones (1989) found that search times were faster for images than for words. Analysis of the search patterns suggests that, while people look for verbal items serially, they detect potential image targets in their peripheral vision and move directly to them. While text must be read in a linear manner, the human visual system is able to process graphics in parallel and reject goal-irrelevant objects as a part of pre-attention processing. Lavie (2005), in his review of the research, concludes "that active cognitive control of visual selective attention may only be needed to resolve conflict between targets and a potent salient distracter that strongly competes with the target" (p. 80).

The idea that images have a more extensive processing by the pre-attention system is consistent with the idea that image search is faster since the burden on working memory has been transformed to the perceptual system. The perceptual system is able to automatically evaluate images rather than having to consciously study them (Wickens & Carswell, 1995). On the other hand, image searches have a higher rate of missed targets, which is also consistent with the view that images are not scanned serially (Lansdale & Ormerod, 1994). Pre-attention system may reject images too quickly without considering the details of image and that the relevant information exists in the details. The basic problem is that the pre-attention system can only address high-level search processing, such as finding red balls in a midst of green balls or finding stars in circles. It cannot help identify specific types of red balls or specific faces in a photograph.

When a graphical target is defined on one level of a salient feature, the search time to detect the target does not depend on how many non-targets are in the visual field. In other words, a whole set of non-target items could be processed in parallel in the search for the target (Wickens, 1992). This observation explains why it is easy to find a single red object in a collection of various colored objects. The red provides a salient feature which the pre-attention processor can use to reject all the non-red objects. The time will be almost the same for finding a red object within a field whether the field contains 2 objects or 50 objects.

Obviously, text is read in a linear fashion; however, that same consistency does not carry over to searching through images. People do not seem to display consistent search patterns.

The fact that much of visual search behavior is internally driven by cognitive factors means that there are no highly consistent physical patterns of display scanning and no optimal scan pattern in search, beyond the fact that search should be guided by the expectancy of target location (Wickens, 1992, p. 81).

The search pattern people use is based on the expectations of where the useful information will be found. Eye tracking studies have found these areas are fixated first and frequently. As such, the scan path will change based on the information people expect to find; each time they looks at the same information set, they may scan it differently. However, it seems people rarely have an optimal scan pattern. They will look at the same areas repeatedly even though they know the information will not have changed and will skip other areas. In addition, images in visually competitive environments tend to receive less attention (Janiszewski, 1998). High visual complexity can distract readers from acquiring the intended message as they are forced to sift through more irrelevant information.

How people scan an image for areas of interest strongly depends on experience. Kundel and La Follett (1972) studied experienced and novice radiologists looking at x-rays to detect tumors. They found novice radiologists looked at the entire film evenly while the experienced radiologists focused on the areas which were most likely to contain tumors. Stagar and Angus (1978) had search and rescue experts study photographs of crash sites. The experts only scanned about 50% of the terrain and missed relevant clues even in the areas they did look at.

Learning how to search images requires dedicated training. For example, when pilots are learning how to scan control panels or radiologists learning how to evaluate x-rays. Besides learning what to look for, they also need to learn *how* to control their scan path while looking at the image.

Of particular interest in how people search within and across graphical objects:

- Attention can be captured by salient but task-irrelevant information. The chance of this undesirable attention capture increased when people worked in high cognitive load conditions (Lavie & De Fockert, 2005)

- Instructing people to ignore goal-irrelevant objects is not sufficient to prevent the objects from being processed (Lavie, 2005). They may be disregarded after processing, but they still require cognitive resources.

- People fixate on the areas that contain the most information. For example, in a photograph, people look at the face or other areas of high detail.

- The eye will be drawn to large, bright, or blinking areas. While this might help draw attention to warnings, it can also bias the information interpretation. Excessive use of high contrasting elements will also result in people ignoring the area. Consider banner blindness and how people ignore the blinking ads which appear on the right-hand side of many web sites; this ignoring effect is so strong that some research has found designs where a warning was displayed as flashing text in boxes, but the users ignored it as irrelevant and later didn't recall the flashing element.

- People try to minimize eye movements as part of their information seeking. When asked to evaluate six different models of cars based on multiple criteria, the comparisons were done between adjacent sets of information with less comparison as the data sets were farther apart (Russo & Rosen, 1975).

EXAMPLES

Astronomical Information

People never search for data, they search for information to apply to their situation. Yet, many websites provide little more than data dumps.

On the webpage describing the Cassini Orbiter instruments (http://saturn.jpl.nasa.gov/spacecraft/cassiniorbiterinstruments/), there is one link for each of the 12 instruments. The link goes a page with dedicated information about that specific instrument. The amount of text on each of those pages seems to directly connect to the interest a more general reader will want. The page for the imaging systems has 647 words that explain the cameras on the spacecraft. The page for the Ion and Neutral Mass Spectrometer has 87 words.

Most readers want to nice pictures and know what cameras are, but most do not know what a spectrometer is or what it does. This could mean that the site should spend time educating people about spectrometers; however, this is not an information need of the people coming to the site. Chances are good they will not even click on a link to the Ion and Neutral Mass Spectrometer if they don't understand the heading.

Business Reports

Business reports often get used in meetings, whether formal or ad hoc, where people must quickly search through them and refind information to support a discussion point. Clearly, the information must be easy to refind so that it does not bog the discussion down. If it can't be found quickly, then people will use what they t remember reading which can lead to improper decisions.

Here is an example of poor HII with everything buried in a long paragraph. The paragraph contains the criteria which were used to evaluate two textbooks (just the evaluation criteria, not the analysis itself). *Question: was the white space around figures part of the evaluation?* The information to answer that question is in the paragraph and a design team can find it since they wrote it. But a person sitting in a meeting who needs that one piece of information will not be able to refind it, even if she is very sure she read it.

Topic coverage was selected as a point of interest because it is critical for the subject material to be thoroughly covered. The student needs enough detail within the text to grasp the ideals and concepts being discussed. Level of complexity was chosen because the author of the books should strive to keep the tone as simple as possible within reason. The material within electrical engineering textbooks is complex as it stands with all of the formulas, calculations, and figures without adding to the complexity. The chapter exercises are of special interest as well because they are a great way for students to practice the new ideals that they just learned. The chapters should contain enough problems so that the students feel that they have had plenty of practice. The problems should start off easy and then progress to harder problems. This helps the students feel more comfortable with their abilities to do the problems. The figures within the chapters were also evaluated because of the importance of good and abundant figures. Within the electrical engineering curriculum figures are vital to the learning of the material, because the students are dealing with things like voltage and current which cannot be visualized. Therefore, an adequate amount of figures should be present and the figures should be easy to understand. The figures should have enough white space around them to distinguish them from the text, have good captions clearly describing the content, and proper placement within the chapter. Next, the example problems were evaluated because the example problems are so important for visualizing the concepts just learned in the chapter. The majority of students learn the most from the example problems, because they show how to apply the information just learned. The example problems should also closely resemble the exercises. Lastly, the organization and layout of both books were compared because this is the overall impression of the books.

Redesigned with lists, the same information is easy to skim and supports refinding information. All this second version does is add bullets, none of the text has changed. With this design, a person can find the section on evaluating figures much quicker than having to skim through a long paragraph. With some rewriting, which this text needs, refinding information to answer the question would be even easier.

- Topic coverage was selected as a point of interest because it is critical for the subject material to be thoroughly covered. The student needs enough detail within the text to grasp the ideals and concepts being discussed.
- Level of complexity was chosen because the author of the books should strive to keep the tone as simple as possible within reason. The material within electrical engineering textbooks is complex as it stands with all of the formulas, calculations, and figures without adding to the complexity.
- The chapter exercises are of special interest as well because they are a great way for students to practice the new ideals that they just learned. The chapters should contain enough problems so that the students feel that they have had plenty of practice. The problems should start off easy and then progress to harder problems. This helps the students feel more comfortable with their abilities to do the problems.
- The figures within the chapters were also evaluated because of the importance of good and abundant figures. Within the electrical engineering curriculum figures are vital to the learning of the material, because the students are dealing with things like voltage and current which cannot be visualized. Therefore, an adequate amount of figures should be present and the figures should be easy to understand. The figures should have enough white space around them to distinguish them from the text, have good captions clearly describing the content, and proper placement within the chapter.
- The example problems were evaluated because the example problems are so important for visualizing the concepts just

learned in the chapter. The majority of students learn the most from the example problems, because they show how to apply the information just learned. The example problems should also closely resemble the exercises.
- The organization and layout of both books were compared because this is the overall impression of the books.

This example is dealing with printed reports, but the same problem exists on web pages. Too much information too packed in for easy access, easy reading, and, most importantly, easy refinding. Supporting HII and people's information needs means using useful headings and lists, not just heading and lists for their own sake or because the design team was told to use lots of them. They have a purpose in supporting the HII. Misused, they fail to accomplish that and become more noise for a reader to struggle though.

SUMMARY

The Web contains a vast amount of information relevant to a specific task or goal as well as a vast amount of irrelevant or downright wrong/fraudulent information about a specific task or goal. Finding and interpreting this information requires working within a complex search environment. The information search process of any text, whether printed page or web site, can be viewed as HII which combines visual perception of the information presentation, the processes of mentally manipulating the information in working memory and long-term memory, and the decision-making processes of defining relevant information and interpreting it with respect to the situation

Models of How People Search

There have been several models of how people search for information, such as the eight-phase models of Marchionini (1995) and the four-phase model of Shneiderman et al. (1998). In general, the all consist of steps that deal with formulating the information need, searching for the information, reviewing and evaluating the search results, and refining/iterating the search.

The choice of which model design teams should use depend on their view of how people view the situation and look for information within it, the detail level required of the information, and the stage the search occupies in the HII process.

Factors of Successful Search

People's goals and information needs directly influence the search strategies they use. It also means they do not always use the same strategies, but vary them to fit the context of the situation. Four aspects of how people search for and interact with information include their: goals and context, memory, attention, and mental model.

People search strategies can be classified into one of six types: searching, browsing, scanning, exploring, wandering, and structured. These types can be combined as modified within the overall search cycle.

People tend to approach information seeking using one of two approaches: active or passive engagement. Experience levels showed little difference in the search strategy for Internet information, even at the level of novices and experts search strategy is constant. However, the more experienced people do have more success since they are able to implement the strategy better.

Search can be impaired by slow performance or improper salience. Page load and system response times impede the HII. Slow system responses lead to frustration: times of less than 1 second don't break people's trains of thought and they will accept delays of up to 8–10 seconds. Over the 8–10 seconds and quality HII is compromised. Poor information salience can lead to missed information or false alarms (wrong information viewed as correct/applicable).

Finding Relevant Information

People search for information to fill an information gap between what they currently know and what they feel they should know about the situation. When people search for relevant information, at a simplistic level, they only need to find information to fill their information need. However, they often don't know what information they need or what information is available in the system.

Besides helping people to find information, high quality HII must help people *refind information.* Most of the time, people are not looking for new information, they are *refinding* information which they previously have seen.

Searching Graphical Images

Searching for graphical objects or images is easier than searching for text. Images are processed with the pre-attention system which lessens the load on working memory.

REFERENCES

Ackoff, R. (1967). Management misinformation systems. *Management Science, 14,* 147–156. doi:10.1287/mnsc.14.4.B147

Albers, M. (2004). *Communication of complex information: User goals and information needs for dynamic Web information.* Mahwah, NJ: Erlbaum.

Alvarado, C., Jeevan, J., Ackerman, M., & Karger, D. (2003). *Surviving the information explosion: How people find their electronic information* (pp. 1–9). MIT AI Memo AIM-2003-006. Retrieved from http://www.csail.mit.edu/~teevan/work/publications/papers/aim03.pdf

Armbruster, B., & Armstrong, J. (1993). Locating information in text: A focus on children in the elementary grades. *Contemporary Educational Psychology, 18*, 139–161. doi:10.1006/ceps.1993.1015

Arora, N., Hesse, B., Rimer, B., Viswanath, K., Clayman, M., & Croyle, R. (2008). Frustrated and confused: The American public rates its cancer-related information seeking experiences. *Journal of General Internal Medicine, 23*, 223–228. doi:10.1007/s11606-007-0406-y

Barreau, D., & Nardi, B. (1995). Finding and reminding: File organization from the desktop. *SIGCHI Bulletin, 27*(3), 66–69.

Barrick, J., & Spilker, B. (2003). The relations between knowledge, search strategy, and performance in unaided and aided information search. *Organizational Behavior and Human Decision Processes, 90*, 1–18. doi:10.1016/S0749-5978(03)00002-5

Ben Zur, H., & Breznitz, S. (1981). The effect of time pressure on risky choice behavior. *Acta Psychologica, 47*, 89–104. doi:10.1016/0001-6918(81)90001-9

Bowie, J. (1996). Information engineering: Communicating with technology. *Intercom, 43*(5), 6–9.

Brand-Gurwel, S., Wopereis, I., & Vermetten, Y. (2005). Information problem solving by experts and novices: Analysis of a complex cognitive skill. *Computers in Human Behavior, 21*, 487–508. doi:10.1016/j.chb.2004.10.005

Bruce, H., Jones, W., & Dumais, S. (2004). *Refinding information on the web: What do people do and what do they need*. Retrieved from http://kftf.ischool.washington.edu/

Campagnoni, F. R., & Ehrlich, K. (1989). Information retrieval using hypertext-based help system. *Proceedings of the 12th Annual International ACMSIGIR Conference,* (pp. 212–220).

Canter, D., Rivers, R., & Storrs, G. (1985). Characterising user navigation through complex data structures. *Behaviour & Information Technology, 4*, 93–102. doi:10.1080/01449298508901791

Carlson, R., Wenger, J., & Sullivan, M. (1993). Coordinating information from perception and working memory. *Journal of Experimental Psychology. Human Perception and Performance, 19*(3), 531–548. doi:10.1037/0096-1523.19.3.531

Casner, S. (1994). Understanding the determinants of problem-solving behavior in a complex environment. *Human Factors, 34*(4), 580–596.

Chalmers, P. (2003). The role of cognitive theory in human-computer interface. *Computers in Human Behavior, 19*, 593–607. doi:10.1016/S0747-5632(02)00086-9

Chevalier, A., & Kicka, M. (2006). Web designers and web users: Influence of the ergonomic quality of the web site on the information search. *International Journal of Man-Machine Studies, 64*(10), 1031–1048.

Chli, M., & De Wilde, P. (2006). Internet search: Subdivision-based interactive query expansion and the soft Semantic Web. *Applied Soft Computing, 6*(4), 372–383. doi:10.1016/j.asoc.2005.11.003

Cockburn, A., & McKenzie, B. (2001). What do web users do? An empirical analysis of Web use. *International Journal of Human-Computer Studies, 54*, 903–922. doi:10.1006/ijhc.2001.0459

Dennis, A., & Taylor, N. (2004). Information foraging on the Web: The effects of "acceptable" Internet delays on multi-page information search behavior. *Decision Support Systems, 42*, 810–824. doi:10.1016/j.dss.2005.05.032

Downing, R., Moore, J., & Brown, S. (2005). The effects and interaction of spatial visualization and domain expertise on information seeking. *Computers in Human Behavior, 21*, 195–209. doi:10.1016/j.chb.2004.03.040

Dreher, M. (1992). Searching for information in textbooks. *Journal of Reading, 35*, 364–371.

Eheman, C., Berkowitz, Z., Lee, J., Mohile, S., Purnell, J., & Rodriguez, E. (2009). Information-seeking styles among cancer patients before and after treatment by demographics and use of information sources. *Journal of Health Communication, 14*(5), 487–502. doi:10.1080/10810730903032945

Englmeier, K., & Mang, E. (1997). For information patters to information architecture. In M. Smith, G. Salvendy, & R. Koubek (Eds.), *Proceedings of the 7th International Conference on Human-Computer Interaction* (pp. 35–38). New York, NY: Elsevier.

Fennema, M., & Kleinmuntz, D. (1995). Anticipation of effort and accuracy in multi-attribute choice. *Organizational Behavior and Human Decision Processes, 63*(1), 21–32. doi:10.1006/obhd.1995.1058

Guthrie, J. (1988). Locating information in documents: Examination of a cognitive model. *Reading Research Quarterly, 23*, 178–199. doi:10.2307/747801

Gwizdka, J., & Spence, I. (2007). Implicit measures of lostness and success in Web navigation. *Interacting with Computers, 19*(3), 357–369. doi:10.1016/j.intcom.2007.01.001

Hsieh-Yee, I. (1993). Effects of search experience and subject knowledge on the search tactics of novice and experienced searchers. *Journal of the American Society for Information Science American Society for Information Science, 44*, 161–174. doi:10.1002/(SICI)1097-4571(199304)44:3<161::AID-ASI5>3.0.CO;2-8

Hsieh-Yee, I. (2001). Research on Web search behavior. *Library & Information Science Research, 23*, 167–185. doi:10.1016/S0740-8188(01)00069-X

Janiszewski, C. (1998). The influence of display characteristics on visual exploratory search behavior. *The Journal of Consumer Research, 25*, 290–301. doi:10.1086/209540

Jeevan, J. (2004). *How people re-find information when the Web changes.* MIT AI Memo 2004-012.

Johnson, E., Payne, J., & Bettman, J. (1988). Information displays and preference reversals. *Organizational Behavior and Human Decision Processes, 42*, 1–21. doi:10.1016/0749-5978(88)90017-9

Jones, W., Bruce, H., & Dumais, S. (2004). *Re-finding information on the Web: What do people do and what do they need.* Retrieved from http://kftf.ischool.washington.edu/

Jung Lee, Y., Park, J., & Widdows, R. (2009). Exploring antecedents of consumer satisfaction and repeated search behavior on e-health information. *Journal of Health Communication, 14*, 160–173. doi:10.1080/10810730802659830

Ketamo, H., Kiili, K., & Haaparanta, H. (2003). Empirical basis for navigation framework. *Journal of Digital Contents, 2*(1), 96–101.

Khan, K., & Locatis, C. (1998). Searching through cyberspace: The effects of link display and link density on information retrieval from hypertext on the World Wide Web. *Journal of the American Society for Information Science American Society for Information Science, 49*, 176–182. doi:10.1002/(SICI)1097-4571(199802)49:2<176::AID-ASI7>3.0.CO;2-8

Kim, J., & Lee, J. (2002). Critical design factors for successful e-commerce systems. *Behaviour & Information Technology, 21*(3), 185–199. doi:10.1080/0144929021000009054

Kim, K. (2001). Implications of user characteristics in information seeking on the World Wide Web. *International Journal of Human-Computer Interaction, 13*(3), 323–340. doi:10.1207/S15327590IJHC1303_3

Klein, G. (1999). *Sources of power: How people make decisions*. Cambridge, MA: MIT.

Kundel, H., & La Follett, P. (1972). Visual search patterns and experience with radiological images. *Radiology, 103*, 523–528.

Kunst-Wilson, W., & Zajonc, R. (1980). Affective discrimination of stimuli that cannot be recognized. *Science, 207*, 557–558. doi:10.1126/science.7352271

Kwasitsu, L. (2001). Information-seeking behavior of design process and manufacturing engineers. *Library and Information Science, 25*, 459–476. doi:10.1016/S0740-8188(03)00054-9

Lansdale, M., Jones, M., & Jones, M. (1989). Visual search in iconic and verbal interfaces. In Megaw, E. (Ed.), *Contemporary ergonomics* (pp. 422–429). London, UK: Taylor and Francis.

Lansdale, M., & Ormerod, T. (1994). *Understanding interfaces: A handbook of human-computer dialogue*. London, UK: Academic Press.

Lavie, N. (2005). Distracted and confused? Selective attention under load. *Trends in Cognitive Sciences, 9*(2), 75–82. doi:10.1016/j.tics.2004.12.004

Lavie, N., & De Fockert, J. (2005). The role of working memory in attentional capture. *Psychonomic Bulletin & Review, 12*(4), 669–674. doi:10.3758/BF03196756

Lawless, K., & Kulikowich, J. (1998). Domain knowledge, interest, and hypertext navigation: A study of individual differences. *Journal of Educational Multimedia and Hypermedia, 7*, 51–70.

Lazonder, A., & Rouet, J. (2008). Information problem solving instruction: Some cognitive and metacognitive issues. *Computers in Human Behavior, 24*, 753–765. doi:10.1016/j.chb.2007.01.025

Lin, D., & Su, Y. (1998). The effect of time pressure on expert system based training for emergency management. *Behaviour & Information Technology, 17*(4), 195–202. doi:10.1080/014492998119409

Maglio, P., & Barret, R. (1997). On the trail of information searchers. *Proceedings of the Nineteenth Annual Conference of the Cognitive Science Society,* (pp. 466–471). Stanford University, Palo Alto, CA, LEA, Mahwah, NJ.

Marchionini, G. (1995). *Information seeking in electronic environments*. New York, NY: Cambridge UP. doi:10.1017/CBO9780511626388

Maule, A., & Mackie, P. (1990). A componential investigation of the effects of deadlines on individual decision making. In Borchering, K., Larichev, O., & Messick, D. (Eds.), *Contemporary issues in decision making* (pp. 449–461). Amsterdam, The Netherlands: North-Holland.

McEneaney, J. (2001). Graphic and numerical methods to assess navigation in hypertext. *International Journal of Human-Computer Studies, 55*, 761–786. doi:10.1006/ijhc.2001.0505

McGovern, G. (2010). *Navigation is more important than search*. Retrieved from http://www.gerrymcgovern.com/nt/2010/ nt-2010-04-26-Navigation-search.htm

Mirel, B. (1998). Applied constructivism for user documentation. *Journal of Business and Technical Communication, 12*(1), 7–49. doi:10.1177/1050651998012001002

Mirel, B., Feinberg, S., & Allmendinger, L. (1991). Designing manuals for active learning styles. *Technical Communication, 38*(1), 75–87.

Navarro-Prieto, R., Scaife, M., & Rogers, Y. (1999). Cognitive strategies in Web searching. *Proceeding of the Fifth Conference on Human Factors and the Web,* (pp. 43–56). Gaithersburg, MD.

Newell, A., & Simon, H. (1972). *Human problem solving*. Englewood Cliffs, NJ: Prentice Hall.

Nielsen, J. (2001). *The 3Cs of critical Web use: Collect, compare, choose*. Retrieved December 3, 2008, from http://www.useit.com/ alertbox/20010415.html

Nielsen, J. (2010). *Website response times*. Retrieved August 8, 2010, from http://www.useit.com/alertbox//response-times.html

Nilsson, R., & Mayer, R. (2002). The effects of graphic organizers giving cues to the structure of a hypertext document on users' navigation strategies and performance. *International Journal of Human-Computer Studies, 57*, 1–26. doi:10.1006/ijhc.2002.1011

O'Malley, C. (1986). Helping users help themselves. In Norman, D., & Draper, S. (Eds.), *User centered system design: New perspectives on human-computer interaction* (pp. 377–398). Mahwah, NJ: Erlbaum.

Orasanu, J., & Connolly, T. (1993). The reinvention of decision making. In Klein, G., Orasanu, J., Calderwood, R., & Zsambok, C. (Eds.), *Decision making in action: Models and methods* (pp. 3–20). Norwood, NJ: Ablex.

Pauker, S., & Pauker, S. (1999). What is a good decision? *Effective Clinical Practice, 2*, 1994–1946.

Payne, J., Bettman, J., & Johnson, E. (1988). Adaptive strategy selection in decision making. *Journal of Experimental Psychology. Learning, Memory, and Cognition, 14*, 534–552. doi:10.1037/0278-7393.14.3.534

Payne, J., Bettman, J., & Johnson, E. (1993). *The adaptive decision maker*. Cambridge, UK: Cambridge University Press.

Penrose, J., & Seiford, L. (1988). Microcomputer users' preferences for software documentation: An analysis. *Journal of Technical Writing and Communication, 18*(4), 355–366.

Pollock, A., & Hockley, A. (1997). What's wrong with Internet searching? *D-Lib Magazine, 3*(3). Retrieved from http://www.dlib.org/dlib/march97/bt/03pollock.html doi:10.1045/march97-pollock

Proctor, R. (2002). Content preparation and management for web design: Eliciting, structuring, searching, and displaying information. *International Journal of Human-Computer Interaction, 14*(1), 25–92. doi:10.1207/S15327590IJHC1401_2

Qiu, L. (1993). Analytical searching vs. browsing in hypertext information retrieval systems. *Canadian Journal of Information and Library Science, 18*, 1–13.

Rein, G., McDue, D., & Slein, J. (1997). A case for document management functions on the Web. *Communications of the ACM, 40*(9), 81–89. doi:10.1145/260750.260777

Richards, D. (2000). The reuse of knowledge: A user-centered approach. *International Journal of Human-Computer Studies, 52*, 553–579. doi:10.1006/ijhc.1999.0342

Roske-Hofstrand, R., & Paap, K. (1986). Cognitive networks as a guide to menu organization: An application in the automated cockpit. *Ergonomics, 29*, 1301–1311. doi:10.1080/00140138608967247

Rouet, J. (2003). What was I looking for? The influence of task specificity and prior knowledge on students' search strategies in hypertext. *Interacting with Computers, 15*, 409–428. doi:10.1016/S0953-5438(02)00064-4

Rouet, J., & Tricot, A. (1996). Task and activity models in hypertext usage. In van Oostendorp, H., & de Mul, S. (Eds.), *Cognitive aspects of electronic text processing* (pp. 239–264). Norwood, NJ: Ablex.

Russo, J., & Rosen, L. (1975). An eye fixation analysis of multialternative choice. *Memory & Cognition, 3*, 267–276. doi:10.3758/BF03212910

Savolainen, R., & Kari, J. (2004). Placing the Internet in information source horizons. A study of information seeking by Internet users in the context of self-development. *Library & Information Science Research, 26,* 415–433. doi:10.1016/j.lisr.2004.04.004

Schwartz, L. (2010). Making informed decisions about mammograms. *Science News, 177*(4), 32. doi:10.1002/scin.5591770426

Shenton, A., & Dixon, P. (2004a). Issues arising from youngsters' information-seeking behavior. *Library & Information Science Research, 26,* 177–200. doi:10.1016/j.lisr.2003.12.003

Shneiderman, B., Byrd, D., & Croft, W. (1998). Sorting out searching: A user-interface framework for text searches. *Communications of the ACM, 41*(4), 95–98. doi:10.1145/273035.273069

Simon, H. (1979). *Models of thought.* New Haven, CT: Yale UP.

Slone, D. (2003). Internet search approaches: The influence of age, search goals, and experience. *Library & Information Science Research, 25,* 403–418. doi:10.1016/S0740-8188(03)00051-3

Song, G., & Salvendy, G. (2003). A framework for reuse of user experience in Web browsing. *Behaviour & Information Technology, 22*(2), 79–90. doi:10.1080/0144929031000092231

Sonnenwald, D., & Wildemuth, B. (2001). A research method to investigate information seeking using the concept of information horizons: An example from a study of lower socio-economic student's information seeking behaviour. *New Review of Information Behaviour Research, 2,* 65–86.

Spink, A., Wolfram, D., Jansen, B. J., & Saracevic, T. (2001). Searching the Web: The public and their queries. *Journal of the American Society for Information Science American Society for Information Science, 5*(3), 226–234.

Spink, A., & Xu, J. (2000). Selected results from a large study of Web searching: The excite study. *Information Research, 6*(1). Retrieved from http://InformationR.net/ir/ 6-1/paper90.html

Spool, J. (1997). *Why on-site searching stinks.* Retrieved December 28, 2005, from http://www.uie.com/ articles/search_stinks/

Stagar, P., & Angus, R. (1978). Locating crash sites in simulated air-to-ground visual search. *Human Factors, 20,* 453–466.

Stanney, K., & Salvendy, G. (1995). Information visualization: Assisting low spatial individuals with information access tasks through the use of visual mediators. *Ergonomics, 38,* 1184–1198. doi:10.1080/00140139508925181

Stoop, A., van't Riet, A., & Berg, M. (2004). Using information technology for patient education: Realizing surplus value? *Patient Education and Counseling, 54,* 187–195. doi:10.1016/S0738-3991(03)00211-8

Tauscher, L., & Greenberg, S. (1997). Revisitation patterns in World Wide Web navigation. *Proceeding of the ACM CHI 97: Conference on Human Factors in Computing Systems* Atlanta, GA (pp. 399–406).

The future of online search. (2005). Interview with John Batelle, Wired editor. Retrieved from http://www.cnn.com/2005/TECH/12/ 23/john.bartelle/index.html

Trimmel, M., Meixner-Pendleton, M., & Haring, S. (2003). Stress response caused by system response time when searching for information on the Internet. *Human Factors, 45*(4), 615–621. doi:10.1518/hfes.45.4.615.27084

Vakkari, P. (2001). Changes in search tactics and relevance judgments when preparing a research proposal: A summary of findings of a longitudinal study. *Information Retrieval, 4*(3), 295–310.

Walraven, A., Brand-Gruwel, S., & Boshuizen, H. (2008). Information-problem solving: A review of problems students encounter and instructional solutions. *Computers in Human Behavior, 24,* 623–648. doi:10.1016/j.chb.2007.01.030

Warwick, C., Rimmer, J., Blandford, A., Gow, J., & Buchanan, G. (2009). Cognitive economy and satisficing in information seeking: A longitudinal study of undergraduate information behaviour. *Journal of the American Society for Information Science and Technology, 60*(12), 2402–2415. doi:10.1002/asi.21179

Weller, D. (2004). The effects of contrast and density on visual web search. *Usability News, 6*(2). Retrieved from http://psychology.wichita.edu/surl/ usabilitynews/62/density.htm

Whittaker, S., & Hirshberg, J. (2001). The character, value, and management of personal paper archives. *ACM Transactions on Computer-Human Interaction, 8*(2), 150–170. doi:10.1145/376929.376932

Wickens, C. (1992). *Engineering psychology and human performance.* New York, NY: HarperCollins.

Wickens, C., & Carswell, C. (1995). The proximity compatibility principle: Its psychological foundations and its relevance to display design. *Human Factors, 37,* 473–494. doi:10.1518/001872095779049408

Wickens, C., & Hollands, J. (2000). *Engineering psychology and human performance.* Upper Saddle River, NJ: Prentice Hall.

Wright, P. (1974). The harassed decision maker: Time pressure, distractions, and the use of evidence. *The Journal of Applied Psychology, 59*(5), 555–561. doi:10.1037/h0037186

Zhang, H., & Salvendy, G. (2001). The implications of visualization ability and structure preview design for Web information search tasks. *International Journal of Human-Computer Interaction, 13*(1), 75–95. doi:10.1207/S15327590IJHC1301_5

Zipf, G. (1949). *Human behavior and the principle of least effort.* New York, NY: Addison-Wesley.

ADDITIONAL READING

Brand-Gurwel, S., Wopereis, I., & Vermetten, Y. (2005). Information problem solving by experts and novices: Analysis of a complex cognitive skill. *Computers in Human Behavior, 21,* 487–508. doi:10.1016/j.chb.2004.10.005

Marchionini, G. (1995). *Information seeking in electronic environments.* New York, NY: Cambridge UP. doi:10.1017/CBO9780511626388

Mirel, B., Feinberg, S., & Allmendinger, L. (1991). Designing manuals for active learning styles. *Technical Communication, 38*(1), 75–87.

Rouet, J. (2003). What was I looking for? The influence of task specificity and prior knowledge on students' search strategies in hypertext. *Interacting with Computers, 15,* 409–428. doi:10.1016/S0953-5438(02)00064-4

Walraven, A., Brand-Gruwel, S., & Boshuizen, H. (2008). Information-problem solving: A review of problems students encounter and instructional solutions. *Computers in Human Behavior, 24,* 623–648. doi:10.1016/j.chb.2007.01.030

Warwick, C., Rimmer, J., Blandford, A., Gow, J., & Buchanan, G. (2009). Cognitive economy and satisficing in information seeking: A longitudinal study of undergraduate information behaviour. *Journal of the American Society for Information Science and Technology, 60*(12), 2402–2415. doi:10.1002/asi.21179

Chapter 13
How People Make Decisions and Take Action

ABSTRACT

The earlier chapters of this book have looked at how people interact with and interpret information. This chapter looks at the factors that influence how people use that information to make a decision. In the end, effective communication depends on people doing something with the information; a decision needs to be made and actions taken. Those decisions and actions feed back into the overall situation, which modifies the available information. People then interpret the changes and makes more decisions, even if the decision is that everything is ok and no further actions are required (Figure 1).

BACKGROUND

Executives do not need help with decision making; they need help with gathering information—Tom Murray

The old school of software interface design and document writing took the view that if people could find the information somewhere within the system or manual, then they could use it for decision making and the design requirements had been met (Albers, 1996). But simply ensuring that all the information is available ignores how people process information to make a decision., Orasanu and Connolly (1993) discuss how, while research typically looks at decision making in isolation, in reality decision making occurs as part of larger tasks and is only a single part of achieving a larger goal of interacting with a situation. They place decisions within a cycle which "consist[s] of defining what the problem is, understanding what a reasonable solution would look like, taking action to reach that goal, and evaluating the effects of that action" (p. 6). As Figure 1 shows, decision making is a part of a long cycle of collecting information from the situation, integrating it into prior knowledge, making choices and actions, and monitoring the results.

Decisions within an HII context never exist in isolation, but are embedded in the larger tasks that the decision maker is trying to accomplish. Laboratory-based decision research in the labora-

DOI: 10.4018/978-1-4666-0152-9.ch013

Figure 1. How people make decisions

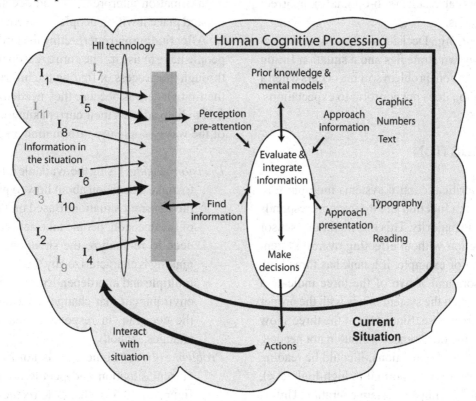

tory tends to require decisions apart from any meaningful context. In natural settings, making a decision is not an end in itself but, rather, a means to achieving a broader goal. Hollnagel (1993) places decision making neatly into context.

Work in a natural environment requires a mixture of skilled actions, established routines or procedures, and more or less complex decisions. Here decisions occur as a natural part of the way in which the situation develops or as part of a context. Decision making is only one of several activities that the operator must carry out, and decisions are made whenever the situation requires it. This means that the natural decision making is prepared, that the context and the conditions are known, and that the decision is integrated in the overall pattern of activities. The need to make a decision is not suddenly forced upon the operator, *but can be anticipated and fitted into the natural flow of work. (p. 32)*

The main areas covered in this chapter are:

Models of decision making: Describes the classical decision making model and recognition primed model of decision making.

How people make situation-specific decisions: Describes the strategies that people use to interpret information and make predictions about the future development of the situation based on hypothetical decisions. It also considers how the way information is presented and framed has a significant effect on how people understand a situation and the decisions they make.

Decision-making influences and biases: Describes the various factors that exert an influence on how people reach decisions and how those factors can result in sub-optimal or incorrect decisions.

Problem solving: Decisions often get make using known strategies and a situation fitting expectation; problem solving occurs when a situation does not conform to expectations.

INTRODUCTION

In system-critical control systems multiple sensors monitor a function and the systems responds based on the majority. This allows for one sensor to malfunction without effecting overall system reliability. For example, if a tank has three high level sensors and if two of the three indicate a high level, then the system reacts with the proper high level response. Since two of the three show high level, the third sensor's input in not needed. If one of three malfunctions, it could be reading anything from low to normal to high-high level, but it would not impact system operation. Unfortunately, people do not respond to multiple inputs as reliably as mechanical or electronic systems. A sensor input operates totally independent of the other sensors and a system always gives the same response to the same inputs. People's evaluation of the inputs, decision, and potential errors lack the consistency of a mechanical system. On the other hand, lacking that rigid consistency means people can adjust to changes within the inputs and goals and, consequently, are not limited to system-design constraints.

Decision making occurs as a result of comparing what is perceived in the environment and what is known by the decision maker (Mason & Mitroff, 1973). Essentially all of our current literature discusses considering the needs of people when designing information. However, current practice does not typically consider how people's questions depend on how they make decisions and interact with the system (Gerlach & Kuo, 1991; Woods & Roth, 1988). HII attempts to take the entire cycle

of information interpretation and decision making and place it within people's current situation.

After finding and interpreting the information, people have to use it. The entire reason they went through the process of finding the information in the first place was because they needed information to help address their current situation. Some of the ways people use information are:

Decision Making: Using the available information to make a decision about how to proceed in their current situation. Based on the results of the decision, people take action and then need to re-analyze the situation. Decision making is characterized by the need to make multiple and interdependent decisions in an environment that changes as a function of the decision, in response to environment changes, or both.

Problem Solving: Something is not right in the current situation and people are trying to figure out what to change to fix the problem. As portrayed in this book, problem solving differs from decision making by focusing on determining and adjusting a situation as a single stand-alone event. Also, problem solving tends to happen when people do not understand what caused the issue. Much of decision-making is rule-based with a "when X happens, then do Y" structure. With problem-solving, the rule-based situation has broken down and people need to shift to a knowledge-based analysis to understand what is happening in the situation. Once they understand the situation, they can make decisions. For example, a business analysis working to figure out the reason for dropping sales in a region. First, she needs to use problem-solving to figure out the problems and then make decisions on how to fit them.

Monitoring: Watching the current situation and ensuring it continues along the present path. It is part of the cyclic nature of HII. If the information fits the expected progress,

Figure 2. Decision process diagram

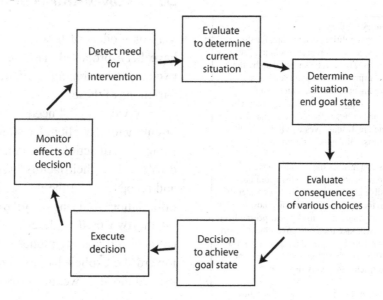

then a decision of "do nothing" is correct. However, if the information indicates that it is deviating, then people move into decision making or problem solving.

Rasmussen (1986) considers how people interact with many physical systems and how they make decisions to maintain those systems. Figure 2 provides a basic visual of the process he describes.

For control of a physical system such as an industrial process plant, a normative model of the necessary decision phases can be suggested. This sequence has been developed from analysis of decision making in a power plant control room and includes the following phases. First, the decision maker has to detect the need for intervention and has to look around and observe some important data in order to have direction for subsequent activities. He or she then has to analyze the evidence available in order to identify the present state of affairs, and to evaluate their possible consequences with reference to the established operational goals and company policies. Based on the evaluation, a target state into which

the system should be transferred is chosen, and the task that the decision maker has to perform is selected from a review of the resources available to reach the target state...When the task has thus been identified, the proper procedure, i.e., how to do it, must be planned and executed. It will be noticed that the nature of the information processes changes during the sequence. In the beginning, it is an analysis of the situation to identify the problem, then a prediction and value judgment and, finally, a selection and planning of the proper control actions. Depending upon the context in which the control decisions have to be made, in particular whether it is control of a physical system governed by causal physical laws, or a social system governed by human intentions, the breakdown of the decision task may result in different elementary phases (Rasmussen, 1986, p. 6)

Although Rasmussen was focused on decisions for physical system control, such as industrial control rooms, the same ideas apply to most HII situations. Granted, HII situations tend to have a stronger social element, so they are harder to predict and control, but the decision-making process

Box 1.

Decision making for policy makers

Policy making is built upon a political system that, for the most part, seeks to resolve value differences, not scientific differences, between groups. This can be summed up by the statement "the somewhat grim truth that good science and the presence of a rational argument do not guarantee that policymakers will do the "right thing" when crafting policy. The intersection of science and politics is fraught with compromise and trade-offs, and elected representatives will always seek to balance competing interests" (Wilson & Harsha, 2008, p. 24).

The list of compromises emphasizes the need to consider more than just the audience information needs—which could be defined as the best possible information—, but to consider the entire situation in which the audience operates and how they will be interpreting the information. Consider how people from different political parties will take the same government report and claim it proves either there is no cause for concern or the world is about to end. Although the information is the same, the overall audience interpretation is very different.

Wilson and Harsha (2008) further position the information and resulting decisions by saying:

> *Although it is a worthwhile goal to present the best science, simply providing the best science will not necessarily lead to a more 'scientifically based' decision (p. 26)*

For design teams striving to provide the best information, such a quote may be discouraging, but it is the reality of many decision-making environments, not just national policy as Wilson and Harsha were discussing. Decisions get made with information filtered through both the presentation design choices and a large set of human biases. High quality HII needs to take into account all of those factors which operate within the situation and consider how they will influence both the interpretation and decision process.

---

remains the same. When monthly business reports are analyzed, the analyst is performing essentially the same task as a plant operator, with the major difference being that the business reports are not in real-time. But both people are working to maintain their situation awareness or contextual awareness of what it happening, to understand what factors are most volatile so they require close scrutiny, and to evaluate the overall situation to make decisions about how to maintain it on the preferred track. This chapter examines the factors which influence decision makers and either support or distract them from making effectives decisions for the situation.

DECISION-MAKING MODELS

Various models of how people make decisions have been proposed. This section looks at the two most common; many of the other models are variations of these.

Any valid model needs to consider two different factors: explicit decision factors based on using rules of action (when the value exceeds X, do Y) and implicit factors based on knowledge and recognition of the unique interaction of the information within the situation (Gonzalez, 2005). Of the two models described here, the classical decision-making model is heavily weighted toward the explicit factors and the recognition-primed model is weighted toward the implicit.

Classical Decision-Making Model

The classical decision-making model attempts to quantitatively evaluate the optimal or best solution to the problem. In theory, it is very simple. All of the possible choices/solutions are determined, the factors or criteria which influence the solutions are determined, and weighting values are assigned to each of the criteria. In this model, people are expected to evaluate all the various alternative solutions with respect to the factors that influence the solutions. The result is a matrix with factors across the top and possible solutions down the side. By assigning weighting functions to each factor, the optimal solution can be found by simply summing over the factors; the solution with the highest value is the optimal solution. Figure 2 shows a hypothetical example for evaluating PCs.

Classical decision making assumes people define a set of criteria, evaluate all the possible options against the criteria, and then make the optimal choice. While looking nice from a theoretical viewpoint, research has shown that people simply don't evaluate situations in this manner (Klein, 1999; Klein, et al., 1993). The obvious problems with the classical model are: (1) determining all the alternative solutions in advance,

Table 1. Example of classical decision matrix. This matrix shows the evaluation of 5 PCs based on four criteria. The numbers under the criteria name are the weights assigned to each. By multiplying each value by the weight and adding the resulting scores, the best choice can be determined. In this example, there is a tie between PC 4 and PC 5.

	Speed (.2)	Memory (.3)	Drive (.1)	Cost (.4)	Total
PC 1	10	7	7	8	8.0
PC 2	10	6	6	6	6.8
PC 3	12	6	6	7	7.6
PC 4	8	9	8	8	8.3
PC 5	11	6	7	9	8.3

(2) determining the factors which influence them, and (3) setting the weighting factors (Klein, 1993; Klein et al, 1993).

In addition, most real-world situations either are not analytic in nature, thus not lending fitting analytical task analysis, or situation complexity results in more data than can possibly be handled or broken down into effective criteria. In healthcare, patients are asked to make treatment decisions, in some case with life-threatening decisions such as cancer treatments. But, because of lack of medical knowledge, they are unable to clearly define options or analytically evaluate them. Also, how would weighting factors be assigned in an analytical manner for factors such as "quality of life" and "life expectancy?"

Another problem with the classical model is that there are no methods to prove that all possible solutions or factors have been defined, or that the factor weights are realistic. In many instances, where the matrix of Table 1 is actually used, rather than evaluating the options, it becomes a game of manipulating the criteria weights until the desired option emerges as optimal. Many people respond to this type of analysis by adjusting the weighting factors until the totals on the matrix matches the decision which was initially desired (the boss wants to buy PC2, so play with the numbers until that is the best choice). If the criteria or the weights are manipulated to get a desired option, then there is no actual evaluation. But it does bring to light how the desired choice is often made. In

reality, people reach a preferred choice early in the decision-making process and working with a matrix tends to become an exercise in justifying that decision, rather than arriving at a decision.

In general, the classical decision-making model has been discredited as a model of how people actually make decisions. However, it is still prevalent in many texts and is often the only model presented. People seem to want the rigorous methodology it seems to contain as a means of justifying a decision. But the lack confidence in collecting all the attributes and the difficulty of assigning weights leads to a much higher level of apparent rigorousness that reality gives it.

Naturalistic Decision Making (Recognition Primed Model)

Instead of an analytic analysis, Hollnagel (1993) considers how most people handle decision-making situations in a reactive manner with decision making going through four stages:

- Define the principle objective
- Outline a few obvious alternatives
- Select an alternative that is a reasonable compromise
- Repeat the procedure if the result is unsatisfactory or if the situation changes too much

Agreeing with Hollnagle, Klein (1993, 1999) has been highly critical of the classical model and has advanced a recognition-primed model which more closely describes real-world decision making. The recognition-primed model assumes that people perform assessments of situations based on experience and that they attempt to make satisfactory, rather than optimal, decisions.

Field research indicates the recognition primed model fits how people reach decisions much better than the classical model. The weighting factors of the classical model focused on defining the 'best possible' solution, but people don't typically work toward the best. Instead, decision making operates as a satisfying process rather than an optimal path process (Orasanu & Connolly, 1993; Simon, 1979). When people search for information, they suffice rather than attempt to find all or the best information. The same performance occurs with decision making. People often settle for less than optimal performance; instead of maximizing output, they economize on cognitive resource allocation and attempt to produce satisfactory output with minimal effort. Based on how they view the situation, they rely on intuitive thinking, which rapidly leads to an answer but which follows a route that gives little information on how or why it was chosen (Rasmussen, 1986; Klein, 1999).

Most theories about how people make decisions or follow a process, assume they start with a planning segment. The models assume people take the time to carefully plan out their course of action. However, research into how people actually proceed reveals a different picture. The recognition primed model fits the real-world process of people quickly looking a situation over and almost immediately knowing what to do based on past experience. In Klein's studies (1999), he looked at people who had to make rapid decisions, such as fire commanders at a major building fire. Although many decisions relevant to HII may not proceed as quickly as the situations Klein studied, people still tend to quickly develop a preferred solution or, at least, a partial solution.

Often people follow first impressions or stereotypical actions and going with initial judgments and their general knowledge about this type of situation, rather than evaluating the situation (Webster & Kruglanski, 1994). People almost immediately come up with a potential solution fitting the active mental model and examine it for possible problems. If none are found, then that is the decision. On the basis of experience, a set of rules is progressively refined and tuned until it triggers the mental model only for the relevant cases. If a choice worked last time or a solution to another problem can be adapted for reuse (Besnard & Cacitti, 2005), they will use that one. Other options are not considered, including an evaluation of whether or not the decision is the best. Rather, as long as it works, it is considered sufficient.

In terms of reading information, going with stereotypical actions means people will often have reached some decisions long before they finish reading an entire text. Klein (1999) found people evaluate based on the order in which they receive information. Part of Wright's (1974) research on decision making under time pressure shows how people want to quickly reach closure and will to jump to a conclusion before seeing all of the information. Design teams need to consider how these factors play into information presentation and potential error conditions if decisions are reached too soon.

HOW PEOPLE MAKE SITUATION-SPECIFIC DECISIONS

Decision-making is rarely the logical process design teams would like it to be (Stewart, 1994). Nor does it completing conform to any single decision-making model. Instead, it revolves around people obtaining an understanding of the situation and doing something with that understanding. Decision making is a satisfying process rather than an optimal path process (Orasanu & Connolly,

1993); people do not carefully analyze a situation and try to reach an optimal solution, rather they accept the first available solution which is "close enough." Design teams need to move away from a "rational and logical view of decision-making and focus instead on such things as problem structuring/framing, creativity and idea processing, post-decision, and feedback analysis" (Parker & Sinclair, 2001, p. 450; Angehrn & Jelassi (1994).

A significant part of people's decision-making ability seems to depend on their tacit knowledge about the general situation (Gonzalez, 2005). When asked to explain how a decision was reached or even the main elements in performing a task, many people are unable to provide clear, coherent answers (Berry & Broadbent, 1987, 1988).

In a study of decisions made by emergency medical dispatchers at this control centre, Blandford, and Wong (2004) found that, like decision making in any complex situation, decisions are not made in isolation but within the context of a dynamically changing situation. Mentally constructing the situation model requires integrating information from multiple sources, different modalities, and different times. In additions, there can be ambiguous or conflicting information, which must be tracked for future resolution. When decision making situations are viewed in this way, the problems of the classical model become apparent; there is simply no time or method to methodically analyze the information. A significant part of a design team's job is to understand the underlying factors driving the dynamically-changing situation and how the information needs and information flow change within it with respect to how people make decisions.

Decision making efficiency is, of course, a requirement in most system designs when decision making is one of their goals. However, measuring that efficiency can be difficult. A classic method is timing how long it takes to reach a decision. However, what factors to measure must be carefully considered. For example, pilots who are good decision makers take longer to understand a situa-

tion, but are faster at executing their actions once they made a decision (Orasanu & Fischer, 1997). With pilots, making decisions and controlling their plane are seen as a single response/system. However, with many informational systems, after people reach a decision, the actions are performed independent of the system. In many cases, the decision maker may have to depend on other people to perform the actions which will change the situation. For example, an executive sends out memos to various business units about how to implement his decision. In that case, time measurements of just the information system interaction might be misleading, even though that is the only element under a design team's control.

The design analysis needs to define what will be good predictors for understanding the situation or supporting the decisions. Roberts (1989) studied how well people comprehend information and found that their understanding level can be discerned from how they respond to it. When they understand information, people make direct confirmation statements. On the other hand, when unsure of their understanding, they make assumptions or place the information into their own words. With low understanding, they will repeat text almost verbatim. Applying this research to the wording of people's responses can provide valuable information during usability testing. How

Box 2.

Patient's medical decisions
Healthcare is moving toward a model where the patient is supposed to be an active participant in the treatment decision-making process. Of course, this book has already had many examples were lack of understanding impacts quality participation in that process. The process is not straightforward. Although it is relatively easy to draw up a flowchart of actions, people do not respond in lockstep with that flowchart. Réach et al, (2005) found that diabetics did not perform insulin adjustments as they should, but were highly influenced by their health knowledge and beliefs and a fear of hypoglycemia. This was born out by a significant difference between what they said they did and what their diabetic logbook showed they actually did. One of the strongest factors was uncertainty, a factor which is present to some level in essentially every decision-making situation.

people explain the reason for their decision or their comprehension of a text can be as important as the completeness/accuracy of their explanation. The cognitive overload of many systems results from design teams trying to provide everything rather than providing what people need and giving information proper salience.

Information Needs and Presentation

Rather than a lack of information, the failure to anticipate people's needs forms the basis of most information problems and poor decision making. Overall information content, whether of documentation or web systems) is often high, but poor design destroys the content's ability to transmit that information (Albers, 1996). Ackoff (1967) suggests that managers typically suffer from a shortage of decision-relevant information and a simultaneous overabundance of irrelevant information. In a study where the task was to compare features of cars so they could make a recommendation to their boss about new company cars, most people gave up on using a car corporation web site and simply said they would go talk to a dealer. While the site provided abundant information on individual models, it gave no way to view comparable information across models or to easily answer some of the specific questions the boss wanted answered (Albers, 2000).

With cars, people can go to a dealer, but many times there is no significant external resource. The information provided in the report or on the corporate website is essentially all of the available information. If that information leaves concepts or causal relationships unexplained, then people have a choice of using their prior knowledge to fill in the gaps or performing additional research. But time and access often prevent any additional research. Thus, people resort to using prior knowledge to fill in gaps. And, of course, people often do not realize they lack all of the information they need. In the end, people are far less likely to try and find information when it requires effort to

search for the it (Mao & Benbasat, 2001). Design teams must understand what is needed and must provide it within the situation's context and when people need it.

Providing information within the situation's context and people's information needs is difficult. Information which supports decision-making needs to be flexible to accommodate the variability in information needs. Research on how patients make health care treatment decisions found that patients show a wide variation in their priorities. This brings into question the normal information design idea that addressing the information needs of the "majority of people" will provide individuals with the information that they need for an informed decision. Instead, to support high quality decision making these wide variations uncovered during the early analysis need to be accommodated in the design (Feldman-Stewart & Brundage, 2004). Personas provide one method ensuring different audiences are considered.

Klein (1999) found that people evaluate based on the order in which they receive information, accentuating the importance of information salience and of information being presented in an order relevant the situation. Wright (1974) revealed that under time pressure people will to jump to a conclusion before seeing all of the information, much less taking the time to interpret it. People evaluate information in different ways. For example, looking at a brand and then comparing within that brand, or looking at an attribute (such as price or a specific feature) and comparing various brands with respect to it. In a mismatch, marketing tends to focus on brand-level comparisons, while people tend to use mostly attribute-level comparisons or an even split between attribute and brand processing (Bettman & Zins, 1979). Design teams need to explicitly determine how people want the information ordered while still being flexible to allow different ordering. The best ordering of data is by type of decision, and not by data category, problem, source, or date, all of which tend to be database fields which are easy

Box 3.

Tailor information to individual needs

As much as possible, information needs to be designed to fit an individual person's needs and not be a one-size-fits-all solution. The problem is that different people respond differently and want different pieces of information. A study on providing information about prostate cancer screening found:

> *Our study suggests that men react differently to each piece of information. To ensure good decision-making, we therefore believe all men should receive information that there is a decision to be made regarding prostate cancer screening, that decisions may vary depending on individual preferences, and that screening can be both helpful and harmful (Sheridan et al., 2004, p. 350).*

To be fully relevant for decision making, the information presentation needs to fit the context and the people's prior knowledge. The importance of explanation of the information, rather than simply stating what to do, plays a crucial role in quality HII as people work to fit the new information into their existing situational models and make decisions.

---

to display but not highly relevant to the situation. Although displays which map directly to the underlying database makes for efficient programming, the presentation must reflect people's needs, not system architecture.

Combining these various research findings emphasizes the importance of carefully considering the information presentation (see chapter 10: *How people interact with information presentation*) and how it can influence people's decision making. There is a large chance that people may only read the first part of a text before reaching a decision; a long carefully built argument fails if its conclusions depend strongly on the later parts of a text. People may not read the ending sections or may only skim it, showing a confirmation bias as they look for support for their already-made decisions which were inspired by the beginning of the text.

A common presentation in business reports is to show numbers across time, predict how a trend will continue, and make appropriate decisions to adjust a predicted trend to the optimal trend. Besides just looking at the data series, people bring in other causal information to help with the decision: for example, knowing sales were down

at one store for a month because a competitor opened across the street. However, people are very poor at using the extra information to improve their decisions, and decisions based strictly on the numbers are often as accurate. When they are not as accurate, it becomes obvious and serious problems can occur. This was explained as a minimal cognitive effort effect since merging the causal information with numbers would require a high cognitive effort, something people try to avoid (Slovic, 1972).

Acquiring decision support information is subject to costly errors of two kinds: over-acquiring and incurring excessive informational costs; and under-acquiring and incurring excessive risks of decisional error. People often want an excess of information. They do not feel comfortable basing a decision on a single reason, but attempt to gather additional supporting material, even when it is not needed (Newell, Weston, & Shanks, 2003). Effective use of the extra information does not improve with experience (Lim & O'Connor, 1996).

Irrelevant Information and Presentation

People need to be able to distinguish relevant from irrelevant information and to group information elements together. Although this sounds obvious, relevance and proper grouping are situation-dependent and not a function of either the person or the information. Proper visual momentum of the presentation focuses people's attention to the salient elements and helps people build this grouping (Woods, 1984). Brooke & Duncan (1981) found, in studies of fault-finding performance, that display format affects "the ability of the diagnostician to perceive what is relevant and what is not" (p. 188). At the best, the focus on irrelevant information will waste time and, at the worst, can mislead the person into making incorrect decisions.

People want to use all of the available information and consider the most salient information as the most important. Irrelevant information which is salient strongly and predictably affects decisions even when people consciously admit the information is irrelevant. Chinander and Schweitzer (2003) explain this finding as arising from the ease of manipulating the information, which creates an input bias. People process it in ways that fit the presentation without restructuring it (Bettman & Zins, 1979) and adjust and create their strategies for making decisions opportunistically, based on the HII (Payne et al., 1992). But this means that if the presentation contains irrelevant information, especially if it is highly salient, it will negatively contribute to the decision-making process.

Decision Aids

People need information within subjective and highly dynamic domains. Decision aids are some type of text or computer-based program designed to help people through the decision-making process.

Modern information systems no longer just provide a set of fixed answers, instead they try to provide support for people with the ability to give explanations and detailed information about a desired topic with respect to the current situation (or at least, the progressive systems and research worlds are working toward this goal). While providing this support may sound like an expert system, expert systems have been criticized as being designed to fit the machine's viewpoint, as too brittle, and designed from an assumption that the computer can provide *the* answe. Expert system design typically starts with an assumption of removing people from the decision loop, or at least minimizing their input. Instead, high quality HII for decision aids needs to provide information and support people in reaching a decision, rather than asking questions and making the decision.

Decision aids for assisting patient decisions have been extensively researched within healthcare. The design has changed from paper-based flowcharts to the wizards used by many software

programs. Regardless of format, they have three main components: "(1) a structured presentation of information, (2) exercises to help the patient determine what attributes of the choices are important to their particular decision, and (3) exercises to help the patient integrate those important aspects, in order to arrive at a single preferred option" (Feldman-Stewart & Brundage, 2004, p. 266). Some examples are:

- Prostate cancer screening (Sheridan et al., 2004)
- Breast cancer (Stalmeier & van Roosmalen, 2009)
- Chronic obstructive pulmonary disease (Wilson et al, 2005)

When creating a decision aid, design teams need to consider four areas:

- Defining the information to include and justifying why it should be included to avoid dumping everything into the decision aid.
- Defining the information presentation. Poor presentation will compromise the quality of the information.
- Understanding how the decision aid will be used and how it fits within the situational context of people as they work within a complex and dynamic decision-making situation.
- Defining how the decision aid will be evaluated and what constitutes successful use.

Many decision aids focus on providing a single option or recommendation, often without clear justification for why to accept it. Dalala and Bonaccio (2010) found that an important factor in people accepting a recommendation is understanding the alternatives and why they are not the best choice. People don't want to be told to "do X" or "buy X." They need to understand why X is the best option rather than Y or Z.

Presenting Alternatives

Because people rarely base a decision on simple data look up (i.e., the table says 6, so the answer is no), the potential choices and reasoning behind those choices are necessary for communicating information that meets people's needs.

For many years, there was a belief that a computer would be able to analyze the entire situation and present people with *the* solution for approval. A significant part of early expert system research and the information engineering of the late 1990s worked toward this goal. The results of the computer analysis tended to be less than people desired and its acceptance of the suggestions was even lower. People do not like a computer to dictate actions to them, actions which were presented without explanation. Instead, people want alternatives and explanations that are presented within the situation's context.

When comparing information, people normally want to see a range of options rather than just an optimal (however defined) solution. Many people unconsciously demand any presentation which requires them to make an action-based decision to have at least 2 different options. For example, a study of physicians found they strongly resisted suggestions to not carry out an action when they were not offered an alternative, even if the action they intended to perform was virtually always counterproductive (Bates et al., 2003). The information communicated to people needs to say more than "don't do X" but must also say what to do and why.

When evaluating alternatives, decision makers need to make accurate predictions of how the choice will fit into and influence the overall situation. But this is often not the case; instead, they often show a range of problems which significantly impact the quality of the decision (Hsee & Hastie, 2006).

- Rather than alternatives closely matching the optimal one, people prefer a diverse set that provides a basis for comparison. The issue is that if a second or third solution is very similar to the optimal one, it provides little on which to make a comparison, as opposed to options with distinct differences (Lökketangen & Woddruff, 2005). However, it seems as if "decision makers will not be able to correctly anticipate the simultaneous influence of more than one task feature" (Fennema & Kleinmuntz, 1995, p. 23). Trying to show the effect of multiple changes at once will confuse people as they have trouble dividing out the influence of each factor. On the other hand, understanding the interrelation of those factors is essential to making good decisions.

- People evaluate based on the order in which they receive information; accentuating the importance for information salience and for information to be presented in an order relevant to understanding the situation (Klein, 1999).

- When presented with multiple options, people tended to focus on the differences between the options and ignore their common features. When asked about their dormitory assignments, college students focused on the physical rather than the social aspects when asked to predict their future happiness. However, when explicitly asked, they said the social was more important than the physical aspects. The students focused on the features which varied between dorms and ignored the social factors, which varied only slightly between dorms (Dunn et al., 2003).

- When confronted with many choices (for example, 30 types of sunscreen), people fall back to using heuristics rather than logically working out the best option. In a speed dating study, when interacting with a large number of people, choices were based on easy-to-evaluate physical char-

Box 4.

Determining relative value of an attribute

In most decision-making situations, the choices are not equal, but a choice must be made on which one is best for the situation. One way design teams can assess how people perceive the relative values of attributes is to have them adjust them until the choices are seen as equal.

For instance, imagine a decision-maker who expresses indifference between job A (16 days vacation and $33,000 salary) and job B (10 days vacation and $36,000 salary). For this decision-maker, the advantage of having 6 more vacation days in job A equals the advantage of having $3000 higher salary in job B (alternatively, losing 6 days equals losing $3000). (Willemsen & Keren, 2003, p. 343)

In this example, jobs A and B with their salaries could be presented and people asked to adjust the vacation days until they perceived the jobs as equivalent. Likewise, the price of a piece of equipment could be adjusted until it is perceived as equal to another one with more or fewer features. The end result for the design team is an understanding of the relative value people assign to the attributes.

Two factors influence the interpretation of the results.

- Downward adjustments are more inconsistent than upward adjustments (Willemsen & Keren, 2003). In other words, across multiple people, increasing values of a lower valued item is more consistent than decreasing the value of the higher valued item. The downward adjustments tend to be less than the upward adjustments. Assume one product was $100 with 5 features and another was $66 with 3 features. People would adjust the $100 product down $20 ($80) to make then equivalent or adjust the $66 product up $18 ($84).
- Choosing and rejecting are not cognitively handled the same. For example, pick the best of these five or pick the top three of these five (reject two). Positive attributes are weighted more heavily for choosing the best and negative attributes are weighted more heavily for rejecting the bottom two (Shafir, 1993).

---

acteristics such as weight and height. With smaller groups, people based their choices on factors that were harder to obtain, such as whether the other person had a college degrees or was a smoker (Lenton & Francesconi, 2010).

Interestingly, people feel regret if they choose a probabilistically favored option and then the outcome is unfavorable. The unfavorable outcome does not even have to stem from the choice itself; it can stem from outside factors such as weather or orders being shipped late. In future decisions they are less willing to again make that choice, even when they continue to believe that the option was the best for the situation (Ratner & Herbst, 2005). While this feeling of regret is an apparent contradiction to what should be expected with the classical decision model, it does fit with decision-making biases and how people handle uncertainty and incomplete information in decision making, topics which will be discussed later in the chapter.

DECISION-MAKING INFLUENCES AND BIASES

The decision-making models portray decision making as a simple process of collecting and analyzing information followed by making a decision based upon the analyzed information. Unfortunately, like most HII, the actual process is much more complex and many human attributes exert an influence on the final decision. This section looks at some of these factors.

To make a good choice, decision makers need to predict the consequences of their choice, but this proves to be a difficult task (Hsee & Hastie, 2006). A number of biases contribute to these effects when evaluating alternatives.

Impact Bias: People often overestimate the impact (both intensity and duration) of an event. Previously good or bad experiences exert a strong influence on future choices, since people work with an implicit assumption that the previous event's experiences will be repeated.

Projection Bias: People project their feelings and emotions onto any group they are making a decision for. Parents assume their teenagers will feel the same way. Corporate decision makers assume the various departments or groups within the corporation will react to the decision as they would.

Figure 3. Factors interfering with evaluating alternatives (adapted from Hsee & Hastie 2006, p. 32). Different biases affect each stage of the decision making process. Design teams need to consider how those biases may affect the HII.

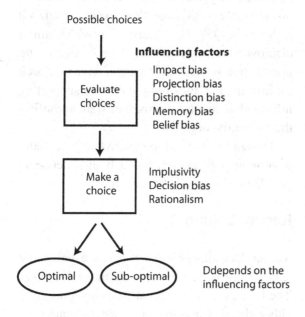

Judgment Bias or Predecisional Distortion Bias: Evaluating the alternatives with respect to the desired answer or choice; essentially, deciding on the answer before beginning the evaluation. The positive or negative attributes of the alternatives get distorted so that that final choice corresponds to the best choice. Carlson and Pearo (2004) found that most of the distortion occurs on attributes which were previously valued by the decision maker. For example, if operations-per-minute was a highly valued attribute, a decision maker would distort or explain away the value to make the desired choice seem to have the best value. Judgment bias has also been seen in studies of ship control decisions made by Naval officers (Perrin et al, 2001).

Overvaluation Bias: People want items with lots of features and make their choices based on the relative number of features, but then rarely use most of them. The disconnect arises because the decision fails to consider how the features will be used in the future (Zhao, Meyer, & Han, 2006).

Memory Bias: Predictions of future experiences are often based on memories of past experiences. Unfortunately, people's memory of past events tends to very distorted (Mather & Johnson, 2000; Mather, Shafir, & Johnson, 2000). Memory-based evaluations are strongly influenced by the event's peak and end experiences.

The factors which can interfere with evaluating multiple options and making decisions are summed up in Figure 3.

Effort and Accuracy Trade Off

During the decision-making process, there is a cost tradeoff between the value of the information and the cognitive cost implied by remembering/analyzing it. In situations which require cognitive effort, such as decision making, people engage in what is called an "effort-accuracy tradeoff framework" (Payne et al., 1993). According to this theory, an individual balances the effort/cost of a particular course of action against the benefits of taking that action. Interestingly, people focus more on reducing the cognitive effort than on maximizing decision quality. Rather than expend extra effort to achieve an optimal solution, reaching a satisfactory solution is sufficient (Russo & Dosher, 1983; Beach & Mitchell, 1978). Gregor and Benbasat (1999) found the "effort-accuracy tradeoff" could also be applied to how people use explanatory text. People would ignore explanatory information unless they felt it was worth the effort to read and interpret it. Usability tests of procedural documents consistently find people skipping blocks of text because "it's just information." They want to complete a task and not read about it, thus they do not exert the effort.

As part of minimizing cognitive effort,

- People tend to minimize the amount of new information they remember and maximize the use of existing information (Vassilakis & Moustakis, 1996).
- As time pressure increases, people base their decisions on first impressions or stereotypical actions (Webster & Kruglanski, 1994) since that reduces effort. Instead of reading an entire text, the content of the first paragraph may be the total basis of the decision.

People's evaluation of the cost-benefit depends strongly on their perceptions of accuracy-effort (Chu & Spires, 2003). However, the effort used for these perceptions is not actual effort, but anticipated effort (how difficult does it seem to be). People are very poor at estimating anticipated effort (Fennema & Kleinmuntz, 1995). Typically, effort estimates in areas where people have low knowledge are much higher than the actual effort.

Search for Supporting Information

People rationalize their interpretation of information to fit with their desired or expected outcome. According to the naturalistic decision model, people will first classify and understand a situation and then will immediately select an action (Endsley, 1995; Klein, 1999). As they gain experience, they can make finer classifications based on their knowledge of critical cues in the environment. Supporting people's tendency to make an immediate decision means that the information required to prove/disprove the decision must be quick and easy to obtain.

Expectancy bias already leads to giving preference to information which supports the expected result. As the complexity of the information increases, the impact of this bias increases. The problem is that people do not increase their mental

analysis to match the increased complexity of the information. People very quickly reach some sort of potential decision, which they then try to prove/disprove by looking at more information. However, they increasingly ignore information incompatible with what they expect (Ganzach & Schul, 1995). The information which might disprove a choice is ignored and only supporting information is viewed. If people have to search for information, they only search for supporting information. In other words, they want to confirm their potential decision.

Design teams need to ensure that potentially disproving information has a high salience so people must mentally process it.

Recent Events

Recent decisions or news of recent events has a strong influence on how people make decisions. The influence of the recent past can come from either the decision-maker's past (a manager's recent performance) or from relevant events (stories from a colleague or news events which had lots of press). A choice that turns out favorable leads to people making similar choices, and they will actually make decisions supporting riskier choices than if the initial favorable event had not occurred. In gambling, this occurs as making bigger bets after winning a big pot. In business, if a product-based decision worked well, a riskier decision for the same or similar product will get approved. Likewise, if a decision had a bad outcome, people will resist making a similar decision and only want to make 'safe' choices.

In a study of business managers (Ratner & Herbst, 2005), besides failing to attempt exact results (they were content to suffice), they exhibited decision-making that showed a mix of risk taking and avoiding behavior. Rather than consider each situation individually, the managers tended to base decisions on recent events with the greatest risk-taking appearing after a gain brought about by a good decision. Having just had a success caused them to engage in risky decisions; the same effect is seen in gamblers who will place riskier bets after a win. The reverse happens after loss. Then the managers were risk-adverse and made decisions with an extremely conservative mindset.

The gambler's fallacy that a game is ready to pay off since it hasn't paid off recently, reflects the influence of recent events. The basic HII problem with the recent event effect is that many decisions carry a probabilistic outcome and chance influences whether or not a gain occurs. Random factors which are beyond the control of the decision maker often influence the outcome, but the decision maker implicitly assumes those same factors will happen the next time. The same mix of risk taking and risk avoiding behavior is found in situations driven by pure chance, such as with gambling. After a loss people are less willing to repeat a decision again. An interesting point is people will avoid repeating a decision with a negative outcome even when they believe that the option is more likely than the alternatives to produce a successful outcome.

In the longer term, the recent event effect tends to fade. Norman (2009) discusses how the bad experiences people have are typically overshadowed by the good ones and even though people complain, they are ready to repeat the experience (whether to take a trip or to use a product). He attributes this to memories fading at different rates. Memories of emotional distress or frustrations fade faster than positive memories. People may give a litany of horror stories about various experiences, such as long slow lines at a theme park or poor instructions which made product assembly almost impossible, yet they intend to return to the theme park or buy that manufacturer's product again. Since negative and positive emotion memories fade a different rates, design teams need to consider this when part of the audience analysis consists of discussing past experiences. The people receiving the communication or the decision maker's approving the project may reject

negative analysis or, at least, claim it wasn't really that bad. In their memory, the bad aspects have faded; they are suffering from *rosy remembrance* (Mitchell et al, 1997).

Hindsight Bias

In retrospect, many events and occurrences seem to be predictable and inevitable. *Hindsight bias* is people's tendency, after learning about the actual outcome of a situation or the correct answer to a question, to distort their previous judgments to be consistent with the new (post-event) information.

For example, hindsight on stock market trades either show a stock that gains or losses was inevitable based on various factors which were known at the time of purchase (Louie, 2005). Perhaps the company had a major lawsuit pending, but believing it would be resolved favorably, the stock was bought. If the lawsuit is resolved favorably, the increased value is seen as inevitable based on the terms of the lawsuit. If lawsuit is resolved unfavorably, the drop in stock value is rationalized away as inevitable based on the terms of the lawsuit.

Post-event analysis of major problems tends to find the same hindsight factors. Engineering memos or maintenance decisions which were justified at the time they were made are seen in hindsight to have been problematical and lead to the major problem. The Challenger investigation found memos where the engineers questioned the o-ring performance. A more interesting point here is that, if the investigation had determined a different cause of the explosion, the o-ring memos would be ignored and other memos about the faulty part would almost certainly have been found. In a highly complex system, a post-event analysis will find indications that people knew about the problem. But the report skips over the often 100s or 1000s indications of other problem.

From an HII view, designs teams cannot control for hindsight. However, it does feed into the recent event bias and can strongly affect future decisions.

Emotions and Logic

From a design view, the analysis typically assumes the information will be evaluated from a logical view and emotions will not be involved. However, in many cases, this assumption is not true. The recent events' effects are one example with the risk taking or risk avoidance often driven by the emotional low/high of the decision makers. People are more willing to take risks after a success than a failure, even when they acknowledge the success/failure of the current decision situation is independent of the past one. Emotional reactions to situations can lead people away from the better choices and instead they will accept lower value but safer choices. Emotional reaction to a negative outcome can lead people to switch away from the options that they believe are most likely to be successful on the next occasion (Ratner & Herbst, 2005).

A significant problem for HII is that single, uncommon events have a profound influence on the emotional forces people engage when making decisions. Events which people admit are not common, such an airplane crash or a house fire, coupled with the event occurring in the recent past make it almost impossible for people to not to make decisions strongly influenced by it. For example, after a major airline crash many people avoid flying. They will even admit that they know the airplane is safe, but still don't want to fly. Likewise, having a relative die during surgery makes people leery of having any surgery, even though it may be different type surgery with a different surgeon. People may even admit the relative was a high-risk surgery candidate, but they still let emotions dominate their surgical decisions. Or a manager may reject a proposal because he doesn't want to work with that person or department; the manager's emotions override quality of the proposal.

In general, design teams should assume that emotions dominate when reason and emotions conflict with each other (Loewenstein, 1996).

However, some research does find that the emotional response can be reduced if the design forces people to think through the choices and makes the important information highly salient (Ratner & Herbst, 2005; Shiv & Fedorikhin, 1999).

Heuristics

As the decision task increases in complexity, contrary to intuition, the decision maker does not increase the complexity of the decision-making strategy. Heuristics are used since they save mental effort, but no single heuristic works across all situations (Payne, Bettman, & Johnson, 1988). In complex situations, rather trying to integrate multiple features, people tend to adapt decision-making strategies which use relatively simple, error-prone heuristics (Fennema & Kleinmuntz, 1995). "Easy to use" seems to be a dominant factor in heuristic choice. When people meet up with complex situations with documents that do not effectively assist in solving, contrary to the desired result, their decision-making ability tends to decrease and they make decisions based on simple heuristic rules. Unfortunately, these decisions often lead to non-optimal solutions and may lead to incorrect solutions since the use of the heuristic may oversimplify the analysis and ignore key information specific to the situation.

The heuristic people use depends on both information presentation and how they estimate the anticipated effort of extracting the desired information. The main heuristics people employ tend to rely on the availability of information or frequency of information appearance (Tversky & Kahneman 1981). Essentially, any information already in short-term memory receives excessive weight. People want to use information which is easily/quickly available rather than have to search for it, including mentally retrieving it from long term memory. As a result, information salience has a major effect on the decision process since it can maintain information (relevant or irrelevant) in short-term memory. Although this seems to sup-

Box 5.

> **Statistical heuristics**
> People can attempt to use statistics for judgments about everyday problems using statistical heuristics, which are rough approximations of statistical principles. The decision logic may proceed with comments about a 50-50 chance or a 75% chance. However, most people are unable to clearly explain what a 75% chance actually means with respect to the situation and their decision. Also, framing issues interact with the statistical heuristic: decisions are different if the information is presented as spend $250,000 for a 75% chance of a increasing productivity or spend $250,000 for a 25% chance of a no change in productivity.
>
> Statistical heuristics work best when the information space and process are clear and when chance clearly plays into the result (Nisbett et al., 1983). The real problem is that most people actually lack the skill set to reason via statistics. They tend to overlook good statistical practice which accounts for factors such as sample size, correlation, and base rate. On the other hand, people with formal statistical training do tend to avoid the logical reasoning errors that stem from faulty statistical analysis (Fong, 1988).

port a highly compact information presentation, Rubens and Rubens (1988) found that making the information too compact or concise hindered performance. Rather, information in context and how it relates to understanding the situation must occupy a prominent position in design considerations and the information structure must enhance its usability.

Management by PowerPoint or having everything condensed into five bullet points is one method of management by heuristics. The executives only wants enough information so they can apply a set of rules and make a rapid decision about the situation.

The extensive use of heuristics in decision making brings the concept of "exact results" into question. Besides sufficing on information seeking, it seems decision makers are willing to accept that their decisions are not perfect, but good enough. Larichev et al (1995) claim that since the decision maker is not concerned with exact answers, it makes no sense to measure systems based on exactness of results. Yet, many design guidelines and usability tests use exactness as their definition of effectiveness.

Time Pressure

Time pressure, like other stresses, reduces people's ability to process complex information and to use it to reach decisions. The number of factors they consider is reduced as they try to rush to a decision. A major decision influencing factor with time pressure is that people want to quickly reach closure on the problem. Rather than working to understand the entire situation, they want to make some type of decision. How quickly they reach a decision occurs as a trade-off between amount of effort expended to reach a decision and desired accuracy. As time pressure increases, people base their decision on first impressions or stereotypical actions (Webster & Kruglanski, 1994). Thus, instead of reading an entire text, the content of the first paragraph may be the sole basis of the decision.

People are highly adaptive when making decisions under time pressure (Payne, Bettman, & Johnson, 1988).

- Rate of information search increases.
- Heuristic-based decision-making increases.
- Options are rejected based on single aspects.
- Confirmation bias increases where information which does not support the desired decision is ignored (Ganzach & Schul, 1995).

HII which involves decisions under time pressure should try to focus the decision maker on breadth of evaluation, rather than depth of evaluation (Payne, Bettman, & Luce, 1996).

For example, reviews of communication in cancer care have noted that patients frequently display high anxiety when they are diagnosed with cancer. The high anxiety is understandable, but it also results in self-imposed time pressure to reach a treatment decision. Rather than working to understand the options, people either avoid a decision by asking the physician to make a recommendation or go with a simple heuristic of using the survival rate numbers. Unfortunately, survival rates can be described in multiple ways and most people lack the statistical training to properly understand them. Thus, small differences in numeric rates, such as 1%, can have a major influence on the treatment decision (Feldman-Stewart & Brundage, 2004) and factors such as treatment side effects and quality of life are ignored.

Framing

Framing effects occur when the same information is evaluated differently when it is presented in gain or loss frames. Essentially any information situation can be framed in either positive or negative terms. People respond differently depending on a positive or negative framing (Figure 4). Consider two different carnival games which gave their odds

as having a 70% chance of winning a teddy bear or a 30% chance of losing. Although these two games have the same odds of winning, expressing the information in positive or negative terms effects how people respond to it. If asked to justify the choice of which game to play to win a teddy bear, most people do not consider the games to be equivalent and would state the game with a 70% chance of willing was better to play than the one with a 30% chance of losing.

Framing affects the factors people consider when analyzing a situation and making decisions, and how the information gets framed has a strong effect on the type of decision people reach. Framing takes one or more aspects of a situation and increases the relative salience of the common and the distinctive features, even when they don't necessarily deserve that increase (Tversky, 1977). For example, Levin and Gaeth (1988) found that

Figure 4. Gain-loss frame. You are given $50. Then you have two choices: (1) You can keep $20 or gamble all or nothing, or (2) lose $30 or gamble all or nothing. People perceive the gain frame as a better bet, but the two choices are identical. They keep the $20 and quit, while they gamble rather than lose $30.

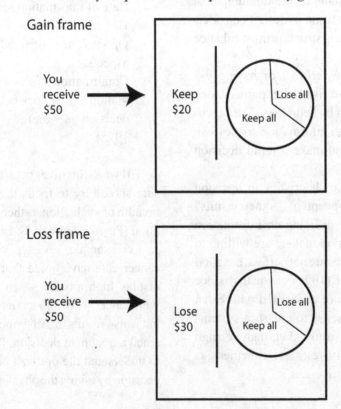

perceptions of the quality of ground beef depended on whether the beef was labeled as "75% lean" or "25% fat." The beef was rated as better tasting and less greasy when described as 75% lean.

How design teams frame the information presentation as negative or positive has a strong influence on how people interpret the information. When people use heuristics, the chosen heuristic depends heavily upon how the information gets presented.

Uncertainty

Most decisions do not have an absolute correct answer. External factors play a role in how the actions will be carried out and the information available to the decision maker is incomplete. Consequently, people must make decisions knowing there is an element of uncertainty which they cannot eliminate. This can have a profound effect on the long-term decision-making process.

Consider a decision maker who has made, under conditions of uncertainty, a chain of normatively optimal, but practically unsuccessful decisions (namely, wise decisions that have turned out badly). The decision maker can be a business person, a physician, whatever. Decision making under uncertainty is tantamount to gambling, and in gambling there are no guarantees of success. Suppose the unfortunate outcomes were just a coincidence, namely, were brought about "by chance." Though the decision maker cannot be faulted, her superiors erroneously perceive the long run of failures as evidence of incompetence. Unfair as this may sound, to the extent that it happens, it alters the nature of the distributions to which observers are then exposed: if decision makers are replaced after a bad run, they do not get the chance to have their bad run diluted by more typical future runs. Thus, their final track record, being based on a truncated career, is indeed poorer, on average, than that of a luckier, though

not better, decision maker who did not have such a bad run. (Bar-Hillel & Wagenaar, 1991, p. 449)

Interestingly, people feel regret if they choose a probabilistically favored option (the probability numerically expresses the uncertainty in the information) and then the outcome is unfavorable. In future decisions they are less willing to again make that choice, even when they believe that the option is the best (Ratner & Herbst, 2005).

When faced with uncertainty, people will fall back on what is familiar to them and will try to avoid moving outside of their comfort zones. A study of novice stock traders found that with uncertain information, they tended to recommend familiar stocks (Fox & Weber, 2002).

Risk Avoidance

Risk is the term for handicapping the probability that a desired outcome will occur. If a morning weather forecast has a 0% chance of rain, people don't take an umbrella. If there's a 100% chance of rain, people carry an umbrella. Anywhere in between—and the vast majority of decisions are in between—it's a judgment call. But even if the weather forecasters get the percentages right, it may not help an individual. The chance of rain was 70%, but that means a 30% chance of carrying an umbrella all day and not having rain. Recent event bias may mean that two days later, they will not take an umbrella when the rain chance is again 70% and this time it does rain.

Chapter 9: *How people approach numbers, statistics, and risks,* "Risk perception" discussed risk and probabilities at greater length than this section, which focuses on people's risk-avoidance behavior. The risk avoidance arises from the interaction of some of the factors in earlier sections, primarily: recent event bias and use of heuristics.

Regulatory focus theory sees decision-making as being focused on one of two factors: promotion and prevention (Higgins, 1997). The promotion focus privileges accomplishments and positive outcomes. The prevention focus privileges safety, responsibilities, and negative outcomes. People with promotion focus tend to strive toward making gains while those with a try to ensure non-loss.

In general, people operate with a prevention focus and, thus, show a preference to avoid risk. Studies of business decision-makers consistently reveal they take the 'safe bet' with small gains or assured no-loss rather than making a riskier, higher return decision. When making choices, people tend to pick the more conservative choice or go for what they feel is a sure thing. Often, these risk avoidance choices lead to sub-optimal performance.

In a study of business managers, besides failing to attempt exact results, they exhibited decision-making that showed both risk taking and avoiding behavior. Rather than consider each situation individually, the managers tended to base decisions on recent events with the greatest risk taking appearing after a gain. Also, rather than fully analyzing the situation, people result to heuristics to make rapid decisions. Overall there appeared to be a greater underlying tendency toward risk avoidance (Sullivan & Kida, 1995, p. 82). Besides making choices that tend to avoid risk, business managers also typically fail to anticipate losses, or exploit gains. Instead, they adapt a less-than-optimal strategy that assumes neither a loss nor gain will occur (Langholtz et al., 1995). Langholtz et al. attributed part of the less-than-optimal behavior to an equal-scheduling tendency for resource-allocation problems. Rather than partitioning resources by their importance, managers tended to make decisions which divide them equally. As a result, some areas have too many resources and other too few.

PROBLEM SOLVING

When people are familiar with the problem environment, they don't use a goal-oriented approach. Rather, they use a set of rules based on what has previously worked (Rasmussen, 1986). Most decision making can be rule-based; people have seen similar situations before and know what to do. On the basis of experience, the mental model develops a set of rules which are progressively refined and tuned. When presented with a new problem, people based their interaction on their mental models and past experience (Roediger, 1980; Randel and Pugh, 1996) and tried to reuse what has worked in the past (Besnard & Cacitti, 2005). However, sometimes those rules fail to apply and what has worked before fails to work this time. At this point, people must engage in problem solving. Problem solving "rarely arises straightforwardly, but rather results from a long and recursive process with backtracking and erratic switching among the following activities: thinking about ideas, production, reorganization, modification, and evaluation" (Nanard & Nanard, 1995, p. 50).

Kintsch (1998) points out that people tend to understand problems very quickly. After gaining an understanding, they can make decisions about how to proceed. Only when they are unable to resolve or comprehend the situation do people shift to a problem-solving mode. In unfamiliar situations when proven rules are not available, people shift to a goal-oriented approach where they consider different methods that will achieve their goal. Typically, multiple attempts are not actually made, but are performed as a mental exercise. Rasmussen (1986) points out that "the efficiency of humans in coping with complexity [in problem solving] is largely due to the availability of a large repertoire of different mental representations of the environment from which rules to control behavior can be generated ad hoc (p. 100).

As people gain experience with the situation, they develop routines. These routines may start as a problem-solving strategy, but over time they become a rule-based method of addressing a familiar problem (Cary & Carlson, 1999). The research literature often makes a distinction (e.g., Payne, Bettman, & Johnson, 1988) between skill-as-procedures and skill-as-understanding. Some skills involve the reproduction of rehearsed procedures to carry out known tasks, while others require developing new sequences of actions based on people understanding of the sitaution. Instructions are written for skill-as-procedure, while troubleshooting guides, even those written as step by step instructions, depend on skill-as-understanding. Skill-as-understanding is problem solving; taking prior knowledge, applying to the current situation, and arriving at a decision about why the situation is not responding as desired. Much of the decision making in business and healthcare can be described as rule-based and skills-as-procedures. From experience, the decision maker knows how to interpret the current data set and how to proceed. Only when some of the data significantly fails to conform to their expectations do they shift to problem-solving.

Solving a problem is a multi-stage process. The literature contains many different models of how people solve problems and each model has a different number of steps. However, the main differences tend to be the granularity of the individual steps in the model. Norman (1984) identifies four stages in the problem-solving process.

Intention: Clarifying the goal mentally. People have to consider what they really want to achieve.
Selection: Translating the intention into an action. Based on the situation, the steps which are needed to interact with it need to be planned out.
Execution: Performing the interaction with the situation.
Evaluation: Looking at the results and determining if the action had the desired effect. If not, the process repeats.

Although Norman's model is described as a simple linear sequence, problem-solving research reveals that people rarely plan out complete sequences before executing them (Suchman, 1987;

Anderson, 1990). Instead, they are performed in a cyclic manner with constant backtracking and moving toward the goal by small steps. Payne (1991) showed how a lack of knowledge typically limits the selection step (if you don't know the full affects of an action, you can't predict its effect). But even when people do know the affect, they still tend to interweave the steps (Payne, Howes, & Reader, 2001). Rather than trying to reach the goal in a single major change, many small changes are made and after each change the situation is re-evaluated.

Part of the reason for interweaving is that people have a hard time manipulating multiple items in memory at the same time. While Miller's (1956) work on 7 +/- 2 is often quoted, that quote is out of context and not really applicable to problem solving. Halford et al, (2005). shows that when problem solving, people have difficulty mentally maintaining four variables and find five nearly impossible when analyzing graphical representations. Research on plant monitoring has found similar results, with error rates increasing rapidly when the number of variables exceeds three (Lightner, 2001)

For design teams developing high quality HII,

The more critical question for effective human performance may be how knowledge is activated and utilized in the actual problem-solving environment. The question concerns not merely whether the problem solver knows some particular piece of domain knowledge, such as the relationship between two entities. Does he or she know' that it is relevant to the problem at hand, and does he or she know how to utilize this knowledge in problem solving? (Woods & Roth, 1988, p. 420)

Expert and Novice Level Problem Solving

Greeno (1973) has suggested that problem solving involves accessing and transferring information from short-term memory and long-term memory to "working memory" and combining or restructuring that information to arrive at an understanding of the situation. Of course, having the information in long-term memory requires experience. Domain knowledge is a major factor in problem-solving and leads to people show expert problem-solving skills in one field and novice skills in another, and can actually show these characteristics at the level of specific tasks within a field. Without the prior knowledge, they cannot fully address the situation (Shanteau, 1992).

There has been a substantial amount of research into the difference between expert and novice problem solving (Wickens & Hollands, 2000 give a good overview). Also, see chapter 4: *How people approach information*, "Novice to expert continuum." Obviously, one substantial difference is the amount prior knowledge. Another factor is the level of people's problem solving skills. With poor problem solving skills, people rely on surface level features of the information and use an means-ends approach (Corbalan, Kester, & Van Merriënboer, 2009; Simon, Langley, & Bradshaw, 1981). With more knowledge or skill, they look for or address the deeper underlying principles and try to reshape the problem into something understandable. How the problem gets mentally represented has a significant effect on how easy it is to solve (Jonassen, 2003).

EXAMPLES

Astronomical Information

At some point, many people research information on buying a telescope. If they have minimal exposure, they start with thinking in terms of the telescope's magnification, which is prominently listed on low-end telescopes. But after that point, other than price, they don't know what to look at next.

The people have a goal (buy a telescope), but they don't know what information they need to accomplish that goal. High quality HII will work to both provide information and explicitly dispel any myths or misinformation they have. The information needs are broader than most people would initial think, such as:

- What will you observe?
- How will it be transported?
- Will you be setting it up alone?
- Buy a telescope or binoculars?

The myths and misinformation include topics, such as:

- What magnification really means and is it useful.
- How far can you see.
- Mirror size is the most important thing.

Design teams need to consider the numerous biases will influence the telescope decision making.

- *Recent event bias.* If the person has recently interacted with a particular type of telescope, they may show a preference for that style.
- *Framing bias.* Depending on how the research the information and especially if they have already searched on marketing sites, the prior information they have found will strongly frame how they interpret the information on this site.
- *Risk avoidance and uncertainty bias.* They want a telescope and know it will be expensive. Thus they want a sure thing, but uncertainty in their use and lack of knowledge about observing methods complicates the decision.

Business Reports

After a report is created, it is sent to the decision-makers who bring it to a meeting. Often, they have not read it before the meeting or have only read the executive summary. Thus, they do not fully understand all of the logic which went into the report. The design team needs to consider how many factors will start to influence the decisions based on the report.

- *Recognition primed decision making.* The reader sees a valid option with no apparent negatives, and thus is ready to go with that option. The report body may clearly layout those negatives, but that part hasn't been read. The negative factors must be salient to help avoid a discussion centered around "so why not go with option B? I like that one" instead of a discussion on the value of all the options.
- *Risk avoidance.* The decision makers want assurances they are making the right decision and that there is minimal risk. The risks need to be explain and focused on what they consider important. Time delay versus costs versus employee productivity improvements all have risk factors, but depending on the situation, will vary in their importance.
- *Heuristics.* If the report is describing a situation similar to ones from the past, the decision makers will use a heuristic approach and go with what worked before. The unique aspects of the current situation may not support and those unique aspects must receive salience.
- *Alternatives.* People are more confidence in a decision if they have alternatives. The report should provide different options.

The decision makers have many other things to do and do not want to spend time on the current discussion. They want to make a decision and move on. The report design must provide alternatives and give the information related to those alternatives with proper salience levels to support rapid decision making. At the same time, it needs to work to minimize the effects of decision making biases which could result in a highly sub-optimal or incorrect decision.

SUMMARY

This chapter looks at the factors which influence how people use that information to make decisions. Decision making occurs as a result of comparing what is perceived in the environment, what is known by the decision maker, and the desired state of the situation. Decisions within an HII context never exist in isolation, but are embedded within the larger tasks that the person needs to accomplish.

Models of Decision Making

The chapter looked at two different models of decision making.

The classical decision-making model attempts to quantitatively evaluate the optimal or best solution to the problem. All of the possible choices/solutions are determined, the factors or criteria which influence the solutions are determined, and weighting values are assigned to each of the criteria. The solution with the highest value is optimal. However, people don't make decisions in this manner and exhaustively determining the criteria and weights is almost impossible.

The recognition primed model fits the real-world process of people quickly looking a situation over and almost immediately knowing what to do based on past experience. When people need to make a decision, they suffice rather than attempt to find all or the best information.. People almost immediately come up with a potential solution fitting the active mental model and examine it for possible problems. If none are found, then that is the decision. Often they follow first impressions or stereotypical actions and go with initial judgments and their general knowledge about this type of situation, rather than fully evaluating the situation

How People Make Situation-Specific Decisions

People use a range of strategies to interpret information and make predictions about the future development of the situation on which to base their decisions.

Good HII for decision making revolves around people obtaining an understanding of the situation and doing something with that understanding. Decision making is a satisfying process rather than an optimal path process; instead, they accept the first available solution which is "close enough." A significant part of people's decision-making ability seems to depend on their tacit knowledge about the general situation.

Rather than a lack of information, the failure to anticipate people's needs forms the basis of most poor decision making. People typically suffer from a shortage of decision-relevant information and a simultaneous overabundance of irrelevant information. Overall information content is often high, but poor design destroys the content's ability to transmit that information.

People need to be able to group information elements together and to distinguish relevant from irrelevant information. They want to use all of the available information and consider the most salient information as the most important. Salient but irrelevant information can strongly and predictably affects decisions even when people consciously admit the information is irrelevant.

Decision aids are some type of text or computer-based program designed to help people through the decision-making process. High quality decision aids must give people alternatives and explanations of the suggested choice. People do not like a computer to dictate actions to them, actions which were presented without explanation. They don't want to be told to "do X" or "buy X." They need to understand why X is the best option rather than Y or Z.

Decision-Making Influences and Biases

Many factors exert an influence on how people reach decisions.

Effort-Accuracy Trade Off: During the decision-making process, there is a cost tradeoff between the accuracy or value of the information, and the cognitive effort of finding and analyzing it.

Search for Supporting Information: People very quickly reach some sort of potential decision, which they then try to prove/disprove by looking at more information. They rationalize their interpretation of information to fit with their desired or expected outcome and, as information quantity increases, ignore information incompatible with what they desire to find.

Recent Events: Recent decisions or news of recent events have a strong influence on how people make decisions.

Hindsight Bias: Hindsight bias is people's tendency, after learning about the actual outcome of a situation or the correct answer to a question, to distort their previous judgments to be consistent with the new (post-event) information.

Emotions: People's risk taking or risk avoidance often driven by the emotional low/high resulting from recent decisions. People are more willing to take risks after a success than a failure. Emotional reactions to situations can lead people away from the better choices and instead they will accept lower value but safer choices. Emotional reaction to a negative outcome can lead people to switch away from the options that they believe are more likely to be successful.

Heuristics: Heuristics are used since they save the mental effort of fully understanding the situation. As the decision task increases in complexity, contrary to intuition, the decision maker does not increase the complexity of the decision-making strategy.

Framing: Framing effects occur when the same information is evaluated differently when it is presented in gain or loss frames. Essentially any information situation can be framed in either positive or negative terms. People respond differently depending on a positive or negative framing.

Risk Avoidance: People operate with a prevention focus and, thus, show a preference to avoid risk. Studies of business decision-makers consistently reveal they take the 'safe bet' with small gains or assured no-loss rather than making a riskier, higher return decision.

Problem Solving

People tend to understand situations very quickly and make decisions about how to proceed. When they are unable to resolve or comprehend the situation, people shift to a problem-solving mode. Problem solving has four stages: intention to achieve a goal, selection of possible plan/route to the goal, execution of the plan, and evaluation of the execution phase.

REFERENCES

Ackoff, R. (1967). Management misinformation systems. *Management Science, 14,* 147–156. doi:10.1287/mnsc.14.4.B147

Albers, M. (1996). Decision-making: A missing facet of effective documentation. *Proceedings of the 14th Annual International Conference on Computer Documentation* (pp. 1–6). New York, NY: ACM.

Albers, M. (2000a). *Information design for web sites which support complex decision making.* Presented at STC 2000 Annual Conference, Orlando FL. May 21–24, 2000.

Anderson, J. R. (1990). *Cognitive psychology and its implications.* New York, NY: Freeman.

Angehrn, A., & Jelassi, T. (1994). DSS research and practice in perspective. *Decision Support Systems, 12,* 267–275. doi:10.1016/0167-9236(94)90045-0

Bar-Hillel, M., & Wagenaar, W. (1991). The perception of randomness. *Advances in Applied Mathematics, 12*(4), 428–454. doi:10.1016/0196-8858(91)90029-I

Bates, D. (2003). Ten commandments for effective clinical decision support: Making the practice of evidence-based medicine a reality. *Journal of the American Medical Informatics Association, 10*(6), 523–530. doi:10.1197/jamia.M1370

Beach, L., & Mitchell, T. (1978). A contingency model for the selection of decision strategies. *Academy of Management Review, 3,* 439–449.

Berry, D., & Broadbent, D. (1987). The combination of explicit and implicit learning processes in task control. *Psychological Research, 49*(1), 7–15. doi:10.1007/BF00309197

Berry, D., & Broadbent, D. (1988). On the relationship between task performance and associated task knowledge. *The Quarterly Journal of Experimental Psychology. A, Human Experimental Psychology, 36,* 209–231. doi:10.1080/14640748408402156

Besnard, D., & Cacitti, L. (2005). Interface changes causing accidents. An empirical study of negative transfer. *International Journal of Human-Computer Studies, 62,* 103–125. doi:10.1016/j.ijhcs.2004.08.002

Bettman, J., & Zins, M. (1979). Information format and choice task effects in decision making. *The Journal of Consumer Research, 6*(2), 141–153. doi:10.1086/208757

Blandford, A., & Wong, B. (2004). Situation awareness in emergency medical dispatch. *International Journal of Human-Computer Studies, 61*, 421–452. doi:10.1016/j.ijhcs.2003.12.012

Brooke, J., & Duncan, K. (1981). Effects of system display format on performance in a fault location task. *Ergonomics, 24*, 175–189. doi:10.1080/00140138108559232

Carlson, K., & Pearo, L. (2004). Limiting predecisional distortion by prior valuation of attribute components. *Organizational Behavior and Human Decision Processes, 94*, 48–59. doi:10.1016/j.obhdp.2004.02.001

Cary, M., & Carlson, R. (1999). External support and the development of problem solving routines. *Journal of Experimental Psychology. Learning, Memory, and Cognition, 25*, 1053–1070. doi:10.1037/0278-7393.25.4.1053

Chinander, K., & Schweitzer, M. (2003). The input bias: The misuse of input information in judgments of outcomes. *Organizational Behavior and Human Decision Processes, 91*, 243–253. doi:10.1016/S0749-5978(03)00025-6

Chu, P., & Spires, E. (2003). Perceptions of accuracy and effort of decision strategies. *Organizational Behavior and Human Decision Processes, 91*(2), 203–214. doi:10.1016/S0749-5978(03)00056-6

Corbalan, G., Kester, L., & Van Merriënboer, J. (2009). Combining shared control with variability over surface features: Effects on transfer test performance and task involvement. *Computers in Human Behavior, 25*, 290–298. doi:10.1016/j.chb.2008.12.009

Dalala, R., & Bonaccio, S. (2010). What types of advice do decision-makers prefer? *Organizational Behavior and Human Decision Processes, 112*, 11–23. doi:10.1016/j.obhdp.2009.11.007

Dunn, E., Wilson, T., & Gilbert, D. (2003). Location, location, location: The misprediction of satisfaction in housing lotteries. *Personality and Social Psychology Bulletin, 29*, 1421–1432. doi:10.1177/0146167203256867

Endsley, M. (1995). Toward a theory of situation awareness in dynamic systems. *Human Factors, 37*(1), 32–64. doi:10.1518/001872095779049543

Feldman-Stewart, D., & Brundage, M. (2004). Challenges for designing and implementing decision aids. *Patient Education and Counseling, 54*, 265–273. doi:10.1016/j.pec.2003.09.007

Fennema, M., & Kleinmuntz, D. (1995). Anticipation of effort and accuracy in multi-attribute choice. *Organizational Behavior and Human Decision Processes, 63*(1), 21–32. doi:10.1006/obhd.1995.1058

Fox, C., & Weber, M. (2002). Ambiguity aversion, comparative ignorance, and decision context. *Organizational Behavior and Human Decision Processes, 88*(1), 476–498. doi:10.1006/obhd.2001.2990

Ganzach, Y., & Schul, Y. (1995). The influence of quantity of information and goal framing on decisions. *Acta Psychologica, 89*, 23–36. doi:10.1016/0001-6918(94)00004-Z

Gerlach, J., & Kuo, F. (1991). Understanding human-computer interaction for information system design. *Management Information Systems Quarterly, 15*(4), 527–550. doi:10.2307/249456

Gonzalez, C. (2005). Decision support for real-time, dynamic decision-making tasks. *Organizational Behavior and Human Decision Processes, 96*, 142–154. doi:10.1016/j.obhdp.2004.11.002

Greeno, J. (1973). The structure of memory and the process of solving problems. In R. L. Rolso (Ed.), *Contemporary Issues in Cognitive Psychology: The Loyola Symposium*. New York, NY: Wiley.

Gregor, S., & Benbasat, I. (1999). Explanations from intelligent systems: Theoretical foundations and implications for practice. *Management Information Systems Quarterly, 23*(4), 497–530. doi:10.2307/249487

Halford, G., Baker, R., McCredden, J., & Bain, J. (2005). How many variables can humans process? *Psychological Science, 16*(1), 70–76. doi:10.1111/j.0956-7976.2005.00782.x

Higgins, E. (1997). Beyond pleasure and pain. *The American Psychologist, 52*(12), 1280–1300. doi:10.1037/0003-066X.52.12.1280

Hollnagel, E. (1993). Decision support and task nets. In Klein, G., Orasanu, J., Calderwood, R., & Zsambok, C. (Eds.), *Decision making in action: Models and methods* (pp. 31–36). Norwood, NJ: Ablex.

Hsee, C., & Hastie, R. (2006). Decision and experience: Why don't we choose what makes us happy? *Trends in Cognitive Sciences, 10*(1), 31–37. doi:10.1016/j.tics.2005.11.007

Jonassen, D. (2003). Using cognitive tools to represent problems. *Journal of Research on Technology in Education, 35*(3), 362–381.

Kintsch, W. (1998). *Comprehension: A paradigm for cognition*. New York, NY: Cambridge University Press.

Klein, G. (1993). A recognition-primed decision (RPD) model of rapid decision making. In Klein, G., Orasanu, J., Calderwood, R., & Zsambok, C. (Eds.), *Decision making in action: Models and methods* (pp. 138–147). Norwood, NJ: Ablex.

Klein, G. (1999). *Sources of power: How people make decisions*. Cambridge, MA: MIT.

Klein, G., Orasanu, J., Calderwood, R., & Zsambok, C. (1993). *Decision making in action: Models and methods*. Norwood, NJ: Ablex.

Langholtz, H., Gettys, C., & Foote, B. (1995). Are resource fluctuations anticipated in resource allocation tasks? *Organizational Behavior and Human Decision Processes, 64*(3), 274–282. doi:10.1006/obhd.1995.1105

Larichev, O., Olson, D., Moshkovich, H., & Mechitov, A. (1995). Numerical vs. cardinal measurements in multiattribute decision making: How exact is exact enough? *Organizational Behavior and Human Decision Processes, 64*(1), 9–21. doi:10.1006/obhd.1995.1085

Lenton, A., & Francesconi, M. (2010). How humans cognitively manage an abundance of mate options. *Psychological Science, 21*(4), 528–533. doi:10.1177/0956797610364958

Levin, I., & Gaeth, G. (1988). How consumers are affected by the framing of attribute information before and after consuming the product. *The Journal of Consumer Research, 15*, 374–378. doi:10.1086/209174

Lightner, N. (2001). Model testing of users' comprehension in graphical animation: The effect of speed and focus areas. *International Journal of Human-Computer Interaction, 13*(1), 53–73. doi:10.1207/S15327590IJHC1301_4

Lim, J., & O'Connor, M. (1996). Judgmental forecasting with time series and causal information. *International Journal of Forecasting, 12*, 139–153. doi:10.1016/0169-2070(95)00635-4

Loewenstein, G. (1996). Out of control: Visceral influences on behavior. *Organizational Behavior and Human Decision Processes, 65*, 272–292. doi:10.1006/obhd.1996.0028

Lökketangen, A., & Woddruff, D. (2005). A distance function to support optimized selection decisions. *Decision Support Science, 39*, 345–354. doi:10.1016/j.dss.2004.01.001

Mao, J., & Benbasat, I. (2001). The effects of contextualized access to knowledge on judgment. *International Journal of Human-Computer Studies*, *55*, 787–814. doi:10.1006/ijhc.2001.0507

Mason, R., & Mitroff, I. (1973). A program for research on management information systems. *Management Science*, *19*, 475–487. doi:10.1287/mnsc.19.5.475

Mather, M., & Johnson, M. (2000). Choice-supportive source monitoring: Do our decisions seem better to us as we age? *Psychology and Aging*, *15*, 596–606. doi:10.1037/0882-7974.15.4.596

Mather, M., Shafir, E., & Johnson, M. K. (2000). Misrememberance of options past: Source monitoring and choice. *Psychological Science*, *11*, 132–138. doi:10.1111/1467-9280.00228

Miller, G. (1956). The magical number seven, plus or minus two: Some limits on our capacity for processing information. *Psychological Review*, *63*, 81–97. doi:10.1037/h0043158

Mitchell, T., Thompson, L., Peterson, E., & Cronk, R. (1997). Temporal adjustments in the evaluation of events: The rosy view. *Journal of Experimental Social Psychology*, *33*(4), 421–448. doi:10.1006/jesp.1997.1333

Nanard, J., & Nanard, M. (1995). Hypertext design environments and the hypertext design process. *Communications of the ACM*, *38*(8), 49–56. doi:10.1145/208344.208347

Newell, B. R., Weston, N. J., & Shanks, D. R. (2003). Empirical tests of a fast-and-frugal heuristic: Not everyone "takes-the-best." *Organizational Behavior and Human Decision Processes*, *91*, 82–96. doi:10.1016/S0749-5978(02)00525-3

Nisbett, R., Krantz, D., Jepson, C., & Kunda, Z. (1983). The use of statistical heuristics in everyday inductive reasoning. *Psychological Review*, *90*, 339–363. doi:10.1037/0033-295X.90.4.339

Norman, D. (1984). Stages and levels in human-machine interaction. *International Journal of Man-Machine Studies*, *21*, 365–375. doi:10.1016/S0020-7373(84)80054-1

Norman, D. (2009). Memory is more important than actuality. *Interaction*, *16*(2), 24–26. doi:10.1145/1487632.1487638

Orasanu, J., & Connolly, T. (1993). The reinvention of decision making. In Klein, G., Orasanu, J., Calderwood, R., & Zsambok, C. (Eds.), *Decision making in action: Models and methods* (pp. 3–20). Norwood, NJ: Ablex.

Orasanu, J., & Fischer, U. (1997). Finding decisions in natural environments: The view from the cockpit. In Zsambok, C., & Klein, G. (Eds.), *Naturalistic decision making* (pp. 343–357). Hillsdale, NJ: Erlbaum.

Parker, C., & Sinclair, M. (2001). User-centred design does make a difference. The case of decision support systems in crop production. *Behaviour & Information Technology*, *20*(6), 449–460. doi:10.1080/01449290110089570

Payne, J., Bettman, J., Coupey, E., & Johnson, E. (1992). A constructive process view of decision making: Multiple strategies in judgment and choice. *Acta Psychologica*, *80*, 107–141. doi:10.1016/0001-6918(92)90043-D

Payne, J., Bettman, J., & Johnson, E. (1988). Adaptive strategy selection in decision making. *Journal of Experimental Psychology. Learning, Memory, and Cognition*, *14*, 534–552. doi:10.1037/0278-7393.14.3.534

Payne, J., Bettman, J., & Johnson, E. (1993). *The adaptive decision maker*. Cambridge, UK: Cambridge University Press.

Payne, J., Bettman, J., & Luce, M. (1996). When time is money: Decision behavior under opportunity-cost time pressure. *Organizational Behavior and Human Decision Processes*, *66*, 131–152. doi:10.1006/obhd.1996.0044

Payne, S. (1991). Display-based action at the user interface. *International Journal of Man-Machine Studies, 35*, 275–289. doi:10.1016/S0020-7373(05)80129-4

Perrin, B., Barnett, B., Walrath, L., & Grossman, J. (2001). Information order and outcome framing: An assessment of judgment bias in a naturalistic decision-making context. *Human Factors, 43*(2), 227–238. doi:10.1518/001872001775900968

Randel, J., & Pugh, L. (1996). Differences in expert and novice situation awareness in naturalistic decision making. *International Journal of Human-Computer Studies, 45*, 579–597. doi:10.1006/ijhc.1996.0068

Rasmussen, J. (1986). *Information processing and human-machine interaction: An approach to cognitive engineering.* New York, NY: North-Holland.

Ratner, R., & Herbst, K. (2005). When good decisions have bad outcomes: The impact of affect on switching behavior. *Organizational Behavior and Human Decision Processes, 96*, 23–37. doi:10.1016/j.obhdp.2004.09.003

Réach, G., Zerrouki, A., Leclercq, D., & d'Ivernois, J. (2005). Adjusting insulin doses: From knowledge to decision. *Patient Education and Counseling, 56*, 98–103. doi:10.1016/j.pec.2004.01.001

Roberts, D. (1989). Readers' comprehension responses in informative discourse: Toward connecting reading and writing in technical communication. *Journal of Technical Writing and Communication, 19*(2), 135–148. doi:10.2190/A1JA-0L9H-YLMH-YUE4

Roediger, H. (1980). Memory metaphors in cognitive psychology. *Memory & Cognition, 8*, 231–246. doi:10.3758/BF03197611

Rubens, P., & Rubens, B. (1988). Usability and format design. In Doheny-Farina, S. (Ed.), *Effective documentation: What we have learned from research* (pp. 213–234). Cambridge, MA: MIT.

Russo, J., & Dosher, B. (1983). Strategies for multiattribute binary choice. *Journal of Experimental Psychology. Learning, Memory, and Cognition, 9*, 676–696. doi:10.1037/0278-7393.9.4.676

Shafir, E. (1993). Choosing versus rejecting: Why some options are both better and worse than others. *Memory & Cognition, 21*, 546–556. doi:10.3758/BF03197186

Shanteau, J. (1992). Competence in experts: The role of task characteristics. *Organizational Behavior and Human Decision Processes, 53*(2), 252–266. doi:10.1016/0749-5978(92)90064-E

Sheridan, S., Felix, K., Pignone, M., & Lewis, C. (2004). Information needs of men regarding prostate cancer screening and the effect of a brief decision aid. *Patient Education and Counseling, 54*, 345–351. doi:10.1016/j.pec.2003.12.003

Shiv, B., & Fedorikhin, A. (1999). Heart and mind in conflict: Interplay of affect and cognition in consumer decision making. *The Journal of Consumer Research, 26*, 278–282. doi:10.1086/209563

Simon, H. (1979). *Models of thought.* New Haven, CT: Yale UP.

Simon, H., Langley, P., & Bradshaw, G. (1981). Scientific discovery as problem solving. *Synthese, 47*, 1–27. doi:10.1007/BF01064262

Slovic, P. (1972). From Shakespeare to Simon: Speculations—and some evidence—about man's ability to process information. *Oregon Research Institute Research Bulletin, 12*, 1–29.

Stalmeier, P., & van Roosmalen, M. (2009). Concise evaluation of two decision aids. *Patient Education and Counseling, 74*, 104–109. doi:10.1016/j.pec.2008.07.043

Stewart, J. (1994). The psychology of decision making. In Jennings, D. (Ed.), *Decision making: An integrated approach* (pp. 54–95). London, UK: Pitman Publishing.

Suchman, L. (1987). *Plans and situated actions: The problem of human-machine communication.* Cambridge, UK: Cambridge.

Tversky, A. (1977). Features of similarity. *Psychological Review, 84*, 327–352. doi:10.1037/0033-295X.84.4.327

Tversky, A., & Kahneman, D. (1981). The framing of decisions and the psychology of choice. *Science, 211*, 453–458. doi:10.1126/science.7455683

Vassilakis, P., & Moustakis, V. (1996). Identifying decision maker's preferences through a prototype based inductive learning method: A medical case study. *Behaviour & Information Technology, 15*(2), 113–122. doi:10.1080/014492996120328

Webster, D., & Kruglanski, A. (1994). Individual differences in need. for cognitive closure. *Journal of Personality and Social Psychology, 67*(6), 1049–1672. doi:10.1037/0022-3514.67.6.1049

Wickens, C., & Hollands, J. (2000). *Engineering psychology and human performance.* Upper Saddle River, NJ: Prentice Hall.

Willemsen, M., & Keren, G. (2003). The meaning of indifference in choice behavior: Asymmetries in adjustments embodied in matching. *Organizational Behavior and Human Decision Processes, 90*, 342–359. doi:10.1016/S0749-5978(02)00521-6

Wilson, C., & Harsha, P. (2008). IT policy—Advising policymakers is more than just providing advice. *Communications of the ACM, 51*(12), 24–26. doi:10.1145/1409360.1409370

Wilson, K., Aaron, S., Vandemheen, K., Hebert, P., McKim, D., & Fiset, V. (2005). Evaluation of a decision aid for making choices about intubation and mechanical ventilation in chronic obstructive pulmonary disease. *Patient Education and Counseling, 57*, 88–95. doi:10.1016/j.pec.2004.04.004

Woods, D. (1984). Visual momentum: A concept to improve the cognitive coupling of person and computer. *International Journal of Man-Machine Studies, 21*, 229–244. doi:10.1016/S0020-7373(84)80043-7

Woods, D., & Roth, E. (1988). Cognitive engineering: Human problem solving with tools. *Human Factors, 30*(4), 415–430.

Wright, P. (1974). The harassed decision maker: Time pressure, distractions, and the use of evidence. *The Journal of Applied Psychology, 59*(5), 555–561. doi:10.1037/h0037186

Zhao, S., Meyer, R., & Han, J. (2006). *A tale of two judgments: Biases in prior valuations and subsequent utilization of novel technological product attributes.* Retrieved from http://knowledge.wharton.upenn.edu/ article/1292.cfm

ADDITIONAL READING

Klein, G. (1999). *Sources of power: How people make decisions.* Cambridge, MA: MIT.

Newell, B. R., Weston, N. J., & Shanks, D. R. (2003). Empirical tests of a fast-and-frugal heuristic: Not everyone "takes-the-best." *Organizational Behavior and Human Decision Processes, 91*, 82–96. doi:10.1016/S0749-5978(02)00525-3

Ratner, R., & Herbst, K. (2005). When good decisions have bad outcomes: The impact of affect on switching behavior. *Organizational Behavior and Human Decision Processes, 96*, 23–37. doi:10.1016/j.obhdp.2004.09.003

Suchman, L. (1987). *Plans and situated actions: The problem of human-machine communication.* Cambridge, UK: Cambridge University Press.

Chapter 14
Conclusion

ABSTRACT

People process information on three levels: readability, understandability, and comprehension (Warren, 1993). Readability, how people perceive individual words, has been the focus of the majority of the research, but does not guarantee people understand the content. But the other two carry the information's meaning. Comprehension, the highest level, is extracting the intending meaning from the text and being able to relate it to the world and use it in the situation. Fitting information to the situation requires comprehension, not just being able to read the content. HII works to focus design teams at the comprehension level for maximally effective communication.

BACKGROUND

When I'm working on a problem, I never think about beauty. I think only how to solve the problem. But when I have finished, if the solution is not beautiful, I know it is wrong.—R. Buckminster Fuller

Communication is rhetorical and "nothing can be taken out of its rhetorical context and that items in that context must work in harmony to achieve purpose" (Gribbons & Elsar, 1998, p. 471). However, a rhetorical approach relies on a descriptive theory which has minimal predictive power. Like too many design guidelines, a strict rhetorical approach works in too broad of

strokes. Statements of "write appropriately for the audience" are best understood in hindsight, when analyzing why a communication failed. They provide little guidance to determine what is appropriate for the audience and how to present it. A guideline of "The information is easy to comprehend" appears on many heuristic evaluations but is of questionable quality since it provides nothing to aid people creating or evaluating the information in determining if readers will be able to comprehend it.

For example, Hargis et al (1998) stated, "Use graphics that are meaningful and appropriate. Ensure that each illustration accurately depicts the object, concept, or function it is designed to illustrate, and that it does so as simply as possible" (p. 201). Rodriguez (2002) questions how these guidelines can possibly be fulfilled since the

DOI: 10.4018/978-1-4666-0152-9.ch014

methods for accomplishing them are not available. Or more precisely, how can design teams know they are meeting the objective. What defines that the graphic is as simple as possible? The answer varies dramatically between audiences and between different information needs for the same audience. In one situation, a cardiac surgeon needs a highly anatomically correct view of the heart and in another a simple line drawing will suffice, even thought the two graphics might be presenting the same information. But the situation and information needs of that specific situation are different. I'm sure that authors of dense obtuse documents would claim the writing conforms to the guidelines they were given, probably by claiming it's a very dense topic and it can't be made any clearer without losing important material.

HII does not strive to eliminate rhetorical principles or design guidelines, but rather to allow design teams to work within the limitations imposed by the design guidelines. A problem with guidelines and their associated descriptive approaches, and a staple comment on various Internet lists for information design and usability, is the mantra of "it depends on the specifics of the situation." This is a true statement, but it does not help with creating content which can be effectively communicated. By understanding the underlying theory, then design teams have a better grip on analyzing the specifics of the situation and predicting how people will respond. Effective communication decisions require design teams to understand both the specifics of the situation and of human behavior so they understand how to communicate information to meet people's information needs. Guidelines provide basic guidance about designing information, but were never designed to address how people interact with information in a specific situation. Design teams must extend them to provide the situation-level detail. Ensuring communication and comprehension requires understanding the HII aspects of the situation.

The remainder of this chapter sums up the HII model which forms the foundation of this book with a focus on the cyclic nature of that model. It then takes the process of determining people's goals and information needs from my earlier work (Albers, 2004) and applies the HII concepts to that process to provide a robust framework for developing content.

CYCLIC NATURE OF THE HII MODEL

The HII model for this book is presented in Figure 1. It shows the cyclic interaction information between the situation and people interacting with the information and situation. Chapter 1 described the overall model and each chapter has examined one aspect in detail. Now, as a way of concluding, we will look at the overall model and how information flows in cycles through it.

A brief summary of the main elements.

- Information exists in the environment and is available to people.
- Movement of information via the gate-keeping functions of a system or, principally, human perception, selects the information which will receive consideration.
- People bring prior knowledge and mental models to a situation which forms a base for their interpretation and selection of the information.
- People approach information in a wide range of ways and are influenced by many psychological factors.
- People interact with information in ways that depend on the presentation and different presentations can radically change the interpretation.
- Decisions and performance of actions implementing those decisions change both the situation and the information which people must understand.

The overall model is cyclic. In actually operation, it would contain many internal cycles.

Figure 1. Human-information interaction model

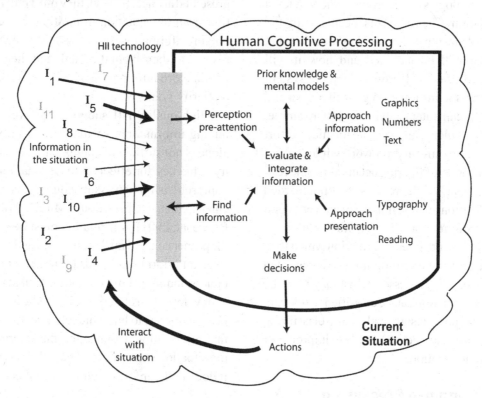

For example, all of the necessary information is rarely collected initially. Instead, as people build the relationships, they realize based on their mental model that more information is required. The interaction then cycles back to collecting information from the world.

Information in the Situation

The relevant information about a situation exists in the world. As part of comprehending a situation, people have to take in the relevant information and exclude irrelevant information. Thus first part of comprehending a situation is identifying which information exists and which is relevant. Unfortunately, the relevant information is mixed with lots of irrelevant information which makes it difficult for people to extract the relevant information.

Interacting and extracting information from a situation tends to change the situation. In ad-

dition, the information evolves and changes as the situation evolves and changes. As a result, the information in the situation form their own open-ended cycles which people must deal with as they work to extract information.

HII and Extracting Information

Any real-world situation contains too much information to process. Unfortunately, people often cannot easily see that they either have too much or irrelevant information. Instead, they try to process all of it. The filtering controls the flow so only the relevant information for the current stage is processed. Processing too much information at once leads to cognitive overload and processing information in the wrong order/time impairs comprehension and interpretation. In both cases, decision making ability is seriously compromised.

Filtering occurs at the system design level and in how people perceive information.

The technology system provides the first level of information filtering. This occurs with the decisions of design teams as they decide what information will be included and how it will be presented. The HCI provided by the system controls how the information gets displayed and how people can interact with it. For example, navigation problems may require too much effort to make finding information worthwhile.

A second level of filtering occurs as people read the information. People are constantly bombarded with information all day; thus, they are very good at ignoring information. When looking at information, they only tend to see information which they feel is relevant. Other information is disregarded and never mentally processed. Obviously, all of the available information can be classified as relevant or irrelevant; poor design leads to misclassifying information and subjecting people to improper or irrelevant information.

HII and Cognitive Processing

Prior knowledge reflects what people bring to the situation (which may be minimal or incorrect). It has a profound effect on how new information gets interpreted, since it gets interpreted with respect to the prior knowledge and not as stand-alone information. As a result, prior knowledge imposes a limitation on the situation model that it is built from a mental model. Misconceptions in the mental model are reflected in the situation model. Constructing a situation model, which is a instantiated mental model, is a major element of understanding a situation. The situation model has shifted from the mental model's stereotypical description to one that contains the actual values and concepts for the current situation.

People search for information to meet specific needs which they think will enable them to meet their situational goals (Slone, 2002). They read, interact with, and interpret information as part of comprehending it and relating it to their current information needs. That information is rarely all presented at once. Instead, they must pull information from the situation in multiple cycles. They obtain information, process it, review it with respect to their mental model, and then work to obtain more information to fill in missing pieces or clarify points of confusion.

High quality HII supports the cycles of obtaining information. Availability of information alone is not sufficient; contextualized accessibility is the key for effective dissemination, proper comprehension, and subsequent performance enhancement (Albers, 2004; Mirel, 1998; Mao & Benbasat, 2001). Information must be viewed in the proper context, information isolated from other relevant information leads to limited or distorted understanding (Ahn et al., 2005). A substantial part of developing an understanding of the information in a situation is to build the relationships between that information. Connecting the information to the situation exists more in the relationships than it does in the information itself (Albers, 2010)

HII and Decisions/Actions

The final goal of cognitively processing the information is to do something with it; to take an action. The information leads to a decision about how to affect a change in the situation. Decisions lead to actions which change the information in the situation. This leads to a cyclic interaction with people having to comprehend the changed information in the situation so they can monitor the changes and potentially engage in more decision-making/actions cycles.

In the final analysis, high quality HII exists to support people in making decisions and monitoring those changes in the situation. Everything else is simply a part of the process leading to a decision.

USING THE HII MODEL

As part of early development, design teams have to take the HII model in figure xx and perform the analysis to instantiate it. The audience analysis, task analysis, and requirement design all contribute to building an HII model of the situation. They bring in the details of the specific situations of interest to create a model which can move forward with the design process. "The purpose of any representation or model is to allow one to abstract over much of the complexity of real world behaviour while retaining an unambiguous description of the essential elements needed to explain that behaviour" (Monk, 1999, p. 129).

Throughout the design process, in addition to the HII model, there exist three different models which design teams must consider.

Reader Model: The reader model represents the readers' preconceived notions of the situation based on beliefs, goals, emotions, and prior experience. Some of their beliefs may actually be superstitions—representing mistaken or incorrect interpretations of their prior experience.

Designer Model: The designer model contains what is designed and what the designer intends for the reader to understand. It includes the information given to the reader, the interaction behavior between the information and the reader, and the information relationships between information elements.

Implementation Model: The implementation model reflects how the designer model actually gets transformed into a working system. This includes the font and layout choices, and button-pushing and mouse clicking interaction design decisions. It also includes the under-the-covers design elements (database schemas, software objects, etc.) which should never be seen by the people interacting with the information, but which are essential to effective HII.

The HII model works to integrate elements of the reader and designer model as it captures not the design requirements per se, but people's goals,

information needs, and required interactions to achieve their goals. As such, it is an abstraction of the presentation and interaction needs which is independent of the implementation details.

When asked to rate the influence on using a source of information, engineers listed (in order): accessibility, availability, technical quality, and relevance (Kwasitsu, 2001). Such a list order is somewhat troubling since it puts simply being able to get to information above the quality of information. But it shows the importance of high quality HII; design teams must ensure the technical quality and relevance match the accessibility. All three models: reader, designer, and implementation, must coherently mesh for high quality communication of information.

Figure 2 shows a cyclic model which highlights the cyclic nature of how people interact with information. The HII model (Figure 1) used as the foundation of this book contains a strong cyclic interaction component. Unlike most HCI models, it acknowledges that all of the required information is not within the system and the HII occurs in a broader range that just with the system. In addition, the HII model has a strong focus on what happens in people's heads as opposed to focusing on how they interact with the system. HII deals with how people mentally process the information and interacts with the overall situation, not just how people interact with a computer system.

Vicente (1999a) clearly laid out the need for allowing for the cyclic nature of design focused on HII techniques.

Perhaps even more important, however, is the fact that it is not possible to determine the limits on our knowledge....Each iteration is a data-driven step, and we have no knowledge of the overall space of possibilities in which we are searching. (p. 106)

As Vicente points out, when design teams start on the analysis, they often have only a sketchy idea of what they will find. Only by performing the analysis and examining the goals information

Figure 2. Cyclic interaction of goals, information, and the situation (adapted from Monk, 1999, p. 128)

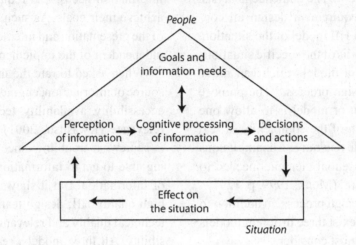

needs can they clearly understand people's goals, information needs, and the HII requirements as they work within the information space.

The focus on clear communication for information needs and supporting how people interact with information throughout the cycle must be a part of the entire design team's mission. Any design team working with an information system tasked with providing information to a group of people must ensure the interaction and content makes sense within those people's knowledge domain. We are many years past simply providing data and letting people figure it out (Mirel 1998, 2003). Most people involved in communicating technical information readily acknowledge this statement, but find that putting it into practice is much harder.

Fields such as HCI and IA recognize the communication problems inherent in HII. Practitioners in those fields know to start with information needs and tasks. However, the nature of these fields tends to lead to deliverables which do not go down to the information/content level. They focus on the audience needs at a higher level since they are not producing the actual content to be communicated. HII gives a framework for connecting the work of HCI and IA to the content and ensuring

the overall design effectively communicates the content to a reader.

Different groups of people approach information differently. What they want from it and how they expect to acquire it differs. Understanding what they desire and their expectations are essential in meeting the information needs and the communication goals. As such, a design needs to ensure the information source conforms to the situational context that best fits how people approach the information. There is often an assumption by design teams that the information can be captured in one situation and used across many others, with the approaches used in one situation applicable to all. However, this assumption has proved problematic (Bechky 2003; Szulanski, 1996; von Hippel, 2001). We are getting much better at arranging the information, but the arrangement controls how to present the information. Missing are the elements of when and why to present the information. Basically, our understanding of how humans mentally represent the information and manipulate information has not kept up with the technology to provide information (Nilsson & Mayer, 2002).

FRAMEWORK FOR HII IN COMPLEX SITUATIONS

Complex Situations

Chapter 1 defined a complex situation as one that fits these characteristics:

- Total situation is more than just the sum of the parts (a complete description of the situation cannot be given).
- Multiple paths to a solution exist.
- Information requirements to answer a question cannot be predefined.
- Effect on the overall system of a change to one factor cannot be predicted (nonlinear response).
- Part of an open system. Difficult to break out and study a section in isolation.

For real-world complex situations—most qualify as complex—good HII depends on uncovering the people's goals and information needs. In this process, the design team must remember the characteristics of a complex situation (Albers, 2004):

No single answer: The questions people ask don't have a single answer. Multiple answers can be correct even within the same situation. Some answers maybe more correct than others, but with satisficing and good enough reasoning, people are satisfied when the answer works.

Open-ended questions: The questions lack any clear end point at which a person can say that they now have all of the information. Instead, the amount of available and relevant information greatly exceeds people's ability or desire to process it all.

Multi-dimensional strategies: There is no single method or path that people follow to reach an answer they are satisfied with.

Dynamic: The information changes, often on time scales that matter to understanding the situation.

Has a history: The situation has a past and those past events influence how the situation will develop in the future.

Nonlinear response: Situation responses to decisions and actions often display a non-linear response. This means that at times small changes to some parts result in large changes while at other times large changes have minimal effects. A linear response would give a consistent and proportional change to the action.

Understanding the HII of Complex Situations

Determining people's goals and information needs and shaping the information for presentation follows several basic steps. This section provides a high level framework of the process for developing a system with high quality HII. It looks at a eight step process for working with complex information and considers the HII issues which design teams must address in each step.

When faced with a complex situation, design teams need to do more than just define the information needs and collect/display that information. Granted, many current systems have taken that approach, but they also suffer from various levels low usability and poor HII. Instead of just providing information, design teams need to allow for the HII—how will the people actually interact with that information and what factors drive that interaction. Besides being a visual of a complex situation, Figure 3 also can be considered a visual of how design teams should approach the analysis. It places the person and the HII squarely in the center and the other forces all work to shape and influences the person and the HII. But none of those areas should capture the majority of a design team's attention.

Figure 3. HII in a complex situation. Design teams need to focus their attention on the inside of the gray area and not allow the outside factors to gain a disproportional share of their attention.

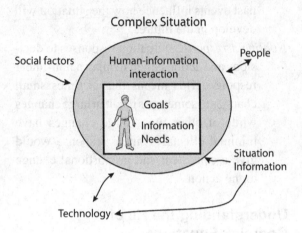

The complex interactions and relationships of a complex situation must be built up and cannot be captured in a single pass analysis. The HII analysis must be performed in an iterative manner to allow for deeper analysis of points uncovered during any one cycle. The cyclic approach provides better overall usability than attempting to design the perfect system on the first attempt (Bailey, 1993). The cyclic nature of the data collection and analysis allows verification of the information relationships and gathers a deeper understanding of how people interact with the information. On the other hand, whereas an iterative cycle is important, too much iteration wastes time and adds little to the final results; two or three cycles probably will reach the point of diminishing returns (Hartson & Boehm-Davis, 1993).

The remainder of this section takes the eight step process defined in my earlier work (Albers, 2004) and extends it by applying HII concepts. The result is one potential route which design teams can use to capture the goals and information needs to provide high quality HII in complex situations. As with the HII model, these eight steps are not a linear sequence, but are a cyclic model which requires multiple passes to refine and flesh out the

answers. Extensive backtracking and refinement are expected as a design team works through the steps to uncover the goals, information needs, and information relationships which must be presented for the final system to provide high quality HII.

The eight steps are:

1. Plan the scope of the information product.
2. Identify the audience groups of the final information product.
3. Define the people's goals by audience group.
4. Define the information needs of each audience group or role to achieve the goals.
5. Define the information relationships that connect the information to goals.
6. Determine the source of each information element.
7. Build a visual model.
8. Define the presentation requirements.

The discussion will describe the basic analysis for the step and consider the HII concepts which must receive extra attention. Most of the HII concepts described in this book apply to all of the steps, but that would result in high repetition.

This section ignores implementation factors that are critical for a successful and functional HII information system, but that from the viewpoint of this book do not directly influence the HII. Although by no means a complete list, this includes factors such as:

- Time to produce the information.
- Who will be writing and maintaining the information.
- Choice of tools for development, data storage, and presentation.
- Implementation issues such as bandwidth, data format, storage and retrieval methods.

Design teams must not discount the importance of these factors. A successful implementation requires them, but they part of the technical implementation and are outside the scope of HII.

Plan the Scope of the Information Product

The situation contains an over-abundance of information, even within the information in the situation area of Figure 1. Design teams need to define the scope of both the overall project and, as they refine individual information needs, the scope of each concept to be presented. Without clearly defining the scope, the HII can be significantly impacted because it will be difficult to present an integrated view. Scope must come from the people using the information and fit within their goals and information needs. The all-too-frequent methods of talking to their managers or being "the corporate approved way" does not provide the information needed to truly understand situational context and make informed decisions. The scope statements must be created in terms of the people's vocabulary, their reasons for using the system and their problems.

Scope statements must be specific enough to be used as a guideline for separating relevant and irrelevant information.

- Define the context and situations for which the content is relevant.
- Connect the scope to the audience group definitions. The scope of relevant information is highly interconnected with specific audience groups. Often these groups are too diverse to work with as a single unit. For example, consider physician information and patient information. The basic prior knowledge and information needs of the two groups (actually medical and non-medical groups in general) are very different.
- Scope needs to consider the prior knowledge and mental models the people bring to the situation. When the scope matches up to these elements, it is easier to draw the lines of what information fits within the situation. The prior knowledge and mental

model defines how they see and interpret the information. It also provides a base for determining the proper graphics and numbers to communicate the information.

Without a clear scope of the individual goals and information needs, the final design risks presenting whatever information was easiest to obtain. Notice that this paragraph deals with goals and information needs which, on the first cycle, are not yet defined. The first cycle defines the over-arching scope with the lower-level scope statements being defined in additional iterations of the analysis.

Identify the Audience Groups

Define all the potential audience groups. Different audience groups bring different mental models and prior knowledge to the information. They also want different levels of information detail and may have different information needs even for the same high-level goal. High quality HII must be tailored to the different audience groups and not force all of the audience groups to adjust to a single presentation. A major objective of the audience analysis is to provide the design team with the base for ensuring the system view matches the reader view rather than forcing the reader to match the system view.

Various effective methods of both defining and fleshing out the audience groups have been proposed, such as:

- Personas (Cooper, 1999).
- Usage cases. (Constantine & Lockwood, 1999).
- Scenarios (Carroll, 1995).

Audience groups are defined with respect to the situation and not job role. The same people often appear in different audience groups depending on how or when they interact with the information. For example, "production manager" may fail to be an audience group because situations they address in their office may be very different from the situations they address on the production floor. The final analysis may list two audience groups of "production management group" to handle office-based issues and "production control group" to handle production-based issues, a group that may also include production workers.

Defining the audience groups allows design teams to more clearly grasp the abilities, attitudes, and aspirations of those groups. These factors all strongly influence how they approach information and how they will work with it. It help clarify the amount of effort different audience groups will exert to understand the situation, what information they consider most salient, and what factors may limit their ability to interact with the information and the system.

Define the Goals by Audience Group

Collect the goals for each audience group. A coherent set of goals is actually major aspect for what defines an audience group. Because of differences in individual needs and prior knowledge, each person within an audience group may not articulate the exact same set of goals, but there will be high similarity and they will generally need information about the same goals. The final presentation design will have to handle presenting information relevant to those selected goals.

The audience and task analysis methods in current use work well for the analysis of complex situations; the major change is design teams must shift from thinking in terms of tasks to thinking in terms of goals. The data collection doesn't change, but the analysis of that data does have to change. Any of the following methods—probably a combination of them—build up a picture of the goals and information needs people bring to a situation.

- Personas
- Contextual Inquiry
- Scenarios
- Focus groups
- Critical Incident
- Crystal-ball method

Defining the goals is not a matter of finding them whole laying around, but require a dedicated effort to assemble them from the bits and pieces of the analysis. The design must provide for a deeper understanding of people, their goals and their work processes than is common in current design (Kuutti, 1995). "The best analysts have always known that settling requirements is neither a matter of simply finding out from users or clients exactly what to build nor a matter of our simply telling them what it is we are going to do for them" (Constantine & Lockwood, 1999, p. 486). The final result is not an assembly of collected information, but a synthesis which is much greater than the original whole.

Figure 4 shows a visual model of the scope and goals for information about a molecular cloud. The scope of the information and the goals closely map onto each other. The high level scope in this figure deals with understanding the collapse of the cores in the cloud to form stars. Inside of that scope individual goals have been defined (in the figure G1, G2, and G3). When it comes to defining information needs and content creation, only the areas within the goal circles are needed. The star collapse area contains all known information about star collapse inside a molecular cloud. However, much of that is highly technical and only suitable for professional astronomers doing that research. There are other areas that overlap—the two shown here are cooling of cores and cloud movement—which have as subset of information relevant to core collapse.

Design teams will find that keeping the definition of goals and information needs separate is difficult and in most analysis situations the two will be done simultaneously. However, they serve very different purposes and they must not be conflated in either the design documents or the

Figure 4. Goals and scope for core collapse in a molecular cloud. Only the information within the gray goal circles needs to be presented. Those circles cover different area for a general audience and an advanced audience. Design teams need to allow for this difference in information needs.

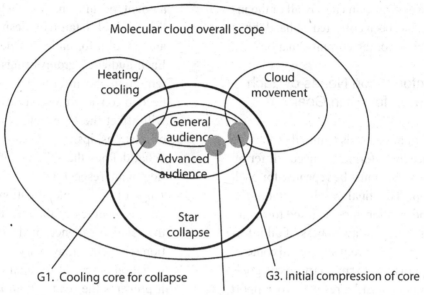

final design. Without the goals, design teams risks obtaining a huge stack of information needs that lack a clear user-defined association between the information elements or relevance to a specific situation.

A major design task for defining the goals is understanding the logical relationships between goals and information needs, the reasons that information is seen as connected to the goal, and when the connections are relevant.

- How do people see the goal and what information defines that they are on track to solve it? That information must be perceived during the first glance evaluation so the information will be read.
- Goals form a hierarchy with sub-goals for each goal. What sub-goals need to be achieved to declare a goal achieved. How are the connections and relationships between those goals and sub-goals viewed by the readers.

- How are people going to be using the achieved goal or sub-goals? If they are moving toward decisions and taking actions, the design team needs to ensure the HII keeps them on track toward appropriate decisions.
- How active or passive are the people at working to obtain the information? The overall design and layout need to lead to estimates of effort for understanding the information that fit how the people expect to work with it. Typeface choices and paragraph design have a strong influence.
- What order of presentation is best and how can framing effects be minimized?
- What defines that the goal is relevant to understanding the situation? People may form goals which can be proper in some circumstances and not others. How can the presentation communicate if pursuing this goal is relevant in the current situation?

- How does the person know they have achieved the goal? In a complex situation there is no end point where either the person or the design team can say all of the information has been collected. What defines it is sufficient for the current situation?

Define the Information Needs of Each Audience Group for Each Goal

Define the information needs required to achieve each goal. Since the information needs differ by audience groups, this must be repeated for each audience group. The final result contains the information and relationships required to ensure people can enhance their awareness of all information relevant to the current situational context.

The overlaps of the information needs for goals or audience groups must be resolved to support efficient content development. Although different audience groups may have the same goal, the information they require may differ based on factors such as prior knowledge and how they approach the situation. For quality HII, the information must be matched to the audience group and not defined as the information needs of any one specific group. For example, only dealing with the novice level and just letting more advanced audience groups use the novice level information.

Using the same methods used for defining goals (and probably at the same time), design teams must collect the information needed to achieve and verify those goals. They should attempt to construct as complete as possible a set of information required to fully understand and evaluate a situation. Just as importantly, they must define the order in which the information must be presented, how it should be presented, and what makes it important to the situation and goal.

The information needs collected for each goal need to be collected with a focus on supporting quality HII, which requires ensuring these points are considered.

- What information is needed to achieve the goal. Different audience groups have different prior knowledge which changes the amount of information they need. Also, the depth of detail they desire changes the amount of information needed.
- Each audience group brings biases to interpreting the information. Design teams need to consider those biases and how they will affect the interpretation and building of relationships.
- What defines the salience of the information with respect to the goal across the range of applicable situations. Depending on the specifics of the situational context, the relative salience of different information elements may vary. Capturing this variation is crucial for quality HII because it prevents the reader from having to perform extensive mental analysis to reshape the information to reflect that relative importance. Many readers will not perform this mental analysis, compromising the communication.
- How the information should be presented (text, graphs, etc.). Different audience groups have different expectations about how they want to receive the information. They also have different abilities to interpret graphics and diagrams.
- How will people respond to different presentations (text, graphs, equations, etc.)? Some people will skip any text with equations or tables; some will only look at the graphics.
- What information is needed to verify the goal is proceeding as expected or has been achieved? Information salience must allow people to verify the situation is developing as expected. What information relationships should people be forming and how can a failure to form these relationships be flagged to indicate to readers that they are having a problem.

- What information shows the goal has reached a critical point or a decision point? People need to know they have acquired enough information or that the situation has reached a point at which they must make some type of decision, regardless of their comfort level. This requires clearly understanding how the information needs connect to the situation and how the information will change as the situation develops.

- What detail level needs to be communicated. Different audience groups want different amounts of detail and the same audience group may want different amounts of detail for the same goal in different situational contexts.

- Order in which information is needed. Building a coherent mental image of a situation requires acquiring the information in the proper order. Framing effects and biases can be introduced when the information gets presented in a more or less haphazard manner.

The information needs are not simply the pile of data that a person requires to achieve a goal or understand a situation. The information needs analysis also carries with it the metadata of how the information relates to the situation, to itself, and to the different audience groups. Often, the difference between a system with high quality HII and poor HII is not the information content, but that the poor system analysis never captured the proper level of metadata which allows the content developers to make the information relevant to the readers.

Define the Information Relationships that Connect the Information to Goals

Information does not stand alone. Information does not exist independently; it only makes sense with respect to the situation when viewed within the web of information relationships (Figure 5). The relationships define what makes the information relevant to the goal and how it either influences or relates to other information (Albers, 2010). The relationships a person forms results from reworking the information into a mental structure which fits the current situation. The design must move those relationships from the model to the content people see and interact with to help them build those relationships.

Basden and Hibberd (1996) criticize the belief that all the information needed can be defined in advance and then collected into a database. The system simply needs to retrieve the pertinent data and present it. In this view, the data speaks for itself and information acquisition becomes little more than simply reading the facts provided by the system. But data only becomes relevant information within a specific context. It never exists simply to be read, rather readers need to connect the information into a set of relationships which construct their understanding of the situation.

The design team must uncover the relationships that exist within and between information elements and various aspects of the situation. They must understand what makes the information relevant to the goal and how it either influence or relates to other information. Readers will always form a variation of the web in Figure 5C. The ease with which they can form that web depends on how clearly the design team has uncovered the relationships during the analysis and supported them in the design. The interconnection of information relationships should not be separated for the convenience of the design team when creating content. A "divide & conquer" analysis philosophy is a fast-track to HII failure.

HII issues about the information relationships design teams must uncover include:

- Mental models contain default relationships, which is one of their major advantages in cognition. People will take the provided information and assign those relationships. Design teams need to ensure

Figure 5. Information relationships reflect how people think about the information and do not reflect a simple hierarchy structure. The hierarchy in (A) may make it easy to display, but does not support good HII. Instead, the design team must understand how all of the information relates within a situation (B) and how to connects to specific goals (C).

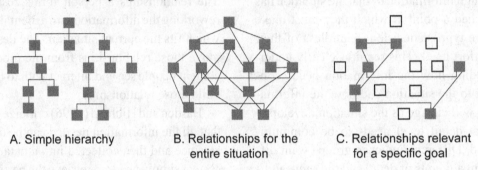

A. Simple hierarchy

B. Relationships for the entire situation

C. Relationships relevant for a specific goal

the early analysis uncovers them and that the content merges well. Otherwise, people are likely to ignore part of the information and use any defaults provided by the mental model.

- Irrelevant information will be integrated into people's view of the situation, causing a distorted view. Design teams need to prevent the irrelevant information from appearing so that it does not become part of the relationships people build.

- Many biases arise not from the information itself, but from how that information gets related to other information. Considering potential biases during design can help prevent them by making salient relationships clearer.

- Framing and ordering effects build the relationships based on the first information presented. The choice of this presentation order must fit the situation. Design teams need to worry about preference reversals.

- Information relationships include information values that should track together. Design teams need to capture how people mentally relate various information elements. For example, various factors on a sales report should move up/down in proportion to each other. One action might be appropriate when two values are both in-

creasing, while a different action is appropriate when one increases while the other decreases.

- Information relationships are build based on the system display. Ease of use and task complexity must be balanced to support relationship building versus simple data display.

- Graphs are a standard method of displaying trend relationships. The proper graph with proper scaling needs to be used to allow for seeing the real trend.

Determine the Source of Each Information Element

In a modern corporate environment, the information will never be in a single repository. The design teams need to define where the information is located and who is responsible for its maintenance. Tannenbaum (2002) points out this simple sounding step is often forgotten and "the location of data an information was never considered an issue" (p. 55) until incorrect or out-of-date information start routinely appearing.

The textual information provided to people requires constant updates as the bigger environment changes. Ensuring the information is up-to-date requires tracking it, which implies knowing its source. In addition, much of the numerical information may be coming from multiple transactional databases, with their own maintenance groups. Design teams need to be cognizant of the information sources so they can ensure any changes in those sources get properly reflected in the information system.

Build a Visual Model

Create a visual model for each major concept for each audience group that contains the overall goal structure, the information needs for the goal, and the relationships between the information elements. This model is comparable to various forms of information modeling, although they tend to be more focused on development of procedure-based texts.

For some goals, the visual model will make it apparent that different audience groups can be collapsed and for other goals it will highlight the areas of different information needs and relationships between them. The model gives design teams a clear vision of how to structure the content to support people's information needs and how to build the relationships between information elements.

Define the Presentation Requirements

Design teams must define how the information fits together to give an integrated presentation and how people need to receive it. In chapter 1, Figure 3 contained an area labeled "user text goes here." This step begins the process of taking the goals and information need previously uncovered and resolving what goes there and how it goes there. The focus here is not on information creation, but on deciding what information elements go together and how they interact with other information elements. It answers the all important question of "what is the system's HII." A poor answer nullifies all of the information analysis and results in poor HII and an unusable system.

Notice that defining the presentation is the final step in the cycle, not the first. Many systems with poor HII start designing the presentation layer too early without understanding what/how people need the information. Supporting good HII and improving people's performance means structuring the analysis and resulting design to reflect the people's practices and not the technical aspects of the implementation (Bodker, 1991).

Design teams need to take the information elements uncovered in the analysis and fit them together to give an integrated presentation. Effectively communicating information by connecting goals and information needs to an interface is an extremely difficult task. A computer screen is too limited and impoverished to effectively support the highly parallel processing human mind. A small display area (even large monitors have small display areas compared to the total information volume) complicates the communication process, taxes people's memory, and leads to information overload (Johnson, 1997). The recent move to mobile devices with their very small screens greatly complicates the design team's task.

The presentation must fit people's information needs. This sounds like a trivial statement, but has many levels of complexity buried within it. Consider how Woods and Roth (1988) address the issue of providing proper information by saying:

The critical question is not to show that the problem solver possesses domain knowledge, but rather that more stringent criterion that situation relevant knowledge is accessible under the conditions in which the task is performed (p. 420).

Achieving the goal of meeting people's goals and information needs means presenting information when and how they want it. Meeting people's goals and information needs can require slightly different information or information in a slightly different form. Perhaps someone wants a graph and another wants a table. Or the detail level of the text needs to change. Once the goals, information needs, and relationships are defined for each audience group, then the design team can figure out what constitutes the proper presentation for that group. There is no single "correct" presentation format for complex situations. Just as there is no single format to help solve open-ended problems because there is no single answer; rather the answer to open-ended questions depend on people's ability, their prior knowledge of the task, how much information they want, and their expectations about the situation.

Rather than being something people focus on, the content and the design must communicate the message in a clear manner without interfering with that communication. Once the design begins to be noticed, the amount of information conveyed decreases because the cognitive resources devoted to handling the design (often interface interaction issues), rather than information, increases. Each mouse click must be an obvious one; readers must always be clear on what information is currently displayed, what sits behind each link, and how all of the information fits together.

HII issues of concern for defining the presentation include the following. All contribute to people's acceptance of the information and the overall quality of the resulting system.

- Information relationships be maintained and clearly presented. The visual momentum must be maintained between screens. Information which is not currently being viewed has a lower salience and importance level than the currently viewed information, regardless of the actual relative importance. Design teams must balance this trade-off.
- The information must be presented in the most effective manner: video clip, graphics, or text only. Every presentation method has its plus and minuses and affects the overall communication of that information. They all have different perceived efforts to comprehend it and different ways they interrelate with the rest of the information.

- Clear information organization emphasizes the need to follow effective layout principles: formatting of lists and headings, visual cues, lots of white space, generous leading, and readable fonts. Proper choices disappear as people read while improper choices can make people refuse to read by making the text look too dense.
- The most important information must be the most salient information. It must not get lost in large amounts of other information.
- People need to be cued to relevant information not currently visible or that has recently changed.
- People have a hard time handling information that arrives at the wrong time. Just as important as getting it in the right way, it also needs to arrive at the right time. It can be neither too soon nor too late. Too soon and the person either forgets it or must go back and find it again; too late, and the information might as well have not existed. It will either be ignored or can cause problems as people try to undo a decision to make use of the new, but late, information.

Enhancing people's understanding of the situation requires information which clearly communicates the required information that supports people's goals and gives them an understanding of the situation and the possible solutions. Any non-trivial system has a high level of complexity, but the design must hide it (Eden, 1988). Design teams must capture and understand the complexity with respect to the business strategy and reader viewpoints to have a starting place for hiding the complexity and to create the HII that clearly communicates the information via an appropriate presentation method.

FINAL THOUGHTS

The focus of this book and HII, in general, emphasizes communicating information, and not writing documents or designing web sites, or other methods of generating content. Throughout this book I tried to take the theoretical and applied research that has been done across several different fields and transform it into a form that supports developing high quality HII which is accessible to a wide range of readers. The goal was to provide design teams with a sound theoretical foundation from which they can make decisions with respect to designing and communicating information.

HII focuses on communicating information, not creating information. Developing information which clearly communicates and fits people's needs requires understanding how people think and what drives their decision processes. People interact with information to understand situations. They do not want to interact with computers; the computer is only an intermediary to the desired information.

The major goal of this book has been to bring into focus the many issues that impede people from comprehending information and understanding a situation as they move along the path of forming their goals about understanding a situation, and transforming data to information. It works to clarify the issues which must be considered by design teams tasked with communicating information which maximizes people's comprehension of that information.

Post-hoc analysis of information systems consistently uncovers stories of how systems went unused or were used in ways quite different from initially envisioned. In unused systems, the HII failed to meet people needs, regardless of the content. When the system is used in un-envisioned ways, the high quality HII allowed people take over the technology and turn it to their own uses (Dourish, 1999; Mirel, 1998). As with so many other people-oriented processes, HII is fundamentally dynamic and nonlinear with the actually path of the information interaction impossible to predict. Design teams cannot pick one communication path, but they can and must maintain the general route. Then the information will be communicated to the reader, which is the overall goal of any system.

The following quote gives a description of the problems HCI works to address:

We believe that the problems HCI seeks to solve are complex ones. Designing to support human activity is a hard problem, and when you have a difficult problem it is necessary to use every available resource. HCI is contributing to the understanding, design, and evaluation of human interaction with and through computing devices, and through this seeking to improve both the artifacts and the quality of human activity that they support. (Johnson, May, & Johnson, 2003, p. 278).

This quote can be easily paraphrased (below) into the purposes which HII works to address. It should be clear that communicating complex information is a complex process (Albers, 2004). More importantly, HII moves beyond interactions with computing devices and focuses on information and the situation.

Communication problems relevant to HII are complex ones. Designing to support how people interact with information is a hard problem and when you have a difficult problem, you must use all available resources. HII contributes to understanding, designing, and evaluating how people interact with information and their environment, and seeks to improve the quality of that interaction.

Combine this 57 word statement with the 119 word elevator definition of HII given at start of chapter 1 and they succinctly sum up the entire purpose of this book, of HII, and design team's communication goals.

REFERENCES

Ahn, H., Lee, H., Cho, K., & Park, S. (2005). Utilizing knowledge context in virtual collaborative work. *Decision Support Systems*, *39*, 563–582. doi:10.1016/j.dss.2004.03.005

Albers, M. (2004). *Communication of complex information: User goals and information needs for dynamic Web information*. Mahwah, NJ: Erlbaum.

Albers, M. (2010). Usability and information relationships: Considering content relationships when testing complex information. In Albers, M., & Still, B. (Eds.), *Usability of complex Information Systems: Evaluation of user interaction* (pp. 109–131). Boca Raton, FL: CRC Press. doi:10.1201/EBK1439828946-9

Bailey, G. (1993). Iterative methodology and designer training in human-computer interface design. [Washington, DC: ACM.]. *Proceedings of INTERCHI*, *93*, 198–205.

Basden, A., & Hibberd, P. (1996). User interface issues raised by knowledge refinement. *International Journal of Human-Computer Studies*, *45*, 135–155. doi:10.1006/ijhc.1996.0046

Bechky, B. (2003). Sharing meaning across occupational communities: The transformation of understanding on a production floor. *Organization Science*, *14*(3), 312–330. doi:10.1287/orsc.14.3.312.15162

Bodker, S. (1991). *Through the interface: A human activity design approach to computer interface design*. Mahwah, NJ: Erlbaum.

Carroll, J. (1995). (Ed.). *Scenario-based design: Envisioning work and technology in system development*. New York, NY: Wiley.

Constantine, L., & Lockwood, L. (1999). *Software for use: A practical guide to the models and methods of usage-centered design*. New York, NY: ACM Press.

Cooper, A. (1999). *The inmates are running the asylum*. Indianapolis, IN: Sams.

Dourish, P. (1999). Where the footprints lead: Tracking down other roles for social navigation. In Munro, A., Hook, K., & Denyon, D. (Eds.), *Social navigation of information space* (pp. 15–34). London, UK: Springer. doi:10.1007/978-1-4471-0837-5_2

Eden, C. (1988). Cognitive mapping. *European Journal of Operational Research*, *36*, 1–13. doi:10.1016/0377-2217(88)90002-1

Gribbons, W., & Elsar, A. (1998). Visualizing information: An overview of this special issue. *Technical Communication*, *45*(4), 467–472.

Hargis, G., Hernandez, A., Hughes, P., Ramaker, J., Rouiller, S., & Wilde, E. (1998). *Developing quality technical information: A handbook for writers and editors*. New York, NY: Prentice Hall.

Hartson, R., & Boehm-Davis, D. (1993). User interface development process and methodologies. *Behaviour & Information Technology*, *12*(2), 98–114. doi:10.1080/01449299308924371

Johnson, P., May, J., & Johnson, H. (2003). Introduction to multiple and collaborative tasks. *ACM Transactions on Computer-Human Interaction*, *10*(4), 277–280. doi:10.1145/966930.966931

Johnson, S. (1997). *Interface culture*. New York, NY: Basic Books.

Kuutti, K. (1995). Work processes: Scenarios as a preliminary vocabulary. In Carroll, J. (Ed.), *Scenario-based design: Envisioning work and technology in system development* (pp. 19–36). New York, NY: Wiley.

Kwasitsu, L. (2001). Information-seeking behavior of design process and manufacturing engineers. *Library and Information Science*, *25*, 459–476. doi:10.1016/S0740-8188(03)00054-9

Mao, J., & Benbasat, I. (2001). The effects of contextualized access to knowledge on judgment. *International Journal of Human-Computer Studies*, *55*, 787–814. doi:10.1006/ijhc.2001.0507

Mirel, B. (1998). Applied constructivism for user documentation. *Journal of Business and Technical Communication*, *12*(1), 7–49. doi:10.1177/1050651998012001002

Mirel, B. (2003). *Interaction design for complex problem solving: Developing useful and usable software*. San Francisco, CA: Morgan Kaufmann.

Monk, A. (1999). Modeling cyclic interaction. *Behaviour & Information Technology*, *18*(2), 127–139. doi:10.1080/014492999119165

Nilsson, R., & Mayer, R. (2002). The effects of graphic organizers giving cues to the structure of a hypertext document on users' navigation strategies and performance. *International Journal of Human-Computer Studies*, *57*, 1–26. doi:10.1006/ijhc.2002.1011

Rodriguez, M. (2002). Development of diagrammatic procedural instructions for performing complex one-time tasks. *International Journal of Human-Computer Interaction*, *14*(3&4), 405–422.

Slone, D. (2002). The Influence of mental models and goals on user search patterns during Web interaction. *Journal of the American Society for Information Science and Technology*, *53*(13), 1152–1169. doi:10.1002/asi.10141

Szulanski, G. (1996). Exploring internal stickiness: Impediments to the transfer of best practice within the firm. *Strategic Management Journal*, *17*, 27–43.

Tannenbaum, A. (2002). *Metadata solutions: Using metamodels, repositories, XML and enterprise portals to generate information on demand*. Boston, MA: Addison-Wesley.

Vicente, K. (1999). *Cognitive work analysis*. Mahway, NJ: Erlbaum.

von Hippel, E. (2001). Innovation by user communities: Learning from open-source software. *MIT Sloan Management Review*, *42*(4), 82–86.

Warren, T. (1993). Three approaches to reader analysis. *Technical Communication*, *40*(1), 81–87.

Woods, D., & Roth, E. (1988). Cognitive engineering: Human problem solving with tools. *Human Factors*, *30*(4), 415–430.

Compilation of References

Ackoff, R. (1967). Management misinformation systems. *Management Science*, *14*, 147–156. doi:10.1287/mnsc.14.4.B147

Aggelidis, V., & Chatzoglou, P. (2009). Using a modified technology acceptance model in hospitals. *International Journal of Medical Informatics*, *78*(2), 115–126. doi:10.1016/j.ijmedinf.2008.06.006

Ahn, H., Lee, H., Cho, K., & Park, S. (2005). Utilizing knowledge context in virtual collaborative work. *Decision Support Systems*, *39*, 563–582. doi:10.1016/j.dss.2004.03.005

Albers, M. (1996). Decision-making: A missing facet of effective documentation. *Proceedings of the 14th Annual International Conference on Computer Documentation* (pp. 1–6). New York, NY: ACM.

Albers, M. (2000). Information design for web sites which support complex decision making. *Proceedings of the STC 2000 Annual Conference*, Orlando FL. May 21–24, 2000.

Albers, M. (2004b). Signal to noise ratio of information in documentation. *Proceedings of 22nd Annual International Conference on Computer Documentation* (pp. 41–44). New York, NY: ACM.

Albers, M. (2008). *Human-information interaction*. 28th Annual International Conference on Computer Documentation, Lisbon Portugal. Sept 22–24, 2008.

Albers, M. (2009). Information relationships: The source of useful and usable content. *Proceedings of 29th Annual International Conference on Computer Documentation* (pp. 171–178). New York, NY: ACM.

Albers, M. (2003). Complex problem solving and content analysis. In Albers, M., & Mazur, B. (Eds.), *Content and complexity: Information design in software development and documentation* (pp. 263–284). Mahwah, NJ: Erlbaum.

Albers, M. (2004). *Communication of complex information: User goals and information needs for dynamic Web information*. Mahwah, NJ: Erlbaum.

Albers, M. (2010). Design and usability: Beginner interactions with complex software. *Journal of Technical Writing and Communication.*, *41*(3), 273–289.

Albers, M. (2010). Usability and information relationships: Considering content relationships when testing complex information. In Albers, M., & Still, B. (Eds.), *Usability of complex Information Systems: Evaluation of user interaction* (pp. 109–131). Boca Raton, FL: CRC Press. doi:10.1201/EBK1439828946-9

Albers, M. (2010). Usability of complex Information Systems. In Albers, M., & Still, B. (Eds.), *Usability of complex Information Systems: Evaluation of user interaction* (pp. 3–16). Boca Raton, FL: CRC Press. doi:10.1201/EBK1439828946-3

Albers, M., & Still, S. (2010). *Usability of complex Information Systems: Evaluation of user interaction*. Boca Raton, FL: CRC Press. doi:10.1201/EBK1439828946

Albright, S. (1993). A statistical analysis of hitting streaks in baseball. *Journal of the American Statistical Association*, *88*(424), 1175–1183. doi:10.2307/2291254

Allen, B. (1996). *Information tasks: Toward a user-centered approach to Information Systems*. San Diego, CA: Academic Press.

Allen, N. (1996). Ethics and visual rhetorics: Seeing's not believing anymore. *Technical Communication Quarterly*, *5*(1), 87–105. doi:10.1207/s15427625tcq0501_6

Allen, P. (1996). User attitudes toward corporate style guides: A survey. *Technical Communication*, *43*(3), 237–243.

Alvarado, C., Jeevan, J., Ackerman, M., & Karger, D. (2003). *Surviving the information explosion: How people find their electronic information* (pp. 1–9). MIT AI Memo AIM-2003-006. Retrieved from http://www.csail.mit.edu/~teevan/ work/publications/papers/aim03.pdf

American National Standards Institute. (1998). *Warning signs, labels, tags, colours and symbol standards Z535* (pp. 1–5). Arlington, VA: National Electrical Manufacturers Association.

Anderson, J. R. (1990). *Cognitive psychology and its implications*. New York, NY: Freeman.

Anderson, R., & Pearson, P. (1984). A schema-theoretic view of basic processes in reading comprehension. In Pearson, P. (Ed.), *Handbook of reading research* (pp. 255–291). New York, NY: Longman.

Andriole, S., & Adelman, L. (1995). *Cognitive system engineering for user–computer interface design, prototyping, and evaluation*. Mahwah, NJ: Erlbaum.

Angehrn, A., & Jelassi, T. (1994). DSS research and practice in perspective. *Decision Support Systems*, *12*, 267–275. doi:10.1016/0167-9236(94)90045-0

Antonides, G., Verhoef, P., & Van Aalst, M. (2002). Consumer perception and evaluation of waiting time: A field experiment. *Journal of Consumer Psychology*, *12*(3), 193–202. doi:10.1207/S15327663JCP1203_02

Antony, S., Batra, D., & Santhanam, R. (2005). The use of a knowledge-based system in conceptual data modeling. *Decision Support Systems*, *41*, 176–188. doi:10.1016/j.dss.2004.05.011

Arditi, A., & Cho, J. (2005). Serifs and font legibility. *Vision Research*, *45*, 2926–2933. doi:10.1016/j.visres.2005.06.013

Armbruster, B., & Armstrong, J. (1993). Locating information in text: A focus on children in the elementary grades. *Contemporary Educational Psychology*, *18*, 139–161. doi:10.1006/ceps.1993.1015

Arning, K., & Ziefle, M. (2007). Understanding age differences in PDA acceptance and performance. *Computers in Human Behavior*, *23*, 2904–2927. doi:10.1016/j.chb.2006.06.005

Arnott, D., & O'Donnell, P. (2008). A note on an experimental study of DSS and forecasting exponential growth. *Decision Support Systems*, *45*, 180–186. doi:10.1016/j.dss.2007.11.006

Arora, N., Hesse, B., Rimer, B., Viswanath, K., Clayman, M., & Croyle, R. (2008). Frustrated and confused: The American public rates its cancer-related information seeking experiences. *Journal of General Internal Medicine*, *23*, 223–228. doi:10.1007/s11606-007-0406-y

Ashby, F., & O'Brien, J. (2005). Category learning and multiple memory systems. *Trends in Cognitive Sciences*, *9*(2), 83–89. doi:10.1016/j.tics.2004.12.003

Ash, J., Berg, M., & Coiera, E. (2004). Some unintended consequences of Information Technology in health care: The nature of patient care information system-related errors. *Journal of the American Medical Informatics Association*, *11*(2), 104–112. doi:10.1197/jamia.M1471

Atkins, P., Wood, R., & Rutgers, P. (2002). The effects of feedback format on dynamic decision making. *Organizational Behavior and Human Decision Processes*, *88*, 587–604. doi:10.1016/S0749-5978(02)00002-X

Atwood, J. (2005). Comparing font legibility. *Coding Horror*. Retrieved from http://www.codinghorror.com/blog/ 2005/11/comparing-font-legibility.html

Austin, P., Matlack, R., Dunn, K., Kosler, C., & Brown, C. (1995). Discharge instructions: Do illustrations help our patients understand them? *Annals of Emergency Medicine*, *25*, 317–320. doi:10.1016/S0196-0644(95)70286-5

Baddeley, A. (1986). *Working memory*. Oxford, England: Oxford UP.

Baddeley, A. (1995). Working memory. In Gazzaniga, M. S. (Ed.), *The cognitive neurosciences* (pp. 755–764). Cambridge, MA: MIT Press.

Baddeley, A. (2000). The episodic buffer: A new component of working memory? *Trends in Cognitive Sciences*, *4*(11), 417–423. doi:10.1016/S1364-6613(00)01538-2

Baddeley, A. (2001). Is working memory still working? *The American Psychologist*, *56*, 851–864. doi:10.1037/0003-066X.56.11.851

Baddeley, A., & Hitch, G. (1974). Working memory. In Bower, G. (Ed.), *The psychology of learning and motivation: Advances in research and theory* (Vol. 8, pp. 47–89). New York, NY: Academic Press.

Bagozzi, R. (2007). The legacy of the technology acceptance model and a proposal for a paradigm shift. *Journal of the Association for Information Systems*, *8*, 244–254.

Bailey, R. (2000). *Link affordance*. Retrieved April 27, 2009, from http://webusability.com/ article_link_affordance_11_2000.htm

Bailey, G. (1993). Iterative methodology and designer training in human-computer interface design. [Washington, DC: ACM.]. *Proceedings of INTERCHI*, *93*, 198–205.

Bailey, R. (1989). *Human performance engineering*. New York, NY: Prentice-Hall.

Baker, H., Uus, K., Bamford, J., & Marteau, T. (2004). Increasing knowledge about a screening test: preliminary evaluation of a structured, chart-based, screener presentation. *Patient Education and Counseling*, *52*, 55–59. doi:10.1016/S0738-3991(02)00249-5

Balakrishnan, R., & Hinckley, K. (2002). Symmetric bimanual interaction. *ACM CHI2002 Conference, CHI Letters, 2*(1), (pp. 33–40). New York, NY: ACM

Bar-Hillel, M., & Wagenaar, W. (1991). The perception of randomness. *Advances in Applied Mathematics*, *12*(4), 428–454. doi:10.1016/0196-8858(91)90029-I

Barnum, C., & Palmer, L. (2010). Tapping into desirability in user experience. In Albers, M., & Still, B. (Eds.), *Usability of complex Information Systems: Evaluation of user interaction* (pp. 253–280). Boca Raton, FL: CRC Press. doi:10.1201/EBK1439828946-17

Baron, J. (2000). *Thinking and deciding* (Vol. 3). Cambridge, UK: Cambridge UP.

Barreau, D., & Nardi, B. (1995). Finding and reminding: File organization from the desktop. *SIGCHI Bulletin*, *27*(3), 66–69.

Barrick, J., & Spilker, B. (2003). The relations between knowledge, search strategy, and performance in unaided and aided information search. *Organizational Behavior and Human Decision Processes*, *90*, 1–18. doi:10.1016/S0749-5978(03)00002-5

Barshi, I. (1997). *Effect of message length in ATC communication: Linguistic and cognitive aspects*. Paper presented at the Ninth International Symposium on Aviation Psychology, Columbus, OH.

Basden, A., & Hibberd, P. (1996). User interface issues raised by knowledge refinement. *International Journal of Human-Computer Studies*, *45*, 135–155. doi:10.1006/ijhc.1996.0046

Bates, D. (2003). Ten commandments for effective clinical decision support: Making the practice of evidence-based medicine a reality. *Journal of the American Medical Informatics Association*, *10*(6), 523–530. doi:10.1197/jamia.M1370

Bazerman, C. (2001). Nuclear information: One rhetorical moment in the construction of the information age. *Written Communication*, *18*(3), 259–295. doi:10.1177/0741088301018003002

Beach, L., & Mitchell, T. (1978). A contingency model for the selection of decision strategies. *Academy of Management Review*, *3*, 439–449.

Bechky, B. (2003). Sharing meaning across occupational communities: The transformation of understanding on a production floor. *Organization Science*, *14*(3), 312–330. doi:10.1287/orsc.14.3.312.15162

Becker, S. (2004). A study of web usability for older adults seeking online health resources. *ACM Transactions on Computer-Human Interaction*, *11*(4), 387–406. doi:10.1145/1035575.1035578

Becker, S. (2005). E-government usability for older adults. *Communications of the ACM*, *48*(2), 102–104. doi:10.1145/1042091.1042127

Bedell, S., Agrawal, A., & Petersen, L. (2004). A systematic critique of diabetes on the World Wide Web for patients and their physicians. *International Journal of Medical Informatics*, *73*, 687–694. doi:10.1016/j.ijmedinf.2004.04.011

Beene, L. (1988). How can technical writing be made more cohesive and coherent? In Beene, L., & White, P. (Eds.), *Solving problems in technical writing* (pp. 108–129). New York, NY: Oxford UP.

Belkin, N. (1980). Anomalous states of knowledge as a basic for information retrieval. *The Canadian. Journal of Information Science*, *5*, 133–143.

Belmore, S. (1985). Reading computer-presented text. *Bulletin of the Psychonomic Society*, *23*, 12–14.

Ben Zur, H., & Breznitz, S. (1981). The effect of time pressure on risky choice behavior. *Acta Psychologica*, *47*, 89–104. doi:10.1016/0001-6918(81)90001-9

Benbasat, I., Dexter, A., & Todd, P. (1986a). An experimental program investigating color-enhanced. and graphical information presentation: An integration of findings. *Communications of the ACM*, *29*(11), 1094–1105. doi:10.1145/7538.7545

Benbasat, I., Dexter, A., & Todd, P. (1986b). The influence of color and graphical information presentation in a managerial decision simulation. *Human-Computer Interaction*, *2*, 65–92. doi:10.1207/s15327051hci0201_3

Benedek, J., & Miner, T. (2002). *Measuring desirability: New methods for measuring desirability in the usability lab setting*. Retrieved from http://www.microsoft.com/ usability/ UEPostings/DesirabilityToolkit.doc

Bennett, K., & Flacch, (2011). *Display and interface design: Subtle science, exact art*. Boca Raton, FL: CRC Press.

Bennett, K., & Walters, B. (2001). Configural display design techniques considered at multiple levels of evaluation. *Human Factors*, *43*(3), 415–434. doi:10.1518/001872001775898304

Benson, J., Olewiler, K., & Broden, N. (2005). *Typography for mobile phone devices: The design of the Qualcomm sans font family*. Retrieved April 9, 2010, from http://www.aiga.org/resources/ content/2/0/9/3/documents/typography_for_mobile_phone_devices.pdf

Benway, J., & Lane, D. (1998). Banner blindness: Web searchers often miss "obvious" links. *Internetworking*, *1*(3). Retrieved May 4, 2006, from http://www.internettg.org/newsletter/ dec98/banner_blindness.html

Berg, M. (1998). Medical work and the computer based patient record: A sociological perspective. *Methods of Information in Medicine*, *38*, 294–301.

Bernard, M., & Mills, M. (2000). So, what size and type of font should I use on my website? *Usability News*, *2*(2). Retrieved from http://psychology.wichita.edu/surl/usabilitynews/22/font.asp

Bernard, M., Lida, B., Riley, S., Hackler, T., & Janzen, K. (2002). A comparison of popular online fonts: which size and type is best? *Usability News*, *4*(1). Retrieved from http://www.surl.org/usabilitynews/ 41/onlinetext.asp

Bernhardt, S. (2002). *Technical writing for adults*. ATTW discussion list Sept 26, 2002.

Bernstam, E., Sagaram, S., Walji, M., Johnson, C., & Meric-Bernstam, F. (2005). Usability of quality measures for online health information: Can commonly used technical quality criteria be reliably assessed? *International Journal of Medical Informatics*, *74*, 675–683. doi:10.1016/j.ijmedinf.2005.02.002

Berry, L. (1991). The interaction of color realism and pictorial recall memory. *Proceedings of Selected Research Presentations at the Annual Convention of the Association for Educational Communications and Technology*. (ERIC Document Reproduction Service No. ED334974.)

Berry, D., & Broadbent, D. (1987). The combination of explicit and implicit learning processes in task control. *Psychological Research*, *49*(1), 7–15. doi:10.1007/BF00309197

Berry, D., & Broadbent, D. (1988). On the relationship between task performance and associated task knowledge. *The Quarterly Journal of Experimental Psychology. A, Human Experimental Psychology*, *36*, 209–231. doi:10.1080/14640748408402156

Berry, D., Knapp, P., & Raynor, T. (2005). Expressing medicine side effects: Assessing the effectiveness of absolute risk, relative risk, and number needed to harm, and the provision of baseline risk information. *Patient Education and Counseling*, *63*, 89–96. doi:10.1016/j.pec.2005.09.003

Besnard, D., & Cacitti, L. (2005). Interface changes causing accidents. An empirical study of negative transfer. *International Journal of Human-Computer Studies*, *62*, 103–125. doi:10.1016/j.ijhcs.2004.08.002

Best, R., Rowe, M., Ozuru, Y., & McNamara, D. (2005). Deep-level comprehension of science texts: The role of the reader and the text. *Topics in Language Disorders*, *25*, 65–83. doi:10.1097/00011363-200501000-00007

Betrancourt, M., & Bisseret, A. (1998). Integrating textual and pictorial information via pop-up windows: An experimental study. *Behaviour & Information Technology*, *17*(5), 263–273. doi:10.1080/014492998119337

Bettman, J., Johnson, E., & Payne, J. (1990). A componential analysis of cognitive effort in choice. *Organizational Behavior and Human Decision Processes*, *45*, 111–139. doi:10.1016/0749-5978(90)90007-V

Bettman, J., & Zins, M. (1979). Information format and choice task effects in decision making. *The Journal of Consumer Research*, *6*(2), 141–153. doi:10.1086/208757

Beyer, H., & Holtzblatt, K. (1998). *Contextual design: Defining customer-centered systems*. San Francisco, CA: Morgan-Kaufmann.

Beyth-Marom, R., & Dekel, S. (1983). A curriculum to improve thinking under uncertainty. *Instructional Science*, *12*, 67–82. doi:10.1007/BF00120902

Bhavnani, S., & John, B. (2000). The strategic use of complex computer systems. *Human-Computer Interaction*, *15*, 107–137. doi:10.1207/S15327051HCI1523_3

Birdi, K., & Zapf, D. (1997). Age differences in reactions to errors in computer-based work. *Behaviour & Information Technology*, *16*(6), 309–319. doi:10.1080/014492997119716

Bix, L., Lockhart, H., Selke, S., Cardoso, F., & Olejnik, M. (2003). Is x-height a better indicator of legibility than type size for drug labels? *Packaging Technology and Science*, *16*(5), 199–207. doi:10.1002/pts.625

Blandford, A., & Wong, B. (2004). Situation awareness in emergency medical dispatch. *International Journal of Human-Computer Studies*, *61*, 421–452. doi:10.1016/j.ijhcs.2003.12.012

Block, R., Hancock, P., & Zakay, D. (2000). Sex differences in duration judgments: A meta-analytic review. *Memory & Cognition*, *28*(8), 1333–1346. doi:10.3758/BF03211834

Boag, A. (1996). Typographic measurement: A chronology. [Department of Typography and Graphic Communication: University of Reading.]. *Typography Papers*, *1*, 105–121.

Bodker, S. (1991). *Through the interface: A human activity design approach to computer interface design*. Mahwah, NJ: Erlbaum.

Bohnenblust, H., & Slovic, P. (1998). Integrating technical analysis and public values in risk-based decision-making. *Reliability Engineering & System Safety*, *59*, 151–159. doi:10.1016/S0951-8320(97)00136-1

Boland, P., & Pawitan, Y. (1999). Trying to be random in selecting numbers for Lotto. *Journal of Statistics Education*, *7*(3). Retrieved May 10, 2009, from http://www.amstat.org/publications/ jse/secure/v7n3/boland.cfm

Booth, K., Beaver, K., Kitchener, H., O'Neill, J., & Farrell, C. (2005). Women's experiences of information, psychological distress and worry after treatment for gynecological cancer. *Patient Education and Counseling*, *56*, 225–232. doi:10.1016/j.pec.2004.02.016

Bootsmaa, R., Fernandeza, L., & Mottet, D. (2004). Behind Fitts' law: Kinematic patterns in goal-directed movements. *International Journal of Human-Computer Studies*, *61*, 811–821. doi:10.1016/j.ijhcs.2004.09.004

Borgman, C. (1985). The user's mental model of an information retrieval system. *Proceedings of the 8th International ACM Special Interest Group on Information Retrieval Conference*, (pp. 268–273). New York, NY: ACM.

Bouch, A., Kuchinsky, A., & Bhatti, N. (2000). Quality is in the eye of the beholder: Meeting users' requirements for Internet quality of service. *Proceedings of the SIGCHI Conference on Human Factors in Computing Systems* (pp. 297–304). New York, NY: ACM.

Bowie, J. (1996). Information engineering: Communicating with technology. *Intercom*, *43*(5), 6–9.

Boyarsk, D., Neuwirth, C., Forlizzi, J., & Regli, S. H. (1998). A study of fonts designed for screen display. *Proceedings of the SIGCHI Conference on Human Factors in Computing Systems* (pp. 87–94). New York, NY: ACM.

Bracy, G. (1998). Tips for readers of research—No causation from correlation. *Phi Delta Kappan, 79*(9), 711–712.

Brand-Gurwel, S., Wopereis, I., & Vermetten, Y. (2005). Information problem solving by experts and novices: Analysis of a complex cognitive skill. *Computers in Human Behavior, 21*, 487–508. doi:10.1016/j.chb.2004.10.005

Bransford, J. D., & Schwartz, D. L. (1999). Rethinking transfer: A simple proposal with multiple implications. In Iran-Nejad, A., & Pearson, P. D. (Eds.), *Review of research in education* (*Vol. 24*, pp. 61–101). Washington, DC: American Educational Research Association. doi:10.2307/1167267

Bransford, J., & Johnson, M. (1972). Contextual prerequisites for understanding: Some investigations of comprehension and recall. *Journal of Verbal Learning and Verbal Behavior, 11*, 717–726. doi:10.1016/S0022-5371(72)80006-9

Brasseur, L. (2003). *Visualizing technical information: A cultural critique*. Amityville, NY: Baywood.

Brazier, F., & Veer, G. (1991). Design decisions for a user interface. In Ackerman, D., & Tauber, M. (Eds.), *Mental models and human computer interaction* (pp. 159–178). Amsterdam, The Netherlands: North Holland.

Brinkman, W., Buil, V., Cullen, R., Gobits, R., & Van Nes, F. (2001). Design and evaluation of online multimedia maintenance manuals. *Behaviour & Information Technology, 20*(1), 47–52. doi:10.1080/01449290010020639

Brooke, J. (1996). SUS: A "quick and dirty" usability scale. In Jordan, P., Thomas, B., Weerdmeester, B., & McClelland, A. (Eds.), *Usability evaluation in industry* (pp. 189–194). London, UK: Taylor and Francis.

Brooke, J., & Duncan, K. (1981). Effects of system display format on performance in a fault location task. *Ergonomics, 24*, 175–189. doi:10.1080/00140138108559232

Brown, S. (1985). Time perception and attention: The effect of prospective and retrospective paradigms and task demands on perceived duration. *Perception & Psychophysics, 38*, 115–124. doi:10.3758/BF03198848

Bruce, H., Jones, W., & Dumais, S. (2004). *Re-finding information on the web: What do people do and what do they need*. Retrieved from http://kftf.ischool.washington.edu/

Bruine de Bruin, W., & Keren, G. (2003). Order effects in sequentially judged options due to the direction of comparison. *Organizational Behavior and Human Decision Processes, 92*, 91–101. doi:10.1016/S0749-5978(03)00080-3

Brumberger, E. (2003a). The rhetoric of typography: The awareness and impact of typeface appropriateness. *Technical Communication, 50*(2), 224–231.

Brumberger, E. (2004). The rhetoric of typography: Effects on reading time, reading comprehension, and perceptions of ethos. *Technical Communication, 51*(1), 13–24.

Buckland, M. (1991). Information as thing. *Journal of the American Society for Information Science American Society for Information Science, 42*(5), 351–360. doi:10.1002/(SICI)1097-4571(199106)42:5<351::AID-ASI5>3.0.CO;2-3

Burgess, P. W., Veitch, E., De Lacy Costello, A., & Shallice, T. (2000). The cognitive and neuroanatomical correlates of human multitasking. *Neuropsychologia, 38*, 848–863. doi:10.1016/S0028-3932(99)00134-7

Buxton, W., & Myers, B. (1987). A study in two-handed input. *Proceedings of the ACM Conference on Human Factors in Computing Systems*, (pp. 321–326). New York, NY: ACM.

Byrne, R. (1989). Human deductive reasoning. *The Irish Journal of Psychology, 10*, 216–231.

Calisir, F., Eryazici, M., & Lehto, M. (2008). The effects of text structure and prior knowledge of the learner on computer-based learning. *Computers in Human Behavior, 24*, 439–450. doi:10.1016/j.chb.2007.01.032

Calvo, M., Castillo, M., & Estevez, A. (1999). On-line predictive inferences in reading: Processing time during versus after the priming context. *Memory & Cognition, 27*, 834–843. doi:10.3758/BF03198536

Campagnoni, F. R., & Ehrlich, K. (1989). Information retrieval using hypertext-based help system. *Proceedings of the 12th Annual International ACM SIGIR Conference*, (pp. 212–220).

Campbell, K. (1994). *Coherence, continuity, and cohesion*. Mahwah, NJ: Erlbaum.

Canter, D., Rivers, R., & Storrs, G. (1985). Characterising user navigation through complex data structures. *Behaviour & Information Technology, 4*, 93–102. doi:10.1080/01449298508901791

Card, S., Robertson, G., & Mackinlay, J. (1991). The information visualizer: An information workspace. *Proceedings of the SIGCHI Conference on Human Factors in Computing Systems*, (pp. 181–188). New York, NY: ACM.

Card, S., English, W., & Burr, B. (1978). Evaluation of mouse, rate-controlled isometric joystick, step keys, and text keys for text selection on a CRT. *Ergonomics, 21*, 601–613. doi:10.1080/00140137808931762

Card, S., Moran, T., & Newell, A. (1983). *The psychology of human-computer interaction*. Hillsdale, NJ: Erlbaum.

Carey, J., & White, E. (1991). The effects of graphical versus numerical response on the accuracy of graph-based forecasts. *Journal of Management, 17*(1), 77–96. doi:10.1177/014920639101700106

Carliner, S. (2000). A three-part framework for information design. *Technical Communication, 49*, 561–576.

Carlson, K., Meloy, M., & Russo, J. (2006). Leader-driven primacy: Using attribute order to affect consumer choice. *The Journal of Consumer Research, 32*, 513–518. doi:10.1086/500481

Carlson, K., & Pearo, L. (2004). Limiting predecisional distortion by prior valuation of attribute components. *Organizational Behavior and Human Decision Processes, 94*, 48–59. doi:10.1016/j.obhdp.2004.02.001

Carlson, R., Wenger, J., & Sullivan, M. (1993). Coordinating information from perception and working memory. *Journal of Experimental Psychology. Human Perception and Performance, 19*(3), 531–548. doi:10.1037/0096-1523.19.3.531

Carney, R., & Levin, J. (2002). Pictorial illustrations still improve students' learning from text. *Educational Psychology Review, 14*(1), 5–26. doi:10.1023/A:1013176309260

Carpenter, D., DeVellis, R., Fisher, E., DeVallis, B., Hogan, S., & Jordan, J. (2010). The effect of conflicting medication information and physician support on medication adherence for chronically ill patients. *Patient Education and Counseling, 81*(2), 169–176. doi:10.1016/j.pec.2009.11.006

Carpenter, P., & Shah, P. (1998). A model of the perceptual and conceptual processes in graph comprehension. *Journal of Experimental Psychology. Applied, 4*, 75–100. doi:10.1037/1076-898X.4.2.75

Carretti, B., Borella, E., Cornoldi, C., & De Beni, R. (2009). Role of working memory in explaining the performance of individuals with specific reading comprehension difficulties: A meta-analysis. *Learning and Individual Differences, 19*, 246–251. doi:10.1016/j.lindif.2008.10.002

Carroll, J. (1995). (Ed.). *Scenario-based design: Envisioning work and technology in system development*. New York, NY: Wiley.

Carroll, J., & Rosson, M. (1987). The paradox of the active user. In Carroll, J. (Ed.), *Interfacing thought: Cognitive aspects of human-computer interaction* (pp. 80–111). Cambridge, MA: MIT Press.

Carroll, J., Smith-Kerker, P., Ford, J., & Mazur-Rimetz, S. (1988). The minimal manual. *Human-Computer Interaction, 3*, 123–153. doi:10.1207/s15327051hci0302_2

Carswell, C., Frankenberger, S., & Bernhard, D. (1991). Graphing in depth: Perspectives on the use of three dimensional graphs to represent lower-dimensional data. *Behaviour & Information Technology, 10*(6), 459–474. doi:10.1080/01449299108924304

Carswell, C., & Ramzy, C. (1997). Graphing small data sets: Should we bother? *Behaviour & Information Technology, 16*(2), 61–71. doi:10.1080/014492997119905

Carswell, C., & Wickens, C. (1987). Information integration and the object display: An interaction of task demands and display superiority. *Ergonomics, 30*, 511–527. doi:10.1080/00140138708969741

Cary, M., & Carlson, R. (1999). External support and the development of problem solving routines. *Journal of Experimental Psychology. Learning, Memory, and Cognition, 25*, 1053–1070. doi:10.1037/0278-7393.25.4.1053

Cary, M., & Carlson, R. (2001). Distributing working memory resources in problem solving. *Journal of Experimental Psychology. Learning, Memory, and Cognition*, *27*, 836–848. doi:10.1037/0278-7393.27.3.836

Casaday, G. (1991). Balance. In Karat, J. (Ed.), *Taking software design seriously: Practical techniques for HCI design* (pp. 45–62). New York, NY: Academic Press.

Casner, S. (1994). Understanding the determinants of problem-solving behavior in a complex environment. *Human Factors*, *34*(4), 580–596.

Cerella, J. (1985). Information processing rates in the elderly. *Psychological Bulletin*, *98*, 67–83. doi:10.1037/0033-2909.98.1.67

Chadwick-Dias, A., McNulty, M., & Tullis, T. (2003). Web usability and age: How design changes can improve performance. *Proceedings of the 2003 Conference on Universal usability*, (pp. 30–37). New York, NY: ACM

Chalmers, P. (2003). The role of cognitive theory in human-computer interface. *Computers in Human Behavior*, *19*, 593–607. doi:10.1016/S0747-5632(02)00086-9

Chandler, P., & Sweller, J. (1996). Cognitive load while learning to use a computer program. *Applied Cognitive Psychology*, *10*, 151–170. doi:10.1002/(SICI)1099-0720(199604)10:2<151::AID-ACP380>3.0.CO;2-U

Chao, C., Salvendy, G., & Lightner, N. (1999). Development of a methodology for optimizing elicited knowledge. *Behaviour & Information Technology*, *18*(6), 413–430. doi:10.1080/014492999118841

Chaparro, B. Baker, J., Shaikh, A., Hull, S., & Brady, L. (2004). Reading online text: A comparison of four white space layouts. *Usability News*, *6*(2). Retrieved April 14, 2010, from http://www.surl.org/usabilitynews/ 62/whitespace.asp

Chaparro, B., Shaikh, A., & Baker, J. (2005). Reading online text with a poor layout: Is performance worse? *Usability News*, *7*(1). Retrieved from http://psychology.wichita.edu/surl/ usabilitynews/71/page_setting.html

Chaparro, A., Bohan, M., Fernandez, J. E., Choi, S. D., & Kattel, B. (1999). The impact of age on computer input device use: Psychophysical and physiological measures. *International Journal of Industrial Ergonomics*, *24*, 503–513. doi:10.1016/S0169-8141(98)00077-8

Chase, W., & Simon, H. (1973). The mind's eye in chess. In Chase, W. (Ed.), *Visual information processing* (pp. 215–281). New York, NY: Academic Press.

Chen, M., Anderson, J., & Sohn, M. (2001). What can a mouse cursor tell us more? Correlation of eye/mouse movements on Web browsing. *Conference on Human Factors in Computing Systems*, (pp. 281–282). Seattle, WA.

Cheng, P., Cupit, J., & Shadbold, N. (2001). Supporting diagrammatic knowledge acquisition: An ontological analysis of Cartesian graphs. *International Journal of Human-Computer Studies*, *54*, 457–494. doi:10.1006/ijhc.2000.0455

Cheng, P., & Simon, H. (1995). Scientific discovery and creative reasoning with diagrams. In Smith, S., Ward, T., & Finke, R. (Eds.), *The creative cognition approach* (pp. 205–228). Cambridge, MA: MIT Press.

Chen, Z., & Mo, L. (2004). Schema induction in problem solving: A multidimensional analysis. *Journal of Experimental Psychology. Learning, Memory, and Cognition*, *30*, 583–600. doi:10.1037/0278-7393.30.3.583

Chevalier, A., & Kicka, M. (2006). Web designers and web users: Influence of the ergonomic quality of the web site on the information search. *International Journal of Man-Machine Studies*, *64*(10), 1031–1048.

Chiesi, H., Spilich, G., & Voss, J. (1979). Acquisition of domain-related information in relation to high and low domain knowledge. *Journal of Verbal Learning and Verbal Behavior*, *18*, 257–273. doi:10.1016/S0022-5371(79)90146-4

Chinander, K., & Schweitzer, M. (2003). The input bias: The misuse of input information in judgments of outcomes. *Organizational Behavior and Human Decision Processes*, *91*, 243–253. doi:10.1016/S0749-5978(03)00025-6

Chli, M., & De Wilde, P. (2006). Internet search: Subdivision-based interactive query expansion and the soft Semantic Web. *Applied Soft Computing*, *6*(4), 372–383. doi:10.1016/j.asoc.2005.11.003

Choi-Kwon, S., Lee, S., Park, H., Kwon, S., Ahn, J., & Kim, J. (2005). What stroke patients want to know and what medical professionals think they should know about stroke: Korean perspectives. *Patient Education and Counseling*, *56*, 85–92. doi:10.1016/j.pec.2003.12.011

Chung, J. (2000). Signals and reading comprehension. Theory and practice. *System*, *28*, 247–259. doi:10.1016/S0346-251X(00)00010-5

Chu, P., & Spires, E. (2003). Perceptions of accuracy and effort of decision strategies. *Organizational Behavior and Human Decision Processes*, *91*(2), 203–214. doi:10.1016/S0749-5978(03)00056-6

Chu, S., Paul, N., & Ruel, L. (2009). Using eye tracking technology to examine the effectiveness of design elements on news websites. *Information Design Journal*, *17*(1), 31–43. doi:10.1075/idj.17.1.04chu

Chu, Y., & Chu, R. (1990). The subsidence of preference reversals in simplified and market-like experimental settings: A note. *The American Economic Review*, *80*, 902–911.

Clark, H., & Brownell, H. (1975). Judging up and down. *Journal of Experimental Psychology. Human Perception and Performance*, *1*, 339–352. doi:10.1037/0096-1523.1.4.339

Clark, H., & Haviland, S. (1977). Comprehension and the given-new contract. In Freedle, R. (Ed.), *Discourse production and comprehension* (pp. 1–40). Norwood, NJ: Ablex.

Cleveland, W., & McGill, R. (1984). Graphical perception: Theory, experimentation, and application to the development of graphical methods. *Journal of the American Statistical Association*, *79*, 531–554. doi:10.2307/2288400

Cockburn, A., & McKenzie, B. (2001). What do web users do? An empirical analysis of Web use. *International Journal of Human-Computer Studies*, *54*, 903–922. doi:10.1006/ijhc.2001.0459

Cohen, M., & Bacdayan, P. (1994). Organizational routines are stored as procedural memory: Evidence from a laboratory study. *Organization Science*, *5*(4), 554–568. doi:10.1287/orsc.5.4.554

Collett, J. (2004). Automaticity. *The encyclopedia of educational technology.* Retrieved September 6, 2010, from http://edweb.sdsu.edu/eet/ articles/autoskills/index.htm

Collister, D., & Tversky, B. (2005). *Nonanalytic inference*. Retrieved April 24, 2010, from http://www-psych.stanford.edu/~bt/ concepts_categories/papers/cogscidc01.doc.pdf

Collyer, C., Stanley, K., & Bowater, C. (1990). Perceiving scattergrams: Is visual line fitting related to estimation of the correlation co-efficient. *Perceptual and Motor Skills*, *71*, 371–378.

Conklin, J. (2003). *Wicked problems and fragmentation*. Retrieved March 7, 2003, from http://www.cognexus.org/id26.htm

Constantine, L., & Lockwood, L. (1999). *Software for use: A practical guide to the models and methods of usage-centered design*. New York, NY: ACM Press.

Conway, A., Tuholski, S., Shisler, R., & Engle, R. (1999). The effect of memory load on negative priming: An individual differences investigation. *Memory & Cognition*, *27*, 1042–1050. doi:10.3758/BF03201233

Cooke, N., & Rowe, A. (1994). Evaluating mental model elicitation methods. *Proceedings of the Human Factors and Ergonomics Society 38th Annual Meeting*, (pp. 261–265).

Cooper, A. (1999). *The inmates are running the asylum*. Indianapolis, IN: Sams.

Corbalan, G., Kester, L., & Van Merriënboer, J. (2009). Combining shared control with variability over surface features: Effects on transfer test performance and task involvement. *Computers in Human Behavior*, *25*, 290–298. doi:10.1016/j.chb.2008.12.009

Cottrell, K., & McNamara, D. (2002). Cognitive precursors to science comprehension. In W. D. Gray & C. D. Schunn (Eds.), *Proceedings of the Twenty-fourth Annual Meeting of the Cognitive Science Society* (pp. 244–249). Mawah, NJ: Erlbaum.

Coury, B., & Boulette, M. (1992). Time stress and the processing of visual displays. *Human Factors*, *34*, 707–726.

Cuevas, H., Fiore, S., Bowers, C., & Salas, E. (2004). Fostering constructive cognitive and metacognitive activity in computer-based complex task training environments. *Computers in Human Behavior*, *20*, 225–241. doi:10.1016/j.chb.2003.10.016

Cypher, A. (1986). The structure of users' activities. In Norman, D., & Draper, S. (Eds.), *User centered system design: New perspectives on human-computer interaction* (pp. 243–264). Mahwah, NJ: Erlbaum.

Cyr, D., Head, M., & Larios, H. (2010). Colour appeal in website design within and across cultures: A multi-method evaluation. *International Journal of Human-Computer Studies, 68*(1-2), 1–21. doi:10.1016/j.ijhcs.2009.08.005

Czerwinski, M., Horvitz, E., & Wilhite, S. (2004). A diary study of task switching and interruptions. Retrieved December 10, 2008, from http://research.microsoft.com/users/marycz/chi2004diarystudyfinal.pdf

Dahlbäck, O. (1990). An experimental analysis of risk taking. *Theory and Decision, 20*(3), 183–202. doi:10.1007/BF00126801

Dalala, R., & Bonaccio, S. (2010). What types of advice do decision-makers prefer? *Organizational Behavior and Human Decision Processes, 112*, 11–23. doi:10.1016/j.obhdp.2009.11.007

Davidson, J., Deuser, R., & Sternberg, R. (1994). The role of metacognition in problem solving. In Metcalfe, J., & Shimamura, A. (Eds.), *Metacognition: Knowing about knowing* (pp. 207–226). Cambridge, MA: MIT Press.

Davis, F. (1989). Perceived usefulness, perceived ease of use, and user acceptance of Information Technology. *Management Information Systems Quarterly, 13*(3), 319–339. doi:10.2307/249008

Davis, F., Bagozzi, R., & Warshaw, P. (1989). User acceptance of computer technology: A comparison of 2 theoretical models. *Management Science, 35*, 982–1003. doi:10.1287/mnsc.35.8.982

De Angeli, A., Matera, M., Costabile, M., Garzotto, F., & Paolini, P. (2003). On the advantages of a systematic inspection for evaluating hypermedia usability. *International Journal of Human-Computer Interaction, 15*(3), 315–335. doi:10.1207/S15327590IJHC1503_01

De Martino, B., Kumaran, D., Seymour, B., & Dolan, R. (2006). Frames, biases, and rational decision-making in the human brain. *Science, 313*, 684–687. doi:10.1126/science.1128356

de Vries, H., Mesters, I., van de Steeg, H., & Honing, C. (2005). The general public's information needs and perceptions regarding hereditary cancer: An application of the integrated change model. *Patient Education and Counseling, 56*, 154–165. doi:10.1016/j.pec.2004.01.002

DeKay, M., Patiño-Echeverri, D., & Fischbeck, P. (2009). Distortion of probability and outcome information in risky decisions. *Organizational Behavior and Human Decision Processes, 109*, 79–92. doi:10.1016/j.obhdp.2008.12.001

Delp, C., & Jones, J. (1996). Communicating information to patients: The use of cartoon illustrations to improve comprehension of instructions. *Academic Emergency Medicine, 3*, 264–270. doi:10.1111/j.1553-2712.1996.tb03431.x

Dennis, A., & Taylor, N. (2004). Information foraging on the Web: The effects of "acceptable" Internet delays on multi-page information search behavior. *Decision Support Systems, 42*, 810–824. doi:10.1016/j.dss.2005.05.032

Derr, R. (1983). A conceptual analysis of information need. *Information Processing & Management, 19*(5), 273–278. doi:10.1016/0306-4573(83)90001-8

DeSanctis, G. (1984). Computer graphics as decision aids: Directions for research. *Decision Sciences, 15*, 463–487. doi:10.1111/j.1540-5915.1984.tb01236.x

Desouza, K. (2003). Facilitating tacit knowledge exchange. *Communications of the ACM, 46*(6), 85–88. doi:10.1145/777313.777317

Devroop, K. (2000). *Correlation versus causation: Another look at a common misinterpretation.* ED 445 078.

Diaper, D., & Sanger, C. (2006). Tasks for and tasks in human-computer interaction. *Interacting with Computers, 18*, 117–138. doi:10.1016/j.intcom.2005.06.004

Dickson, G., DeSanctis, G., & McBride, D. (1986). Understanding the effectiveness of computer graphics for decision support: A cumulative experimental approach. *Communications of the ACM, 29*, 40–47. doi:10.1145/5465.5469

Dienes, Z., & Fahey, R. (1995). Role of specific instances in controlling a dynamic system. *Journal of Experimental Psychology. Learning, Memory, and Cognition, 21*(4), 848–862. doi:10.1037/0278-7393.21.4.848

Dillon, A., Kleinman, L., Choi, G., & Bias, R. (2006). Visual search and reading tasks using ClearType and regular displays: Two experiments. *Proceedings of the SIGCHI Conference on Human Factors in Computing Systems,* April 22–27, 2006, Montréal, Québec, Canada.

Dillon, A. (1992). Reading from paper versus screens: A critical review of the empirical literature. *Ergonomics, 35*, 1297–1326. doi:10.1080/00140139208967394

DiVita, J., Obermayer, R., Nugent, W., & Linville, J. (2004). Verification of the change blindness phenomenon while managing critical events on a combat information display. *Human Factors, 46*(2), 205–218. doi:10.1518/hfes.46.2.205.37340

Djajadiningrat, T., Overbeeke, K., & Wensveen, S. (2002). But how, Donald, tell us how? On the creation of meaning in interaction design through feedforward and inherent feedback. [London, England.]. *Proceedings of, DIS2002*, 285–291.

Doane, S., Pellegrino, J., & Klatzky, R. (1990). Expertise in a computer operating system: Conceptualization and performance. *Human-Computer Interaction, 5*, 267–304. doi:10.1207/s15327051hci0502&3_5

Doheny-Farina, S. (1998). *Effective documentation: What we have learned from research*. Cambridge, MA: MIT.

Doumont, J. (2002). Choosing the right graph. *IEEE Transactions on Professional Communication, 45*(1), 1–6. doi:10.1109/47.988358

Dourish, P. (1999). Where the footprints lead: Tracking down other roles for social navigation. In Munro, A., Hook, K., & Denyon, D. (Eds.), *Social navigation of information space* (pp. 15–34). London, UK: Springer. doi:10.1007/978-1-4471-0837-5_2

Downing, R., Moore, J., & Brown, S. (2005). The effects and interaction of spatial visualization and domain expertise on information seeking. *Computers in Human Behavior, 21*, 195–209. doi:10.1016/j.chb.2004.03.040

Dreher, M. (1992). Searching for information in textbooks. *Journal of Reading, 35*, 364–371.

Druckman, J. (2001). On the limits of framing effects: Who can frame? *The Journal of Politics, 63*(4), 1041–1066. doi:10.1111/0022-3816.00100

Dufty, D., Graesser, A., Louwerse, M., & McNamara, D. (2006). Is it just readability, or does cohesion play a role? In R. Sun & N. Miyake (Eds.), *Proceedings of the 28th Annual Conference of the Cognitive Science Society* (p. 1251). Mahwah, NJ: Erlbaum.

Duggan, G., & Payne, S. (2001). Interleaving reading and acting while following procedural instructions. *Journal of Experimental Psychology. Applied, 7*(4), 297–307. doi:10.1037/1076-898X.7.4.297

Duin, A. (1991). Reading to learn and do. *Proceedings of 38th STC Conference.*

Duin, A. (1989). Factors that influence how readers learn from test: Guidelines for structuring technical documents. *Technical Communication, 36*(2), 97–101.

Duncan, J. (1984). Selective attention and the organization of visual information. *Journal of Experimental Psychology. General, 113*(4), 501–517. doi:10.1037/0096-3445.113.4.501

Dunlosky, J., Rawson, K., & Middleton, E. (2005). What constrains the accuracy of metacomprehension judgments? Testing the transfer-appropriate-monitoring and accessibility hypotheses. *Journal of Memory and Language, 52*, 551–565. doi:10.1016/j.jml.2005.01.011

Dunn, E., Wilson, T., & Gilbert, D. (2003). Location, location, location: The misprediction of satisfaction in housing lotteries. *Personality and Social Psychology Bulletin, 29*, 1421–1432. doi:10.1177/0146167203256867

Dye, K. (1988). When is document accurate and complete. *Professional Communication Conference, 1988* (pp. 269–272). Seattle, WA. October 5–7, 1988.

Dyson, M., & Haselgrove, M. (2001). The influence of reading speed and line length on the effectiveness of reading from screen. *International Journal of Human-Computer Studies, 54*, 585–612. doi:10.1006/ijhc.2001.0458

Dyson, M., & Kipping, G. (1998). The effects of line length and method of movement on patterns of reading from screen. *Visible Language, 32*, 150–181.

Eden, C. (1988). Cognitive mapping. *European Journal of Operational Research, 36*, 1–13. doi:10.1016/0377-2217(88)90002-1

Edwards, A., & Elwyn, G. (2001). Understanding risk and lessons for clinical risk communication about treatment preferences. *Quality in Health Care, 10*, 9–13. doi:10.1136/qhc.0100009

Eheman, C., Berkowitz, Z., Lee, J., Mohile, S., Purnell, J., & Rodriguez, E. (2009). Information-seeking styles among cancer patients before and after treatment by demographics and use of information sources. *Journal of Health Communication, 14*(5), 487–502. doi:10.1080/10810730903032945

Eichenbaum, H. (1997). Declarative memory: Insights from cognitive neurobiology. *Annual Review of Psychology, 48*, 547–572. doi:10.1146/annurev.psych.48.1.547

Einhorn, H. J., & Hogarth, R. M. (1981). Behavioral decision theory: Processes of judgment and choice. *Annual Review of Psychology, 32*, 53–88. doi:10.1146/annurev.ps.32.020181.000413

Einstein, G., McDaniel, M., Owen, P., & Cote, N. (1990). Encoding and recall of texts: The importance of material appropriate processing. *Journal of Memory and Language, 29*, 566–581. doi:10.1016/0749-596X(90)90052-2

Emerson, M., & Miyake, A. (2003). The role of inner speech in task switching: A dual-task investigation. *Journal of Memory and Language, 48*, 148–168. doi:10.1016/S0749-596X(02)00511-9

Endsley, M. (1995). Toward a theory of situation awareness in dynamic systems. *Human Factors, 37*(1), 32–64. doi:10.1518/001872095779049543

Engle, R., & Bukstel, L. (1978). Memory processes among bridge players of differing expertise. *The American Journal of Psychology, 91*, 673–689. doi:10.2307/1421515

Engle, R., Conway, A., Tuholski, S., & Shisler, R. (1995). A resource account of inhibition. *Psychological Science, 6*, 122–125. doi:10.1111/j.1467-9280.1995.tb00318.x

Englmeier, K., & Mang, E. (1997). For information patters to information architecture. In M. Smith, G. Salvendy, & R. Koubek (Eds.), *Proceedings of the 7th International Conference on Human-Computer Interaction* (pp. 35–38). New York, NY: Elsevier.

Epps, B. (1986). Comparison of six cursor control devices based on Fitts' law models. *Proceedings of the Human Factors Society 30th Annual Meeting*, (pp. 327–331). Santa Monica, CA: Human Factors Society.

Estrada, C., Martin-Hryniewicz, M., Peek, B., Collins, C., & Byrd, J. (2004). Literacy and numeracy skills and anticoagulation control. *The American Journal of the Medical Sciences, 328*, 88–93. doi:10.1097/00000441-200408000-00004

Evans, D., Blair, V., Greenhalgh, R., Hopwood, R., & Howell, A. (1994). The impact of genetic counselling on risk perception in women with a family history of breast cancer. *British Journal of Cancer, 70*, 934–938. doi:10.1038/bjc.1994.423

Eylon, D., & Allison, S. (2002). The paradox of ambiguous information in collaborative and competitive settings. *Group & Organization Management, 27*, 172–208. doi:10.1177/10501102027002002

FAA. (n.d.). *Character and symbol size.* Retrieved November 25, 2008, from http://www.hf.faa.gov/Webtraining/VisualDisplays/text/size1a.htm

Fabre, J., Howard, S., & Smith, R. (2000). Designing time at the user interface. *Behaviour & Information Technology, 19*(6), 451–463. doi:10.1080/014492900750052705

Fallowfield, L. (1997). Offering choice of surgical treatment to women with breast cancer. *Patient Education and Counseling, 30*, 209–214. doi:10.1016/S0738-3991(96)00947-0

Fallowfield, L. (2001). Participation of patients in decisions about treatment for cancer. *British Medical Journal, 323*, 1144. doi:10.1136/bmj.323.7322.1144

Farkas, G. (1998). Reading one-to-one: An intensive program serving a great many students while still achieving large effects. In Crane, J. (Ed.), *Social programs that work* (pp. 75–109). New York, NY: Russell Sage Foundation.

Farris, J., Jones, K., & Elgin, P. (2002). Users' schemata of hypermedia: What is so spatial about a website? *Interacting with Computers, 14*, 487–502. doi:10.1016/S0953-5438(02)00011-5

Fawcett, H., Ferdinand, S., & Rockley, A. (1991). *Organizing information.* Presented at the 38th STC Conference.

Feldman-Stewart, D., & Brundage, M. (2004). Challenges for designing and implementing decision aids. *Patient Education and Counseling, 54*, 265–273. doi:10.1016/j.pec.2003.09.007

Feltwell, A., & Rees, C. (2004). The information-seeking behaviors of partners of men with prostate cancer: A qualitative pilot study. *Patient Education and Counseling, 54*, 179–185. doi:10.1016/S0738-3991(03)00212-X

Fennema, M., & Kleinmuntz, D. (1995). Anticipation of effort and accuracy in multi-attribute choice. *Organizational Behavior and Human Decision Processes, 63*(1), 21–32. doi:10.1006/obhd.1995.1058

Ferguson, E. (1977). The mind's eye: Nonverbal thought in technology. *Science, 197*, 827–836. doi:10.1126/science.197.4306.827

Few, S. (2009). *Data presentation: Tapping the power of visual perception.* Retrieved May 1, 2009, from http://www.intelligententerprise.com/ showArticle.jhtml?articleID=31400009

Fezzani, K., Albinet, C., Thon, B., & Marquie, J. (2010). The effect of motor difficulty on the acquisition of a computer task: A comparison between young and older adults. *Behaviour & Information Technology, 29*(2), 115–124. doi:10.1080/01449290701825139

Fillippatou, D., & Pumfrey, P. (1996). Pictures, titles, reading accuracy and reading comprehension: A research review (1973–95). *Educational Research, 38*, 259–291. doi:10.1080/0013188960380302

Fiore, S., Cuevas, H., & Oser, R. (2003). A picture is worth a thousand connections: The facilitative effects of diagrams on mental model development and task performance. *Computers in Human Behavior, 19*(2), 185–199. doi:10.1016/S0747-5632(02)00054-7

Fisher, D. (1975). Reading and visual search. *Memory & Cognition, 3*, 188–196. doi:10.3758/BF03212897

Fitts, P. (1954). The information capacity of the human motor system in controlling the amplitude of movement. *Journal of Experimental Psychology, 47*(6), 381–391. doi:10.1037/h0055392

Foss, D., Smith-Kerker, P., & Rosson, M. (1987). On comprehending a computer manual: Analysis of variables affecting performance. *International Journal of Man-Machine Studies, 26*(3), 277–300. doi:10.1016/S0020-7373(87)80064-0

Fox, C., & Weber, M. (2002). Ambiguity aversion, comparative ignorance, and decision context. *Organizational Behavior and Human Decision Processes, 88*(1), 476–498. doi:10.1006/obhd.2001.2990

Freudenthal, D. (2001). The role of age, foreknowledge and complexity in learning to operate a complex device. *Behaviour & Information Technology, 20*(1), 23–35. doi:10.1080/01449290010020666

Frownfelter-Lohrke, C., & Fulkerson, C. (2001). The incident and quality of graphics in annual reports: An international comparison. *Journal of Business Communication, 38*(3), 337–368. doi:10.1177/002194360103800308

Fu, L., Salvendy, G., & Turley, L. (2002). Effectiveness of user testing and heuristic evaluation as a function of performance classification. *Behaviour & Information Technology, 21*(2), 137–143. doi:10.1080/02699050110113688

Fu, W., & Gray, W. (2004). Resolving the paradox of the active user: Stable suboptimal performance in interactive tasks. *Cognitive Science, 28*, 901–935. doi:10.1207/s15516709cog2806_2

Galliers, J., Sutcliffe, A., & Minocha, S. (1999). An impact analysis method for safety critical user interface design. *ACM Transactions on Computer-Human Interaction, 6*, 341–369. doi:10.1145/331490.331493

Gallo, D., Weiss, J., & Schacter, D. (2004). Reducing false recognition with criterial recollection tests: Distinctiveness heuristic versus criterion shifts. *Journal of Memory and Language, 51*, 473–493. doi:10.1016/j.jml.2004.06.002

Ganzach, Y., & Schul, Y. (1995). The influence of quantity of information and goal framing on decisions. *Acta Psychologica, 89*, 23–36. doi:10.1016/0001-6918(94)00004-Z

Garcia, F., & Tissiani, G. (2003). Guideline for adaptive graphical user interfaces using universal networking language. *Journal of Digital Contents, 1*(1), 51–55.

Garcia, M., & Caldera, C. (1996). The effect of color and typeface on the readability of on-line text. *Computers & Industrial Engineering, 31*(1-2), 519–524. doi:10.1016/0360-8352(96)00189-1

Garfield, J., & del Mas, R. (1991). Students' conceptions of probability. In D. Vere-Jones (Ed.). *Proceedings of the Third International Conference on Teaching Statistics*, (Vol. 1, pp. 340–349). Voorburg, The Netherlands: International Statistical Institute.

Garfield, J., & Ahlgren, A. (1988). Difficulties in learning basic concepts in probability and statistics: Implications for research. *Journal for Research in Mathematics Education*, *19*, 46–63. doi:10.2307/749110

Garrett, S., & Caldwell, B. (2002). Describing functional requirements for knowledge sharing communities. *Behaviour & Information Technology*, *21*(5), 359–364. doi:10.1080/0144929021000050265

Gerlach, J., & Kuo, F. (1991). Understanding human-computer interaction for information system design. *Management Information Systems Quarterly*, *15*(4), 527–550. doi:10.2307/249456

Gery, G. (2002). Task support, reference, instruction, or collaboration? Factors in determining electronic learning and support options. *Technical Communication*, *49*(4), 420–427.

Gibson, J. (1977). The theory of affordances. In Shaw, R., & Bransford, J. (Eds.), *Perceiving, acting and knowing* (pp. 67–82). Hillsdale, NJ: Erlbaum.

Gigerenzer, G., Hertwig, R., van den Broek, E., Fasolo, B., & Katsikopoulos, K. (2005). A 30% chance of rain tomorrow: How does the public understand probabilistic weather forecasts? *Risk Analysis*, *25*(3), 623–629. doi:10.1111/j.1539-6924.2005.00608.x

Gilad, D., & Kliger, D. (2008). Priming the risk attitudes of professionals in financial decision making. *Review of Finance*, *12*(3), 567–586. doi:10.1093/rof/rfm034

Giles, T., & Still, B. (2005). A syntactic approach to readability. *Journal of Technical Writing and Communication*, *35*(1), 47–70. doi:10.2190/PHUC-GY8L-JRLE-VMNN

Gilovich, T., Vallone, R., & Tversky, A. (1985). The hot hand in basketball: On the misperception of random sequences. *Cognitive Psychology*, *17*, 295–314. doi:10.1016/0010-0285(85)90010-6

Glaser, R., & Chi, M. (1988). Overview. In Chi, M. T. H., Glaser, R., & Farr, M. J. (Eds.), *The nature of expertise* (pp. xv–xxviii). Hillsdale, NJ: Erlbaum.

Gloria Mark, G., Gonzalez, V., & Harris, J. (2005). No task left behind? Examining the nature of fragmented work. *Proceedings of the SIGCHI Conference on Human Factors in Computing Systems*, April 2–7, 2005. Portland, Oregon.

Goetz, E., Anderson, R., & Schallert, D. (1981). The representation of sentences in memory. *Journal of Verbal Learning and Verbal Behavior*, *20*, 369–385. doi:10.1016/S0022-5371(81)90506-5

Golbeck, A. L., Ahlers-Schmidt, C. R., Paschal, A. M., & Dismuke, S. E. (2005). A definition and operational framework for health numeracy. *American Journal of Preventive Medicine*, *29*, 375–376. doi:10.1016/j.amepre.2005.06.012

Golub, L., & Kidder, C. (1974). Syntactic density and the computer. *Elementary English*, *51*, 1128–1131.

Gonzalez, C. (2005). Decision support for real-time, dynamic decision-making tasks. *Organizational Behavior and Human Decision Processes*, *96*, 142–154. doi:10.1016/j.obhdp.2004.11.002

González-Vallejo, C., & Moran, E. (2001). The evaluability hypothesis revisited: Joint and separate evaluation preference reversal as a function of attribute importance. *Organizational Behavior and Human Decision Processes*, *86*(2), 216–233. doi:10.1006/obhd.2001.2953

Gorry, G. (2005). As simple as possible, but not simpler. *Communications of the ACM*, *48*(9), 119–122. doi:10.1145/1081992.1082026

Gough, P. (1972). One second of reading. In Kavanagh, J. F., & Mattingley, I. G. (Eds.), *Language by ear and by eye* (pp. 331–358). Cambridge, MA: MIT Press.

Gould, J., Alfaro, L., Finn, R., Haupt, B., & Minuto, A. (1987). Reading from CRT displays can be as fast as reading from paper. *Human Factors*, *29*(5), 497–517.

Graesser, A. C., Singer, M., & Trabasso, T. (1994). Constructing inferences during narrative text comprehension. *Psychological Review*, *101*, 371–395. doi:10.1037/0033-295X.101.3.371

Graesser, A., Gernsbacher, M., & Goldman, S. (2003). *Handbook of discourse processes*. Mahwah, NJ: Erlbaum.

Graham, W., Smith, P., Kamal, A., Fitzmaurice, A., Smith, N., & Hamilton, N. (2000). Randomised controlled trial comparing effectiveness of touch screen system with leaflet for providing women with information on prenatal tests. *British Medical Journal, 320*(7228), 155–160. doi:10.1136/bmj.320.7228.155

Grainger, J., Rey, A., & Dufau, S. (2008). Letter perception: From pixels to pandemonium. *Trends in Cognitive Sciences, 12*(10), 381–387. doi:10.1016/j.tics.2008.06.006

Grayling, T. (2002). If we build it, will they come? A usability test of two browser-based embedded help systems. *Technical Communication, 49*(2), 193–209.

Gray, W., & Boehm-Davis, D. (2000). Milliseconds matter: An introduction to microstrategies and to their use in describing and predicting interactive behavior. *Journal of Experimental Psychology. Applied, 6*(4), 322–335. doi:10.1037/1076-898X.6.4.322

Gray, W., & Fu, W. (2004). Soft constraints in interactive behavior: The case of ignoring perfect knowledge in-the-world for imperfect knowledge in-the-head. *Cognitive Science, 28*, 359–382.

Gray, W., John, B., & Atwood, M. (1993). Project Ernestine: Validating a GOMS analysis for predicting and explaining real-world performance. *Human-Computer Interaction, 8*(3), 237–309. doi:10.1207/s15327051hci0803_3

Gray, W., Schoelles, M., & Sims, C. (2005). Adapting to the task environment: Explorations in expected value. *Cognitive Systems Research, 6*, 27–40. doi:10.1016/j.cogsys.2004.09.004

Greeno, J. (1973). The structure of memory and the process of solving problems. In R. L. Rolso (Ed.), *Contemporary Issues in Cognitive Psychology: The Loyola Symposium.* New York, NY: Wiley.

Gregor, S., & Benbasat, I. (1999). Explanations from intelligent systems: Theoretical foundations and implications for practice. *Management Information Systems Quarterly, 23*(4), 497–530. doi:10.2307/249487

Gribbons, W. (1991). Visual literacy in corporate communication: Some implications for information design. *IEEE Transactions on Professional Communication, 34*(1), 42–50. doi:10.1109/47.68427

Gribbons, W., & Elsar, A. (1998). Visualizing information: An overview of this special issue. *Technical Communication, 45*(4), 467–472.

Grice, H. (1975). Logic and conversation. In Cole, P., & Morgan, J. (Eds.), *Syntax and semantics* (pp. 41–58). New York, NY: Academic Press.

Griffin, J., & Wright, P. (2009). Older readers can be distracted by embellishing graphics in text. *The European Journal of Cognitive Psychology, 21*(5), 740–757. doi:10.1080/09541440802155627

Grissom, S., & Dunagan, L. (2001). Improved satisfaction during rehabilitation after hip and knee arthroplasty: A retrospective analysis. *American Journal of Physical Medicine & Rehabilitation, 80*, 798–803. doi:10.1097/00002060-200111000-00002

Gross, M. (1998). The imposed query: Implications for library service evaluation. *Reference and User Services Quarterly, 37*, 290–299.

Grudin, J. (1990). Interface. *Proceedings of Conference on Computer-Supported Cooperative Work 90,* (pp. 269–278). New York, NY: ACM.

Grudin, J. (1989). The case against user interface consistency. *Communications of the ACM, 32*, 1164–1173. doi:10.1145/67933.67934

Guiard, Y. (1987). Asymmetric division of labor in human skilled bimanual action: The kinematic chain as a model. *Journal of Motor Behavior, 19*, 486–517.

Guimaraes, T., Igbaria, M., & Lu, M. (1992). The determinants of DSS success: An integrated model. *Decision Sciences, 23*, 409–429. doi:10.1111/j.1540-5915.1992.tb00397.x

Gulliksen, J., & Lantz, A. (2003). Design versus design—From the shaping of product to the creation of user experience. *International Journal of Human-Computer Interaction, 15*(1), 5–20. doi:10.1207/S15327590IJHC1501_02

Gurmankin, A. D., Baron, J., & Armstrong, K. (2004). The effect of numerical statements of risk on trust and comfort with hypothetical physician risk communication. *Medical Decision Making, 24*, 265–271. doi:10.1177/0272989X04265482

Guthrie, J. (1988). Locating information in documents: Examination of a cognitive model. *Reading Research Quarterly*, 23, 178–199. doi:10.2307/747801

Guynes, J. (1988). Impact of system response time on state anxiety. *Communications of the ACM*, 31(3), 342–347. doi:10.1145/42392.42402

Gwizdka, J., & Spence, I. (2007). Implicit measures of lostness and success in Web navigation. *Interacting with Computers*, 19(3), 357–369. doi:10.1016/j.intcom.2007.01.001

Gyselinck, V., & Tardieu, H. (1999). The role of illustrations in text comprehension: What, when, for whom, and why? In van Oostenddorp, H., & Goldman, S. (Eds.), *The construction of mental representations during reading* (pp. 195–218). Mahwah, NJ: LEA.

Haber, R., & Schindler, R. (1981). Errors in proofreading: Evidence of syntactic control of letter processing? *Journal of Experimental Psychology. Human Perception and Performance*, 7, 573–579. doi:10.1037/0096-1523.7.3.573

Hackos, J., & Redish, J. (1998). *User and task analysis for interface design*. New York, NY: Wiley.

Haider, H., & Frensch, P. (1999). Information reduction during skill acquisition: The influence of task instruction. *Journal of Experimental Psychology. Applied*, 5, 129–151. doi:10.1037/1076-898X.5.2.129

Halasz, F. G., & Moran, T. P. (1983). Mental models and problem solving in using a pocket calculator. In *Proceedings of the Association for Computing Machinery, Special Interest Group on Computer and Human Interaction and the Human Factors Society*, (pp. 212–216). New York, NY: ACM.

Halford, G., Baker, R., McCredden, J., & Bain, J. (2005). How many variables can humans process? *Psychological Science*, 16(1), 70–76. doi:10.1111/j.0956-7976.2005.00782.x

Hallgren, C. (1997). Using a problem focus to quickly aid users in trouble. *Proceedings of the 1997 STC Annual Conference*. Washington, DC: STC.

Halpern, D., Blackman, S., & Salzman, B. (1989). Using statistical risk information to assess oral contraceptive safety. *Applied Cognitive Psychology*, 3, 251–260. doi:10.1002/acp.2350030305

Halvey, M., Keane, M., & Smyth, B. (2006). Mobile web surfing is the same as Web surfing. *Communications of the ACM*, 49(3), 76–81. doi:10.1145/1118178.1118179

Hamilton, M., & Rajaram, S. (2001). The concreteness effect in implicit and explicit memory tests. *Journal of Memory and Language*, 44, 96–117. doi:10.1006/jmla.2000.2749

Handmer, J., & Proudley, B. (2007). Communicating uncertainty via probabilities: The case of weather forecasts. *Environmental Hazards*, 7, 79–87. doi:10.1016/j.envhaz.2007.05.002

Hargis, G., Hernandez, A., Hughes, P., Ramaker, J., Rouiller, S., & Wilde, E. (1998). *Developing quality technical information: A handbook for writers and editors*. New York, NY: Prentice Hall.

Harris, R. (1996). *Information graphics: A comprehensive reference*. Atlanta, GA: Management Graphics.

Hart, S., & Staveland, L. (1988). Development of NASA-TLX (task load index): Results of empirical and theoretical research. In Hancock, P., & Meshkati, N. (Eds.), *Human mental workload* (pp. 239–250). Amsterdam, The Netherlands: North-Holland. doi:10.1016/S0166-4115(08)62386-9

Hartson, R., & Boehm-Davis, D. (1993). User interface development process and methodologies. *Behaviour & Information Technology*, 12(2), 98–114. doi:10.1080/01449299308924371

Hartwick, J., & Barki, H. (1994). Explaining the role of user participation in Information System use. *Management Science*, 40, 440–465. doi:10.1287/mnsc.40.4.440

Harvey, N., & Bolger, F. (1996). Graphs versus tables: Effects of data presentation format on judgmental forecasting. *International Journal of Forecasting*, 12, 119–137. doi:10.1016/0169-2070(95)00634-6

Haskins, J. (1958). Testing suitability of typefaces for editorial subject matter. *The Journalism Quarterly*, 35, 186–194. doi:10.1177/107769905803500205

Hawley, S., & Zkmund-Fisher, B., Ubel, Pl, Jancovic, A., Lucas, T., & Fagerlin, A. (2008). The impact of the format of graphical presentation on health-related knowledge and treatment choices. *Patient Education and Counseling*, 73, 448–455. doi:10.1016/j.pec.2008.07.023

Hawley, S., Zkmund-Fisher, B., Ubel, P., Jancovic, A., Lucas, T., & Fagerlin, A. (2008). The impact of the format of graphical presentation on health-related knowledge and treatment choices. *Patient Education and Counseling, 73*, 448–455. doi:10.1016/j.pec.2008.07.023

Hayes, C., & Akhavi, F. (2008). Creating effective decision aids for complex tasks. *Journal of Usability Studies, 3*(4), 152–172.

Hayes-Roth, B., & Thorndyke, P. (1979). Integration of knowledge from text. *Journal of Verbal Learning and Verbal Behavior, 18*, 91–108. doi:10.1016/S0022-5371(79)90594-2

Healey, C. (2007). *Perception in visualization*. Retrieved May 1, 2009, from http://www.csc.ncsu.edu/ faculty/ healey/PP/index.html

Healey, C., Booth, K., & Enns, J. (1996). High-speed visual estimation using preattentive processing. *ACM Transactions on Human Computer Interaction, 3*(2), 107–135. doi:10.1145/230562.230563

Heba, G. (1997). Digital architectures: A rhetoric of electronic document structures. *IEEE Transactions on Professional Communication, 40*(4), 275–283. doi:10.1109/47.650005

Hefley, W. (1995). Helping users help themselves. *IEEE Software, 12*(2), 93–95. doi:10.1109/52.368272

Hegarty, M. (1992). Mental animation: Inferring motion from static diagrams of mechanical systems. *Journal of Experimental Psychology. Learning, Memory, and Cognition, 18*, 1084–1102. doi:10.1037/0278-7393.18.5.1084

Hegland, F. (2006). *Welcome page*. Retrieved June 12, 2006, from http://www.liquidinformation.org/ index-fr.html

Heiser, J., & Tversky, B. (2006). Arrows in comprehending and producing mechanical diagrams. *Cognitive Science, 30*(3), 581–592. doi:10.1207/s15516709cog0000_70

Helfenstein, S., & Pertti Saariluoma, P. (2007). Apperception in primed problem solving. *Cognitive Processing, 8*, 211–232. doi:10.1007/s10339-007-0189-4

Herbig, P., & Kramer, H. (1992). The phenomenon of innovation overload. *Technology in Society, 14*, 441–461. doi:10.1016/0160-791X(92)90038-C

Herndl, C., Fennell, B., & Miller, C. (1991). Understanding failures in organizational discourse: The accident at Three Mile Island and the shuttle Challenger disaster. In Bazerman, C., & Paradis, J. (Eds.), *Textual dynamics of the profession* (pp. 279–305). Madison, WI: University of Wisconsin.

Hertzum, M., & Frøkjær, E. (1996). Browsing and querying in online documentation: A study of user interfaces and the interaction process. *ACM Transactions on Computer-Human Interaction, 3*(2), 136–161. doi:10.1145/230562.230570

Hess, S., Detweiler, M., & Ellis, R. (1999). The utility of display space in keeping-track of rapidly changing information. *Human Factors, 41*(2), 257–281. doi:10.1518/001872099779591187

Hicks, M., O'Malley, C., Nichols, S., & Anderson, B. (2003). Comparison of 2D and 3D representations for visualising telecommunication usage. *Behaviour & Information Technology, 22*(3), 185–201. doi:10.1080/0144929031000117080

Hick, W. (1952). On the rate of gain of information. *The Quarterly Journal of Experimental Psychology, 4*, 11–26. doi:10.1080/17470215208416600

Higgins, E. (1997). Beyond pleasure and pain. *The American Psychologist, 52*(12), 1280–1300. doi:10.1037/0003-066X.52.12.1280

Hinds, C., Streater, A., & Mood, D. (1995). Functions and preferred methods of receiving information related to radiotherapy. *Cancer Nursing, 18*, 374–383. doi:10.1097/00002820-199510000-00007

Hix, D., & Hartson, R. (1993). *Developing user interfaces: Ensuring usability through product and process*. New York, NY: Wiley.

Hochhauser, M. (1998). Writing for staff, employees, patients, and family members. *Hospital Topics, 76*(1), 5–12. doi:10.1080/00185869809596484

Holden, R., & Karsh, B. (2010). The technology acceptance model: Its past and its future in health care. *Journal of Biomedical Informatics, 43*, 159–172. doi:10.1016/j.jbi.2009.07.002

Hollands, J., & Spence, I. (1992). Perception of graphical displays: The stacking model. In *Proceedings of the 25th Annual Conference of the Human Factors Association of Canada* (pp. 187–192). Mississauga, Canada: Human Factors Association of Canada.

Holleran, P., & Bauersfeld, K. (1993). Vertical spacing of computer-presented text. *INTERCHI Adjunct Proceedings, 179–180.*

Hollnagel, E. (1988). Mental models and model mentality. In L. P. Goodstein, H. B. Andersen & S. E. Olsen (Eds.), *Task errors and mental models* (pp. 261–268). RisÃ National Laboratory, Denmark: Taylor & Francis.

Hollnagel, E. (1993). Decision support and task nets. In Klein, G., Orasanu, J., Calderwood, R., & Zsambok, C. (Eds.), *Decision making in action: Models and methods* (pp. 31–36). Norwood, NJ: Ablex.

Hollnagel, E., & Woods, D. (1983). Cognitive systems engineering: New wine in new bottles. *International Journal of Man-Machine Studies, 18,* 583–600. doi:10.1016/S0020-7373(83)80034-0

Hornik, J. (1984). Subjective vs. objective time measures: A note on the perception of time in consumer behavior. *The Journal of Consumer Research, 11,* 615–618. doi:10.1086/208998

Hornof, A., & Kieras, D. E. (1997). Cognitive modeling reveals menu search is both random and systematic. *Proceedings of the SIGCHI Conference on Human Factors in Computing Systems,* (pp. 107–114), New York, NY: ACM.

Horton, W. (1990). *Designing and writing online documentation.* New York, NY: Wiley.

Horton, W. (1993). Dump the dumb screen dumps. *Technical Communication, 40,* 146–148.

Hourcade, J., Bederson, B., Druin, A., & Guimbretière, F. (2004). Differences in pointing task performance between preschool children and adults using mice. *ACM Transactions on Computer-Human Interaction, 11*(4), 357–386. doi:10.1145/1035575.1035577

Houston, D., & Sherman, S. (1995). Cancellation and focus: The role of shared and unique features in the choice process. *Journal of Experimental Social Psychology, 31*(4), 357–378. doi:10.1006/jesp.1995.1016

Houston, D., Sherman, S., & Baker, S. (1989). The influence of unique features and direction of comparison on preferences. *Journal of Experimental Social Psychology, 25,* 121–141. doi:10.1016/0022-1031(89)90008-5

Houts, P., Doak, C., Doak, L., & Loscalzo, M. (2006). The role of pictures in improving health communication: A review of research on attention, comprehension, recall, and adherence. *Patient Education and Counseling, 61,* 173–190. doi:10.1016/j.pec.2005.05.004

Howard, T. (2007). Unexpected complexity in a traditional usability study. *Journal of Usability Studies, 3*(4), 189–205.

Hoxmeier, J., & Dicesare, C. (2000). System response time and user satisfaction: An experimental study of browser based applications. *Proceedings of the Americas Conference on Information Systems,* (pp. 140–145). August 10–13, 2000. Long Beach, CA: Association for Information Systems.

Hoyer, W., Rebok, G., & Sved, S. (1979). Effects of varying irrelevant information on adult age differences in problem solving. *Journal of Gerontology, 34*(4), 553–560.

Hsee, C. (1995). Elastic justification: How tempting but task irrelevant factors influence decisions. *Organizational Behavior and Human Decision Processes, 62*(3), 330–337. doi:10.1006/obhd.1995.1054

Hsee, C. (1996). The evaluability hypothesis: An explanation of preference reversals between joint and separate evaluations of alternatives. *Organizational Behavior and Human Decision Processes, 67*(3), 247–257. doi:10.1006/obhd.1996.0077

Hsee, C. K., & Zhang, J. (2004). Distinction bias: Misprediction and mischoice due to joint evaluation. *Journal of Personality and Social Psychology, 86*(5), 680–695. doi:10.1037/0022-3514.86.5.680

Hsee, C., & Hastie, R. (2006). Decision and experience: Why don't we choose what makes us happy? *Trends in Cognitive Sciences, 10*(1), 31–37. doi:10.1016/j.tics.2005.11.007

Hsia, J. (2007). An enhanced technology acceptance model for e-learning systems in high-tech companies. *Proceedings of the 7th WSEAS International Conference on Distance Learning and Web Engineering* (pp. 338–343). Beijing, China. New York, NY: ACM Press.

Hsieh-Yee, I. (1993). Effects of search experience and subject knowledge on the search tactics of novice and experienced searchers. *Journal of the American Society for Information Science American Society for Information Science, 44*, 161–174. doi:10.1002/(SICI)1097-4571(199304)44:3<161::AID-ASI5>3.0.CO;2-8

Hsieh-Yee, I. (2001). Research on Web search behavior. *Library & Information Science Research, 23*, 167–185. doi:10.1016/S0740-8188(01)00069-X

Huang, A. (2009). Science needs ace communicators and politicians. *Science News, 175*(9), 32. doi:10.1002/scin.2009.5591750922

Huberman, B., Pirolli, P., Pitkow, J., & Lukose, R. (1998). Strong regularities in World Wide Web surfing. *Science, 280*, 95–97. doi:10.1126/science.280.5360.95

Huff, D., & Geis, I. (1993). *How to lie with statistics.* New York, NY: Norton.

Hughes, M. (2002). Moving from information transfer to knowledge creation: A new value proposition for technical communicators. *Technical Communication, 49*(3), 275–285.

Hutchins, E. (1995). *Cognition in the wild.* Cambridge, MA: MIT.

Hutchins, E., Hollan, J., & Norman, D. (1985). Direct manipulation interfaces. *Human-Computer Interaction, 1*(4), 311–338. doi:10.1207/s15327051hci0104_2

Hyman, R. (1953). Stimulus information as a determinant of reaction time. *Journal of Experimental Psychology, 45*, 188–196. doi:10.1037/h0056940

Jackson, M., & McClelland, J. (1979). Processing determinants of reading speed. *Journal of Experimental Psychology. General, 108*, 151–181. doi:10.1037/0096-3445.108.2.151

Jagacinski, R. (1977). A qualitative look at feedback control theory as a style of describing behavior. *Human Factors, 19*, 331–347.

Janiszewski, C. (1998). The influence of display characteristics on visual exploratory search behavior. *The Journal of Consumer Research, 25*, 290–301. doi:10.1086/209540

Janssen, D., & Neutelings, R. (2001). *Reading and writing public documents.* Amsterdam, The Netherlands: John Benjamins.

Jansson, D., & Smith, S. (1991). Design fixation. *Design Studies, 12*, 3–11. doi:10.1016/0142-694X(91)90003-F

Jaspers, M., Steen, T., Bos, C., & Geenen, M. (2004). The think aloud method: A guide to user interface design. *International Journal of Medical Informatics, 73*, 781–795. doi:10.1016/j.ijmedinf.2004.08.003

Jeevan, J. (2004). *How people re-find information when the Web changes.* MIT AI Memo 2004-012.

Jeffries, R., Turner, A., Polson, P., & Atwood, M. (1981). *The processes involved in designing software.* Hillsdale, NJ: Erlbaum.

Jenkins, V., Fallowfield, L., & Saul, J. (2001). Information needs of patients with cancer: Results from a large study of UK cancer centres. *British Journal of Cancer, 84*, 48–51. doi:10.1054/bjoc.2000.1573

Johansson, K., Salantera, S., Katajisto, J., & Leino-Kilpi, H. (2004). Written orthopedic patient education materials from the point of view of empowerment by education. *Patient Education and Counseling, 52*, 175–181. doi:10.1016/S0738-3991(03)00036-3

John, B., & Kieras, D. (1996). The GOMS Family of user interface analysis techniques: Comparison and contrast. *ACM Transactions on Computer-Human Interaction, 3*(4), 320–351. doi:10.1145/235833.236054

Johnson, E., Payne, J., & Bettman, J. (1988). Information displays and preference reversals. *Organizational Behavior and Human Decision Processes, 42*, 1–21. doi:10.1016/0749-5978(88)90017-9

Johnson, J. D., Andrews, J. E., & Allard, S. (2001). A model for understanding and affecting genetics information seeking. *Library & Information Science Research, 23*(4), 335–349. doi:10.1016/S0740-8188(01)00094-9

Johnson, J., Andrews, J., & Allard, S. (2001). A model for understanding and affecting genetics information seeking. *Library & Information Science Research, 23*(4), 335–349. doi:10.1016/S0740-8188(01)00094-9

Johnson-Laird, P. (1983). *Mental models.* Cambridge, UK: Cambridge UP.

Johnson, P. (1992). *Human computer interaction: Psychology, task analysis and software engineering.* London, UK: McGraw-Hill.

Johnson, P., & Afflerback, P. (1985). The process of constructing mean ideas from text. *Cognition and Instruction, 2*(3&4), 207–232. doi:10.1080/07370008.1985.9648917

Johnson, P., May, J., & Johnson, H. (2003). Introduction to multiple and collaborative tasks. *ACM Transactions on Computer-Human Interaction, 10*(4), 277–280. doi:10.1145/966930.966931

Johnson, S. (1997). *Interface culture.* New York, NY: Basic Books.

Johnson-Sheehan, R., & Baehr, C. (2001). Visual-spatial thinking in hypertexts. *Technical Communication, 48*(1), 22–30.

Jonassen, D. (2003). Using cognitive tools to represent problems. *Journal of Research on Technology in Education, 35*(3), 362–381.

Jones, W., Bruce, H., & Dumais, S. (2004). *Re-finding information on the Web: What do people do and what do they need.* Retrieved from http://kftf.ischool.washington.edu/

Jones, E., & Nisbett, R. (1971). *The actor and the observer: Divergent perceptions of the causes of behavior.* New York, NY: General Learning Press.

Jones, K., Farris, J., & Johnson, B. (2005). GUI Objects with impenetrable borders: Instructions (not practice) makes perfect. *International Journal of Human-Computer Studies, 62*(6), 687–712. doi:10.1016/j.ijhcs.2005.02.002

Jordan, M. (1989). Beyond impression: Evaluating causal connections. In Fearing, B., & Sparrow, K. (Eds.), *Technical writing: Theory and practice* (pp. 102–114). New York, NY: MLA.

Judge, J., Field, T., DeFlorio, M., Laprino, J., Auger, J., & Rochon, P. (2006). Prescribers' responses to alerts during medication ordering in the long term care setting. *Journal of the American Medical Informatics Association, 13*(4), 385–390. doi:10.1197/jamia.M1945

Jung Lee, Y., Park, J., & Widdows, R. (2009). Exploring antecedents of consumer satisfaction and repeated search behavior on e-health information. *Journal of Health Communication, 14*, 160–173. doi:10.1080/10810730802659830

Just, M. A., & Carpenter, P. A. (1980). A theory of reading: From eye fixations to comprehension. *Psychological Review, 87*, 329–354. doi:10.1037/0033-295X.87.4.329

Kahneman, D. (1973). *Attention and effort.* Englewood Cliffs, NJ: Prentice-Hall.

Kahneman, D., & Tversky, A. (1979). Prospect theory: An analysis of decision under risk. *Econometrica: Journal of the Econometric Society, 47*, 263–291. doi:10.2307/1914185

Kahneman, D., & Tversky, A. (1982). The psychology of preferences. *Scientific American, 246*, 160–173. doi:10.1038/scientificamerican0182-160

Kalyuga, S., Chandler, P., & Sweller, J. (2004). When redundant on-screen text in multimedia technical instruction can interfere with learning. *Human Factors, 46*, 567–581. doi:10.1518/hfes.46.3.567.50405

Kammersgaard, J. (1988). Four different perspective on human-computer interaction. *International Journal of Man-Machine Studies, 28*, 343–362. doi:10.1016/S0020-7373(88)80017-8

Kang, N., & Yoon, W. (2008). Age- and experience-related user behavior differences in the use of complicated electronic devices. *International Journal of Human-Computer Studies, 66*, 425–437. doi:10.1016/j.ijhcs.2007.12.003

Kaplan, S. (1995). The restorative benefits of nature: Toward an integrative framework. *Journal of Environmental Psychology, 15*, 169–182. doi:10.1016/0272-4944(95)90001-2

Karat, J., & Karat, C. (2003). The evolution of user-centered focus in the human-computer interaction field. *IBM Systems Journal, 42*(4), 532–541. doi:10.1147/sj.424.0532

Karger, D., & Quan, D. (2004). Prerequisites for a personalizable user interface. *Proceedings. of Intelligent User Interface 2004 Conference,* Ukita, 2004.

Karpinski, A. (2009). *Facebook users get worse grades in college.* Retrieved from http://www.livescience.com/culture/090413-facebook-grades.html

Kearsley, G. (2006). *Mental models.* Retrieved July 13, 2006, from http://tip.psychology.org/models.html

Kehoe, E., Bednall, T., Yin, L., Olsen, K., Pitts, C., Henry, J., & Bail, P. (2009). Training adult novices to use computers: Effects of different types of illustrations. *Computers in Human Behavior*, *25*, 275–283. doi:10.1016/j.chb.2008.12.005

Keller, C., Siegrist, M., & Gutscher, H. (2006). The role of the affect and availability heuristics in risk communication. *Risk Analysis*, *26*, 631–639. doi:10.1111/j.1539-6924.2006.00773.x

Kerzman, H., Baron-Epel, O., & Toren, O. (2005). What do discharged patients know about their medication? *Patient Education and Counseling*, *56*, 276–282. doi:10.1016/j.pec.2004.02.019

Ketamo, H., Kiili, K., & Haaparanta, H. (2003). Empirical basis for navigation framework. *Journal of Digital Contents*, *2*(1), 96–101.

Khan, K., & Locatis, C. (1998). Searching through cyberspace: The effects of link display and link density on information retrieval from hypertext on the World Wide Web. *Journal of the American Society for Information Science American Society for Information Science*, *49*, 176–182. doi:10.1002/(SICI)1097-4571(199802)49:2<176::AID-ASI7>3.0.CO;2-8

Kieras, D., & Bovair, S. (1984). The role of a mental model in learning to operate a device. *Cognitive Science*, *8*, 255–273. doi:10.1207/s15516709cog0803_3

Kieras, D., Meyer, D., Ballas, J., & Lauber, E. (2000). Modern computational perspectives on executive mental processes and cognitive control: Where to from here? In Monsell, S., & Driver, J. (Eds.), *Control of cognitive processes: Attention and performance XVIII* (pp. 681–712). Cambridge, MA: MIT Press.

Kieras, D., & Polson, P. (1985). An approach to the formal analysis of user complexity. *International Journal of Man-Machine Studies*, *22*, 365–394. doi:10.1016/S0020-7373(85)80045-6

Kiger, J. (1984). The depth/breadth trade-off in the design of menu-driven user interfaces. *International Journal of Man-Machine Studies*, *20*, 201–213. doi:10.1016/S0020-7373(84)80018-8

Kim, J., & Lee, J. (2002). Critical design factors for successful e-commerce systems. *Behaviour & Information Technology*, *21*(3), 185–199. doi:10.1080/0144929021000009054

Kim, K. (2001). Implications of user characteristics in information seeking on the World Wide Web. *International Journal of Human-Computer Interaction*, *13*(3), 323–340. doi:10.1207/S15327590IJHC1303_3

Kim, L., & Albers, M. (2003). Presenting information on the small-screen interface: Effects of table formatting. *IEEE Transactions on Professional Communication*, *46*(2), 94–103. doi:10.1109/TPC.2003.813165

King, W., & He, J. (2006). A meta-analysis of the technology acceptance model. *Information & Management*, *43*, 740–755. doi:10.1016/j.im.2006.05.003

Kintsch, W. (1980). Learning from text, levels of comprehension, or: Why anyone would read a story anyway. *Poetics*, *9*, 87–98. doi:10.1016/0304-422X(80)90013-3

Kintsch, W. (1988). The role of knowledge in discourse comprehension: A construction-integration model. *Psychological Review*, *95*, 163–182. doi:10.1037/0033-295X.95.2.163

Kintsch, W. (1998). *Comprehension: A paradigm for cognition*. New York, NY: Cambridge University Press.

Kintsch, W., & Keenan, J. (1973). Reading rate and retention as a function of the number of propositions in the base structure of sentences. *Cognitive Psychology*, *5*, 257–274. doi:10.1016/0010-0285(73)90036-4

Kintsch, W., & Welsch, D. (1991). The construction–integration model: A framework for studying memory for text. In Hockley, W. E., & Lewandowsky, S. (Eds.), *Relating theory and data: Essays on human memory in honor to Bennet B. Murdock* (pp. 367–385). Hillsdale, NJ: Erlbaum.

Kirsch, I. S., Jungeblut, A., Jenkins, L., & Kolstad, A. (2002). *Adult literacy in America: A first look at the findings of the national adult literacy survey* (3rd ed., NCES 1993-275). Washington, DC: U.S. Department of Education, Office of Educational Research and Improvement, National Center for Education Statistics.

Klare, G. (2000). The measurement of readability: Useful information for communicators. *ACM Journal of Computer Documentation, 24*(3), 107–121. doi:10.1145/344599.344630

Klein, G. (1988). Do decision biases explain too much? *Human Factors Society Bulletin, 32*(5), 1–3.

Klein, G. (1993). A recognition-primed decision (RPD) model of rapid decision making. In Klein, G., Orasanu, J., Calderwood, R., & Zsambok, C. (Eds.), *Decision making in action: Models and methods* (pp. 138–147). Norwood, NJ: Ablex.

Klein, G. (1999). *Sources of power: How people make decisions.* Cambridge, MA: MIT.

Klein, G., Orasanu, J., Calderwood, R., & Zsambok, C. (1993). *Decision making in action: Models and methods.* Norwood, NJ: Ablex.

Klingbeil, C., Speece, M., & Schubiner, H. (1995). Readability of pediatric patient education materials. Current perspectives on an old problem. *Clinical Pediatrics, 34*(2), 96–102. doi:10.1177/000992289503400206

Knauff, M., & Johnson-Laird, P. (2002). Visual imagery can impede reasoning. *Memory & Cognition, 30,* 363–371. doi:10.3758/BF03194937

Koester, H., & Levine, S. (1994). Validation of a keystroke-level model for a text entry system used by people with disabilities. *Proceedings of the First ACM Conference on Assistive Technologies,* (pp. 115–122). New York, NY: ACM.

Kolodner, J. (1983). Towards an understanding of the role of experience in the evolution from novice to expert. *International Journal of Man-Machine Studies, 19,* 497–518. doi:10.1016/S0020-7373(83)80068-6

Konold, C. (1989). An outbreak of belief in independence? In C. Maher, G. Goldin & B. Davis (Eds.), *Proceedings of the 11th Annual Meeting of the North American Chapter of the International Group for the Psychology of Mathematics Education* (Vol. 2, pp. 203-209), Rutgers, NJ: Rutgers.

Koriat, A. (1995). Dissociating knowing and the feeling of knowing: Further evidence for the accessibility model. *Journal of Experimental Psychology. General, 124*(3), 311–333. doi:10.1037/0096-3445.124.3.311

Korzenko, J., Robins, D., & Holmes, J. (2008). *What are your users REALLY thinking? An objective way to uncover the subjective.* Presentation at IA Summit 2008.

Kosslyn, S. (1994). *Elements of graph design.* New York, NY: Freeman.

Kostelnick, C. (1988). Conflicting standards for designing data displays: Following, flouting, and reconciling them. *Technical Communication, 45*(4), 473–482.

Kostelnick, C. (1990). The rhetoric of text design in professional communication. *The Technical Writing Teacher, 17*(3), 189–202.

Kostelnick, C. (1993). Viewing functional pictures in context. In Blyler, N., & Thralls, C. (Eds.), *Professional communication: The social perspective* (pp. 243–256). Newbury Park, CA: Sage.

Kostelnick, C. (1996). Supra-textual design: The Visual rhetoric of whole documents. *Technical Communication Quarterly, 5*(1), 9–33. doi:10.1207/s15427625tcq0501_2

Kotovsky, K., Hayes, J., & Simon, H. (1985). Why are some problems hard? Evidence from Tower of Hanoi. *Cognitive Psychology, 17,* 248–294. doi:10.1016/0010-0285(85)90009-X

Koyani, S., Balley, R., & Nall, J. (2006). *Research based Web design.* Washington, DC: National Cancer Institute. Retrieved from http://www.usability.gov/guidelines/

Kress, G. (2005). Gains and losses: New forms of texts, knowledge, and learning. *Computers and Composition, 22,* 5–22. doi:10.1016/j.compcom.2004.12.004

Krug, S. (2000). *Don't make me think! A common sense approach to Web usability.* Berkeley, CA: New Riders.

Kuhn, T. (1962). *The structure of scientific revolutions.* Chicago, IL: University of Chicago Press.

Kumsaikaew, P., Jackman, J., & Dark, V. (2006). Task relevant information in engineering problem solving. *Journal of Engineering Education, 95,* 227–239.

Kundel, H., & La Follett, P. (1972). Visual search patterns and experience with radiological images. *Radiology, 103,* 523–528.

Kunst-Wilson, W., & Zajonc, R. (1980). Affective discrimination of stimuli that cannot be recognized. *Science, 207*, 557–558. doi:10.1126/science.7352271

Kurosu, M., & Kashimura, K. (1995). Apparent usability vs. inherent usability. *CHI '95 Conference Companion*, (pp. 292–293). New York, NY: ACM.

Kushleyeva, Y., Salvucci, D., & Lee, F. (2005). Deciding when to switch tasks in time-critical multitasking. *Cognitive Systems Research, 6*, 41–49. doi:10.1016/j.cogsys.2004.09.005

Kushniruk, A., Triola, M., Borycki, E., Stein, B., & Kannry, J. (2005). Technology induced error and usability: The relationship between usability problems and prescription errors when using a handheld application. *International Journal of Medical Informatics, 74*, 519–526. doi:10.1016/j.ijmedinf.2005.01.003

Kuutti, K. (1995). Work processes: Scenarios as a preliminary vocabulary. In Carroll, J. (Ed.), *Scenario-based design: Envisioning work and technology in system development* (pp. 19–36). New York, NY: Wiley.

Kwan, M., & Balasubramanian, P. (2003). KnowledgeScope: Managing knowledge in context. *Decision Support Services, 35*, 467–486. doi:10.1016/S0167-9236(02)00126-4

Kwasitsu, L. (2001). Information-seeking behavior of design process and manufacturing engineers. *Library and Information Science, 25*, 459–476. doi:10.1016/S0740-8188(03)00054-9

Kwasnik, B. (1992). A descriptive study of the functional components of browsing. In J. Larson & C. Unger (Eds.), *Engineering for Human-Computer Interaction: Proceedings of the IFIP TC2/WG2.7 Working Conference on Engineering for Human-Computer Interaction*, (pp. 191–203). Amsterdam, The Netherlands: North-Holland.

Laberge, D., & Samuels, S. (1974). Towards a theory of automatic information processing in reading. *Cognitive Psychology, 6*, 293–323. doi:10.1016/0010-0285(74)90015-2

Labiale, G. (2001). Visual search and preferences concerning different types of guidance displays. *Behaviour & Information Technology, 20*(3), 149–158. doi:10.1080/01449290110048025

Landauer, T., & Nachbar, D. (1985). Selection from alphabetic and numeric menu trees using a touch screen: Breadth, depth, and width. *Proceedings of the SIGCHI conference on Human factors in computing systems*, (pp.73–78), New York, NY: ACM.

Lane, D. (2007). Statistical and practical significance. In *HyperStat online statistics textbook*. Retrieved May 12, 2009, from http://davidmlane.com/ hyperstat/B35955.html

Lane, D., Napier, H., Batsell, R., & Naman, J. (1993). Predicting the skilled use of hierarchical menus with the keystroke-level model. *Human-Computer Interaction, 8*, 185–192. doi:10.1207/s15327051hci0802_4

Lang, A., Borse, J., Wise, K., & David, P. (2002). Captured by the World Wide Web: Orienting to structural and content features of computer presented information. *Communication Research, 29*(3), 215–245. doi:10.1177/0093650202029003001

Langholtz, H., Gettys, C., & Foote, B. (1995). Are resource fluctuations anticipated in resource allocation tasks? *Organizational Behavior and Human Decision Processes, 64*(3), 274–282. doi:10.1006/obhd.1995.1105

Lansdale, M., Jones, M., & Jones, M. (1989). Visual search in iconic and verbal interfaces. In Megaw, E. (Ed.), *Contemporary ergonomics* (pp. 422–429). London, UK: Taylor and Francis.

Lansdale, M., & Ormerod, T. (1994). *Understanding interfaces: A handbook of human-computer dialogue*. London, UK: Academic Press.

Laplante, P., & Flaxman, H. (1995). The convergence of technology and creativity in the corporate environment. *IEEE Transactions on Professional Communication, 38*(1), 20–23. doi:10.1109/47.372389

Larichev, O., Olson, D., Moshkovich, H., & Mechitov, A. (1995). Numerical vs. cardinal measurements in multiattribute decision making: How exact is exact enough? *Organizational Behavior and Human Decision Processes, 64*(1), 9–21. doi:10.1006/obhd.1995.1085

Larkin, J., & Simon, H. (1987). Why a diagram is (sometimes) worth ten thousand words. *Cognitive Science, 11*, 65–99. doi:10.1111/j.1551-6708.1987.tb00863.x

Larson, K. (2004). *The science of word recognition*. Retrieved May 28, 2009, from http://www.microsoft.com/typography/ ctfonts/WordRecognition.aspx

Larson, K., & Czerwinski, M. (1998). Web page design: Implications of memory, structure and scent for information retrieval. *Proceedings of the SIGCHI Conference on Human Factors in Computing Systems,* (pp. 25–32). New York, NY: ACM.

Larson, K., van Dantzich, M., Czerwinski, M., & Robertson, G. (2000). Text in 3D: Some legibility results. In *Extended Abstracts of CHI '2000, Human Factors in Computing Systems* (pp. 145–146). New York, NY: ACM. doi:10.1145/633292.633374

Lathrop, G. (1967). Perceived variability. *Journal of Experimental Psychology, 73,* 498–502. doi:10.1037/h0024344

Lavie, N. (2005). Distracted and confused? Selective attention under load. *Trends in Cognitive Sciences, 9*(2), 75–82. doi:10.1016/j.tics.2004.12.004

Lavie, N., & De Fockert, J. (2005). The role of working memory in attentional capture. *Psychonomic Bulletin & Review, 12*(4), 669–674. doi:10.3758/BF03196756

Lawless, K., & Kulikowich, J. (1998). Domain knowledge, interest, and hypertext navigation: A study of individual differences. *Journal of Educational Multimedia and Hypermedia, 7,* 51–70.

Lazonder, A., & Rouet, J. (2008). Information problem solving instruction: Some cognitive and metacognitive issues. *Computers in Human Behavior, 24,* 753–765. doi:10.1016/j.chb.2007.01.025

Lee, F., Teich, J., Spurr, D., & Bates, D. (1996). Implementation of physician order entry: User satisfaction and self-reported usage patterns. *Journal of the American Medical Informatics Association, 3,* 42–55. doi:10.1136/jamia.1996.96342648

Lefevre, J., & Dixon, P. (1986). Do written instructions need examples? *Cognition and Instruction, 3*(1), 1–30. doi:10.1207/s1532690xci0301_1

Lenton, A., & Francesconi, M. (2010). How humans cognitively manage an abundance of mate options. *Psychological Science, 21*(4), 528–533. doi:10.1177/0956797610364958

Lerman, C., Kash, K., & Stefanek, M. (1994). Younger women at increased risk for breast cancer: Perceived risk, psychological well-being and surveillance behavior. *Journal of the National Cancer Institute. Monographs, 16,* 171–176.

Levie, W., & Lentz, R. (1982). Effects of text illustrations: A review of research. *Educational Communication and Technology Journal, 30,* 195–232.

Levin, D., Drivdahl, S., Momen, N., & Beck, M. (2002). False predictions about the detectability of unexpected visual changes: The role of beliefs about attention, memory, and the continuity of attended objects in causing change blindness blindness. *Consciousness and Cognition, 11*(4), 507–527. doi:10.1016/S1053-8100(02)00020-X

Levin, D., & Simons, D. (1997). Failure to detect changes to attended objects in motion pictures. *Psychonomic Bulletin & Review, 4,* 501–506. doi:10.3758/BF03214339

Levin, I., & Gaeth, G. (1988). How consumers are affected by the framing of attribute information before and after consuming the product. *The Journal of Consumer Research, 15,* 374–378. doi:10.1086/209174

Levin, J. (1981). On functions of pictures in prose. In Pirozzolo, F., & Wittrock, M. (Eds.), *Neuropsychological and cognitive processes in reading* (pp. 203–228). New York, NY: Academic Press.

Levin, J., & Mayer, R. (1993). Understanding illustrations in text. In Britton, B., Woodward, A., & Brinkley, M. (Eds.), *Learning from textbooks* (pp. 95–13). Hillsdale, NJ: Erlbaum.

Levy, E., Zacks, J., Tversky, B., & Schiano, D. (1996). Gratuitous graphics? Putting preferences in perspective. In *Proceedings of the SIGCHI conference on human factors in computing systems* (pp. 42–49). New York, NY: ACM Press.

Levy, A., & Hershey, J. (2006). Distorting the probability of treatment success to justify treatment decisions. *Organizational Behavior and Human Decision Processes, 101,* 52–58. doi:10.1016/j.obhdp.2006.04.003

Levy, A., & Hershey, J. (2008). Value-induced bias in medical decision making. *Medical Decision Making, 28,* 269–276. doi:10.1177/0272989X07311754

Lewis, C., & Walker, P. (1989). Typographic influences on reading. *The British Journal of Psychology, 80*, 241–257. doi:10.1111/j.2044-8295.1989.tb02317.x

Lichtenstein, S., & Slovic, P. (1973). Response-induced reversals of preference in gambling: An extended replication in Las Vegas. *Journal of Experimental Psychology, 101*, 16–20. doi:10.1037/h0035472

Lightner, N. (2001). Model testing of users' comprehension in graphical animation: The effect of speed and focus areas. *International Journal of Human-Computer Interaction, 13*(1), 53–73. doi:10.1207/S15327590IJHC1301_4

Lim, J., & O'Connor, M. (1996). Judgmental forecasting with time series and causal information. *International Journal of Forecasting, 12*, 139–153. doi:10.1016/0169-2070(95)00635-4

Lin, D., & Su, Y. (1998). The effect of time pressure on expert system based training for emergency management. *Behaviour & Information Technology, 17*(4), 195–202. doi:10.1080/014492998119409

Linderholm, T., Everson, M. G., van den Broek, P., Mischinski, M., Crittenden, A., & Samuels, J. (2000). Effects of causal text revisions on more- and less-skilled readers' comprehension of easy and difficult texts. *Cognition and Instruction, 18*, 525–556. doi:10.1207/S1532690XCI1804_4

Lindgaard, F., Fernandes, G., Dudek, C., & Brown, J. (2006). Attention Web designers: You have 50 milliseconds to make a good first impression. *Behaviour & Information Technology, 25*(3), 115–126. doi:10.1080/01449290500330448

Lipkus, I., & Holland, J. (1999). The visual communication of risk. *Journal of the National Cancer Institute. Monographs, 25*, 149–163.

Lipkus, I., Klein, W., & Rimer, B. (2001). Communicating breast cancer risks to women using different formats. *Cancer Epidemiology, Biomarkers & Prevention, 10*, 895–898.

Lipson, M. (1982). Learning new information from text: The role of prior knowledge and reading ability. *Journal of Reading Behavior, 14*(3), 243–261.

Liu, X. (1991). Hypotheses testing by fundamental knowledge. *International Journal of Man-Machine Studies, 35*, 409–427. doi:10.1016/S0020-7373(05)80136-1

Loewenstein, G. (1996). Out of control: Visceral influences on behavior. *Organizational Behavior and Human Decision Processes, 65*, 272–292. doi:10.1006/obhd.1996.0028

Lohse, G. (1993). A cognitive model for understanding graphical perception. *Human-Computer Interaction, 8*, 352–388. doi:10.1207/s15327051hci0804_3

Lohse, G. (1997). The role of working memory on graphical information processing. *Behaviour & Information Technology, 16*(6), 297–308. doi:10.1080/014492997119707

Lökketangen, A., & Woddruff, D. (2005). A distance function to support optimized selection decisions. *Decision Support Science, 39*, 345–354. doi:10.1016/j.dss.2004.01.001

Loman, N., & Mayer, R. (1980). Signaling techniques that increase the readability of expository prose. *Journal of Educational Psychology, 75*(3), 402–412. doi:10.1037/0022-0663.75.3.402

Lord, C., Ross, L., & Lepper, M. (1979). Biased assimilation and attitude polarization: The effects of prior theories on subsequent evidence. *Journal of Personality and Social Psychology, 37*, 2098–2110. doi:10.1037/0022-3514.37.11.2098

Lowe, R. (2002). Animation and learning: Selective processing of information in dynamic graphics. *Learning and Instruction, 13*(2), 157–176. doi:10.1016/S0959-4752(02)00018-X

Lukoscheka, P., Fazzarib, M., & Marantz, P. (2003). Patient and physician factors predict patients' comprehension of health information. *Patient Education and Counseling, 50*, 201–210. doi:10.1016/S0738-3991(02)00128-3

Lusk, E., & Kersnick, M. (1979). The effect of cognitive style and report format on task performance: The MIS design consequences. *Management Science, 25*, 787–798. doi:10.1287/mnsc.25.8.787

Lynch, P., & Horton, S. (2002). *Web style guide* (2nd ed.). New Haven, CT: Yale UP.

MacKenzie, I. (2003). Motor behaviour models for human-computer interaction. In Carroll, J. (Ed.), *HCI Models, theories, and frameworks: Toward a multidisciplinary science* (pp. 27–54). San Francisco, CA: Morgan Kaufmann.

Mackiewicz, J. (2005). How to use five letterforms to gauge a typeface's personality: A research-driven method. *Journal of Technical Writing and Communication, 35,* 291–315. doi:10.2190/LQVL-EJ9Y-1LRX-7C95

Mackiewicz, J. (2007). Perceptions of clarity and attractiveness in PowerPoint graph slides. *Technical Communication, 54*(2), 145–156.

Mackiewicz, J. (2007a). Audience perceptions of fonts in projected PowerPoint text slides. *Technical Communication, 54*(3), 295–307.

Mackiewicz, J. (2007b). Perceptions of clarity and attractiveness in PowerPoint graph slides. *Technical Communication, 54*(2), 145–156.

MacLeod, C. (1991). Half a century of research on the Stroop effect: An integrative review. *Psychological Bulletin, 109,* 163–203. doi:10.1037/0033-2909.109.2.163

Maglio, P., & Barret, R. (1997). On the trail of information searchers. *Proceedings of the Nineteenth Annual Conference of the Cognitive Science Society,* (pp. 466–471). Stanford University, Palo Alto, CA, LEA, Mahwah, NJ.

Mahmood, A., Burn, J., Gemoets, L., & Jacquez, C. (2000). Variables affecting Information Technology end-user satisfaction: A meta-analysis of the empirical literature. *International Journal of Human-Computer Studies, 52,* 751–771. doi:10.1006/ijhc.1999.0353

Malenka, D., Baron, J., Johansen, S., & Ross, J. (1993). The framing effect of relative and absolute risk. *Journal of General Internal Medicine, 8,* 543–548. doi:10.1007/BF02599636

Malhotra, Y., & Galletta, D. (2004). Building systems that users want to use. *Communications of the ACM, 47*(12), 89–94. doi:10.1145/1035134.1035139

Maltz, M., & Meyer, J. (2001). Use of warnings in an attentionally demanding detection task. *Human Factors, 43*(2), 217–226. doi:10.1518/001872001775900931

Mannes, S., & Kintsch, W. (1987). Knowledge organization and text organization. *Cognition and Instruction, 4*(2), 91–115. doi:10.1207/s1532690xci0402_2

Manning, A., & Amare, N. (2006). Visual-rhetoric ethics: Beyond accuracy and injury. *Technical Communication, 53,* 195–211.

Mao, J., & Benbasat, I. (2001). The effects of contextualized access to knowledge on judgment. *International Journal of Human-Computer Studies, 55,* 787–814. doi:10.1006/ijhc.2001.0507

Marchionini, G. (1989). Information-seeking strategies of novices using a full-text electronic encyclopedia. *Journal of the American Society for Information Science American Society for Information Science, 29*(3), 165–176.

Marchionini, G. (1995). *Information Seeking in Electronic Environments.* New York, NY: Cambridge UP. doi:10.1017/CBO9780511626388

Marchionini, G. (2008). Human–information interaction research and development. *Library & Information Science Research, 30,* 165–174. doi:10.1016/j.lisr.2008.07.001

Marquie, J., Jourdan-Boddaert, L., & Huet, N. (2002). Do older adults underestimate their actual computer knowledge? *Behaviour & Information Technology, 21*(4), 273–280. doi:10.1080/01449290210000020998

Marsh, R., Bink, M., & Hicks, J. (1999). Conceptual priming in a generative problem-solving task. *Memory & Cognition, 27*(2), 355–363. doi:10.3758/BF03211419

Martin, G., & Corl, K. (1986). System response time effects on user productivity. *Behaviour & Information Technology, 5*(1), 3–13. doi:10.1080/01449298608914494

Mason, R., & Mitroff, I. (1973). A program for research on management information systems. *Management Science, 19,* 475–487. doi:10.1287/mnsc.19.5.475

Masson, M. (1982). Cognitive processes in skimming stories. *Journal of Experimental Psychology. Learning, Memory, and Cognition, 8,* 400–417. doi:10.1037/0278-7393.8.5.400

Mather, M., & Johnson, M. (2000). Choice-supportive source monitoring: Do our decisions seem better to us as we age? *Psychology and Aging, 15,* 596–606. doi:10.1037/0882-7974.15.4.596

Mather, M., Shafir, E., & Johnson, M. K. (2000). Misrememberance of options past: Source monitoring and choice. *Psychological Science*, *11*, 132–138. doi:10.1111/1467-9280.00228

Maule, A., & Mackie, P. (1990). A componential investigation of the effects of deadlines on individual decision making. In Borchering, K., Larichev, O., & Messick, D. (Eds.), *Contemporary issues in decision making* (pp. 449–461). Amsterdam, The Netherlands: North-Holland.

Mayer, R. (1976). Comprehension as affected by structure of problem representation. *Memory & Cognition*, *4*, 249–265. doi:10.3758/BF03213171

Mayer, R., & Gallini, J. (1990). When is an illustration worth ten thousand words? *Journal of Educational Psychology*, *82*, 715–726. doi:10.1037/0022-0663.82.4.715

Mayes, J., Draper, S., McGregor, A., & Oatley, K. (1988). Information flow in a user interface: The effect of experience and context on the recall of MacWrite screens. In Jones, D. M., & Winder, R. (Eds.), *People and Computers IV* (pp. 275–289). New York, NY: Cambridge University Press.

Mazur, D., & Hickam, D. (1991). Patients' interpretations of probability terms. *Journal of General Internal Medicine*, *6*, 237–240. doi:10.1007/BF02598968

McCrory, J. (2006). 800 or 1024 - Which min. display resolution to build for? *Sigia-l discussion list* (May 2, 2006).

McDaniel, M., Hines, R., & Guynn, M. (2002). When text difficulty benefits less-skilled readers. *Journal of Memory and Language*, *46*, 544–561. doi:10.1006/jmla.2001.2819

McDonald, J., Dayton, T., & McDonald, D. (1988). Adapting menu layout to tasks. *International Journal of Man-Machine Studies*, *28*, 417–435. doi:10.1016/S0020-7373(88)80020-8

McEneaney, J. (2001). Graphic and numerical methods to assess navigation in hypertext. *International Journal of Human-Computer Studies*, *55*, 761–786. doi:10.1006/ijhc.2001.0505

McFarlane, D., & Latorella, K. (2002). The scope and importance of human interruption in human-computer interaction design. *Human-Computer Interaction*, *17*, 1–61. doi:10.1207/S15327051HCI1701_1

McGovern, G. (2005). *Why it matters to focus on your reader*. Retrieved from http://www.gerrymcgovern.com/nt/ 2005/nt_2005_06_06_reader.htm

McGovern, G. (2006a). *Making the customer CEO*. Retrieved from http://www.gerrymcgovern.com/nt/ 2006/nt-2006-06-12-customer-ceo.htm

McGovern, G. (2006c). *Is your content a waste of time and money?* Retrieved from http://www.gerrymcgovern.com/nt/ 2006/nt-2006-02-06-content-value.htm

McGovern, G. (2010). *Navigation is more important than search*. Retrieved from http://www.gerrymcgovern.com/nt/2010/ nt-2010-04-26-Navigation-search.htm

McGrenere, J., & Ho, W. (2000). Affordances: Clarifying and evolving a concept. [Montreal, Canada.]. *Proceedings of Graphic Interface*, *2000*, 179–186.

Mckeen, J., & Guimaraes, T. (1997). Successful strategies for user participation in systems development. *Journal of Management Information Systems*, *14*, 133–150.

McKenzie, P. (2002). Communication barriers and information-seeking counterstrategies in accounts of practitioner-patient encounters. *Library and Information Science*, *24*, 31–47. doi:10.1016/S0740-8188(01)00103-7

McKoon, G., & Ratcliff, R. (1992). Inference during reading. *Psychological Review*, *99*(3), 440–466. doi:10.1037/0033-295X.99.3.440

McNamara, D. (2007). (Ed.), *Reading comprehension strategies: Theories, interventions, and technologies*. Mahwah, NJ: Erlbaum.

McNamara, D. (2001). Reading both high and low coherence texts: Effects of text sequence and prior knowledge. *Canadian Journal of Experimental Psychology*, *55*, 51–62. doi:10.1037/h0087352

McNamara, D., Kintsch, E., Songer, N., & Kintsch, W. (1996). Are good texts always better? Interactions of text coherence, background knowledge, and levels of understanding in learning from text. *Cognition and Instruction*, *14*, 1–43. doi:10.1207/s1532690xci1401_1

McNamara, D., & Kintsch, W. (1996). Learning from text: Effects of prior knowledge and text coherence. *Discourse Processes*, *22*, 247–287. doi:10.1080/01638539609544975

McNamara, D., & Scott, J. (2001). Working memory capacity and strategy use. *Memory & Cognition, 29*(1), 10–17. doi:10.3758/BF03195736

McNeil, B., Pauker, S., Sox, H., & Tversky, A. (1982). On the elicitation of preferences for alternative therapies. *The New England Journal of Medicine, 306,* 1259–1262. doi:10.1056/NEJM198205273062103

Medin, D., Lynch, E., & Solomon, K. (2000). Are there kinds of concepts? *Annual Review of Psychology, 51,* 121–147. doi:10.1146/annurev.psych.51.1.121

Meyer, J., Shamo, M., & Gopher, D. (1999). Information structure and the relative efficacy of tables and graphs. *Human Factors, 41*(4), 570–587. doi:10.1518/001872099779656707

Meyer, J., Taieb, M., & Flascher, I. (1997). Correlation estimates of perceptual judgments. *Journal of Experimental Psychology. Applied, 3*(1), 3–20. doi:10.1037/1076-898X.3.1.3

Michielutte, R., Bahnson, J., Digman, M., & Schroeder, E. (1992). The use of illustrations and narrative text style to improve readability of a health education brochure. *Journal of Cancer Education, 7,* 251–260. doi:10.1080/08858199209528176

Miller, R. (1968). Response time in man-computer conversational transactions. *Proceedings of the. AFIPS Fall Joint Computer Conference,* (Vol. 33, pp. 267–277).

Miller, G. (1956). The magical number seven, plus or minus two: Some limits on our capacity for processing information. *Psychological Review, 63,* 81–97. doi:10.1037/h0043158

Miller, J. (1960). Information input overload and psychopathology. *The American Journal of Psychiatry, 116,* 695–704.

Millis, K., & Graesser, A. (1994). The time-course of constructing knowledge-based inferences for scientific texts. *Journal of Memory and Language, 33*(5), 583–599. doi:10.1006/jmla.1994.1028

Minsky, M. (1975). A framework for representing knowledge. In Winston, P. (Ed.), *The psychology of computer vision* (pp. 211–277). New York, NY: McGraw-Hill.

Mirani, R., & King, W. (1994). Impacts of end-user and information center characteristics on end-user computing support. *Journal of Management Information Systems, 11*(1), 141–160.

Mirel, B. (1988). Cognitive processing, text linguistics and documentation writing. *Journal of Technical Writing and Communication, 18*(2), 111–133. doi:10.2190/20JV-5N1E-6LNR-443U

Mirel, B. (1992). Analyzing audiences for software manuals: A survey of instructional needs for real world tasks. *Technical Communication Quarterly, 1*(1), 15–35. doi:10.1080/10572259209359489

Mirel, B. (1998). Applied constructivism for user documentation. *Journal of Business and Technical Communication, 12*(1), 7–49. doi:10.1177/1050651998012001002

Mirel, B. (2002). Advancing a vision of usability. In Mirel, B., & Spilka, R. (Eds.), *Reshaping technical communication* (pp. 165–188). Mahwah, NJ: Erlbaum.

Mirel, B. (2003). Dynamic usability: Designing usefulness into systems for complex tasks. In Albers, M., & Mazur, B. (Eds.), *Content and complexity: Information design in software development and documentation* (pp. 233–261). Mahwah, NJ: Erlbaum.

Mirel, B. (2003). *Interaction design for complex problem solving: Developing useful and usable software.* San Francisco, CA: Morgan Kaufmann.

Mirel, B., Feinberg, S., & Allmendinger, L. (1991). Designing manuals for active learning styles. *Technical Communication, 38*(1), 75–87.

Mitchell, T., Thompson, L., Peterson, E., & Cronk, R. (1997). Temporal adjustments in the evaluation of events: The rosy view. *Journal of Experimental Social Psychology, 33*(4), 421–448. doi:10.1006/jesp.1997.1333

Moll, J. (1986). Doctor–patient communication in rheumatology: Studies of visual and verbal perception using educational booklets and other graphic material. *Annals of the Rheumatic Diseases, 45,* 198–209. doi:10.1136/ard.45.3.198

Monahan, J., & Steadman, H. (1996). Violent storms and violent people. *The American Psychologist, 51,* 931–938. doi:10.1037/0003-066X.51.9.931

Monk, A. (1999). Modeling cyclic interaction. *Behaviour & Information Technology, 18*(2), 127–139. doi:10.1080/014492999119165

Monsell, S. (1993). Task switching. *Trends in Cognitive Sciences, 7*(3), 134–140. doi:10.1016/S1364-6613(03)00028-7

Moore, P. (1995). Information problem solving: A wider view of library skills. *Contemporary Educational Psychology, 20,* 1–31. doi:10.1006/ceps.1995.1001

Moray, N. (1992). Mental models of complex dynamic systems. Mental models and everyday activities. In P. A. Booth & A. Sasse (Eds.), *Proceedings of 2nd Interdisciplinary Workshop on Metal Models,* (pp. 103–131). Cambridge, UK: Robinson College.

Moray, N. (1987). Intelligent aids, mental models and the theory of machines. *International Journal of Man-Machine Studies, 27,* 619–629. doi:10.1016/S0020-7373(87)80020-2

Moriarty, S., & Scheiner, E. (1984). A study of close-set type. *The Journal of Applied Psychology, 69*(4), 700–702. doi:10.1037/0021-9010.69.4.700

Morrison, J., Pirolli, P., & Card, S. (2001). *A taxonomic analysis of what World Wide Web activities significantly impact people's decisions and actions.* Presented at the Association for Computing Machinery's Conference on Human Factors in Computing Systems, Seattle, March 31–April 5, 2001.

Mosteller, F., Siegel, A., Trapido, E., & Youtz, C. (1981). Eye fitting straight lines. *The American Statistician, 35*(3), 150–152. doi:10.2307/2683983

Mueller, N., Odegaard, A., Anderson, K., Yuan, J., Gross, M., Koh, K., & Pereira, M. (2010). Soft drink and juice consumption and risk of pancreatic cancer: The Singapore Chinese health study. *Cancer Epidemiology, Biomarkers & Prevention, 19,* 447–455. doi:10.1158/1055-9965. EPI-09-0862

Müller, M. (2007). Being aware: Where we think the action is. *Cognition Technology and Work, 9*(2), 109–126. doi:10.1007/s10111-006-0047-7

Mumby, D. (1988). *Communication and power in organizations: Discourse, ideology, and domination.* Norwood, N J: Ablex.

Murata, A. (1999). Extending effective target width in Fitts' law to a two-dimensional pointing task. *International Journal of Human-Computer Interaction, 11*(2), 137–152. doi:10.1207/S153275901102_4

Murphy, A. H., & Winkler, R. L. (1971). Forecasters and probability forecasts: Some current problems. *Bulletin of the American Meteorological Society, 52,* 239–247. doi:10.1175/1520-0477(1971)052<0239:FAPFSC>2.0 .CO;2

Murphy, P., Chesson, A., Berman, S., Arnold, C., & Galloway, G. (2001). Neurology patient education materials: Do our education aids fit our patients' needs? *The Journal of Neuroscience Nursing, 2,* 99–104. doi:10.1097/01376517-200104000-00006

Murray, T. (2003). Applying text comprehension and active reading principles to adaptive hyperbooks. *Proceedings of Cognitive Science,* July, 2003, Boston, MA, (pp. 840–845).

Mussweiler, T. (2002). The malleability of anchoring effects. *Experimental Psychology, 49*(1), 67–72. doi:10.1027//1618-3169.49.1.67

Myers, B. A. (1985). The importance of percent-done progress indicators for computer-human interfaces. *Proceedings of the SIGCHI Conference on Human Factors in Computing Systems,* (pp. 11–17). New York, NY: ACM.

Nah, F. (2004). A study on tolerable waiting time: How long are Web users willing to wait? *Behaviour & Information Technology, 23*(3), 153–163. doi:10.1080/01449 290410001669914

Nanard, J., & Nanard, M. (1995). Hypertext design environments and the hypertext design process. *Communications of the ACM, 38*(8), 49–56. doi:10.1145/208344.208347

Narayanan, N., & Hegarty, M. (2002). Multimedia design for communication of dynamic information. *International Journal of Human-Computer Studies, 57,* 279–315. doi:10.1006/ijhc.2002.1019

National Institute of Health. (2002). *Making your web site senior friendly.* Retrieved January 13, 2010, from http://www.nlm.nih.gov/pubs/staffpubs/ od/ocpl/aging-checklist.html

Natter, H., & Berry, D. (2005). Effects of presenting baseline risk when comparing absolute and relative risk presentations. *Psychology Health and Medicine, 10,* 326–334. doi:10.1080/13548500500093407

Navarro-Prieto, R., Scaife, M., & Rogers, Y. (1999). Cognitive strategies in Web searching. *Proceeding of the fifth Conference on Human Factors and the Web,* (pp. 43–56). Gaithersburg, MD.

Naveh-Benjamin, M., Craik, F., Perretta, J., & Tonev, S. (2000). The effects of divided attention on encoding and retrieval processes: The resiliency of retrieval processes. *The Quarterly Journal of Experimental Psychology, 53*(4), 609–625.

Newell, A., & Simon, H. (1972). *Human problem solving.* Englewood Cliffs, NJ: Prentice Hall.

Newell, B. R., Weston, N. J., & Shanks, D. R. (2003). Empirical tests of a fast-and-frugal heuristic: Not everyone "takes-the-best.". *Organizational Behavior and Human Decision Processes, 91,* 82–96. doi:10.1016/S0749-5978(02)00525-3

Newman, W. M., & Lamming, M. G. (1995). *Interactive system design.* Cambridge, MA: Addison-Wesley.

Nicholson, B., & Sahay, S. (2004). Embedded knowledge and offshore software development. *Information and Organization, 14,* 329–365. doi:10.1016/j.infoandorg.2004.05.001

Nickerson, R., & Landauer, T. (1997). Human-computer interaction: Background and issues. In Helander, M., & Landauer, T. K. (Eds.), *Handbook of human-computer interaction* (2nd ed., pp. 3–32). Amsterdam, The Netherlands: Elsevier Science B.V.

Nicols, S., & Ritter, F. (1995). A theoretically motivated tool for automatically generating command aliases. *Proceedings of the SIGCHI Conference on Human Factors in Computing Systems,* (pp. 393–400). New York, NY: ACM.

Nielsen, J. (1989). The matters that really matter for hypertext usability. *Proceedings of the ACM Hypertext Conference,* (pp. 239–248). New York, NY: ACM

Nielsen, J. (1997). *The need for speed.* Retrieved November 17, 2007, from http://www.useit.com/ alertbox/9703a.html

Nielsen, J. (1998). *Electronic books—A bad idea.* Retrieved November 11, 2007, from http://www.useit.com/alertbox/980726.html

Nielsen, J. (1999). *The top ten new mistakes of Web design.* Retrieved from http://www.useit.com/ alertbox/990530.html

Nielsen, J. (2001). *The 3Cs of critical Web use: Collect, compare, choose.* Retrieved December 3, 2008, from http://www.useit.com/ alertbox/20010415.html

Nielsen, J. (2007). *Banner blindness: Old and new findings.* Retrieved November 11, 2007, from http://www.useit.com/alertbox/ banner-blindness.html

Nielsen, J. (2010). *Website response times.* Retrieved August 8, 2010, from http://www.useit.com/ alertbox//response-times.html

Nielsen, J. (1993). *Usability engineering.* San Diego, CA: Academic Press.

Nilsson, R., & Mayer, R. (2002). The effects of graphic organizers giving cues to the structure of a hypertext document on users' navigation strategies and performance. *International Journal of Human-Computer Studies, 57,* 1–26. doi:10.1006/ijhc.2002.1011

Nisbet, M., Scheufele, D., Shanahan, J., Moy, P., Brossard, K., & Lewenstein, B. (2002). Knowledge, reservations, or promise? *Communication Research, 29*(5), 584–608. doi:10.1177/009365002236196

Nisbett, R., Krantz, D., Jepson, C., & Kunda, Z. (1983). The use of statistical heuristics in everyday inductive reasoning. *Psychological Review, 90,* 339–363. doi:10.1037/0033-295X.90.4.339

Nist, S., & Mealey, D. (1991). Teacher-directed comprehension strategies. In Flippo, R., & Caverly, D. (Eds.), *Teaching reading and study strategies at the college level.* Newark, DE: International Reading Association.

Noordman, L., Vonk, W., & Kempff, H. (1992). Causal inferences during the reading of expository texts. *Journal of Memory and Language, 31,* 573–590. doi:10.1016/0749-596X(92)90029-W

Norman, D. (1999). Commentary: Banner blindness, human cognition and Web design. *Internetworking*. Retrieved May 6, 2009, from http://www.internettg.org/newsletter/mar99/commentary.html

Norman, D. (1984). Stages and levels in human-machine interaction. *International Journal of Man-Machine Studies*, *21*, 365–375. doi:10.1016/S0020-7373(84)80054-1

Norman, D. (1998). *The invisible computer*. Cambridge, MA: MIT Press.

Norman, D. (2002). *The design of everyday things*. New York, NY: Basic Books.

Norman, D. (2004). *Emotional design*. New York, NY: Basic Books.

Norman, D. (2009). Memory is more important than actuality. *Interaction*, *16*(2), 24–26. doi:10.1145/1487632.1487638

Norman, D. A. (2002). *The design of everyday things*. New York, NY: Basic Books.

Norman, D., & Draper, S. (1986). *User centered system design: New perspectives on human-computer interaction*. Mahwah, NJ: Erlbaum.

Nowaczyk, R., & James, E. (1993). Applying minimal manual principles for documentation of graphical user interfaces. *Journal of Technical Writing and Communication*, *23*(4), 379–388.

O'Brien, E. J., Cook, A. E., & Peracchi, K. A. (2004). Updating situation models: Reply to Zwaan & Madden. *Journal of Experimental Psychology. Learning, Memory, and Cognition*, *30*, 289–291. doi:10.1037/0278-7393.30.1.289

O'Connor, M., Remus, W., & Griggs, K. (1993). Judgmental forecasting in times of change. *International Journal of Forecasting*, *9*, 163–172. doi:10.1016/0169-2070(93)90002-5

O'Hara, K., & Payne, S. (1998). The effects of operator implementation cost on planfulness of problem solving and learning. *Cognitive Psychology*, *35*, 34–70. doi:10.1006/cogp.1997.0676

O'Malley, C. (1986). Helping users help themselves. In Norman, D., & Draper, S. (Eds.), *User centered system design: New perspectives on human-computer interaction* (pp. 377–398). Mahwah, NJ: Erlbaum.

O'Reilly, T., & McNamara, D. (2006). Reversing the reverse cohesion effect: Good texts can be better for strategic, high-knowledge readers. *Discourse Processes*, *43*, 121–152.

Oberauer, K., & Kliegl, R. (2006). A formal model of capacity limits in working memory. *Journal of Memory and Language*, *55*, 601–626. doi:10.1016/j.jml.2006.08.009

Oberauer, K., Lange, E., & Engle, R. (2004). Working memory capacity and resistance to interference. *Journal of Memory and Language*, *51*, 80–96. doi:10.1016/j.jml.2004.03.003

Ojakaar, E. (2001). *Users decide first; move second*. Retrieved May 16, 2006, from http://www.uie.com/articles/users_decide_first/

Orasanu, J., & Connolly, T. (1993). The reinvention of decision making. In Klein, G., Orasanu, J., Calderwood, R., & Zsambok, C. (Eds.), *Decision making in action: Models and methods* (pp. 3–20). Norwood, NJ: Ablex.

Orasanu, J., & Fischer, U. (1997). Finding decisions in natural environments: The view from the cockpit. In Zsambok, C., & Klein, G. (Eds.), *Naturalistic decision making* (pp. 343–357). Hillsdale, NJ: Erlbaum.

Øritsland, T., & Buur, J. (2003). Interaction styles: An aesthetic sense of direction in interface design. *International Journal of Human-Computer Interaction*, *15*(1), 67–85. doi:10.1207/S15327590IJHC1501_06

Otero, J., & Kintsch, W. (1992). Failures to detect contradictions in a text: What readers believe versus what they read. *Psychological Science*, *3*(4), 229–235. doi:10.1111/j.1467-9280.1992.tb00034.x

Owen, D. (1986). Answers first, then questions. In Norman, D., & Draper, S. (Eds.), *User centered system design: New perspectives on human-computer interaction* (pp. 362–375). Mahwah, NJ: Erlbaum.

Ozok, A., & Salvendy, G. (2004). Twenty guidelines for the design of Web-based interfaces with consistent language. *Computers in Human Behavior*, *20*(2), 149–161. doi:10.1016/j.chb.2003.10.012

Ozuru, Y., Best, R., & McNamara, D. (2004). Contribution of reading skill to learning from expository texts. In K. Forbus, D. Gentner & T. Regier (Eds.), *Proceedings of the 26th Annual Cognitive Science Society* (pp. 1071–1076). Mahwah, NJ: Erlbaum.

Pagendarm, M., & Schaumburg, H. (2001). Why are users banner-blind? The impact of navigation style on the perception of web banners. *Journal of Digital Information, 2*(1). Retrieved May 6, 2006, from http://jodi.tamu.edu/ Articles/ v02/i01/Pagendarm/

Paiva, A. (Ed.). (2000). *Affective interactions: Toward a new generation of computer interfaces*. New York, NY: Springer.

Paivio, A. (1971). *Imagery and verbal processes*. New York, NY: Holt, Rinehart, and Winston.

Paivio, A. (1986). *Mental representations: A dual coding approach*. Oxford, England: Oxford UP.

Palladino, P., Cornoldi, C., De Beni, R., & Pazzaglia, F. (2001). Working memory and updating processes in reading comprehension. *Memory & Cognition, 29*(2), 344–354. doi:10.3758/BF03194929

Paradis, J., Dobrin, D., & Miller, R. (1985). Writing at Exxon ITD. In Odell, L., & Goswami, D. (Eds.), *Writing in nonacademic settings* (pp. 281–307). New York, NY: Guidford.

Parker, H., Roast, C., & Siddiqi, J. (1997). HCI and requirements engineering: Towards a framework for investigating temporal properties in interaction. *SIGCHI Bulletin, 29*(1). http://www.acm.org/sigchi/bulletin/1997.1

Parker, C., & Sinclair, M. (2001). User-centred design does make a difference. The case of decision support systems in crop production. *Behaviour & Information Technology, 20*(6), 449–460. doi:10.1080/01449290110089570

Parker, R. (1997). *Looking good in print*. Research Triangle Park, NC: Ventana Communications Group, Inc.

Park, J., Yoon, W., & Ryu, H. (2000). Users' recognition of semantic affinity among tasks and the effects of consistency. *International Journal of Human-Computer Interaction, 12*(1), 89–105. doi:10.1207/S15327590IJHC1201_4

Parush, A. (2004). *Interview with Donald Norman on mental models*. Retrieved from http://www.carleton.ca/ hotlab/hottopics/ Articles/DonNormanInterview.html

Patel, V., Branch, T., & Arocha, J. (2002). Errors in interpreting quantities as procedures: The case of pharmaceutical labels. *International Journal of Medical Informatics, 65*, 193–211. doi:10.1016/S1386-5056(02)00045-X

Patrick, J., & Haines, H. (1988). Training and transfer of fault-finding skills. *Ergonomics, 31*, 193–210. doi:10.1080/00140138808966661

Pauker, S., & Pauker, S. (1999). What is a good decision? *Effective Clinical Practice, 2*, 1994–1946.

Payne, J., Bettman, J., Coupey, E., & Johnson, E. (1992). A constructive process view of decision making: Multiple strategies in judgment and choice. *Acta Psychologica, 80*, 107–141. doi:10.1016/0001-6918(92)90043-D

Payne, J., Bettman, J., & Johnson, E. (1988). Adaptive strategy selection in decision making. *Journal of Experimental Psychology. Learning, Memory, and Cognition, 14*, 534–552. doi:10.1037/0278-7393.14.3.534

Payne, J., Bettman, J., & Johnson, E. (1993). *The adaptive decision maker*. Cambridge, UK: Cambridge University Press.

Payne, J., Bettman, J., & Luce, M. (1996). When time is money: Decision behavior under opportunity-cost time pressure. *Organizational Behavior and Human Decision Processes, 66*, 131–152. doi:10.1006/obhd.1996.0044

Payne, S. (1991). Display-based action at the user interface. *International Journal of Man-Machine Studies, 35*, 275–289. doi:10.1016/S0020-7373(05)80129-4

Payne, S. (1995). Naive judgments of stimulus-response compatibility. *Human Factors, 37*(3), 495–506. doi:10.1518/001872095779049309

Payne, S. (2002). Balancing information needs: Dilemmas in producing patient information leaflets. *Health Informatics Journal, 8*, 174–179. doi:10.1177/146045820200800402

Payne, S., Howes, A., & Reader, W. (2001). Adaptively distributing cognition: A decision making perspective on human-computer interaction. *Behaviour & Information Technology, 20*(5), 339–346. doi:10.1080/01449290110078680

Pealer, L., Weiler, R., Pigg, R., Miller, D., & Dorman, S. (2001). The feasibility of a Web-based surveillance system to collect health risk behavior data from college students. *Health Education & Behavior, 28*(5), 547–559. doi:10.1177/109019810102800503

Peebles, D., & Cheng, P. (2003). Modeling the effect of task and graphical representation on response latency in a graph reading task. *Human Factors, 45*(1), 28–46. doi:10.1518/hfes.45.1.28.27225

Penrose, J., & Seiford, L. (1988). Microcomputer users' preferences for software documentation: An analysis. *Journal of Technical Writing and Communication, 18*(4), 355–366.

Perfetti, C., & Landesman, L. (2001). *The truth about download times.* Retrieved December 2, 2008, from http://www.uie.com/articles/download_time/

Perrin, B., Barnett, B., Walrath, L., & Grossman, J. (2001). Information order and outcome framing: An assessment of judgment bias in a naturalistic decision-making context. *Human Factors, 43*(2), 227–238. doi:10.1518/001872001775900968

Peters, E., Hibbard, J., Slovic, P., & Dieckmann, N. (2007). Numeracy skill and the communication, comprehension, and use of risk-benefit information. *Health Affairs, 26*, 741–748. doi:10.1377/hlthaff.26.3.741

Peters, E., Västfjäll, D., Slovic, P., Mertz, C., Mazzocco, K., & Dickert, S. (2006). Numeracy and decision making. *Psychological Science, 17*(5), 407–413. doi:10.1111/j.1467-9280.2006.01720.x

Peters, M. (1981). Attentional asymmetries during concurrent bimanual performance. *Quarterly Journal of Experimental Psychology, 33A*, 95–103.

Peterson, C., & Beach, L. (1967). Man as an intuitive statistician. *Psychological Bulletin, 68*, 29–46. doi:10.1037/h0024722

Peterson, C., & Miller, A. (1964). Mode, median and mean as optimal strategies. *Journal of Experimental Psychology, 68*, 363–367. doi:10.1037/h0040387

Pett, D. (1993, October). *White letters on colored backgrounds: Legibility and preference.* Visual Literacy in the Digital Age: Selected Reading from the Annual Conference of the International Visual Literacy Association. ERIC Document Reproduction Service No. ED370559.

Phillips, J., Meehan, J., & Triggs, T. (2003). Effects of cursor orientation and required precision on positioning movements on computer screens. *International Journal of Human-Computer Interaction, 15*(3), 379–389. doi:10.1207/S15327590IJHC1503_04

Pinker, S. (1990). A theory of graph comprehension. In Freedle, R. (Ed.), *Artificial intelligence and the future of testing* (pp. 73–126). Hillsdale, NJ: Erlbaum.

Pirolli, P. (2007). *Information foraging theory: Adaptive interaction with information.* Oxford, UK: Oxford UP. doi:10.1093/acprof:oso/9780195173321.001.0001

Pollatsek, A., Lima, S., & Well, A. (1981). Concept or computation: Students' understanding of the mean. *Educational Studies in Mathematics, 12*, 191–204. doi:10.1007/BF00305621

Pollatsek, A., Well, A., Konold, C., & Hardiman, P. (1987). Understanding conditional probabilities. *Organizational Behavior and Human Decision Processes, 40*, 255–269. doi:10.1016/0749-5978(87)90015-X

Pollock, A., & Hockley, A. (1997). What's wrong with Internet searching? *D-Lib Magazine, 3*(3). Retrieved from http://www.dlib.org/dlib/march97/bt/03pollock.htmldoi:10.1045/march97-pollock

Pomerantz, J., & Schwaitzberg, S. (1975). Grouping by proximity: Selective attention measures. *Perception & Psychophysics, 18*, 355–361. doi:10.3758/BF03211212

Porter, J. (2003). *Testing the three-click rule.* Retrieved May 16, 2010, from http://www.uie.com/articles/three_click_rule/

Potelle, H., & Rouet, J. (2003). Effects of content representation and readers' prior knowledge on the comprehension of hypertext. *International Journal of Human-Computer Studies, 58*(3), 327–345. doi:10.1016/S1071-5819(03)00016-8

Poulton, E. (1958). Time for reading and memory. *The British Journal of Psychology, 49*, 230–245. doi:10.1111/j.2044-8295.1958.tb00661.x

Powe, B., Daniels, E., Finnie, R., & Thompson, A. (2005). Perceptions about breast cancer among African American women: Do selected educational materials .challenge them? *Patient Education and Counseling, 56*, 197–204. doi:10.1016/j.pec.2004.02.009

Powers, M., Lashley, C., Sanchez, P., & Shneiderman, B. (1984). An experimental comparison of tabular and graphic data presentation. *International Journal of Man-Machine Studies, 20*, 545–566. doi:10.1016/S0020-7373(84)80029-2

Poynter, D. (1989). Judging the duration of time intervals: A process of remembering segments of experience. In Levin, I., & Zakay, D. (Eds.), *Time and human cognition: A life-span perspective* (pp. 305–331). Amsterdam, The Netherlands: North-Holland. doi:10.1016/S0166-4115(08)61045-6

Proctor, R. (2002). Content preparation and management for web design: Eliciting, structuring, searching, and displaying information. *International Journal of Human-Computer Interaction, 14*(1), 25–92. doi:10.1207/S15327590IJHC1401_2

Qiu, L. (1993). Analytical searching vs. browsing in hypertext information retrieval systems. *Canadian Journal of Information and Library Science, 18*, 1–13.

Quesenbery, W. (2003). Dimensions of usability. In Albers, M., & Mazur, B. (Eds.), *Content and complexity: Information design in software development and documentation* (pp. 81–102). Mahwah, NJ: Erlbaum.

Rabbitt, P. (1989). Sequential reactions. In Holding, D. (Ed.), *Human skills* (2nd ed.). New York, NY: Wiley.

Rains, S., & Karmikel, C. (2009). Health information-seeking and perceptions of website credibility: Examining Web-use orientation, message characteristics, and structural features of websites. *Computers in Human Behavior, 25*, 544–553. doi:10.1016/j.chb.2008.11.005

Ramsay, J., Barbesi, A., & Preece, J. (1998). A psychological investigation of long retrieval times on the World Wide Web. *Interacting with Computers, 10*, 77–86. doi:10.1016/S0953-5438(97)00019-2

Randel, J., & Pugh, L. (1996). Differences in expert and novice situation awareness in naturalistic decision making. *International Journal of Human-Computer Studies, 45*, 579–597. doi:10.1006/ijhc.1996.0068

Raskin, J. (2003/2004). Silicon superstitions. *ACM Queue; Tomorrow's Computing Today, 1*(9).

Rasmussen, J. (1986). *Information processing and human-machine interaction: An approach to cognitive engineering.* New York, NY: North-Holland.

Rasmussen, J., Pejtersen, A., & Goodstein, L. (1994). *Cognitive systems engineering.* New York, NY: Wiley.

Ratner, R., & Herbst, K. (2005). When good decisions have bad outcomes: The impact of affect on switching behavior. *Organizational Behavior and Human Decision Processes, 96*, 23–37. doi:10.1016/j.obhdp.2004.09.003

Rayner, K., & Pollatsek, A. (1989). *The psychology of reading.* New York, NY: Prentice-Hall.

Réach, G., Zerrouki, A., Leclercq, D., & d'Ivernois, J. (2005). Adjusting insulin doses: From knowledge to decision. *Patient Education and Counseling, 56*, 98–103. doi:10.1016/j.pec.2004.01.001

Readance, J., & Moore, D. (1981). A meta-analytic review of the effect of adjunct pictures on reading comprehension. *Psychology in the Schools, 18*, 218–224. doi:10.1002/1520-6807(198104)18:2<218::AID-PITS2310180219>3.0.CO;2-1

Reason, J. (1990). *Human error.* Cambridge, UK: Cambridge UP.

Recht, D., & Leslie, L. (1988). Effect of prior knowledge on good and poor readers' memory of text. *Journal of Educational Psychology, 80*, 16–20. doi:10.1037/0022-0663.80.1.16

Redish, J. (1988). Reading to learn to do. *The Technical Writing Teacher, 15*(3), 223–233.

Redish, J. (1994). Understanding readers. In Barnum, C., & Carliner, S. (Eds.), *Techniques for technical communicators* (pp. 15–41). New York, NY: Macmillan.

Redish, J. (2000). Readability formulas have even more limitations than Klare discusses. *ACM Journal of Computer Documentation, 24*(3), 132–137. doi:10.1145/344599.344637

Redish, J. (2007). Expanding usability testing to evaluate complex systems. *Journal of Usability Studies, 2*(3), 102–111.

Redish, J. C., & Selzer, J. (1985). The place of readability formulas in technical communication. *Technical Communication, 32*(4), 46–52.

Redish, J., & Schell, D. (1989). Writing and testing instructions for usability. In Fearing, B., & Sparrow, K. (Eds.), *Technical writing: Theory and practice* (pp. 63–71). New York, NY: Modern Language Association of America.

Reicher, G. (1969). Perceptual recognition as a function of meaningfulness of stimulus material. *Journal of Experimental Psychology, 81*, 275–280. doi:10.1037/h0027768

Rein, G., McDue, D., & Slein, J. (1997). A case for document management functions on the Web. *Communications of the ACM, 40*(9), 81–89. doi:10.1145/260750.260777

Remus, W. (1984). An empirical investigation of the impact of graphical and tabular data presentations on decision making. *Management Science, 30*(5), 533–542. doi:10.1287/mnsc.30.5.533

Remus, W. E., O'Connor, M. J., & Griggs, K. (1995). Does reliable information improve the accuracy of judgmental forecasting? *International Journal of Forecasting, 11*, 285–293. doi:10.1016/0169-2070(94)00578-Z

Rensink, R., O'Regan, J., & Clark, J. (1997). To see or not to see: The need for attention to perceive changes in scenes. *Psychological Science, 8*, 368–373. doi:10.1111/j.1467-9280.1997.tb00427.x

Richards, A., Hannon, E., & Kerakshan, N. (2010). Predicting and manipulating the incidence of inattentional blindness. *Psychological Research, 74*, 513–523. doi:10.1007/s00426-009-0273-8

Richards, D. (2000). The reuse of knowledge: A user-centered approach. *International Journal of Human-Computer Studies, 52*, 553–579. doi:10.1006/ijhc.1999.0342

Roberts, D. (1989). Readers' comprehension responses in informative discourse: Toward connecting reading and writing in technical communication. *Journal of Technical Writing and Communication, 19*(2), 135–148. doi:10.2190/A1JA-0L9H-YLMH-YUE4

Robertson, G., Card, S., & Mackinlay, J. (1993). Information visualization: Using 3D interactive animation. *Communications of the ACM, 36*(4), 57–71. doi:10.1145/255950.153577

Robins, D., Holmes, J., & Stansbury, M. (2010). Consumer health information on the Web: The relationship of visual design and perceptions of credibility. *Journal of the American Society for Information Science and Technology, 61*(1), 13–29.

Rodden, K. Fu, X., Aula, A., & Spiro, I. (2008). Eye-mouse coordination patterns on Web search results pages. *CHI '08 Extended Abstracts on Human factors in Computing Systems* (pp. 2997–3002). April 5–10, 2008. Florence, Italy.

Rodriguez, M. (2002). Development of diagrammatic procedural instructions for performing complex one-time tasks. *International Journal of Human-Computer Interaction, 14*(3&4), 405–422.

Roediger, H. (1980). Memory metaphors in cognitive psychology. *Memory & Cognition, 8*, 231–246. doi:10.3758/BF03197611

Rogers, B. (2003). Measuring online experience: It's about more than time! *Usability News, 5*(2). Retrieved from http://psychology.wichita.edu/surl/ usabilitynews/52/experience.htm

Roscoe, S. (1968). Airborne displays for flight and navigation. *Human Factors, 10*, 321–332.

Rosenbaum, S., & Walters, D. (1986). Audience diversity: A major challenge in computer documentation. *IEEE Transactions on Professional Communication, 29*(4).

Rosenfeld, L., & Morville, P. (1998). *Information architecture for the World Wide Web*. Cambridge, MA: O'Reilly.

Roske-Hofstrand, R., & Paap, K. (1986). Cognitive networks as a guide to menu organization: An application in the automated cockpit. *Ergonomics, 29*, 1301–1311. doi:10.1080/00140138608967247

Rosson, M. (1983). Patterns of experience in text editing. *Proceedings of the CHI '83 Human Factors in Computing Systems* (pp. 171–175). New York, NY: ACM.

Rothman, R. L., Housam, R., Weiss, H., Davis, D., Gregory, R., & Gebretsadik, T. (2006). Patient understanding of food labels: The role of literacy and numeracy. *American Journal of Preventive Medicine, 31*, 391–398. doi:10.1016/j.amepre.2006.07.025

Rouet, J. (2003). What was I looking for? The influence of task specificity and prior knowledge on students' search strategies in hypertext. *Interacting with Computers, 15*, 409–428. doi:10.1016/S0953-5438(02)00064-4

Rouet, J., & Tricot, A. (1996). Task and activity models in hypertext usage. In van Oostendorp, H., & de Mul, S. (Eds.), *Cognitive aspects of electronic text processing* (pp. 239–264). Norwood, NJ: Ablex.

Rowan, K. (1991). When simple language fails: Presenting difficult science to the public. *Journal of Technical Writing and Communication, 21*, 369–382. doi:10.2190/D3BD-32RC-FGW0-C5JB

Royer, J. M., & Cunningham, D. J. (1981). On the theory and measurement of reading comprehension. *Contemporary Educational Psychology, 6*, 187–216. doi:10.1016/0361-476X(81)90001-1

Rubens, P. (1986). A reader's view of text and graphics: Implications for transactional text. *Journal of Technical Writing and Communication, 16*(1/2), 73–86.

Rubens, P., & Rubens, B. (1988). Usability and format design. In Doheny-Farina, S. (Ed.), *Effective documentation: What we have learned from research* (pp. 213–234). Cambridge, MA: MIT.

Rubinstein, J., Meyer, D., & Evans, J. (2001). Executive control of cognitive processes in task switching. *Journal of Experimental Psychology. Human Perception and Performance, 27*(4), 763–797. doi:10.1037/0096-1523.27.4.763

Rudnicky, A., & Kolers, P. (1984). Size and case of type as stimuli in reading. *Journal of Experimental Psychology. Human Perception and Performance, 10*, 231–249. doi:10.1037/0096-1523.10.2.231

Rumelhart, D. (1980). Schemata: The building blocks of cognition. In Spiro, R., Bruce, B., & Brewer, W. (Eds.), *Theoretical issues in reading comprehension* (pp. 38–58). Hillsdale, NJ: Erlbaum.

Russell, M. (2005). Using eye-tracking data to understand first impressions of a website. *Usability News, 7*(1). Retrieved from http://psychology.wichita.edu/surl/usabilitynews/71/eye_tracking.html

Russo, J. (1977). The value of unit price information. *JMR, Journal of Marketing Research, 14*, 193–201. doi:10.2307/3150469

Russo, J., Carlson, K., & Meloy, M. (2006). Choosing an inferior alternative. *Psychological Science, 17*, 899–904. doi:10.1111/j.1467-9280.2006.01800.x

Russo, J., & Dosher, B. (1983). Strategies for multiattribute binary choice. *Journal of Experimental Psychology. Learning, Memory, and Cognition, 9*, 676–696. doi:10.1037/0278-7393.9.4.676

Russo, J., & Rosen, L. (1975). An eye fixation analysis of multialternative choice. *Memory & Cognition, 3*, 267–276. doi:10.3758/BF03212910

Russo, J., Staelin, R., Nolan, C., Russell, G., & Metcalf, B. (1986). Nutrition information in the supermarket. *The Journal of Consumer Research, 13*, 48–70. doi:10.1086/209047

Saariluoma, P., & Kalakoski, V. (1998). Apperception and imagery in blindfold chess. *Memory (Hove, England), 6*, 67–90. doi:10.1080/741941600

Salthouse, T., & Babcock, R. (1991). Decomposing adult age differences in working memory. *Developmental Psychology, 72*, 763–776. doi:10.1037/0012-1649.27.5.763

Salvador, T., Barile, S., & Sherry, J. (2004). Ubiquitous computing design principles: Supporting human-human and human-computer transaction. *Proceedings of the SIGCHI Conference on Human Factors in Computing Systems* (pp. 1497–1500). New York, NY: ACM.

Sanbonmatsu, D., Kardes, F., & Gibson, B. (1991). The role of attribute knowledge and overall evaluations in comparative judgment. *Organizational Behavior and Human Decision Processes, 48*(1), 131–146. doi:10.1016/0749-5978(91)90009-I

Sanders, M., & McCormick, E. (1993). *Human factors in engineering and design.* New York, NY: McGraw-Hill.

Santa Clara Grand Jury. (2005). *Problems implementing the San Jose police computer aided dispatch system.* Retrieved June 12, 2006, from http://www.sccsuperiorcourt.org/jury/GJreports/2005/SJPoliceComputerAidedDispatch.pdf

Santhanam, R., & Wiedenbeck, S. (1993). Neither novice nor expert: The discretionary user of software. *International Journal of Man-Machine Studies, 38,* 201–229. doi:10.1006/imms.1993.1010

Sasse, M. (1992). Users' models of computer systems. In Rogers, Y., Rutherford, A., & Bibby, P. A. (Eds.), *Models in the mind: Theory, perspective & application.* London, UK: Academic Press.

Satzinger, J., & Olfman, L. (1998). User interface consistency across end-user applications: The effects on mental models. *Journal of Management Information Systems, 14*(4), 167–194.

Savolainen, R. (1995). Everyday life information seeking: Approaching information seeking in the context of "way of life". *Library & Information Science Research, 17,* 259–294. doi:10.1016/0740-8188(95)90048-9

Savolainen, R., & Kari, J. (2004). Placing the Internet in information source horizons. A study of information seeking by Internet users in the context of self-development. *Library & Information Science Research, 26,* 415–433. doi:10.1016/j.lisr.2004.04.004

Sayago, S., & Blat, J. (2010). Telling the story of older people e-mailing: An ethnographical study. *International Journal of Human-Computer Studies, 68,* 105–120. doi:10.1016/j.ijhcs.2009.10.004

Scaife, M., & Rogers, Y. (1996). External cognition: How do graphical representations work? *International Journal of Human-Computer Studies, 45,* 185–213. doi:10.1006/ijhc.1996.0048

Scanlon, T. (1996). *Making online information usable.* Retrieved from http://www.uie.com/articles/online_information/

Schank, R., & Abelson, R. (1977). *Scripts, plans, goals and understanding.* Mahwah, NJ: Erlbaum.

Schanteau, J. (1992). Competence in experts: The role of tasks characteristics. *Organizational Behavior and Human Decision Processes, 53,* 252–266. doi:10.1016/0749-5978(92)90064-E

Schapira, M., Nattinger, A., & McAuliffe, T. (2006). The influence of graphic format on breast cancer risk communication. *Journal of Health Communication, 11,* 569–582. doi:10.1080/10810730600829916

Scharff, L., & Ahumada, A. (2003). Contrast measures for predicting text readability. In Rogowitz, B., & Pappas, T. (Eds.), *Human Vision and Electronic Imaging VIII* (pp. 463–472). Santa Clara, CA: SPIE.

Scheiter, K., & Gerjets, P. (2002). The impact of problem order: Sequencing problems as a strategy for improving one's performance. In W. D. Gray & C. D. Schunn (Eds.), *Proceedings of the 24th Annual Conference of the Cognitive Science Society* (pp. 798–803). Mahwah, NJ: Erlbaum.

Schlesinger, J. (1970). *Planning, programming, budgeting.* Inquiry of the subcommittee on national security and international operations for the Senate Committee on Government Operations, 91 Cong. 1 Sess., 482.

Schneider, V., Healy, A., & Bourne, L. (2002). What is learned under difficult conditions is hard to forget: Contextual interference effects in foreign vocabulary acquisition, retention, and transfer. *Journal of Memory and Language, 46,* 419–440. doi:10.1006/jmla.2001.2813

Schneider, W., & Chein, J. (2003). Controlled & automatic processing: Behavior, theory, and biological mechanisms. *Cognitive Science, 27,* 525–559.

Schneider, W., & Fisk, A. (1982). Concurrent automatic and controlled visual search: Can processing occur without resource cost? *Journal of Experimental Psychology. Learning, Memory, and Cognition, 8,* 261–278. doi:10.1037/0278-7393.8.4.261

Schnotz, W., & Bannert, M. (2003). Construction and interference in learning from multiple representation. *Learning and Instruction, 13*(2), 141–156. doi:10.1016/S0959-4752(02)00017-8

Scholtz, J. (2006). Metrics for evaluating human information interaction systems. *Interacting with Computers, 18,* 507–527. doi:10.1016/j.intcom.2005.10.004

Schriver, K. (1997). *Dynamics in document design: Creating texts for readers*. New York, NY: Wiley.

Schwartz, D., & Teleni, D. (2000). Tying knowledge to action with kMail. *IEEE Intelligent Systems and Their Applications*, *15*, 33–39. doi:10.1109/5254.846283

Schwartz, L. (2010). Making informed decisions about mammograms. *Science News*, *177*(4), 32. doi:10.1002/scin.5591770426

Schyns, P., & Rodet, L. (1997). Categorization creates functional features. *Journal of Experimental Psychology. Learning, Memory, and Cognition*, *23*, 681–696. doi:10.1037/0278-7393.23.3.681

Seger, C. A. (1994). Implicit learning. *Psychological Bulletin*, *115*, 163–196. doi:10.1037/0033-2909.115.2.163

Seibel, R. (1972). Data entry devices and procedures. In Van Cott, H., & Kinkade, R. (Eds.), *Human engineering guide to equipment design*. Washington, DC: US Government Printing.

Selker, T. (2005). Fostering motivation and creativity for computer users. *International Journal of Human-Computer Studies*, *63*, 410–421. doi:10.1016/j.ijhcs.2005.04.005

Shafir, E. (1993). Choosing versus rejecting: Why some options are both better and worse than others. *Memory & Cognition*, *21*, 546–556. doi:10.3758/BF03197186

Shah, P., & Carpenter, P. (1995). Conceptual limitations in comprehending line graphs. *Journal of Experimental Psychology. General*, *124*, 43–61. doi:10.1037/0096-3445.124.1.43

Shah, P., & Hoeffner, J. (2002). Review of graph comprehension research: Implications for instruction. *Educational Psychology Review*, *14*(1), 47–69. doi:10.1023/A:1013180410169

Shaikh, D. (2005). The effects of line length on reading online news. *Usability News, 7*(2). Retrieved April 13, 2010, from http://www.surl.org/usabilitynews/ 72/LineLength.asp

Shalev, V., Chodick, G., & Heymann, A. (2009). Format change of a laboratory test order form affects physician behavior. *International Journal of Medical Informatics*, *78*, 639–644. doi:10.1016/j.ijmedinf.2009.04.011

Shannon, C. (1948). A mathematical theory of communication. *The Bell System Technical Journal*, *27*, 379–423.

Shanteau, J. (1992). Competence in experts: The role of task characteristics. *Organizational Behavior and Human Decision Processes*, *53*(2), 252–266. doi:10.1016/0749-5978(92)90064-E

Shearer, H. (2010). An activity-theoretical approach to the usability testing of information products meant to support complex use. In Albers, M., & Still, B. (Eds.), *Usability of complex Information Systems: Evaluation of user interaction* (pp. 181–206). Boca Raton, FL: CRC Press. doi:10.1201/EBK1439828946-13

Shears, C., & Weiss, E. (2005). Inference vs control sentences: Are readers able to detect our intended differences? *Brain and Cognition*, *57*, 195–197. doi:10.1016/j.bandc.2004.08.044

Shenton, A., & Dixon, P. (2004a). Issues arising from youngsters' information-seeking behavior. *Library & Information Science Research*, *26*, 177–200. doi:10.1016/j.lisr.2003.12.003

Sheridan, S., Felix, K., Pignone, M., & Lewis, C. (2004). Information needs of men regarding prostate cancer screening and the effect of a brief decision aid. *Patient Education and Counseling*, *54*, 345–351. doi:10.1016/j.pec.2003.12.003

Shih, H. (2004). Extended technology acceptance model of internet utilization behavior. *Information & Management*, *41*(6), 719–729. doi:10.1016/j.im.2003.08.009

Shinoda, H., & Ikeda, M. (1998). Visual acuity depends on perceived size. *Optical Review*, *5*(1), 65–68. doi:10.1007/s10043-998-0065-1

Shiv, B., & Fedorikhin, A. (1999). Heart and mind in conflict: Interplay of affect and cognition in consumer decision making. *The Journal of Consumer Research*, *26*, 278–282. doi:10.1086/209563

Shneiderman, B. (1984). Response time and display rate in human performance with computers. *Computing Surveys*, *16*, 265–285. doi:10.1145/2514.2517

Shneiderman, B. (1997). *Designing the user interface: Strategies for effective human-computer interaction*. Reading, MA: Addison-Wesley.

Shneiderman, B. (1998). *Designing the user interface.* Boston, MA: Addison-Wesley.

Shneiderman, B. (2000). Universal usability. *Communications of the ACM, 43*(5), 85–91. doi:10.1145/332833.332843

Shneiderman, B., Byrd, D., & Croft, W. (1998). Sorting out searching: A user-interface framework for text searches. *Communications of the ACM, 41*(4), 95–98. doi:10.1145/273035.273069

Shu, K., Boyle, D., Spurr, C., Horsky, J., Heiman, H., & O'Connor, P. (2001). Comparison of time spent writing orders on paper with computerized physician order entry. *Studies in Health Technology and Informatics, 84*(2), 1207–1121.

Shushan, R., & Wright, D. (1994). *Desktop publishing by design.* Redmond, WA: Microsoft Press.

Siegfried, T. (2010). Odds are, it's wrong: Science fails to face the shortcomings of statistics. *Science News, 177*(7), 26. doi:10.1002/scin.5591770721

Siegrist, M., & Cvetkovich, G. (2001). Better negative than positive? Evidence of a bias for negative information about possible health hazards. *Risk Analysis, 21*(2), 199–206. doi:10.1111/0272-4332.211102

Silvestri, P. (1989). A note on cause and correlation. *Psychological Reports, 64*(2), 445–446. doi:10.2466/pr0.1989.64.2.445

Simkin, D., & Hastie, R. (1987). An information processing analysis of graph perception. *Journal of the American Statistical Association, 82*, 454–465. doi:10.2307/2289447

Simon, H. (1976). *Administrative behavior* (3rd ed.). New York, NY: Free Press.

Simon, H. (1979). *Models of thought.* New Haven, CT: Yale UP.

Simon, H. (1981). *Sciences of the artificial* (2nd ed.). Cambridge, MA: MIT Press.

Simon, H., Langley, P., & Bradshaw, G. (1981). Scientific discovery as problem solving. *Synthese, 47*, 1–27. doi:10.1007/BF01064262

Simons, D., & Levin, D. (1997). Change blindness. *Trends in Cognitive Sciences, 1*, 261–267. doi:10.1016/S1364-6613(97)01080-2

Simons, D., & Rensink, R. (2005). Change blindness: Past, present, and future. *Trends in Cognitive Sciences, 9*(1), 16–89. doi:10.1016/j.tics.2004.11.006

Sinclair, H. (1971). Digital versus conventional clocks: A review. *Applied Ergonomics, 2*, 178–181. doi:10.1016/0003-6870(71)90044-5

Singer, M., & O'Connell, G. (2003). Robust inference processes in expository text comprehension. *The European Journal of Cognitive Psychology, 15*, 607–631. doi:10.1080/095414400340000079

Sjöberg, L. (2000). Factors in risk perception. *Risk Analysis, 20*(1), 1–12. doi:10.1111/0272-4332.00001

Slone, D. (2002). The influence of mental models and goals on user search patterns during Web interaction. *Journal of the American Society for Information Science and Technology, 53*(13), 1152–1169. doi:10.1002/asi.10141

Slone, D. (2003). Internet search approaches: The influence of age, search goals, and experience. *Library & Information Science Research, 25*, 403–418. doi:10.1016/S0740-8188(03)00051-3

Slovic, P. (1972). From Shakespeare to Simon: Speculations—and some evidence—about man's ability to process information. *Oregon Research Institute Research Bulletin, 12*, 1–29.

Slovic, P. (1993). Perceived risk, trust, and democracy: A systems perspective. *Risk Analysis, 13*, 675–682. doi:10.1111/j.1539-6924.1993.tb01329.x

Slovic, P. (2000). *The perception of risk.* London, UK: Earthscan.

Slovic, P., Finucane, M., Peters, E., & MacGregor, D. (2004). Risk as analysis and risk as feelings: Some thoughts about affect, reason, risk, and rationality. *Risk Analysis, 24*, 311–322. doi:10.1111/j.0272-4332.2004.00433.x

Slovic, P., Monahan, J., & MacGregor, D. (2000). Violence risk assessment and risk communication: The effects of using actual cases, providing instruction and employing probability versus frequency formats. *Law and Human Behavior, 24*, 271–296. doi:10.1023/A:1005595519944

Smith, E., & Goodman, L. (1984). Understanding written instructions: The role of an explanatory schema. *Cognition and Instruction, 1*(4), 359–396. doi:10.1207/s1532690xci0104_1

Snyder, M., & Campbell, B. (1980). Testing hypotheses about other people: The role of the hypothesis. *Personality and Social Psychology Bulletin, 6*, 421–426. doi:10.1177/014616728063015

Song, G., & Salvendy, G. (2003). A framework for re-use of user experience in Web browsing. *Behaviour & Information Technology, 22*(2), 79–90. doi:10.1080/0144929031000092231

Sonnenwald, D., & Wildemuth, B. (2001). A research method to investigate information seeking using the concept of information horizons: An example from a study of lower socio-economic student's information seeking behaviour. *New Review of Information Behaviour Research, 2*, 65–86.

Speier, C., & Morris, M. (2003). The influence of query interface design on decision-making performance. *Management Information Systems Quarterly, 27*(3), 397–423.

Spence, I. (2004). The apparent and effective dimensionality of representations of objects. *Human Factors, 46*(4), 738–747. doi:10.1518/hfes.46.4.738.56809

Spence, I., & Lewandowsky, S. (1991). Displaying proportions and percentages. *Applied Cognitive Psychology, 5*, 61–77. doi:10.1002/acp.2350050106

Spink, A., & Xu, J. (2000). Selected results from a large study of Web searching: The excite study. *Information Research, 6*(1). Retrieved from http://InformationR.net/ir/ 6-1/paper90.html

Spink, A., Wolfram, D., Jansen, B. J., & Saracevic, T. (2001). Searching the Web: The public and their queries. *Journal of the American Society for Information Science American Society for Information Science, 5*(3), 226–234.

Spool, J. (1997). *Why on-site searching stinks.* Retrieved December 28, 2005, from http://www.uie.com/ articles/search_stinks/

Spool, J. (1998). *As the page scrolls.* Retrieved May 25, 2010, from http://www.uie.com/articles/ page_scrolling/

Spool, J. (2009). Deciding when graphics will help (and when they won't). *UIEtips.* Retrieved April 30, 2010, from http://www.uie.com/articles/deciding_when_graphics_help/

Spool, J., Scanlon, T., Schroeder, W., Snyder, C., & DeAngelo, T. (1997). *Web site usability: A designer's guide.* Andover, MA: User Interface Engineering.

Sprague, R. (1995). Electronic document management: Challenges and opportunities for information system managers. *Management Information Systems Quarterly, 19*(1), 29–50. doi:10.2307/249710

Spyradakis, J. (1989a). Signaling effects: A review of the research—Part I. *Journal of Technical Writing and Communication, 19*(3), 227–240.

Spyradakis, J. (1989b). Signaling effects: Increased content retention and new answers—Part II. *Journal of Technical Writing and Communication, 19*(4), 395–415.

Spyridakis, J., & Wenger, M. (1992). Writing for human performance: Relating reading research to document design. *Technical Communication, 39*(2), 202–215.

Spyridakis, J., & Wenger, M. (1992). Writing for human performance: Relating reading research to document design. *Technical Communication, 39*(2), 202–215.

Stagar, P., & Angus, R. (1978). Locating crash sites in simulated air-to-ground visual search. *Human Factors, 20*, 453–466.

Staggers, N., & Norcio, A. (1993). Mental models: Concepts for human-computer interaction research. *International Journal of Man-Machine Studies, 38*, 587–605. doi:10.1006/imms.1993.1028

Stalmeier, P., & van Roosmalen, M. (2009). Concise evaluation of two decision aids. *Patient Education and Counseling, 74*, 104–109. doi:10.1016/j.pec.2008.07.043

Stanford, J., Tauber, E., Fogg, B., & Marable, L. (2002). Experts vs. online consumers: A comparative credibility study of health and finance Web sites. *Consumer WebWatch Research Report.* Retrieved from http://www.consumer-webwatch.org/dynamic/web-credibility-reports-experts-vs-online-abstract.cfm

Stanney, K., & Salvendy, G. (1995). Information visualization: Assisting low spatial individuals with information access tasks through the use of visual mediators. *Ergonomics*, *38*, 1184–1198. doi:10.1080/00140139508925181

Start, J. (1989). The best colors for audio-visual materials for more effective instruction. *Proceedings of Selected Research Papers presented at the Annual Meeting of the Association for Educational Communications and Technology in Dallas, TX*. ERIC Document Reproduction Service No. ED308842.

Stary, C. (1999). Toward the task-complete development of activity-oriented user interfaces. *International Journal of Human-Computer Interaction*, *11*(2), 153–182. doi:10.1207/S153275901102_5

Sternberg, S. (1966). High speed scanning in human memory. *Science*, *153*, 652–654. doi:10.1126/science.153.3736.652

Stevens, K., Stevens, K., & Stevens, W. (1992). Measuring the readability of business writing: The Cloze procedure versus readability formulas. *Journal of Business Communication*, *29*(4), 367–382. doi:10.1177/002194369202900404

Stewart, J. (1994). The psychology of decision making. In Jennings, D. (Ed.), *Decision making: An integrated approach* (pp. 54–95). London, UK: Pitman Publishing.

Stone, E., Sieck, W., Bull, B., Yates, J., Parks, S., & Rush, C. (2003). Foreground:background salience: Explaining the effects of graphical displays on risk avoidance. *Organizational Behavior and Human Decision Processes*, *90*, 19–36. doi:10.1016/S0749-5978(03)00003-7

Stone, E., Yates, J., & Parker, A. (1994). Risk communication: Absolute versus relative expressions of low probability risks. *Organizational Behavior and Human Decision Processes*, *60*, 387–408. doi:10.1006/obhd.1994.1091

Stone, E., Yates, J., & Parker, A. (1997). Effects of numerical and graphical displays on professed risk-taking behavior. *Journal of Experimental Psychology. Applied*, *3*, 243–256. doi:10.1037/1076-898X.3.4.243

Stoop, A., van't Riet, A., & Berg, M. (2004). Using information technology for patient education: Realizing surplus value? *Patient Education and Counseling*, *54*, 187–195. doi:10.1016/S0738-3991(03)00211-8

Stopke, J., & Staley, C. (1994). *An eye for type*. Ann Arbor, MI: Promotional Perspectives.

Storch, N. (1992). Does the user interface make interruptions disruptive? A study of interface style and form of interruption. *Proceedings of the SIGCHI Conference on Human Factors in Computing Systems*, (pp. 14–14). New York, NY: ACM.

Stroop, J. (1935). Studies of interference in serial verbal reactions. *Journal of Experimental Psychology*, *18*, 643–662. doi:10.1037/h0054651

Stvilia, B., Mon, L., & Yi, Y. (2009). A model for online consumer health information quality. *Journal of the American Society for Information Science and Technology*, *60*(9), 1781–1791. doi:10.1002/asi.21115

Suchman, L. (1987). *Plans and situated actions: The problem of human-machine communication*. Cambridge, UK: Cambridge.

Sundstrom, G., & Salvador, A. (1994). Cooperative human-computer decision making: An experiment and some design implications. *Proceedings of the Human Factors and Ergonomics Society 38th Annual Meeting*, (pp. 220–224). Nashville, Tennessee Oct. 24–28, 1994.

Sutcliffe, A., Karat, J., Bodker, S., & Gaver, B. (2006). Can we measure quality in design and do we need to? *Proceedings of Designing Interactive Systems: Processes, Practices, Methods, &* [New York, NY: ACM.]. *Techniques*, *2006*, 119–121.

Sutcliffe, A., & Maiden, N. (1992). Analyzing the novice analyst: Cognitive models in software engineering. *International Journal of Man-Machine Studies*, *36*, 719–740. doi:10.1016/0020-7373(92)90038-M

Swarts, J. (2004). Textual grounding: How people turn texts into tools. *Journal of Technical Writing and Communication*, *34*(1 & 2), 67–89. doi:10.2190/EG0C-QUEY-F9FK-2V0D

Sweller, J. (1988). Cognitive load during problem solving: Effects on learning. *Cognitive Science*, *12*, 257–285. doi:10.1207/s15516709cog1202_4

Sweller, J., Chandler, P., Tierney, P., & Cooper, M. (1990). Cognitive load as a factor in the structuring of technical material. *Journal of Experimental Psychology. General*, *119*, 176–192. doi:10.1037/0096-3445.119.2.176

Szameitat, A., Rummel, J., Szameitat, D., & Ster, A. (2009). Behavioral and emotional consequences of brief delays in human-computer interaction. *International Journal of Human-Computer Studies, 67*, 561–570. doi:10.1016/j.ijhcs.2009.02.004

Szulanski, G. (1996). Exploring internal stickiness: Impediments to the transfer of best practice within the firm. *Strategic Management Journal, 17*, 27–43.

Tabor, W., & Hutchins, S. (2004). Evidence for self-organized sentence processing: Digging-in effects. *Journal of Experimental Psychology. Learning, Memory, and Cognition, 30*(2), 431–450. doi:10.1037/0278-7393.30.2.431

Tannenbaum, A. (2002). *Metadata solutions: Using metamodels, repositories, XML and enterprise portals to generate information on demand*. Boston, MA: Addison-Wesley.

Tantillo, J., Di Lorenzo-Aiss, J., & Mathisen, R. E. (1995). Quantifying perceived differences in type styles: An exploratory study. *Psychology and Marketing, 12*, 447–457. doi:10.1002/mar.4220120508

Tapiero, I. (2007). *Situation models and levels of coherence*. Mahwah, NJ: Erlbaum.

Tauscher, L., & Greenberg, S. (1997). Revisitation patterns in World Wide Web navigation. *Proceeding of the ACM CHI 97: Conference on Human Factors in Computing Systems* Atlanta, GA (pp. 399–406).

Taylor, C. (1934). The relative legibility of black and white print. *Journal of Educational Psychology, 25*(8), 561–578. doi:10.1037/h0074746

Thatcher, A., & Greyling, M. (1998). The use and meaning of the "computer experience" variable. In Scott, P., & Bridger, R. (Eds.), *Global ergonomics* (pp. 541–546). Amsterdam, The Netherlands: Elsevier.

The future of online search. (2005). Interview with John Batelle, Wired editor. Retrieved from http://www.cnn.com/2005/TECH/12/ 23/john.bartelle/index.html

Thompson, C., & Mingay, D. (1991). Estimating the frequency of everyday events. *Applied Cognitive Psychology, 5*, 497–510. doi:10.1002/acp.2350050605

Thuring, M., Hannemann, J., & Haake, J. (1995). Hypermedia and cognition: Designing for comprehension. *Communications of the ACM, 38*, 57–66. doi:10.1145/208344.208348

Timmermans, D., Molewijk, B., Stiggelbout, A., & Kievit, J. (2004). Different formats for communicating surgical risks to patients and the effect on choice of treatment. *Patient Education and Counseling, 54*, 255–263. doi:10.1016/S0738-3991(03)00238-6

Tinker, M. (1963). *Legibility of print*. Ames, IA: Iowa State University Press.

Tobin, S., & Grondin, S. (2009). Video games and the perception of very long durations by adolescents. *Computers in Human Behavior, 25*, 554–559. doi:10.1016/j.chb.2008.12.002

Tole, J., Stephens, A., Harris, R., & Ephrath, A. (1982). Visual scanning behavior and mental workload in aircraft pilots. *Aviation, Space, and Environmental Medicine, 53*, 54–61.

Toleman, M., & Welsh, J. (1996). Can design choices for language-based editors be analysed with keystroke-level models? *Proceedings of the HCI '96 Conference on People and Computers,* (pp. 97–112). Surrey, UK: Springer-Verlag.

Tomasi, J., & Menlenbacker, B. (1999). Re-engineering online documentation: Designing example-based online support systems. *Technical Communication, 46*(1), 55–66.

Toms, E. (2002). Information interaction: Providing a framework for information architecture. *Journal of The American Society for Information Science and Technology, 53.1*. 855–862.

Topi, H., Valacich, J., & Hoffer, J. (2005). The effects of task complexity and time availability limitations on human performance in database query tasks. *International Journal of Human-Computer Studies, 62*, 349–379. doi:10.1016/j.ijhcs.2004.10.003

Tractinsky, N., & Meyer, J. (1999). Chartjunk or goldgraph? Effects of presentation objectives and content desirability on information presentation. *Management Information Systems Quarterly, 23*(3), 397–420. doi:10.2307/249469

Tractinsky, N., & Meyer, J. (2001). Task structure and the apparent duration of hierarchical search. *International Journal of Human-Computer Studies*, *55*, 845–860. doi:10.1006/ijhc.2001.0506

Tracy, J., & Albers, M. (2006). *Measuring cognitive load to test the usability of web sites.* Society for Technical Communication 53rd Annual Conference, Las Vegas, NV. May 7–10, 2006.

Treisman, A. (1982). Perceptual grouping and attention in visual search for features and for objects. *Journal of Experimental Psychology. Human Perception and Performance*, *8*(2), 194–214. doi:10.1037/0096-1523.8.2.194

Treisman, A. (1985). Preattentive processing in vision. *Computer Vision Graphics and Image Processing*, *31*, 156–177. doi:10.1016/S0734-189X(85)80004-9

Treisman, A. (1991). Search, similarity, and integration of features between and within dimensions. *Journal of Experimental Psychology. Human Perception and Performance*, *1*(3), 652–676. doi:10.1037/0096-1523.17.3.652

Treisman, A., & Gelade, G. (1980). A feature-integration theory of attention. *Cognitive Psychology*, *12*, 97–136. doi:10.1016/0010-0285(80)90005-5

Treisman, A., & Gormican, S. (1988). Feature analysis in early vision: Evidence from search asymmetries. *Psychological Review*, *95*(1), 15–48. doi:10.1037/0033-295X.95.1.15

Treu, S. (1992). Interface structures: Conceptual, logical, and physical patterns applicable to human-computer interaction. *International Journal of Man-Machine Studies*, *37*, 565–593. doi:10.1016/0020-7373(92)90024-F

Triesch, J., Ballard, D., Hayhoe, M., & Sullivan, B. (2003). What you see is what you need. *Journal of Vision (Charlottesville, Va.)*, *3*, 86–94. doi:10.1167/3.1.9

Trimmel, M., Meixner-Pendleton, M., & Haring, S. (2003). Stress response caused by system response time when searching for information on the Internet. *Human Factors*, *45*(4), 615–621. doi:10.1518/hfes.45.4.615.27084

Tufte, E. (1983). *The visual display of quantitative information.* Cheshire, CT: Graphics Press.

Tufte, E. (1990). *Envisioning information.* Cheshire, CT: Graphics Press.

Tufte, E. (1997). *Visual explanations: Images and quantities, evidence and narrative.* Cheshire, CT: Graphics Press.

Tullis, T. (1993). Is user interface design just common sense? In G. Salvendy & M. Smith, (Eds.), *Proceedings of the 5th International Conference on Human-Computer Interaction*, (Vol. 2, pp. 9–14). New York, NY: Elsevier.

Tulving, E. (2002). Episodic memory: From mind to brain. *Annual Review of Psychology*, *53*, 1–25. doi:10.1146/annurev.psych.53.100901.135114

Tversky, A. (1977). Features of similarity. *Psychological Review*, *84*, 327–352. doi:10.1037/0033-295X.84.4.327

Tversky, A., & Kahneman, D. (1971). The belief in the law of small numbers. *Psychological Bulletin*, *76*, 105–110. doi:10.1037/h0031322

Tversky, A., & Kahneman, D. (1974). Judgment under uncertainty: Heuristics and biases. *Science*, *185*, 1124–1130. doi:10.1126/science.185.4157.1124

Tversky, A., & Kahneman, D. (1981). The framing of decisions and the psychology of choice. *Science*, *211*, 453–458. doi:10.1126/science.7455683

Tversky, A., Slovic, P., & Kahneman, D. (1990). The causes of preference reversals. *The American Economic Review*, *80*, 204–217.

Tversky, B. (2002). Some ways that graphics communicate. In Allen, N. (Ed.), *Words and images: New steps in an old dance* (pp. 57–74). Westport, CT: Ablex.

Tversky, B., Zacks, J. M., Lee, P. U., & Heiser, J. (2000). Lines, blobs, crosses and arrows. In Anderson, M., Cheng, P., & Haarslev, V. (Eds.), *Theory and application of diagrams* (pp. 221–230). Edinburgh, UK: Springer. doi:10.1007/3-540-44590-0_21

Tyre, M. J., & von Hippel, E. (1997). The situated nature of adaptive learning in organizations. *Organization Science*, *8*(1), 71–83. doi:10.1287/orsc.8.1.71

Vakkari, P. (2001). Changes in search tactics and relevance judgments when preparing a research proposal: A summary of findings of a longitudinal study. *Information Retrieval*, *4*(3), 295–310.

Valero, P., & Sanmartiân, J. (1999). Methods for defining user groups and user adjusted information structures. *Behaviour & Information Technology, 18*(4), 245–259. doi:10.1080/014492999119002

van den Broek, P., Lorch, R., Linderholm, T., & Gustafson, M. (2001). The effects of readers' goals on inference generation and memory for texts. *Memory & Cognition, 29*(8), 1081–1087. doi:10.3758/BF03206376

van der Meij, H., & Gellevij, M. (1998). Screen captures in software documentation. *Technical Communication, 45*, 529–543.

van der Meij, H., & Gellevij, M. (2002). Effects of pictures, age, and experience on learning to use a computer program. *Technical Communication, 49*(3), 330–339.

Van Dijk, T., & Kintsch, W. (1983). *Strategies of discourse comprehension.* New York, NY: Academic Press.

van Hees, M. (1996). User instructions for the elderly: What the literature tells us. *Journal of Technical Writing and Communication, 26*(4), 521–536.

Van Nimwegen, C., Van Oostendorp, H., & Tabachneck-Schijf, H. (2005). The role of interface style in planning during problem solving. In *Proceedings of the 27th Annual Cognitive Science Conference* (pp. 2771–2776). Mahwah, NJ: Erlbaum.

Van Schaik, P. (1999). Involving users in the specification of functionality using scenarios and model-based evaluation. *Behaviour & Information Technology, 18*(6), 455–466. doi:10.1080/014492999118878

Vanderbeeken, M. (2009). Taking a broader view of the human experience. *Interaction,* (March/April): 54–57. doi:10.1145/1487632.1487645

Vassilakis, P., & Moustakis, V. (1996). Identifying decision maker's preferences through a prototype based inductive learning method: A medical case study. *Behaviour & Information Technology, 15*(2), 113–122. doi:10.1080/014492996120328

Venkatesh, V., & Davis, F. (2000). A theoretical extension of the technology acceptance model: Four longitudinal field studies. *Management Science, 46*, 186–204. doi:10.1287/mnsc.46.2.186.11926

Venkatesh, V., Morris, M., Davis, G., & Davis, F. (2003). User acceptance of Information Technology: Toward a unified view. *Management Information Systems Quarterly, 27*(3), 425–478.

Vicente, K. (1999). *Cognitive work analysis.* Mahway, NJ: Erlbaum.

Visser, W., & Morals, A. (1991). Concurrent use of different expertise elicitation methods applied to the study of the programming activity. In Ackermann, D., & Tauber, M. J. (Eds.), *Mental models and human-computer interactions* (pp. 97–114). Amsterdam, The Netherlands: North Holland.

von Hippel, E. (2001). Innovation by user communities: Learning from open-source software. *MIT Sloan Management Review, 42*(4), 82–86.

Vu, K., Hanley, G., Strybel, T., & Proctor, R. (2000). Metacognitive processes in human-computer interaction: Self-assessments of knowledge as predictors of computer expertise. *International Journal of Human-Computer Interaction, 12*(1), 43–71. doi:10.1207/S15327590IJHC1201_2

Wachtel, P. (1967). Conceptions of broad and narrow attention. *Psychological Bulletin, 68*, 417–419. doi:10.1037/h0025186

Wade, S., Schraw, G., Buxton, W., & Hayes, M. (1993). Seduction of the strategic reader: Effects of interest on strategies and recall. *Reading Research Quarterly, 28*, 93–111. doi:10.2307/747885

Waern, Y. (1989). *Cognitive aspects of computer supported tasks.* New York, NY: Wiley.

Wagar, B., & Dixon, M. (2005). Past experience influences object representation in working memory. *Brain and Cognition, 57*, 248–256. doi:10.1016/j.bandc.2004.08.054

Wagenaar, W., & Sagaria, S. (1975). Misperception of exponential growth. *Perception & Psychophysics, 18*(6), 416–422. doi:10.3758/BF03204114

Wagenaar, W., & Timmers, H. (1977). Inverse statistics and misperception of exponential growth. *Perception & Psychophysics, 21*(6), 558–562. doi:10.3758/BF03198737

Wagenaar, W., & Timmers, H. (1978). Extrapolation of exponential time series is not enhanced by having more data points. *Perception & Psychophysics*, *24*(2), 182–184. doi:10.3758/BF03199548

Wagenaar, W., & Timmers, H. (1979). The pond-and-duckweed problem: Three experiments on the misperception of exponential growth. *Acta Psychologica*, *43*(3), 239–251. doi:10.1016/0001-6918(79)90028-3

Wagner, R., & Sternberg, R. (1987). Executive control in reading comprehension. In Britton, B. K., & Glynn, S. M. (Eds.), *Executive control processes in reading* (pp. 1–21). Hillsdale, NJ: Erlbaum.

Walker, N. Millians, J., & Worden, A. (1996). Mouse accelerations and performance of older computer users. *Proceedings of the Human Factors and Ergonomics Society 40th Annual Meeting*, (pp. 151–154). Santa Monica, CA: HFES.

Walker, N., & Smelcer, J. (1990). A comparison of selection time from walking and bar menus. *Proceedings of the SIGCHI Conference on Human Factors in Computing Systems*, (pp. 221-225). New York, NY: ACM.

Walker, N., Millians, J., & Worden, A. (1996). Mouse accelerations and performance of older computer users. *Proceedings of the Human Factors and Ergonomics Society 40th Annual Meeting*, (pp.151–154). Santa Monica, CA: HFES.

Wallsten, T. (1981). Physician and medical student bias in evaluating diagnostic information. *Medical Decisión Making*, *1*(2), 145–164. doi:10.1177/0272989X8100100205

Wallsten, T., & Barton, C. (1982). Processing probabilistic multidimensional information for decisions. *Journal of Experimental Psychology. Learning, Memory, and Cognition*, *8*, 361–384. doi:10.1037/0278-7393.8.5.361

Walraven, A., Brand-Gruwel, S., & Boshuizen, H. (2008). Information-problem solving: A review of problems students encounter and instructional solutions. *Computers in Human Behavior*, *24*, 623–648. doi:10.1016/j.chb.2007.01.030

Wang, H., Johnson, T., & Zhang, J. (2006). The order effect in human abductive reasoning: An empirical and computational study. *Journal of Experimental & Theoretical Artificial Intelligence*, *18*(2), 215–247. doi:10.1080/09528130600558141

Warren, T. (1993). Three approaches to reader analysis. *Technical Communication*, *40*(1), 81–87.

Warwick, C., Rimmer, J., Blandford, A., Gow, J., & Buchanan, G. (2009). Cognitive economy and satisficing in information seeking: A longitudinal study of undergraduate information behaviour. *Journal of the American Society for Information Science and Technology*, *60*(12), 2402–2415. doi:10.1002/asi.21179

Watters, C., Duffy, J., & Duffy, K. (2003). Using large tables on small display devices. *International Journal of Human-Computer Studies*, *58*, 21–37. doi:10.1016/S1071-5819(02)00124-6

Weber, B., & Chapman, G. (2005). The combined effects of risk and time on choice: Does uncertainty eliminate the immediacy effect? Does delay eliminate the certainty effect? *Organizational Behavior and Human Decision Processes*, *96*(2), 104–118. doi:10.1016/j.obhdp.2005.01.001

Webster, D., & Kruglanski, A. (1994). Individual differences in need. for cognitive closure. *Journal of Personality and Social Psychology*, *67*(6), 1049–1672. doi:10.1037/0022-3514.67.6.1049

WebTorque. (2011). *Movement and change in user interfaces*. Retrieved from http://webtorque.org/?p=1141

Weigand, H. (2006). Two decades of the language-action perspective. *Communications of the ACM*, *49*(5), 45–26.

Weinstein, N. (1980). Unrealistic optimism about future life events. *Journal of Personality and Social Psychology*, *39*, 806–820. doi:10.1037/0022-3514.39.5.806

Weinstein, N. (1987). Unrealistic optimism about illness susceptibility: Conclusions from a community wide sample. *Journal of Behavioral Medicine*, *10*, 481–500. doi:10.1007/BF00846146

Weiss, E. (1985). *Writing a Usable User Manual*. Philadelphia, PA: ISI Press.

Well, A., Pollatsek, A., & Boyce, S. (1990). Understanding the effects of sample size in the mean. *Organizational Behavior and Human Decision Processes*, *47*, 289–312. doi:10.1016/0749-5978(90)90040-G

Weller, D. (2004). The effects of contrast and density on visual web search. *Usability News*, *6*(2). Retrieved from http://psychology.wichita.edu/surl/ usabilitynews/62/density.htm

Wenger, M., & Payne, D. (1996). Human information processing correlates of reading hypertext. *Technical Communication, 43*, 51–60.

Wharton, C., & Kintsch, W. (1991). An overview of construction-integration model: A theory of comprehension as a foundation for a new cognitive architecture. *ACM SIGART Bulletin, 2*(4), 169–173. doi:10.1145/122344.122379

Whitburn, M. (1984). The ideal orator and literary critic as technical communicators: An emerging revolution in English departments. In Lundsford, A., & Ede, L. (Eds.), *Essays in classical rhetoric and modern discourse* (pp. 230–248). Carbondale, IL: Southern Illinois University Press.

Whitmire, E. (2003). Epistemological beliefs and the information-seeking behavior of undergraduates. *Library & Information Science Research, 25*, 127–142. doi:10.1016/S0740-8188(03)00003-3

Whitmire, E. (2004). The relationship between undergraduates' epistemological reflection, reflective judgment and their information seeking behavior. *Information Processing & Management, 40*(1), 97–111. doi:10.1016/S0306-4573(02)00099-7

Whittaker, S., & Hirshberg, J. (2001). The character, value, and management of personal paper archives. *ACM Transactions on Computer-Human Interaction, 8*(2), 150–170. doi:10.1145/376929.376932

Whitworth, B., & Moor, A. (2003). Legitimate by design: Towards trusted socio-technical systems. *Behaviour & Information Technology, 22*(1), 31–51. doi:10.1080/01449290301783

Wickens, C. (1992). *Engineering psychology and human performance*. New York, NY: HarperCollins.

Wickens, C., & Carswell, C. (1995). The proximity compatibility principle: Its psychological foundations and its relevance to display design. *Human Factors, 37*, 473–494. doi:10.1518/001872095779049408

Wickens, C., & Hollands, J. (2000). *Engineering psychology and human performance*. Upper Saddle River, NJ: Prentice Hall.

Wiley, J., & Myers, J. (2003). Availability and accessibility of information and causal inferences from scientific text. *Discourse Processes, 36*(2), 109–129. doi:10.1207/S15326950DP3602_2

Willemsen, M., & Keren, G. (2003). The meaning of indifference in choice behavior: Asymmetries in adjustments embodied in matching. *Organizational Behavior and Human Decision Processes, 90*, 342–359. doi:10.1016/S0749-5978(02)00521-6

Williams, D., & Noyes, J. (2007). How does our perception of risk influence decision-making? Implications for the design of risk information. *Theoretical Issues in Ergonomics Science, 8*(1), 1–35. doi:10.1080/14639220500484419

Williams, L. (1989). Foveal load affects the functional field of view. *Human Performance, 2*, 1–28. doi:10.1207/s15327043hup0201_1

Wills, C., & Holmes-Rovner, M. (2003). Patient comprehension of information for shared treatment decision making: State of the art and future directions. *Patient Education and Counseling, 50*, 285–290. doi:10.1016/S0738-3991(03)00051-X

Wills, C., & Moore, C. (1996). Perspective-taking judgments of medication acceptance: Inferences from relative importance about the impact and combination of information. *Organizational Behavior and Human Decision Processes, 66*(3), 251–267. doi:10.1006/obhd.1996.0054

Wilson, C., & Harsha, P. (2008). IT policy—Advising policymakers is more than just providing advice. *Communications of the ACM, 51*(12), 24–26. doi:10.1145/1409360.1409370

Wilson, J., & Rutherford, A. (1989). Mental models: Theory and application in human factors. *Human Factors, 31*, 617–634.

Wilson, K., Aaron, S., Vandemheen, K., Hebert, P., McKim, D., & Fiset, V. (2005). Evaluation of a decision aid for making choices about intubation and mechanical ventilation in chronic obstructive pulmonary disease. *Patient Education and Counseling, 57*, 88–95. doi:10.1016/j.pec.2004.04.004

Winkleman, W., Leonard, K., & Rossos, P. (2005). Patient-perceived usefulness of online electronic medical records. *Journal of the American Medical Informatics Association, 12,* 306–314.

Winograd, E., Smith, A., & Simon, E. (1982). Aging and the picture superiority effect in recall. *Journal of Gerontology, 37,* 70–75.

Winograd, T., & Flores, F. (1986). *Understanding computers and cognition: A new foundation for design.* Norwood, NJ: Ablex.

Winslow, E. (2001). Patient education materials. *The American Journal of Nursing, 10,* 33–39. doi:10.1097/00000446-200110000-00021

Witkin, H. (1978). *Cognitive styles in personal and cultural adaptation.* Washington, DC: Clark UP.

Wogalter, M., Jarrard, S., & Simpson, S. (1994). Influence of warning label signal words on perceived hazard level. *Human Factors, 36*(3), 547–556.

Wogalter, M., & Silver, N. (1990). Arousal strength of signal words. *Forensic Reports, 3,* 407–420.

Wolfe, J. (1994). Guided search 2.0: A revised model of visual search. *Psychonomic Bulletin & Review, 1*(2), 202–238. doi:10.3758/BF03200774

Wolfe, R. M., Sharp, L. K., & Lipsky, M. S. (2002). Content and design attributes of antivaccination websites. *Journal of the American Medical Association, 287,* 3245–3248. doi:10.1001/jama.287.24.3245

Wong, K., & Kwong, J. (2005). Comparing two tiny giants or two huge dwarfs? Preference reversals owing to number size framing. *Organizational Behavior and Human Decision Processes, 98,* 54–65. doi:10.1016/j.obhdp.2005.04.002

Woods, D. (1984). Visual momentum: A concept to improve the cognitive coupling of person and computer. *International Journal of Man-Machine Studies, 21,* 229–244. doi:10.1016/S0020-7373(84)80043-7

Woods, D. (1984). Visual momentum: A concept to improve the cognitive coupling of person and computer. *International Journal of Man-Machine Studies, 21,* 229–244. doi:10.1016/S0020-7373(84)80043-7

Woods, D., & Cook, R. (1999). Perspectives and human error. In Durso, F. (Ed.), *Handbook of applied cognition* (pp. 141–172). West Sussex, UK: Cambridge UP.

Woods, D., Patterson, E., & Roth, E. (2002). Can we ever escape from data overload? A cognitive systems diagnosis. *Cognition Technology and Work, 4,* 22–36. doi:10.1007/s101110200002

Woods, D., & Roth, E. (1988). Cognitive engineering: Human problem solving with tools. *Human Factors, 30*(4), 415–430.

Wright, P. (1974). The harassed decision maker: Time pressure, distractions, and the use of evidence. *The Journal of Applied Psychology, 59*(5), 555–561. doi:10.1037/h0037186

Wyatt, J., & Wright, P. (1998). Design should help use of patients' data. *Lancet, 352,* 1375–1378. doi:10.1016/S0140-6736(97)08306-2

Yang, H., & Yoo, Y. (2004). It's all about attitude: Revisiting the technology acceptance model. *Decision Support Systems, 38,* 19–31. doi:10.1016/S0167-9236(03)00062-9

Yarett, I. (2010). *Does soda cause pancreatic cancer? What the latest study really says.* Retrieved May 13, 2010, from http://blog.newsweek.com/blogs/ thehumancondition/archive/2010/02/18/ does-soda-cause-pancreatic-cancer-what-the-latest-study-really-says.aspx

Young, H., & Miller, J. (1991). Visual-discrimination on color VDTs at 2 viewing distances. *Behaviour & Information Technology, 10,* 191–205. doi:10.1080/01449299108924282

Zacks, J. M., Levy, E., Tversky, B., & Schiano, D. (2002). Graphs in print. In Anderson, M., Meyer, B., & Olivier, P. (Eds.), *Diagrammatic representation and reasoning* (pp. 187–206). London, UK: Springer-Verlag. doi:10.1007/978-1-4471-0109-3_11

Zacks, J., Levy, E., Tversky, B., & Schiano, D. (1998). Reading bar graphs: Effects of depth cues and graphical context. *Journal of Experimental Psychology. Applied, 4,* 119–138. doi:10.1037/1076-898X.4.2.119

Zacks, J., & Tversky, B. (1999). Bars and lines: A study of graphic communication. *Memory & Cognition, 27,* 1073–1079. doi:10.3758/BF03201236

Zakay, D., & Hornik, J. (1991). How much time did you wait in line? A time perception perspective. In Chebat, J. C., & Venkatesan, V. (Eds.), *Time and consumer behaviour* (pp. 1–18). Montreal, Canada: University of Quebec at Montreal.

Zaphiris, P., & Kurniawan, S. (2001). Effects of information layout on reading speed: Differences between paper and monitor presentation. *Proceedings of the Human Factors and Ergonomics Society 45th Annual Meeting*, (pp. 1210–1214). Santa Monica, CA: HFES.

Zeff, C. (1965). Comparison of conventional and digital time displays. *Ergonomics*, 8, 339–345. doi:10.1080/00140136508930811

Zeng, Q., Kogan, S., Plovnick, R., Crowell, J., Lacroix, E., & Greenes, R. (2004). Positive attitudes and failed queries: An exploration of the conundrums of consumer health information retrieval. *International Journal of Medical Informatics*, 73(1), 45–55. doi:10.1016/j.ijmedinf.2003.12.015

Zeng, Q., Kogan, S., Plovnick, R., Crowell, J., Lacroix, E., & Greenes, R. (2004). Positive attitudes and failed queries: An exploration of the conundrums of consumer health information retrieval. *International Journal of Medical Informatics*, 73(1), 45–55. doi:10.1016/j.ijmedinf.2003.12.015

Zhang, H., & Salvendy, G. (2001). The implications of visualization ability and structure preview design for Web information search tasks. *International Journal of Human-Computer Interaction*, 13(1), 75–95. doi:10.1207/S15327590IJHC1301_5

Zhang, J. (1996). A representational analysis of relational information displays. *Journal of Human-Computer Studies*, 45(1), 59–74. doi:10.1006/ijhc.1996.0042

Zhang, Y., Goonetilleke, R., Plocher, T., & Liang, S. (2005). Time-related behaviour in multitasking situations. *International Journal of Human-Computer Studies*, 62, 425–455. doi:10.1016/j.ijhcs.2005.01.002

Zhao, S., Meyer, R., & Han, J. (2006). *A tale of two judgments: Biases in prior valuations and subsequent utilization of novel technological product attributes*. Retrieved from http://knowledge.wharton.upenn.edu/article/1292.cfm

Zimmermann, G., & Vanderheiden, G. (2005). *Creating accessible applications with RUP*. Retrieved April 28, 2006, from http://www.128.ibm.com/developerworks/rational/library/jul05/zimmerman/index.html#notes

Zipf, G. (1949). *Human behavior and the principle of least effort*. New York, NY: Addison-Wesley.

Zumbach, J., & Mohraz, M. (2008). Cognitive load in hypermedia reading comprehension: Influence of text type and linearity. *Computers in Human Behavior*, 24(3), 875–887. doi:10.1016/j.chb.2007.02.015

Zwaan, R., & Singer, M. (2003). Text comprehension. In Graesser, A., Gernsbacher, M., & Goldman, S. (Eds.), *Handbook of discourse processes* (pp. 83–121). Mahwah, NJ: Erlbaum.

About the Author

Michael J. Albers is a Professor at East Carolina University where he teaches in the professional writing program. Before coming to ECU, he taught for eight years at the University of Memphis. His primary teaching areas are editing, information design, and usability. In 1999, he completed his PhD in Technical Communication and Rhetoric from Texas Tech University. Before earning his PhD, he worked for 10 years as a technical communicator, writing software documentation and performing interface design. His research interests include designing information focused on answering real-world questions, presentation of complex information, and human-information interaction. He has two edited collections and one book published, with another book under contract. In addition, he has published 15 peer-reviewed journal articles and book chapters and guest-edited special issues of four journals. He is an STC Fellow and an active member of ACM/SIGDOC. He has presented at both organizations' conferences multiple times and has worked on the organizing committees of both conferences. He has served as ACM/SIG-DOC Secretary for six years.

Index